CIMA Official
Learning System

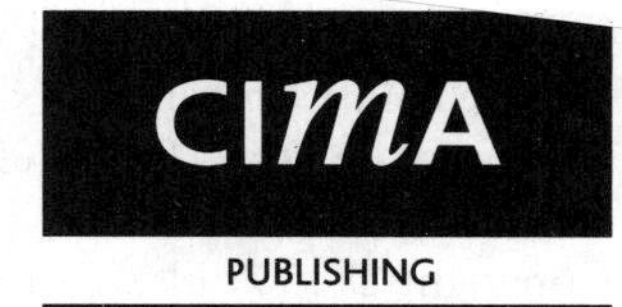

Managerial Level

F2 – Financial Management

Luisa Robertson

ELSEVIER

AMSTERDAM BOSTON HEIDELBERG LONDON NEW YORK OXFORD
PARIS SAN DIEGO SAN FRANCISCO SINGAPORE SYDNEY TOKYO

CIMA Publishing is an imprint of Elsevier
Linacre House, Jordan Hill, Oxford OX2 8DP, UK
30 Corporate Drive, Suite 400, Burlington, MA 01803, USA

British Library Cataloguing in Publication Data
A catalogue record for this book is available from the British Library

Library of Congress Catalog in Publication Data
A catalog record for this book is available from the Library of Congress

ISBN: 978-1-85617-784-9

Typeset by Macmillan Publishing Solutions
(www.macmillansolutions.com)

Printed and bound in Hungary

09 10 11 11 10 9 8 7 6 5 4 3 2 1

Contents

The CIMA *Learning System*

Acknowledgements

Every effort has been made to contact the holders of copyright material, but if any here have been inadvertently overlooked the publishers will be pleased to make the necessary arrangements at the first opportunity.

How to use the CIMA *Learning System*

This *Financial Management Learning System* has been devised as a resource for students attempting to pass their CIMA exams, and provides:

- a detailed explanation of all syllabus areas;
- extensive 'practical' materials, including readings from relevant journals;
- generous question practice, together with full solutions;
- an exam preparation section, complete with exam standard questions and solutions.

This Learning System has been designed with the needs of home-study and distance-learning candidates in mind. Such students require very full coverage of the syllabus topics, and also the facility to undertake extensive question practice. However, the Learning System is also ideal for fully taught courses.

The main body of the text is divided into a number of chapters, each of which is organised on the following pattern:

- *Detailed learning outcomes.* It is expected after your studies of the chapter are complete. You should assimilate these before beginning detailed work on the chapter, so that you can appreciate where your studies are leading.
- *Step-by-step topic coverage.* This is the heart of each chapter, containing detailed explanatory text supported where appropriate by worked examples and exercises. You should work carefully through this section, ensuring that you understand the material being explained and can tackle the examples and exercises successfully. Remember that in many cases knowledge is cumulative: if you fail to digest earlier material thoroughly, you may struggle to understand later chapters.

- *Question practice.* The test of how well you have learned the material is your ability to tackle exam-standard questions. Make a serious attempt at producing your own answers, but at this stage don't be too concerned about attempting the questions in exam conditions. In particular, it is more important to absorb the material thoroughly by completing a full solution than to observe the time limits that would apply in the actual exam.
- *Solutions.* Avoid the temptation merely to 'audit' the solutions provided. It is an illusion to think that this provides the same benefits as you would gain from a serious attempt of your own. However, if you are struggling to get started on a question you should read the introductory guidance provided at the beginning of the solution, and then make your own attempt before referring back to the full solution.

Having worked through the chapters you are ready to begin your final preparations for the examination. The final section of the CIMA *Learning System* provides you with the guidance you need. It includes the following features:

- A brief guide to revision technique.
- A note on the format of the examination. You should know what to expect when you tackle the real exam, and in particular the number of questions to attempt, which questions are compulsory and which optional, and so on.
- Guidance on how to tackle the examination itself.
- A table mapping revision questions to the syllabus learning outcomes allowing you to quickly identify questions by subject area.
- Revision questions are of exam standard and should be tackled in exam conditions, especially as regards the time allocation.
- Solutions to the revision questions. As before, these indicate the length and the quality of solution that would be expected of a well-prepared candidate.

If you work conscientiously through this CIMA *Learning System* according to the guidelines above you will be giving yourself an excellent chance of exam success. Good luck with your studies!

Guide to the Icons used within this Text

Key term or definition

Equation to learn

Exam tip to topic likely to appear in the exam

Exercise

Question

Solution

Comment or Note

Study technique

Passing exams is partly a matter of intellectual ability, but however accomplished you are in that respect you can improve your chances significantly by the use of appropriate study and revision techniques. In this section we briefly outline some tips for effective study during the earlier stages of your approach to the exam. Later in the text we mention some techniques that you will find useful at the revision stage.

Planning

To begin with, formal planning is essential to get the best return from the time you spend studying. Estimate how much time in total you are going to need for each subject that you face. Remember that you need to allow time for revision as well as for initial study of the material. The amount of notional study time for any subject is the minimum estimated time that students will need to achieve the specified learning outcomes set out earlier in this chapter. This time includes all appropriate learning activities, for example, face-to-face tuition, private study, directed home study, learning in the workplace and revision time. You may find it helpful to read *Better exam results* by Sam Malone, CIMA Publishing, ISBN: 075066357X. This book will provide you with proven study techniques. Chapter by chapter it covers the building blocks of successful learning and examination techniques.

The notional study time for Managerial level – *Financial Analysis* is 200 hours. Note that the standard amount of notional learning hours attributed to one full-time academic year of approximately 30 weeks is 1,200 hours.

By way of example, the notional study time might be made up as follows:

	Hours
Face-to-face study: up to	60
Personal study: up to	100
'Other' study – e.g., learning in the workplace, revision, etc.: up to	40
	200

Note that all study and learning-time recommendations should be used only as a guideline and are intended as minimum amounts. The amount of time recommended for face-to-face tuition, personal study and/or additional learning will vary according to the type of course undertaken, prior learning of the student, and the pace at which different students learn.

Now split your total time requirement over the weeks between now and the examination. This will give you an idea of how much time you need to devote to study each week. Remember to allow for holidays or other periods during which you will not be able to study (e.g., because of seasonal workloads).

With your study material before you, decide which chapters you are going to study in each week, and which weeks you will devote to revision and final question practice.

Prepare a written schedule summarising the above – and stick to it!

The amount of space allocated to a topic in the study material is not a very good guide as to how long it will take you.

It is essential to know your syllabus. As your course progresses you will become more familiar with how long it takes to cover topics in sufficient depth. Your timetable may need to be adapted to allocate enough time for the whole syllabus.

Tips for effective studying

1. Aim to find a quiet and undisturbed location for your study, and plan as far as possible to use the same period of time each day. Getting into a routine helps to avoid wasting time. Make sure that you have all the materials you need before you begin so as to minimise interruptions.
2. Store all your materials in one place, so that you don't waste time searching for items around the house. If you have to pack everything away after each study period, keep them in a box, or even a suitcase, which won't be disturbed until the next time.
3. Limit distractions. To make the most effective use of your study periods you should be able to apply total concentration, so turn off the TV, set your phones to message mode, and put up your 'do not disturb' sign.
4. Your timetable will tell you which topic to study. However, before diving in and becoming engrossed in the finer points, make sure you have an overall picture of all the areas that need to be covered by the end of that session. After an hour, allow yourself a short break and move away from your books. With experience, you will learn to assess the pace you need to work at. You should also allow enough time to read relevant articles from newspapers and journals, which will supplement your knowledge and demonstrate a wider perspective.
5. Work carefully through a chapter, making notes as you go. When you have covered a suitable amount of material, vary the pattern by attempting a practice question. Preparing an answer plan is a good habit to get into, while you are both studying and revising, and also in the examination room. It helps to impose a structure on your solutions, and avoids rambling. When you have finished your attempt, make notes of any mistakes you made, or any areas that you failed to cover or covered only skimpily.
6. Make notes as you study, and discover the techniques that work best for you. Your notes may be in the form of lists, bullet points, diagrams, summaries, 'mind maps', or the written word, but remember that you will need to refer back to them at a later date, so they must be intelligible. If you are on a taught course, make sure you highlight any issues you would like to follow up with your lecturer.
7. Organise your paperwork. There are now numerous paper storage systems available to ensure that all your notes, calculations and articles can be effectively filed and easily retrieved later.

Paper F2
Financial Management

Syllabus Overview

Paper F2 extends the scope of Paper F1 Financial Operations to more advanced topics in financial accounting (preparation of full consolidated financial statements and issues of principle in accounting standards dealing with more complex areas) and to developments in external reporting. With the advanced level of financial accounting and reporting achieved in this paper, the analysis and interpretation of accounts becomes more meaningful and this constitutes a substantial element.

Syllabus Structure

The syllabus comprises the following topics and study weightings:

A	Group Financial Statements	35%
B	Issues in Recognition and Measurement	20%
C	Analysis and Interpretation of Financial Accounts	35%
D	Developments in External Reporting	10%

Assessment Strategy

There will be a written examination paper of 3 hours, plus 20 minutes of pre-examination question paper reading time. The examination paper will have the following sections:

Section A – 50 marks
Five compulsory medium answer questions, each worth 10 marks. Short scenarios may be given, to which some or all questions relate.

Section B – 50 marks
One or two compulsory questions. Short scenarios may be given, to which questions relate.

Learning Outcomes and Indicative Syllabus Content

F2 – A. Group Financial Statements (35%)

Learning Outcomes On completion of their studies students should be able to: Lead	Component	Indicative Syllabus Content
1. Prepare the full consolidated statements of a single company and the consolidated statements of financial position and comprehensive income for a group (in relatively complex circumstances). (3)	(a) prepare a complete set of consolidated financial statements, as specified in IAS 1(revised), in a form suitable for publication for a group of companies; (b) identify and demonstrate the impact on group financial statements where: there is a minority interest; the interest in a subsidiary or associate is acquired or disposed of part way through an accounting period (to include the effective date of acquisition and dividends out of pre-acquisition profits); shareholdings, or control, are acquired in stages; intra-group trading and other transactions occur; the value of goodwill is impaired; (c) explain and apply the concept of a joint venture and how their various types are accounted for.	• Relationships between investors and investees, meaning of control and circumstances in which a subsidiary is excluded from consolidation. (A) • The preparation of consolidated financial statements (including the group cash flow statement and statement of changes in equity) involving one or more subsidiaries, sub-subsidiaries and associates (IAS 1(revised), 7 & 27, IFRS 3). (A) • The treatment in consolidated financial statements of minority interests, pre- and post-acquisition reserves, goodwill (including its impairment), fair value adjustments, intra-group transactions and dividends, piece-meal and mid-year acquisitions, and disposals to include sub-subsidiaries and mixed g roups. (A, B) • The accounting treatment of associates and joint ventures (IAS 28 & 31) using the equity method and proportional consolidation method. (A, C)
2. Explain the principles of accounting for capital schemes and foreign exchange rate changes.	(a) explain the principles of accounting for a capital reconstruction scheme or a demerger; (b) explain foreign currency translation principles, including the difference between the closing rate/net investment method and the historical rate method; (c) explain the correct treatment for foreign loans financing foreign equity investments.	• Accounting for reorganisations and capital reconstruction schemes. (A) • Foreign currency translation (IAS 21), to include overseas transactions and investments in overseas subsidiaries. (B, C)

F2 – B. Issues in Recognition and Measurement (20%)

Learning Outcomes

On completion of their studies students should be able to:

Lead	Component	Indicative Syllabus Content
1. Discuss accounting principles and their relevance to accounting issues of contemporary interest. (4)	(a) discuss the problems of profit measurement and alternative approaches to asset valuations; (b) discuss measures to reduce distortion in financial statements when price levels change; (c) discuss the principle of substance over form applied to a range of transactions; (d) discuss the possible treatments of financial instruments in the issuer's accounts (i.e. liabilities versus equity, and the implications for finance costs); (e) identify discuss circumstances in which amortised cost, fair value and hedge accounting are appropriate for financial instruments, explain the principles of these accounting methods and discuss considerations in the determination of fair value; (f) discuss the recognition and valuation issues concerned with pension schemes (including the treatment of actuarial deficits and surpluses) and share-based payments.	• The problems of profit measurement and the effect of alternative approaches to asset valuation; current cost and current purchasing power bases and the real terms system; Financial Reporting in Hyperinflationary Economies (IAS 29). (A, B) • The principle of substance over form and its influence in dealing with transactions such as sale and repurchase agreements, consignment stock, debt factoring, securitised assets, loan transfers and public and private sector financial collaboration. (C) • Financial instruments classified as liabilities or shareholders funds and the allocation of finance costs over the term of the borrowing (IAS 32 & 39). (D, E) • The measurement, including methods of determining fair value, and disclosure of financial instruments (IAS 32 & 39, IFRS 7). (D, E) • Retirement benefits, including pension schemes – defined benefit schemes and defined contribution schemes, actuarial deficits and surpluses (IAS 19). (F) • Share-based payments (IFRS 2): types of transactions, measurement bases and accounting; determination of fair value. (F)

F2 – C. Analysis and Interpretation of Financial Accounts (35%)

Learning Outcomes On completion of their studies students should be able to:		
Lead	**Component**	**Indicative Syllabus Content**
1. Produce a ratio analysis from financial statements and supporting information, and explain its limitations. (4)	(a) calculate and interpret a full range of accounting ratios; (b) explain and discuss the limitations of accounting ratio analysis and analysis based on financial statements.	• Ratios in the areas of performance, profitability, financial adaptability, liquidity, activity, shareholder investment and financing, and their interpretation. (A) • Calculation of Earnings per Share under IAS 33, to include the effect of bonus issues, rights issues and convertible stock. (A) • The impact of financing structure, including use of leasing and short-term debt, on ratios, particularly gearing. (A) • Limitations of ratio analysis (e.g. comparability of businesses and accounting policies). (B)
2. Analyse and evaluate performance and position, and discuss the results. (4)	(a) analyse financial statements in the context of information provided in the accounts and corporate report; (b) evaluate performance and position based on analysis of financial statements; (c) prepare and discuss segmental analysis, with inter-firm and international comparisons taking account of possible aggressive or unusual accounting policies and pressures on ethical behaviour; (d) discuss the results of an analysis of financial statements and its limitations in a concise report.	• Interpretation of financial statements via the analysis of the accounts and corporate reports. (A, B) • The identification of information required to assess financial performance and the extent to which financial statements fail to provide such information. (A, B, D) • Interpretation of financial obligations included in financial accounts (e.g. redeemable debt, earn-out arrangements, contingent liabilities). (A, B, D) • Segment analysis: inter-firm and international comparison (IFRS 8). (C) • The need to be aware of aggressive or unusual accounting policies ('creative accounting'), e.g. in the areas of cost capitalisation and revenue recognition, and threats to the ethics of accountants from pressure to report 'good results'. (C) • Reporting the results of analysis. (D)

F2 – D. Developments in External Reporting (10%)

Learning Outcomes On completion of their studies students should be able to:		
Lead	**Component**	**Indicative Syllabus Content**
1. Explain and discuss contemporary developments in financial and non-financial reporting. (4)	(a) discuss pressures for extending the scope and quality of external reports to include prospective and non-financial matters, and narrative reporting generally; (b) explain how information concerning the interaction of a business with society and the natural environment can be communicated in the published accounts; (c) identify and discuss social and environmental issues which are likely to be most important to stakeholders in an organisation; (d) explain the process of measuring, recording and disclosing the effect of exchanges between a business and society – human resource accounting; (e) identify and discuss major differences between IFRS and US GAAP, and the measures designed to contribute towards their convergence.	• Increasing stakeholder demands for information that goes beyond historical financial information and frameworks for such reporting, including, as an example of national requirements and guidelines, the UK's Business Review and the Accounting Standard Board's best practice standard, RS1, and the Global Reporting Initiative. (A, B) • Environmental and social accounting issues, differentiating between externalities and costs internalised through, for example, capitalisation of environmental expenditure, recognition of future environmental costs by means of provisions, taxation and the costs of emissions permit trading schemes. (B, C) • Non-financial measures of social and environmental impact. (B, C) • Human resource accounting. (D) • Major differences between IFRS and US GAAP, and progress towards convergence. (E)

Introduction to F2 *Financial Management*

Introduction to F2 *Financial Management*

1

Learning Outcomes

After completing the work in this *Learning System* students should be able to:

- prepare the full consolidated statements of a single company and the consolidated statements of financial position and comprehensive income for a group (in relatively complex circumstances);
- explain the principles of accounting for capital schemes and foreign exchange rate changes;
- discuss accounting principles and their relevance to accounting issues of contemporary interest;
- produce ratio analysis from financial statements and supporting information;
- evaluate performance and position;
- discuss contemporary developments in financial and non-financial reporting.

1.1 Introduction

The learning outcomes of this course are achieved through study of four principal syllabus areas, given below with the related syllabus weighting:

Group financial statements	35%
Issues in recognition and measurement	20%
Analysis and interpretation of financial accounts	35%
Developments in external reporting	10%

The *Learning System* has been organised in the same way as this listing:

Chapters 2–9	Group financial statements
Chapters 10–13	Recognition and measurement issues
Chapters 14–16	Analysis and interpretation of financial accounts
Chapters 17–18	Developments in external reporting

This introductory chapter of the Learning System contains the following sections:

1.2 International financial reporting standards covered by the Financial Management syllabus

1.3 Advice and guidance for F2 candidates.

1.2 International Financial Reporting Standards covered by the Financial Management syllabus

To successfully achieve the learning aims of F2, we must study aspects of specific international accounting standards. The indicative syllabus content provided in the syllabus highlights the areas we must be familiar with. The relevant standards are covered in the forthcoming chapters, however for additional clarity a list is provided below:

Financial Management candidates are expected to have studied the following standards in preparation for the exam:

IAS 1	*(revised)*	*Presentation of Financial Statements**
IAS 7		*Statement of Cash Flow*
IAS 19		*Employee Benefits*
IAS 21		*The Effects of Changes in Foreign Exchange Rates*
IAS 27	*(revised)*	*Consolidated and Separate Financial Statements*
IAS 28		*Investments in Associates*
IAS 29		*Financial Reporting in Hyperinflationary Economies*
IAS 31		*Interests in Joint Ventures*
IAS 32		*Financial Instruments: Presentation*
IAS 33		*Earnings per Share*
IAS 39		*Financial Instruments: Recognition and Measurement*
IFRS 2		*Share-based Payment*
IFRS 3	*(revised)*	*Business Combinations*
IFRS 5		*Non-current Assets Held for Sale and Discontinued Operations (Note: In respect only of subsidiaries held exclusively for disposa)l*
IFRS 7		*Financial Instruments: Disclosure*
IFRS 8		*Operating Segments*

*Note: Candidates will not be examined specifically on knowledge of IAS 1. However, they are expected to be able to present financial statements prepared in accordance with IAS 1, and to that extent it is examinable and specifically mentioned in the indicative syllabus content for F2.

1.3 Advice and guidance for F2 candidates

The part of the book preceding this chapter (The CIMA *Learning System*) contains some useful general advice on study techniques. Candidates are advised to take notice of this. The syllabus for F2 is similar in content to its predecessor P8 Financial Analysis. The comments below refer to candidates performance on the recent diets of P8, however as they mostly refer to exam technique and style of answers, they are fully relevant to all F2 candidates.

The best source of detailed feedback about the examinations is found in the Post-Examination Guides (PEGs). PEGs are available on the CIMA website at www.cimaglobal.com (look under the section 'Studying'). This area of the website will contain other useful information about F2. It is updated frequently, so candidates should refer to it on a regular basis during their period of study.

Some common themes emerge in the (P8) PEGs particularly with reference to exam technique:

- Candidates often do not address the question asked. This is especially true of written questions.
- In questions requiring analysis and interpretation of financial statements candidates often demonstrate a lack of commercial awareness. It is not sufficient to state blandly that figures have gone up or down, or to calculate a long list of accounting ratios. In order to find out what is required by these questions, candidates are advised to spend some time studying the questions and answers very carefully. General commercial awareness can be improved by reading the financial press and specific awareness of the type of information given by financial statements could be addressed by careful reading of a lot of examples of real-life statements.
- Candidates do not allocate their time properly. Often there is evidence of one or more questions having been rushed because too long has been spent on some other question. Sometimes, for example, answers to written questions for 10 marks are as long, or longer, than the answers provided for written questions for 25 marks. In order to increase their chances of a pass, candidates should practise working past exam questions within the time allowance (NB – past papers for P8 are available on the CIMA website, also within the Studying section and as they are testing similar technical areas as F2, many will be relevant to your studying). While sitting the examination they should be absolutely rigorous with themselves about not exceeding the time allowed on any question.
- Workings for calculation questions, especially consolidated financial statements questions, are sometimes virtually illegible because they are so untidy. If poor handwriting or organisation are a problem, candidates should make it part of their exam preparation to practise being neater. Sometimes, in order to save time, it seems that candidates take short-cuts by doing the calculation on their calculators without writing down their workings. Often this means that no marks can be awarded for questions. An extract from the May 2007 PEG explains:

  Some candidates '. . . produce very lengthy and cumbersome workings for consolidation questions, using many T accounts, or 'tree' diagrams (or, occasionally, both). Errors are penalised only once, and markers give credit for figures that, while incorrect because of earlier errors, show the correct application of principles. However, the nature of some candidates' workings can make it very difficult, even impossible, to follow through the figures. Sometimes the workings are so complicated that it is clear that the candidate himself or herself has become thoroughly confused by them'.

- Some candidates do not prepare, apparently, for all sections of the syllabus. It is quite common to find, for example, that they are apparently ignorant of anything to do with financial instruments or other parts of syllabus area B. Candidates who go into the exam knowing about only part of the syllabus are very likely to fail. The examination is designed so as to cover the syllabus according to the syllabus weightings set out earlier in this chapter. There is very little variation from this and so candidates can be confident that syllabus area B will account for 20% of the question content, and syllabus area D for another 10%.
- Some candidates are much given to repetition in written questions. Markers will not give additional marks for the same point expressed in a slightly different way.

In each examination it is clear that a minority of candidates is significantly under-prepared for the examination. Such candidates, who have virtually no chance of passing, bring down the average pass rate. Well-prepared candidates who have conscientiously studied all syllabus areas and who have done plenty of practice questions, will be able to pass, and should not be deterred by apparently low historic pass rates.

It is important to read the PEGs as they provide useful guidance on what not to do if you wish to pass the examination. They are likely to be of particular use and relevance to those candidates who are not able to attend any formal tuition sessions and whose studying comprises this *Learning System* only.

1.4 Summary

This introductory chapter lists the examinable accounting standards.

All candidates are advised to read the post-examination guidance (PEGs) which are made available on the CIMA website. Section 1.3 of the chapter identifies some of the key points from the PEGs covering the 2005, 2006 and 2007 Financial Analysis examinations; however, many of the points cover issues relating to examinable areas that are vital in F2 and so are highly relevant.

Accounting for Investments

Accounting for Investments

2

Learning Outcomes

After studying this chapter students should be able to:

- explain the relationships between investors and investees;
- explain the different levels of investment and the conditions required for significant influence, control and joint control;
- explain the circumstances in which a subsidiary is excluded from consolidation;
- explain and apply the principles of recognition of goodwill based on the fair value of assets at the date of acquisition.

Achievement of the above learning outcomes will contribute to the overall learning aim of syllabus area A.

2.1 Introduction

This chapter introduces the appropriate accounting for investments in other entities. The extent of the investment will often determine the appropriate accounting treatment and this chapter examines the investments that will be accounted for as:

- Simple investments
- Investments in associates
- Investments in subsidiaries
- Investments in joint ventures

The focus is mainly on accounting for subsidiaries as the rules and requirements outlined will form the basis of the applications in Chapters 3 and 4.

The accounting for fair values in consolidation and the recognition of goodwill are also covered in this chapter.

2.2 Accounting for investments

Entities will often invest in the equity of other businesses. The extent of the equity shareholding will normally determine how the investment is accounted for. The accounting treatment applied for investments is intended to reflect the importance of the investment in the financial statements of the investee and how the future performance and financial position might be affected by these investments. It follows then that the greater the level of investment the more detailed the financial information will be. A significant investment in another entity may require additional financial statements to be produced.

The accounting in the investees' *individual accounts* for all investments and for *simple investments* (commonly less than 20% of the total equity share capital of the entity invested in), will be determined by applying the recognition, measurement and disclosure requirements of the accounting standards that specifically deal with investments:

- IAS 32 Financial instruments: presentation
- IAS 39 Financial instruments: recognition and measurement
- IFRS 7 Financial instruments: disclosure

The provisions of these standards are dealt with in more detail in Chapter 11, however the basic impact on the financial statements will involve one entry in the statement of financial position (balance sheet) for *investments* and one entry in the income statement for *income* earned from these investments (dividend received).

2.3 Investment in associates

If an investor holds, directly or indirectly, 20% of the voting rights of an entity then it is normally considered an associated entity and is accounted for in accordance with IAS 28 *Investments in Associates*. IAS 28 states that there is a presumption that the investor has significant influence over the entity, unless it can be clearly demonstrated that this is not the case.

The key concept in the definition is 'significant influence'. IAS 28 explains that significant influence is the power to participate in the financial and operating policy decisions of the entity but is not control over those policies. The existence of significant influence by an investor is usually evidenced in one or more of the following ways:

- representation on the board of directors
- participation in policy-making processes
- material transactions between the investor and the entity
- interchange of managerial personnel
- provision of essential technical information.

The impact of this level of investment on the investing entity is likely to be greater than that of a simple investment. There is greater exposure to the results of the associate and a decline in its value will have a greater negative impact on the statement of financial position of the investing entity. The information provided therefore is a step further than that provided for simple investments.

The investment in the associate is equity accounted (covered in depth in Chapter 5) and the investment shown in the statement of financial position will include the investing entity's share of the gains of the associate from the date the investment was made. The investing entity will show the share of realised and recognised gains it is entitled to by virtue of this investment rather than just the dividend received.

2.4 Investment in subsidiaries

It is often the case that businesses conduct part of their operations by making investments in other business entities. For example, a business that aims to expand its market share could opt to purchase one or more of its competitors, rather than taking the slower route of building market share by gradual organic growth. Another example is where a business purchases an investment in one or more of its suppliers of key goods and services in order to integrate and secure its supply chain.

In order to fulfil the needs of investors and other users, additional information is likely to be required, and therefore the IASB has in issue several accounting standards setting out the principles and practices that must be followed where an investment comprises a significant proportion of the total equity of the investee entity.

2.4.1 The principle of control

This chapter will start to examine the accounting required under IFRS for investments in subsidiaries. The accounting standard that sets out the requirements for recognition of an entity as a subsidiary is IAS 27 *Consolidated and Separate Financial Statements*. This standard was revised in January 2008, but its basic principles have been part of IFRS for many years.

First, some relevant definitions taken from the standard:

A *parent* is an entity that has one or more subsidiaries.
A *subsidiary* is an entity, including an unincorporated entity such as a partnership, which is controlled by another entity (known as the parent).

The key concept in determining whether or not an investment constitutes a subsidiary is that of *control*.

Control is the power to govern the financial and operating policies of an entity so as to obtain benefit from its activities.

There is a presumption that control exists where the investor entity owns over half of the voting power of the other entity. If an investor entity, ABC, owns 55% of the voting share capital of entity DEF, in the absence of any special circumstances, ABC is presumed to be in control of DEF. The maximum investment that could be held by another investor is 45%, and so ABC will always have the capacity to win a vote over the other investor(s). The nature of the relationship between ABC and DEF is that of parent and subsidiary.

In most cases, control can be easily determined by looking at the percentage ownership of the ordinary share capital in the investee entity. Provided ownership is greater than 50% a parent/subsidiary relationship can be assumed. However, there are exceptions. A parent/ subsidiary relationship can exist even where the parent owns less than 50% of the voting power of the subsidiary since the key to the relationship is control. IAS 27 supplies the following instances:

When there is:

(a) power over more than half of the voting rights by virtue of an agreement with other investors;
(b) power to govern the financial and operating policies of the entity under a statute or agreement;
(c) power to appoint or remove the majority of the members of the board of directors or equivalent governing body and control of the entity is by that board or body; or
(d) power to cast the majority of votes at meetings of the board of directors or equivalent governing body and control of the entity is by that board or body.

The reason for describing the nature of control in such detail in IAS 27 is that entities have sometimes created ownership structures designed to evade the requirements for accounting for subsidiaries.

In the Financial Management examination, questions may be set that test understanding of the principle of control, and it is possible that you will be required to explain these conditions in a written question.

2.4.2 The requirement to prepare consolidated financial statements

Where a parent/subsidiary relationship exists, IAS 27 requires that the parent should prepare consolidated financial statements. It is important to realise from the outset that this is an additional set of financial statements. The parent and subsidiary continue to prepare their own financial statements. Therefore in a group comprising one parent and one subsidiary, a total of three sets of financial statements are required. Where a group comprises, say, the parent and four subsidiaries, a total of six sets of financial statements are required: one for the parent, one for each of the four subsidiaries and one set of consolidated financial statements.

2.4.3 Exclusion from preparing consolidated accounts

A full set of financial statements in addition to those already prepared is, of course, quite an onerous requirement. IAS 27 includes some exemptions, as follows:

A parent need not present consolidated financial statements if and only if:

(a) the parent is itself a wholly owned subsidiary, or is a partially-owned subsidiary of another entity and its other owners, including those not otherwise entitled to vote, have been informed about, and do not object to, the parent not presenting consolidated financial statements;
(b) the parent's debt or equity instruments are not traded in a public market (a domestic or foreign stock exchange or an over-the-counter market, including local and regional markets);

(c) the parent did not file, nor is it in the process of filing, its financial statements with a securities commission or other regulatory organisation for the purpose of issuing any class of instruments in a public market;
(d) the ultimate or any intermediate parent of the parent produces consolidated financial statements available for public use that comply with IFRS.

These provisions have been spelt out in some detail so as to minimise the risk of entities evading the accounting requirements. It will be apparent, though, that quite a lot of groups are not, in fact, required to prepare consolidated financial statements. This is particularly relevant where there are 'vertical' group structures, such as the one illustrated below:

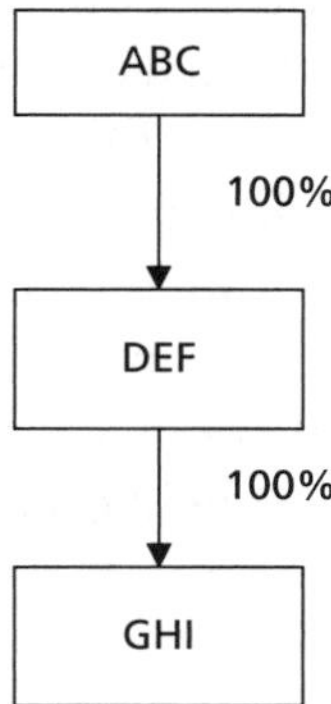

There are two groups within this structure:
the DEF group, where DEF owns 100% of its subsidiary, GHI.
the ABC group, where ABC owns 100% of its subsidiary DEF.

The IAS 27 exemption means that only one set of consolidated financial statements has to be prepared: for the ABC group. DEF is exempted from the requirement. If only 55% of the voting capital of DEF was owned by ABC, and non-controlling interests held the remaining 45%, DEF can still be exempted from the requirement to prepare consolidated financial statements provided that the non-controlling interests do not object.

The only other exemption from the requirement to consolidate is in respect of an investment in subsidiary that has been acquired exclusively with the intention of reselling it. The provisions of **IFRS 5** ***Non-current Assets Held for Sale and Discontinued Operations*** apply: the sale must be highly probable, i.e. there must be a plan to sell the asset and the asset must be actively marketed. The sale should be expected to qualify for recognition as a completed sale within one year of its classification as held for sale. It is not therefore possible for a parent's management to decide not to consolidate a subsidiary that has previously been consolidated on the grounds that they intend to sell it at some point in the future. It is obviously important to prevent this approach so that unscrupulous managers do not remove loss-making subsidiaries from the consolidation process.

2.4.4 Goodwill

When a controlling investment is made the parent is investing in the net assets of the subsidiary. The value of the assets presented on the statement of financial position is unlikely to be what is paid by the investing entity.

Usually, the owners of a profitable business will expect to receive more in exchange for the investment than its net asset value. This additional amount arises for various reasons. It is quite likely that the assets recognised in the statement of financial position do not represent all the assets of the firm but intangibles such as good reputation and customer loyalty may be worth something to the purchaser. The difference between the cost of investment and the fair value of the net assets acquired is known as **goodwill on acquisition**, and the accounting standard IFRS 3 *Business Combinations* requires its recognition in consolidated financial statements.

2.4.5 IFRS 3 *Business combinations*

IFRS 3 was originally issued in March 2004 replacing an earlier standard. However, it was just the first stage in a longer term IASB project on accounting for business combinations. The next stage culminated in the issue, in January 2008, of the revised version of IFRS 3.

IFRS 3 requires that entities should account for business combinations by applying the **acquisition method of accounting**. This involves recognising and measuring the identifiable assets acquired, the liabilities assumed and any non-controlling interest in the acquiree entity (the recognition and measurement of non-controlling interests will be explained in Chapter 3). Measurement should be at fair value on the date of acquisition. Where 100% of the equity of a subsidiary is acquired, goodwill on acquisition is calculated as follows:

Goodwill on acquisition is the aggregate of:
Consideration, measured at fair value
LESS
Net assets acquired (the fair value of identifiable assets acquired less liabilities assumed)

This measures goodwill on acquisition which is recognised in the consolidated financial statement of position within non-current assets. Goodwill on acquisition is an asset of the group (not of the individual entities within the group) and is subject to impairment reviews to ensure its value is not overstated. The goodwill arises at the date of acquisition and will not change unless impairment is identified, whereby it will be held net of impairment losses (which should be recognised in accordance with IAS 36 *Impairment of Assets*).

Practical application of recognising and measuring goodwill will be covered in the remaining chapters for Syllabus section A.

2.4.6 Fair values in acquisition accounting

IFRS 3 requires that whenever a group entity is consolidated for the first time the purchase consideration and the group share of the net assets of the acquired entity are measured at fair values. The difference between these two figures is goodwill. The purpose of a fair-value exercise is to apportion the consideration given by the parent to purchase the shares in the newly acquired entity to the net assets of the newly acquired entity for consolidation purposes. Any difference between the fair value of the consideration given and the fair values of the net assets acquired is goodwill on acquisition.

As far as the net assets of the acquired entity are concerned, the amounts that are initially consolidated should normally be restricted to net assets of the acquired entity that existed at the date of the acquisition. They should be recognised separately as at the date of acquisition if they satisfy IFRS 3's criteria for recognition:

- In the case of an asset other than an intangible asset, it is probable that any associated future economic benefits will flow to the acquirer, and its fair value can be measured reliably.

- In the case of a liability other than a contingent liability, it is probable that an outflow of resources embodying economic benefits will be required to settle the obligation, and its fair value can be measured reliably.
- It is an intangible asset that meets the IAS 38 *Intangible Assets* definition.
- In the case of a contingent liability, its fair value can be measured reliably.

General principles

Fair value is defined in IFRS 3 as:

> . . . the amount for which an asset could be exchanged or a liability settled between knowledgeable, willing parties in an arm's-length transaction.

As a general rule, fair value is market value. More detail regarding the fair valuation of specific assets and liabilities is given below.

The cost of a business combination should represent the fair values of assets given, liabilities incurred or assumed, and equity instruments issued by the acquirer, in exchange for control of the acquiree.

Fair value of consideration

Fair value must be measured at the date of the exchange. In cases where the acquisition is for the asset of cash, measurement of fair value is straightforward. However, in some cases the consideration offered will comprise equity shares, wholly or in part. Where this is the case, the shares must be valued at fair value. The published price at the date of exchange is the best evidence of fair value where the equity instruments are listed on a stock exchange. The only exception to this is if, for some reason, the market value of the relevant instrument at the date of acquisition is unusually high or low (e.g. if world events have resulted in a temporary significant downturn in market values of securities). In such circumstances it would be necessary to consider the market value of the instrument around the date of acquisition to arrive at a representative and realistic figure for fair value.

A special case involves contingent consideration:

Entity A might pay $8 million to acquire the shares of entity B, but the contract may be subject to a clause relating to contingent consideration which stipulates that if certain criteria are met in the first year of ownership (relating perhaps to profitability), a further $1 million will be payable to the former shareholders of B. Where an element of the consideration is contingent on future events, that element should be included in the overall cost of the acquisition if the adjustment is probable and can be measured reliably. Occasionally the terms of the agreement may be such that it is impossible to say whether, and if so how much, additional consideration will be paid, and in such circumstances, the group accounts may have to simply disclose the matter, rather than by making provision. The fair value of the contingent consideration should be based on the present value of future consideration payable.

Any costs incurred in the business combination (legal fees, etc.) will be written off as expenses in the period.

Costs of issuing financial instruments in connection with the acquisition should *not* be included as part of the fair value of consideration. Instead, they are included as part of the initial measurement of the financial instrument, in accordance with IAS 39 (see Chapter 11).

Property, plant and equipment

Fair value should be based on depreciated market value unless (in the case of plant and equipment) there is no evidence of market value because of the specialised nature of the plant and equipment or because it is rarely traded, except as part of a continuing business. In such cases fair value should be based on depreciated replacement cost.

Inventories

Where inventories are replaced by purchases in a ready market, the fair value = market value. However, where, as in the case of manufactured inventories, there is no ready market fair value is the current cost to the acquiring entity of obtaining the same inventories. If no current cost figure is readily available (as may well be the case) it can be approximated by taking inventories at sales values less:

- costs to complete (for work-in-progress inventories)
- incidental costs of disposal
- a realistic allowance for profit.

Listed investments

In most cases, the price quoted at the date of exchange will represent fair value.

Intangible assets

The acquirer should recognise an intangible asset of the acquiree at the date of acquisition provided that it meets the definition of an intangible asset provided by IAS 38 *Intangible Assets*, and that it can be measured reliably. Intangible assets must be separable (i.e. must be capable of being separated and divided from the entity and of being sold) or they must arise from contractual or legal rights.

Monetary assets and liabilities

The fair value should be based on the amounts due to be received or paid. For many monetary assets and liabilities, the fair value will be the amount at which they are stated in the subsidiary undertaking's statement of financial position at the date of exchange. However, the fair value of some long-term monetary items may be materially different from book value, for example, where an acquired entity is carrying material amounts of long-term borrowings at fixed rates that are not representative of current interest rates. Where fair value is materially different from book values, fair value should be used. It may be necessary, in respect of unlisted financial instruments, to estimate fair value by discounting to present value amounts expected to be received or paid.

Example 2.A

A newly acquired subsidiary has in issue $10 million 5% loan stock that is redeemable at par in 5 years' time. Current market interest rates are 8%. The relevant cash flows are $500,000 per year for 5 years in respect of interest and then a repayment of $10 million in 5 years' time. In order to approximate the fair value of the instrument these cash flows are discounted at 8%, as follows:

An annuity of $500, 000 for 5 years:
3.993 × 500, 000 = $1, 996, 500
Plus a payment of $10m in 5 years' time:
0.681 × $10m = $6, 810, 000
Total fair value = $8, 806, 500.

Provisions for restructuring

Only the identifiable assets, liabilities and contingent liabilities of the acquiree that exist at the year end date can be recognised separately by the acquirer as part of allocating the cost of the combination. IFRS 3 states that: 'future losses or other costs expected to be incurred as a result of a combination are not liabilities incurred or assumed by the acquirer in exchange for control of the acquiree, and are not, therefore, included as part of the cost of the combination'.

Contingent liabilities

Contingent liabilities, in accordance with IAS 37 *Provisions, Contingent Liabilities and Contingent Assets,* are not recognised in financial statements. However, by contrast, IFRS 3 requires that the contingent liabilities of an acquiree are recognised at fair value at the date of acquisition provided that their fair value can be measured reliably. Therefore, when calculating goodwill on acquisition, it is important to remember to include all measurable contingent liabilities. Note that contingent assets are not recognised by the acquiring entity.

2.5 Investment in joint ventures

Where an entity enters into an arrangement whereby control over an economic activity is shared between it and other parties, a joint venture arrangement exists. A joint venture can take a number of forms (will be covered in depth in Chapter 5), however one of those is where a new entity is formed and since that entity is under joint control it will be consolidated.

Again the method of accounting reflects the level of the investment made – it is greater than significant influence (associate) but not as much as full control (subsidiary). The joint venture will be consolidated but not using the full consolidation method. Instead IAS 31 *Interests in Joint Ventures* requires that joint ventures be proportionally consolidated. This will involve only aggregating the parent's share of the JV's assets, liabilities, revenues and expenses.

The practical application of proportionate consolidation will be covered in depth in Chapter 5.

2.6 Summary

This chapter has reviewed the accounting for investments and looked at how the different levels of investment warrant different accounting treatment. The introduction to accounting for subsidiaries included a review of the principles of control, how to determine fair values of assets and liabilities acquired and how to recognise goodwill on acquisition. The requirements that have to be met to be excluded from preparing consolidated financial statements were also covered.

This chapter covered some key principles in the consolidation process and you may find that you refer back to it as you progress through Chapters 3 to 9.

Revision Questions 2

The questions below are intended to be tests of understanding. They are not of exam standard as this area is likely to be tested within a question that also covers other technical areas.

Question 1

Where the purchase price of an acquisition is less than the aggregate fair value of the net assets acquired, which ONE of the following accounting treatments of the difference is required by IFRS 3 *Business Combinations*?

(A) Deduction from goodwill in the consolidated statement of financial position?
(B) Immediate recognition as a gain in the statement of changes in equity?
(C) Recognition in the statement of comprehensive income over its useful life?
(D) Immediate recognition as a gain in profit or loss.

Question 2

PQR holds several investments in subsidiaries. In December 20X5 it acquired 100T of the ordinary share capital of STU. PQR intends to exclude STU from consolidation in its group financial statements for the year ended 28 February 20X6, on the grounds that it does not intend to retain the investment in the longer term.

Explain, with reference to the relevant International Financial Reporting Standard, the conditions relating to exclusion of this type of investment from consolidation.

Question 3

On 30 September 20X5 GHI purchased 80% of the ordinary share capital of JKL for $1.45 million. The book value of JKL's net assets at the date of acquisition was $1.35 million. A valuation exercise showed that the fair value of JKL's property, plant and equipment at that date was $100,000 greater than book value, and JKL immediately incorporated this revaluation into its own books. JKL's financial statements at 30 September 20X5 contained notes referring to a contingent liability (with a fair value of $200,000).

GHI acquired JKL with the intention of restructuring the latter's production facilities. The restructuring plan, including a detailed estimate of costs, was well advanced at 30 September 20X5. The estimated costs totalled $115,000.

Calculate goodwill on acquisition, and identify any of the above items that should be excluded from the calculation in accordance with IFRS 3 *Business Combinations*.

Question 4

AB purchase 100% of the equity share capital of CD and at the date of acquisition the net assets of CD were reviewed and the following is discovered:

1. The intangible non-current assets of CD at the acquisition date, consist of the estimated value of a brand that is associated with the entity. This estimate has been made by the directors and no reliable external estimate of the market value of the brand is available.
2. Relevant details of tangible non-current assets of CD are:

Description	*SOFP carrying value* $'000	*Market value* $'000	*Depreciated replacement cost* $'000	*Recoverable amount* $'000
Property	10,000	12,000	Not given	13,500
Plant	10,000	Not given	11,000	14,000

3. Inventories of CD comprise:
   - Obsolete inventory (year end value: $500,000). This inventory has a net realisable value of $300,000.
   - The balance of inventory (statement of financial position value: $3,500,000). This inventory has a net realisable value of $4,200,000. A reasonable profit allowance for the sale of the inventory would be $400,000.
4. The provision of $1 million in the statement of financial position of CD is against the reorganisation costs expected to be incurred in integrating the entity into the Sea group. These costs would not be necessary if CD were to remain outside the group. Although the plan was agreed by the board of directors before the acquisition date, it was not made known to those affected by the plan until after that date.

Discuss how the above will affect the fair value of the identifiable net assets in calculating goodwill.

Question 5

On 31 July 20X7, AGR acquired 80% of the ordinary share capital of its subsidiary BLK. The book value of BLK's net assets at the date of acquisition was $1,300,000. This value included $300,000 in respect of certain specialised items of plant, which were bought on 31 July 20X4. The plant is being depreciated on a straight line basis over 6 years with an assumption of nil residual value. No estimate of market value at the date of acquisition is available, but it would cost $700,000 to replace the plant at current prices.

Since 20X5, BLK has been developing a specialised industrial process. Following registration of the patent and some coverage in the trade press, BLK received an offer for the patent of $150,000 in April 20X7. The offer was rejected. BLK does not recognise the patent as an asset. AGR's directors think it probable that other processes developed by BLK have a market value, and they have made a broad estimate of $75,000 to cover such items which have not been capitalised by BLK.

Shortly before the acquisition of BLK took place, its directors had started a programme to rationalise production. The estimate cost of the programme was $250,000, but no provision for it was recognised in the entity's financial statements at 31 July 20X7. The programme has continued and is now (November 20X7) substantially complete.

Calculate the fair value of BLK's net assets that would be included in the consolidated statement of financial position of AGR at 31 July 20X7, assuming that there are no relevant issues other than those given above. If appropriate, explain your reasons for excluding any of the possible adjustments to fair value.

Solutions to Revision Questions

Solution 1

The correct answer is (D).

Solution 2

According to IFRS 5 *Non-Current Assets held for Sale and Discontinued Operations*, a subsidiary that has been acquired and is held exclusively with a view to its subsequent disposal, does not require consolidation. However, the investment can be regarded as 'held for sale' only if its disposal is intended to take place within 12 months of the date of statement of financial position. In the case of PQR's investment in STU, the disposal would have to take place before 28 February 20X7.

Solution 3

Goodwill on acquisition

	$	$
Investment in JKL		1,450,000
Acquired:		
Net assets at book value	1,350,000	
Revaluation	100,000	
Contingent liability	(200,000)	
	1,250,000	
80% of fair value of net assets		1,000,000
Goodwill on acquisition		450,000

According to IFRS 3, restructuring provisions can be taken into account only if the acquiree has an existing liability for restructuring recognised in accordance with IAS 37 *Provisions, Contingent Liabilities and Contingent Assets*. This condition is not met in this case.

Solution 4

1. No value should be attached to the intangible asset when determining fair value of net assets acquired since there is no reliable market value.
2. The fair value of the property should be based on the market value of $12,000,000.

3. The obsolete inventories should be included at the NRV of $300,000. The remaining inventories are carried at $3,500,000, however the fair value can be taken as the sales value less realistic allowance for profit. The fair value of these inventories is therefore $3,800,000.
4. No amount should be included for the provision. Although the plan is approved it has not been communicated to those that will be affected (e.g. employees, customers, suppliers, etc.) and so as per IAS 37 no constructive obligation exists. IFRS 3 only allows provisions where there is a constructive obligation.

Solution 5

	$'000
Book value before adjustment	1,300
Fair value adjustment for PPE: replacement cost of $700,000 less 3/6 years depreciation = $350,000	
Uplift in value: $350,000 − 300,000	50
Recognition of intangible asset	150
Provision for rationalisation programme	(250)
Fair value at 31 July 20X7	1,250

The director's valuation of $75,000 in respect of other patents has been excluded from the fair value calculation because (i) there appears to be insufficient evidence that the intangibles are separable; and (ii) the broad general estimate probably does not meet the requirement that such assets should be measured reliably.

The Consolidated Statement of Financial Position

The Consolidated Statement of Financial Position

3

Learning Outcomes

After studying this chapter students should be able to:

- prepare a consolidated statement of financial position;
- account for non-controlling interests;
- account for the effects of intra-group balances and transactions in the consolidated statement of financial position;
- apply the concepts of fair value at the date of acquisition.

3.1 Introduction

This chapter builds upon the foundations established in Chapter 2, and applies the principles of full consolidation in Section 3.2 and prepares a consolidated statement of financial position, firstly for a simple group scenario, including:

- Elimination of the investment on consolidation
- Recognition goodwill on acquisition.

The chapter continues with the preparation of the consolidated statement of financial position, incorporating the more common complexities in group accounting, including:

- Accounting for partly owned subsidiaries (Section 3.3)
- Accounting for the effects of transactions between group entities Sections (3.4 and 3.5)
- Accounting for adjustments to fair values at the date of acquisition (Section 3.7).

Adjustments may be required to achieve uniform accounting policies between parent and subsidiary, and this is covered in Section 3.6.

3.2 Applying the principles of consolidation: the consolidated statement of financial position

Consolidated financial statements represent the performance and position of the combined group entities as if they were a single economic entity. All the results and the assets and liabilities that are under the control of the parent are combined together to show single totals for each item in the financial statements. This means that the revenue and expenses, assets and liabilities of the entities in the group are added together, line by line. So, if a parent's revenue for the year is $2m and its only subsidiary has revenue for the year of $1m, group revenue is reported on a single line in the consolidated income statement at $3m.

Of course, the process involved is not quite as simple as this implies, and various complexities will be gradually explained in the next few chapters of the *Learning System*. For the moment, however, we will concentrate on only one of the financial statements: the consolidated statement of financial position, and the figures and facts in the example below will be kept very simple so that the basic principles can be demonstrated.

Example 3.A

On 31 December 20X0 A purchased all of the shares of B for $25,000. The statements of financial positions of the individual entities at that date were:

	A	*B*
	$	$
Non-current assets		
Property, plant and equipment	60,000	20,000
Investment	25,000	–
	85,000	20,000
Net current assets	15,000	5,000
	100,000	25,000
Equity		
Share capital	50,000	10,000
Retained earnings	50,000	15,000
	100,000	25,000

Solution

In this introductory example A has paid $25,000 for the investment in 100% of B. B's equity has a book value of $25,000. The objective is to prepare a consolidated statement of financial position that recognises the assets and liabilities over which A now has control. This means combining the asset and liability figures. For example, the consolidated figure for property, plant and equipment is calculated by adding across that line: $60,000 + $20,000 = $80,000.

However, it is important to ensure that assets and liabilities are not double counted. It would be incorrect to include both A's investment in B and the assets and liabilities represented by that investment, and so the investment in B is eliminated. The net asset side of the statement of financial position therefore is as follows:

A Group: consolidated statement of financial position at 31 December 20X0

	$	Comment
Non-current assets		
Property, plant and equipment	80,000	A + B
Investment in B	–	Eliminated – B's net assets recognised instead
Net current assets	20,000	A + B
	100,000	

The equity side of the consolidated statement of financial position shows the share capital of the parent only. Consolidated retained earnings consist of the total of:

The retained earnings of the parent

The post-acquisition retained earnings of the subsidiary

	$	*Comment*
Equity		
Share capital	50,000	A only
Retained earnings	50,000	A + post-acquisition retained earnings of B-$50,000 + $0
	100,000	

Because the investment was bought on the last day of the financial year, post-acquisition earnings in the subsidiary are $0. This will, of course, not usually be the case.

This consolidated statement of financial position shows the effect of a single consolidation adjustment: the investment in B shown in A's statement of financial position has been eliminated against the share capital and retained earnings of B:

DR Share capital and retained earnings of B	25,000
CR Investment in B	25,000

After the initial acquisition, earnings will be made in B. The group share of post-acquisition earnings (in this case 100%) will form part of the total of consolidated retained earnings, balanced by increases in net assets on the other side of the statement of financial position in the future.

The example below demonstrates the preparation of the consolidated statement of financial position one year after the initial acquisition.

Example 3.B

Statement of financial positions at 31 December 20X1

	A	*B*
	$	$
Non-current assets		
Property, plant and equipment	65,000	24,000
Investment	25,000	–
	90,000	24,000
Net current assets	20,000	6,000
	110,000	30,000
Equity		
Share capital	50,000	10,000
Retained earnings	60,000	20,000
	110,000	30,000

Solution

Note that the investment has remained exactly the same in the individual statement of financial position of A. This would normally be the case, unless impairment had taken place.

This means, however, that the elimination of the investment against the equity of B leaves a difference of $5,000 ($25,000 is set against a total of $30,000). This difference is post-acquisition retained earnings which will be reflected as part of consolidated retained earnings.

The same principles as before are following in preparing the consolidated statement of financial position for the A Group:

A Group: consolidated statement of financial position at 31 December 20X1

	$	*Comment*
Non-current assets		
Property, plant and equipment	89,000	A + B
Investment in B	–	Eliminated – B's net assets recognised instead
Net current assets	26,000	A + B
	115,000	
Equity		
Share capital	50,000	A only
Retained earnings	65,000	A ($60,000 + post-acquisition reserves in B $5,000)
	110,000	

3.2.1 Goodwill

In Example 3.A a subsidiary with a net asset value of $25,000 was acquired for exactly $25,000. This involved two simplifying assumptions:

(a) the investment in B could be acquired from its owners for exactly the amount of net assets in the statement of financial position; and
(b) the carrying value of net assets was equivalent to its fair value.

It will, in practice, hardly ever be the case that both of these conditions exist. Usually, the owners of a profitable business will expect to receive more in exchange for the investment than its net asset value. This additional amount arises for various reasons. It is quite likely that the assets recognised in the statement of financial position do not represent all the assets of the firm but intangibles such as good reputation and customer loyalty may be worth something to the purchaser. The difference between the cost of investment and the fair value of the net assets acquired is known as goodwill on acquisition. The requirements of IFRS 3 relating to the recognition of goodwill were discussed in Chapter 2.

Where 100% of the equity of a subsidiary is acquired, goodwill on acquisition is calculated as follows:

The aggregate of: consideration, measured at fair value
LESS
Net assets acquired (the fair value of identifiable assets acquired less liabilities assumed)

Example 3.C

C acquired 100% of the equity share capital of D on 31 December 20X2. The statements of financial positions of the two entities at that date were as shown below:

Statement of financial position at 31 December 20X2

	C	D
	$	$
Non-current assets		
Property, plant and equipment	100,000	30,000
Investment	50,000	–
	150,000	30,000
Net current assets	50,000	10,000
	200,000	40,000
Equity		
Share capital	50,000	10,000
Retained earnings	150,000	30,000
	200,000	40,000

Note: The fair value of D's net current assets was the same as carrying value at 31 December 20X2. The fair value of the property, plant and equipment was $32,000.

Prepare the consolidated statement of position at 31 December 20X2.

Solution

Working
1. Calculation of goodwill on acquisition

	$	$
Consideration		50,000
Net assets acquired, at fair value		
Property, plant and equipment	32,000	
Net current assets	10,000	
Total identifiable net assets		42,000
Goodwill		8,000

C Group: consolidated statement of financial position at 31 December 20X2

	$	*Comment*
Non-current assets		
Goodwill	8,000	See working 1
Property, plant and equipment	132,000	100,000 + 30,000 + 2,000 (Fair value adjustment)
Investment in D	–	Eliminated – D's net assets recognised instead
		50,000 + 10,000
Net current assets	60,000	
	200,000	
Equity		
Share capital	50,000	C only
Retained earnings	150,000	Retained earnings of C
Total assets	200,000	

Some points to note:

1. The revaluation of D's property, plant and equipment has been accounted for in the calculation of goodwill. No revaluation reserve is required in the consolidated financial statements. The adjustment to fair value has been recognised in the consolidated financial statements in order to comply with IFRS 3. However, it need not necessarily be recognised in D's own financial statements – recognition will depend upon D's accounting policies.
2. The retained earnings at 31 December 20X2 are those of C, the parent, only. This is because the acquisition has taken place on that day. Remember that in subsequent consolidated statements of position consolidated retained earnings will comprise the retained earnings of the parent plus its share of the post-acquisition retained earnings in the subsidiary.
3. An alternative way of calculating goodwill is to deduct the value of equity plus or milnus any adjustments in respect of fair value from the consideration:

	$	$
Consideration		50,000
Less:		
Equity acquired	40,000	
Fair value adjustment	2,000	
		42,000
Goodwill		8,000

This method is likely to be quicker than listing all the assets and liabilities acquired.

3.2.2 Bargain purchases

Occasionally, it happens that the amount of consideration paid for an investment in a subsidiary is less than the aggregate of the fair value of net assets acquired. The difference between the two amounts, rather than giving rise to an asset, goodwill, is a credit balance. This difference is sometimes referred to as 'negative goodwill'. Where this occurs, the acquiring entity must reassess the assets and liabilities acquired to ensure that all are included, and that they are appropriately measured. If, after this exercise, there is still a credit balance, IFRS 3 requires that the acquirer should recognise the credit as a gain through profit or loss on the date of acquisition.

3.3 Non-controlling interests

The examples in this chapter so far have all involved a parent company acquiring 100% of the voting share capital of a subsidiary. However, control of a subsidiary can be acquired with a partial acquisition (which will usually involve a purchase of something in excess of 50% of the issued equity share capital). The consequence of a partial acquisition is that a part of the shareholding in the subsidiary continues to be held by one or more parties external to the group. This part of the shareholding is designated as 'non-controlling interests' (NCI) by IFRS 3 (revised). (Note: Prior to the revision of IFRS 3 in January 2008 'non-controlling interests' were referred to as 'minority interests' and this may be the term you find used in older examples and other textbooks.)

3.3.1 Accounting for non-controlling interests

Earlier in the chapter the following accounting technique for acquisitions was explained:

All the results and the assets and liabilities that are under the control of the parent are combined together to show single totals for each item in the financial statements. This means that the revenue and expenses, assets and liabilities of the entities in the group are added together, line by line.

The existence of NCI makes no difference at all to the application of the principle of control. The assets and liabilities of the subsidiary are under the control of the parent regardless of the fact that NCI exist, and therefore the revenue and expenses, assets and liabilities of the entities in the group are added together, line by line.

NCI are recognised within equity in the consolidated financial statements. IFRS (revised) permits a choice of accounting treatment for the measurement of NCI:

Either:

(a) NCI should be measured at fair value; or
(b) NCI should be measured at the proportionate share of the acquiree's identifiable net assets.

A great deal of discussion preceded the issue of IFRS 3 (revised) on the issue of measurement of NCI. The IASB would have preferred to have option (a) as the only treatment, however many of its constituents objected because it would be difficult and expensive to undertake this measurement exercise. Where the equity instruments of the subsidiary are themselves quoted on an active market, the exercise of valuing NCI is straightforward. If not, it is likely to involve estimation and assumptions about (eg.) an appropriate discounting for the fact the interests are non-controlling and therefore worth less.

Because of the controversy, IFRS 3 (revised) offers a choice of accounting treatments as illustrated in the example below.

Example 3.D

The statements of financial positions of E and its subsidiary F at 31 December 20X3 were as follows:

	E	*F*
	$	$
Non-current assets		
Property, plant and equipment	90,000	25,000
Investment	32,000	–
	122,000	25,000
Net current assets	38,000	14,000
	160,000	39,000
Equity		
Share capital ($1 shares)	80,000	20,000
Retained earnings	80,000	19,000
	160,000	39,000

E acquired 18,000 shares in F on 31 December 20X0 when F's retained earnings were $10,000.

Required: prepare the consolidated statement of financial position for the E group as at 31 December 20X3, under each of the two following assumptions:

1. It is the E group's policy to value non-controlling interests at acquisition at its proportionate share of the fair value of the subsidiary's identifiable net assets.
2. It is the E group's policy to value non-controlling interests at fair value. The fair value of the NCI in F at the date of acquisition was estimated to be $2,500.

Note: It can be assumed that no fair value adjustments were required to F's net assets at the date of acquisition.

Solution – assumption 1

First, the group structure must be established. E owns 18,000 of the 20,000 shares of F: a shareholding of 90%. This means that the NCI is 10% (100% – 90%).

Workings

1. *Non-controlling interests*
   This is 10% of the net assets of F at 31 December 20X3: 10% × $39,000 = $3,900.
2. *Goodwill on consolidation*

	$	$
Consideration		32,000
Net assets at date of acquisition:		
Share capital ($1 shares)	20,000	
Retained earnings	10,000	
Group share (90%)		27,000
Goodwill		5,000

3. *Retained earnings*

	$
Retained earnings of E	80,000
90% of post-acquisition retained earnings of F: 90% × ($19,000 – $10,000)	8,100
	88,100

E Group: consolidated statement of financial position at 31 December 20X3

	$	*Comment*
Non-current assets		
Goodwill	5,000	See working 2
Property, plant and equipment	115,000	90,000 + 25,000
	120,000	
Net current assets	52,000	38,000 + 14,000
	172,000	
Equity attributable to owners of the parent		
Share capital	80,000	E only
Retained earnings	88,100	See working 3
	168,100	
Non-controlling interests	3,900	See working 1
	172,000	

Solution – assumption 2

Workings

1. *Goodwill on consolidation*

	$
Consideration transferred	32,000
NCI at fair value	2,500
	34,500
Net assets at acquisition:	
Share capital	(20,000)
Retained earnings	(10,000)
Goodwill on acquisition	4,500

2. *Non-controlling interests*
NCI at 31 December 20X3 = NCI at date of acquisition + share of post-acquisition profits:

At date of acquisition	2,500
Post-acquisition profit share:	
10% × ($19,000 − $10,000)	900
At 31 December 20X3	3,400

3. *Retained earnings*

	$
Retained earnings of E	80,000
Post-acquisition retained earnings:	
($19,000 − $10,000) × group share 90%	8,100
	88,100

E Group: consolidated statement of financial position at 31 December 20X3

	$	*Comment*
Non-current assets		
Goodwill	4,500	See working 1
Property, plant and equipment	115,000	90,000 + 25,000
	119,500	
Net current assets	52,000	38,000 + 14,000
	171,500	
Equity attributable to owners of the parent		
Share capital	80,000	E only
Retained earnings	88,100	See working 3
	168,100	
Non-controlling interest	3,400	See working 1
	171,500	

It should be noted that NCI are treated as part of total equity. The other constituent part of equity is described in the statement of financial position above as 'equity attributable to owners of the parent', which is the description used in IAS 1.

Note also that the value of goodwill changes because of the valuation at fair value of NCI. This is because the fair value of NCI is lower (in this example) than the attributable share of net assets worked out on a simple percentage basis. This means that, in fair value terms, the value of net assets acquired by E is greater, and therefore goodwill on consolidation is lower.

In F2, the examination questions will state which of the permitted treatments is to be applied. Where the fair value option is to be followed, the fair value of NCI will be given.

3.4 The elimination of intra-group balances

IAS 27 requires that:

'Intragroup balances, transactions, income and expenses should be eliminated in full'.

Intragroup balances are likely to arise where the parent and subsidiary entities trade with each other. The consolidated financial statements present the results and position of the parent entity and its subsidiary (or subsidiaries) as if they were a single combined entity. Therefore, where balances appear in both a parent and subsidiary statement of financial position, they must be eliminated against each other on consolidation. If this were not done, elements such as receivables and payables would be overstated.

The balances should be cancelled out against each other as part of the consolidation process. Where there are items in transit (usually cash or inventory) the balances may not cancel entirely. Any surplus must be recognised as an in-transit item in the consolidated statement of financial position.

Example 3.E

The statements of financial positions of A and B as at 31.12.X7 are as follows:

	A		*B*	
	$	$	$	$
ASSETS				
Non-current assets				
Investment in B (note 1)		15,000		
Property, plant and equipment		30,000		15,000
Current assets				
Inventories	10,000		5,000	
Receivables (note 2)	12,000		6,000	
		22,000		11,000
		67,000		26,000
EQUITY + LIABILITIES				
Equity				
Issued capital		40,000		10,000
Retained earnings		14,000		8,000
Current liabilities		54,000		18,000
Trade payables (note 2)	8,000		4,000	
Bank overdraft	5,000		4,000	
		13,000		8,000
		67,000		26,000

Notes

1. A bought 75% of the shares in B on 31.12.X4 when the retained earnings of B stood at $4,000. Since that date, there has been no impairment of goodwill on consolidation.
2. The receivables of A include $3,000 in respect of goods supplied to B in the last few months of the year. The payables of B include $2,000 payable to A. You ascertain that on 30.12.X7 B sent a payment of $1,000 to A. This payment was received and recorded by A on 3.1.X8.
3. It is the group's policy to value non-controlling interests at acquisition at its proportionate share of the fair value of the subsidiary's identifiable net assets. (i.e. not at fair value)

Prepare the consolidated statement of financial position as at 31.12.X7.

Solution

Before starting to prepare the consolidated statement of financial position it is worth noting that:

- Since B is a 75% subsidiary, the non-controlling interests is 25%.
- The intra-group balances differ by $1,000 ($3,000 − $2,000). The difference is clearly caused by the cash in transit of $1,000.

  We now proceed to prepare the consolidated statement of financial position.

A Group: Consolidated statement of financial position at 31 December 20X7

	$	$	
ASSETS			
Non-current assets			
Goodwill		4,500	See working 2
Property, plant and equipment		45,000	A + B
		49,500	

Current assets			
Inventories	15,000		A + B
Receivables	15,000		A + B − $3,000
Cash in transit	1,000		The reconciling item
		31,000	
		80,500	
EQUITY + LIABILITIES			
Equity			
Issued capital		40,000	A only
Retained earnings		17,000	See working 3
		57,000	
Non-controlling interests		4,500	See working 1
		61,500	
Current liabilities			
Trade payables	10,000		A + B − $2,000
Bank overdraft	9,000		A + B
		19,000	
		80,500	

Workings

1. *Non-controlling interests*
   25% × $18,000 = $4,500
2. *Goodwill*

	$	$
Cost of investment		15,000
Net assets at the date of acquisition		
Issued capital	10,000	
Retained earnings	4,000	
	14,000	
Group share (75%)		(10,500)
Total goodwill		4,500

3. *Retained earnings*

	$
Retained earnings of A	14,000
75% of post-acquisition retained earnings of B ($8,000 − $4,000)	3,000
	17,000

3.4.1 Intragroup loans and preference shares

Example 3.A deals with intragroup balances that arise in respect of trading. It is also, however, possible that intragroup balances arise because one group entity holds loans or preference shares in another group entity.

Changes brought about by IAS 32 *Financial Instruments: Presentation* regarding classifications of financial instruments resulted in the majority of preference shares being classified as loan instruments (liabilities) rather than equity instruments (this is explained in more detail in Chapter 11 of this *Learning System*. This means that loans and preference shares in practice are likely to be dealt with in the same way. The long-term receivable in one entity corresponds with the long-term payable in another and for group accounting purposes they cancel each other out. (Example 3.F in the next section of this chapter demonstrates how this is done.)

3.5 The treatment of unrealised profits on assets bought from group companies

IAS 27 explains that profits and losses arising from intra-group transactions that are recognised in assets, such as inventory and non-current assets, should be eliminated in full. These are commonly known as unrealised profits because, from a group point of view, the profit on such transactions has not yet been realised. Suppose that an entity D habitually purchases inventory from its parent, A. A makes a profit on the sale which is recognised upon despatch of the goods to D. This is fine for the purposes of entity-level financial statements for A and D. However, the A group accounts present the results and position of the group as if it were a single entity. It would be incorrect to artificially boost the profits of this single entity by including profit made on transfers of inventories or other assets between the constituent entities, and therefore they must be eliminated as part of the consolidation process. Profit on such transactions cannot be recognised until the inventories or other assets are sold outside the group, at which point the profits are realised from a group point of view.

Taking the example of A and D a little further:

Example 3.F

D sells inventories to A at a standard profit margin of 25%. At the group's year end of 31 December, the inventories of A include goods purchased from D at cost to A of $12,500.

Assumption 1: D is a wholly owned subsidiary of A.
What is the amount of the adjustment to eliminate intra-group profits?

Solution

First, the amount of profit made by D must be established. The goods at cost to A are $12,500. D's profit margin is 25% which means that the value in A of $12,500 represents 125% of cost to D.

Profit made by D = 25/125 × $12,500 = $2,500

Inventories in A, from a group accounting perspective, are therefore overstated by $2,500 as is profit in D. The consolidation adjustment required is:

DR Consolidated profits	2,500	
CR Consolidated inventories		2,500

Assumption 2: D is 80% owned by A and non-controlling interests (NCI) hold the remaining 20% of the equity share capital of D. All other facts remain the same.

Solution

The amount of profit in D arising from the intra-group transaction is as before. However, only 80% of the profits arising in the subsidiary are attributable to the group, and the NCI take credit for the remainder of 20%. IAS 27 requires that profits and losses arising from this type of transaction are eliminated in full which means that the credit to consolidated inventories must be for the full $2,500. In this case, though, because of the existence of NCI, the debit entry is split to give the following consolidation adjustment:

DR Consolidated profits	2,000	
DR NCI	500	
CR Consolidated inventories		2,500

In this example the sale has been from the subsidiary to the parent entity, which potentially brings in the complication of non-controlling interests. Where the position is reversed and the parent sells to the subsidiary, the intra-group profit is recorded in the parent entity, and therefore the issue of non-controlling interests is irrelevant.

If the positions had been reversed in this example, with A selling to D, the consolidation adjustment would be simply:

DR Consolidated profits	2,500	
CR Consolidated inventories		2,500

The example below is a comprehensive example that includes consolidation adjustments in respect of elimination of intra-group payables and receivables, both long term and short term and the elimination of intra-group profits.

Example 3.G

The statements of financial positions of A and B as at 31.12.X7 are as follows:

	C		*D*	
	$	$	$	$
ASSETS				
Non-current assets				
Property, plant and equipment		145,000		50,000
Investments		53,000		–
		198,000		50,000
Current assets				
Inventories	40,000		30,000	
Trade receivables	45,000		17,600	
Intra-group receivables	–		2,500	
Cash at bank	17,000		9,900	
		102,000		60,000
		300,000		110,000
EQUITY AND LIABILITIES				
Equity				
Ordinary ($1) shares		100,000		40,000
Retained earnings		90,000		32,000
		190,000		72,000
Non-current liabilities				
Preference shares	50,000		10,000	
5% borrowings	20,000		10,000	
		70,000		20,000
Current liabilities				
Trade payables	39,000		18,000	
Intra-group payables	1,000		–	
		40,000		18,000
		300,000		110,000

Notes

1. The investment by C in D was acquired as follows:

	$
30,000 ordinary shares of $1	44,000
4,000 preference shares	4,000
5,000 5% borrowings	5,000
	53,000

   The ordinary shares were acquired when the retained earnings of D were $12,000. Since acquisition there has been no impairment of goodwill.

2. A remittance of $1,500, sent by C to D on 30.12.X2, was not recorded in the books of D until 4.1.X3.
3. Goods had been sold at normal selling price by D to C during the year. The total sales of such goods during the year were $80,000. The inventory of C at 31.12.X2 contained goods purchased from D at a selling price of $16,000. D earns 20% profit margin on its sales to H.
4. At the year end there was no liability outstanding in respect of loan interest or preference share dividends payable.
5. It is the group's policy to value non-controlling interests at acquisition at its proportionate share of the fair value of the subsidiary's identifiable net assets.

Requirement: prepare a consolidated statement of financial position at 31.12.X2.

Solution

The following points are important:

1. C owns 75% of the ordinary shares, 40% of the preference shares and 50% of the borrowings in D. Only the ordinary shares are relevant for determining C's interest in its subsidiary. The preference shares and borrowings are both liabilities, which will be eliminated in part. The balances left over after elimination represent the investment by investors outside of the group, and will be included in the group's long-term liabilities.
2. There is a difference on intra-group balances of $1,500 (the receivable of D is $2,500 while the payable of C is $1,000. The difference is due to cash in transit between C and D).
3. The inventory of C contains goods costing C $16,000 that were purchased from D. D made a profit of $3,200 on these goods ($16,000 × 20%). From the group's perspective the profit on these goods will not be realised until the goods are sold outside the group. Therefore an adjustment must be made to the closing consolidated inventory figure to ensure that it is included at cost to the group. There is no need to adjust consolidated inventory for goods that have been sold by one group company to another and that have been then sold on outside the group. As far as the group is concerned, profit on the sale of these inventories has been recognised. The unrealised profit adjustment is made in respect only of inventories sold intra-group that remain in the group at the year end.

The consolidated statement of financial position of the C group as at 31.12.X2 is as follows:

	$	$	*Comments*
ASSETS			
Non-current assets			
Goodwill		5,000	See working 1
Property, plant and equipment		195,000	C + D
		200,000	
Current assets			
Inventories	66,800		$40,000 + $30,000 − $3,200 (see note 3 above)
Trade receivables	62,600		C + D
Cash in transit	1,500		See note 2 above
Cash at bank	26,900		
		157,800	
		357,800	
EQUITY AND LIABILITIES			
Equity			
Share capital		100,000	C only
Consolidated retained earnings		102,600	See working 2
		202,600	
Non-controlling interests		17,200	See working 3
Non-current liabilities			
Preference shares	56,000		See working 4
5% borrowings	25,000		See working 4
		81,000	
Current liabilities			
Trade payables		57,000	C + D
		357,800	

Workings

1. *Goodwill*

	$	$
Cost of investment in ordinary shares		44,000
Net assets at the date of acquisition:		
Share capital (75% × $40,000)	30,000	
Reserves (75% × $12,000)	9,000	
		(39,000)
Goodwill		5,000

2. *Consolidated retained earnings*

	$
C	90,000
D (75% × 32,000 − 12,000)	15,000
75% × unrealised profit in inventory (75% × $3,200)	(2,400)
	102,600

3. *Non-controlling interests*

	$
25% × net assets (25% × 72,000)	18,000
25% × unrealised profit in inventory (25% × $3,200)	(800)
	17,200

4. *Non-current liabilities*

	$ *Preference Shares*	$ *Borrowings*
C	50,000	20,000
D ($10,000 − 4,000)	6,000	
D ($10,000 − 5,000)		5,000
	56,000	25,000

3.5.1 Intra-group trading in non-current assets

The same principles are followed as explained above in respect of inventory. However, inventory is usually sold quickly, and can be expected to leave the group, thus realising profit to the group, shortly after the date of the statement of financial position.

The consequences of intra-group trading are somewhat more complicated where non-current assets are involved, because they are likely to continue to be recognised within the group entity for more than one accounting period.

Where there is unrealised profit on the intra-group sale of a non-current asset item consolidation adjustments must be made over the life of the asset in order to ensure that unrealised profit is eliminated.

The example below explains the required adjustments.

Example 3.H

E owns 75% of the equity shares of F. On 31.12.X0 (the year end date) E sold an item of plant to F for $120,000. The plant cost E $100,000 to manufacture. F depreciated the plant over a 5-year period starting from 1.1.X1. Show the carrying value of the plant in the consolidated statement of financial position as at 31.12.X0, 31.12.X1 and 31.12 .X2 and explain the relevant consolidation adjustments.

Solution

- 31.12.X0. The profit made by E is $20,000. This is unrealised from a group perspective since the asset has merely been transferred from one group entity to another. The cost *to the group* of this asset is $100,000 and this is what should appear in group property, plant and equipment. However, the property, plant and equipment of F will (quite correctly from the viewpoint of F as a separate entity) include the asset at a cost of $120,000. Therefore, given that we start the consolidated statement of financial position by aggregating the assets and liabilities from the individual statement of financial positions of the group companies, we need to make the following consolidation adjustment:

Credit	Property, plant and equipment	$20,000
Debit	Retained earnings	$20,000

There is no adjustment to the non-controlling interests since since the unrealised profit is made by the parent.

- **31.12.X1.** The asset will appear in the statement of financial position of F at a carrying amount of $96,000 [(4/5) × $120,000]. The carrying amount based on cost to the group is $80,000 [(4/5) × $100,000]. Therefore a consolidation adjustment of $16,000 is required at 31.12.X1. Once again the adjustment is to property, plant and equipment and consolidated retained earnings. Notice that the adjustment we are making on 31.12.X1 does not *add to* the adjustment made on 31.12.X0. This is the *equivalent adjustment* that is required on 31.12.X1.
- **31.12.X2.** The carrying amount of the asset in the books of F is $72,000 [(3/5) × $120,000] and the carrying amount based on cost to the group $60,000 [(3/5) × $100,000]. This means that the consolidation adjustment to property, plant and equipment and retained earnings on 31.12.X2 is $12,000. Over time the required adjustment reduces as the asset is used; the adjustment in this case reduces by $4,000 each year. This is the difference between the depreciation that will have been charged by F [(1/5) × $120,000 = $24,000] each year and the required amount based on cost to the group [(1/5) × $100,000 = $20,000].

The additional depreciation has been charged by the partly owned subsidiary and so the NCI is affected by its share of the adjustment for depreciation.

3.6 Adjustments to achieve uniformity of accounting policy

IAS 27 requires that consolidated financial statements should be prepared using uniform accounting policies for like transactions and other events.

It is quite possible to have a group in which entities adopt different accounting policies in their own financial statements, and there is nothing to prevent them from doing so. However, where this is the case consolidation adjustments are required in order to ensure that the consolidated financial statements all reflect the accounting policies of the parent.

Example 3.I demonstrates the adjustments required to align accounting policies.

Example 3.I

The statements of financial positions of G and its subsidiary H as at 31 December 20X3 are as follows:

	G	*H*
	$	$
Intangible asset (note)		15,000
Property, plant and equipment	40,000	35,000
Investment in H	50,000	
Net current assets	20,000	20,000
	110,000	70,000
Ordinary share capital	60,000	50,000
Retained earnings	50,000	20,000
	110,000	70,000

Note

1. G purchased 40,000 of the $1 shares of H on 1.1.X0 for $50,000 when the retained earnings of H showed a balance of $10,000. There has been no impairment of goodwill on consolidation since acquisition.
2. H has all the same accounting policies as G except as regards intangible assets. The intangible assets of H are all of a type whose recognition would not be permitted under IAS 38. IAS 38 is to be followed in preparing the consolidated financial statements. When G made its investment in H on 1.1.X0 the intangible assets of H included $7,500 that would not qualify for recognition under IAS 38.
3. It is the group's policy to value non-controlling interests at acquisition at its proportionate share of the fair value of the subsidiary's identifiable net assets.

Prepare the consolidated statement of financial position as at 31.12.X3. No adjustments are needed for intra-group balances or unrealised profit on inventory.

Solution

Before we proceed to the consolidated statement of financial position it is worth noting that G owns 80% of the shares of H (40,000 out of a total of 50,000). The adjustment required in respect of H to reflect the accounting policy difference has the following effects:

- Closing net assets and closing retained earnings are overstated by $15,000. This means that restated closing net assets are $55,000 ($70,000 – $15,000) and restated closing retained earnings are $5,000 ($20,000 – $15,000).
- Pre-acquisition retained earnings are overstated by $7,500. This means that restated pre-acquisition retained earnings are $2,500 ($10,000 – $7,500).

We now have a relatively straightforward consolidated statement of financial position.

	$	*Comments*
Goodwill	8,000	See working 2
Property, plant and equipment	75,000	G + H
Net current assets	40,000	G + H
	123,000	
Share capital	60,000	G only
Retained earnings	52,000	See working 3
	112,000	
Non-controlling interests	11,000	See working 1
	123,000	

Workings

1. *Non-controlling interests*
   20% × $55,000 (the restated net assets of H).
2. *Goodwill*

	$	$
Cost of investment		50,000
Net assets at the date of acquisition:		
Share capital	50,000	
Retained earnings – *as restated*	2,500	
	52,500	
Group share (80%)		(42,000)
Goodwill		8,000

3. *Retained earnings*

	$
G	50,000
H – based on restated figures [80% ($5,000 – $2,500)]	2,000
	52,000

3.7 Adjustments for fair value at the date of acquisition

In Chapter 2 it was noted that goodwill was calculated using fair value measurements for assets and liabilities in the subsidiary at the date of acquisition, in accordance with the requirements of IFRS 3. Chapter 2, introduced the principles of fair value measurement on acquisition of a subsidiary. For the moment, in this chapter, we will examine the implications of measurement at fair value on the financial statements subsequent to acquisition.

Sometimes the fair values of net assets at the point of acquisition are recognised in the subsidiary at the date of consolidation, where the accounting policy of the entity itself permits this. However, where the subsidiary adopts the cost model of valuation, there will be continuing differences on consolidation arising from the fact that the net assets of the subsidiary are recognised at fair value upon acquisition. In the latter case, consolidation adjustments will be required.

The example below illustrates the adjustments required.

Example 3.J

The statements of financial positions of Star and its subsidiary entity Ark as at 31 December 20X7 were as follows:

	Star	*Ark*
	$'000	$'000
Property, plant and equipment	120	177
Investment in Ark	134	
Inventory	10	5
Receivables	30	25
Bank	10	5
	304	212
Ordinary share capital	100	75
Retained earnings	144	120
	244	195
Current liabilities	60	17
	304	212

Additional information

1. On 1 January 20X5, when the retained earnings of Ark showed a balance of $60,000, Star purchased 60,000 ordinary shares in Ark for $134,000.
2. Star sold goods to Ark during the year for $10,000 at a mark-up of 25% on cost. At the year-end, half of these goods were still held in inventory by Ark.
3. On 1 January 20X5 the net assets of Ark had a fair value of $155,000. The excess of fair value over the carrying value in the individual financial statements of Ark was due to plant included in property, plant and equipment. This plant had a useful economic life of 5 years from 1 January 20X5. None of the plant that was subject to a fair-value adjustment at 1 January 20X5 had been sold by 31 December 20X7. Property plant and equipment is measured in Ark's own financial statements at depreciated cost.
4. Since acquisition there has been no impairment of goodwill on consolidation.
5. It is the group's policy to value non-controlling interests at acquisition at its proportionate share of the fair value of the subsidiary's identifiable net assets.

Prepare the consolidated statement of financial position for the group as at 31.12.X7.

Solution

Before we prepare the consolidated statement of financial position, let us consider the implications of each of the additional pieces of information we have been given (the numbers below correspond with the numbered pieces of information):

1. This tells us that Star owns 80% (60/75) of the shares of Ark. At the date of acquisition the individual financial statements of Ark showed net assets of $135,000 (share capital $75,000 plus retained earnings $60,000).
2. This tells us that there is unrealised profit in the closing inventory of Ark. The closing inventory of Ark that was bought from Star is $5,000 [(1/2) × $10,000]. The profit element in this inventory is $1,000 [(25/125) × $5,000]. We need to take care when computing this figure – the profit is expressed as a percentage of the group cost, not the intra-group selling price.
3. This tells us that the fair value of the net assets of Ark was $20,000 ($155,000 – $135,000) greater than the carrying value in the individual statement of financial position of Ark at the date of acquisition. Since the excess is due to plant that is being depreciated over 5 years the fair-value adjustment will have an impact on closing net assets as well (the acquisition took place three years ago). The impact on closing net assets is an increase of $8,000 [$20,000 × (2/5)].We can summarise the effect as:
   - pre-acquisition retained earnings increased by $20,000 to $80,000;
   - closing property, plant and equipment increased by $8,000 to $185,000;
   - closing net assets increased by $8,000 to $203,000;
   - closing retained earnings increased by $8,000 to $128,000.

We now prepare the consolidated statement of financial position:

	$'000	*Comment*
Goodwill	10	See working 2
Property, plant and equipment	305	120 + 185 – using *adjusted* figure
Inventory	14	10 + 5 – 1 (unrealised profit)
Receivables	55	S + A
Bank	15	S + A
	399	
Share capital	100	Star only
Retained earnings	181.4	See working 3
	281.4	
Non-controlling interests	40.6	See working 1
Current liabilities	77	60 + 17
	399	

Workings

1. *Non-controlling interests*
   20% × $203,000 (the *adjusted* net assets of Ark at 31.12.X7). There is no need to charge the minority shareholders with any unrealised profit in this example because the profit is made by the *parent*.

2. *Goodwill*

	$'000	$'000
Cost of investment		134
Net assets at the date of acquisition:		
Share capital	75	
Retained earnings – *as amended*	80	
	155	
Group share (80%)		(124)
Total goodwill		10

3. *Retained earnings*

	$'000
Star	144
Ark using *amended* figures:	
80% ($128,000 – $80,000)	38.4
Unrealised profit on inventory – made by the *parent*	(1)
	181.4

3.8 Summary

This chapter introduced the application of the rules for full consolidation. The IFRS 3 requirements for recognition of goodwill were applied and the consolidation was completed for fully owned and partially owned subsidiaries. The consolidated statement of financial position was prepared.

The chapter also covered several additional complexities involved in the preparation of the consolidated statement of financial position, including intra-group trading and balances, fair value adjustments and adjustment to achieve uniformity of accounting policy.

Students should be sure that they have completely understood the chapter and its examples, and should have worked through the revision questions that follow, before moving on to Chapter 4.

A brief note about workings: it was noted in Chapter 1 that a common mistake made by candidates was that of producing untidy and illegible workings for more complex questions. It is important to get into the habit of producing logical and neat workings for consolidation questions. The style of working used throughout this *Learning System* involves the use of a columnar approach. Some candidates use double entry consolidation workings, showing T accounts, and others use a diagrammatic method. To some extent, the style of working used depends upon that demonstrated by your tutor (where applicable). However, it is strongly recommended that students learn to use the columnar method. Completely accurate answers can be obtained by using other methods, but the problem is that using T accounts or diagrams takes longer. Columnar workings also tend to be easier for markers to follow.

The preparation of the consolidated statement of financial position could be tested in either the shorter style questions or the Long questions (i.e. for 25 marks). The long style questions are likely to contain further complications such as acquisitions or disposals, or the incorporation into consolidated statements of joint venture or associate interests. These are dealt with in subsequent chapters in this *Learning System*.

Revision Questions 3

Note: The questions that are included in the early part of the study system are not usually of exam standard. Tests of knowledge are essential early on in the study process to ensure the basics have been grasped – the exam standard questions will come in later chapters. Please ensure you complete the revision questions in this chapter as they are a fundamental test of your understanding of consolidation, which is essential before moving onto more complex consolidation.

Question 1

On 31 December 20X4 AB acquired 100% of the ordinary share capital of its subsidiary, CD for $50,000. The statements of financial positions of the individual entities at that date were:

	AB	*CD*
	$	**$**
Non-current assets		
Property, plant and equipment	70,000	30,000
Investment	50,000	–
	120,000	30,000
Net current assets	30,000	15,000
	150,000	45,000
Equity		
Share capital	50,000	20,000
Retained earnings	100,000	25,000
	150,000	45,000

Requirement

Prepare the consolidated statement of financial position for the AB Group at 31 December 20X4.

Question 2

This question relates to AB and CD (facts of the acquisition as in Question 1) one year on from the acquisition. The statements of financial positions of the two entities at 31 December 20X5 were as follows:

	AB	*CD*
	$	$
Non-current assets		
Property, plant and equipment	75,000	32,000
Investment	50,000	–
	125,000	32,000

Net current assets	37,000	17,000
	162,000	49,000
Equity		
Share capital	50,000	20,000
Retained earnings	112,000	29,000
	162,000	49,000

Requirement

Prepare the consolidated statement of financial position for the AB Group at 31 December 20X5.

Question 3

AX acquired 30,000 of the 50,000 issued ordinary voting shares of CY on 1 April 20X7, for $60,000. Retained earnings of CY at that date were $25,000. The acquisition was sufficient to give it control over CY's operating and financial policies.

The statements of financial positions of the two entities were as follows on 31 March 20X8:

	AX	*CY*
	$	**$**
Non-current assets		
Property, plant and equipment	125,000	50,000
Investment	60,000	–
	185,000	50,000
Net current assets	40,000	30,000
	225,000	80,000
Equity		
Share capital	100,000	50,000
Retained earnings	125,000	30,000
	225,000	80,000

It is the group's policy to value non-controlling interests at its proportionate share of the fair value of the subsidiary's identifiable net assets.

Requirement

Prepare the consolidated statement of financial position for the AX Group at 31 March 20X8.

Question 4 (same detail as Q 3 but non-controlling interest at fair value)

AX acquired 30,000 of the 50,000 issued ordinary voting shares of CY on 1 April 20X7, for $60,000. Retained earnings of CY at that date were $25,000. The acquisition was sufficient to give it control over CY's operating and financial policies.

The statements of financial positions of the two entities were as follows on 31 March 20X8:

	AX	*CY*
	$	**$**
Non-current assets		
Property, plant and equipment	125,000	50,000
Investment	60,000	–
	185,000	50,000
Net current assets	40,000	30,000
	225,000	80,000
Equity		
Share capital	100,000	50,000
Retained earnings	125,000	30,000
	225,000	80,000

It is the group's policy to value non-controlling interests at fair value. The fair value of the NCI in CY at the date of acquisition was $28,000.

Requirement

Prepare the consolidated statement of financial position for the AX Group at 31 March 20X8.

Question 5

The statements of financial positions as at 30 June 20X4 of A and its subsidiary entity B is summarised below.

	A		*B*	
	$	$	$	$
ASSETS				
Non-current assets				
Property, plant and equipment		9,000		4,800
Investment in subsidiary		10,000		–
		19,000		4,800
Current assets				
Inventories	12,000		18,000	
Trade receivables	25,000		21,000	
Current account with B	4,000		–	
Bank balance	20,000		–	
		61,000		39,000
		80,000		43,800
EQUITY + LIABILITIES				
Equity				
Issued capital ($1 each)		40,000		8,000
Retained earnings		24,000		9,800
		64,000		17,800
Current liabilities				
Trade payables	16,000		18,000	
Current account with A	–		2,000	
Bank overdraft	–		6,000	
		16,000		26,000
		80,000		43,800

Notes

1. A acquired 6,400 ordinary shares in B many years ago. The balance on B's retained earnings at the date of acquisition by A was $1,000. Goodwill on consolidation had been written off following an impairment review before the start of the current financial year.
2. On 30 June 20X4 there was cash in transit from B to A of $2,000.
3. It is the group's policy to value non-controlling interests at its proportionate share of the fair value of the subsidiary's identifiable net assets.

Requirement

Prepare a consolidated balance sheet for the A group as at 30 June 20X4.

Question 6

The statements of financial positions as at 31 December 20X4 of X and its subsidiary entity Y are summarised below:

	X		Y	
	$	$	$	$
ASSETS				
Non-current assets				
Intangible assets				2,000
Property, plant and equipment		29,000		24,800
Investment in Y		21,000		
		50,000		26,800
Current assets				
Inventories	12,000		18,000	
Trade receivables	24,750		21,000	
Trading account with Y	4,000			
Interest receivable from Y	250			
Bank balance	20,000			
		61,000		39,000
		111,000		65,800
EQUITY + LIABILITIES				
Equity				
Ordinary shares of $1 each		40,000		8,000
Retained earnings		21,000		11,000
		61,000		19,000
Non-current liabilities				
Interest bearing borrowings		30,000		20,000
Current liabilities				
Trade payables		20,000	18,300	
Interest payable			500	
Current account with X			2,000	
Bank overdraft			6,000	
				26,800
		111,000		65,800

Notes

1. X acquired 6,000 ordinary shares in Y on 1 January 20X1. The price paid was $11,000. The balance on Y's retained earnings at the date of acquisition by X was $5,000. This included an intangible asset of $1,000 (see note 4 below). Goodwill on consolidation is retained at cost in the group statement of financial position. There has been no

evidence of impairment since acquisition. X made a long-term loan of $10,000 to Y on the same date.

2. On 31 December 20X4 there was cash in transit from Y to X of $2,000.
3. On 31 December 20X4 the inventory of Y included $4,800 of goods purchased from X. X had invoiced these goods at cost plus 25%.
4. The intangible asset of Y does not satisfy the recognition criteria laid down in IAS 38. IAS 38 is to be followed in preparing the consolidated accounts.
5. It is the group's policy to value non-controlling interests at its proportionate share of the fair value of the subsidiary's identifiable net assets.

Requirement

Prepare a consolidated statement of financial position for the X group as at 31 December 20X4.

Question 7

STV owns 75% of the ordinary share capital of its subsidiary TUW. At the group's year end, 28 February 20X7, STV's payables include $3,600 in respect of inventories sold to it by TUW.

TUW's receivables include $6,700 in respect of inventories sold to STV. Two days before the year end STV sent a payment of $3,100 to TUW that was not recorded by the latter until two days after the year end.

Explain, briefly, how the in-transit item should be dealt with as follows in the consolidated statement of financial position at 28 February 20X7.

Question 8

LPD buys goods from its 75% owned subsidiary QPR. QPR earns a mark-up of 25% on such transactions. At the group's year end, 30 June 20X7. LPD had not yet taken delivery of goods, at a sales value of $100,000, which were despatched by QPR on 29 June 20X7. Calculate the value of the goods in transit that would appear in the consolidated statement of financial position of the LPD group at 30 June 20X7?

Solutions to Revision Questions

 Solution 1

Working 1: Goodwill

	$
Consideration	50,000
Net assets acquired:	
100% × $45,000	(45,000)
Goodwill	5,000

AB Group: consolidated statement of financial position at 31 December 20X4

	$	*Comment*
Non-current assets		
Goodwill	5,000	See working 1
Property, plant and equipment	100,000	70,000 + 30,000
Net current assets	45,000	30,000 + 15,000
	150,000	
Equity		
Share capital	50,000	AB only
Retained earnings	100,000	Retained earnings of AB
	150,000	

 Solution 2

Working 1: Retained earnings

Retained earnings for the group = retained earnings of the parent + post-acquisition retained earnings in the subsidiary:

Retained earnings of the parent	112,000
Post-acquisition retained earnings in the subsidiary (29,000 − 25,000)	4,000
	116,000

Tutorial note: goodwill on acquisition is calculated once – upon acquisition.

AB Group: Consolidated statement of financial position at 31 December 20X5

	$	*Comment*
Non-current assets		
Goodwill	5,000	As in solution 1
Property, plant and equipment	107,000	75,000 + 32,000
Net current assets	54,000	37,000 + 17,000
	166,000	
Equity		
Share capital	50,000	AB only
Retained earnings	116,000	See working 1
	166,000	

Solution 3

First, the group structure must be established. AX owns 30,000 of the 50,000 shares of F: a shareholding of 60%. This means that the NCI is 40% (100% − 60%).

Workings

1. *Non-controlling interests*
   This is 40% of the net assets of CY at 31 March 20X8: 40% × $80,000 = $32,000.
2. *Goodwill on consolidation*

	$	$
Consideration		60,000
Net assets at date of acquisition:		
Share capital ($1 shares)	50,000	
Retained earnings	25,000	
	75,000	
Group share (60%)		45,000
Goodwill		15,000

3. *Retained earnings*

	$
Retained earnings of AX	125,000
60% of post-acquisition retained earnings of CY: 60% × ($30,000 − $25,000)	3,000
	128,000

AX Group: consolidated statement of financial position at 31 March 20X8

	$	*Comment*
Non-current assets		
Goodwill	15,000	See working 2
Property, plant and equipment	175,000	125,000 + 50,000
	190,000	
Net current assets	70,000	40,000 + 30,000
	260,000	
Equity attributable to owners of the parent		
Share capital	100,000	AX only
Retained earnings	128,000	See working 3
	228,000	
Non-controlling interests	32,000	See working 1
	260,000	

Solution 4

Workings

1. *Goodwill on consolidation*

	$
Consideration transferred	60,000
NCI at fair value	28,000
	88,000
Net assets at acquisition:	
Share capital	(50,000)
Retained earnings	(25,000)
Goodwill on acquisition	13,000

2. *Non-controlling interests*

NCI at 31 March 20X8 = NCI at date of acquisition + share of post-acquisition profits:

At date of acquisition	28,000
Post-acquisition profit share:	
40% × ($30,000 − $25,000)	2,000
At 31 March 20X8	30,000

3. *Retained earnings*

	$
Retained earnings of AX	125,000
Post acquisition retained earnings:	
($30,000 − $25,000) × group share 60%	3,000
	128,000

	$	*Comment*
Non-current assets		
Goodwill	13,000	See working 1
Property, plant and equipment	175,000	125,000 + 50,000
	188,000	
Net current assets	70,000	40,000 + 30,000
	258,000	
Equity attributable to owners of the parent		
Share capital	100,000	AX only
Retained earnings	128,000	See working 3
	228,000	
Non-controlling interest	30,000	See working 1
	258,000	

Solution 5

A – consolidated statement of financial position as at 30 . 6 . X4

	$	$
ASSETS		
Non-current assets		
Goodwill (W3)		–
Property, plant and equipment		13,800
		13,800
Current assets		
Inventories	30,000	
Trade receivables	46,000	
Cash in transit	2,000	
Bank balance	20,000	
		98,000
		111,800
EQUITY + LIABILITIES		
Equity		
Issued capital		40,000
Retained earnings (W4)		28,240
		68,240
Non-controlling interests (W2)		3,560
Current liabilities		
Trade payables	34,000	
Bank overdraft	6,000	
		40,000
		111,800

Workings

1. *Group structure*
   A owns 6,400 of B's 8,000 shares. This represents a holding of 80%.
2. *Non-controlling interests*
   20% × $17,800 = $3,560
3. *Goodwill on consolidation (all written off)*
   $10,000 – 80% ($8,000 + $1,000) = $2,800
4. *Consolidated retained earnings*

	$
Retained earnings of A	24,000
80% of post-acquisition retained earnings of B ($9,800 – $1,000 = $8,800)	7,040
Goodwill written off (W3)	(2,800)
	28,240

Solution 6

X – consolidated statement of financial position as at 31.12 . X4

	$	$
ASSETS		
Non-current assets		
Goodwill on consolidation (W5)		2,000
Property, plant and equipment		53,800
		55,800
Current assets		
Inventories (W3)	29,040	
Trade receivables	45,750	
Cash in transit (W7)	2,000	
Bank balance	20,000	
		96,790
		152,590
EQUITY + LIABILITIES		
Equity		
Ordinary shares of $1		40,000
Retained earnings (W6)		23,790
		63,790
Non-controlling interest (W4)		4,250
Non-current liabilities		
Interest bearing borrowings (X + Y − 10,000)		40,000
Current liabilities		
Trade payables	38,300	
Interest payable (W8)	250	
Bank overdraft	6,000	
		44,550
		152,590

Workings

1. *Group structure*
   X owns 6,000 out of 8,000 Y shares and so owns 75%.

2. *Pre-consolidation adjustment*
   Group policy does not recognise the intangible assets that are in Y's own statement of financial position. This makes the retained earnings of Y at the year end date $9,000 ($11,000 − $2,000) and the retained earnings of Y at the date of acquisition $4,000 ($5,000 – $1,000).

3. *Unrealised profit in inventory*
   Profit element is 25% of the cost to X, or 25/125 of the selling price charged by X, which is also the cost to Y.

   Therefore the unrealised profit is 25/125 × $4,800 = $960. There is no Non-controlling interest since the profit is made by the parent. Consolidated inventories are reduced by $960.

4. *Non-controlling interests*
   25% × ($19,000 − $2,000) = $4,250. Remember the accounting policy adjustment!

5. *Goodwill*
   Total goodwill is $11,000 − [75% ($8,000 + $4,000)] = $2,000. Pre-acquisition retained earnings are reduced by $1,000 for the intangible asset.

6. *Consolidated retained earnings*

	$
retained earnings of X	21,000
75% of post-acquisition retained earnings of Y as adjusted ($9,000 – $4,000)	3,750
Unrealised profit in inventory (W3)	(960)
	23,790

7. *Intra-group balances*
   The intra-group balances (receivables/payables) are cancelled out on consolidation and cash in transit of $2000 represents the difference.
8. *Interest payable*
   Half of the interest payable by Y is due to X as X invested $10,000 in the borrowings of Y. This intercompany amount ($250) is eliminated on consolidation.

Solution 7

The payment of $3,100 is correctly deducted from STV's bank but the corresponding payable held by TUW does not yet reflect it. The cash in transit should be recognised at $3,100 and the intra-company accounts agreed and eliminated in the consolidated accounts (dr payables, cr receivables).

Solution 8

The value of the goods in transit should be at the cost to the group, ie less any inrealised profit. The profit on $100,000 sales is $20,000 ($100,000 × 25/125) and so the goods in transit should be held at $80,000.

The Consolidated Income Statements of Comprehensive Income and Changes in Equity

The Consolidated Income Statements of Comprehensive Income and Changes in Equity

4

Learning Outcomes

After studying this chapter students should be able to:

- prepare a consolidated income statement and a consolidated statement of comprehensive income;
- prepare a consolidated statement of changes in equity;
- account for intra-group transactions;
- apply the concepts of fair value at the point of acquisition.

4.1 Introduction

The previous two chapters introduced some of the basic principles of consolidation accounting and applied them to the preparation of a consolidated statement of financial position. This chapter extends the application of the principles to the preparation of a consolidated statement of comprehensive income and statement of changes in equity.

Section 4.2 introduces the changes made by IAS 1 (revised) in respect of the income statement. Section 4.3 examines the basic principles of preparing the consolidated statements. Section 4.4 looks at the treatment of intra-group finance costs arising from investments in preference shares and loans. Section 4.5 covers the elimination of intra-group trading in the consolidated income statement. Section 4.6 revisits the issue of adjusting for fair value and changes in accounting policy, applied to the consolidated statement of comprehensive income.

4.2 IAS 1 (revised) Presentation of financial statements

IAS 1 has been in issue in one form or another for many years. The content of IAS 1 does not form part of the F2 syllabus, and its provisions will not be examined directly in the form of specific questions. However, its presentation requirements will affect the way many F2 questions and answers are set out, and to that extent it is pervasive.

IAS 1 was revised in September 2007 and entities are required to apply it for accounting periods beginning on or after 1 January 2009. The requirements of the revised standard will be followed in this study system.

The principal changes in financial statement presentation are briefly explained below.

Presentation of the income statement and statement of changes in equity (SOCIE).

Prior to the issue of the revised IAS 1, entities were required to present an income statement that included items of income and expense recognised in profit or loss. Any other items of income and expenditure, i.e. those not recognised in profit or loss, were to be presented in the SOCIE, together with owner changes in equity (such as increases in share capital and dividends paid).

IAS 1 (revised) draws a distinction between owner changes in equity and all other items of income and expense (which are known as 'comprehensive income'). IAS 1 (revised) requires that all non-owner changes in equity should be **presented either in**:

- A single statement of comprehensive income

Or

- Two statements, one being an income statement and the other a statement of comprehensive income.

The SOCIE is to be used exclusively for presenting changes in owner equity.

The lower part of the single statement or the statement of comprehensive income are used to present items of income or expense that IFRS require to be recognised outside profit or loss such as translation differences relating to foreign operations and gains or losses on available-for-sale investments.

The IASB would have preferred a single statement of comprehensive income, but the Board's constituents who responded to the exposure draft preceding IAS 1 (revised) mostly preferred the use of two statements.

A pro-forma example showing the headings to be used in a statement of comprehensive income is shown below. This is taken from the illustrative examples in IAS 1 (revised).

Statement of comprehensive income

	$
Revenue	X
Cost of sales	X
Gross profit	X
Other income	X
Distribution costs	X
Administrative expenses	X
Other expenses	X
Finance costs	X
Share of profit of associates	X
Profit before tax	X
Income tax expense	X
PROFIT FOR THE YEAR	X
Other comprehensive income:	X
Exchange differences on translating foreign operations	
Available-for-sale financial assets	X
Cash flow hedges	X
Gains on property revaluation	X
Actuarial gains/(losses) on defined benefit pension plans	X

Share of other comprehensive income of associates	X
Income tax relating to components of other comprehensive income	X
Other comprehensive income for the year, net of tax	X
TOTAL COMPREHENSIVE INCOME FOR THE YEAR	X
Profit attributable to:	
Owners of the parent	X
Non-controlling interests	X
	X
Total comprehensive income attributable to:	X
Owners of the parent	X
Non-controlling interests	X

Where the two statement option is adopted, the statement above is split after PROFIT FOR THE YEAR. The upper part of the statement is the income statement, followed by a split of profit attributable to the owners of the parent and non-controlling interests. The lower part of the statement is the statement of comprehensive income, followed by a split of the total comprehensive income attributable to the owners of the parent and the non-controlling interests.

For the purposes of this study system an income statement will be presented unless the questions or example specifically includes an item or transaction that would be recorded in other comprehensive income, whereby we will adopt the single statement approach of producing a statement of total comprehensive income.

4.3 Basic principles

We discussed the underlying rationale for consolidated financial statements in Chapter 2. The objective is to present one set of financial statements for all entities under common control. In the context of the income statement, this means presenting the results of all group entities in one income statement. As far as the consolidated statement of changes in equity is concerned, this means just one statement dealing with all the entities in the group.

The majority of the figures are simple aggregations of the results of the parent entity and all the subsidiaries. Non-controlling interests are ignored in the aggregations, as with the statement of financial positions we have already studied in chapter 3.

Intra-group investment income is eliminated. This is because intra-group investment income is replaced by the underlying profits and losses of the group entities.

The figure of profit for the period is split into the amounts attributable to equity holders of the parent and to non-controlling interest. IAS 1 requires that the split should be disclosed on the face of the income statement or statement of comprehensive income.

The statement of changes in equity, according to IAS 1, should show amounts attributable to the equity holders of the parent, and, in a separate column, the amounts attributable to non-controlling interest.

Example 4.A

Draft income statements for the year ended 31 December 20X4

	Acquirer	*Swallowed*
	$	$
Revenue	600,000	300,000
Cost of sales	(420,000)	(230,000)
Gross profit	180,000	70,000
Distribution costs	(50,000)	(25,000)

Administrative expenses	(50,000)	(22,000)
Profit from operations	80,000	23,000
Investment income	4,000	–
Finance cost	(8,000)	(3,000)
Profit before tax	76,000	20,000
Income tax expense	(30,000)	(8,000)
Profit for the year	46,000	12,000

Summarised statements of changes in equity for the year ended 31 December 20X4

	Acquirer	*Swallowed*
	$	$
Balance at start of year	78,000	48,000
Profit for the year	46,000	12,000
Dividends	(20,000)	(5,000)
Balance at end of year	104,000	55,000

Acquirer purchased 16,000 of the 20,000 issued $1 shares in Swallowed on 31 December 20X1 for $33,000. The balance on Swallowed's equity at that date was $35,000 (issued share capital $20,000 plus retained earnings $15,000). There has been no impairment of goodwill since acquisition.

Prepare a consolidated income statement and a consolidated statement of changes in equity for the Acquirer group for the year ended 31 December 20X4.

Solution

Before we prepare the income statement itself we should note that:

- Acquirer owns 16,000 of Swallowed's 20,000 issued $1 shares so this makes Swallowed an 80% subsidiary.

Consolidated income statement

	$	*Comments*
Revenue	900,000	A + S
Cost of sales	(650,000)	A + S
Gross profit	250,000	
Distribution costs	(75,000)	A + S
Administrative expenses	(72,000)	A + S
Profit from operations	103,000	
Finance cost	(11,000)	A + S: investment income eliminated as inter-group
Profit before tax	92,000	
Income tax expense	(38,000)	A + S
Profit for the period	54,000	
Attributable to:	$	
Equity holders of the parent	51,600	
Non-controlling interest (20% × profit of S only)	2,400	
	54,000	

Consolidated statement of changes in equity

	Attributable to equity holders of the parent	*Non-controlling interestt*	*Total equity*
	$	$	$
Balance at start of year (W1)	88,400	9,600	98,000
Profit for the period	51,600	2,400	54,000
Dividends (W2)	(20,000)	(1,000)	(21,000)
Balance at end of year	120,000	11,000	131,000

Workings

1. *Balance at the start of the year*

   Attributable to equity holders of the parent:

	$
Acquirer	78,000
Swallowed (80% × [$48,000 − $35,000])	10,400
	88,400

   The balance attributable to the non-controlling interest is 20% of Swallowed's brought forward balance: $48,000 × 20% = $9,600

2. *Dividends*

   The amount paid to the minority was $5,000 × 20% = $1,000

   Note that the non-controlling interest carried forward represents 20% of the equity in Swallowed: $55,000 × 20% = $11,000.

The disclosure requirements in IAS 1 require that the amounts attributable to equity holders of the parent are broken down into share capital and the different categories of reserves. However, this question does not provide sufficient information for full disclosure.

4.4 Investments in preference shares and loans

Investment by the parent in loans to its subsidiary means that there will be an intra-group finance cost as well as intra-group dividends. These will cancel out in the same way. The only difference is that loan interest receivable from a subsidiary will cancel out against the finance cost of that subsidiary rather than against dividends. The same principle is followed in respect of preference shares. Preference shares, as noted in Chapter 3, will almost always be classfied as liabilities, rather than equity, and so preference dividends constitute part of the finance cost.

> ! Note to illustrate the format of the statement of comprehensive income, the following example includes other comprehensive income in the period, being a revaluation gain. The format followed, therefore is that of the single statement of comprehensive income.

Example 4.B

Statements of comprehensive income for the year ended 31 December 20X5

	A	*B*
	$	$
Profit from operations	100,000	30,000
Investment income	6,000	–
Finance cost	(11,000)	(7,000)
Profit before tax	95,000	23,000
Income tax expenses	(38,000)	(10,000)
Profit for the period	57,000	13,000
Other comprehensive income:		
Gain on revaluation of property (net of tax)	5,000	2,000
Total comprehensive income	62,000	15,000

Summarised statements of changes in equity for the year ended 31 December 20X5

	A	*B*
	$	$
Balance at start of period	152,000	65,000
Total comprehensive income for the period period	62,000	15,000
Dividends – ordinary shares	(10,000)	(5,000)
Balance at end of period	204,000	75,000

Additional information

A made its investments in B on 1 January 20X3 when the statement of financial position of B showed the following:

	$
Ordinary share capital – $1 shares	25,000
Preference share capital – $1 shares	20,000
Reserves	12,000
	57,000

The cost of investing in the shares of B was:

- $27,700 for 15,000 ordinary shares;
- $5,200 for 5,000 preference shares.

On 1 January 20X3 A provided 50% of B's loans. The finance cost of $7,000 in B relates both to the preference share dividend (2,000) and loan interest (5,000).

Solution

The first step is to establish the group structure and reconcile the investment income that is included in A's income statement. You may ask: Why bother with the reconciliation if we're going to eliminate A's investment income anyway? There are two reasons:

- We only eliminate intra-group investment income. Entity A may have some income from trade investments.
- When the investment income is partly interest and partly dividends then the elimination has different consequences.

The table below shows the position regarding A's three-part investment in B.

Investment type	*A's share*	*Total finance cost/dividend*	*A's share of total*
		$	$
Loans	50%	5,000	2,500
Preference shares	25%	2,000	500
Ordinary shares	60%	5,000	3,000
			6,000

You can see that in this case all of the investment income is intra-group and so should be eliminated.

Consolidated statement of comprehensive income

	$	*Comments*
Profit from operations	130,000	A + B
Finance cost	(15,000)	A + B 2 inter-group finance cost of $2,500 + $500
Profit before tax	115,000	
Tax	(48,000)	A + B
Profit for the period	67,000	
Other comprehensive income:		
Gain on revoluation of property (net of tax)	7,000	
Total comprehensive income (TCI)	74,000	

Profit attributable to:	$	
Owners of the parent	61,800	
Non-controlling interest	5,200	See working 1
	67,000	

TCI attributable to:	$	
Owners of the parent	68,000	
Non-controlling interest	6,000	See working 1
	74,000	

Consolidated statement of changes in equity

	Attributable to equity holders of the parent	*Non-controlling interestt*	*Total equity*
	$	$	$
Balance at the start of the year (W2)	156,800	18,000	174,800
Total comprehensive income for the period	68,000	6,000	74,000
Dividends (W3)	(10,000)	(2,000)	(12,000)
Balance at the end of the year	214,800	22,000	236,800

Workings

1. *Non-controlling interest in consolidated statement of comprehensive income*
   In profit for the period $13,000 × 40% = $5,200
   In total comprehensive income for the period = $5,200 + (40% × $2,000) = $6,000
   The owners share of TCI is the balance $74,000 − $6,000 = $68,000 and represents their share of the profit of $61,800 + A's revaluation gain $5,000 + 60% of B's gain $1,200
2. *Balance of equity at the start of the period*
   Attributable to equity shareholders of the parent:

	$
A	152,000
B [60% × ($65,000 − $57,000)]	4,800
	156,800

Attributable to NCI:

	$
Share of balance of equity [40% × ($65,000 − $20,000)]	18,000

3. *Dividends paid to the NCI:*

   Ordinary shares ($5,000 × 40%) 2,000

   The closing balance in respect of the NCI in the statement of changes in equity can be proved as follows:

   Share of balance of equity (40% × [75,000 − 20,000 preference shares]) 22,000

4.5 Intra-group trading

There is no need to worry about cancellation of intra-group balances for the consolidated income statement. This is clearly a statement of financial position issue. Intra-group trading will be of relevance in the consolidated income statement to the extent that one group entity provides goods or services for another group entity. In these circumstances there are clearly income and costs that are wholly intra-group.

Intra-group revenue must be eliminated *in full* from revenue. This is the case whatever has subsequently happened to any goods that are sold by one group entity to another. Unless there is unrealised profit on unsold inventory (see below) then the adjustment to costs is the same as the adjustment to revenue.

We have already seen from our studies of the consolidated statement of financial position (see Chapter 3) that unrealised profit on intra-group revenue must be eliminated from closing inventory and profit. Unrealised profit on intra-group revenue is deducted from gross profit. The adjustment to cost of sales is the difference between the adjustment to revenue and the adjustment to gross profit.

Where there is unrealised profit brought forward then this amount will have been charged against the consolidated reserves of previous years. Therefore the charge to gross profit for the year is the *movement* on the provision for unrealised profit.

Where the unrealised profit is made by a subsidiary in which there is a non-controlling interest then a share of the charge to the consolidated income statement is made against the non-controlling interest.

Example 4.C

Income statements of PQR and its subsidiary XYZ for the year ended 31 December 20X1

	PQR	*XYZ*
	$'000	$'000
Revenue	125,000	50,000
Cost of sales	(50,000)	(20,000)
Gross profit	75,000	30,000
Distribution costs	(10,000)	(4,000)
Administrative expenses	(8,000)	(3,200)
Profit from operations	57,000	22,800
Investment income	3,180	–
Finance cost	(24,500)	(7,750)
Profit before taxation	35,680	15,050
Income tax	(14,000)	(7,000)
Profit for the period	21,680	8,050

Summarised statements of changes in equity for PQR and XYZ

	PQR	*XYZ*
	$'000	$'000
Balance at 1 January 20X1	76,700	50,300
Profit for the period	21,680	8,050
Ordinary dividends	(8,000)	(2,100)
Balance at 31 December 20X1	90,380	56,250

Other information

1. Included in the revenue of XYZ is $5 million in respect of sales to PQR. XYZ earns a profit of 25% on cost. These are sales of components that XYZ has been supplying to PQR on a regular basis for a number of years. The amount included in the inventory of PQR in respect of goods purchased from XYZ at the beginning and end of the year was as follows:

Date	*Inventory of components in PQR's books*
	$'000
31.12.X1	800
31.12.X0	600

2. At the date of PQR's investment in XYZ the statement of financial position of XYZ showed:

	$'000
Ordinary share capital (1$ shares)	25,000
Reserves	22,500
	47,500

PQR bought 20 million ordinary shares in XYZ at a cost of $27 million. On the same date PQR purchased 25% of the loan stock of XYZ.

XYZ's finance cost for the year ended 31 December 20X1 comprised the following:

	$'000
Loan stock interest	6,000
Interest payable on short-term borrowings	1,750
	7,750

Solution

1. PQR owns 80% of the ordinary shares of XYZ and 25% of the loans. The intra-group investment income that PQR credits in its own income statement is:
   - Loan stock interest $1,500,000 (25% × $6,000,000)
   - Dividends $1,680,000 (80% × $2,100,000)
   - Total = $3,180,000
2. Intra-group sales of $5 million will be eliminated from revenue and cost of sales:
   DR Group revenue $5,000,000
   CR Group cost of sales $5,000,000
   There is unrealised profit on both opening and closing inventory:
   - Unrealised profit on closing inventory = $160,000 (25/125 × $800,000)
   - Unrealised profit on opening inventory = $120,000 (25/125 × $600,000)
   So the movement on unrealised profit and the deduction from gross profit for the year is $40,000.
   - DR Group cost of sales $40,000
   - CR Provision for unrealised profit $40,000

Consolidated income statement of the PQR Group for the year ended 31 December 20X1

	$'000	*Comments*
Revenue	170,000	PQR + XYZ − $5 million
Cost of sales	(65,040)	PQR + XYZ − $5 million + $40,000
Gross profit	104,960	
Distribution costs	(14,000)	PQR + XYZ
Administrative expenses	(11,200)	PQR + XYZ
Finance costs	(30,750)	PQR + XYZ + ($6 million × 75%)
Profit before tax	49,010	
Income tax	(21,000)	PQR + XYZ
Profit for the period	28,010	

Attributable to:		
Equity holders of parent	26,408	
Non-controlling interest	1,602	(working 1)
	28,010	

Consolidated statement of changes in equity of the PQR Group for the year ended 31 December 20X1

	Attributable to equity holders of parent	*Non-controlling interest*	*Total*
	$'000	$'000	$'000
Balance at start of period (working 2)	78,844	10,036	88,880
Profit for the period	26,408	1,602	28,010
Dividends (working 3)	(8,000)	(420)	(8,420)
Balance at end of period	97,252	11,218	108,470

Working 1

Profit attributable to non-controlling interest in income statement:

	$'000
Profit for the period per XYZ income statement	8,050
Less: increase in provision for unrealised profit	(40)
	8,010
Non-controlling interest (20%)	1,602

Working 2

Balance at start of period: attributable to equity holders of parent:

	$'000
In PQR's own statement of changes in equity	76,700
Share of XYZ's post-acquisition earnings (50,300 − 47,500 − 120) × 80%	2,144
	78, 844

Balance at start of period: attributable to non-controlling interest

	$'000
(50,300 − 120) × 20%	10, 036

Working 3

Dividends paid to non-controlling interest: ($2,100 × 20%) = 420

4.6 Adjustments for fair value or to reflect changes in accounting policy

We saw when we studied these aspects in the preparation of the consolidated statement of financial position that the consolidation technique to apply was essentially the same.

The effects of the adjustments will frequently impact on the profit for the year. This may be because, for example, the group charge for depreciation needs to be increased due to the fair value of the non-current assets of an acquired subsidiary being larger than the carrying value on acquisition.

As we saw in Chapter 3 such adjustments affect the retained earnings of the subsidiary for consolidation purposes, both at the date of acquisition and at the statement of financial position date. Therefore we will need to allow for the effect of these adjustments when computing goodwill on consolidation and opening consolidated equity.

Example 4.D

Income statements of A and its subsidiaries B and C for the year ended 31 December 20X8

	A	B	C
	$'000	$'000	$'000
Revenue	56,000)	52,000)	44,000
Cost of sales	(30,000)	(28,000)	(24,000)
Gross profit	26,000)	24,000)	20,000
Other operating expenses	(13,000)	(12,000)	(10,000)
Investment income	4,000		
Finance cost	(3,000)	(2,000)	(1,800)
Profit before tax	14,000	10,000)	8,200
Tax	(5,000)	(3,000)	(2,500)
Profit for the period	9,000	7,000	5,700

Notes
A acquired 80% of the ordinary shares of B on 1 January 20X5 and 75% of the ordinary share capital of C on 1 January 20X6. Details of the cost of the investments and the net assets at the date of acquisition as shown in the statement of financial positions of B and C are given below.

	B	*C*
	$'000	$'000
Cost of investment	36,000	25,500
Net assets at the date of acquisition		
Share capital	20,000	15,000
Share premium	10,000	6,000
Retained earnings	8,000	6,000
	38,000	27,000

At the dates of acquisition of B and C the fair values of the non-current assets of the companies were $4 million and $3 million respectively in excess of their carrying values in their financial statements. The non-current assets had an estimated future useful economic life of 5 years. The non-current assets are fully depreciable and the depreciation is charged to cost of sales. None of these non-current assets had been sold by 31 December 20X8. Goodwill on both acquisitions has remained unimpaired. B and C paid a dividend to ordinary shareholders of $3 million and $2 million respectively in the year to 31 December 20X8.

Prepare the consolidated income statement of the A group for the year ended 31 December 20X8.

Solution

The question gives us the group structure. The key issue we need to resolve prior to actually preparing the consolidated income statement is the calculation of the fair value adjustments. The fair-value adjustments will affect goodwill and depreciation. Since the non-current assets that caused the fair-value adjustment have a useful economic life of 5 years the total additional depreciation is $1,400,000, that is, ($4,000,000 + $3,000,000)/5.

The intra-group investment income that is eliminated is:

- $2,400,000 from B (80% × $3 million);
- $1,500,000 from C (75% × $2 million);

This means that $100,000 remains.

We now proceed to the consolidated income statement.

	$'000	*Comments*
Revenue	152,000	A + B + C
Cost of sales	(83,400)	A + B + C + $800,000 + $600,000 (extra dep'n)
Gross profit	68,600	
Other operating expenses	(35,000)	A + B + C
Investment income	100	A's income from trade investments
Finance cost	(6,800)	A + B + C
Profit before tax	26,900	
Tax	(10,500)	A + B + C
Profit for the period	16,400	
Attributable to:	$'000	
Equity holders of the parent	13,885	
Non-controlling interest	2,515	(See working)
	16,400	

Working: *Non-controlling interest*

- B – 20% × ($7,000,000 – $800,000) = $1,240,000.
- C – 25% × ($5,700,000 – $600,000) = $1,275,000.

Total $2,515,000.

4.7 Summary

This chapter has explained various aspects involved in preparing a consolidated statement of comprehensive income, the consolidated income statement and a statement of changes in equity. Students will have noted that the treatment of these items is consistent with their treatment in the consolidated statement of financial position.

This examination may contain long questions (25 or 50 marks) that require the preparation of a consolidated income statement/statement of comprehensive income and possibly a consolidated statement of changes in equity only. It is likely that such questions would contain additional complications that we will be covering in later chapters, such as acquisitions or disposals part-way through the year, and the inclusion of interests in joint ventures or associates. The long questions at the end of this chapter are, therefore, not fully representative of the range of issues that would arise in a practical consolidation questions. They are included here because they are useful for practice. The examination standard questions are contained in the section called preparing for the examination.

Revision Questions

4

Question 1

Draft statements of comprehensive income and summarised statements of changes in equity of H and its subsidiary S for the year ended 31 December 20X4

	H	*S*
	$'000	$'000
Revenue	2,100	1,200
Cost of sales	(1,850)	(1,066)
Gross profit	250	134
Distribution costs	(50)	(20)
Administrative expenses	(30)	(14)
Investment income	16	–
Profit before tax	186	100
Income tax expense	(80)	(40)
Profit for the period	106	60
Other comprehensive income:		
Gains from revaluation (net of tax)	16	10
Total comprehensive income (TCI)	122	70
Opening equity	140	70
TCI for the period	122	70
Dividends	(40)	(20)
Closing equity	222	120

H purchased 80% of the shares in S when S's equity (share capital plus retained earnings) was $40,000. Goodwill of $12,000 was fully written off to consolidated retained earnings at 31.12 . X3, following an impairment review.

Requirement

Prepare the consolidated income statement and the consolidated statement of changes in equity of the H group for the year ended 31 December 20X4.

(10 marks)

Question 2

Draft income statements and summarised statements of changes in equity of Hope and its subsidiary Despair for the year ended 30 June 20X7

	Hope	*Despair*
	$	$
Revenue	159,800	108,400
Cost of sales	(79,200)	(61,600)
Gross profit	80,600	46,800
Administrative expenses	(27,000)	(16,000)
Investment income:		
Ordinary dividend	9,000	–
Loan interest	1,000	1,500
Finance cost	(6,000)	(4,000)
Profit before tax	57,600	28,300
Income tax expense	(29,400)	(14,800)
Profit for the period	28,200	13,500
Opening equity	133,400	53,600
Profit for the period	28,200	13,500
Ordinary dividends	(15,000)	(10,000)
Closing equity	146,600	57,100

Other information

1. Hope acquired its interest in Despair as follows:

   9,000 of the 10,000 $1 ordinary shares on 30 June 20X3 when the equity of Despair was $35,000 (ordinary shares $10,000 plus retained earnings $25,000).

2. Hope has not provided Despair with any of its loan capital.
3. The revenue of Hope includes $19,000 in respect of goods sold to Despair at a price that yielded a profit of 20% on selling price. $8,000 of these goods were in the inventory of Despair at 30 June 20X7. Inventories of such goods at 30 June 20X6 amounted to $6,000.

Requirements

(a) Explain how the investment in Despair should be accounted for the group accounts.
(3 marks)

(b) Produce the consolidated income statement and statement of changes in equity.
(17 marks)

(c) Explain the treatment of the intra-group sales between Hope and Despair.
(5 marks)

(Total = 25 marks)

Question 3

(a) On 1 September 20X6, BLT held 60% of the ordinary share capital of its only subsidiary CMU. The consolidated equity of the group at that date was $576,600, of which $127,000 was attributable to the non-controlling interest.

On 28 February 20X7, exactly halfway through the financial year, BLT bought a further 20% of the ordinary share capital of CMU. In the year ended 31 August 20X7 BLT's profits for the period were $98,970 and CMU's were $30,000. BLT paid a divided of $40,000 on 1 July 20X7. There were no other movements in equity. It can be assumed that profits accrue evenly throughout the year.

Prepare a consolidated statement of changes in equity for the BLT group for the year ended 31 August 20X7. **(6 marks)**

(b) GPT regularly sells goods to its subsidiary in which it owns 60% of the ordinary share capital. During the group's financial year ended 31 August 20X7. GPT sold goods to its subsidiary valued at $100,000 (selling price) upon which it makes a margin of 20%. By the group's year end 70% of the goods had been sold to parties outside the group.

Explain, with calculations, the adjustments required to correctly deal with the intra-group trading.

(4 marks)
(Total = 10 marks)

Solutions to Revision Questions

Solution 1

(a) Consolidated statement of comprehensive income

	$'000
Revenue (H + S)	3,300
Cost of sales (H + S)	(2,916)
Gross profit	384
Distribution costs (H + S)	(70)
Administrative expenses (H + S)	(44)
Income tax expense	(120)
Profit for the period	150

Profit attributable to:	$'000
Equity holders of the parent	138
Non-controlling interest (20% × $60)	12
	150

TCI attributable to:	$'000
Equity holders of the parent	162
Non-controlling interest (20% × $60) + (20% × $10)	14
	176

Consolidated statement of changes inpp equity

	Attributable to equity holders of the parent $'000	*NCI* $'000	*Total equity* $'000
Balance at the start of the year (W1)	152	14	166
TCI for the period	162	14	176
Dividends (W2)	(40)	(4)	(44)
Balance at the end of the year	274	24	298

Workings

1. *Balance at the start of the year*

   Attributable to equity holders of the parent:

	$'000
H	140
S (80% × [70 − 40])	24
Less: goodwill impairment	(12)
	152

The balance attributable to the non-controlling interest is 20% of the brought forward balance of S (i.e., \$70,000 × 20%) = \$14,000

2. *Dividends*
   The amount paid to the NCI was \$20,000 × 20% = \$4,000

Solution 2

(a) Hope owns 90% of the equity share capital of Despair and therefore is presumed to have control over the operating and financial policies of the entity. Under IAS 27, Despair should be accounted for as a subsidiary of Hope and should be fully consolidated. 100% of the assets and liabilities of Despair should be included and the 10% interest held outwith the group should be included separately in both the income statement and the statement of financial position as "non-controlling interests".

(b) **Hope Group: Consolidated income statement for the year ended 30 June 20X7**

	$
Revenue (H + D − \$19,000 [W1])	249,200
Costs of sales (balancing figure)	(122,200)
Gross profit (H + D − \$400 [W1])	127,000
Administrative expenses (H + D)	(43,000)
Investment income (external only) W2	2,500
Finance cost (H + D)	(10,000)
Profit before taxation	76,500
Income tax expense (H + D)	(44,200)
Profit for the period	32,300
Attributable to:	
Equity holders of parent	30,950
Non-controlling interest (W3)	1,350
	32,300

Hope Group: Consolidated statement of changes in equity for the year ended 30 June 20X7

	Attributable to equity holders of the parent $	*Non-controlling interest* $	*Total equity* $
Balance at the start of the year (W4)	148,940	5,360	154,300
Profit for the period	30,950	1,350	32,300
Dividends (W5)	(15,000)	(1,000)	(16,000)
Balance at the end of the year	164,890	5,710	170,600

Workings

1. Intra-group sales of \$19 million are adjusted in the consolidated income statement. The adjustment at gross profit level is the movement in the provision for unrealised profit:
   - Unrealised profit on closing inventory is 20% × \$8,000 = \$1,600
   - Unrealised profit on opening inventory is 20% × \$6,000 = \$1,200

   So, the movement is \$1,600 − \$1,200 = \$400.
2. The cancellation of investment income is of the intra-group element only (the dividend received by Hope from Despair). The interest income of both entities is not intra-group and so it remains in the consolidated income statement: \$1,000 + \$1,500 = \$2,500.
3. Profit for the period of Despair × 10% = \$13,500 × 10% = \$1,350

4. The opening equity attributable to the equity shareholders of the parent is:

	$
Hope	133,400
Despair (90% × $53,600 – $35,000)	16,740
Opening PUP on inventory (W1)	(1,200)
	148,940

The opening equity attributable to the non-controlling interest is:
10% × $53,600 5,360

5. Dividends paid to the NCI: $10,000 × 10% = $1,000.

(c) The correct treatment of the intra-group sale is to eliminate it in full from revenue in the consolidated income statement. Where the goods have not been sold on outside the group at the year-end then it is necessary to eliminate any profit made on those goods by the supplying entity (Hope in this case). Where the profit elimination is required at the beginning and end of the year then a net adjustment is required in the consolidated income statement, since the opening provision for unrealised profit will be reversed in the year, assuming that the goods are sold on outside the group. The charge is shared between the group and the non-controlling interest depending on the group interest in the entity making the unrealised profit. In this case the unrealised profit is made by the parent, so no adjustment is required against the non-controlling interest .

Solution 3

(a) **BLT Group: Statement of changes in equity for the year ended 31 August 20X7**

	Attributable to equity holders of parent	*Non-controlling interest*	*Total*
	$	$	$
Brought forward	449,600	127,000	576,600
Profit for the period (W1)	119,970	9,000	128,970
Transfer in respect of shares purchased by BLT	66,500	(66,500)	
Dividend	(40,000)	———	(40,000)
Carried forward	596,070	69,500	665,570

W1 Profit shares

NCI share of profit

$30,000 × 6/12 × 40%	6,000
$30,000 × 6/12 × 20%	3,000
	9,000

Group share

$98,970 + ($30,000 – 9,000) = $119,970

W2 Transfer in respect of share purchase

Value of non-controlling interest at date of transfer: $127,000 + 6,000 = $133,000
50% of shareholding transferred: $133,000/2 = $66,500

(b) The full value of the intra-group sales must be eliminated from the group accounts. \$100,000 will be deducted from both revenue and cost of sales in the consolidated income statement. The unrealised profit of \$6,000 (30% × profit (\$100,000 × 20%)) will be deducted from inventories and charged to cost of sales. (note the goods flow from the parent to the subsidiary and do as the parent has earned the unrealised profits, the NCI of Despair is not affected).

Associates and Joint Ventures

Associates and Joint Ventures

5

Learning Outcomes

After studying this chapter students should be able to:

- explain the conditions required to be an associate of another entity and the accounting treatment for associates;
- explain the conditions required to account for an operation as a joint venture, the different forms the venture can take, and how they should be accounted for;
- prepare consolidated financial statements including an associate;
- prepare consolidated financial statements including a joint venture.

5.1 Introduction

In Chapter 2 we discussed how cost information about investments and investment income is sometimes insufficient to give the investors appropriate information does not just hold good in situations where the investor has control. Where the investor has a degree of influence over the operations of the investment, but not outright control, then there is an argument for saying that the 'normal' method of accounting for investments is inappropriate.

In this chapter we consider the effect on an investor's financial position and performance of its interest in two specific kinds of investments – associates and joint ventures. In both cases, the investor can exercise a degree of influence over the affairs of the investment but cannot direct its operating and financial policies (as is the case with subsidiaries). In these circumstances one of the two alternative forms of accounting may well be appropriate in the consolidated financial statements of the investor. These two forms are *equity accounting* and *proportionate consolidation*.

Section 5.2 looks at accounting for associates and the detailed application of equity accounting. Section 5.3 examines accounting for joint ventures, firstly looking at the types of ventures and how they are accounted for. Proportionate consolidation will be applied in this section. Section 5.4 uses a detailed worked example to illustrate the different impact on financial statements of the three types of accounting for investments we have learned about so far; full consolidation, proportionate consolidation and equity accounting.

5.2 IAS 28 *Accounting for associates*

The IAS 28 defines an associate as:

> An entity, including an unincorporated entity such as a partnership, over which the investor has significant influence and that is neither a subsidiary nor an interest in a joint venture.

The key concept in the definition is 'significant influence'. IAS 28 says that significant influence is the power to participate in the financial and operating policy decisions of the entity but is not control over those policies. The existence of significant influence by an investor is usually evidenced in one or more of the following ways:

- representation on the board of directors,
- participation in policy-making processes,
- material transactions between the investor and the entity,
- interchange of managerial personnel,
- provision of essential technical information.

If an investor holds, directly or indirectly, 20% of the voting rights of an entity, IAS 28 states that there is a presumption that the investor has significant influence over the entity, unless it can be clearly demonstrated that this is not the case.

5.2.1 Equity accounting

IAS 28 requires that associates are accounted for using equity accounting. This is not a method of consolidation, the assets and liabilities of the associate are not aggregated on a line-by-line basis in the group accounts. Instead, only selected items are included in the consolidated financial statement:

The consolidated statement of comprehensive income:

- The investor will include **its share of the results of the associate for the period** in its consolidated statement of comprehensive income (or income statement depending on how the statements have been prepared).
- The share of results is based on the associate's profit after tax, but is included in the consolidated profit before tax in the group accounts.
- The investor will also include its share of any other comprehensive income of the associate in the 'Income from associate, net of tax' section of the income statement.

The consolidated statement of financial position:

- The investor will include one figure within non-current assets in the consolidated statement of financial position, entitled **Investment in associat**e. The balance to be included under this heading is calculated as follows:

Investment at cost; plus
Share of profits or losses since acquisition; plus
Share of any other changes to shareholders' funds e.g. other comprehensive income (maybe from revaluation of non-current assets); less
Impairment of goodwill; less
Dividends received.

This calculation makes sense if we think about the value of the investment to the investor; the investment increases in value as profits are generated and as other gains are recognised, but reduces in value if impairment is required. Dividends received from an associate reduce the value of the associate by the amount of the distribution but this is balanced by an increase to cash in the books of the investor.

Goodwill on acquisition

Note that the starting point for this calculation is cost of investment. This means the value of any goodwill on acquisition is already included. Goodwill is part of the value of investment. It may have to be calculated if any impairment is to be recorded; however, it will not appear under the heading of goodwill in the group statement of financial position. The impairment will simply be deducted from the value of the investment.

Example 5.A

On 1 May 20X6 AB purchased 40% of the share capital of GH for $375,000. The retained earnings of GH at that date were $400,000.

The consolidated financial statements of AB are presented below together with the accounts of GH for the year to 31 May 20X8.

Income statements for the year ended 31 May 20X8	AB	GH
	$000	$000
Profit from operations	1,270	290
Interest paid	(130)	(40)
Profit before tax	1,140	250
Income tax	(140)	(50)
Profit for the period	1,000	200

Statements of financial position as at 31 May 20X8	AB	GH
	$000	$000
Assets		
Non-current assets		
Investment in GH	375	
Other assets	2,100	900
	2,475	900
Capital and liabilities		
Share capital	500	250
Retained earnings	1,875	550
	2,375	800
Liabilities	100	100
	2,475	900

Additional information:

1. GH paid a dividend of $100,000 in the year. AB has incorporated its share of this dividend in profit from operations.
2. Goodwill is impaired by 20% in the year. No impairment was considered necessary in previous years.

Requirement

Prepare the consolidated statement of financial position and consolidated income statement for the AB group for the year ended 31 May 20X8.

Solution

Consolidated Income statement for the year ended 31 May 20X8	AB
	$000
Profit from operations ($1,270 − W1 $23 − W2 $40)	1,207
Interest paid	(130)
	1,077
Share of profit of associate (W3)	80
Profit before tax	1,157
Income tax	(140)
Profit for the period	1,017

Consolidated statement of financial position as at 31 May 20X8	AB
	$000
Assets	
Non-current assets	
Investment in associate (W4)	372
Other assets	2,100
	2,472
Capital and liabilities	
Share capital	500
Retained earnings (W5)	1,872
	$2,372
Liabilities	100
	2,472

Workings

W1 Impairment of goodwill – the impairment is given as a percentage so we will have to calculate goodwill to determine the impairment.

Goodwill on acquisition:

Consideration paid		$375
Net assets acquired:		
Share capital	$250	
Retained earnings at acquisition	$400	
40% acquired		260
Goodwill on acquisition		115

Impairment of goodwill is therefore 20% × £115,000 = $23,000. This will be charged to the group income statement in the year and will reduce the value of the investment:

Dr	Profit from operations		$23,000
	Cr	Investment in associate	$23,000

Being the impairment of goodwill on associate

W2 40% of the dividend of $100,000 paid by GH will have been received by AB. This is currently included in the profit from operations. Dividends received reduce the value of the investment in associate, and the only figure that should be included in the income statement in respect of the associate is the share of results for the year. The dividend received should be adjusted in the group accounts as:

Dr	Investment in associate	$40,000	
	Cr Profit from operations		$40,000

Being elimination of dividends from the income statement

W3 Share of profit of associate

AB is entitled to 40% of the profit after tax of GH, 40% × $200,000 = $80,000.

W4 Investment in associate

	$000
Cost of investment	375
Plus share of post-acquisition profits 40% × ($550,000 − $400,000)	60
Less dividend received	(40)
Less impairment	(23)
Investment in associate	372

W5 Retained earnings

	Group $000	GH $000
Retained earnings of AB	1,875	
Retained earnings of GH		550
RE of GH at acquisition		(400)
		150
40% group share of GH	60	
Impairment of goodwill	(23)	
Less elimination of dividend	(40)	
	1,872	

5.2.2 Treatment of unrealised profits on intra-group trading

You will already be aware that, under full consolidation, intra-group profits and losses are eliminated in full in the consolidated financial statements.

Example 5.B

Suppose that in the year ended 31 December 20X0 Predator (see Example 5.A) sold goods to Victim having a sales value of $2 million, making a profit of $500,000. 20% of these goods were unsold by Victim at the year-end.

The unrealised profit at the year-end is 20% × $500,000 = $100,000. Therefore, in the consolidated financial statements, this unrealised profit is eliminated from retained earnings and inventories as shown below:

	DR	*CR*
	$'000	$'000
Retained earnings	100	
Inventories		100

In the consolidated income statement, revenue would be reduced by $2 million (removing the intra-group element) and cost of sales by $1.9 million. The net effect of this adjustment is of course to adjust gross profit by $100,000.

However, when we equity account our associate we are not aggregating the assets and liabilities on a line-by-line basis – we don't have its inventories and retained earnings figures included in our statement of financial position. There is no adjustment to remove sales and cost of sales, as we have not aggregated the associate's income statement with the group's income statement.

When we use equity accounting the associate is only reflected in one line in the group income statement and one line in the group statement of financial position therefore any adjusting entries for intra-group trading will have to be affecting either; share of associate's profits or investment in associate. The entry required will depend on which direction the goods are going; to the associate or from the associate.

Sale by parent (or subsidiary) to associate (equity method of consolidation)

If Predator is consolidated using the equity method of consolidation then the inventories of Victim will not appear on the consolidated statement of financial position. Therefore crediting inventories would be inappropriate. The *group share* of the net assets of Victim will appear under the heading 'Investments'. Therefore the correct consolidation adjustment will be:

	DR	*CR*
	$'000	$'000
Retained earnings	50	
Investment in Victim		50

In the consolidated income statement, gross profit would be reduced by $50,000. The issue of whether or not any adjustment should be made to revenue is not made clear in IAS 28 *Investments in associates*. It could be argued that given the margin that is earned on the intra-group sales (25%) then revenue should be adjusted by $200,000 ($50,000 × 100/25). This would lead to a reduction in cost of sales of $150,000 to give the required adjustment of $50,000 to gross profit. Given that Predator makes a profit of 25% on sales, this is the sales value that corresponds to an unrealised profit adjustment of $50,000.

Sale to parent (or subsidiary) from associate (equity method of consolidation)

Where the transaction (using the same details as above) is going in the other direction, the overstated inventories are sitting in the parent's accounts, so inventories are adjusted. The unrealised profit is made by the associate and so the share of the profit of associate is overstated; corrected by:

	DR	*CR*
	$'000	$'000
Share of profit of associate	50	
Inventories		50

Note: If you are only asked to prepare the consolidated statement of financial position then the debit would be straight to retained earnings.

5.3 IAS 31 *Interests in joint ventures*

The IAS states that a joint venture is:

A contractual arrangement whereby two or more parties undertake an economic activity that is subject to joint control.

A joint venture can take a number of forms and the appropriate form of accounting depends on the form of the joint venture. However, IAS 31 states that whatever form the joint venture takes there are two common characteristics:

- Two or more venturers are bound by a contractual arrangement.
- The contractual arrangement establishes joint control.

5.3.1 Accounting for joint ventures

Jointly controlled operations

Some joint ventures do not involve the establishment of an entity that is separate from the venturers themselves, but rather the joint uses of the assets and other resources of the individual venturer. An example given in IAS 31 of such an arrangement is the joint manufacture of an aircraft by two or more entities. In such situations the *individual* financial statements of each entity will show:

- The assets that it controls and the liabilities that it incurs.
- The expenses that it incurs and its share of the income that it earns from the sale of goods or services by the joint venture.

No further adjustments will be required in the consolidated financial statements.

Jointly controlled assets

Some joint ventures involve the joint control and ownership of one or more assets used exclusively for the purpose of the joint venture. IAS 31 gives the joint ownership and control of an oil pipeline by two or more oil companies as an example of this type of joint venture. Accounting is very similar to jointly controlled operations in that, both in the separate financial statements of the venturers and in their consolidated financial statements each venturer will recognise:

- its share of the jointly controlled assets and jointly incurred liabilities, classified according to their nature;
- any liabilities that it has incurred;
- its share of the income generated by the venture, less any joint expenses of the venture;
- any expenses that it has incurred itself in respect of its interest in the joint venture.

Jointly controlled entities

A jointly controlled entity involves the establishment of a corporation, partnership or other entity in which each venturer has an interest. An example given of such a joint venture in IAS 31 is where an entity commences business in a foreign country in conjunction with the government or other agency in that country by establishing a separate entity that is jointly controlled by the entity and the government or agency. IAS 31 provides for two alternative treatments of such ventures in the consolidated financial statements of the investors. In all cases the individual financial statements of the investors will show the contributions made in cash or other assets as an investment in the jointly controlled entity.

5.3.2 Accounting for jointly controlled entities

The recommended treatment for such joint ventures in the consolidated financial statements is that the venturer should use **proportionate consolidation**. IAS 31 states that this best represents the economic reality of the arrangement, which is that the venturer has control over its share of future economic benefits through its shares of the assets and liabilities of the joint venture. Proportionate consolidation may either:

- aggregate the appropriate share of net assets and net income with those of the group on a line-by-line basis (as we did in our earlier example); or
- show separately the appropriate share of net assets and net income on a line-by-line basis.

Example 5.C

GHK prepares its group accounts to 31 December. The accounts for GHK and its fully owned subsidiaries are shown below for GHK excluding its joint venture LM.

GHK acquired its interest in LM in 2006. GHK is one of 4 venturers who exercise joint control over the operations of LM. A contractual agreement details the terms of the arrangement. At the date the interest was acquired the retained earnings of LM totalled $400,000.

The consolidated financial statements of GHK are presented below together with the accounts of LM for the year to 31 December 20X8.

Income statements for the year ended 31 December 20X8	**GHK**	**LM**
	$000	$000
Revenue	2,700	1,460
Cost of sales	2,000	1,000
Gross profit	700	460
Net operating expenses	400	200
Profit before tax	300	260
Income tax expense	100	60
Profit for the period	400	200

Statements of financial position as at 31 December 20X8	**GHK**	**LM**
	$000	$000
Assets		
Non-current assets		
Property, plant and equipment	1,320	900
Investment in LM	450	-
Current assets	1,770	900
Inventories	100	120
Receivables	730	380
	2,600	1,400
Capital and liabilities		
Share capital	1,000	500
Retained earnings	1,200	700
	2,200	1,200
Liabilities		
Current liabilities	400	200
	2,600	1,400

Additional information:

1. There is no impairment of goodwill.
2. LM paid a dividend of $100,000 in the year to 31 December 20X8. GHK has included its share of this dividend in net operating expenses.
3. GHK incorporates LM in the group accounts using proportionate consolidation.

Requirement

Prepare the consolidated income statement and the consolidated statement of financial position for GHK incorporating the joint venture, LM for the year to 31 December 20X8.

Solution

The share of revenues, costs, assets and liabilities of the JV are aggregated with the group figures. There is no non-controlling interest as only the group share (25% as GHK is 1 of 4 venturers) is included.

Consolidated income statement for the year ended 31 December 20X8	GHK
	$000
Revenue $2,700 + (25% × $1,460)	3,065
Cost of sales $2,000 + (25% × $1,000)	(2,250)
Gross profit	815
Net operating exps $400 + (25% × $200) + W1 $25	(475)
Profit before tax	340
Income tax expense $100 + (25% × $60)	(115)
Profit for the period	225

Statement of financial position as at 31 December 20X8	GHK
	$000
Assets	
Non-current assets	
Property, plant and equipment $1320 + (25% × 900)	1,545
Goodwill (W2)	225
	1,770
Current assets	
Inventories $100 + (25% × $120)	130
Receivables $730 + (25% × $380)	825
	2,725
Capital and liabilities	
Share capital (parent only)	1,000
Retained earnings (W3)	1,275
Liabilities	
Current liabilities $400 + (25% × $200)	450
	2,725

Workings

W1 Elimination of internal dividend

25% of the $100,000 dividend paid by LM has been received by GHK. This must be eliminated by:

Dr Net operating expenses	$25,000	
Cr Retained earnings		$25,000

Being the group share of the dividend paid by the JV

The group retained earnings include 25% of the post-acquisitions earnings of the JV so the net impact on retained earnings is nil as we have reduced GHK's retained earnings and increased LM's retained earnings by the same amount. The amount is correctly deducted from the income statement.

W2 Goodwill on acquisition

Consideration paid		$450
Net assets acquired:		
Share capital	$500	
Retained earnings at acquisition	$400	
25% acquired	$900	225
Goodwill on acquisition		225

W3 Retained earnings

	Group $000	LM $000
Retained earnings of GHK	1,200	
Retained earnings of LM		700
RE of LM at acquisition		(400)
		300
25% group share of LM	75	
	1,275	

5.3.3 Treatment of unrealised profits on intra-group trading

When we have used proportionate consolidation, the group share of the inventory of the relevant entity *is* included in consolidated inventory.

Example 5.D

Suppose that in the year ended 31 December 20X0 Predator (see Example 5.B) sold goods to Victim having a sales value of $2 million, making a profit of $500,000. 20% of these goods were unsold by Victim at the year-end. The unrealised profit at the year-end is 20% × $500,000 = $100,000.

Therefore the appropriate journal adjustment would be:

	DR	*CR*
	$'000	$'000
Retained earnings	50	
Inventory		50

In the consolidated income statement, revenue would be reduced by $1 million (50% × $2 million) and cost of sales by $950,000 (50% × $1,900,000). The net effect is to achieve an adjustment of $50,000 at gross profit level.

In the case of proportionate consolidation it makes no difference which way the sale goes (from parent/subsidiary or vice versa), the consolidation adjustment is the same.

5.3.4 Alternative treatment

However, IAS 31 permits an alternative treatment: the interest is consolidated using the equity method, as for associates. If this treatment is adopted, or if the first form of proportionate consolidation is used (see above), then IAS 31 required that entities disclose the aggregate amounts of each of current assets, long-term assets, current liabilities, long-term liabilities, income and expenses related to its interest in joint ventures.

The IASB has continued to permit both the recommended and the alternative treatment of joint ventures: the revised IAS 31 that follows the improvements project is unchanged in this respect. It therefore provides an interesting example of a case where some degree of choice is available to reporting entities.

5.4 The impact of different methods of accounting for investments

---

Example 5.E

Statement of financial positions of Predator and Victim as on 31 December 20X0

	Predator	*Victim*
	$'000	$'000
Non-current assets		
Investment in Victim	7,200	–
Other	16,500	10,000
Current assets	14,800	8,800
	38,500	18,800
Issued capital ($1 shares)	20,000	12,000
Retained earnings	12,500	3,000
	32,500	15,000
Current liabilities	6,000	3,800
	38,500	18,800

Notes

1. The investment in Victim comprises 6 million shares acquired on 31 December 20X4 when Victim's equity was $13 million (issued capital $12 million plus retained earnings $1 million).
2. Predator sells a product that is used by Victim. The total sales of the product in 20X4 were $1,000,000. None of the goods were in the inventory of Victim at the year-end. However, the trade receivables of Predator and the trade payables of Victim include $100,000 in respect of the sale of these goods.

Income statements for the year ended 31 December 20X0

	Predator	*Victim*
	$'000	$'000
Revenue	9,000	4,500
Operating costs	(4,500)	(2,250)
Investment income	400	–
Profit before tax	4,900	2,250
Income tax expense	(1,300)	(750)
Profit for the period	3,600	1,500

Summarised statements of changes in equity for the year ended 31 December 20X0

	Predator	*Victim*
	$'000	$'000
Opening equity	30,900	14,300
Profit for the period	3,600	1,500
Dividends	(2,000)	(800)
Closing equity	32,500	15,000

We will now prepare the consolidated financial statements of the group under the three possible methods of consolidation: full consolidation, equity method of consolidation and proportionate consolidation.

Consolidated statement of financial position

	Full	*Equity*	*Proportionate*
	$'000	$'000	$'000
Goodwill	700		700
Investment in Victim		8,200	
Other non-current assets	26,500	16,500	21,500
Current assets	23,500	14,800	19,150
	50,700	39,500	41,350
Issued capital	20,000	20,000	20,000
Retained earnings	13,500	13,500	13,500
	33,500	33,500	33,500
Non-controlling interest	7,500	–	–
Current liabilities	9,700	6,000	7,850
	50,700	39,500	41,350

Workings

	Full	*Equity*	*Proportionate*
	$'000	**$'000**	**$'000**
1. *Goodwill on consolidation*			
Cost of investment	7,200	7,200	7,200
Share of net assets at date of acquisition	(6,500)	(6,500)	(6,500)
Total goodwill	700	700	700
2. *Investment under equity method*			
Investment at cost		7,200	
Share of post-acquisition profits ($2,000 × 50%)		1,000	
		8,200	
3. *Consolidated retained earnings*			
Predator	12,500	12,500	12,500
Victim [50% ($3 m – $1 m)]	1,000	1,000	1,000
	13,500	13,500	13,500

4. *Current assets*			
Predator	14,800	14,800	14,800
Victim	8,800	–	4,400
Intra-group balance	(100)	–	(50)
	23,500	14,800	19,150
5. *Current liabilities*			
Predator	6,000	6,000	6,000
Victim	3,800	–	1,900
Intra-group balance	(100)	–	(50)
	9,700	6,000	7,850

Notes explaining the methods of consolidation

(a) *Full consolidation* is the method used to deal with most subsidiaries. You should be familiar with the mechanics of this method from previous chapters. This method is also known as *line-by-line consolidation*.

(b) *Equity accounting* (or *one-line consolidation*) deals only with the *group share* of the assets, and so on, of Victim. The group's interest in Victim is shown as one amount in the consolidated financial statements.

(c) Under equity accounting the carrying amount of the investment is based on the underlying assets and liabilities of the investment, plus any goodwill not written off. It can be compared with the full consolidation method as follows:

	$'000
Full consolidation	
Underlying net assets at BS date	15,000
Goodwill	700
	15,700
Non-controlling interest	(7,500)
	8,200
Equity method	
Investment at cost	7,200
Share of post-acquisition profits	1,000
	8,200

Under equity accounting intra-group balances do not cancel out because the assets and liabilities of Victim are not shown in group receivables and payables.

(d) *Proportionate consolidation* is a cross between full consolidation and the equity method. The method is similar to full consolidation in that the assets and liabilities are aggregated on a line-by-line basis. However it is similar to the equity method in that only the group share of assets and liabilities is included and there is no need for a non-controlling interest.

(e) Notice that whatever method of consolidation is used, goodwill and consolidated reserves are the same.

Consolidated income statement

	Full	*Equity*	*Proportionate*
	$'000	$'000	$'000
Revenue	12,500	9,000	10,750
Operating costs	(5,750)	(4,500)	(5,125)
Share of profits of Victim		750	
Profit before tax	6,750	5,250	5,625
Income tax expense	(2,050)	(1,300)	(1,675)
Profit for the period	4,700	3,950	3,950
Attributable to:	$		
Equity holders of the parent	3,950		
Non-controlling interest	750		
	4,700		

Workings

1. *Revenue*			
Predator	9,000	9,000	9,000
Victim	4,500		2,250
Intra-group sales eliminated	(1,000)		(500)
	12,500	9,000	10,750
2. *Operating costs*			
Predator	4,500	4,500	4,500
Victim	2,250		1,125
Intra-group sales eliminated	(1,000)		(500)
	5,750	4,500	5,125
3. *Share of profits of Victim*			
		Equity	
		$'000	
50% of profit for the period		750	

Notice that the principle used here mirrors that used in the statement of financial position. Under full consolidation, income and expenses are aggregated on a line-by-line basis, with full elimination of intra-group transactions. Under the equity method there is one-line consolidation of operating profits, with no elimination of intra-group transactions (unless there is any unrealised profit – see later in the chapter). Under the proportionate consolidation method there is line-by-line consolidation of the group share of Victim's balances, with proportionate elimination of intra-group transactions.

Consolidated statement of changes in equity attributable to equity holders of the parent

	Full	*Equity*	*Proportionate*
	$'000	$'000	$'000
Opening equity	31,550	31,550	31,550
Profit for the period	3,950	3,950	3,950
Dividends – Predator	(2,000)	(2,000)	(2,000)
Closing equity	33,500	33,500	33,500
Working: Opening equity			
Predator	30,900	30,900	30,900
Victim [50% × (14,300 − 13,000)]	650	650	650
	31,550	31,550	31,550

The fairly obvious comment here is that the statement in respect of changes in equity attributable to equity holders of the parent is identical whatever method of consolidation is used.

5.5 Fair values and accounting policies

Where, at the date of acquisition, the fair value of the net assets of an investment that is equity accounted or proportionally consolidated is significantly different from their carrying values in the financial statements of the acquired entity, the initial consolidated carrying values should be based on fair values

In addition, wherever possible the financial statements of the investee entity should be prepared to the same date, and using the same accounting policies, as the rest of the group. If the financial statements are not prepared to the same date, the difference between the dates should be no more than 3 months.

5.6 Summary

This chapter has reviewed the methods of accounting that are appropriate where an investor does not have complete control over an investee's activities. Generally, it is appropriate to use the equity method of accounting for associates. As a general rule of thumb, associate status is often indicated where an investor holds between 20% and 50% of the equity capital of the investee entity.

Joint ventures involve two or more parties in an economic activity subject to joint control. The recommended accounting treatment for jointly controlled entities is proportionate consolidation, but IAS 31 also permits use of the equity method.

Revision Questions 5

Question 1

(a) The following statements refer to a situation where an investing entity (D) seeks to exert control or influence over another entity (E). Assume that D is required to prepare consolidated accounts because of other investments.

(i) if D owns more than 20% but less than 50% of the equity shares in E, then E is bound to be an associate of D.
(ii) if D controls the operating and financial policies of E, then E cannot be an associate of D.
(iii) if E is an associate of D, then any amounts payable by E to D are not eliminated when preparing the consolidated statement of financial position of D.

Which of the above statements are true?

(b) Briefly explain the preferred treatment of jointly controlled entities in accordance with IAS 31 *Interests in Joint Ventures*.

Question 2

On 30 June 20X3, Sugar entered into an agreement with two other investors to establish a new entity, Spice. All three investors subscribed for 1/3 of the equity shares in Spice and each share carries one vote. All three investors appointed two representatives to the six-member board of directors of Spice. All key policy decisions require the agreement of five of the six board members.

The following statements refer to the treatment of the investment in Spice in the consolidated financial statements of Sugar for the year ended 30 September 20X3:

(i) Spice will be treated as a joint venture simply because the three investors hold 1/3 of the shares each.
(ii) Spice will be treated as a joint venture in this case, but only because of the requirement that key policy decisions require the consent of at least five of the directors.
(iii) If Spice carries on a business that is distinct from that of its investors, then it will be consolidated using proportional consolidation.
(iv) Spice is only a joint venture if the requirement that key policy decisions require the consent of five directors is established by contract.

Assuming that the recommended treatment set out in IAS 31 *Interests in Joint Ventures* is used, which of the above statements are true?

Question 3

On 1 January 20X5, CD purchased 30% of the ordinary share capital of EF for $280,000, which gave it significant influence over EF's activities. In the financial year ended 31 December 20X5. EF reported pre-tax profits of $62,000. The tax charge was $20,000. During the financial year ended 31 December 20X5, EF paid a total divided of $5,000 to its shareholders.

In the year ended 31 December 20X6, EF made a pre-tax loss of $18,000, with a tax credit of $4,000. A review of CD's investment in EF at 31 December 20X6 concluded that impairment had taken place. An impairment loss of $45,000 was charged in CD's consolidated financial statements for the year.

Calculate the carrying amount of the investment in EF to be included in CD's consolidated statement of financial position at 31 December 20X6.

Question 4

AB owns a controlling interest in another entity, CD, and exerts significant influence over EF, an entity in which it holds 30% of the ordinary share capital. During the financial year ended 30 April 2005, EF sold goods to AB valued at $80,000. The cost of the goods to EF was $60,000. Twenty-five per cent of the goods remained in AB's inventory at 30 April 2005. Briefly explain how the intra-group trading will be dealt with in the consolidated accounts of AB.

Question 5

The income statements of ST and two entities in which it holds investments are shown below for the year ended 31 January 20X6:

	ST	*UV*	*WX*
	$'000	$'000	$'000
Revenue	1,800	1,400	600
Cost of sales	(1,200)	(850)	(450)
Gross profit	600	550	150
Operating expenses	(450)	(375)	(74)
Profit from operations	150	175	76
Finance cost	(16)	(12)	–
Interest income	6	–	–
Profit before tax	140	163	76
Income tax expense	(45)	(53)	(26)
Profit for the period	95	110	50

Notes

1. *Investments by ST*

Several years ago ST acquired 70% of the issued ordinary share capital of UV. On 1 February 20X5 ST acquired 50% of the issued share capital of WX, an entity set up under a contractual arrangement as a joint venture between ST and one of its suppliers. The directors of ST have decided to adopt a policy of proportionate consolidation wherever appropriate and permitted by International Financial Reporting Standards.

2. *UV's borrowings*
During the financial year ended 31 January 20X6, UV paid the full amount of interest due on its 6% debenture loan of $200,000. ST invested $100,000 in the debenture when it was issued three years ago.

3. *Intra-group trading*
During the year WX sold goods to ST for $20,000. Half of the goods remained in ST's inventories at 31 January 20X6. WX's gross profit margin on the sale was 20%.

Requirement

Prepare the consolidated income statement of the ST group for the year ended 31 January 20X6. (Exam standard questions for **10 marks**)

Question 6

AJ is a law stationery business. In 20X2 the majority of the entity's board of directors were replaced. The new board decided to adopt a policy of expansion through acquisition. The statements of financial position as at 31 March 20X5 of AJ and of two entities in which it holds significant investments are shown below.

	AJ		*BK*		*CL*	
	$'000	$'000	$'000	$'000	$'000	$'000
ASSETS						
Non-current assets						
Property, plant and equipment	12,500		4,700		4,500	
Investments	18,000		–		1,300	
		30,500		4,700		5,800
Current assets						
Inventories	7,200		8,000		–	
Trade receivables	6,300		4,300		3,100	
Financial assets	–		–		2,000	
Cash	800		–		900	
		14,300		12,300		6,000
		44,800		17,000		11,800
EQUITY + LIABILITIES						
Equity						
Called up share capital ($1 shares)		10,000		5,000		2,500
Retained earnings		14,000		1,000		4,300
		24,000		6,000		6,800
Non-current liabilities						
Loan notes		10,000		3,000		–
Current liabilities						
Trade payables	8,900		6,700		4,000	
Tax	1,300		100		600	
Short-term borrowings	600		1,200		400	
		10,800		8,000		5,000
		44,800		17,000		11,800

Notes to the statement of financial positions

1. *Investment by AJ in BK*

On 1 April 20X2, AJ purchased $2 million loan notes in BK at par.

On 1 April 20X3, AJ purchased 4 million of the ordinary shares in BK for $7.5 million in cash, when BK's retained earnings were $1.5 million.

BK is an unquoted entity and so the investment is classified as an available for sale asset in AJ's own accounts. No reliable measure of fair value can be ascertained and so the investment remains at cost in the individual accounts of AJ.

At the date of acquisition of the shares, BK's property, plant and equipment included land recorded at cost of $920,000. At the date of acquisition the land was valued at $1,115,000. No other adjustments in respect of fair value were required to BK's assets and liabilities upon acquisition. BK has not recorded the revaluation in its own accounting records.

2. *Investment by AJ in CL*

On 1 October 20X4, AJ acquired 1 million shares in CL, a book distributor, when the retained earnings of CL were $3.9 million. The purchase consideration was $4.4 million. Since the acquisition, AJ has the right to appoint one of the five directors of CL. The remaining shares in CL are owned principally by three other investors.

No fair value adjustments were required in respect of CL's assets or liabilities upon acquisition. The investment in CL is held at cost (as with BK) as no reliable measure can be made of its fair value.

3. *Goodwill on consolidation*

Since acquiring its investment in BK, AJ has adopted the requirements of IFRS 3 *Business Combinations* in respect of goodwill on consolidation. During March 20X5, it has conducted an impairment review of goodwill. As a result the value of goodwill on consolidation in respect of BK is now $1.7 million.

It is the group's policy to value the non-controlling interest at acquisition at the proportionate share of the fair value of the subsidiary's identifiable net assets.

4. *Intra-group trading*

BK supplies legal books to AJ. On 31 March 20X5, AJ's inventories included books purchased at a total cost of $1 million from BK. BK's mark-up on books is 25%.

Requirements

(a) Explain, with reasons, how the investments in BK and CL will be treated in the consolidated financial statements of the AJ group. **(5 marks)**

(b) Prepare the consolidated statement of financial position for the AJ group at 31 March 20X5.

(20 marks)

(Exam standard question-Total marks = 25)

Question 7

You are the accountant responsible for training at Develop, an entity with a number of investments throughout the world. A key financial reporting task is to prepare consolidated financial statements and this forms an important aspect of the training of new accountants.

A recently-employed trainee has sent you this memorandum.

I have just attended my first training course and have learned the mechanics of how to treat subsidiaries, associates and trade investments in the consolidated accounts. I'm reasonably comfortable with the numbers, but the concepts baffle me. Why does the exercise of adding together the statement of financial position of our entity with those of our subsidiaries give our shareholders useful financial information? Why do we treat associates differently – I find the concept of adding together all the net assets and showing our share as one amount particularly confusing? I'm happier with the treatment of trade investments, at least I can see that the figure is what we paid to buy the shares. Why not do this for all our investments. I don't need a detailed explanation of the mechanics, which I'm already reasonably happy with.

Requirement

Draft a reply to your trainee that explains the principles underpinning the preparation of consolidated financial statements. You should clearly explain why subsidiaries, associates and trade investments are treated differently and why the information is of benefit to the shareholders of the investor. **(Exam standard question - 10 marks)**

Solutions to Revision Questions 5

Solution 1

(a) The first statement is not true; a simple ownership test does not categorically determine the nature of the relationship between an investor and investee entity. However, the second and third statements are correct.

(b) The preferred treatment for jointly controlled entities is to account for them using proportional consolidation. This involves including the venturer's share of the assets, liabilities, income and expenses, and aggregating that share in the group accounts. As only the appropriate share has been included, there is no need to account for non-ontrolling interest.

Solution 2

The first statement is not true; in all cases the nature of the relationship and the degree of control exerted must be examined in order to assess whether or not a joint venture exists. The other statements are true.

Solution 3

	$'000	$'000
Cost of investment		280
20X5 profit after tax (62 − 20)	42	
20X5 dividend	(5)	
20X6 loss after tax (18 − 4)	(14)	
	23	
Group share = 30% × $23		6.9
		286.9
Less: impairment		(45)
		241.9

Solution 4

Unrealised profit = ($80,000 − $60,000) × 25% = $5,000.

The group share of the figure is 30%:$1,500. The profit and inventory are located in the holding entity, so therefore the adjustment is to consolidated reserves and consolidated inventory.

Solution 5

ST Group: consolidated income statement for the year ended 31 January 20X6

	$'000
Revenue {1,800 + 1,400 + [(600 − 20)/2]}	3,490
Cost of sales [1,200 − (20/2) + 850 + (450/2) + 1(W1)]	(2,266)
Gross profit	1,224
Operating expenses [450 + 375 + (74/2)]	(862)
Profit from operations	362
Finance cost [16 + (12 − 6)]	(22)
Profit before tax	340
Income tax expense [45 + 53 + (26/2)]	(111)
Profit for the period	229
	$'000
Attributable to:	
Equity holders of the parent	196
Non-controlling interest [110 (profit of UV for the period) × 30%]	33
	229

(W1) Provision for unrealised profit
$10,000 × 20% = $2,000.
Fifty per cent of this is treated as realised, and the remainder ($1,000) as unrealised.

Solution 6

(a) AJ owns 80% of the shares of BK, which points to the existence of a parent/subsidiary relationship. Provided that AJ controls the activities of BK (and there is nothing to suggest that it does not have control), AJ will account for its investment in BK as a subsidiary and will prepare consolidated financial statements, using the acquisition method.

AJ acquired 40% of the shares in CL. An investment of 40% in another entity would normally indicate that the investor has a significant influence over (but not control of) the entity's activities. The fact that AJ has the power to appoint one director to the board tends to support this conclusion. Also, the fact that three other investors hold most of the remainder of the shares make it unlikely that another investor in CL would be able to control the entity's activities. AJ will account for CL as an associate using the equity accounting method.

(b) **AJ: Consolidated statement of financial position at 31 March 20X5**

	$'000	$'000
Non-current assets		
Property, plant and equipment [12,500 + 4,700 + 195 (FV)]	17,395	
Goodwill	1,700	
Investment in associate (W3)	4,560	
Other financial assets (W1)	4,100	
		27,755
Current assets		
Inventories [7,200 + 8,000 − 200 (W4)]	15,000	
Trade receivables (6,300 + 4,300)	10,600	
Cash	800	
		26,400
		54,155

Capital and reserves		
Share capital	10,000	
Consolidated reserves (W6)	13,156	
		23,156
Non-Controlling interest (W5)		1,199
Non-current liabilities		
Loan notes [10,000 + 3,000 − 2,000 (intra-group)]		11,000
Current liabilities		
Trade payables (8,900 + 6,700)	15,600	
Tax (1,300 + 100)	1,400	
Short term borrowings (600 + 1,200)	1,800	
		18,800
		54,155

Workings

1. *AJ's investments*

	$'000
As stated	18,000
Purchase of BK's loan notes	(2,000)
Purchase of BK's shares	(7,500)
Purchase of CL's shares	(4,400)
Balance: other financial assets	4,100

2. *Goodwill on consolidation of BK*

	$'000
Purchase consideration	7,500
Share of net assets acquired:	
[5,000 + 1,500 + 195 (FV adjustment)] × 80%	(5,356)
Goodwill as originally calculated	2,144
Impairment loss (balancing figure)	(444)
Goodwill carried forward	1,700

3. *Investment in associate*

	$'000
Purchase consideration	4,400
Group share of post-acquisition profits [($4,300 − $3,900) × 40%]	160
	4,560

4. *Intra-group trading*

Total provision for unrealised profit (PURP) = $1 million × 25/125 = $200,000

	$'000	$'000
DR Minority share (20%)	40	
DR Consolidated reserves	160	
CR Consolidated inventories		200

5. *Non-controlling interest*

	$'000
Share of net assets in BK:	
(6,000 + 195) × 20%	1,239
Less: PURP (W4)	(40)
	1,199

6. *Consolidated reserves*

	$'000
AJ	14,000
BK – share of post-acquisition loss:	
(1,500 − 1,000) × 80%	(400)
CL – share of post-acquisition profits:	
(4,300− 3,900) × 40%	160
Impairment loss (W2)	(444)
PURP (W4)	(160)
	13,156

Solution 7

Consolidated financial statements show the resources deployed by a single economic entity and the return generated by those resources. The boundary of the single economic entity is determined by common control. Control is essentially the ability to direct the operating and financial policies of an entity. IAS 27 *Consolidated and separate financial statements* – defines a subsidiary in terms of the ability of the parent to exercise control. That is why a group consists of a parent undertaking and its subsidiary undertakings. Because this single economic entity (comprising more than one separate legal entities) is under common control, it is logical to show one statement of financial position containing 100% of the controlled resources and one income statement containing 100% of the returns earned by those resources. However, a further function of financial statements is to show the interests of the investors in the resources under common control, so the ownership interests section of the statement of financial position needs to separately identify the interests of the parent undertaking's shareholders from those of other 'non-controlling interests' in the economic entity.

It is inappropriate to treat associates and trade investments the way we treat subsidiaries because they are outside the boundary of control. However, associates do qualify for special treatment. Although the parent undertaking cannot control the deployment of resources, it is in a position to exercise a significant degree of influence over their deployment. If they actively exercise this significant influence, then mere inclusion of the amount invested, plus the amounts that happen to be received as dividends, is unlikely to adequately reflect the extent of the investor's interest. Therefore, although full consolidation is inappropriate, because control is not present, a special form of treatment is needed. This treatment, known as the equity method of consolidation, shows the investor's share of the net assets of the associate and its share of the profits.

Trade investments do not qualify for special treatment because control of significant influence is not present. If there is no control or influence over resources, then it is inappropriate to show those resources in any way in the consolidated statement of financial position and it is better to show the initial amount invested. Similarly, if there is not control or influence over the distribution of profits then it is better to restrict amounts included in the consolidated income statement to dividends received.

Consolidated Statement of Cash Flows

Consolidated Statement of Cash Flows

6

LEARNING OUTCOME

After studying this chapter students should be able to:

- prepare a consolidated statement of cash flow for a group of entities.

6.1 Introduction

Section 6.2 outlines the requirements of IAS 7 *Cash Flow Statements (note IAS 1 revised the title of the statement to 'statement of cash flows')*. Section 6.3 works through detailed examples to explain the preparation of group cash flow statements including the following complexities:

- acquisition of a subsidiary during the year;
- disposal of a subsidiary during the year;
- exchange differences arising on the translation of a foreign operation.

6.2 IAS 7 – the general principles

A cash flow statement is an integral part of a complete set of financial statements. It presents information that is not available from the income statement and the statement of financial position.

One of the key features of the cash flow statement is that it gives an indication of the relationship between the profitability of an entity and the cash-generating ability of that entity. Profitability and cash-generating ability are both important but distinct aspects of corporate performance. Additionally, of course, the cash flow statement provides information on how an entity has used the cash it has generated.

While a cash flow statement is an extremely important and useful document taken on its own, it is of most relevance when considered in conjunction with the income statement and the statement of financial position. This is because some of the cash flows for a period will result from transactions that took place in earlier years and some cash flows may well result in further cash flows in a future period. It is usually necessary to refer to the profit and loss account and statement of financial position to evaluate the cash flows in this way.

Before we briefly describe the cash flows that are included under each heading, it is worth stating exactly how 'cash flow' is defined for the purposes of IAS 7. Cash flow is defined as inflows and outflows of cash and cash equivalents:

- Cash is regarded as cash on hand and demand deposits.
- Cash equivalents are short-term, highly liquid investments that are readily convertible to known amounts of cash and which are subject to an insignificant risk of changes in value.

6.2.1 IAS 7 – standard headings

The standard headings under which the cash flows should be reported are given below:

(a) cash flow from operating activities;
(b) cash flow from investing activities, returns on investments and servicing of finance;
(c) cash flow from financing activities;
(d) net change in cash and cash equivalents for the period.

6.3 Cash flow statements for groups

Cash flow statement preparation for groups will be considered under the following headings:

- general principles;
- treatment of subsidiaries with non-controlling interests;
- treatment of investments that are equity-accounted;
- treatment of investments acquired during the year;
- treatment of investments disposed of during the year;
- treatment of foreign subsidiaries.

6.3.1 General principles

The cash flows need to be analysed under the same major headings as for a single entity and cash is defined in the same way.

The statement should report only cash flows that are external to the group. This can effectively be achieved by working with the figures from the consolidated income statement and statement of financial position.

6.3.2 Treatment of subsidiaries with non-controlling interests

One hundred per cent of the cash flows of all subsidiaries that are line-by-line consolidated should be included in the consolidated cash flow statement.

Dividends paid to non-controlling interests are cash flows that are external to the group, and will therefore be shown as a cash outflow under the heading 'cash flow from operating activities'.

Therefore we need to calculate the dividend, as the following example (that will be used to illustrate a number of the points of principle in this unit) will show.

Example 6.A

We are given the following information concerning the Investor group for the year to 31 December 20X3.

Consolidated income statement

	$'000	$'000
Profit from operations		
Group entities		16,600
Associate		980
Profit before tax		17,580
Income tax expense		
Group entities	7,900	
Associate	420	
		(8,320)
Profit for the period		9,260
Attributable to:		
Equity holders of the parent		7,710
Non-controlling interest		1,550
		9,260

Summarised consolidated statement of changes in equity (in respect of equity holders of the parent)

	$'000
Balance at 1 January 20X3	21,845
Profit for the period	7,710
Dividends paid	(2,100)
New shares issued	2,000
Balance at 31 December 20X3	29,455

Consolidated statements of financial position

	31.12.X3		*31.12.X2*	
ASSETS	$'000	$'000	$'000	$'000
Non-current assets				
Investment in associate		6,200		5,700
Goodwill on acquisition		680		280
Property, plant and equipment		21,200		16,900
		28,080		22,880
Current assets				
Inventories	16,600		12,200	
Receivables	15,000		9,300	
Cash	50		1,445	
		31,650		22,945
		59,730		45,825
EQUITY & LIABILITIES				
Share capital		14,000		13,000
Share premium		2,645		1,645
Retained earnings		12,810		7,200
		29,455		21,845
Non-controlling interests		8,200		6,600
		37,655		28,445
Long-term loans		1,655		5,280
Current liabilities				
Trade payables	7,700		5,800	
Taxation	9,100		4,900	
Bank overdraft	3,620		1,400	
		20,420		12,100
		59,730		45,825

Notes

1. On 1 July 20X3 the Investor group acquired 80% of the issued capital of Vulnerable, whose net assets at that date were as follows:

	$'000
Property, plant and equipment	2,600
Inventories	900
Receivables	980
Cash	200
Trade payables	(1,380)
Tax	(300)
	3,000

   The purchase consideration was $2.8 million in cash.

2. Depreciation charged in the year amounted to $2,200,000. There were no disposals of property, plant and equipment during the year.

Given the information concerning Investor, we can calculate the dividend that was paid to the non-controlling interest by reconciling the movement in the non-controlling interest per the statement of financial position to profits credited to the non-controlling interest per the income statement. This reconciliation is provided below:

	$'000
Non-controlling interest as at 1 January 20X3	6,600
Non-controlling interest in profits for the year	1,550
Increase in non-controlling interest due to acquisition*	600
Dividend paid to non-controlling interest (balance)	(550)
Non-controlling interest as at 31 December 20X3	8,200

*The identifiable net assets of Vulnerable at the date of acquisition were $3 million. Because Vulnerable becomes an 80% subsidiary we then have a non-controlling interest of 20% of $ 3 million, which is $600,000.

6.3.3 Treatment of investments that are equity-accounted

The cash flows of such entities should not be included in the cash flow statement for the group. The only time the cash flows of the group are affected by investments that are equity-accounted is when the entity in which the investment is made makes a dividend payment.

Dividends received from such investments should be shown as a cash inflow. These dividends should be shown under the heading 'cash flow from investing activities'.

The dividend figure can be derived in a similar way to dividends paid to non-controlling interest, as the working below indicates.

	$'000
Investment in associates at 1 January 20X3	5,700
Share of profit before taxation for the year	980
Share of tax charge for the year	(420)
Dividend received in the year (to balance)	(60)
Investment in associates at 31 December 19X3	6,200

6.3.4 Treatment of investments acquired during the year

If the investment is line-by-line consolidated, then the cash flows from the investment will be included in the consolidated cash flow statement *from the date of acquisition.* IAS 7 requires that the *cash* paid to acquire the investment, net of any cash or overdrafts that the investment brings to the group, be shown as an *outflow* of cash under the heading 'investing activities'.

When computing cash flows in a year when a new investment has been acquired, it is important to ensure that the net assets of the new investment at the date of acquisition are not double counted. We will show below the consolidated cash flow statement of the Investor group (see Section 6.3.1) to demonstrate this procedure.

Investor – statement of cash flows for the year ended 31 December 20X3

	$'000	$'000
Cash flow from operating activities		
Net profit from group entities before tax	16,600	
Depreciation	2,200	
Increase in inventory (W2)	(3,500)	
Increase in receivables (W2)	(4,720)	
Increase in payables (W2)	520	
Tax paid (W3)	(4,000)	
Dividends paid		
Parent shareholders	(2,100)	
Non-controlling interest	(550)	
		4,450
Cash flow from investing activities		
Dividend received from associate	60	
Purchase of property, plant and equipment (W4)	(3,900)	
Purchase of subsidiary (net of cash acquired – W2)	(2,600)	
		(6,440)
Cash flow from financing activities		
Issue of shares	2,000	
Repayment of loans	(3,625)	
		(1,625)
		(3,615)
Decrease in cash		
Cash in hand		(1,395)
Bank overdraft		(2,220)
		(3,615)

Workings

1. The goodwill account can be reconciled as follows:

	$'000
Opening balance	280
Increase due to acquisition	
$2.8 m − 80% × $3 m	400
Closing balance	680

2. The cash outflow in respect of the purchase of Vulnerable in the accounting period is the amount paid ($2.8 million) minus the cash balance of Vulnerable at the date of acquisition ($0.2 million). This cash outflow effectively entitles the group to consolidate the net assets of Vulnerable and so, *to the extent that increases in the net assets of the group were due to the acquisition of Vulnerable*, they are taken into account in the cash outflow of $2.6 million. Therefore, in reconciling movements on working capital that

are added back in determining the cash flow from operating activities, the net assets at the date of acquisition should *not* be double counted. Therefore we have the following:

Item	*Overall movement*	*Vulnerable at date of acquisition*	*As per cash flow statement*
	$'000	$'000	$'000
Inventories	4,400	900	3,500
Receivables	5,700	980	4,720
Payables	1,900	1,380	520

3. Movements in the tax account can be reconciled as follows (remembering once again not to double count the tax liability assumed on acquisition of Vulnerable):

	$'000
Tax balance at 1 January 20X3	4,900
Increase due to acquisition of Vulnerable	300
Income statement for the year	7,900
Cash paid (to balance)	(4,000)
Tax balance at 31 December 20X3	9,100

4. In a similar way, we can reconcile movements in property, plant and equipment:

	$'000
Balance as 1 January 20X3	16,900
Additions in the year	
Due to acquisition of Vulnerable	2,600
Other (to balance)	3,900
Depreciation charge for the year	(2,200)
Balance as at 31 December 20X3	21,200

Acquisitions of investments that are equity accounted or treated as a trade investment present few problems as far as the preparation of the consolidated cash flow statement is concerned. Since none of the net assets are line-by-line consolidated the *only* amount that is included in the cash flow statement is to show the cash paid to purchase the investment as a cash outflow under the heading 'cash flow from investing activities'. Any dividends received after the date of acquisition will be shown as a cash inflow under the heading 'cash flow from financing activities'.

6.3.5 Treatment of investments disposed of during the year

As far as the consolidated cash flow statement is concerned, disposals are very much the mirror image of acquisitions.

If the investment was line-by-line consolidated prior to the disposal, and is no longer line-by-line consolidated after the disposal, then the proceeds of disposal of the investment (net of any cash and overdrafts of the investment at the date of disposal) will be shown as a cash inflow under the heading 'acquisitions and disposals'.

The principles regarding the reconciliation of the movements on net assets apply here as applied in the case of the acquisition of investments.

Example 6.B

The consolidated income statement and extracts from the consolidated statement of changes in equity of the JCN group for the year ended 31 December 20X0, and the consolidated statements of financial position of the group at the beginning and end of 20X0, are given below:

Consolidated income statement – year ended 31 December 20X0

	$'000
Profit from operations	20,000
Finance cost	(1,400)
Profit on disposal (N1)	700
Profit before tax	19,300
Income tax expense	(6,500)
Profit for the period	12,800
Attributable to:	
Equity holders of the parent	11,800
Non-controlling interests	1,000
	12,800

Summarised consolidated statement of changes in equity – year ended 31 December 20X0 (in respect of equity holders of the parent)

	$'000
Balance at 1 January 20X0	49,500
Profit for the period	11,800
Dividends paid	(3,000)
Balance at 31 December 20X0	58,300

Consolidated statements of financial position – as at 31 December:

	20X0		*20W9*	
ASSETS	$'000	$'000	$'000	$'000
Property, plant and equipment (N2)		51,350		50,000
Current assets				
Inventories	25,000		23,000	
Trade receivables	21,000		19,000	
Cash in hand	6,000		2,000	
		52,000		44,000
		103,350		94,000
EQUITY & LIABILITIES				
Share capital		20,000		20,000
Retained earnings		38,300		29,500
		58,300		49,500
Non-controlling interests		5,050		5,750
		63,350		55,250
Long-term loans		9,500		12,500
Current liabilities				
Trade payables	18,500		16,250	
Tax	6,000		5,000	
Bank overdraft	6,000		5,000	
		30,500		26,250
		103,350		94,000

Notes

1. On 30 June 20X0 JCN disposed of its investment in Pear, a subsidiary in which it had a shareholding of 80%. The proceeds of the disposal were $5.5 million. Details of the disposal were as follows:

	$'000
Net assets at the date of disposal	
Property, plant and equipment	4,000
Inventories	2,000
Receivables	2,500
Trade payables	(1,500)
Tax	(300)
Bank overdraft	(200)
Long-term loan	(500)
	6,000

JCN had acquired its investment on 30 June 20V8 for $1.9 million when the net assets of Pear were $2 million. Goodwill was found to be impaired several years ago, and so was fully written off before the start of the current financial year.

2. Depreciation charged during the period in the consolidated income statement amounted to $10.1 million. There were no disposals of property, plant and equipment by the group other than those effectively made upon disposal of the investment in Pear.

The consolidated cash flow statement for the group for the year ended 31 December 20X0 would be as follows:

	$'000	$'000
Cash flow from operating activities		
Profit before tax	19,300	
Finance cost	1,400	
Profit on disposal	(700)	
Depreciation	10,100	
Increase in inventories (W1)	(4,000)	
Increase in receivables (W1)	(4,500)	
Increase in payables (W1)	3,750	
Interest paid	(1,400)	
Tax paid (W3)	(5,200)	
		18,750
Cash flow from investing activities		
Purchase of property, plant and equipment (W5)	(15,450)	
Sale of Pear (W4)	5,700	
		(9,750)
Cash flow from financing activities		
Repayment of long-term loan	(2,500)	
Dividends paid:		
Non-controlling interest (W2)	(500)	
Parent shareholders	(3,000)	
Increase in cash and cash equivalents		
Cash in hand		6,000
Bank overdraft		(3,000)
		3,000

Workings

1. As with acquisitions, care must be taken not to double count working capital movements when an investment is disposed of during the year. When we have disposed of a subsidiary, we have already accounted for a working capital *reduction* (the working capital of the subsidiary which is removed from the group statement of financial position on disposal). Therefore we must take care to add this movement back so as to derive the movement from operating sources. Therefore the figures in the cash flow statement can be derived as follows:

Item	*Net movement per the statement of financial position*	*Movement due to the disposal*	*Movement per the cash flow statement*
	$'000	$'000	$'000
Inventories	2,000	2,000	4,000
Receivables	2,000	2,500	4,500
Trade payables	(2,250)	(1,500)	(3,750)

2. The movement in the non-controlling interest account is as follows:

	$'000	
Non-controlling interest as at 1 January 20X0	5,750	
Reduction due to disposal (20% × $6 m)	(1,200)	
Non-controlling interest in the profits of the year	1,000	
So dividend paid to non-controlling interest	(500)	(to balance)
Non-controlling interest as at 31 December 20X0	5,050	

3. The movement in the tax account is:

	$'000
Tax liability as at 1 January 20X0	5,000
Reduction due to disposal	(300)
Tax charge for the year	6,500
Cash paid (to balance)	(5,200)
Tax liability as at 31 December 20X0	6,000

4. The cash outflow shown in the cash flow statement that is caused by the disposal of Pear is the proceeds of sale ($5.5 million) *plus* the bank overdraft of Pear at the date of disposal. A *reduction* in a bank overdraft is a *reduction* in a *negative* component of cash and so *increases* the cash of the group.
5. The outflow of cash in respect of the purchase of property, plant and equipment can be computed by reconciling the statement of financial position movement in property, plant and equipment as shown below:

	$'000
Balance at 1 January 20X0	50,000
Reduction due to disposal of Pear	(4,000)
Depreciation charge for the year	(10,100)
Additions for the year (to balance)	15,450
Balance at 31 December 20X0	51,350

6. While the overall loans balance has been reduced by $3 million, there was a reduction of $500,000 due to the disposal of Pear. Therefore there must have been a repayment of $2.5 million.

Disposals of investments that are *not* line-by-line consolidated do not cause any particular problems. The proceeds of sale are shown as a cash inflow under the heading 'cash flow from investing activities'. *No allowance* needs to be made when reconciling individual assets and liabilities, since the assets and liabilities of the investment that is being disposed of were not line-by-line consolidated prior to disposal.

6.3.6 Treatment of foreign subsidiaries

Where the investment is in a foreign undertaking, exchange differences are quite likely to arise. Exchange differences (covered in more depth in Chapter 8) arising on the translation of a foreign operation are recognised within equity, and are reported in other comprehensive income in the period in which they occur.

Where consolidated net assets are increased or decreased by the effect of exchange differences then this needs to be allowed for in reconciling their movement in the cash flow statement. The workings for this look similar to those prepared for acquisition/disposal in the period.

Example 6.C

The consolidated income statement and extracts from the statement of changes in equity of Etac for the year ended 31 December 20X0 and the consolidated statement of financial positions at that date and at the beginning of the year are given below:

Consolidated statement of comprehensive income – year ended 31 December 20X0

	$'000
Revenue	30,000
Cost of sales	(20,000)
Gross profit	10,000
Other operating expenses	(6,000)
Finance cost	(1,000)
Profit before tax	3,000
Income tax expense	(1,000)
Profit for the period	2,000
Other comprehensive income:	
Exchange difference (N1)	310
Total comprehensive income	2,310
Profit attributable to:	
Equity holders of parent	1,700
Non-controlling interest	300
	2,000
Total comprehensive income attributable to:	
Equity holders of parent	1,950
Non-controlling interest $300 + (310-250)	360
	2,310

Extract from consolidated statement of changes in equity (parent only) – year ended 31 December 20X0

	$'000
Balance at 1 January 20X0	6,200
TCI for the period	1,950
Dividends paid	(1,200)
Balance at 1 January 20X0	6,950

Statements of financial position – as at 31 December

	20X0		20W9	
ASSETS	$'000	$'000	$'000	$'000
Property, plant and equipment (N2)		15,450		11,500
Current assets				
Inventories	4,000		3,500	
Receivables	5,000		4,500	
Cash in hand	600		500	
		9,600		8,500
		25,050		20,000
EQUITY & LIABILITIES				
Share capital		4,000		4,000
Retained earnings		2,950		2,200
		6,950		6,200
Non-controlling interests		3,300		3,050
		10,250		9,250
Long-term loan		6,000		3,000
Current liabilities				
Trade payables	4,200		3,900	
Tax	1,000		850	
Bank overdraft	3,600		3,000	
		8,800		7,750
		25,050		20,000

Notes

1. The exchange differences on retranslation of the opening net assets and profits of the foreign subsidiary were as follows:

	$'000
On property, plant and equipment	225
On inventories	75
On receivables	95
On cash in hand	10
On trade payables	(65)
On taxation payable	(20)
On bank overdraft	(60)
On profits for the period	50
	310

The group share of these differences is included in consolidated equity. The exchange difference on profits all relate to operating items excluding depreciation.
2. The depreciation of property, plant and equipment for the year was $1,600,000. No disposals took place during the year.
3. Goodwill on acquisition was fully written off several years before the start of the current financial year.

Consolidated statement of cash flows for the year to 31 December 20X0

	$'000	$'000
Cash flow from operating activities		
Profit before tax	3,000	
Finance cost	1,000	
Depreciation	1,600	
Inventory increase	(500)	
Receivables increase	(500)	
Payables increase	300	
Exchange differences on working capital	105	
Exchange differences on profit	50	
Interest paid	(1,000)	
Tax paid (W2)	(870)	
Dividends paid*		
Non-controlling interest (W1)	(110)	
Parent shareholders	(1,200)	
		1,875
Cash flow from investing activities (W3)		(5,325)
Cash flow from financing activities		
Increase in long-term loan		3,000
		(450)
Increase/decrease in cash		
Cash in hand		90
Bank overdraft (600 – 60)		(540)
		(450)

*Tutorial note: Dividends paid may be shown as either operating cash flows or cash flows from financing activities according to IAS 7

Workings

1. *Reconciliation of non-controlling interest*

	$'000
Non-cnontrolling interest at 1 January 20X0	3,050
Exchange differences	60
Profit for the year	300
Dividends (balancing figure)	(110)
Non-controlling interest at 31 December 20X0	3,300

2. *Reconciliation of tax*

	$'000
Tax liability at 1 January 20X0	850
Exchange difference	20
Income statement	1,000
Cash paid (balancing figure)	(870)
Tax liability at 31 December 20X0	1,000

3. *Reconciliation of property, plant and equipment*

	$'000
Balance at 1 January 20X0	11,500
Exchange difference	225
Depreciation	(1,600)
Additions (balancing figure)	5,325
Balance at 31 December 20X0	15,450

6.4 Summary

This chapter contains some detailed calculations and explanations relating to the preparation of a cash flow statement for a group of entities. Where questions in this area are set in the examination students will often find that they incorporate an addition and/or a disposal during the year. It is also quite possible that questions will be set that involve exchange differences arising on the translation of a foreign operation.

Students should note that the basic principles involved in preparing a group cash flow statement are the same as for the other consolidated financial statements: the statement should show 100 per cent of the cash flows arising from the assets and liabilities that the group controls, and intra-group cash flows should be eliminated.

Revision Questions

Note that a few short questions are included as tests of understanding. Exam standard questions have the mark allocation noted.

Question 1

STB is preparing its consolidated statement of cash flows for the year ended 31 October 20X7. Its consolidated opening balance at net book value for property, plant and equipment was $207,000. During the year the STB group disposed of plant for proceeds of $8,500 that had cost $62,000 several years ago and which was fully written down at 1 November 20X6. There were no other disposals. The depreciation charge for the year ended 31 October 20X7 was $32,000. The consolidated closing book value for property, plant and equipment was $228,000.

Calculate the cash outflow in respect of purchases of property, plant and equipment for inclusion in the consolidated cash flow statement of STB group for the year ended 31 October 20X7?

Question 2

GPX's financial statements included an investment in associate at $6,600,000 in its consolidated statement of financial position at 30 September 20X5. At 30 September 20X6, the investment in associate had risen to $6,750,000. GPX's pre-tax share of profit in the associate was $420,000, with a related tax charge of $180,000. The net amount of $240,000 was included in the consolidated income statement for the year ended 30 September 20X6.

There were no impairments to the investment in associate, or acquisitions or disposals of shares during the financial year.

Calculate the amount of the cash flow related to this investment for inclusion in the consolidated cash flow statement for the year ended 30 September 20X6?

Question 3

On 1 March 20X4, NS acquired 30% of the shares of TP. The investment is accounted for as an associate in NS's consolidated financial statements. Both NS and TP have an accounting year end of 31 October. NS has no other investments in associates.

Net profit for the year in TP's income statement for the year ended 31 October 20X4 was $230,000. It declared and paid a dividend of $100,000 on 1 July 20X4. No other dividends were paid in the year.

Calculate the amount that will have been included as an inflow in respect of earnings from the associate in the consolidated cash flow statement of NS for the year ended 31 October 20X4?

Question 4

Extracts from the consolidated financial statements of the AH Group for the year ended 30 June 20X5 are given below.

AH Group: Consolidated income statement for the year ended 30 June 20X5

	20X5
	$'000
Revenue	85,000
Cost of sales	(59,750)
Gross profit	25,250
Operating expenses	(5,560)
Finance cost	(1,400)
Profit before disposal of property	18,200
Disposal of property (N2)	1,250
Profit before tax	19,450
Income tax	(6,250)
Profit for the period	13,200
	$'000
Attributable to:	
Non-controlling interests	655
Equity holders of parent	12,545
	13,200

AH Group: Extracts from statement of changes in equity for the year ended 30 June 20X5

	Share capital	*Share premium*	*Retained earnings*	*Total*
	$'000	$'000	$'000	$'000
Opening balance	18,000	10,000	18,340	46,340
Issue of share capital	2,000	2,000	4,000	
Profit for period			12,545	12,545
Dividends			(6,000)	(6,000)
Closing balance	20,000	12,000	24,885	56,885

AH Group: Statement of financial position, with comparatives, as at 30 June 20X5

	20X5		*20X4*	
	$'000	$'000	$'000	$'000
Non-current assets				
Property, plant and equipment	50,600		44,050	
Intangible assets (N3)	6,410		4,160	
		57,010		48,210

Current assets				
Inventories	33,500		28,750	
Trade receivables	27,130		26,300	
Cash	1,870		3,900	
		62,500		58,950
		119,510		107,160
Equity and liabilities				
Share capital	20,000		18,000	
Share premium	12,000		10,000	
Retained earnings	24,885		18,340	
		56,885		46,340
Non-controlling interests		3,625		1,920
Non-current liabilities				
Interest-bearing borrowings		18,200		19,200
Current liabilities				
Trade payables	33,340		32,810	
Interest payable	1,360		1,440	
Tax	6,100		5,450	
		40,800		39,700
		119,510		107,160

Notes

1. Several years ago AH acquired 80% of the issued ordinary shares of its subsidiary, BI. On 1 January 20X5, AH acquired 75% of the issued ordinary shares of CJ in exchange for a fresh issue of 2 million of its own $1 ordinary shares (issued at a premium of $1 each) and $2 million in cash. The net assets of CJ at the date of acquisition were assessed as having the following fair values:

	$'000
Property, plant and equipment	4,200
Inventories	1,650
Receivables	1,300
Cash	50
Trade payables	(1,950)
Tax	(250)
	5,000

2. During the year, AH disposed of a non-current asset of property for proceeds of $2,250,000. The carrying value of the asset at the date of disposal was $1,000,000. There were no other disposals of non-current assets. Depreciation of $7,950,000 was charged against consolidated profits for the year.
3. Intangible assets comprise goodwill on acquisition of BI and CJ (20X4: BI only). Goodwill has remained unimpaired since acquisition.

Requirement

Prepare the consolidated cash flow statement of the AH Group for the financial year ended 30 June 20X5 in the form required by IAS 7 *Cash Flow Statements*, and using the indirect method. Notes to the cash flow statement are not required, but full workings should be shown. **(25 marks)**

Question 5

Carver is an entity incorporated in 20R8 to produce models carved from wood. In 20U5 it acquired a 100% interest in Olio, a wood importing entity. In 20V9 it acquired a 40% interest in a competitor, Multi-Products. On 1 October 20W9 it acquired a 75% interest in Good Display. It is planning to make a number of additional acquisitions over the next 3 years. The draft consolidated accounts for the Carver group are as follows:

Consolidated income statement for the year ended 30 September 20X0

	$'000	$'000
Profit from operations		1,485
Share of profits of associates		495
Income from trade investments		155
Finance costs		(150)
Profit before tax		1,985
Income tax expense		
Group tax on profits	391	
Deferred tax	104	
Share of tax of associates	145	
		(640)
Profit for the period		1,345
Attributable to:		
Equity holders of parent		1,245
Non-controlling interest		100
		1,345

Summarised consolidated statement of changes in equity for the year ended 30 September 20X0 (in respect of the equity holders of the parent)

	$'000
Balance at 1 October 20W9	6,395
Profit for the period	1,245
Dividends	(400)
Issue of share capital	2,728
Balance at 30 September 20X0	9,968

Consolidated statement of financial position as at 30 September

	20W9		*20X0*	
	$'000	$'000	$'000	$'000
Non-current assets				
Goodwill on consolidation				100
Buildings – net book value		2,200		2,075
Machinery				
Cost	1,400		3,000	
Aggregate depreciation	(1,100)		(1,200)	
		300		1,800
		2,500		3,975
Investments in associate		1,000		1,100
Other long-term investments		410		410
Current assets				
Inventories	1,000		1,975	
Trade receivables	1,275		1,850	
Short-term investments	1,500		2,675	
Cash at bank	1,080		1,890	
Cash in hand	10		15	
		4,865		8,405

		8,775		13,890
Share capital (25¢ shares)		2,000		3,940
Share premium account		2,095		2,883
Retained earnings		2,300		3,145
		6,395		9,968
Non-controlling interests		–		115
Non-current liabilities				
Obligations under finance leases	170		710	
Loans	500		1,460	
Deferred tax	13		30	
		683		2,200
Current liabilities				
Trade payables	480		800	
Bank overdrafts	770		65	
Obligations under finance leases	200		240	
Corporation tax	217		462	
Accrued interest and finance charges	30		40	
		1,697		1,607
		8,775		13,890

Notes

1. *Non-current assets*
   - There had been no acquisitions or disposals of buildings during the year.
   - Machinery costing $500,000 was sold for $500,000 resulting in a profit of $100,000. New machinery was acquired in 20X0 including additions of $850,000 acquired under finance leases.

2. *Investments*
   All current asset investments are readily convertible into cash and are not subject to significant market price risk.
3. *Information relating to the acquisition of Good Display*

	$'000
Net assets at date of acquisition	
Machinery	165
Inventories	32
Trade receivables	28
Cash	112
Trade payables	(68)
Tax	(17)
	252
Non-controlling interest	(63)
Group share	189
Goodwill on consolidation	100
Purchase consideration	289
Satisfied by	
880,000 shares	275
Cash	14
	289

Goodwill on consolidation of all acquisitions, except that of Good Display had been found to be impaired prior to the current financial year and had been fully written off.

4. *Loans*

   Loans were issued at a discount in 20X0 and the carrying amount of the loans at 30 September 20X0 included $40,000, representing the finance cost attributable to the discount and allocated in respect of the current reporting period.

Requirement

Prepare a consolidated cash flow statement for the Carver group for the year ended 30 September 20X0. **(25 marks)**

Solutions to Revision Questions

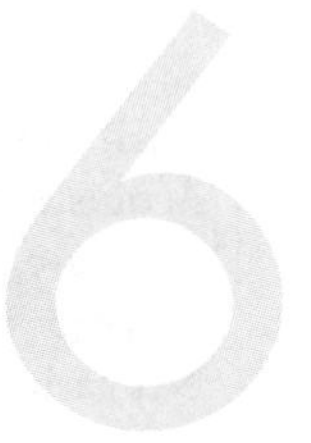

Solution 1

	$'000
Opening balance	207
Less: depreciation	(32)
Add: purchases (balancing figure)	53
Closing balance	228

Solution 2

	$'000
Opening investment in associate	6,600
Add: share of profit of associate	240
Cash flow (dividend paid) (balancing figure)	(90)
Closing investment in associate	6,750

Solution 3

The amount that should appear in the cash flow statement is the cash inflow from the associate. This is the dividend received by the holding entity:

$100,000 × 30% = $30,000

Solution 4

AH Group: Consolidated statement of cash flows for the year ended 30 June 20X5

	$'000	$'000	Ref. to working
Cash flows from operating activities			
Profit before taxation	19,450		
Adjustments for:			
Profit on disposal of property	(1,250)		
Depreciation	7,950		
Finance cost	1,400		
Decrease in receivables	470		1
(Increase) in inventories	(3,100)		1
(Decrease) in trade payables	(1,420)		1
Cash generated from operations	23,500		
Interest paid	(1,480)		2
Income taxes paid	(5,850)		2
Net cash from operating activities		16,170	

Cash flows from investing activities			
Acquisition of subsidiary (net of cash)	(1,950)		3
Purchase of property, plant and equipment	(11,300)		4
Proceeds from sale of property	2,250		
Net cash used in investing activities		(11,000)	
Cash flows from financing activities			
Repayment of interest-bearing borrowings	(1,000)		
Dividends paid by AH	(6,000)		
Dividends paid to non-controlling interests	(200)		5
Net cash used in financing activities		(7,200)	
Net decrease in cash		(2,030)	
Cash at beginning of period		(3,900)	
Cash at end of period		1,870	

Workings

1. *Working capital changes*

	Receivables $'000	*Inventories* $'000	*Trade payables* $'000
Closing balance	(27,130)	(33,500)	(33,340)
Less: acquired with CJ	1,300	1,650	1,950
	(25,830)	(31,850)	(31,390)
Opening balance	26,300	28,750	32,810
Decrease/increase/decrease	470	(3,100)	1,420

2. *Interest and income taxes*

	Interest $'000	*Income taxes* $'000
Liability brought forward	1,440	5,450
Liability acquired with CJ	–	250
Charge to income statement	1,400	6,250
Liability carried forward	(1,360)	(6,100)
Balance: amount paid	1,480	5,850

3. *Acquisition of subsidiary*

	$'000
Cash element of consideration	2,000
Less: cash acquired with CJ	(50)
	1,950

4. *Purchase of property, plant and equipment*

	$'000
Balance brought forward	44,050
Acquired with CJ	4,200
Disposal at net book value	(1,000)
Depreciation for year	(7,950)
Less: balance carried forward	(50,600)
Balance: purchased	(11,300)

5. *Dividend paid non-controlling interests*

	$'000
Balance brought forward	1,920
Profit attributable to non-controllign intersts	655
Acquired with CJ ($5,000 × 25%)	1,250
Less: balance carried forward	(3,625)
Balance: dividend paid	200

Solution 5

Carver: statement of cash flows for the year ended 30 September 20X0

	$'000
Cash flow from operating activities (W1)	122
Cash flow from investing activities (W5)	(82)
Cash flow from financing activities (W9)	2,655
Increase in cash (W13)	2,695

Workings

1. *Reconciliation of operating profit to net cash flow from operating activities*

	$'000
Profit before tax from group entities (1,985 − 495)	1,490
Income from trade investments	(155)
Finance costs	150
Depreciation of buildings (reduction in NBV)	125
Depreciation of machinery (see below)	200
Profit on sale of machinery	(100)
Increase in inventory (975 − 32)	(943)
Increase in receivables (575 − 28)	(547)
Increase in trade payables (320 − 68)	252
Interest paid (W2)	(100)
Tax paid (W4)	(250)
Net cash outflow from operating activities	122

Note

Depreciation of machinery	
Increase in provision	100
Provision on sold machinery no longer needed	100
	200

2. *Interest paid*

	$'000
Charge in income statement	150
Less: charge due to amortisation of discount	(40)
Increase in liability	(10)
So cash flow	100

3. *Dividends paid to non-controlling interest*

	$'000
Share of profit	100
Increase due to acquisition	63
Movement in statement of financial position	(115)
Dividend paid	48

4. *Taxation paid*

	$'000
Charge in income statement (current plus deferred)	495
Increase due to acquisition	17
Movement in statement of financial position	
Current tax	(245)
Deferred tax	(17)
Cash paid	250

5. *Cash flow from investing activities*

	$'000
Dividends received from associates (W6)	250
Dividends received from other long-term investments	155
Sale of non-current assets	500
Purchase of non-current assets (W7)	(1,085)
Acquisition of Good Display (W8)	98
	(82)

6. *Dividends received from associates*

	£'000
Share of profit after tax	350
Movement in investment	(100)
Dividend received	250

7. *Purchase of non-current assets (machinery)*

	$'000
Increase in cost per statement of financial position	1,600
Acquired under finance leases	(850)
Disposed of in year	500
Increase due to acquisition	(165)
Cash flow	1,085

8. *Purchase of Good Display*

	$'000
Cash paid to purchase subsidiary undertaking	(14)
Cash balances acquired with subsidiary	112
	98

9. *Cash flow from financing activities*

	$'000
Issue of loans (W10)	920
Capital repayments under finance leases (W11)	(270)
	650
Dividends paid	
Non-controlling interest (W3)	(48)
Parent shareholders	(400)
Issue of ordinary shares (W12)	2,453
	2,655

10. *Issue of loans*

	$'000
Increase per balance sheet	960
Less increase due to amortisation of discount	(40)
Cash flow	920

11. *Repayment of loans under leasing obligations*

	$'000
New obligations	850
Less increase in liability	
within 1 year	(40)
after more than 1 year	(540)
Cash outflow	270

12. *Issue of shares*

	$'000
Increase per statement of financial position	
Share capital	1,940
Share premium	788
Increase due to non-cash consideration	(275)
Cash flow	2,453

13. *Movement in cash in the period*

	$'000
Increase in cash in hand	5
Decrease in bank overdrafts	705
Increase in bank balances	810
Increase in short-term investments	1,175
Increase in cash	2,695

Changes to Group Structures

Changes to Group Structures

7

Learning Outcomes

After studying this chapter students should be able to:

- demonstrate the impact on group financial statements when a subsidiary is acquired part way through an accounting period, and where shareholdings, or control, are acquired in stages;

7.1 Introduction

In this chapter we look specifically at where there have been changes to the group structure in the period. We will consider acquisitions, disposals and business reorganisations. There will be more opportunities in this chapter to practice the basic principles of consolidation, being the calculation of goodwill on acquisition, group retained earnings and non-controlling interest; however, time apportionment within these calculations will be necessary.

Acquisitions will be covered in the following way:

- In Section 7.2 we will introduce acquisitions in the period with a simple example.
- In Section 7.3 we will apply the fair value requirements of IFRS 3 *Business Combinations*, introduced in Chapter 2, in a worked example and look at how that impacts the calculation of goodwill and non-controlling interest, and adjusts consolidated net assets.
- The last area of acquisitions that we will consider is the impact on the group accounts where the investment in another entity is built up over time, known as piecemeal acquisitions (Section 7.4).

Disposals in the accounting period will be covered in Section 7.5 and again the accounting treatment will depend on the amount of the investment being disposed of. We will consider:

- Full disposal
- Disposal resulting in a subsidiary becoming an associate
- Disposal resulting in a subsidiary becoming a trade investment
- Disposal resulting in the controlling interest being retained

Business reorganisations will be covered in Section 7.6.

7.2 Acquisitions in the accounting period

7.2.1 Introduction

When a group entity is acquired during the accounting period it is not consolidated for the whole period, only from the date of acquisition. This means that, when preparing the consolidated income statement, the profits must be time-apportioned and only post-acquisition profits included. Unless the question clearly indicates to the contrary, you can assume the profits accrue on a time basis.

An additional problem is that the figure for pre-acquisition profits is unknown. This is needed to compute the goodwill on acquisition. However, the figure can be calculated: accumulated profit in the entity brought forward at the beginning of the year is added to profit for the year up to the date of acquisition.

Example 7.A

Income statements for the year ended 31 March 20X0

	Pig	*Pinky*	*Perky*
	$'000	$'000	$'000
Revenue	80,700	25,000	11,000
Operating expenses	(49,000)	(20,000)	(8,000)
Profit from operations	31,700	5,000	3,000
Investment income	1,400	–	–
Profit before taxation	33,100	5,000	3,000
Income tax expense	(13,500)	(2,000)	(1,200)
Profit for the period	19,600	3,000	1,800

Summarised statements of changes in equity for the year ended 31 March 20X0

	Pig	*Pinky*	*Perky*
	$'000	$'000	$'000
Equity at 1 April 20W9	56,000	23,000	20,200
Profit for the period	19,600	3,000	1,800
Dividends paid in March 20X0	(10,000)	(1,000)	(800)
Equity at 31 March 20X0	65,600	25,000	21,200

The equity of the three entities in the statement of financial positions as at 31 March 20X0 showed the following:

	Pig	*Pinky*	*Perky*
	$'000	$'000	$'000
Share capital ($1 shares)	20,000	15,000	10,000
Share premium account	8,000	5,000	3,000
Retained earnings	37,600	5,000	8,200
	65,600	25,000	21,200

On 30 June 20W7, when the retained earnings of Pinky showed a balance of $1.5 million and the equity of Pinky showed a balance of $21.5 million, Pig bought 12 million shares in Pinky for a cash price of $18 million. On 1 October 20W9 Pig bought 7.5 million shares in Perky for a cash price of $16 million. The share premium accounts of Pinky and Perky both arose prior to the investment by Pig.

The main point of principle to bear in mind when preparing the consolidated income statement (see below) is that only the *post*-acquisition profits of subsidiaries should be included. Therefore, for *the year ended 31 March 20X0 only* the results of Perky must be time apportioned, and only 6 months' worth included in the consolidated income statement.

Consolidated income statement

	$'000
Revenue (Pig + Pinky + 6/12 × Perky)	111,200
Operating expenses (Pig + Pinky + 6/12 × Perky)	(73,000)
Profit from operations before tax	38,200
Income tax expense (Pig + Pinky + 6/12 × Perky)	(16,100)
Profit for the period	22,100
Attributable to:	
Equity holders of parent	21,275
Non-controlling interest (W1)	825
	22,100

Consolidated statement of changes in equity

	Attributable to equity holders of the parent	*Non-controlling interest*	*Total equity*
	$	$	$
Balance at the start of the year (W2)	57,200	4,600	61,800
Non-controlling interest upon acquisition of Perky (W3)		5,275	5,275
Profit for the period	21,275	825	22,100
Dividends (W4)	(10,000)	(400)	(10,400)
Balance at the end of the year	68,475	10,300	78,775

Workings

1. *Non-controlling interest*

	$'000
Pinky ($3,000,000 × 20%)	600,000
Perky ($1,800,000 × 6/12 × 25%)	225,000
	825,000

2. *Balance at the start of the period*
   Attributable to equity shareholders of the parent:

	$'000
Pig	56,000
Pinky [80% × ($23 m − $21.5 m)]	1,200
	57,200

The balance attributable to the non-controlling interest is 20% of the brought forward balance in Pinky of $23 million: $23 m × 20% = $4.6 m.

3. *Non-controlling interest upon acquisition of Perky*
   Equity in Perky at the date of acquisition on 1 October 20W9:

	$'000
Brought forward at the beginning of the year	20,200
6/12 × profit for the year ($1.8 × 6/12)	900
	21,100

Minority share (25% × $21.1 m) = $5,275,000

4. *Dividends*

	$'000
Pinky (20% × $1 m)	200
Perky (25% × $0.8 m)	200
	400

The closing balance in respect of the minority in the statement of changes in equity can be proved as follows:

	'000
Pinky (20% × $25 m)	5,000
Perky (25% × $21,200)	5,300
	10,300

7.2.2 Dividends paid by the subsidiary out of profits earned in the year of acquisition in the financial statements of the parent

Dividend paid after date of acquisition

Treatment of dividends paid in the year of acquisition depends on whether or not the new parent has *received* (or is to receive) the dividend. If the parent is to receive the dividend, then (as shown in the above example) the group share is regarded as income of the parent.

Dividend causing a reduction in the carrying value of the investment

There is a minor exception to the general treatment mentioned in the previous paragraph. If a subsidiary pays a large dividend to its parent just after acquisition it may well be that the value of the subsidiary would be considerably diminished by the outflow of cash that was required. If this diminution in value were such as to lead to a reduction in the carrying value of the investment in the books of the parent then the dividend received would be regarded as a payment from the subsidiary in respect of the reduction in carrying value. The parent would account for this as a reduction in the carrying value of the investment rather than as income.

> ! ... It is important to realise that the above matter affects the accounts of the parent but not the consolidated accounts – an intra-group dividend that cancels out on consolidation clearly cannot have an effect on the consolidated financial statements.

7.2.3 Dividend paid before the date of acquisition

If the dividend is paid out *before* the parent makes its investment, then it is clearly paid out of pre-acquisition profits, and so will not be income of the parent at all. However, in computing the goodwill figure in these circumstances, the dividend must be deducted in computing the net assets of the subsidiary at the date of acquisition since the cash has left the subsidiary before the date of acquisition.

7.3 Fair value in acquisition accounting

7.3.1 The requirements of IFRS 3 *Business Combinations* ('IFRS 3')

IFRS 3 requires that whenever a group entity is consolidated for the first time the purchase consideration and the group share of the net assets of the acquired entity are measured at fair values. The difference between these two figures is goodwill.

Net assets of the acquired entity should be recognised separately as at the date of acquisition if they satisfy IFRS 3's criteria for recognition:

- In the case of an asset other than an intangible asset, it is probable that any associated future economic benefits will flow to the acquirer, and its fair value can be measured reliably;

- In the case of a liability other than a contingent liability, it is probable that an outflow of resources embodying economic benefits will be required to settle the obligation, and its fair value can be measured reliably;
- It is an intangible asset that meets the IAS 38 *Intangible Assets* definition;
- In the case of a contingent liability, its fair value can be measured reliably.

7.3.2 Summary of points given in Chapter 2 regarding fair value for individual assets and liabilities

Fair value of consideration

Fair value must be measured at the date of the exchange. In cases where the acquisition is for the asset of cash, measurement of fair value is straightforward. However, in some cases the consideration offered will comprise equity shares, wholly or in part. Where this is the case, the shares must be valued at fair value.

Property, plant and equipment

Fair value should be based on depreciated market value unless (in the case of plant and equipment) there is no evidence of market value. In such cases fair value should be based on depreciated replacement cost.

Inventories

Where inventories are replaced by purchases in a ready market, the fair value = market value. However, where there is no ready market fair value is the current cost to the acquiring entity of obtaining the same inventories. If no current cost figure is readily available it can be approximated by taking inventories at sales values less:

- costs to complete (for work-in-progress inventories)
- incidental costs of disposal
- a realistic allowance for profit.

Listed investments

In most cases, the price quoted at the date of exchange will represent fair value.

Intangible assets

The acquirer should recognise an intangible asset of the acquiree at the date of acquisition provided that it meets the definition of an intangible asset provided by IAS 38 *Intangible Assets*, and that it can be measured reliably. Intangible assets must be separable or they must arise from contractual or legal rights.

Monetary assets and liabilities

The fair value should be based on the amounts due to be received or paid.

Provisions for restructuring

Only the identifiable assets, liabilities and contingent liabilities of the acquiree that exist at the statement of financial position date can be recognised separately by the acquirer as part of allocating the cost of the combination. IFRS 3 states that: 'future losses or other costs expected to be incurred as a result of a combination are not liabilities incurred or assumed by the acquirer in exchange for control of the acquiree, and are not, therefore, included as part of the cost of the combination' (para. 28).

Contingent liabilities

IFRS 3 requires that the contingent liabilities of an acquiree are recognised at fair value at the date of acquisition provided that their fair value can be measured reliably.

The following example illustrates the application of the requirements to incorporate fair value.

7.3.3 Application of fair value adjustments

Example 7.B

The statement of financial positions of Sea and its subsidiaries River and Stream as at 31 March 20X0 – the accounting reference date for all three entities – are given below:

	Sea		*River*		*Stream*	
ASSETS	$'000	$'000	$'000	$'000	$'000	$'000
Non-current assets						
Intangible assets						5,000
Tangible assets		41,000		30,000		20,000
Investments		17,000				
		58,000		30,000		25,000
Current assets						
Inventories	8,000		6,000		4,000	
Receivables	7,000		5,250		1,500	
Cash	2,000		500		300	
		17,000		11,750		5,800
		75,000		41,750		30,800
EQUITY AND LIABILITIES						
Equity:						
Issued capital ($1 shares)		20,000		17,000		12,000
Share premium account		15,000				1,500
Retained earnings		11,600		18,450		5,948
		46,600		35,450		19,448
Non-current liabilities						
Long-term loans		20,000				8,052
Current liabilities						
Trade payables	5,200		4,000		5,752	
Income tax	3,200		2,300		2,600	
Provision	–		–		3,000	
		8,400		6,300		11,352
		75,000		41,750		30,800

Notes

1. Sea subscribed for 100% of the issued capital of River on the date of its incorporation. No changes have taken place to the issued share capital of River since that date.
2. River supplies a component that is used by Sea in its manufacturing process. River applies a 20% mark-up to the cost of manufacture of the component to arrive at the selling price to Sea. At 31 March 20X0 the inventories of Sea included $600,000 in respect of components purchased from River.
3. Intra-group trading is meant to cease on 25 March each year to enable agreement of intra-group balances at the year-end. On 24 March 20X0 Sea made a payment of $200,000 to River in respect of components purchased in February 20X0. This payment cleared the balances due for purchases up to February 20X0. Purchases of the component from 1 March to 24 March 20X0 by Sea amounted to $180,000. This amount was included in the payables of Sea and the receivables of River at 24 March 20X0. On 30

March 20X0, contrary to normal practice, River despatched goods having an invoiced price of $150,000 and entered the transaction in its books. The transaction was not recorded by Sea in its statement of financial position that is given above.

4. Following protracted negotiations the directors of Sea concluded an agreement whereby Sea acquired 9 million $1 shares in Stream on 31 March 20X0. The terms of the acquisition were that Sea would issue two new $1 shares for every three shares acquired in Stream. On 31 March 20X0 the market value of a $1 share of Sea was $3. The share issue by Sea on 31 March 20X0 is not reflected in the statement of financial position of Sea that appears above.
5. The intangible non-current assets of Stream at 31 March 20X0, consist of the estimated value of a brand that is associated with the entity. This estimate has been made by the directors and no reliable external estimate of the market value of the brand is available.
6. Relevant details of tangible non-current assets of Stream at 31 March 20X0 are:

Description	*Statement of financial position carrying value*	*Market value*	*Depreciated replacement cost*	*Recoverable amount*
	$'000	$'000	$'000	$'000
Property	10,000	12,000	Not given	13,500
Plant	10,000	Not given	11,000	14,000

7. Inventories of Stream at 31 March 20X0 comprise:
   - Obsolete inventory (statement of financial position value: $500,000). This inventory has a net realisable value of $300,000.
   - The balance of inventory (statement of financial position value: $3,500,000). This inventory has a net realisable value of $4,200,000. A reasonable profit allowance for the sale of the inventory would be $400,000.
8. The provision of $1 million in the statement of financial position of Stream is against the reorganisation costs expected to be incurred in integrating the entity into the Sea group. These costs would not be necessary if Stream were to remain outside the group. Although the plan was agreed by the board of directors before 31 March 20X0, it was not made known to those affected by the plan until after 31 March 20X0.
9. No impairment of the goodwill on acquisition of Stream has taken place.

Requirements

(a) Calculate the goodwill that arises on the acquisition of Stream by Sea on 31 March 20X0, providing a brief explanation for each calculation.

(b) Prepare the consolidated statement of financial position of Sea as at 31 March 20X0.

Solution

(a) Goodwill on consolidation of Stream

1. Fair value of investment by Sea:

$$9 \text{ million} \times \frac{2}{3} \times \$3.00 = \$18 \text{ million}$$

2. Fair value of net assets of Stream as at 31 March 20X0:

Asset	*Fair value*	*Reason*
	$'000	
Intangible asset	–	No ascertainable market value
Property	12,000	Market value – less than recoverable amount
Plant	11,000	Depreciated replacement cost – less than recoverable amount
Obsolete inventory	300	Net realisable value (no profit allowance)
Other inventory	3,800	Net realisable value less profit allowance
Other current assets	1,800	Monetary assets that are 'short term'
Trade payables	(5,752)	A short-term liability at carrying value
Taxation	(2,600)	As above
Provision	–	Prohibited by IFRS 3 – also per IAS 37 a 'constructive obligation' does not exist at the statement of financial position date
Net assets at FV	20548	

3. *Goodwill calculation:*
   $18,000,000 – (75% × $20,548,000) = $2,589,000

(b) *Consolidated statement of financial position of Sea as at 31 March 20X0*
Note: Unless otherwise indicated, the figures are a simple aggregation of the balance of Sea, River and Stream – with fair-value adjustments as per part (a).

	$'000
Goodwill on consolidation – from part (a)	2,589
Tangible non-current assets	94,000
Inventory (W1)	18,125
Receivables (W2)	13,420
Cash	2,800
	130,934
Issued capital (W4)	26,000
Share premium (W4)	27,000
Retained earnings (W5)	29,925
	82,925
Non-controlling interest (W6)	5,137
	88,062
Loan	20,000
Trade payables (W3)	14,772
Taxation	8,100
	130,934

Workings

1. *Consolidated inventory figure*

	$'000
Sea + River + Stream	18,100
Inventory in transit	150
Unrealised profit on goods in inventory (20/120 × $60)	(100)
Unrealised profit on inventory in transit	(25)
Per consolidated statement of financial position	18,125

2. *Consolidated receivables figure*

Sea + River + Stream	13,750
Amount owed by Sea per River's accounts	(330)
Per consolidated statement of financial position	13,420

3. *Consolidated trade payables figure*

Sea + River + Stream	14,952
Amount owed to River per Sea's accounts	(180)
Per consolidated statement of financial position	13,420

4. *Consolidated issued capital and share premium*
   Sea only – the figure in the CBS reflect the issue of six million $1 shares at a price of $3.
5. *Retained earnings*

Sea 1 River (Stream all pre-acquisition)	30,050
Unrealised profit on inventory (W1)	(125)
Per consolidated statement of financial position	29,925

6. *Non-controlling interest*

   25% × net assets @ fair value (as part (a)) = 25% × $20,548,000 = $5,137,000

Recording movements in fair value adjustments

The acquisition of Stream was at the end of the year so there was no movement in respect of the non-current assets. Where depreciable assets have had uplift in value on acquisition the movement should represent the cumulative additional depreciation the group will have charged from the acquisition date to the statement of financial position date. It is the net balance (FV at acquisition date less movement) that should be included in group non-current assets and the non-controlling interest calculation. The retained earnings figure will be adjusted for the cumulative movement.

Example 7.C

The fair value adjustment at 31 December 20X6 for non-current assets was $500,000 and the depreciation policy of the group was 20% straight line. Let's consider the impact of this as at 31 December 20X8.

	At acquisition date 31 December 20X6 $'000	Movement $'000	At reporting date 31 December 20X8 $'000
Non-current assets	500	(200)	300

The additional depreciation charged on the uplift in value is $100,000 per annum. The impact on the statement of financial position will be as follows:

- $500,000 will be included in the goodwill calculation as the fair value adjustment at the date of acquisition
- $300,000 will be added to the net assets for non-controlling interest calculation
- $300,000 will be added to consolidated non-current assets
- $200,000 will be deducted from consolidated retained earnings

---

7.4 Piecemeal acquisitions

7.4.1 General principles

Up until this point, the explanations and exercises have assumed that an investment is made in a subsidiary or associate in a single transaction. While this is often the case in practice, it is also quite common for an acquisition to consist of two or more investments made on different dates. This process, involving successive purchases, is sometimes referred to as 'piecemeal acquisition'.

IFRS 3 prescribes the following treatment for a business combination achieved in stages: '... each exchange transaction shall be treated separately by the acquirer, using the cost of the transaction and fair value information at the date of each exchange transaction, to determine the amount of any goodwill associated with that transaction. This results in a step-by-step comparison of the cost of the individual investments with the acquirer's interest in the fair values of the acquiree's identifiable assets, liabilities and contingent liabilities at each step'.

A further investment transaction to acquire the shares of another entity may involve any of the following:

- increasing a stake so that an entity changes from a simple investment to a subsidiary;
- increasing a stake in an entity that is already a subsidiary;
- increasing a stake so that an entity changes from an associate to a subsidiary;

In the next section of the chapter, a detailed example is examined which involved the increase of a stake in an entity that is accounted for as a simple investment to a subsidiary. It should be noted that the principles involved in changing from an associate are the same as explained below.

The following worked example assumes that the investment held in the investor's own accounts is accounted for in accordance with IAS 39 *Financial Instruments: recognition and measurement.* This area is covered in depth in Chapter 11, however to allow effective illustration, the accounting treatment that is adopted is fully explained in the example below.

7.4.2 Piecemeal acquisitions: increasing a stake from a simple investment to a subsidiary

Example 7.D

The simplified income statements for Tiny and its investee entity, Teeny, for the year ended 31 December 20X8, together with simplified statements of financial position at that date, are as follows:

Statements of financial position as at 31 December 20X8

	Teeny $'000	*Tiny* $'000
Investment in Tiny	21,800	
Non-current assets	15,000	21,000
Current assets	11,200	9,000
	48,000	30,000
Issued capital ($1 shares)	12,000	15,000
Retained earnings	29,000	12,000
	41,000	27,000
Current liabilities	7,000	3,000
	48,000	30,000

Income statements for the year ended 31 December 20X8

	Teeny $'000	*Tiny* $'000
Revenue	18,000	6,000
Costs	(12,000)	(4,000)
Profit before tax	6,000	2,000
Income tax	(1,500)	(500)
Profit for the period	4,500	1,500

Investment in Tiny

- Three million shares on 31 December 20X2 when the retained earnings of Tiny were $7.5 million. Although this gave Teeny a 20% equity holding, there was one controlling shareholder and as a result Teeny was unable to exert significant influence over the operating and finanicial policies of Tiny. The investment was therefore held as a simple investment in the consolidated financial statements. The cost of the investment was $5.4 million.
- Six million shares on 30 June 20X8 when the retained earnings of Tiny were $11.25 million. The cost of investment was $15 million.

Fair value of net assets

The fair value and book values of Tiny's net assets on 31 December 20X2 were the same except for a non-current asset of land (non-depreciable). The fair value of the land exceeded its book value by $400,000.

The fair value and book values of Tiny's net assets on 30 June 20X8 were the same except for the same non-current asset of land. The fair value of the land now exceeded book value by $600,000.

Treatment of the investment

The investment in Tiny was accounted for in accordance with IAS 39. It was classified as an available for sale asset and held at fair value from its acquisition. The gains resulting from the fair value assessments totalled $1.2 million up to 30 June 20X8. A further $200,000 was recognised for the 6 months to 31 December 20X8. In line with IAS 39 the gains have been recognised in equity.

The standard requires that any gains recognised at the date of derecognition be transferred to the profit for the period.

The non-controlling interest is measured at the date of acquisition as the proportionate share of the fair value of the net assets of the business.

Requirement

Prepare the consolidated statement of financial position (SOFP) for the Teeny Group as at 31 December 20X8.

Solution

The first investment gave Teeny a 20% holding but without significant influence. The second investment resulted in an increase in the stake to 60 per cent halfway through the year ended 31 December 20X8. This is the point where Teeny gained control over Tiny.

IFRS 3 (revised) requires that the fair value of the net assets be assessed, only at the date that control is gained. The uplift of $600,000 should therefore be included in the net assets acquired. The workings illustrate the point.

Teeny Group: Consolidated statement of financial position as at 31 December 20X8

	$'000
Goodwill (W1)	5,490
Non-current assets (15 + 21 + 0.6)	36,600
Current assets (11.2 + 9)	20,200
	62,290
Issued capital ($1 shares)	12,000
Retained earnings (W2)	29,250
	41,250
Non-controlling interest (W3)	11,040
	52,290
Current liabilities (7 + 3)	10,000
	62,290

Workings

1. *Goodwill on consolidation*

   Calculated at the date control is gained:

	$'000	60% stake $'000
Consideration transferred (paid for 40% stake)		15,000
Fair value of previously held interest of 20% (FV at date control is gained)		6,600 ?
Net assets at date of acquisition:		
Issued capital	15,000	
Retained earnings	11,250	
Fair value uplift	600	
	26,850	
Group share (60%)		(16,110)
Goodwill		5,490

2. *Consolidated retained earnings as at 31 December 20X8*

   Retained earnings:

	Teeny $000	Tiny $000
Retained earnings as per SOFP	29,000	12,000
Profit on derecognition of AFS investment (W3)	1,200	
Retained earnings at date control gained		11,250
		750
Share of post-acq (60% × $750)	450	
Less FV gains recognised in Teeny's own retained earnings ($1,200 + $200)	(1,400)	
Consolidated retained earnings	29,250	

3. From the group's perspective the 20% investment is derecognised at the date that control is gained, i.e. 30 June 20X8. On derecognition the gains up to that date must be included in the consolidated retained earnings. We must remember, however to remove the total gains of $1,400 (up to 31 December 20X8) that would have been included in Teeny retained earnings to avoid double counting.
4. *Non-controlling interest*

   40% × net assets of Tiny at 31 December 20X8

   40% × ($27,000 + FV adj 0.6) = $11,040

The NCI in the SOFP is based on the % holding at the year end, as the balance sheet is intended to show the position of the group at the year end date.

The consolidated income statement is relatively straightforward:

Teeny Group: Consolidated income statement for the year ended 31 December 20X8

	$'000
Revenue (18 + 6)	24,000
Costs (12 + 4)	(16,000)
Profit from operation	8,000
Gain on derecognition of AFS investment	1,200
Profit before tax	9,200
Income tax (1.5 + 0.5)	(2,000)
Profit for the period	7,200
Attributable to:	
Equity holders of the parents	6,750
Non-controlling interest (W)	450
	7,200

Working
Non-controlling interest

$$(\$1.5\text{m} \times 6/12 \times 40\%) + (\$1.5\text{m} \times 6/12 \times 20\%) = \$450{,}000$$

The calculation of the NCI in the consolidated income statement is time apportioned as the income statement shows the profits accruing throughout the year.

7.4.3 Piecemeal acquisitions: from associate to subsidiary

Where a piecemeal acquisition takes a stake from that of associate to a subsidiary, the principles of the accounting treatment remain the same as explained in Section 7.4.2. The fair value of the investment previously held in this case would be the carrying value of the associate. The date that control is gained is the trigger for any fair value adjustment for the net assets of the subsidiary acquired.

7.4.4 Piecemeal acquisitions: increasing a controlling interest

The treatment is different where the parent already holds a controlling interest in the subsidiary as it is merely increasing this interest. No gain or loss on derecognition is recorded, instead it is treated as a transaction between owners and any adjustment is to parent's equity (the parent's interest has increased and the non-controlling interest has decreased).

The calculation would be as follows:

FV of consideration paid	(X)
Decrease in NCI in net assets at date of acquisition	X
Decrease in NCI goodwill (only if NCI is held at FV and goodwill has been calculated on their share)	X
= adjustment to parent's equity	(X)

Example 7.E

Using the details of example 7D. Teeny currently holds 60% of the equity shares and purchases a further 3 million equity shares in Tiny at a cost $5.5m on 30 June 20X9. The net assets of Tiny at that date were $28m.

The adjustment to equity in respect of this additional investment is:

	$00
FV of consideration paid	(5,500)
Decrease in NCI in net assets at date of acquisition (20% × 28 m)	5,600
Adjustment to parent's equity	(100)

This will be credited to retained earnings in the period.

7.5 Disposals in the period

The accounting for disposals in the period depends on the amount of the investment that is being sold. There are four possible scenarios:

1. Full disposal
2. Disposal resulting in a subsidiary becoming an associate
3. Disposal resulting in a subsidiary becoming a trade investment
4. Disposal resulting in the controlling interest being retained

7.5.1 Accounting treatment

Full and partial disposals

Partial disposals in the accounting period will usually still require all the basic consolidation adjustments to be made if the group accounts are to be prepared. Where the classification of the investment changes in the group accounts the calculations will include:

- Calculating consolidated profit/loss on the disposal, which will be included in the group income statement:

  Where the parent loses control of a subsidiary it should:
  - Derecognise the assets and liabilities of the subsidiary (including goodwill) at the date control is lost.
  - Derecognise any balance on NCI in the former subsidiary at the date control is lost.
  - Recognise the fair value of the consideration received (proceeds received on disposal).
  - Recognise any investment retained (associate or trade investment) at fair value at date control is lost (this FV will effectively provide a transfer value which will act as the opening cost for investment in associate or trade investment. The loss of control triggers a fair value assessment for the investment retained.
  - Reclassify any gains recognised previously through other comprehensive income relating to the investment, to profit or loss, for example:
    - A revaluation gain of the subsidiary previously recorded in OCI – the whole of this gain can be realised at the date control is lost.
    - A gain recorded in the parent's individual financial statements within equity and included in OCI, on the available for sale investment – can be transferred from equity to profit or loss on the date that control is lost.
  - Recognise any resulting gain or loss in profit or loss attributable to the parent.
- Time apportioning the calculations for subsidiary, associate and trade investment depending on the level of investment is retained.

Disposal where control is retained

A disposal of part of an investment where the controlling interest is retained is accounted for as an adjustment to parent's equity. No gain or loss on disposal is recorded. It is a transaction between owners (the parent and the non-controlling interest) similar to the treatment adopted for increases in controlling interests in piecemeal acquisitions. Any difference between the consideration received and the increase in the NCI amount is recognised directly in the equity and attributed to the owners of the parent.

The table below summarises what will be required – ***read this through carefully and think about each box*** *before working through the example below, a lot of what it says you will know by this stage in your studies*:

	Consolidated income statement /TCI	**Consolidated statement of financial position**
Full disposal	• Consolidate sub and show NCI up to date of disposal • Include profit or loss on disposal	• No consolidation as disposed of at year end date
Sub to associate	• Consolidate sub and show NCI up to date of disposal • Include profit or loss on disposal • Equity account for associate from disposal date to year end (time apportion results)	• Calculate FV of remaining investment (this will act as opening value of investment) • The investment is equity accounted at year end date
Sub to trade investment	• Consolidate sub and show NCI up to date of disposal • Include profit or loss on disposal • Include dividend income from date of disposal to year end date	• Calculate FV of remaining investment (this will act as opening cost of investment) • Account for investment under IAS 39.
Sub to reduced sub	• Full consolidation for whole period • Time apportion the NCI based on % holding × number of months • **No** profit or loss on disposal	• Full consolidation • NCI at % held at year end date • Calculate adjustment to parent's equity

The following example illustrates the treatment for a complete disposal and for a partial disposal resulting in an associate.

Example 7.F

The following extracts are from the draft accounts of A Group. The figures presented for A represents A and its fully owned subsidiary (goodwill for this subsidiary is fully impaired). The extracts shown for B are for the year to 31 December 20X8. None of these figures have yet been included in the group, which is why the figures for A Group are still showing an investment in B.

Extracts from draft income statements	*A Group*	*B*
	$'000	$'000
Revenue	155,500	25,800
Operating costs	(97,750)	(13,900)
Profit before tax	57,750	11,900
Income tax	(25,250)	(4,300)
Profit for period	32,500	7,600

Extracts from draft statements of financial position	*A Group*	*B*
	$000	$000
Investment in B (held at cost)	11,000	-
Other assets	83,400	22,000
	94,400	22,000
Equity and liabilities		
Share capital	30,000	10,000

Retained earnings	54,400	10,000
	84,400	20,000
Liabilities	10,000	2,000
	94,400	22,000

Additional information:

1. A owns 80% of the 10 million equity shares of B, an unlisted entity, which it purchased for £11 m when the retained earnings were $1.4 m. There has been no goodwill impairment since the date of acquisition.
2. The NCI of B is valued at the proportionate share of the fair value of the net assets.
3. B is an unlisted entity and the fair value of the investment cannot be reliably measured. As a result it is classified as an available for sale investment and is held at cost in the individual accounts of A.

Requirements

Prepare the consolidated statement of income and consolidated statement of financial position for A group assuming the following scenarios:

(a) A Group sells its entire shareholding in B for $18.9 million on 1 October 20X8. Tax arising on the sale amounts to $1.3 million.
(b) A Group sells 5,000 of its 8,000 shares in B for $14 million on 1 October 20X8. Tax arising on the sale amounts to $1 million.
(c) A Group sells 1,000 shares in B for $1.9 million on 1 October 20X8.

The junior accountant who was drafting the accounts was unsure how to record the disposal so none of the entries have been processed.

Solution

(a) The sale will be recorded in A's own accounts as:

Dr	Bank	$18,900
Cr	Investment	$11,000
Cr	Tax liability	$1,300
Cr	Profit on sale	$6,600

This will be the profit in A's own accounts and these entries are included in the consolidated figures below, calculated as proceeds less carrying value. The group profit on sale however will be calculated on the group's share of the carrying value of the subsidiary. See below.

Consolidated income statement for A Group for year ended 31 December 20X8

	$
Revenue ($155,500 + (9/12 × $25,800)) (W1)	174,850
Operating costs ($97,750 + (9/12 × $13,900))	(108,175)
Profit from operations	66,675
Profit on disposal of investment (W2)	2,540
Profit before tax	69,215
Income tax ($25,250 + (9/12 × $4,300) + 1,300 tax on disposal	(29,775)
Profit for the period	39,440
Attributable to:	
Owners of the parent	38,300
Non-controlling interest (W3)	1,140

B is not a subsidiary at the year end date and so the assets and liabilities of B are not included in the group SOFP.

Consolidated statement of financial position for A group as at 31 December 20X8

	$
Assets ($83,400 + proceeds $18,900)	102,300
Equity and liabilities	
Share capital	30,000
Retained earnings (W4)	61,000
	91,000
Liabilities ($10,000 + tax on gain $1,300)	11,300
	102,300

Workings

1. B was a subsidiary until 30 September 20X8 and so the income statement has been consolidated including 9 months of B's trading.
2. *Goodwill on acquisition*

	$'000	$'000
FV of consideration transferred		11,000
Less share of FV of the net assets acquired:		
Share capital	10,000	
Retained earnings at acquisition	1,400	
	11,400	
Group share	80%	(9,120)
Goodwill on acquisition		1,880

3. *Consolidated profit on disposal of investment*

	$'000	$'000
FV of consideration received (proceeds)		18,900
Less share of FV of the consolidated carrying value of the sub at the date of disposal: Share capital	10,000	
Retained earnings at 30 December 20X8	10,000	
Less earnings from 1 Oct to 31 Dec (3/12 × 7600)	(1,900)	
	18,100	
Group share	80%	(14,480)
Goodwill (W2)		(1,880)
Consolidated profit on disposal		2,540

4. *Non-controlling interest*

20% × B's profit for first 9 months = 20% × ($7,600 × 9/12) = 1,140.

5. *Consolidated retained earnings*

	A
	$'000
As per SOFP	54,400
Plus profit on sale (in individual accounts – as was not recorded in the retained earnings of A)	6,600
	61,000

(b) A Group sells 5,000 of its 8,000 shares in B for $14 million on 1 October 20X8. Tax arising on the sale amounted to $1 million.

The sale will be recorded in A's own accounts as:

Dr	Bank	$14,000
Cr	Investment (50/80 × 11,000)	$6,875
Cr	Tax liability	$1,000
Cr	Profit on sale	$6,125

This will be the profit in A's own accounts and these entries are included in the consolidated figures below, calculated as proceeds less carrying value. The group profit on sale however will be calculated on the group's share of the carrying value of the subsidiary. See below.

B was a subsidiary for 9 months and an associate for the remaining 3 months. The consolidated income statement below reflect that.

Consolidated income statement for A Group for year ended 31 December 20X8

	$
Revenue ($155,500 + (9/12 × $25,800)) (W1)	174,850
Operating costs ($97,750 + (9/12 × $13,900))	(108,175)
Profit from operations	66,675
Share of profit of associate 30% × ($7,600 × 3/12)	570
Profit on disposal of investment (W3)	1,765
Profit before tax	69,010
Income tax ($25,250 + (9/12 × $4,300) + 1,000 tax on disposal	(29,475)
Profit for the period	39,535
Attributable to:	
Owners of the parent	38,395
Non-controlling interest (W4)	1,140

B is not a subsidiary at the year end date and so the assets and liabilities of B are not included in the group SOFP. The 30% shareholding retained is equity accounted.

Consolidated statement of financial position for A group as at 31 December 20X8

	$
Assets ($83,400 + proceeds $14,000)	97,400
Investment in associate (W5)	4,695
	102,095
Equity and liabilities	
Share capital	30,000
Retained earnings (W6)	61,095
	91,095
Liabilities ($10,000 + tax on gain $1,000)	11,000
	102,095

Workings

1. *B was a subsidiary until 30 September 20X8 and so the income statement has been consolidated including 9 months of B's trading.*
2. *Goodwill on acquisition*

	$'000	$'000
FV of consideration transferred		11,000
Less share of FV of the net assets acquired:		
Share capital	10,000	
Retained earnings at acquisition	1,400	
	11,400	
Group share	80%	(9,120)
Goodwill on acquisition		1,880

3. *Consolidated profit on disposal of investment*

	$'000	$'000
FV of consideration received (proceeds)		14,000
Plus FV of 30% retained (30/80 × $11m)		4,125
Less share of FV of the consolidated carrying value of the sub at date control is lost		
Share capital	10,000	
Retained earnings at 30 December 20X8	10,000	
Less earnings from 1 Oct to 31 Dec (3/12 × 7600)	(1,900)	
	18,100	
Group share	80%	(14,480)
Goodwill (W2)		(1,880)
Consolidated profit on disposal		1,765

4. *Non-controlling interest*

20% × B's profit for first 9 months = 20% × ($7,600 × 9/12) = 1,140.

5. *Investment in associate*

	$'000
Cost of investment – amount transferred to investment in associate on disposal (30/80 × $11m)	4,125
Plus group share of post acquisition retained earnings (30% × $7,600 × 3/12)	570
	4,695

6. *Consolidated retained earnings*

	Group
Parent retained earnings as per SOFP	54,000
Plus profit on sale not yet recorded	6,125
Plus post-acquisition retained earnings of associate (30% × $7,600 × 3/12)	570
	61,095

(c) A Group sells 1,000 shares in B for $1.9 million on 1 October 20X8.

Adjustment to parent's equity on disposal of 1,000 shares	$000
FV of consideration received	(1,900)
Increase in NCI in net assets at date of disposal (10% × $18,100)	1,810
Adjustment to parent's equity	(90)

The $90,000 will be credited to A Group's retained earnings.

Disposal resulting in a trade investment

The principles are the same as those adopted for the disposal resulting in an associate. The FV of the interest retained forms the cost transferred as the opening value of the investment e.g. equivalent cost of retaining 1,000 shares in the example above would result in $1,800,000 being transferred to cost of investment. The gain of $175,000 ($1,800,000 less $1,625,000 (1,000/8,000 × $13 million)) would be recognised. The investment would then be accounted for in accordance with IAS 39 *Financial instruments: recognition and measurement*.

Disposals and IAS 39 Financial instruments: recognition and measurement

The above examples have been slightly simplified for illustrative purposes. The treatment of the investments in the parent's own accounts will be in accordance with IAS 39. IAS 27 requires that where a parent loses control of a subsidiary, it will be treated as a disposal of an IAS 39 investment. If gains on that investment have, to date, been recognised through other comprehensive income (i.e. it is classified as an available for sale asset in the parent's own accounts) then all previously recognised gains will be reclassified through the income statement and included in realised retained earnings.

IAS 39 is covered in depth in Chapter 11 and a full example will be incorporated in the revision section of this study system.

7.5.2 Interim dividends paid in the year of disposal

Were a dividend to be paid in the year of disposal occurs on a date before the shares were disposed of, the gain on disposal will change as the net assets of the subsidiary at the date of disposal will have reduced by the amount of the dividend paid.

The profits (represented by an increase in net assets) out of which the dividend was paid would have been transferred from the subsidiary to the parent entity, and would form part of the parent's reserves. The fact that a subsequent disposal of shares takes place does not alter the fact that the dividend transfer has already taken place.

It is important to compare the date of disposal with the date of any interim dividend payment, to see whether the disposal preceded the interim payment. In the previous example where full disposal occurs, if B paid a dividend on 30 September 20X8 of $4,000 then the calculations will be as follows:

***Step 1*: Calculate profit or loss on disposal**

The profit on disposal in Wolf's own financial statements remains the same. However, the profit on disposal in the consolidated financial statements differs because the net assets at the date of disposal are lower following the dividend payout.

The calculation is now as follows:

Working

Net assets of B at the date of disposal

	$'000
Net assets at date of disposal (calc above)	18,100
Dividend paid 30 Sept 20X8	(4,000)
Revised NA 1 Oct 20X8	14,100

Profit on disposal in the consolidated financial statements:

	$'000
Sale proceeds	18,900
Less: share of net assets at date of disposal [$14,100 (W1) × 80%]	(11,280)
Less goodwill	(1,800)
Consolidated profit on disposal	5,820

The gain recorded in part (a) in Example 7.F above was $2,620 based on share of consolidated net assets of $18,100. If a dividend is paid by the subsidiary immediately prior to the disposal then the profit reported increases as the net assets have reduced.

7.6 Business reorganisations

Motives for reorganisation

Reorganisations are likely to be undertaken in the following circumstances:

- There is a debit balance on retained earnings.
- Reorganisation is forced by a group of stakeholders, for example, by lenders where debt covenants are breached or are in danger of breach.
- A group that has grown by haphazard acquisition requires an improved management structure or a more logical hierarchy of ownership.
- A new structure will facilitate flotation.
- A new structure will facilitate the disposal of an investment in a subsidiary.
- Part of a business or of a group of entities is hived off into a separate group (this would be an example of a 'demerger' arrangement).

In many jurisdictions entities are permitted to:

- reduce their share capital or share premium;
- enter into a scheme of arrangement with their stakeholders;
- liquidate an entity and transfer its business to a new entity;
- purchase their own shares.

Any of these mechanisms may be involved in a reorganisation scheme.

Little guidance on reconstructions is currently offered by international accounting standards. IFRS 3 *Business combinations* discusses reverse acquisitions relatively briefly. Reverse acquisitions are a type of business combination where, for example, a business entity arranges to have itself 'acquired' by a smaller public entity as a means of obtaining a stock exchange listing. It is usually the case that entities have to build up a respectable record of regular and timely reporting in order to obtain a listing. Arranging for a reverse acquisition via a smaller public entity can be a short-cut to listing. IFRS 3 counsels careful consideration of the pertinent facts of the case when determining which party, in substance, is the parent. Although in this type of example legal form suggests that the smaller listed entity is the parent, it may be that the legal subsidiary is the acquirer, if it has control over the financial and operating policies of the legal parent.

7.6.1 Future developments

The IASB's project on business combinations is complete only as to phase I (which resulted in the issue of IFRS 3). More guidance on accounting for business combinations can be expected in due course in phase II of the project, and some of the issues relating to reconstructions and demergers are likely to be covered in a future financial reporting standard. These may include:

- Accounting for business combinations in which separate legal entities or parts of businesses are brought together to form a joint venture. The IASB has discussed the possibility of applying 'fresh start' accounting to such combinations. 'Fresh start' accounting is based on the principle that such business combinations result in a completely new entity. Therefore, the assets and liabilities of each of the combining entities should be recorded by the new entity at their fair value. Contrast this approach with the 'purchase' or 'acquisition' method of accounting that is set out in IFRS 3. 'Purchase' method accounting requires only that the net assets of a new subsidiary should be measured at fair value; the net assets of the parent continue to be measured in line with its existing policies. Therefore, in a typical group, consolidated net assets comprise net assets that have been brought in at fair value together with net assets at outdated values from earlier acquisitions and the net assets of the parent that may be valued at depreciated historical cost.
- Issues arising in respect of business combinations achieved by contractual arrangements only (i.e. not involving ownership). For example, business entities may be brought together by contractual arrangements to form a reporting entity that obtains dual listing on a stock exchange.

7.6.2 Intra-group reconstructions

In this section we will consider four reconstruction scenarios that may occur within a group of entities.

The transfer of a shareholding in a subsidiary from one group entity to another

---

Example 7.G

Subsidiary moved down

Suppose A, B and C have the following statement of financial positions at the date of reconstruction. A's investments in B and C were made at the dates of incorporation of B and C.

	A	B	*C*	*Consolidated*
	$'000	$'000	$'000	$'000
Investment in B (8 m shares)	8,000			
Investment in C (4 m shares)	4,000			
Other net assets	9,000	12,000	9,000	30,000
	21,000	12,000	9,000	30,000
$1 equity shares	10,000	8,000	5,000	10,000
Reserves	11,000	4,000	4,000	18,200
	21,000	12,000	9,000	28,200
Non-controlling interest (20% × $9 m)				1,800
	21,000	12,000	9,000	30,000

The investment in C is transferred to B by B issuing 3 million new shares to A in return for A's investment in C.

The group structure before the reconstruction would be as follows:

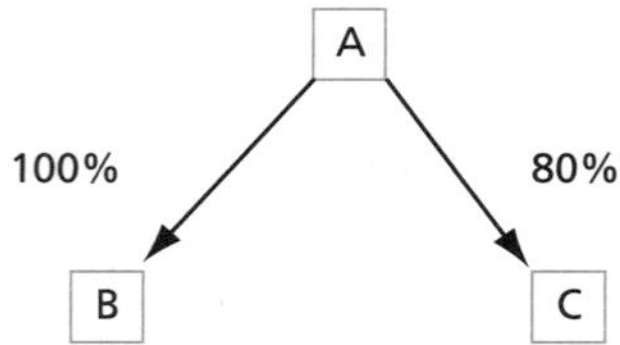

The group structure after the reconstruction would then be:

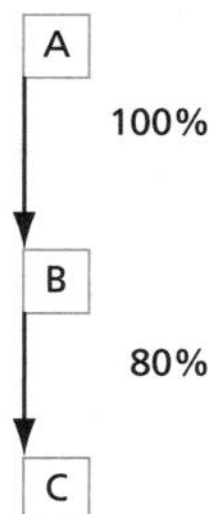

It should be clear that the overall effect on the A group is nil and the consolidated statement of financial position would not change. Such a reorganisation might be appropriate if:

- the directors of A wished to change the operating and reporting structure of the group to reduce the number of direct subsidiaries and achieve a more 'hierarchical' style of management;
- the directors of A wished to create a sub-group to sell off as a separate economic entity.

Where the new owner of the transferred investment issues shares in exchange for the investment then the consolidation is made easier if the investment can be transferred across at its existing carrying value.

In the above example this means that B would take the investment in C at cost from A ($4 million). Since B issues 3 million $1 shares then the credit to share premium will be $1 million ($4 million–$3 million). The statement of financial positions would be as shown below:

	A	*B*	*C*	*Consolidated*
	$'000	$'000	$'000	$'000
Investment in B	12,000			
Investment in C		4,000		
Other net assets	9,000	12,000	9,000	30,000
	21,000	16,000	9,000	30,000
$1 equity shares	10,000	11,000	5,000	10,000
Share premium		1,000		
Reserves	11,000	4,000	4,000	18,200
	21,000	16,000	9,000	28,200
Non-controlling interest				1,800
	21,000	16,000	9,000	30,000

Example 7.H

Subsidiary moved up

Suppose D, E and F have the following statement of financial positions at the date of incorporation (once again the investments are both made at the date of incorporation of the relevant entity).

	D	*E*	*F*	*Consolidated*
	$'000	$'000	$'000	$'000
Investment in E (8 m shares)	8,000			
Investment in F (3 m shares)		3,000		
Other net assets	8,000	10,000	7,000	25,000
	16,000	13,000	7,000	
$1 equity shares	10,000	8,000	4,000	10,000
Reserves	6,000	5,000	3,000	13,250
	16,000	13,000	7,000	23,250
Non-controlling interest (25% × $7 m)				1,750
	16,000	13,000	7,000	25,000

The initial group structure was:

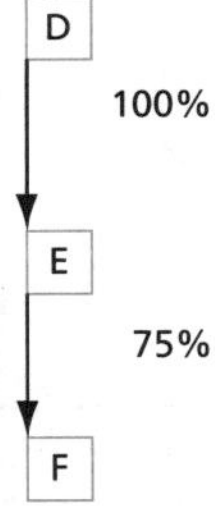

The group reconstruction transfers E's shareholding in entity F to entity D and the group structure becomes:

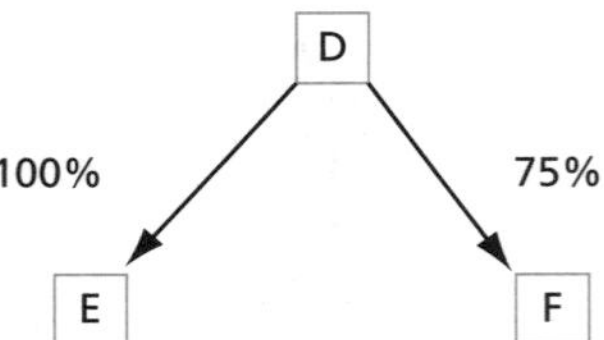

A reconstruction of this type *cannot* be effected by entity D making a share issue to entity E in exchange for its investment in entity F. This is because entity E is entity D's subsidiary and it is illegal for a parent to issue shares to its subsidiary. Therefore in these situations the investment would be transferred by entity E declaring a special dividend, known as a *dividend in specie*. The effect on the individual statement of financial positions and on the consolidated statement of financial position will be as shown below:

	D	*E*	*F*	*Consolidated*
	$'000	$'000	$'000	$'000
Investment in E	8,000			
Investment in F	3,000			
Other net assets	8,000	10,000	7,000	25,000
	19,000	10,000	7,000	25,000
$1 equity shares	10,000	8,000	4,000	10,000
Reserves	9,000	2,000	3,000	13,250
	19,000	10,000	7,000	23,250
Non-controlling interest (25% × $7 m)				1,750
	19,000	10,000	7,000	25,000

This type of reconstruction might be appropriate if:

- the group wished to move to a 'flatter' management style. The sub-subsidiaries could become 'direct' subsidiaries through a reorganisation;
- the group wished to dispose of the subsidiary (entity E in the above example) but keep the sub-subsidiary (entity F in the above example).

Note that the reserves of entity D are increased and the reserves of entity E reduced by the *dividend in specie*. This dividend is often very large in practice so the 'paying' entity might need to internally reconstruct its statement of financial position (see the beginning of this unit) to create sufficient distributable reserves (not necessary in the above example, though).

The addition of a new parent entity to the group

- Suppose a group has a parent entity, P, that is a private entity. If the group is expanding quickly it may wish to obtain a listing and so would need the ultimate parent to be a public limited entity. This *could* be achieved by incorporating a new parent public limited entity that gained ownership of the shares in entity P by 'purchasing' them from the existing shareholders, probably by an issue of its own equity shares.
- One method of combining two separate economic entities is for the two entities to form a group that has a newly incorporated parent.

Example 7.I

Two separate existing groups, group A and group B, become a single group by the shareholders of the parents of the two individual groups exchanging their shares for shares in the new parent to create a group as shown below:

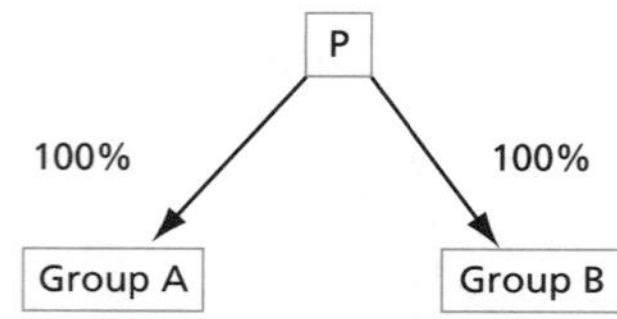

The transfer of shares in one or more subsidiary undertakings of a group to a new entity that is not a group entity, but whose shareholders are the same as those of the group's parent

Suppose a parent entity, A, has a subsidiary, B. Entity A transfers its shares in entity B to a new entity, C, whose shareholders are the same as the *shareholders* of entity A. Entity C will typically issue equity shares to finance this reconstruction but to the shareholders of entity A rather than to the entity itself. The diagram below shows the change in the group structure.

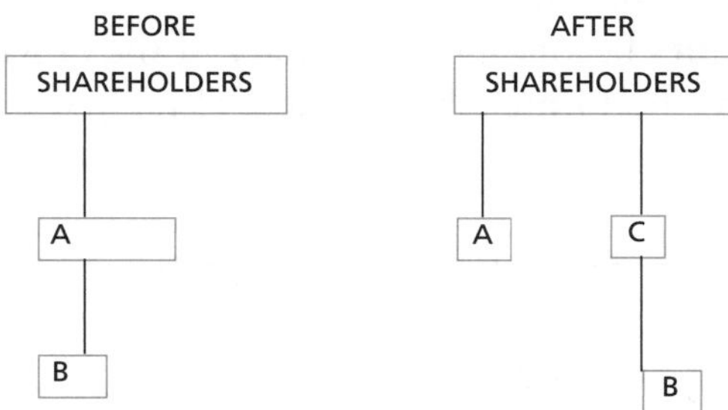

It is clear that, as far as the ultimate shareholders are concerned, little has happened other than a wholly internal rearrangement of their shareholdings, perhaps to facilitate running companies A and B as separate economic entities. As far as the consolidated accounts of A are concerned, though, there has been a disposal of shares in B. The disposal has effectively been made to the *shareholders* of A so the reduction in net assets is treated as a distribution to the shareholders – known as a *dividend in specie.*

Example 7.J

A has two 100% subsidiaries, B and C, which it has owned since their incorporation. The statement of financial positions of the three companies on 31 December 20X0 are as follows:

	A	*B*	*C*
	$'m	$'m	$'m
Investment in B	50		
Investment in C	45		
Property, plant and equipment	60	65	70
Net current assets	30	32	25
	185	97	95
Share capital ($1 shares)	100	50	45
Reserves	85	47	50
	185	97	95

- On 31.12 . X0 A transfers its shares in C to a new entity, D. D issues 60 million $1 shares to the *shareholders* of A.
- The net assets of the A group will be reduced by $95 million as a result of this disposal. This will be reflected in the *consolidated* accounts as a distribution (a dividend in specie) of $95 million. The individual accounts of entity A will show a dividend in specie of $45 million (the cost of the investment). The consolidated statement of financial position of the A group will no longer include any net assets of C and the individual statement of financial positions will be as follows:

	A	*B*	*Consolidated*
	$'m	$'m	$'m
Investment in B	50		
Investment in C	Nil		
Tangible fixed assets	60	65	125
Net current assets	30	32	62
	140	97	187

Share capital ($1 shares)	100	50	100
Reserves (reserves of A reduced by $45 m)	40	47	87
	140	97	187

The combination into a group of two or more entities that before the combination had the same shareholders

This is essentially the reverse of the scenario in the previous example, perhaps where controlling shareholders wish to manage their interests within a single structure. It might be achieved by one of the entities becoming a subsidiary of the other and the new parent issuing further equity shares to the former shareholders of its new subsidiary (who, of course, are also existing shareholders of the new parent).

Example 7.K

Two groups, groups C and D, have the same shareholders. The two groups combine so that D becomes a subsidiary of C. C issues more equity shares to the shareholders of D and the structure changes as follows:

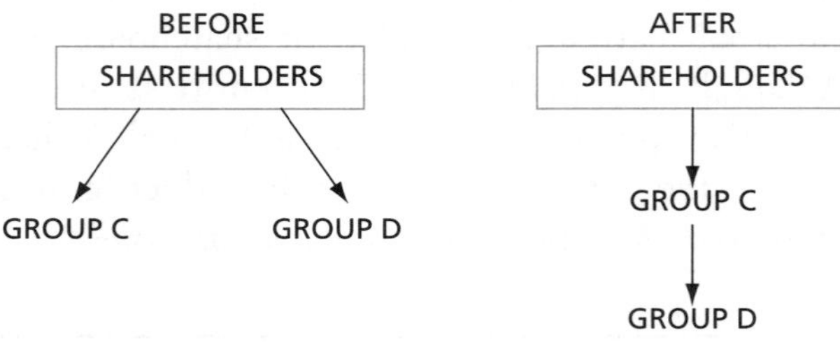

7.7 Summary

This module has looked at various aspects of changes in group structures. Firstly we covered acquisitions in the accounting period, taking account of FV adjustments required at the date of acquisition. We also looked at piecemeal acquisitions where the shareholding had been built up in stages.

The module covered disposals of investments in depth, looking at complete disposals and partial disposals where an investment is retained either as a trade investment or an associate. In all three cases the gain/loss on disposal was included in the group income statement. Where a disposal in the period had resulted in a controlling interest being retained, no gain or loss was recognised. Instead an adjustment was made to equity, representing the amount of the consideration received less the increase in the value of the net assets held by the non-controlling interest.

Business reorganisations were also covered, looking briefly at the different forms the reorganisation can take.

Revision Questions

The list below provides details of what each question covers, to help with your revision of this area.

Acquisitions

Question 1 Preparation of a statement of financial position (SOFP), including detailed fair value adjustments. **(25 marks)**

Question 2 Calculation and explanation of fair value adjustments. **(10 marks)**

Question 3 Preparation of SOFP with a piecemeal acquisition and a FV adjustment. **(15 marks)**

Disposals

Question 4 Calculation of profit/loss on disposal (sub to trade investment). **(5 marks)**

Question 5 Calculation of profit/loss on disposal (controlling interest retained. **(5 marks)**

Question 6 Preparation of income statement with disposal (sub to associate). **(10 marks)**

Question 7 Preparation of SOFP with disposal (sub to associate). **(25 marks)**

Reorganisations

Question 8 Preparation of SOFP after reorganisation **(15 marks)**

Question 1

The statements of financial position of George and its subsidiary entities Zippy and Bungle at 30 June 20X3 (the accounting date for all three entities) are given below:

	George		*Zippy*		*Bungle*	
	$'000	$'000	$'000	$'000	$'000	$'000
ASSETS						
Non-current assets:						
Property, plant and equipment (*Note 3*)	45,000		25,000		20,000	
Financial assets (*Notes 1* and *2*)	20,000		Nil		Nil	
		65,000		25,000		20,000
Current assets:						
Inventories (*Notes 3* and *4*)	18,000		12,000		11,000	
Trade and other receivables (*Notes 3* and *4*)	15,000		10,000		9,000	
		33,000		22,000		20,000
Total assets		98,000		47,000		40,000

EQUITY AND LIABILITIES						
Equity:						
Issued ordinary share capital ($1 shares)	25,000		20,000		10,000	
Share premium account	10,000		Nil		4,000	
Retained earnings	24,000		8,000		9,300	
		59,000		28,000		23,300
Non-current liabilities						
Deferred tax (*Note 3*)	2,000		1,000		1,500	
		22,000		6,000		1,500
Current liabilities						
Trade payables (*Note 4*)	10,000		7,500		8,000	
Tax payable	2,000		1,500		1,000	
Bank overdraft	5,000		4,000		5,000	
Provisions (*Note 3*)	Nil		Nil		1,200	
		17,000		13,000		15,200
Total equity and liabilities		98,000		47,000		40,000

Notes to the statements of financial position

1. On 1 July 20W0, the date of incorporation of Zippy, George subscribed for all the ordinary shares of Zippy at par.
2. On 30 June 20X3, George purchased eight million $1 shares in Bungle. The terms of the purchase consideration were as follows:
   (a) On 30 June 20X3, George issued three $1 ordinary shares for every four shares purchased in Bungle. The market value of the ordinary shares at 30 June 20X3 was $4 per share.
   (b) On 30 June 20X5, George will pay the former shareholders of Bungle $1 in cash for every share in Bungle they have purchased. This payment is contingent on the cumulative profits after tax of Bungle for the 2 years ending 30 June 20X5 being at least $3 million. At the date of carrying out the fair value exercise (see *Note 3* below), the directors of George considered it probable that this cash payment would be made.
   (c) No entries in respect of the purchase of shares in Bungle have been made in the statements of financial position of George.
3. Following the acquisition of Bungle, the directors of George carried out a fair value exercise as required by IFRS 3 – *Business Combinations*. The following matters are relevant and all potential fair value adjustments are material:
   (a) Property, plant and equipment comprise land and buildings and plant and machinery. At 30 June 20X3, the land and buildings had a carrying value of $12 million and a market value of $18 million. The plant and machinery had a carrying value of $8 million. All the plant and machinery was purchased on 30 June 20X0 and was being depreciated on a straight-line basis over eight years. No reliable estimate was available of the current market value of the plant and machinery, but at 30 June 20X3, the plant would have cost $22 million to replace with new plant.
   (b) The inventory at 30 June 20X3 comprised:
      - Finished goods which could be sold for $14.5 million. A reasonable profit allowance for the selling effort of the group would be $3 million.
      - Finished goods that had been damaged and could only be sold for $100,000, representing a significant loss on sale.

(c) Trade receivables includes an amount of $400,000 that the directors of George consider doubtful.

(d) The other provisions of Bungle comprise:
- $400,000 in respect of the closure of various retail outlets to which the directors of Bungle became committed prior to entering into acquisition negotiations with the directors of George.
- $800,000 in respect of the estimated cost of integrating Bungle into the George group. No detailed integration plans had been formulated by 30 June 20X3.

(e) The additional deferred tax that needs to be provided on the adjustments that are necessary as a result of the fair value exercise is a liability of $3 million.

4. George supplies a component to Zippy at cost plus a mark up of 20%. At 30 June 20X3, the inventories of Zippy included $1.5 million in respect of this component. At 30 June 20X3, the receivables of George showed an amount receivable from Zippy of $1.2 million, while the trade payables of Zippy showed an amount payable to George of $600,000. On 29 June 20X3, George sent a consignment of components to Zippy at an invoiced price of $600,000. The consignment was received and recorded by Zippy on 2 July 20X3.

Requirements

(a) Compute the goodwill on consolidation of Bungle that will be shown in the consolidated statement of financial position of George at 30 June 20X3. Provide justification for your figures where you consider this is needed. **(10 marks)**

(b) Prepare the consolidated statement of financial position of George at 30 June 20X3. **(15 marks)**

(Total marks = 25)

? Question 2

ABC is currently expanding its portfolio of equity interests in other entities. On 1 January 20X5, it made a successful bid for a controlling interest in DEF, paying a combination of shares and cash in order to acquire 80% of DEF's 100,000 issued equity shares. The terms of the acquisition were as follows:

In exchange for each $1 ordinary share purchased, ABC issued one of its own $1 ordinary shares plus $1.50 in cash. In addition to the consideration paid, ABC agreed to pay a further $1 per share on 1 January 20X7, on condition that the profits of DEF for the year ended 31 May 20X6 will exceed $6,000,000. ABC's directors consider that it is more likely than not that the additional consideration will be paid. The market value of a $1 share in ABC at 1 January 2005 was $3.50, rising to $3.60 at ABC's 31 May 20X5 year end.

Legal costs were $40,000 and share issue costs associated with the deal were $20,000.

The carrying value of DEF's net assets at 1 January 20X5 was $594,000. Carrying value was regarded as a close approximation to fair value, except in respect of the following:

1. The carrying value of DEF's property, plant and equipment at 1 January 20X5 was $460,000. Market value at that date was estimated at $530,000.
2. DEF had a contingent liability in respect of a major product warranty claim with a fair value of $100,000.
3. The cost of reorganising DEF's activities following acquisition was estimated at $75,000.

4. DEF's inventories included goods at an advanced stage of work-in-progress with a carrying value of $30,000. The sales value of these goods was estimated at $42,000 and further costs to completion at $6,000.

Requirement

Calculate goodwill on the acquisition of DEF, in accordance with the requirements of IFRS 3 *Business Combinations*, explaining your treatment of the legal costs, share issue costs and reorganisation costs. **(10 marks)**

? Question 3

Extracts from the statements of financial position as at 31 December 20X8 are presented below:

Statements of financial positions as at 31 December 20X8	*MC*	*JD*
ASSETS	$000	$000
Non-current assets	4,000	3,000
Available for sale investments	3,440	–
	7,440	3,000
Current assets	1,720	2,000
	9,160	5,000
EQUITY AND LIABILITIES		
Share capital ($1 shares)	1,000	1,000
Retained earnings	6,160	3,500
	7,160	4,500
LIABILITIES	2,000	500
	9,160	5,000

Additional information

1. The available for sale investments relate to two acquisitions in JD made by MC. The details of the acquisitions are as follows:
   31 October 20X7 100,000 equity shares purchased for $500,000.
   30 June 20X8 500,000 equity shares purchased for $2,800,000.
   The retained earnings of JD at 30 June 20X8 totalled $3,000,000.
   The available for sale investments are accounted for in accordance with IAS 39 and are held at fair value. The cumulative gains recognised in equity as at 30 June 20X8 totalled $100,000. A further $40,000 was recognised by 31 December 20X8.
2. The fair value of the net assets of JD was assessed at 30 June 20X8. The results showed an increase of $650,000 relating to plant and machinery. In line with group policy the related assets will be depreciated on a monthly basis over the remaining useful life, which is estimated at 5 years.
3. There has been no impairment of goodwill.

Requirement:

Prepare the consolidated statement of financial position as at 31 December 20X8 for the MC group.

Question 4

AMY, an entity with a 30 September year end, holds several investments in subsidiaries. On 1 April 20X6, it disposed of 35,000 of its 40,000 $1 shares in its subsidiary BNZ for $320,000. AMY had acquired the shares, which represented 80% of BNZ's ordinary share capital, on 1 April 20X4 for $250,000, when BNZ's reserves totalled $186,000. BNZ's net assets at the date of disposal were $275,000. Since acquisition, there has been no impairment to goodwill. The fair value of the investment retained if $33,000.

Calculate the consolidated profit or loss on disposal of the shares for inclusion in AMY's financial statements for the year ended 30 September 20X6. **(4 marks)**

Question 5

Several years ago DVS acquired 75% of the ordinary share capital of EWT at a cost of $1.7 million. The fair value of the total net assets of EWT at the data of acquisition was $1.8 million. Net assets of EWT at 31 January 20X7 totalled $4.7 million. The non-controlling interest is valued at fair value and the resulting goodwill at the date of acquisition on the NCI's interest is $80,000. There has been no impairment of goodwill since the acquisition of the shares in EWT.

On that date DVS disposed of 10% of the ordinary share capital of EWT, leaving it holding 65% of EWT's ordinary shares. The disposal proceeds were $900,000.

Calculate the adjustment ot parent's equity as a result of this disposal.

Question 6

RW holds 80% of the 1,000,000 ordinary shares of its subsidiary, SX. Summarised income statements of both entities for the year ended 31 December 20X4 are shown below:

	RW	*SX*
	$'000	$'000
Revenue	6,000	2,500
Operating costs	(4,500)	(1,700)
Profit before tax	1,500	800
Income tax	(300)	(250)
Profit for the period	1,200	550

RW purchased 800,000 of SX's $1 shares in 20X3 for $3.2 million, when SX's reserves were $2.4 million. Goodwill has been carried at cost since acquisition and there has been no subsequent impairment.

On 1 July 20X4, RW disposed of 500,000 shares in SX for $3 million. SX's reserves at 1 January 20X4 were $2.9 million, and its profits accrued evenly throughout the year. RW is liable to income tax at 30% on any accounting profits made on the disposal of investments. The fair value of the investment retained is $1.4 million.

The effects of the disposal are not reflected in the income statements shown above.

Requirement

Prepare the summarised consolidated income statement for RW for the year ended 31 December 20X4. **(10 marks)**

Question 7

The statement of financial positions of AZ and two entities in which it holds substantial investments as at 31 March 20X6 are shown below:

	AZ		*BY*		*CX*	
	$'000	$'000	$'000	$'000	$'000	$'000
Non-current assets:						
Property, plant and equipment	10,750		5,830		3,300	
Investments	7,650		–		–	
		18,400		5,830		3,300
Current assets:						
Inventories	2,030		1,210		1,180	
Trade receivables	2,380		1,300		1,320	
Cash	1,380		50		140	
		5,790		2,560		2,640
		24,190		8,390		5,940
Equity:						
Share capital ($1 shares)		8,000		2,300		2,600
Preference share capital		–		1,000		–
Retained earnings		10,750		3,370		2,140
		18,750		6,670		4,740
Current liabilities:						
Trade payables	3,520		1,550		1,080	
Income tax	420		170		120	
Suspense account	1,500		–		–	
		5,440		1,720		1,200
		24,190		8,390		5,940

Notes

1. *Investments by AZ in BY*

   Several years ago AZ purchased 80% of BY's ordinary share capital for $3,660,000 when the retained earnings of BY were $1,950,000. In accordance with the group's policy goodwill was recorded at cost, and there has been no subsequent impairment.

   At the same time as the purchase of the ordinary share capital, AZ purchased 40% of BY's preference share capital at par. The remainder of the preference shares are held by several private investors. The preference shares are classified as equity, in accordance with IAS 32 *Financial Instruments: Presentation,* because of the rights and conditions attaching to the shares.

2. *Investment by AZ in CX*

   Several years ago AZ purchased 60% of CX's ordinary share capital for $2,730,000 when the retained earnings of CX were $1,300,000. Goodwill was recorded at cost and there has been no subsequent impairment.

   On 1 October 20X5 AZ disposed of 520,000 ordinary shares in CX, thus losing control of CX's operations. However, AZ retains a significant influence over the entity's operations and policies. The proceeds of disposal, $1,500,000, were debited to cash and credited to a suspense account. No other accounting entries have been made in respect of the disposal. An investment gains tax of 30% of the profit on disposal will become payable by AZ within the twelve months following the statement of financial position date of 31 March 20X6, and this liability should be accrued. The investments made by AZ were in unlisted entities and were initially classified as available for sale in AZ's own accounts. The fair value of these investments were unable to be measured reliably and so continue to be held at cost in AZ's accounts.

CX's reserves at 1 April 20X5 were $1,970,000. The entity's profits accrued evenly throughout the year.

3. *Additional information*
   No fair value adjustments were required in respect of assets or liabilities upon either of the acquisitions of ordinary shares. The called up share capital of both BY and CX has remained the same since the acquisitions were made. All gains and losses on investments held by AZ have been realised through profit or loss in AZ's own accounts.

4. *Intra-group trading*
   During the year ended 31 March 20X6, BY started production of a special line of goods for supply to AZ. BY charges a mark-up of 20% on the cost of such goods sold to AZ. At 31 March 20X6, AZ's inventories included goods at a cost of $180,000 that had been supplied by BY.

Requirements

(a) Calculate the profit or loss on disposal after tax of the investment in CX that will be disclosed in:
   (i) AZ's own financial statements
   (ii) the AZ group's consolidated financial statements **(6 marks)**

(b) Calculate the consolidated reserves of the AZ group at 31 March 20X6. **(5 marks)**

(c) Prepare the consolidated statement of financial position of the AZ group as at 31 March 20X6.

(14 marks)
(Total marks = 25)

Question 8

The following statements of financial position relate to P, Q, R and S as at 31 May 20X7 immediately before the transaction mentioned below:

	P	*Q*	*R*	*S*
	$'m	$'m	$'m	$'m
Property, plant and equipment	3,500	550	60	90
Investment in Q	900			
Investment in R		90		
Investment in S	50			
Net current assets	1,830	400	70	60
Long-term loans	(130)	(30)	(10)	(5)
	6,150	1,010	120	145
Issued capital ($1 shares)	1,350	100	30	20
Share premium account	1,550	100	10	2
Retained earnings	3,250	810	80	105
	6,150	1,010	120	145

The directors of P decided to reconstruct the group at 31 May 20X7. Under the scheme the existing group was split into two separate groups. This involved P disposing of its shareholding in Q to another company, E. In return, E issued 300 million shares to the shareholders of P.

The following information relates to the dates of acquisition of the investments in group companies:

Investor	*Company acquired*	*% acquired*	*Balance on share premium*	*Balance on accumulated profits*
			$'m	$'m
P	Q	100	100	250
P	S	60	20	90
Q	R	80	10	60

P's investment in Q was made before the other two investments. All goodwill on consolidation had been written off as impaired by 31 May 20X6.

Requirement

Prepare the consolidated statement of financial position of the P and E groups as at 31 May 20X7 immediately after the group reconstruction has been put into effect.

(15 marks)

Solutions to Revision Questions

Solution 1

(a)

Step 1: Fair value of net assets acquired

Description	*Fair value*	*Comment*
	$'000	
Land and buildings	18,000	Market value
Plant and machinery	13,750	Depreciated replacement cost (5/8 × $22 m)
Inventory	11,600	Selling price less profit allowance ($11.5 m) + scrap value ($100,000)
Receivables	8,600	Reduced by provision for doubtful receivable
Current liabilities	(14,000)	Book value
Deferred tax	(4,500)	Book value plus $3 m
Other provisions	(400)	$800,000 a post-acquisition item
	33,050	

Step 2: Fair value of consideration given

Shares: 8,000 × 3/4 × $4	= $24,000
Deferred cash: 8,000 × 0.873	= $6,984
Total	$30,984

Step 3: Compute goodwill

$30,984 − (80% × FV of net assets acquired $33,050) = $4,544

(b)

Consolidated statement of financial position of George at 30 June 20X3

	$'000	$'000
ASSETS		
Non-current assets		
Property, plant and equipment (45,000 + 25,000 + 18,000 + 13,750)	101,750	
Goodwill (requirement a)	4,544	
		106,294
Current assets		
Inventories [18,000 + 12,000 + 11,600 − 250 (W1)]	41,350	
Inventory in transit [600 − 100 (W1)]	500	
Receivables (15,000 + 10,000 + 8,600 − 1,200)	32,400	
		74,250
Total assets		180,544

EQUITY AND LIABILITIES		
Equity		
Ordinary share capital (25,000 + 6,000)		31,000
Share premium account (10,000 + 6,000 × $3)		28,000
Retained earnings (W3)		31,650
		90,650
Non-controlling interest (W2)		6,610
		97,260
Non-current liabilities		
Long-term loan (20,000 + 5,000)	25,000	
Deferred consideration	6,984	
Deferred tax (2,000 + 4,500 + 1,000)	7,500	
Other	400	
		39,884
Current liabilities		
Trade payables (10,000 + 7,500 + 8,000 − 600)	24,000	
Tax payable (2,000 + 1,000 + 1,500)	4,500	
Bank overdraft (5,000 + 4,000 + 5,000)	14,000	
		43,400
Total equity and liabilities		180,544

Workings

1. *Unrealised profit (in $'000)*

On inventory in hand (1,500 × 20/120)	= $250
On inventory in transit (600 × 20/120)	= $100

2. *Non-controlling interest*

	$'000
In Bungle: 20% × $33.050 m [see requirement (a)]	6,610

3. *Consolidated retained earnings*

	$'000
George	24,000
Zippy	8,000
Unrealised profit [250 + 100 (see W1)]	(350)
	31,650

Solution 2

Calculation of goodwill on the acquisition of 80% of the equity shares in DEF:

	$'000	$'000
Fair value of consideration:		
80,000 shares acquired for consideration of $5 each ($1.50 in cash + $3.50 in shares)		400
Contingent consideration: $1 per share		80
Total consideration		480

Fair value of net assets acquired:		
Net assets at carrying value	594	
Adjustments for fair value:		
Property, plant and equipment ($530,000 − $460,000)	70	
Contingent liability	(100)	
Inventories (fair value of $36,000 less carrying value of $30,000)	6	
	570	
80% acquired (80% × $570,000)		456
Goodwill on acquisition		24

According to IFRS 3 (revised), directly attributable costs of acquisition should be written off when incurred and so will be charged as an expense in the income statement. The costs of issuing equity instruments are to be accounted for in accordance with IAS 39 *Financial Instruments: recognition and measurement.*

Solution 3

Consolidated statement of financial position of MC Group at 31 December 20X8

	$'000
ASSETS	
Non-current assets	
Plant and equipment (4,000 + 3,000 + 585 (W1))	7,585
Goodwill (W2)	610
	8,195
Current assets (1,720 + 2,000)	3,720
Total assets	11,915
EQUITY AND LIABILITIES	
Equity	
Ordinary share capital	1,000
Retained earnings (W3)	6,381
	7,381
Non-controlling interest (W4)	2,034
	9,415
Current liabilities (2,000 + 500)	2,500
Total equity and liabilities	11,915

Workings

1. *Fair value adjustment*

	At acquisition date $000	Movement $000	At statement of financial position date $000
Plant & equipment	650	(65)	585

2. *Goodwill on acquisition (30 June 20X8)*

	$000	$000
Consideration transferred (50% paid for)		2,800
FV of the investment held previously (FV at the date control is gained, 30 June)		600
Net assets acquired:		
Share capital	1,000	
Retained earnings	3,000	

FV uplift on non-current assets	650	
	4,650	
Group share of NA (60%)		(2,790)
		610

3. *Retained earnings*

	MC	JD
	$'000	$'000
At statement of financial position date	6,160	3,500
Gains from derecognition of financial asset at 30 June (10% investment held – now fully consolidated)	100	
Pre-acquisition retained earnings		(3,000)
		500
60% share of BD's post acq'n earnings	300	
Less gains on AFS investments recognised in MC's own accounts	(140)	
Group share of FV movement 60% (650/5 yrs × 6/12 months)	(39)	
Group retained earnings	6,381	

4. *Non-controlling interest*

40% × net assets of JD at 31 December 20X8:

	$000
Share capital	1,000
Retained earnings	3,500
Net balance of FV uplift (650 -65)	585
	5,085
40%	2,034

Solution 4

AMY: consolidated profit or loss on disposal

	$
FV of consideration	320,000
FV of 10% investment retained	33,000
Less FV of the consolidated net assets at disposal (80% × $275,000)	(220,000)
Goodwill (W1)	(61,200)
Gain on disposal	71,800

Working 1

Goodwill on consolidation

Investment at cost	250,000
Less: acquired: [$40,000 + (186,000 × 80%)]	(188,800)
Goodwill	61,200

Solution 5

Adjustment to parent's equity

	$
Consideration received	(900,000)
Increase in FV of NCI in net assets at disposal date (10% × $4.7m)	470,000
Increase in NCI in goodwill ($80,000 × 25/35) – $80,000	32,000
Adjustment to parent's equity	(398,000)

Solution 6

RW: Consolidated income statement for the year ended 31 December 20X4

	$'000
Revenue (6,000 (6/12 × $2,500))	7,250.0
Operating costs (4,500 + (6/12 × $1,700))	(5,350.0)
	1,900.0
Share of profit of associate (W3)	82.5
Profit on disposal of investment (W2)	420.0
Profit before tax	2402.5
Income tax [300 + (6/12 × $250)+ (W4) $540	(965.0)
Profit for the period	1,437.5
Attributable to:	
Equity holders of the parent	1382.5
Non-controlling interest (W5)	55
Profit for the period	1437.5

Workings

1. *Goodwill on acquisition*

	$000	$'000
FV of consolidation transferred		3,200
Less FV of consolidated net assets at acquisition:		
Share capital	800	
Retained earnings	2,400	
	3,200	
Group share of 80%		(2,560)
Gain on disposal		640

2. *Consolidated profit on disposal*

	$000	$'000
FV of consolidation received		3,000
FV of 30% retained		1,400
Less FV of consolidated net assets as disposal date:		
Share capital	10,000	
Retained earnings 1 Jan	2,900	
Profit for 6 months to 30 June (6/12 × $550)	275	
	4,175	
Group share of 80%		(3,340)
Goodwill		(640)
Gain on disposal		420

3. *Share of profit of associate*
$550,000 × 6/12 months × 30% = $82,500

4. *Tax on gain on disposal*
This is calculated on RW's own profit:

	$'000
Proceeds of sale	3,000
Less CV of investment sold (30/80 × $3.2m)	1,200
Gain in individual accounts	1,800
Tax on that gain at 30%	540

5. *Non-controlling interest*

	$'000
To 1 July 20X4: ($550 × 6/12) × 20%	55

Solution 7

(a) AZ originally acquired 60% of 2,600,000 shares: 1,560,000. On 1 October 20X5, it disposed of 520,000 shares – that is one third of its holding. After the disposal, AZ retained ownership of 40% of the ordinary share capital of CX.

(i) Profit or loss on disposal in AZ's own financial statements:

	$'000
Proceeds of sale	1,500
Cost: 1/3 × $2,730,000	(910)
Profit before tax	590
Tax charge: $590,000 × 30%	(177)
Profit after tax	413

(ii) Profit on disposal in the AZ group's consolidated financial statements.

Workings

Consolidated gain on disposal	$'000
FV of consideration received	1,500
FV of 40% retained (40/60 × $2,730)	1,820
Less FV of the consolidated NA at disposal date (60% × $4,655 (W2))	(2,793)
Goodwill (W1)	(390)
Consolidated gain	137

1. *Goodwill on the acquisition of CX*

	$'000
Cost of investment	2,730
Less: Acquired (2,600 + 1,300 = 3,900 × 60%)	(2,340)
Goodwill on acquisition	390

2. *CX's net assets at the date of disposal*

	$'000
Share capital	2,600
Retained earnings on 1 April 20X5	1,970
1/2 × profit for the year (2,140 − 1,970)/2	85
	4,655

(b)

1. *Provision for unrealised profit*

Cost structure: cost + (20% × cost) =	selling price ($'000)
Unrealised profit = 20/120 × 180 =	30
Of this, 20% is attributable to the minority:	(6)
The remainder reduces consolidated reserves:	24

2. *Consolidated retained earnings*

	$'000
Reserves of AZ	10,750
Post-acquisition retained earnings of BY: ($3,370 − $1,950) × 80%	1,136
Profit on disposal [see part (a)(i)]	413
Post-acquisition retained earnings in associate entity CX ($2,140 − $1,300) × 40%	336
Provision for unrealised profit (W1)	(24)
	12,611

(c)

AZ: Consolidated statement of financial position as at 31 March 20X6

	$'000	$'000
Non-current assets:		
Property, plant and equipment (10,750 + 5,830)	16,580	
Goodwill (W1)	260	
Investment in associate (W2)	2,156	
Other investments (W3)	860	
		19,856
Current assets:		
Inventories (2,030 + 1,210 − 30 PURP)	3,210	
Trade receivables (2,380 + 1,300)	3,680	
Cash (1,380 + 50)	1,430	
		8,320
		28,176
Equity:		
Share capital	8,000	
Consolidated retained earnings [part (b)]	12,611	
		20,611
Non-controlling interest (W4)		1,728
Current liabilities:		
Trade payables (3,520 + 1,550)	5,070	
Income tax {420 + 170 + 177 [part a (i)]}	767	
		5,837
		28,176

Workings

1. *Goodwill on the acquisition of BY*

	$'000
Cost of investment	3,660
Less: acquired (1,950 + 2,300) × 80%	(3,400)
Goodwill on acquisition	260

2. *Investment in associate CX*

	$'000
Cost of nvestment – amount transferred to investment in associate on disposal (40/80 × 2,730)	1,820
Share of post-acquisition profits [(2,140 − 1,300) × 40%]	336
	2,156

3. *Investments*

	$'000
As stated in AZ's statement of financial position	7,650
Less: investment at cost in BY's ordinary shares	(3,660)
Less: investment at cost in BY's preference shares	(400)
Less: investment at cost in CX's ordinary shares	(2,730)
Balance = other investments	860

4. *Non-controlling interest*

	$'000
In BY's preference shares	600
In BY's other net assets (2,300 + 3,370) × 20%	1,134
Provision for unrealised profit (part b)	(6)
	1,728

Solution 8

After the reconstruction there will be two separate groups. P will have one subsidiary, S, and E two subsidiaries, Q and R.

The initial goodwill on consolidation is as follows:

Q − $900 m − 100%($100 m + $100 m + $250 m) = $450 m
R − $90 m − 80%($30 m + $10 m + $60 m) = $10 m
S − $50 m − 60%($20 m + $20 m + $90 m) = $28 m

Therefore the consolidated statement of financial position of the P group is as follows (unless otherwise indicated, the figures are a simple aggregation of P and S).

	$'m
Property, plant and equipment	3,590
Net current assets	1,890
Long-term loans	(135)
	5,345
Issued capital (P only)	1,350
Share premium (P only)	1,550
Retained earnings (see working)	2,387
Non-controlling interest (40% × net assets of S)	58
	5,345

Working

Retained earnings

	$'m
P's retained earnings	3,250
Investment in Q distributed to shareholders	(900)
S's retained earnings [60% ($105 m − $90 m)]	9
Negative goodwill	28
	2,387

The consolidated statement of financial position of the E group appears below (unless otherwise indicated, the figures are a simple aggregation of Q and R).

	$'m
Property, plant and equipment	610
Net current assets	470
Long-term loans	(40)
	1,040
Share capital (E only)	300
Other reserves (W1)	600
Consolidated retained earnings (W2)	116
Non-controlling interest (20% × net assets of R)	24
	1,040

Working

1. *Other reserves*

   E has issued 300 million shares of $1 to acquire an investment in Q that had a carrying value of $900 million. The issue of shares is recorded at par. Given the fact that the reconstruction has no overall effect on the ultimate shareholders or on the non-controlling interests, there should be no effect on the amounts that are included in the consolidated statement of financial position. The 'other reserve' is the difference between the nominal value of the shares issued and the original carrying value of the investment in Q that was previously in the statement of financial position of P.

2. *Consolidated retained earnings*

	$'m
Q ($810 m − $250 m)	560
R [80% ($80 m − $60 m)]	16
Goodwill written off as impaired:	
Q	(450)
R	(10)
	116

8

Foreign Currency Translations

Foreign Currency Translations

8

Learning Outcomes

After studying this chapter students should be able to:

- explain foreign currency translation principles;
- explain the correct treatment for foreign loans financing foreign equity investments.

8.1 Introduction

This chapter examines the provisions of IAS 21 dealing with the effects of foreign exchange rates. Section 8.2 looks at the objectives of the standard and some of the principal definitions it employs. Section 8.3 covers single transactions in foreign currencies. The most complex section of the chapter, Section 8.4, examines the calculations required to translate and then consolidate the financial statements of a foreign operation. Section 8.5 examines hedging of a foreign equity investment by a foreign loan.

8.2 IAS 21 *The effects of changes in foreign exchange rates*

IAS 21 was revised and reissued in December 2003 as part of the IASB's improvements projects. It incorporates several important alterations and so those students who have previously encountered foreign currency transactions regulated by the provisions of IAS 21 should study this chapter with care.

8.2.1 Foreign currency transactions: the accounting problem

Businesses frequently conduct transactions and make investments using foreign currencies. The accounting problem lies in the fact that the currency used in transactions is not the same as the currency in which the business entity conducts its normal operations. Therefore, in order to reflect the effect of the transactions in its own books and financial statements, the entity must use a method of currency translation.

A feature of foreign currency transactions is that they are subject to exchange risk, and that they may give rise to a loss (or, indeed, a profit) on translation.

8.2.2 IAS 21 Objectives and key definitions

The objective of IAS 21 is stated as follows:

The objective of this standard is to prescribe how to include foreign currency transactions and foreign operations in the financial statements of an entity, and how to translate financial statements into a presentation currency.

Two distinct types of foreign activities are covered by the standard: first, single transactions in foreign currencies, and second, foreign operations.

A *foreign currency* is a currency other than the functional currency of the entity.

A *foreign operation* is an entity that is a subsidiary, associate, joint venture or branch of a reporting entity, the activities of which are based or conducted in a country or currency other than those of the reporting entity.

The standard identifies and defines two types of currency: functional currency and presentation currency. *Functional currency* is the currency of the primary economic environment in which the entity operates. *Presentation currency* is the currency in which the financial statements are presented.

As the distinction between the two implies, it is possible for an entity to report in a presentation currency that is not its functional currency.

Functional currency

Where an entity operates in several different national environments it may not always be a straightforward matter to determine its functional currency. Entities need to consider the following issues in determining their functional currency:

- Which currency principally influences selling prices for goods and services?
- Which country's competitive forces and regulations principally determine the selling prices of the entity's goods and services?
- In which currency are funds for financing activities (debt and equity instruments) generated?
- In which currency are receipts from operations generally kept?
- Which currency influences labour, material and other costs of providing goods or services?

Where consideration of the different factors does not result in a clear identification of the functional currency, the issue becomes a matter of judgement for management.

Presentation currency

The functional currency of an entity is a matter of fact, although identifying it may not be straightforward. By contrast, the entity's presentational currency is a matter of choice. IAS 21 permits an entity to present its financial statements in any currency it chooses; this may differ from the entity's functional currency. Why would an entity choose a presentation currency that is different from its functional currency? One of the following reasons may apply:

- The entity's functional currency is relatively obscure. The entity may then choose to report in a currency such as US dollars or Euros in order to make its financial statements more transparent.
- The entity's principal investors tend to function in another currency from the entity's own functional currency.

- The entity may be seeking investment from potential investors whose functional currency is not the same as the entity's functional currency.

8.3 Single transactions in foreign currencies

A single foreign currency transaction is one that is denominated in a foreign currency, or requires settlement in a foreign currency. Examples include:

- purchase or sale of goods or services where the price is denominated in a foreign currency;
- borrowing or lending of funds denominated in a foreign currency;
- acquisition or disposal of assets denominated in a foreign currency.

IAS 21 requires that the transaction should be recorded by translating the foreign currency amount into the entity's functional currency using the spot exchange rate at the date of the transaction (spot rate is the exchange rate for immediate delivery of the currency).

Example 8.A

On 1 July 20X0 entity A which reports in dollars purchased an asset from an entity reporting in euros for ∈200,000. Payment was made on 31 December 20X0. The entity's year end is 30 September.

Relevant exchange rates are:

Date	*Exchange rate* (as to $1)
1 July 20X0	1.50
30 September 20X0	1.40
1 December 20X0	1.45

How will this transaction be recorded in the books of A?

The initial recognition of the transaction is at spot rate on 1 July 20X0. The value of the transaction at that date is:

200,00/1.50 5 $133,333

The following journal records the transaction at 1 July 20X0:

	$	$
DR Asset	133,333	
CR Liability (supplier)		133,333

By A's year end the liability has still not been settled. IAS 21 requires that foreign currency monetary items should be translated using the closing rate at the entity's year end, and that non-monetary items should be translated using the exchange rate at the date of the transaction.

The asset itself is a non-monetary item; it is already included in the books of A using the rate at the date of the transaction, and so there is no need for any adjustment. The liability, however, is a monetary item, and so it must be retranslated at closing rate, as follows:

200,000/1.40 5 $142,857

This increases the liability at the year end (so there will be an additional credit to the supplier account of $142,857 − $133,333 = $9,524. The matching debit represents a loss on exchange, and IAS 21 requires that this should be taken to profit and loss. The year end journal entry in respect of this transaction, therefore, is:

	$	$
DR Income statement	9,524	
CR Liability (supplier)		9,524

By the settlement date, the exchange rate has moved again. On 31 December 20X0 A is obliged to pay €200,000. The cost of this to A in dollar terms is:

200,00/1.40 5 $142,857

However, the liability recorded in the books is $142,857; because of exchange rate movements, A is obliged to pay a lesser amount in dollar terms and so has realised a gain on exchange. The following journal entry records the transaction:

DR Liability (supplier)	142,857	
CR Cash		137,931
CR Income statement		4,926

8.4 Translating foreign operations

Sometimes, foreign operations such as subsidiaries, branches, associates and joint ventures operate using a different functional currency from that of the reporting entity. Where this is the case, the results, assets and liabilities of the foreign operation must be translated into a presentation currency, that is, the currency of the reporting entity.

The method employed is as follows:

(a) assets and liabilities should be translated using the closing rate at the year end date;
(b) income and expenses should be translated at the exchange rates in force at the date of the transactions;
(c) all resulting exchange differences are recognised as part of equity, until such time as the investment in the foreign operation is realised.

Point (b) could involve a foreign operation in a great deal of time consuming work. Therefore, it is accepted by IAS 21 that, for practical reasons, an average rate for the period may be used instead. However, if there are significant fluctuations in the exchange rate during an accounting period, it may not be acceptable to use the average rate.

Consolidation techniques are the same for foreign operations as for operations reporting under the same functional currency as the investor. The requirements of IFRS 3 *Business Combinations,* IAS 28 *Investments in Associates,* IAS 31 *Interests in Joint Ventures* and IAS 27 *Consolidated and Separate Financial Statements* apply equally to foreign operations.

Goodwill arising on the consolidation of a foreign operation should be recognised according to the requirements of IFRS 3. Such goodwill is treated as being an investment by the reporting entity in an asset, and it should be translated along with all other investee's assets at the closing rate. Fair value adjustments to the carrying amounts of assets and liabilities in the foreign operation should also be translated at the closing rate.

The techniques involved in translating a foreign operation are demonstrated in the following example.

Example 8.B

BLX holds several investments in subsidiaries. One of these, CMY, is located overseas. CMY prepares its financial statements in its local currency, the Crown.

Several years ago, when the exchange rate was 5 Crowns = 1$, CMY purchased land at a cost of 170,000 Crowns. On 1 June 20X5, when the exchange rate was 6.5 Crowns = $1 the land was revalued at a fair value of 600,000 Crowns. The exchange rate at the group's year end, 31 December 20X5, was 7 Crowns = $1.

In accordance with the requirements of IAS 21 *The effects of changes in foreign exchange rates,* at what value in $s should the land be recognised in BLX's group financial statements at 31 December 20X5?

Solution

IAS 21 requires that both the cost and any subsequent revaluiton should be translated at closing rate. The value of the revalued assets would then be 600,000/7 = $85,714.

Example 8.C

On 1 October 20X4 Erasmus acquired 80% of the ordinary issued share capital of Heinrich. Heinrich's functional currency is the groat (G). The cost of the investment was G800,000, and at the date of acquisition Heinrich's accumulated profits were G86,000. It is the group policy to value non-controlling interest at acquisition at the proportionate share of the fair value of the subsidiary's identifiable net assets.

Relevant rates of exchange are as follows:

Date	Gs to $1
1 October 20X4	4.0
30 September 20X8	3.9
30 September 20X9	3.75
Average for the year ended 30 September 20X9	3.8

The draft income statements, summarised statements of changes in equity and statements of financial position of Erasmus and its subsidiary are set out below:

Income statements for the year ended 30 September 20X9

	Erasmus	*Heinrich*
	$'000	G'000
Revenue	10,290	10,650
Cost of sales	(5,145)	(5,325)
Gross profit	5,145	5,325
Other operating expenses	(4,116)	(4,260)
Profit from operations	1,029	1,065
Income from shares in Heinrich	64	–
Profit before tax	1,093	1,065
Income tax expense	(348)	(385)
Profit for the period	745	680

Summarised statements of changes in equity for the year ended 30 September 20X9

	Erasmus	*Heinrich*
	$'000	G'000
Balance at start of period	1,252	1,336
Profit for the period	745	680
Dividends	(350)	(300)
Balance at 30 September 20X9	1,647	1,716

Summarised statements of financial position as at 30 September 20X9

	Erasmus	*Heinrich*
	$'000	G'000
Property, plant and equipment	515	920
Investment in Heinrich	200	–
Net current assets	1,189	901
	1,904	1,821
Share capital	905	850
Retained reserves	742	866
	1,647	1,716
Loans	257	105
	1,904	1,821

Requirement

Prepare the summarised consolidated financial statements for the Eramus Group for the year to 30 September 20X9.

Work to nearest $000.

Solution

Erasmus group: Consolidated statement of financial position as at 30 September 20X9

	$'000
Goodwill on consolidation (W1)	13.7
Property, plant and equipment (515 + 245.3)	760.3
Net current assets (1,189 + 240.3)	1,429.3
	2,203.3
Share capital (Erasmus only)	905.0
Retained reserves (balancing figure)	921.8
	1,826.8
Non-controlling interest (W3)	91.5
Loans (257 + 28)	285.0
	2,203.3

Workings

1. *Goodwill on consolidation*

Goodwill on consolidation in G'000:

	G'000	G'000
Cost of acquisition ($200 × 4)		800
Acquired:		
Share capital	850	
Pre-acq reserves	86	
	936 × 80%	(748.8)
Goodwill on acquisition		51.2

Remember that IAS 21 requires that goodwill on consolidation is treated as an asset like any other, and translated at closing rate. So, goodwill in the consolidated statement of financial position is: G51,200/3.75 = $13,700 (rounded to the nearest $100).

2. *Translation of Heinrich's statement of financial position*

All of Heinrich's assets and liabilities are translated at closing rate:

	G'000	*Rate*	$'000
Property, plant and equipment	920	3.75	245.3
Net current assets	901	3.75	240.3
	1,821		485.6
Share capital	850	4.00	212.5
Pre-acquisition retained reserves	86	4.00	21.5
Post-acquisition retained reserves	780	Bal. fig	223.6
	1,716		457.6
Loans	105	3.75	28.0
	1,821		485.6

Note that share capital and pre-acquisition retained reserves are translated at 4.00, the exchange rate ruling at the date of acquisition. However, IAS 21 does not specify the rate at which equity items should be translated, and so closing rate could be used.

3. *Non-controlling interest*

The non-controlling interest is 20% of Heinrich's net assets: $457,600 × 20% = $91,500 (rounded to the nearest $100).

Note that the consolidation conventions applied are no different from the ones we have covered in previous chapters. The share capital is that of the holding entity only, 100% of the assets and liabilities of the subsidiary are included, and a non-controlling interest is calculated in respect of the 20% of the net assets owned by shareholders other than Erasmus.

The retained reserves figure calculated for the moment is a balancing figure only. We will cover this in more detail when calculating the consolidated statement of changes in equity.

Erasmus group: Consolidated income statement for the year ended 30 September 20X9

	$'000
Revenue (10,290 + 2,802.64)	13,092.6
Cost of sales (5,145 + 1,401.3)	(6,546.3)
Gross profit	6,546.3
Other operating expenses (4,116 + 1,121.1)	(5,237.1)
	1,309.2
Tax (348 + 101.3)	(449.3)
Profit for the period	859.9
Attributable to:	
Equity holders of the parent	824.1
Minority interest (178.9 × 20%)	35.8
	859.9

4. *Translation of Heinrich's income statement*

This is translated throughout at the average exchange rate for the year, as required by IAS 21.

	G'000	*Rate*	$'000
Revenue	10,650	3.8	2,802.6
Cost of sales	(5,325)	3.8	(1,401.3)
Gross profit	5,325		1,401.3
Other operating expenses	(4,260)	3.8	(1,121.1)
Profit before tax	1,065		280.2
Income tax expense	(385)	3.8	(101.3)
Profit for the period	680		178.9

The next stage in the process is to prepare the consolidated statement of changes in equity. Note that this is a summarised statement only. In order to make the example relatively straightforward, equity is that relating only to equity holders of the parent.

A statement prepared in accordance with IAS 1 would require a breakdown into the components of share capital and various reserves, and also a column for non-controlling interests.

Erasmus group: Summarised consolidated statement of changes in equity for the year ended 30 September 20X9

	$'000
Brought forward at 1 October 20X8 (W5)	1,339.2
Profit for the period (see consolidated income statement)	824.1
Dividend (Erasmus only)	(350.0)
Exchange gains (balancing figure)	13.5
Carried forward at 30 September 20X9 (see consolidated statement of financial position)	1,826.8

It is clear from the circumstances of the question that the exchange differences will be gains, because of the direction of movements in the rates since acquisition (over time, fewer groats are required to buy $1, so an asset held in groats will produce gains). However, at the moment, we do not know exactly where the $13,500 in gains originates from. We can prove the figure, as shown in the following workings.

5. *Consolidated equity brought forward*

	$'000
Erasmus	1,252.0
Heinrich: 80% of post-acquisition profits (W6)	86.9
Exchange gain on goodwill on acquisition*	0.3
	1,339.2

	$'000
*Goodwill translated at date of acquisition 51,200/4	12.8
Goodwill at 30 September 20X8: 51,200/3.9	13.1
Exchange gain	0.3

6. *Heinrich: Post-acquisition profits*
Heinrich's opening equity is G1,336,000. Translated at the opening exchange rate of 3.9, the $ equivalent is: 1,336,000/3.9 = $342,600.

Post-acquisition profits at the start of the year = opening equity less share capital less pre-acquisition profits:

	$'000
Heinrich: opening equity	342.6
Share capital (see translated balance sheet in W2)	(212.5)
Pre-acquisition retained reserves (see translated statement of financial position in W2)	(21.5)
Heinrich: post acquisition profits	108.6

The group share of the post acquisition profits is 80%: $108.6 × 80% = $86.9 (figures in $'000).

7. *Proof of exchange gains*
These exchange gains arise because of the retranslation of the net assets of Heinrich. The proof is as follows:

	$'000	$'000
Opening net assets (G1,336,000) translated at:		
Opening exchange rate (1,336,000/3.9)		342.6
Closing exchange rate (1,336,000/3.75)		356.3
Gain on retranslation		13.7
Movement in equity in the year (G380,000)		
Profit for the period at average rate (680,000/3.8)	178.9	
Dividend (300,000/3.75)	(80.0)	
	98.9	
Movement in equity at closing rate (380,000/3.75)	101.3	
Gain on retranslation		2.4
Total gain on retranslation of net assets		16.1
Group share (80%)		12.9
Gain on retranslation of goodwill (working 8)		0.6
Total gain		13.5

8. *Gain for year on retranslation of goodwill*
Goodwill was calculated (see W1) as G51,200.

	$'000
Goodwill translated at 30 September 20X8: 51,200/3.9	13.1
Goodwill at 30 September 20X9 (see W1)	13.7
Exchange gain	0.6

Note that the group is attributed with only 80 per cent of the gain on the translation of net assets in Heinrich. The remainder is attributable to the non-controlling interest, and is included in the statement of financial position figure. However, the group is attributed with 100 per cent of the gain on the retranslation of goodwill. This is logical because the goodwill calculation does not concern the minority.

An examination question might require candidates to prove the exchange differences figure, and if it does, the requisite calculations are built into the time allowance for the question. However, if there is no positive requirement to prove the differences, it is sensible to simply slot them in as a balancing figure.

Note the treatment of the differences on exchange in this example. The differences are taken to the statement of changes in equity, as required by IAS 21.

8.4.1 Change in functional currency

The example of Erasmus and Heinrich demonstrates the procedures involved where the financial statements of a subsidiary entity have to be translated into the presentation currency used by the group as a whole.

Occasionally, an entity's functional currency will change because of alterations in business circumstances. The example given in the standard is where there is a change in the currency that mainly influences the prices of goods and services. Where this is the case, a retranslation exercise must be undertaken. IAS 21 requires that the retranslation must be undertaken *prospectively* from the date of the change. 'Prospectively' in this context means that the translation into the new functional currency takes place using the exchange rate at the date of the change. The resulting translated amounts for non-monetary items are treated as being the historical cost of those items.

8.5 Hedging

Hedging establishes a relationship between a hedging instrument and a hedged item. A *hedged item* in the context of this chapter is a net investment in a foreign operation of the type that we have examined in the Erasmus and Heinrich example.

A *hedging instrument,* in the context of this chapter, is a financial liability whose cash flows are expected to offset cash flows of a designated hedge item.

Hedging relationships are now regulated by IAS 39 *Financial Instruments: Recognition and Measurement*, and the topic is covered in more detail in Chapter 13 of this *Learning System.* The particular kind of hedging relationship that is relevant to this present chapter relates to the financing of an investment in a foreign operation by a foreign currency loan taken out by the investing entity.

Example 8.D

G is an acquisitive entity that decides to purchase 75% of the share capital of H, an entity that operates outside G's country of operation, and whose functional currency is the Euro. The purchase price is €18.7 million, and G takes out a loan in euros to finance the purchase. The loan acts as a hedging instrument: any currency movements which adversely affect the investment in H (an asset) will be offset by currency movements in respect of the Euro loan (a liability). Provided that the hedge is designated as such, the exchange movements on both the investment and the hedge can be recognised as part of equity.

If hedging were not permitted, gains or losses on the investment in the foreign operation would be recognised as part of equity (as required by IAS 21) but gains or losses on the loan would be recognised in profit for the year. Hedging allows for recognition of the substance of the relationship between the investment and the loan that finances it.

8.6 Summary

This chapter has examined the provisions of IAS 21 *The Effects of Changes in Foreign Exchange Rates*, in respect of both single transactions and foreign operations. The distinction between functional and presentation currency is important, and students should ensure that they understand the definitions of each.

The translation and consolidation of foreign operations as part of a group is a significant element in the *Financial Management* syllabus. Students can expect that both the mechanics and the underlying principles of foreign operations translation will be examined on a regular basis. These underlying principles include the hedging of foreign equity investments via a foreign currency loan. The coverage of hedging is continued in more detail in Chapter 11 of this *Learning System* which covers the requirements of IAS 39.

Revision Questions

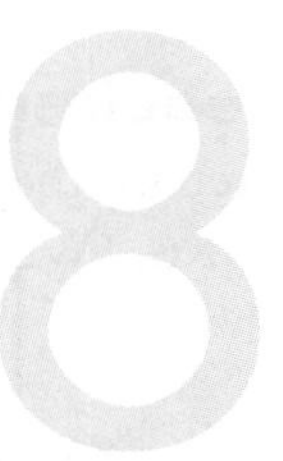

Question 1

The income statements for Home and its wholly owned subsidiary Foreign for the year ended 31 July 20X6 are shown below:

	Home	*Foreign*
	$'000	Crowns '000
Revenue	3,000	650
Cost of sales	(2,400)	(550)
Gross profit	600	100
Distribution costs	(32)	(41)
Administrative expenses	(168)	(87)
Finance costs	(15)	(10)
Profit before tax	385	(38)
Income tax	(102)	10
Profit for the period	283	(28)

Notes

1. The presentation currency of the group is the $, and Foreign's functional currency is the Crown.
2. Home acquired 100% of the ordinary share capital of Foreign on 1 August 20X4 for 204,000 Crowns. Foreign's share capital at that date comprised 1,000 ordinary shares of 1 Crown each, and its reserves were 180,000 Crowns. In view of its subsidiary's losses, Home's directors conducted an impairment review of the goodwill at 31 July 20X6. They concluded that the goodwill had lost 20% of its original value during the year (before taking exchange differences into account). The impairment should be reflected in the consolidated financial statements for the year ended 31 July 20X6. It is the group policy to value non-controlling intrest at acquisition at the proportionate share of the identifiable net assets of the subsidiary.
3. On 1 June 20X6, Home purchased an item of plant for 32,000 Florins. At the year end the payable amount had not yet been settled. No exchange gain or loss in respect of this item is reflected in Home's income statement above.
4. Exchange rates are as follows:

   On 1 August 20X4: 1.7 Crowns = $1
   On 31 July 20X6: 2.2 Crowns = $1
   Average rate for year ended 31 July 20X6: 2.4 Crowns = $1
   On 1 June 20X6: 1.5 Florins = $1
   On 31 July 20X6: 1.6 Florins = $1

5. During the year Foreign made sales of 50,000 Crowns to Home. None of the items remained in inventory at the year end.

Requirement
Prepare the consolidated income statement for the Home group for the year ended 31 July 20X6. (Work to the nearest $100). **(10 marks)**

? Question 2

The statement of financial position of Big and Small as at 31 March 20X3 are given below. The statement of financial position of Small is prepared in florins, the reporting currency for Small.

	Big		*Small*	
	$'000	$'000	Fl'000	Fl'000
Non-current assets				
Property, plant and equipment	60,000		80,000	
Investments	9,500		–––	
		69,500		80,000
Current assets				
Inventories	30,000		40,000	
Trade receivables	25,000		32,000	
Cash	3,000		4,000	
		58,000		76,000
		127,500		156,000
Issued capital and reserves				
Share capital (50 cents/½ florin shares)		30,000		40,000
Revaluation reserve		15,000		–
Retained reserves		34,500		44,000
		79,500		84,000
Non-current liabilities				
Interest-bearing borrowings	15,000		30,000	
Deferred tax	5,000		9,000	
		20,000		39,000
Current liabilities				
Trade payables	12,000		15,000	
Tax	16,000		18,000	
		28,000		33,000
		127,500		156,000

Notes

1. *Investment by Big in Small*
On 1 April 20W7, Big purchased 60 million shares in Small for 57 million florins. The retained reserves of Small showed a balance of 20 million florins at that date. The accounting policies of Small are the same as those of Big except that Big revalues its land, whereas Small carries its land at historical cost. Small's land had been purchased on 1 April 20W4. On 1 April 20W7, the fair value of the land of Small was 6 million florins higher than its carrying value in the individual financial statements of that entity. By 31 March 20X3, the difference between fair value and carrying value had risen to 11 million florins. Apart from this accounting policy difference, no other fair value adjustments were necessary when initially consolidating Small as a subsidiary.

2. *Intra-group trading*
On 6 March 20X3, Big sold goods to Small at an invoiced price of $6,000,000, making a profit of 25% on cost. Small recorded these goods in inventory and payables using an

exchange rate of 5 florins to $1 (there were minimal fluctuations between the two currencies in the month of March 20X3). The goods remained in the inventory of Small at 31 March 20X3 but on 29 March 20X3 Small sent Big a cheque for 30 million florins to clear its payable. Big received and recorded this cash on 3 April 20X3.

3. *Exchange rate*

Date	*Exchange rate* (Fls to $1)
1 April 20W4	7
1 April 20W7	6
31 March 20X2	5.5
31 March 20X3	5
Weighted average for the year to 31 March 20X3	5.2
Weighted average for the dates of acquisition of closing inventory	5.1

Requirements

(a) Translate the statement of financial position of Small as at 31 March 20X3 into $s and prepare the consolidated statement of financial position of the Big group as at 31 March 20X3. **(20 marks)**

(b) IAS 21 *The Effects of Changes in Foreign Exchange Rates* permits an entity to choose a presentation currency that is different from its functional currency.
Identify two possible reasons why an entity might choose to exercise this choice. **(5 marks)**

Total = 25 marks

Question 3

The statement of financial positions of Home and its subsidiary undertaking Away as at 31 March 20X6 and their income statements and statements of changes in equity for the year then ended are as follows (The functional currency of Away is the 'Mint' – the accepted abbreviation for 'Mint' is 'M').

Statement of financial positions as at 31 March 20X6

	Home		*Away*	
	$'000	$'000	M'000	M'000
Non-current assets				
Property, plant and equipment		20,000		30,000
Investment (notes 1 and 2)		5,500		
		25,500		30,000
Current assets				
Inventories	10,000		18,000	
Trade payables	10,000		15,000	
		20,000		33,000
		45,500		63,000
Capital and reserves				
Issued capital (1$/1M shares)		9,000		15,000
Retained reserves		12,500		10,000
		21,500		25,000
Long-term loans		10,000		20,000
Current liabilities				
Trade payables	7,900		10,400	
Bank overdraft	6,100		7,600	
		14,000		18,000
		45,500		63,000

Income statements – year ended 31 March 20X6

	Home	*Away*
	$'000	M'000
Revenue	50,000	60,000
Cost of sales (notes 2 and 4)	(25,000)	(30,000)
Gross profit	25,000	30,000
Other operating expenses	(15,000)	(16,000)
Dividend from Away	1,500	
Finance cost	(1,000)	(2,000)
Profit before tax	10,500	
Income tax expense	(3,600)	(4,200)
Profit for the period	6,900	7,800

Summarised statements of changes in equity – year ended 31 March 20X6

	Home	*Away*
	$'000	M'000
Balance at 1 April 20X5	18,500	21,600
Profit for the period	6,900	7,800
Dividends paid	(3,900)	(4,400)
Balance at 31 March 20X6	21,500	25,000

Notes

1. On 31 March 20X2 Home purchased 11.25 million shares in Away for M16.5 million. The retained reserves of Away on this date stood at M5 million.
2. Since the date of investment by Home the dollar has depreciated against the Mint. Exchange rates at relevant dates have been as follows:

Date	*Exchange rate* (Ms to $1)
31 March 20X2	3.00
31 March 20X5	2.40
Average for the year ended 31 March 20X6	2.35
31 March 20X6	2.20

3. Home received its dividend from Away when the exchange rate was M2.20 to $1.

Requirements

(a) Translate the balance sheet of Away into dollars and prepare the consolidated balance sheet of the Home group as at 31 March 20X6. **(11 marks)**

(b) Translate the income statement of Away into dollars and then prepare the consolidated income statement of the Home group for the year ended 31 March 20X6. **(6 marks)**

(c) Prepare the consolidated statement of changes in equity in respect of the holders of equity shares in the parent, for the Home group for the year ended 31 March 20X6. All figures in the statement should be supported by relevant workings. **(8 marks)**

(Total = 25 marks)

Work to the nearest $'000.

Solutions to Revision Questions

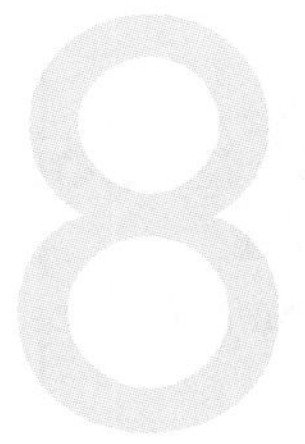

Solution 1

Home group: Consolidated income statement for the year ended 31 July 20X6

	$'000
Revenue [3,000 + (650/2.4) − 20.8] (W1)	3,250.0
Cost of sales [2,400 + (550/2.4) − 20.8] (W1)	(2,608.4)
Gross profit	641.6
Distribution costs [32 + (41/2.4)]	(49.1)
Administrative expenses [168 + (87/2.4)]	(204.3)
Goodwill impairment (W2)	(1.9)
Exchange gain (W3)	1.3
Finance costs [15 + (10/2.4)]	(19.2)
Profit before tax	368.4
Income tax [102 − (10/2.4)]	(97.8)
Profit for the period	270.6

Workings

1. *Intra-group sales*
   Translate at average rate: 50/2.4 = $20.8
   Deduct from both revenue and cost of sales

2. *Goodwill on consolidation and impairment*

	Crowns'000
Cost of investment	204
Acquired	(181)
Goodwill	23

Impairment = 23,000 × 20% = 4,600 Crowns
Translated at average rate: 4,600/2.4 = 1.9 (to nearest $100)

Note: It would be quite acceptable to use closing rate for this calculation.

3. *Exchange difference on payable*

	$'000
Payable recognised on 1 June 2006: 32,000/1.5	21.3
Payable translated at closing rate: 32,000/1.6	(20.0)
Exchange gain	1.3

Solution 2

(a)

Step 1: Pre-adjust net assets for accounting policy change

	Date of acquisition	*Statement of financial position date*
	Fl'000	Fl'000
Share capital	40,000	40,000
Revaluation reserve	6,000	11,000
Retained reserves	20,000	44,000
	66,000	95,000

Step 2: Translate the statement of financial position of Small into $s (after incorporating the above adjustments)

	Fl'000	*Rate*	$'000
Non-current assets	91,000	5	18,200
Inventories	40,000	5	8,000
Receivables	32,000	5	6,400
Cash	4,000	5	800
	167,000		33,400
Share capital	40,000	6	6,667
Revaluation reserve:			
Pre-acquisition	6,000	6	1,000
Post-acquisition	5,000	5	1,000
Retained reserves:			
Pre-acquisition	20,000	6	3,333
Post-acquisition	24,000	Balance	7,000
	95,000		19,000
Interest bearing borrowings	30,000	5	6,000
Deferred tax	9,000	5	1,800
Trade payables	15,000	5	3,000
Tax	18,000	5	3,600
	167,000		33,400

Step 3: Prepare the consolidated statement of financial position

	$'000	$'000
Non-current assets:		
Property, plant and equipment (60,000 + 18,200)	78,200	
Goodwill on acquisition (W4)	1,500	
		79,700
Current assets:		
Inventories [30,000 + 8,000 + 1,200 (W2)]	36,800	
Receivables [25,000 + 6,400 − 6,000 (W2)]	25,400	
Cash [3,000 + 800 + 6,000 (W2)]	9,800	
		72,000
		151,700
Capital and reserves:		
Share capital		30,000
Revaluation reserve [15,000 + (75% × 1,000)]		15,750
Retained reserves (W5)		38,800
Non-controlling interest (W3)		4,750

Non-current liabilities:		
Interest bearing borrowings (15,000 + 6,000)	21,000	
Deferred tax (5,000 + 1,800)	6,800	
		27,800
Current liabilities:		
Trade payables (12,000 + 3,000)	15,000	
Tax (16,000 + 3,600)	19,600	
		34,600
		151,700

Workings

1. *Group structure*
   Big owns 60 million of the 80 million Small shares in issue. This is a 75% subsidiary.
2. *Intra-group trading*
   The unrealised profit made by Big is 25/125 × \$6 million = \$1.2 million. There is cash in transit of \$6 million which needs adding onto consolidated cash and taking out of consolidated receivables.
3. *Non-controlling interest*

   25% × 19,000 = \$4,750
4. *Goodwill*

	Fl'000	Fl'000
Cost of acquisition		57,000
Purchased:		
Share capital	40,000	
Pre-acquisition revaluation reserve	6,000	
Pre-acquisition retained reserves	20,000	
	66,000 × 75%	
		49,500
Goodwill		7,500

Translated at closing rate of 5: 7,500/5 = \$1,500.

5. *Retained reserves*

		\$'000
Big		34,500
Small: post acquisition 7,000 × 75%		5,250
Unrealised profit (W2)		(1,200)
Exchange gain on goodwill:		
Goodwill at acquisition: 7,500/6	1,250	
Goodwill at 31 March 20X3: 7,500/5	1,500	
		250
		38,800

(b) Two of the following reasons:
1. The entity's principal investors tend to function in a currency other than the functional currency of the entity.
2. The entity's functional currency is obscure; it may choose to present its financial statements in a better known currency such as the US dollar or the Euro.
3. The entity may be seeking investment from potential investors whose functional currency is not the same as the entity's.

4. In some jurisdictions, entities are obliged to prepare their financial statements in the local currency, even where this is not the functional currency.

Therefore, to avoid preparing two sets of financial statements, entities may prefer to choose the local currency as their presentation currency.

Solution 3

(a)

Step 1. Translate the balance sheet of Away (note that Away is a 75% subsidiary of Home).

	M'000	*Rate*	$'000
Property, plant and equipment	30,000	2.2	13,636
Inventories	18,000	2.2	8,182
Trade receivables	15,000	2.2	6,818
	63,000		28,636
Issued capital	15,000	3	5,000
Pre-acquisition profits	5,000	3	1,667
Post-acquisition profits	5,000	Balance	4,697
	25,000		11,364
Long-term loans	20,000	2.2	9,091
Trade payables	10,400	2.2	4,727
Bank overdraft	7,600	2.2	3,454
	63,000		28,636

Step 2. Prepare the consolidated balance sheet (notice that most figures are aggregations).

ASSETS	$'000	$'000
Non-current assets		
Goodwill on consolidation (W2)		682
Property, plant and equipment		33,636
		34,318
Current assets		
Inventories	18,182	
Trade receivables	16,818	
		35,000
		69,318
EQUITY AND LIABILITIES		
Equity		
Share capital (Home only)		9,000
Retained reserves (balancing figure)		16,205
		25,205
Non-conrtrolling interest (W1)		2,841
		28,046
Long-term loans		19,091
Current liabilities		
Trade payables	12,627	
Bank overdraft	9,554	
		22,181
		69,318

Workings

1. *Non-controlling interest*
   25% × 11,364 = 2,841

2. *Goodwill*

	M'000	M'000
Investment		16,500
Share capital	15,000	
Pre-acq. reserves	5,000	
	20,000 × 75%	
		15,000
Goodwill		1,500

Translated year end rate:

1,500/2.20 = $682

(b)

Step 1. Translate the income statement of Away into dollars

	M'000	*Rate*	$'000
Turnover	60,000	2.35	25,532
Cost of sales	(30,000)	2.35	(12,766)
Gross profit	30,000		12,766
Other operating expenses	(16,000)	2.35	(6,809)
Finance cost	(2,000)	2.35	(851)
Profit before tax	12,000		5,106
Income tax expense	(4,200)	2.35	(1,787)
Profit for the period	7,800		3,319

Step 2. Prepare the consolidated income statement (most figures are an aggregation)

	$'000
Turnover	75,532
Cost of sales	(37,766)
Gross profit	37,766
Other operating expenses	(21,809)
Finance cost	(1,851)
Profit before tax	14,106
Income tax expense	(5,387)
Profit for the period	8,719
Attributable to:	
Equity holders of the parent	7,889
Non-controlling interest (W1)	830
	8,719

Working

Non-controlling interest

This is 25% of the profit after tax of Away in dollars ($3,319) = $830.

(c)

Consolidated statement of changes in equity (attributable to equity holders of the parent)

	$'000
Balance at the start of the year (W1)	20,375
Profit for the year [see part (b)]	7,889
Dividend of Home	(3,900)
Exchange difference (W2)	841
Balance at the end of the year [see part (a)]	25,205

Workings

1. *Opening consolidated equity*

	$'000
Home	18,500
Away (75% × 2,333 − see below)	1,750
Exchange gain on goodwill*	125
	20,375

	$'000
*Goodwill at 31 March 20X5 $\left(\frac{1500}{2.40}\right)$	625
Goodwill at date of acquisition	500
	125

In order to compute the opening equity (and the post-acquisition change in equity, represented by post-acquisition profits) of Away, we need to translate the opening balance sheet (at last year's closing rate of M2.40 to $1):

	M'000	*Rate*	$'000
Issued capital	15,000	3.00	5,000
Pre-acquisition profits	5,000	3.00	1,667
Post-acquisition profits	1,600	Balance	2,333
Net assets and equity	21,600	2.40	9,000

2. *Exchange difference*

	$'000	$'000
Opening net assets:		
M21.6 m at M2.40 to $1		9,000
Opening net assets: M2.20 to $1		9,818
Increase (exchange gain)		818
Profit for the period:		
M7.8 m at M2.35 to $1	3,319	
Dividend: M4.4 m at M2.20 to $1	(2,000)	
	1,319	
Added to net assets: (M3.4 m) at M2.20 to $1	1,546	
		227
		1,045
Group share (75%) equals		784
Gain for year on retranslation of goodwill		
Goodwill at 31 March 20X5 (see above)	625	
Goodwill at 31 March 20X6 (balance sheet W2)	682	
		57
		841

9 Complex Group Structures

Complex Group Structures

LEARNING OUTCOME

After studying this chapter students should be able to:

- prepare a consolidated income statement and statement of financial position for a group of entities.

9.1 Introduction

Our study of consolidated accounts to date has confined itself to situations where the investments in group entities (whether they be subsidiaries, associates or joint ventures) have been made by the parent entity. Groups where this is the case have a relatively simple structure. In this chapter, we will consider groups where investments in a particular entity are made in whole or in part by an entity other than the parent entity.

The chapter proceeds as follows: Section 9.2 covers complex groups that include sub-subsidiary interests. Section 9.3 looks at mixed groups of entities, that is those in which a parent holds both a direct and indirect investment in a particular entity. Section 9.4 examines a further complexity which arises where a parent has an indirect investment in an associate or joint venture.

9.2 Accounting for sub-subsidiaries

9.2.1 The basics of preparation of the consolidated accounts

The term 'sub-subsidiary' refers to a situation where the ultimate parent P has a subsidiary H and H itself has a subsidiary S. S is regarded as a subsidiary of P as well as a subsidiary of H and must therefore be line-by-line consolidated in P's consolidated financial statements. For accounting purposes, we refer to S as a *sub-subsidiary* of P.

The fact that S is a sub-subsidiary does *not* affect the manner in which it is consolidated. However, certain matters do need to be treated with particular care:

- the computation of the non-controlling interest in the sub-subsidiary;
- the effective date of acquisition of the sub-subsidiary;

- the computation of the goodwill on consolidation of the sub-subsidiary;
- the elimination of intra-group investments and investment income when computing the non-controlling in the *subsidiary*.

Example 9.A

- P made a 75% investment of $20 million in H on 31.12.W6 when the net assets of H were $24 million (issued capital $12 million plus retained earnings $12 million).
- On 31.12.W7 H made a 60% investment of $10 million in S when the net assets of S were $15 million (issued capital $10 million plus retained earnings $5 million).
- None of the entities has issued new shares since 31.12.W6.
- There has been no impairment of goodwill since the acquisitions.
- The group policy is to value non-controlling interest at the proportionate share of net assets of the subsidiary.
- The summarised statement of financial position of the three entities at 31.12.X0 (the latest statement of financial position date) were as shown below:

	P	*H*	*S*
	$m	$m	$m
Investments in subsidiaries	20	10	–
Non-current assets	30	20	20
Net current assets	10	6	5
	60	36	25
Issued capital	30	12	10
Retained earnings	30	24	15
	60	36	25

Solution

The summarised consolidated statement of financial position of the P group at 31.12.X0, together with appropriate workings, is:

	$'000	*Comment*
Goodwill on consolidation	2,750	W2
Non-current assets	70,000	Simple aggregation of P, H and S
Net current assets	21,000	Simple aggregation of P, H and S
	93,750	
Issued capital	30,000	P only
Retained earnings	43,500	W3
	73,500	
Non-controlling interests	20,250	W1
	93,750	

Workings

1. *Non-controlling interests*

The overall group structure is shown in the diagram below:

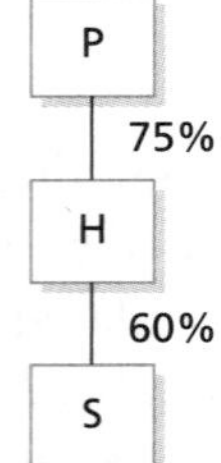

Therefore the effective interest of P in S is (75% × 60% =) 45%. The non-controlling interest is 55%. The non-controlling interest in S should be based on this effective interest of 55%.

The non-controlling interest calculation for H will *not* attribute any of the investment in S to the non-controlling interest. This is because the investment in S does not appear in the consolidated statement of financial position and the purpose of the non-controlling interest calculation is to compute their interest in the net assets that *do* appear there. The cost of the investment in the subsidiary is therefore deducted from the NCI calculation. Therefore the non-controlling interest calculation is:

- In H: 25% × ($36 m − $10 m) = $6.5 m.
- In S: 55% × $25 m = $13.75 m.

So the total non-controlling interest is $20.25 million ($6.5 m + $13.75 m).

2. *Goodwill on consolidation*

	P in H	*H in S*
	$'000	$'000
Cost of investment	20,000	10,000
Investing entity share (75%/60%) of net assets at date of investment	(18,000)	(9,000)
Goodwill	2,000	1,000
Amount attributable to P – the ultimate parent (see below)	2,000	750

The total for goodwill is $2m + $750,000 = $2,750,000. Notice the two-stage approach to the calculation of goodwill relating to S in P's consolidated accounts. First we calculate the goodwill relating to H's investment in S (of 60%). Then we relate the goodwill we have calculated to the *effective* interest of P in S: (75% × 60% =) 45%. P's share of the goodwill being 75% × 1,000,000.

3. *Retained earnings*
   The consolidated retained earnings figure is:

	$'000
From P	30,000
From H [75% × ($24m − 12m)]	9,000
From S [45% × ($15m − $5m)]	4,500
	43,500

The key factor to bear in mind when preparing the consolidated income statement is to use the correct percentage when computing the non-controlling interest in the sub-subsidiary. It is also necessary to eliminate any intra-group investment income when computing the non-controlling interest in the *subsidiary*.

The income statements of P, H and S for the year ended 31 December 20X0 are as follows:

	P	*H*	*S*
	$m	$m	$m
Revenue	100	80	60
Cost of sales	(50)	(40)	(30)
Gross profit	50	40	30
Other operating expenses	(25)	(20)	(15)
Investment income (intra-group)	6	3	–
Profit before tax	31	23	15
Income tax expense	(9)	(6)	(5)
Profit for the period	22	17	10

Solution

Consolidated income statement for the year ended 31 December 20X0

	$m
Revenue (P + H + S)	240
Cost of sales (P + H + S)	(120)
Gross profit	120
Other operating expenses (P + H + S)	(60)
Profit before tax	60
Income tax expense (P + H + S)	(20)
Profit for the peiod	40
Attributable to:	
Equity holders of the parent	31
Non-controlling interest (W1)	9
	40

Workings

1. *Non-controlling interest*

	$m
Non-controlling interest in H is 25% ($17m 2 intra-group investment income of $3m)	3.5
Non-controlling interest in S is 55% (effective interest) 3 $10m	5.5
Total	9.0

The consolidated statement of changes in equity does not cause any particular additional problems. The principle for all subsidiaries (including sub-subsidiaries) is that only the *group* share of any *post*-acquisition changes should be included.

Summarised statements of changes in equity for the three entities for the year ended 31 December 20X0

	P	*H*	*S*
	$m	$m	$m
Balance at start of the period	48	27	20
Net profit for the period	22	17	10
Dividends	(10)	(8)	(5)
Balance at end of the period	60	36	25

Solution

Consolidated statement of changes in equity

	Attributable to equity holders of the parent	Non-controlling interest	Total equity
	$m	$m	$m
Balance at the start of the period (W1)	52.5	15.25	67.75
Profit for the period	31.0	9.0	40.0
Dividends (W2)	(10.0)	(4.0)	(14.0)
Balance at the end of the year	73.5	20.25	93.75

Workings

1. *Balance at the start of the period*

Attributable to equity shareholders of the parent

	$m
P	48.0
H [75% × ($27m − $24m)]	2.25
S [45% × ($20m − $15m)]	2.25
	52.55

Attributable to non-controlling interest

	$m
H [25% × ($27 − $10m)]	4.25
S (55% × $20m)	11.25
	15.25

2. *Dividends paid to the non-controlling interest*

	$m
H (25% × 8)	2
S (40% × 5)	2
	4

9.2.2 Date of acquisition of sub-subsidiary

In the above example, the date P 'acquired' S was 31.12.X7. This was because on that date H bought shares in S and H was at that time a subsidiary of P.

However, if H had bought the shares in S before it became a subsidiary of P (say on 31.12.X5) then this date could not be the date that P 'acquired' S, because on 31.12.X5 H and S were nothing to do with P.

In these circumstances, S would effectively become a subsidiary of P on the same date that H became a subsidiary of P – 31.12.X6 in the above example.

9.3 Mixed groups

A mixed group is one in which a parent has both a direct and an indirect investment in a particular subsidiary. In such situations, both the non-controlling interest and the goodwill must be worked out in two stages.

Example 9.B

Statement of financial position of P, Q and R at 31 December 20X0

	P	*Q*	*R*
	$'000	$'000	$'000
Investment in Q	25,200		
Investment in R	10,000	10,600	
Property, plant and equipment	53,800	53,400	49,000
Current assets	24,000	21,000	15,000
	113,000	85,000	64,000
Issued capital ($) shares)	30,000	20,000	16,000
Share premium account	20,000	10,000	8,000
Retained earnings	35,000	30,000	20,000
	85,000	60,000	44,000
Loans	20,000	18,000	15,000
Current liabilities	8,000	7,000	5,000
	113,000	85,000	64,000

Details regarding intra-group investments are as follows:

Entities	*No. of shares acquired*	*Date shares acquired*	*Accumulated profits at acquisition date*
	£'000		$'000
P in Q	12,000	1.1.X6	10,000
P in R	4,000	1.1.X8	12,000
Q in R	4,800	1.1.X7	8,000

- All share premium accounts arose prior to 1.1.X6.
- There has been no impairment of goodwill on consolidation in respect of any of the acquisitions.
- NCI is valued at the proportionate share of the FV of the net assets of the subsidiary.

Before we prepare the consolidated statement of financial position, note the group structure:

H

45/60 = 75%

S

30/50 = 60%

T

Notice that P *controls* 55% of the voting shares of R so R is a subsidiary. The effective interest of P in R is 25% + [60% × 30%] = 43%. The non-controlling interest percentage is 57.

Solution

The consolidated statement of financial position of the P group at 31 December 20X0 is shown below. Unless otherwise indicated, all the figures on the net assets side are aggregations:

	$'000
ASSETS	
Goodwill on consolidation (W2)	2,800
Property, plant and equipment	156,200
Current assets	60,000
	219,000
EQUITY & LIABILITIES	
Issued capital (P only)	30,000
Share premium account (P only)	20,000
Retained earnings (W3)	51,160
	101,160
Non-controlling interests (W1)	44,840
	146,000
Loans	53,000
Current liabilities	20,000
	219,000

Workings

1. *Non-controlling interest*

	$'000
In Q – 40% ($60,000,000 – $10,600,000)	19,760
In R – 57% × $44,000,000	25,080
Total	44,840

2. *Goodwill on consolidation*

	P in Q		*P in R*		*Q in R*	
	$'000	$'000	$'000	$'000	$'000	$'000
Cost of investment		25,200		10,000		10,600
Net assets at acquisition:						
Issued capital	20,000		16,000		16,000	
Share premium	10,000		8,000		8,000	
Retained earnings	10,000		12,000		8,000	
	40,000		36,000		32,000	
Investor's share		(24,000)		(9,000)		(9,600)
Goodwill		1,200		1,000		1,000
Amount relating to P		1,200		1,000		600

Total goodwill on consolidation = $1,200 + 1,000 + 600 = $2,800 (all figures in $'000s)

3. *Consolidated retained earnings*

	$'000
Reserves of P	35,000
Share of post-acquisition retained earnings of:	
Q [60% ($30m – $10m)]	12,000
R – direct [25% ($20m – $12m)]	2,000
R – indirect [18% ($20m – $8m)]	2,160
	51,160

9.4 Indirect investment in associates or joint ventures

Where there is an indirect investment in an associated undertaking then the question arises as to what proportion of the net assets and profits of the associate should be initially included in the consolidated financial statements of the parent. Where the investor is a group the relevant share is the aggregate of the holdings of the parent and the subsidiaries in the entity. Any holdings of the group's other associates or joint ventures should be ignored for this purpose.

Example 9.C

Summarised statements of financial of H, S and A as at 31 December 20X0

	H	*S*	*A*
	$'000	$'000	$'000
Investments	23,500	10,000	
Property, plant and equipment	20,000	22,000	25,000
Net current assets	8,000	6,000	5,000
	51,500	38,000	30,000
Issued capital ($1 shares)	20,000	15,000	10,000
Retained earnings	31,500	23,000	20,000
	51,500	38,000	30,000

Notes

1. On 31 December 20X5, when the retained earnings of S showed a balance of $11 million, H purchased 12 million shares in S for $23.5 million.
2. On 31 December 20X6, when the retained earnings of A showed a balance of $12 million, S purchased 4 million shares in A for $10 million.
3. There has been no impairment of goodwill on consolidation since the acquisitions took place. Prepare the consolidated balance sheet of H at 31 December 20X0.
4. It is group policy to value non-controlling interest at acquisition at the proportionate share of the fair value of the subsidiary's identifiable net assets.

Requirement

Prepare the summarised consolidated statement of financial position of H at 31 December 20X0.

Solution

Before we prepare the consolidated statement of financial position it is worth identifying the group structure:

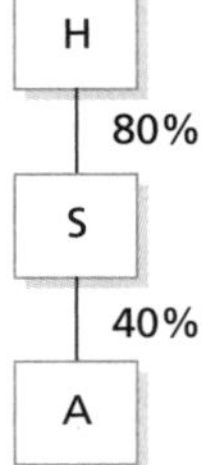

When we calculate share of net assets and share of profits of A in a situation like this, we take the aggregate group share *before* allowing for non-controlling interests. Therefore in this example the group share is 40%. This treatment means that the non-controlling interest in S will need to be credited with their share of the net assets of A at the statement of financial position date.

Summarised consolidated statement of financial position of H as at 31 December 20X0

	$'000
Goodwill on consolidation of S (W2)	2,700
Investment in associate (W3)	12,960
Property, plant and equipment (H + S)	42,000
Net current assets (H + S)	14,000
	71,660
Issued capital (H only)	20,000
Retained earnings (W4)	43,660
	63,660
Non-controlling interest (W1)	8,000
	71,660

Workings

1. *Non-controlling interest*

	$'000
Net assets of S as shown in S's balance sheet	38,000
Deduct cost of investment in A	(10,000)
Add share (40%) of net assets of A at 31.12.X0	12,000
	40,000
Non-controlling interest (20%)	8,000

Notice that the non-controlling interest are credited with an interest in the net assets of A in the same manner that those net assets are reported in the consolidated statement of financial position.

2. *Goodwill on acquisition*

		H in S
	$'000	$'000
Cost of investment		23,500
Net assets at date of investment:		
Share capital	15,000	
Retained earnings	11,000	
	26,000	
Investing entity's share (80%)		(20,800)
Goodwill		2,700

3. *Investment in A*

As a first step we need to calculate the goodwill on acquisition of the associate, and then to calculate the element of it that relates to the 20% non-controlling holders of S's equity.

	$'000	$'000
Cost of investment		10,000
Net assets at date of investment		
Share capital	10,000	
Retained earnings	12,000	
	22,000	
40% of net assets (40% × 22,000)		(8,800)
Goodwill on acquisition		1,200

Of this 20% relates to the non-controlling interest: \$1,200 × 20% = \$240. This is deducted in calculating the investment in associate, as follows:

Investment at cost	10,000
Less: amount of goodwill relating to non-controlling interest	(240)
Add: group share of post-acquisition profits (8,000 × 40%)	3,200
Investment in associate	12,960

It should be noted, however, that IAS 28 is not prescriptive in respect of the treatment of an associate entity over which a subsidiary exerts significant influence. There are other potentially valid approaches that might be taken, and these would be given appropriate credit in an examination.

4. *Retained earnings*

	\$'000
H	31,500
S [80% (\$23m − \$11m)]	9,600
A [32% (\$20m − \$12m)]	2,560
	43,660

Notice that, having attributed the minority shareholders their share of the net assets of A, the final share of retained earnings that is taken to consolidated retained earnings is the effective interest of H in A: (80% × 40% =) 32%.

9.5 Summary

This chapter has examined some relatively complex areas of group accounting. Students should ensure that they understand the principles underlying accounting for complex group structures.

Examination questions can be expected that incorporate various aspects of the material covered in this chapter.

Revision Questions

Question 1

Statement of financial positions as at 31.12.X0

	H	*S*	*T*
	$	$	$
45,000 shares in S	65,000		
30,000 shares in T		55,000	
Net assets	80,000	33,000	75,000
	145,000	88,000	75,000
Issued capital ($1 shares)	100,000	60,000	50,000
Retained earnings	45,000	28,000	25,000
	145,000	88,000	75,000

The intra-group shareholdings were acquired on 1.1.X3 when S retained earnings were $10,000 and T retained earnings were $8,000. Goodwill on consolidation has remained unimpaired since acquisition.

Requirement

Prepare the consolidated statement of financial position as at 31 December 20X0.

(10 marks)

Question 2

Consider the following scenarios regarding disposals:

(a) F owns 70% of the equity shares of G and G owns 30% of the equity shares of H. G is a subsidiary of F and H is an associate of G. All entities prepare financial statements to 31 March. F has no other investments. Ignore goodwill on consolidation.

Just before 31 March 20X5, G sold some goods to F and made a profit of $250,000 on the sale. These goods were in the inventory of F at 31 March 20X5. This is the only trading between the entities during the year ended 31 March 20X5. None of the entities has paid or proposed any dividends in the year. The profit after tax of the three entities in the year ended 31 March 20X5 is:

- F $8 million
- G $4 million
- H $3.2 million

What is the non-controlling interest that will be shown in the consolidated income statement of F for the year ended 31 March 20X5?

(b) The FG group of entities comprises FG and its subsidiaries, HI and JK.

FG acquired 80% of HI's ordinary shares on 31 December 20X3, when the retained earnings of HI stood at $10,000,000, and the retained earnings of JK stood at $7,600,000.

HI acquired 75% of JK's ordinary shares on 31 December 20X2, when the retained earnings of JK stood at $7,000,000.

At 31 December 20X6, HI's retained earnings stood at $12,200,000, and JK's retained earnings stood at $10,600,000.

There have been no other acquisitions and disposals in the group, and no impairments of goodwill or intra-group trading adjustments have been recorded.

How much profit has been added to consolidated retained earnings in the FG group **in respect of the investments in HI and JK** between acquisition and 31 December 20X6?

(c) CXP owns 75% of the ordinary share capital of its subsidiary, DYQ. The shares were acquired on 1 November 20X7 when DYQ's retained earnings stood at $152,000. DYQ acquired a 65% investment in its subsidiary, EZR, on 1 May 20X7. EZR's retained earnings were $189,000 on 1 May 20X7, and $202,000 on 1 November 20X7.

Retained earnings for the three entities at 31 October 20X6, the entities' year end, were as follows:

	$
CXP	266,000
DYQ	178,000
EZR	214,000

There had been no impairment of goodwill in respect of either investment since acquisition.

Calculate the balance of consolidated retained earnings for inclusion in the consolidated statement of financial position of the group at 31 October 20X8. **(10 marks)**

Question 3

On 1 April 20X1 Machinery bought 80% of the issued capital of Components and on 1 April 20X3 Machinery was itself taken over by Sales, which purchased 75% of the ordinary shares in Machinery.

Machinery and Components are unquoted entities. The investments made by Sales are held as Available for Sale investments and since no reliable measure of their fair value is possible, they are subsequently measured at cost.

The statement of financial positions of the three entities as at 31 October 20X5 showed the following position:

	Sales $	*Machinery* $	*Components* $
ASSETS			
Property, plant and equipment			
Freehold land	89,000	30,000	65,000
Buildings	64,000	80,000	23,600
Plant	33,000	84,000	43,800
	186,000	194,000	132,400
Investments			
Investment in Machinery at cost	135,000		
Investment in Components at cost		130,000	
Current assets			
Inventories	108,500	75,500	68,400
Trade receivables	196,700	124,800	83,500
Cash at bank	25,200		25,400
	651,400	524,300	309,700
EQUITY + LIABILITIES			
Equity			
Ordinary shares of $1 each	200,000	120,000	100,000
Retained earnings	154,000	119,000	74,000
	354,000	239,000	174,000
Non-current liabilities			
5% preference shares of $1	–	–	40,000
Current liabilities			
Bank overdraft		37,400	
Trade payables	240,000	200,700	71,200
Income tax	57,400	47,200	24,500
	651,400	524,300	309,700

Additional information

(a) Items purchased by Machinery from Components and remaining in inventory at 31 October 20X5 amounted to $25,000. The profit element is 20% of the selling price for Components.

(b) Included in the plant and equipment of Components is a machine purchased from the manufacturers, Machinery, on 1 January 20X4 for $10,000. Machinery recorded a profit of $2,000 on the sale of the machine.

The group charges depreciation on plant and equipment at the rate of 10% on cost each year, including a full provision in the year of acquisition.

(c) Intra-group balances are included in receivables and payables respectively and are as follows:

		$
Sales	Payables to Machinery	45,600
	Payables to Components	28,900
Machinery	Receivables from Sales	56,900
Components	Receivables from Sales	28,900

(d) A cheque drawn by Sales for $11,300 on 28 October 20X5 was received by Machinery on 3 November 20X5.
(e) At 1 April 20X1, retained earnings in Machinery were $28,000 and in Components were $20,000. At 1 April 20X3 the figures were $40,000 and $60,000 respectively.
(f) Goodwill was completely written off some year ago following an impairment review.

Requirement

Prepare the consolidated statement of financial position as at 31 October 20X5 for Sales and its subsidiaries. **(25 marks)**

Solutions to Revision Questions

 Solution 1

Group structure:

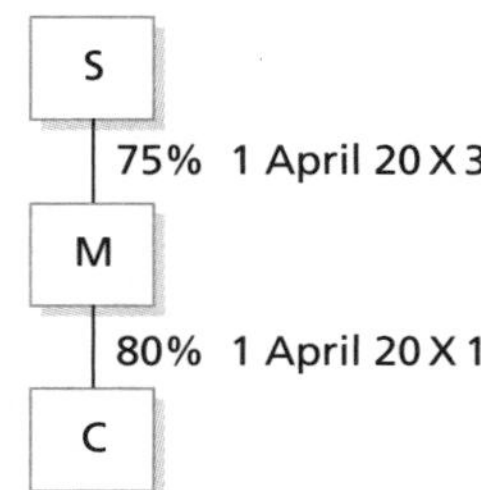

Consolidation %

S	Group share	75%
	Non-controlling interest share	25%
T	Group share 75% × 60%	45%
	Non-controlling interest share	55%

Consolidated statement of financial position at 31 December 20X0

	$	
Net assets	188,000	
Goodwill on consolidation	27,650	(W3)
	215,650	
Capital and reserves		
Issued capital	100,000	
Retained earnings	66,150	(W2)
Non-controlling interest	49,500	(W1)
	215,650	

Workings

1. *Non-controlling interest*

	$
Share of net assets	
S: 25% × 88,000	22,000
T: 55% × 75,000	41,250
Non-controlling share of cost of investment in T	
25% × 55,000	(13,750)
	49,500

2. *Consolidated reserves*

	$
Reserves of H	45,000
Group share of post-acquisition profits	
S: 75% × (28,000 − 10,000)	13,500
T: 45% × (25,000 − 8,000)	7,650
	66,150

3. *Goodwill*

	S $	*T* $
Consideration	65,000	55,000
Net assets acquired		
S: 75% × (60,000 + 10,000)	52,500	
T: 60% × (50,000 + 8,000)		34,800
	12,500	20,200
H's share (100%/75%)	12,500	15,150
Total	27,650	

Solution 2

(a) The non-controlling interest is 30% [($4,000,000 − $250,000) + (30% × $3,200,000)] = $1,413,000.

(b) Since the group was formed on 31 December 2001 the following amounts of profit have been added to consolidated retained earnings in respect of the investments in HI and JK:*Consolidation %*

	$
HI: 80% × ($12.2 m − $10 m) =	1,760,000
JK: 60% × ($10.6 m − $7.6 m) =	1,800,000
	3,560,000

(c) CXP: Consolidated retained earnings

	$
CXP's own retained earnings	266,000
DYQ: ($178,000 − $152,000) × 75%	19,500
EZR: ($214,000 − $202,000) × 75% × 65%	5,850
	291,350

Solution 3

Group structure:

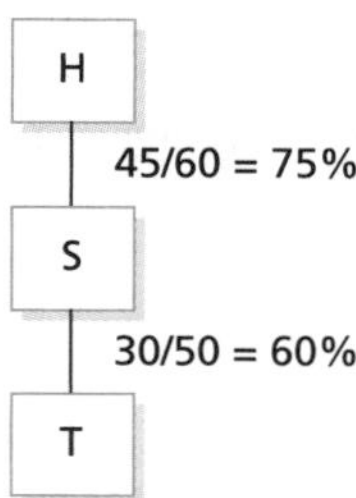

The effective interest is S in C is (75% × 80% =) 60 per cent. The MI is 40 per cent.

Consolidated statement of financial at 31 October 20X5

	$	$
ASSETS		
Property, plant and equipment		
Land		184,000
Buildings		167,600
Plant (160,800 − PUP 1,600)		159,200
		510,800
Current assets		
Inventory (252,400 − PUP 5,000)	247,400	
Receivables		
(405,000 − intra-group 56,900 − 28,900)	319,200	
Cash in hand	50,600	
		617,200
		1,128,000
EQUITY + LIABILITIES		
Equity		
Issued capital		200,000
Retained earnings		200,950
Non-controlling interest		94,450
		495,400
Non-current liabilities		40,000
Current liabilities		
Overdraft (37,400 − cash in transit 11,300)	26,100	
Payables (511,900 − intra-group 45,600 − 28,900)	437,400	
Income tax	129,100	
		592,600
		1,128,000

Workings

1. *Provision for unrealised profit on inventory*

   20% × 25,000 = 5,000

   Adjust reserves of Components – entity that made the sale.

2. *Provision for unrealised profit on plant*

	$
Profit originally recorded	2,000
Realised via extra depreciation charges 2/10 × 2,000	(400)
Provision now required	1,600

Adjust reserves of Machinery – entity that made the sale.

3. *Non-controlling interest*

	$
Machinery 25% × (239,000 − PUP 1,600)	59,350
Components	
Ordinary 40% × (214,000 − 40,000 − PUP 5,000)	67,600
Cost of investment in C made by M	
25% × 130,000	(32,500)
	94,450

4. *Retained earnings*

	$
Sales	154,000
Machinery 75% × (119,000 − 40,000 − PUP 1,600)	58,050
Components 60% × (74,000 − 60,000 − PUP 5,000)	5,400
Less: goodwill written off (W5)	(16,500)
	200,950

5. *Goodwill*

	M $	*C* $
Consideration	135,000	130,000
Net assets acquired		
75% of (120,000 + 40,000)	120,000	
80% of (100,000 + 60,000)		128,000
	15,000	2,000
Amount relating to Sales (100%/75%) (all written off following impairment review)	15,000	1,500

10

Substance Over Form

Substance Over Form

10

Learning Outcomes

- discuss the principle of substance over form applied to a range of transactions; including:
  - Sale and repurchase agreements;
  - Consignment stock;
  - Debt factoring;
  - Securitised assets and loan transfers;

10.1 Introduction

In this chapter we will consider the principles of reporting the substance of transactions and not their legal form. The terms of transactions will be scrutinised to determine how a transaction should be recorded and where appropriate the correcting entries that are required. Specific transactions will then be considered that commonly raise the issue of substance over form.

10.2 Principles of substance over form

There is no specific international financial reporting standard that deals with the topic of substance over form. The IASB *Framework* describes the principle: 'If information is to represent faithfully the transactions and other events that it purports to represent, it is necessary that they are accounted for and presented in accordance with their substance and economic reality and not merely their legal form'.

IAS 18 *Revenue* and IAS 39 *Financial Instruments: Recognition and Measurement* also contain some elements that are relevant to a consideration of substance over form. These will be considered later in the chapter.

10.2.1 Off-balance-sheet financing

Often the motivation behind transactions that require adjustment for substance over form is the avoidance of liabilities on the statement of financial position. Motivations for keeping financing off the statement of financial position include the following:

1. *Effect on the gearing (leverage) ratio.* If an entity is able to exclude liabilities from its statement of financial position it can manipulate the gearing ratio to the lowest possible level. High gearing levels tend to have adverse effects on share prices because the share is perceived by the market as riskier.
2. *Borrowing capacity.* The lower the level of liabilities recorded on the statement of financial position, the greater the capacity for further borrowings.
3. *Borrowing costs.* An entity with an already high level of borrowings will pay a risk premium for further borrowing in the form of a higher interest rate.
4. *Management incentives.* Bonuses and performance-related pay may be based upon reported earnings for a period. If an entity is able to benefit from off-balance-sheet financing arrangements, costs may be lower, thus improving earnings.

10.2.2 Applying substance over form

When assessing the validity of a transaction and its effects, it is important to consider the commercial sense of the transaction. Ask yourself:

- Does this make economic sense? – e.g. selling a property for less than market value.
- With what I know about business, does this make commercial sense? – e.g. why would a financial institution purchase a factory that it will not use and then plans to resell it to the previous owner.
- Which party holds the significant risks and rewards associated with the asset/liability? – has a party recorded a sale but will still be subject to the loss if the asset falls in value?

Often the legal aspects of the transaction are perfectly valid however to achieve a fair presentation of the financial statements we must adopt the principles of substance over form.

Identifying the significant risks and rewards associated with assets and liabilities is the key to establishing the appropriate treatment of transactions.

Consider the following example:

Example 10.A

A sells a machine to B for $20,000 and at the same time agrees to buy it back in 1 year's time for $21,800. The machine remains on A's premises and A continues to use and to insure the machine.

These related transactions are likely to arouse some suspicion. What is actually going on here?

In legal terms, following the first transaction, B is clearly the owner of the machine. However, the substance of the transaction is that A retains the risks and rewards of ownership, and effectively, has taken out a loan for a year at an interest rate of 9%.

Correcting accounting treatment

Applying the principle of substance over form, A should continue to carry the asset in its statement of financial position, with a corresponding liability to B. B would record the loan as a receivable in its own statement of financial position.

Why might this distinction between substance and form matter? What is the motivation for A to keep the loan off the statement of financial position?

Let us extend the example a little further. A is financed partly by long-term borrowing of $30,000. One of the conditions under which the loan was made (the 'covenant') was that A's total liabilities, both long- and short-term should not exceed $80,000. Extracts from two versions of A's statement of financial position, one drawn up to show substance over form and the other to show legal form after the transaction are as follows:

	Substance over form	*Legal form*
	$	$
Non-current assets	100,000	80,000
Current assets	85,000	85,000
	185,000	165,000
Capital and reserves	90,000	90,000
Long-term borrowing	30,000	30,000
Current liabilities	65,000	45,000
	185,000	165,000

The statement of financial position prepared adopting the principle of substance over form shown total liabilities of $30,000 +$65,000 = $95,000. This clearly breached the terms of the covenant. The statement of financial position prepared according to strict legal form, on the other hand, shown total liabilities of $30,000 + $45,000 = $75,000. The terms of the covenant, technically, have not been breached.

The key to applying the principle of substance over form is to fully appreciate the principles of:

- Revenue recognition; and
- Recognition and derecognition of assets and liabilities.

10.3 Recognition of Revenue

The detailed provisions of the IASB's framework and IAS 18 *Revenue* are not specifically tested in F2. The principles they contain, however are often essential benchmarks for deciding substance over form on sale versus financing transactions.

The IASB's *Framework for the Preparation and Presentation of Financial Statements* provides a definition of income, as follows:

> ... income encompasses both revenue and gains. Revenue arises in the course of the ordinary activities of an entity and is referred to by a variety of different names including sales, fees, interest, dividends, royalties and rent. Gains represent other items that meet the definition of income and may, or may not, arise in the course of the ordinary activities of an entity.

IAS 18 specifically concerns itself with revenue and expressly excludes gains from consideration. It encompasses revenue arising from three kinds of transactions and events:

1. the sale of goods;
2. the rendering of services;
3. the use by others of the assets of the entity, yielding interest, royalties and dividends.

10.3.1 Revenue recognition: sale of goods

Revenue is recognised from the sale of goods, provided that all of the conditions below have been satisfied:

- the significant risks and rewards of ownership have been transferred to the buyer;
- the entity retains no effective control over the goods sole, not does it retain any significant degree of the managerial involvement normally associated with ownership;
- revenue can be measured reliably;
- it is probable that the economic benefits associated with the transaction will flow to the entity;
- the costs associated with the transaction can be measured reliably.

The standard notes that, in most cases, the transfer of risks and rewards in the transaction takes place at the same time as the passing of possession to the buyer, or the transfer of legal title. Therefore, when goods are shipped, for example, the point of recognition would normally be the point at which the goods pass into the control of the purchaser. However, the point at which revenue can be recognised may, in some cases, be more difficult to establish. In complex cases it will be necessary to assess carefully where the risks and rewards of ownership reside.

In Example 10.A, there was an apparent sale of a machine, but it was noted that the seller, A, retained the risks and rewards of ownership.

10.3.2 Revenue recognition: sale of services

Revenue associated with transactions involving the rendering of services should be recognised by reference to the state of completion of the transaction at the year end date. Again, a consideration of the substance of the transaction should be undertaken.

A special problem in relation to revenue recognition arises where an agent acts as an intermediary on behalf of a principal, collecting a commission for arranging provision of goods or services.

Example 10.B

X is an advertising agency. It acts as intermediary in arranging magazine advertisements. A single page display in a nationally distributed women's magazine cost $3,000. The magazine publisher invoices the agency $3,000 less the agency's commission of 15%: the net amount of the invoice received by X is, therefore, $2,550 ($3,000 less commission of $450).

X sends an invoice to the advertiser for the full cost of the magazine page, that is, $3,000. There is a related cost of $2,550 payable to the magazine publisher. How much revenue should be recognised by X? There are two possibilities depending upon whether or not X is classed as an agent:

1. Revenue of $3,000 is recognised, together with related costs of $2,550 (presentation of turnover as a principal).
2. Revenue of $450 is recognised (presentation of turnover as an agent).

Clearly, there is quite a significant distinction between the two modes of presentation. In determining which mode is appropriate for X, we can examine the transaction from the risks and benefits perspective. A principal is exposed to all the risks and benefits associated with the selling price of goods and services. Where, by contrast, a seller acts as an agent, it would not normally be associated with the majority of the risks and benefits of the transaction.

In the example of X, the selling price of the services (the cost of a one page display advertisement) is determined by the magazine publisher, not by the advertising agency. The relationship of X to the publisher and to the advertiser appears to be one of agency, and the principles of substance over form would appear to require that X recognises only $450 of revenue in respect of this transaction.

10.4 Recognition and derecognition of assets and liabilities

In order to determine the substance of a transaction it is necessary to identify whether or not it has given rise to new assets or liabilities or has increased or decreased existing assets and liabilities. The existence of an asset may be indicated where an entity derives benefit and is exposed to the element of risk inherent in the benefit. The existence of a liability is indicated where an entity is unable to avoid, legally or commercially, an outflow of economic benefits.

10.4.1 Recognition of assets and liabilities

The recognition of assets and liabilities is covered in the *Framework for the Preparation and Presentation of Financial Statements.* Where a transaction has resulted in an item that meets the definition of an asset or liability, it should be recognised if:

- there is sufficient evidence of the existence of the item;
- the item can be measured at a monetary amount with sufficient reliability.

The *Framework for the Preparation and Presentation of Financial Statements* defines assets and liabilities as follows:

- *assets* are rights or other access to future economic benefits controlled by an entity as a result of past transactions or events;
- *liabilities* are an entity's obligation to transfer economic benefits controlled by an entity as a result of past transactions or events.

10.4.2 Derecognition of assets and liabilities

Where an asset is sold in an outright sale, where all rights and rewards of ownership are transferred and no risks are retained, derecognition (i.e., removal of the asset from the statement of financial position of the transferor) is clearly appropriate. However, where conditions are attached to the transfer, the substance of the transaction must be examined carefully. It may be that each party has access to some of the benefits and subject to some of the risks. In this case it is important to assess which are the significant risks and rewards, e.g. in property the main rewards are the cash flows likely from its operation and the potential for increases in the value of the asset. The main risks are a fall in the value and obsolescence.

In Example 10.A we examined the case of a business (A) that sold a tangible non-current asset to another entity with a right of repurchase at a higher price in 1 year's time. We identified that the substance of this transaction was that of a lending arrangement, not a sale. In that case there was no derecognition of the asset, it should remain in A's financial statements.

Financial assets and liabilities

Derecognition of financial assets and liabilities is covered by IAS 39 *Financial Instruments: Recognition and Measurement.*

Derecognition may arise, under IAS 39, where a financial asset or financial liability is transferred. This will normally occur where the entity has transferred the contractual rights to the cash flows receivable. Financial liabilities should be derecognised only when the obligation which originated the liability is completely extinguished. (See Chapters 11 of this *Learning System* for more on accounting for financial instruments).

A transferred financial asset should not be derecognised where the transferor has a right to reacquire the transferred asset. Consider the details of the examples below:

Example 10.C

In its financial year ending 31 December 20X4, J enters into the following transactions in respect of its mortgage loans portfolio.

1. J transfers a set of mortgage loans to K, in exchange for $250,000. In 1 year's time J will be able to repurchase the loans from K for a fixed sum of $280,000.
2. J transfers a set of mortgage loans to L, in exchange for $250,000. If L decides subsequently to sell the portfolio of mortgage loans, an agreement between J and L stipulates that J has a right of first refusal to reacquire the portfolio and that the re-acquisition price would be the fair value at the time.

Should the mortgage loans be derecognised as financial assets?

In the first case, the answer is almost certainly that the assets should continue to be recognised in the books of J. This is a very similar situation to the one outlined in Example 10.A. In the second case, the financial assets would probably be derecognised. The reacquisition terms are vague and it is by no means certain that any reacquisition would ever take place. Also, the fact that there is no fixed price for a subsequent reacquisition is a influential factor in the decision.

10.5 Substance over form: cases

The following section provides illustrations of how substance over form is applied to specific transactions. The transactions covered are:

- Sale and repurchase agreements
- Consignment stock
- Factoring of receivables
- Securitised assets and loan transfers.

10.5.1 Sale and repurchase agreements

It is important to consider the terms of the arrangement and whether or not a sale has actually taken place. An assessment of the main risks and rewards will normally focus on the value and ultimate use of the asset being 'sold'. Consider the commercial sense of the transaction – would a financing company use the asset itself or is it just lending using the asset as security?

Example 10.D

On 1 February 20X4 BJ sold a freehold interest in land to a financing institution for $7.2 million. The contractual terms require that BJ will repurchase the freehold on 31 January 20X7 for $8.82 million. BJ has the option to repurchase on 31 January 20X5 for $7.7 million or on 31 January 20X6 for $8.24 million. Prior to the disposal the land was recorded at its carrying value of $6 million in BJ's accounting records. The receipt of $7.2 million has been recorded with a credit to suspense account. No other accounting entries have been made in respect of this transaction.

At 31 January 20X5, BJ's directors decide not to take up the option to repurchase.

Requirement

Briefly explain the substance of this transaction, and prepare journal entries to record it correctly in the accounting records of BJ for the year ended 31 January 20X5.

Solution

The substance of the transaction is that BJ has borrowed $7.2 million against the security of freehold land. The land will be repurchased by BJ and the price it will pay increases over time. In this case, the increase each year in the repayable amount reflects an interest charge. IAS 39 *Financial Instruments: Recognition and Measurement* requires initial recognition of the liability, and the related interest expense should be recognised over the relevant period. This is accounted for in the year ended 31 January 20X5 as follows:

	$'000	$'000
DR Suspense account	7,200	
CR Non-current liabilities		7,200
DR Interest expense for year ($7.7 2 7.2 m)	500	
CR Non-current liabilities		500

10.5.2 Consignment stock

Consignment stock is held by one party but owned by another. For example, motor dealers commonly hold inventory in the form of cars on their premises which will be either sold to customers or returned unsold to the manufacturer. There are benefits to both manufacturer and dealer in this type of arrangement. The dealer has access to a wider range of stock than would be possible if he or she were required to make a commitment to purchase, and the manufacturer avoids the costs of holding large quantities of inventory.

Which party, manufacturer or dealer, receives the benefits and is exposed to the risks associated with the inventory? The substance of the commercial arrangement must be examined carefully.

The table below shows the risks and benefits that may arise, depending upon the nature of the contractual arrangements, for the dealer:

Benefits	*Risks*
1. The cash flow arising from sales	1. The risk of having to retain obsolete inventory
2. The right to retain items of inventory to assist in making sales	2. The risk of slow movement of inventory, increasing finance costs and the risk of obsolescence
3. Insulation from price changes after the inventory has been consigned	
4. The right to use the inventory for demonstration purposes	

Based on this analysis of risks and benefits, the substance of the arrangement is identified:

1. Is the substance of the transaction that the inventory is an asset of the dealer?
   If this is the case, inventory is shown in the dealer's statement of financial postion and a corresponding liability to the manufacturer is recognised. The dealer in this case bears all the risks and obtains the rewards of ownership.
2. Is the substance of the transaction that the inventory is an asset of the manufacturer?
   In this case, the dealer will show neither the inventory nor the related liability in his or her statement of financial position.

Example 10.E

AB runs a car dealership. The terms of the agreement between AB and the car manufacturer are as follows:

- The price that AB pays for inventories is fixed at the date the cars arrive on the forecourt
- AB has no right to return the vehicles
- Legal title is not held by AB instead legal title passes when the cars are sold to a third party, or AB uses a car for demonstration purposes
- AB pays a finance charge to the manufacturer between the date of delivery and the date legal title passes or the date of return, whichever is earlier.

Solution

The inventories (cars) should be included in the assets of AB as it is subject to the major risks and rewards associated with the cars. The fact that AB pays the price ruling at the date the cars are delivered suggests that is the date of transfer. AB cannot return the cars and therefore retains the main risk of obsolesce and failure to sell. The finance charge that is payable to the manufacturer again points to AB having taking ownership of the cars but not yet having paid for them. In substance the inventories should be held on the books of AB and a corresponding liability should be shown for the financing element.

10.5.3 Factoring of receivables

Factoring of receivables can be a very useful way of raising cash quickly. However, where such transactions take place it is important to establish their substance. Factoring can be a financing transaction in substance, where cash is advanced against the security of receivables. Or, the transaction may be more in the nature of a working capital shift, where receivables are simply sold on in order to be able to receive cash more quickly.

Factors provide a range of services, and it can be difficult to establish the substance of the transaction. Essentially, the key to understanding lies in the ownership of the receivable. If the provider of the cash has any opportunity of recourse to the seller (i.e., being able to pass receivables back) the deal probably constitutes a financing arrangement.

Example 10.F

A decides to transfer responsibility for collection of its receivables to a factor, B. The arrangement is that B administers the sales ledger and handles all aspects of collection of the receivables in exchange for an administration fee of 1% of all receivables factored. A factoring account is opened, and A is able to draw in cash up to 75% of the receivables factored. The account is credited with cash received when the receivables are realised. It is debited with an interest charge of between 5% and 7.5% depending upon the speed of payment of the receivables. Any receivables not recovered after 90 days are resold to A and credited back to the factoring account.

Solution

In this example, A (the seller) bears the risk of slow payment, as reflected in the interest rate and the repurchase of slow debts. This type of arrangement is essentially a financing one, and should be reflected as a separate asset and liability in the statement of financial postion of A.

10.5.4 Securitised assets and loan transfers

These are similar in nature to factoring of receivables, where a loan asset is transferred to a third party as a way of securitising finance. The benefits associated with the asset are the future cash flows from the repayments and associated interest. The risks would include the risks of slow and non-payment or reduction in future cash flows as a result of early repayment.

10.6 Special purpose entities (SPEs)

The use of special purpose entities (SPEs) was an especially prominent feature of the Enron case in the USA. However, the potential of the SPE for accounting manipulation resulted in the IASC, the predecessor body to the IASB, issuing SIC-12 *Consolidation: special purpose entities* in 1998. The IASB intends to re-examine the problem in the future.

The SIC provides the following examples of an SPE's activities:

- The SPE is principally engaged in providing a source of long-term capital to an entity or funding to support an entity's ongoing major or central operations.
- The SPE provides a supply of goods or services that is consistent with an entity's ongoing major or central operations which, without the existence of the SPE, would have to be provided by the entity itself.

The purpose of SPEs is very often to remove part of a group's activities from the requirement to consolidate. They are often set up using complex legal structures. However, the SIC's guidance on this point is quite straightforward:

An SPE should be consolidated when the substance of the relationship between an entity and the SPE indicates that the SPE is controlled by that entity (para 8).

The true substance of the relationship can be determined by examining where the decision-making powers lie, and which parties benefit from the rewards and bear the risks related to the SPE.

10.7 Summary

There is no separate international financial reporting standard that deals with substance over form. In this chapter we examined various sources of guidance on what is often a complex matter; these include IAS 18, IAS 39, SIC 12 and the *Framework for the Preparation and Presentation of Financial Statements.*

Revision Questions 10

Question 1

On 1 January 20X7, a 70% subsidiary of AB sold a leasehold interest in a property to a bank for $100 million. The property was carried in the financial statements at $80 million and the remaining term of the lease was 20 years from 1 January 20X7. The subsidiary has the option to repurchase the leasehold interest on 31 December 20X7 for $105 million or on 31 December 20X8 for $110 million.

The subsidiary is obliged to repurchase the interest on 31 December 20X9 for $117 million if not repurchased before. The early repurchase option was not exercised on 31 December 20X7.

Your assistant has credited the sales proceeds to a suspense account that is included in current liabilities. In previous years, the leasehold property has been amortised over the lease term with the amortisation expense included in cost of sales. However, no amortisation charge has been made for 20X7 on the grounds that the leasehold interest has been disposed of on the first day of the year.

Requirement

Explain the adjustments that would be required to correctly reflect this transaction in the consolidated financial statements of AB for the year ended 31 December 20X7. You should provide appropriate journal entries to support your adjustment. Refer to the provisions of international accounting standards where relevant. Where no accounting standard exists, you should refer to underlying accounting principles to support your argument.

(10 marks)

Question 2

Z trades in motor vehicles, which are supplied by their manufacturer, X. Trading between the two entities is subject to a contractual agreement, the principal terms of which are as follows:

- Z is entitled to hold on its premises at any one time up to 60 vehicles supplied by X.

X retains legal title to the vehicles until such time as they are sold to a third party by Z.

- Z is required to insure the vehicles on its property, against loss or damage.
- The price at which vehicles are supplied is determined at the time of delivery.

- When Z sells a vehicle to a third party, it is required to inform X within three working days. X submits an invoice to Z at the originally agreed price; the invoice is payable by Z within 30 days.
- Z has the right to return any vehicle to X at any time without incurring a penalty.
- Z is entitled to use any of the vehicles supplied to it for demonstration purposes and road testing. However, if more than a specified number of kilometres is driven in a vehicle, Z is required to pay X a rental charge.

Requirements

(a) Discuss the economic substance of the contractual arrangement between the two entities, in order to identify which entity should recognise the vehicles in inventory once they have been delivered to Z. **(7 marks)**

(b) Identify the point at which X should recognise the sale of its vehicles. **(3 marks)**

(10 marks)

Solutions to Revision Questions 10

Solution 1

This is a sale and repurchase which under the principles of IAS 18 could not be regarded as revenue. In order to identify the appropriate accounting treatment for the 'sales proceeds', it is necessary to apply the principles identified in the IASB *Framework for the Preparation and Presentation of Financial Statements.*

The IASB framework requires entities to account for the economic reality (or substance) of transactions in order to faithfully represent them. It appears that the substance of this transaction is that the entity has a financial liability that would be dealt with according to the requirements of IAS 39 *Financial Instruments: Recognition and Measurement.*

Furthermore, the instrument appears to be held to maturity financial liability which will be dealt with under the 'amortised cost' method. The relevant loan would be regarded as having a maturity date of 31 December 20X9 and therefore the loan would be a non-current liability. Interest charged at the effective interest rate would be included as an expense in the income statement.

Additionally, under the principles of IAS 16 *Property, Plant and Equipment*, the leasehold interest would need to be depreciated since the asset is retained and is consuming economic benefits. The charge to cost of sales would be $4 million ($80 m/20).

The overall impact of the adjustments is shown in the following journal entries:

	DR	*CR*
	$'m	$'m
Cost of sales	4	
Property		4
Being extra depreciation		
Current liabilities	100	
Finance cost	5	
Non-current liabilities		105
Being reallocation of loan and inclusion of finance cost		
Non-controlling interest (SOFP)	2.7	
Non-controlling interest (income statement)		2.7
Being allocation of minority element of adjustments [30% × (4 + 5)]		

Solution 2

(a) The economic substance of the arrangement between the two entities is determined by analysing the risks and benefits of the transaction. The entity that receives the benefits and bears the risks of ownership should recognise the vehicles as inventory. Z, the motor vehicle dealer, appears to derive the following benefits:

- It is free to determine the nature of the inventory it holds, in terms of ranges and models.
- It is protected against price increases between the date of delivery to it and the date of sale because the price is determined at the point of delivery.
- It has access to the inventory for demonstration purposes.

Z incurs the following costs and risks:

- X retains legal title to the goods, so in the case of dispute X would probably be entitled to recover its legal property.
- Z is required to bear the cost of insuring the vehicles against loss or damage.
- Although Z obtains the benefit of using vehicles for demonstration purposes a rental charge may become payable.
- If price reductions occur between the date of delivery and the date of sale, Z will lose out because it will be required to pay the higher price specified upon delivery.

The analysis of the risks and benefits of the transaction does not produce a clear decision as to the economic substance of the arrangement between the two parties. X bears the substantial risk of incurring costs related to slow-moving or obsolete vehicles because Z can return any vehicle to it, without incurring a penalty. This point alone is highly significant and may be sufficient to ensure that X, the manufacturer, should continue to recognise the vehicles in its own inventory. A further relevant point is that X is not paid until the point of sale to a third party, and thus it bears the significant financial risk involved in financing the entity.

(b) In respect of the sale of goods, IAS 18 *Revenue* requires that a sale should be recognised when the selling entity transfers to the buyer the significant risks and rewards of ownership of the goods. As noted above, significant risks and some of the rewards of ownership remain with the manufacturer, X, until such time as the goods are sold by the dealer to a third party. Therefore, revenue should be recognised by X only when a sale to a third party takes place.

Accounting for Financial Instruments

Accounting for Financial Instruments

11

Learning Outcome

After studying this chapter students should be able to:

- explain the possible treatments of financial instruments in the issuer's accounts, including the classification of liabilities and equity, and the implications for the associated finance costs;
- identify circumstances in which amortised cost, fair value and hedge accounting are appropriate for financial instruments, and explain the principles of these accounting methods.

11.1 Introduction

This chapter looks at accounting for financial instruments. Section 11.2 introduces the relevant standards that provide guidance for financial instruments. In Section 11.3 we will look at how to identify and classify financial instruments. Section 11.4 looks at how financial instruments are recognised and measured. We will also study the principles of impairment of financial assets. Section 11.5 looks at the basics of hedging relationships. Section 11.6 will provide a brief overview of the disclosure requirements for financial instruments.

11.2 Financial instruments – relevant accounting standards

The provisions are very detailed as financial instruments make up a large part of our statement of financial position. As a result the accounting and disclosure requirements are contained in three accounting standards:

- IAS 32 *Financial instruments: presentation*
- IAS 39 *Financial instruments: recognition and measurement*
- IFRS 7 *Financial instruments: disclosure*

IAS 39 has been controversial from its original inception. Proposals for changing it have elicited comments and criticisms from many quarters, and several issues remain to be clarified and agreed. The current version of the standard should be regarded as an interim measure only; the IASB is currently undertaking research work that will ultimately lead to the replacement of IAS 39.

The objective of the standard is to establish principles for recognising and measuring financial assets, financial liabilities and contracts to buy or sell a non-financial item that can be settled net in cash or by some other financial instrument.

11.3 IAS 32 *Financial instruments: presentation*

IAS 32 deals mainly with how to identify and classify financial instruments and pays particular note to the issues in classifying debt and equity.

11.3.1 Definitions

IAS 32 defines a financial instrument as:

Any contract that gives rise to both a financial asset of one entity and a financial liability or equity instrument of another entity.

A 'financial asset' can be any of the following:

- cash;
- a contractual right to receive cash or another financial asset from another entity;
- a contractual right to exchange financial instruments with another entity under conditions that are potentially favourable; or
- an equity instrument of another entity;
- a contract that will, or may be, settled in an entity's own financial instruments.

A 'financial liability' can be:
A contractual obligation:

- to deliver cash or another financial asset to another entity;
- to exchange financial instruments with another entity under conditions that are potentially unfavourable.

Or a contract that will, or may be, settled in the entity's own equity instruments.

An equity instrument is: 'any contract that evidences a residual interest in the assets of an entity after deducting all of its liabilities'. To take the most common example, ordinary shares in an entity fall into this category.

Some common examples of financial instruments include the following:

- cash;
- deposits available on demand or after the lapse of a specified period of time;
- commercial debt;
- loans receivable and payable;
- debt and equity securities that are financial instruments from the point of view of both the holder and the issuer;

- asset backed securities, for example, mortgages and other forms of secured loan;
- derivatives, such as options, forward contracts, futures contracts, warrants and other future rights.

Certain types of financial instrument fall outside the scope of the IAS because they are dealt with more fully in other standards. These include: interests in subsidiaries, interests in associates and joint ventures, employee benefit plans and obligations arising under insurance contracts.

11.3.2 Classification of financial instruments

In order to be able to apply the recognition and measurement criteria in IAS 39, we must first decide how a financial instrument should be classified. The classifications of financial instruments are based on the definitions above.

Financial assets should be easy to identify, however a difficulty often arises when classifying debt and equity. Prior to the introduction of this standard, the equity of the business could include all types of shares. The term 'share' being used in the terms of the instrument normally resulted in them being classified as equity.

The definition that IAS 32 introduced describes a financial liability as containing an obligation to transfer economic benefit at a future date. It is this 'obligation' that resulted in many financial instruments being reclassified from equity to debt when IAS 32 was first applied. Classifications as debt as opposed to equity will affect the gearing ratio of the entity.

Gearing is an important measure of an entity's risk and stability. Debt takes priority over shareholders' funds, and interest on debt must be paid otherwise the entity's survival is at risk. The return on shareholders' funds, in the form of dividends, does not have to be paid. The level of payment of dividend, and whether or not a dividend is paid at all, are under the control of the entity's directors.

The importance of the gearing ratio as a measure of the riskiness of the entity means that the classification of financial instruments as debt or equity is of significant importance. Where an entity's gearing ratio is already high, it will probably wish to avoid issuing new financial instruments that fall into the debt category. A straightforward way of doing this is to issue uncontroversial equity in the form of ordinary shares. However, there has been a tendency in recent years to issue complex financial instruments that technically meet the classification of equity but that are actually, in most essential respects, debt. Where these instruments contain any element of obligation they will now be classified as financial liabilities in accordance with IAS 32.

The classification of the instrument has a significant affect on the income statement of the entity. Distributions associated with debt (interest/finance costs) will be deducted from profit, whereas distributions associated with equity (dividends) will be shown as a reduction in equity through the Statement of Changes in Equity. The classification of financial instruments will have an impact on the reported profit for the period and the performance ratios that are subsequently calculated. When determining the classification, IAS 32 requires that the substance of the instrument be considered and not merely its legal form.

Debt or equity?

Some of the basic characteristics of debt and equity are set out in the table below:

	Equity	*Debt*
Return	Dividend	Interest
Rights	Legal ownership of the entity	Repayment of capital
Effect on income statement	Appropriation of profit after tax determined by the directors	Charge against profits before tax
Interest on winding up of the entity	Residual	Preferential, ranking before equity holders
Taxation implications	Appropriation of post-tax profits	Interest payments are tax-deductible

These distinctions appear to be quite straightforward. However, in practice, determining the difference between debt and equity can be quite difficult because of the complexity of some of the financial instruments that have been issued in recent years. IAS 32 provides the following guidance:

IAS 32 requires that the issuer of a financial instrument shall classify it upon initial issue as either a liability or equity, according to the following classification principles:

1. The substance of a financial instrument, rather than its legal form, governs its classification.
2. Where there is a contractual obligation, potentially unfavourable to the issue of the instrument, to deliver either cash or another financial asset to the holder of the instrument, the instrument meets the definition of a financial liability.
3. Where a financial instrument does not give rise to a contractual obligation under potentially unfavourable conditions, then the instrument is classified as equity.
4. Where there is a requirement for mandatory redemption of the instrument by the issuer at a fixed or determinable future data, the instrument meets the definition of a financial liability.

In recent years there has been a trend towards the issue of complex financial instruments whose classification is not immediately obvious, this is when applying substance over form becomes particularly important. In the rest of this section we consider some examples:

Warrants and options

Warrants and options give the holder the right to subscribe for equity shares at a specified time at a specified price. Share option schemes are commonly used as a form of remuneration, especially for senior staff. In February 2004, the IASB issued IFRS 2 on accounting for share-based payment. This financial reporting standard requires that a charge should be made in the income statement to reflect the benefit transferred to the holder of the option, with a credit to share capital. Such instruments therefore have an effect on equity, rather than debt capital. IFRS 2 is covered in Chapter 12 of this *Learning System*.

Perpetual debt

Perpetual debt is an instrument that provides the holder with the right to receive payments in respect of interest at fixed rates, extending into the indefinite future. There is no redemption date for the debt, which makes it rather akin to equity which, similarly, is issued without a redemption date. Perpetual debt, nevertheless, is classified as debt. When such debt is issued, the issuer takes on a financial obligation to make a stream of future interest payments. The payments are regular and fixed in nature, and therefore the capital element is more akin to debt than equity, and should be classified as such.

Redeemable preference shares

Preference shares usually carry a fixed rate of return, and sometimes they are issued with redemption terms attached to them. Where the issuer is obliged to redeem the shares at a fixed or determinable future date, at a fixed or determinable amount, the instrument has the characteristics of a liability, and should be classified as such.

However, a distinction can be drawn between the type of preference share described above, and a preferred share that is redeemable solely at the option of the issuer (i.e. at the point of issue there is no fixed or determinable date of redemption attached to the instrument). In this case, the instrument is probably equity.

Non-redeemable preference shares

Non-redeemable shares may appear to be rather similar to the perpetual debt described earlier. However, the standard makes it clear that classification as debt or equity is determined by the rights attaching to the shares. If distributions are at the discretion of the issuer, then the non-redeemable shares are likely to be classified as equity. However, where distribution is mandatory, the instrument is much more akin to debt.

Example 11.A

On 1 January 20X1 DP issues preference shares at $1 million par value. There is no redemption date attached to the shares. Under the terms of issue, DP has the option of determining the level of distribution to the holders of the preference shares, and the issue document refers to the possibility that in some years no distribution will be made.

In this example, the financial instrument will be classified as equity.

Example 11.B

On 1 January 20X1 EQ issues 7% preference shares at $1 million par value. There is no redemption date attached to the shares. The preference shares are cumulative in nature, that is, if EQ cannot make the distribution of 7% of par value, the distribution liability is carried forward to a future year.

In this example the distribution cannot be avoided (although it can be deferred). Therefore, the instrument is classified as debt.

Preference shares: conflict with national law

One other relevant point about the classification of preference shares is that, in some jurisdictions, national laws require that preference shares are classified as equity. Adherence to the law is, obviously, a matter of some importance, and so compliance with IAS 32 in this respect may not be possible. This conflict exists in respect of the UK, for example. However, it is to be expected that national laws will, in time, be altered in this respect, so that international accounting standards can be adhered to.

Convertible securities with options

Sometimes, debt is issued with an option to convert the debt at some future date into equity shares. So, rather than repaying the debt with cash, the repayment would be with equity shares. Sometimes, such instruments contain an agreement (a put option) which allows holders of the debt to require redemption at a premium; often such securities will carry a low rate of interest to balance a high redemption premium. The put option requires buy-back of the debt by the issuer at a premium price if conversion does not take place.

Example 11.C

C issues $1 million in convertible debt securities in 20X4. The debt carries an annual interest rate of 3%, and conversion is available in 20X9 at the option of the holder at a rate of 1 equity share for every $10 of debt. Alternatively, the holder can opt to exercise a put option in 20X9 to redeem the debt at a premium of 10%. At the time of issue, the market rate of interest for similar debt is 5.5%.

In this case, the annual interest rate is low but is balanced by the availability of a high premium on redemption. If the price of 1 equity share in 20X9 is greater than $11 ($10 of debt plus 10% redemption premium) then the holders of the debt will choose that option. If, however, the price of a share is below $11, holders will choose to exercise the put option and will require redemption at par value + 10%.

In this case, the financial instrument should be classified as debt.

Financial instruments with contingent settlement

Where shares are issued that give the holder the right to require redemption, in cash or another financial asset, upon the occurrence of an uncertain future event (e.g. if the entity fails to achieve a certain level of profits), the instrument should be classified as debt.

Zero coupon bonds

This is a financial instrument that requires no annual payment of interest. Instead, the issuer has a contractual obligation to repay the holders of the bonds a sum on redemption that reflects the fact that they have received no interest (i.e. it is higher than it would have been if annual interest had been paid). The redemption sum represents 'rolled up' finance charges. The obligation is clearly unfavourable to the issuer, it involves the delivery of a financial asset at a fixed or determinable point in the future, and it is therefore classified as debt.

11.3.3 Hybrid instruments

IAS 32 recognises certain categories of financial instrument as having characteristics of both debt and equity. These are known as hybrid financial instruments, and the most common example is that of convertible debt securities. The view taken by IAS 32 is that this type of single financial instrument creates both debt and equity interests. The standard requires that the component parts of the instrument should be classified separately, and the following example demonstrates how this is done.

Example 11.D

An entity issues 5,000 convertible bonds at 1 January 20X0. The bonds have a 5 year term and are issued at par with a face value of $100 per bond. Total proceeds from the bond issue are therefore: 5,000 × $100 = $500,000. The interest rate on the bonds is 5%. Each bond is convertible at any time up to maturity into 100 ordinary shares.

When the bonds are issued the prevailing market interest rate for similar debt without conversion options is 7%. At the issue date, the market price of one ordinary share is $2.50. The dividends expected over the 5 year term of the bonds amount to 10 cents per share at the end of each year.

IAS 32 requires that the liability element is valued by reference, not to the actual interest rate on the convertible bond, but rather by reference to the prevailing market interest rate on similar debt without conversion right – in this case 7%. The calculations are as follows:

	$
Present value of the principal – $500,000 at the end of 5 years discounted to present value: $^{500,000}/_{(1.07)^5}$	356,379
Present value of the interest – $25,000 payable annually in arrears for 5 years:	
$25,000 3 annuity factor for 5 years:	
$\$25,000 \times (^1/_{1.07}) + (^1/_{1.07^2}) + (^1/_{1.07^3}) + (^1/_{1.07^4}) + (^1/_{1.07^5})$	102,500
Total liability component	458,879
Equity component (balancing figure)	41,121
Total value of bond issue	500,000

11.4 IAS 39 *Financial instruments:recognition and measurement*

This standard deals with the recognition and measurement of all financial instruments (except any that are specifically dealt with by a more specific standard).

11.4.1 Initial recognition of financial assets and liabilities

The standard requires recognition of a financial asset or financial liability once the entity becomes **party to the contractual provisions** of the instruments. For example, Entity C enters into a loan agreement with a financial institution, which involves borrowing $50 million. The liability under the agreement will be recognised when, and only when, the contractual arrangements become binding on C.

All financial assets and financial liabilities should be recognised on an entity's statement of financial position. This may seem uncontroversial, but it is important to note that financial assets and financial liabilities include derivative instruments. Prior to IAS 39 being applied, derivatives were not reflected in the financial statements until they were settled. The result of first time application was a significant number of new financial assets and liabilities being included in the accounts of entities, entities that had probably traded in derivatives for years.

The initial recognition criteria is the same for most elements of the financial statements:

- It is probable that economic benefit will flow to or from the entity.
- It can be measured reliabily.

Financial assets
Financial assets must be classified as one of the following:

- fair value through profit or loss
- loans and receivables
- held-to-maturity investments
- available-for-sale financial assets.

It is important that classification should take place immediately because it affects the subsequent measurement rules that apply to the instrument. Each of the categories is described in more detail below.

Fair value through profit or loss

Financial assets categorised as 'fair value through profit or loss' are those that fall into one of these categories:

1. Those that are classified as 'held-for-trading'. This classification is appropriate where financial assets are acquired principally for the purpose of short-term resale, or where the asset is acquired as part of a portfolio where short-term profit taking is the norm.
2. Those that are held as part of a group of financial assets that are managed on a fair value basis in accordance with a documented risk management or investment strategy.

Loans and receivables

These financial assets include non-derivative assets with fixed or determinable payments that are not quoted in an active market, and that are not held as fair value through profit or loss, or as available-for-sale assets. Examples would include loans made to other entities that may be sold on or exchanged at some point before they mature.

Held-to-maturity investments

These are non-derivative financial assets with fixed or determinable payments that an entity intends to hold until they mature. The intention to hold until maturity must be demonstrable. For example, if an entity sells a 'held-to-maturity' investment of a significant amount before its maturity date, the validity of its intentions in respect of other 'held-to-maturity' investments is called into question. The standard requires that in such cases the investments must be reclassified as available-for sale. (Note that this point is important because of differences in approach to measurement of financial assets, which will be discussed in the next section of this chapter.)

Available-for-sale financial assets

A financial asset that is not classified as fair value through profit or loss, or as loans and receivables or as held-to-maturity, will be classified as available-for-sale. Available-for-sale financial assets are held at fair value, with subsequent gains or losses recognised in equity until disposal.

Classification in practice could present some problems. A few examples will help to draw distinctions between the four categories:

Example 11.E

In the course of its normal business, entity D lends $130,000 to entity E at a commercial rate of interest for 5 years. Regular repayments of the loan are scheduled to take place annually. There is no active market for this loan instrument, but in similar circumstances in the past D has sold on such financial assets before they reach maturity.

Initial classification in the books of D: loans and receivables.

Example 11.F

Entity F lends entity G $150,000 for 7 years. The rate of interest on the loan is variable depending on market rates, but there is no commercial market for this financial asset. Regular repayments of the loan are scheduled to take place annually. F will retain the gradually reducing loan in its books until the end of the 7 year period, and intends to hold the asset until maturity.

Initial classification in the books of F: held-to-maturity investments.

Example 11.G

Entity H holds surplus cash of $100,000. Because of the seasonal nature of its business it expects to need the cash to fund investment in inventory in about 6 months' time. In the meantime, the directors of H decide to invest in the listed securities of entity J. After 5 or 6 months the investment will be realised.

Initial classification in the books of H: fair value through profit or loss.

Financial liabilities

Financial liabilities is not specifically mentioned as a category in IAS 39, however it is obviously a very important category as it includes loans, payables, preference shares, debentures, etc.

Financial liabilities can be designated as 'fair value through profit or loss', provided that it is either held for trading, or is designated by the entity as such.

Note that derivatives would normally fall into the 'fair value through profit or loss' category and depending on whether the terms are favourable or unfavourable will determine whether it is shown as a financial asset or liability.

11.4.2 Initial measurement

The initial measurement of all financial instruments should be at fair value. Transactions costs should be included in the initial measurement, except for assets and liabilities held at fair value through profit or loss.

Fair value is the amount for which an asset could be exchanged, or a liability settled, between knowledgeable, willing parties in an arm's-length transaction.

Determining fair value may not be straightforward. IAS 39 provides the following guidance in order of preference:

1. Quoted market prices; these are regarded as the best indicator of fair value and should always be used where available.
2. Where there is no active market, fair value should be established using a valuation technique that refers, where possible, to market conditions. Examples of the type of information that may be used include: recent similar transactions at arm's length, discounted cash flow techniques, reference to the market value of similar instruments, and option pricing models.
3. Where there is no active market and if no reliable estimate of fair value can be made, the entity must measure the financial instrument at cost less any impairment

Transactions costs should be included in the initial measurement of assets and liabilities. The normal recording of costs is:

Dr expenses (income statement)
Cr Bank

IAS 39 requires that transaction costs be included in the initial measurement of the financial instrument.

For financial assets the transaction costs will be:

Dr asset
Cr bank

And for financial liabilities:

Dr liability
Cr bank

Example 11.H

AB acquires a loan investment of $5 million. The transaction costs associated with this acquisition totalled $600,000. In the absence of any other information the investment will be classified as loans and receivables and will be initially recognised by:

Dr	Loans and receivables (financial assets)	$5.6m
Cr	Bank	$5.6m

Example 11.I

CD issues debentures with a value of $4 million. The associated transaction costs were $300,000. The net proceeds of the financial liability will be recorded:

Dr	Bank	$3.7 m
Cr	financial liability	$3.7 m

The treatment of the transaction costs is very important as they are included in the opening carrying value of the instrument. Subsequent measurement rules will then be applied and adjustments made to this initial carrying amount.

11.4.3 Subsequent measurement of financial instruments Financial assets

The regulations in IAS 39 in respect of financial asset categories are as follows:

- *fair value through profit or loss*: fair value;
- *loans and receivables*: amortised cost, using the effective interest rate method;
- *held-to-maturity investments*: amortised cost, using the effective interest rate method;
- *available-for-sale financial assets*: fair value.

Once a decision has been taken on the valuation principles to be applied to a financial asset (i.e., fair value or amortised cost) the entity is not permitted to subsequently change the classification.

Also note that, all derivatives that are not designated as hedging items should be measured at fair value.

Fair value will normally be market value, which in the case of traded instruments will be relatively easy to access (financial press). Where an equity investment cannot be reliably measured (shares in private entities) they must be included in the available for sale category and would be held at cost.

Treatment of gains and losses

Where financial assets are accounted for at fair value, gains and losses on periodic remeasurement (e.g., at the year end date) should be taken straight to the income statement. The exception to this is where financial assets are classified as available-for-sale. Gains and losses arising on these assets should be included in other comprehensive income. Upon their disposal, gains and losses previously taken to equity (and included in OCI) should then be recognised in the income statement.

Example 11.J

Financial asset held at fair value through profit of loss

P purchases 100,000 shares in a listed entity X. The shares were acquired during 20X8 at 118¢ per share, transaction costs were $2,000. X's shares are quoted at 31 December 20X8 date at 112¢. P has classified these financial assets as assets held at fair value through profit or loss.

Initial recording:

Dr	Financial asset	$118,000
Cr	Bank	$118,000

The transaction costs cannot be included for assets and liabilities held at fair value through profit or loss (see Section 11.4.2), there are written off as a period expense:

Dr	Expenses	$2,000
Cr	Bank	$2,000

Subsequent measurement:
Subsequent measurement is at fair value. The 100,000 shares should be held at the year end valuation of 112¢ per share. P has made a loss of $6,000 (112,000 − 118,000). As the asset is classified at fair value through profit or loss so the loss should be recorded in the income statement for the period:

Dr	Loss on financial asset (income statement)	$6,000
Cr	Financial asset	$6,000

Derecognition
If the shares were sold during 20X9 for 119¢ per share, the asset would be derecognised and the gain arising from the 31 December 20X8 until the date of disposal will be recognised in the income statement:

Dr	Bank	$119,000
Cr	Financial asset	$112,000
Cr	Gain on disposal of financial asset	$7,000

Example 11.K

Available for sale asset
If we use the same information about the shares but assume that the shares were classified as available for sale. The initial recording will include transaction costs as it is an available for sale asset (see Section 11.4.2). Subsequent measurement is at fair value with gains and losses being recognised in equity until disposal when the recognised gains are recycled to the income statement.
Initial recording:

Dr	Financial asset	$120,000
Cr	Bank	$120,000

Subsequent measurement:
Subsequent measurement is at fair value. The 100,000 shares should be held at the year end valuation of 112¢ per share. P has made a loss of $8,000 (112,000 − 120,000). As the asset is classified as available for sale the loss goes to equity:

Dr	Other reserves	$8,000
Cr	Financial asset	$8,000

This loss would be included as a loss in other comprehensive income in the year.

Derecognition
If the shares were sold during 20X9 for 119¢ per share, the asset would be derecognised and the gain arising from the 31 December 20X8 until the date of disposal will be recognised in the income statement:

Dr	Bank	$119,000
Cr	Financial asset	$112,000
Cr	Gain on disposal of financial asset	$7,000

The previously recognised loss will be recycled through the income statement on disposal:

Dr	Income statement	$8,000
Cr	Other reserves	$8,000

Loans and receivables and held to maturity assets are held at amortised cost and the principles of calculation are the same for financial liabilities that are held at amortised cost (see below).

Financial liabilities

There are two categories of financial liabilities – those held at fair value through profit or loss; and all other financial liabilities.

The general rule is that financial liabilities should be measured at amortised cost, using the effective interest rate method. The associated finance cost is charged to the income statement.

Derivatives not designated for hedging purposes, however, should be measured at fair value as should those financial liabilities that have been designated at fair value through profit or loss. Profits and losses on subsequent measurement are recognised in the income statement.

Example 11.L

On 1 January 20X0 an entity issues debt of $10 million, incurring issue costs of $100,000. The debt carries a rate of interest of 4% per year (payable on 31 December) and it is repayable on 31 December 20X4 at a premium of $3.5 million (i.e., the capital repayment is $13.5 million). The return to the holder of the debt is therefore partly in the form of periodic interest payments, and partly in the form of a premium on redemption.

The total finance costs associated with the financial instrument can be calculated as follows:

	$'000	$'000
Total amount payable		
Interest (4% × $10m × 5 years)	2,000	
Final repayment	13,500	
		15,500
Net amount receivable		
Issue at par	10,000	
Issue costs	(100)	
		(9,900)
Total finance cost		5,600

Under the amortised cost method it is necessary to calculate the constant percentage rate that would need to be applied to the periodic carrying value of the financial liability to bring the carrying value of the liability up to $13.5 million just before the date of repayment of the principal. In this case, the relevant rate is 10%. In an examination question it is likely that the constant percentage rate would be provided.

The initial recognition of the liability at fair value would be $9.9 million, the proceeds of the issue of the financial instrument. The carrying amount is increased each year by the finance cost, and reduced by any payments made to the holders of the instrument.

Year ended 31 December	*Balance b/fwd* $'000	*Issue* $'000	*Finance cost* $'000	*Payment* $'000	*Balance c/fwd* $'000
20X0	–	9,900	990	(400)	10,490
20X1	10,490	–	1,049	(400)	11,139
20X2	11,139	–	1,113	(400)	11,852
20X3	11,852	–	1,185	(400)	12,637
20X4	12,637	–	1,263	(400)	13,500

Each year the finance cost, which is charged in the income statement, is 10% of the outstanding balance of the financial liability.

The recording in 20X0 would be:

Initial measurement at net proceeds:

Dr	Bank	$9.9m
Cr	Financial liability	$9.9m

Subsequent measurement at amortised cost using the effective interest rate (from table above)

Dr	Finance costs	$990,000
Cr	Bank	$400,000
Cr	Financial liability	$590,000

You can see that the financial liability has been credited with $590,000 which increases the carrying value of the debt to $10,490,000. This includes year 1's apportionment of the total finance cost (see above). This will appear in the statement of financial position, allocated between current and non-current liabilities.

11.4.4 Impairment

Impairment is a potentially significant aspect of the measurement of financial assets. Note, however, that impairment of financial assets applies only to those assets that are measured at amortised cost. Gains and losses on regular remeasurement of financial assets valued at fair value are dealt with as explained earlier in the chapter. Note, however, that where an available-for-sale financial asset has been impaired, the cumulative loss recognised to date in equity, should be transferred to profit or loss (even though the financial asset has not been derecognised).

The rules in the revised IAS 39 are summarised as follows:

- An entity is required to assess at each statement of financial position date whether or not any objective evidence exists of impairment of financial assets (evidence would be e.g. financial distress of the entity you have invested in; an entity you have given a loan to has failed to make a repayment on a due date).
- If there is such evidence a detailed impairment review must be undertaken to assess the extent of any impairment loss.
- If not given the loss amount then the loss is measured as the difference between the carrying amount of the financial asset and the present value of the cash flows estimated to arise from the asset, discounted at the asset's original effective interest rate.
- Impairment losses are recognised through the income statement.

Note that impairment should be recognised only in respect of losses that have already been incurred – not in respect of losses that may take place in the future (the incurred loss model, not the expected loss model).

Example 11.M

A has a financial asset classified as fair value through profit or loss, which has a carrying value of $100,000. The entity to which the investment relates is showing signs of financial distress and the directors of A believe it is prudent to conduct an impairment review on this investment. The review shows the value of the asset to be $88,000. The impairment is taken straight to the income statement:

Dr	Impairment loss (income statement)	$12,000
Cr	Financial asset	$12,000

If we now assume that the investment was initially classified as available for sale and that previously recognised gains to date were $9,000 and had been posted to equity. This amount will be transferred to income statement as it would be inconsistent to charge the income statement with the impairment while a credit balance exists within equity relating to the same asset.

Dr	Impairment loss (income statement)	$12,000
Cr	Financial asset	$12,000
Dr	Other reserves	$9,000
Cr	Income statement	$9,000

11.4.5 Derivatives

The definition of a derivative is as follows:

A derivative is a financial instrument with all three of the following characteristics:

1. its value changes in response to the change in a specified interest rate, security price, commodity price, foreign exchange rate, index of prices or rates, a credit rating or credit index or other variable;

2. it requires no initial net investment;
3. it is settled at a future date.

Examples of derivatives include:

- Forward contracts: contracts to purchase or sell specific quantities of commodities of foreign currencies at a specified price determined at the inception of the contract, with delivery or settlement to take place at a specified future date.
- Options: these are contracts that give a purchaser the right to buy (call option) or to sell (put option) a specified quantity of, for example, a financial instrument, commodity or currency at a specified price.

First, it may be helpful to look at an example of a derivative financial instrument in order to demonstrate accounting at fair value for derivatives.

Example 11.N

On 30 November 20X1, the directors of an entity, Z, decide to enter into a forward foreign exchange contract to buy one million Swiss francs on 31 March 20X2. This is a promise to purchase which, at the time it is taken out, has a cost of zero.

This contract fulfils all three requirements to be classified as a derivative. Until the revised version of IAS 39 was issued this type of stand alone derivative would not have been recorded at all before the date at which the transaction takes place (31 March 20X2). However, IAS 39 now requires that derivatives are recorded at fair value. How is this effected?

More information is required:

The balance sheet date of Z is 31 December 20X1. The exchange rate specified in the forward contract is Sw Fr.2.3 = $1. Therefore, on 31 March Z will be required to pay 1,000,000/2.3 = $434,783. At 31 December, the fair value of the derivative could be more or less than that figure. If it is less, Z will have to record a loss on the derivative, but if it is more, there will be a gain. Let us examine both possibilities:

(1) The exchange rate at 31 December = Sw Fr.2.4 = $1. The fair value of the derivative is therefore 1,000,000/2.4 = $416,667. The best way of looking at this is to say that, if this exchange rate persists until settlement of the contract, Z will have made a loss. It will be obliged to spend $434,783 to buy Sw Fr. 1,000,000, but if the actual exchange rate on that date is Sw Fr.2.4 = $1 it will have made a loss on the deal which could have been done, without the forward contract, for $416,667. The difference between the two figures of $434,783 − $416,667 = $18,116 at 31 December will be recorded, under the provisions of revised IAS 39 as follows:

DR	Income statement (loss)	$18,116
CR	Derivative liability	$18,116

(2) The exchange rate at 31 December = Sw Fr.2.1 = $1. The fair value of the derivative is therefore 1,000,000/2.1 = $476,190. At 31 March Z will be obliged to spend $434,783 to buy Sw Fr.1,000,000, but if the actual exchange rate on that day is Sw Fr.2.1 = $1, it will have made a gain on the deal. The difference between the two figures of $476,190 − $434,783 = $41,407 at 31 December will be recorded, under the provisions of revised IAS 39 as follows:

DR	Derivative asset	$41,407
CR	Income statement (gain)	$41,407

The ultimate gain or loss will be determined by the actual exchange rate on 31 March 20X2.

Assume that the actual rate is Sw Fr.2.35 = $1. Under the terms of the forward contract Z actually pays $434,783. However, if the contract did not exist, it would have paid Sw Fr.1,000,000/2.35 = $425,532. The directors' actions have resulted in Z incurring an overall loss by taking out the contract of $434,783 − $425,532 = $9,251. This is the overall fair value of the derivative liability.

How will the transaction be accounted for at 31 March 20X2? This depends upon the fair value of the derivative that is already accounted for in the books. Two possibilities were examined above at 31 December 20X2. Assume that the exchange rate at that date was Sw Fr.2.4 = $1. As we saw this resulted in the recognition of a derivative liability of $18,116. The final fair value of the derivative liability at 31 March 20X2 has been calculated at $9,251. The derivative ceases to exist at this date and so it must be removed from the books. The accounting entries at 31 March 20X2 are as follows:

DR Derivative liability	$18,116	
CR Gain (income statement) $18,116 − $9,251		$8,865
CR Cash		$434,783
DR Swiss francs cash account* $434,783 − $9,251	$425,532	

**Note*: this is obviously the dollar value of the Swiss franc account. The Swiss franc value of 31 March 20X2 is Sw Fr. 1,000,000.

Understanding this type of complex transaction is easier if the reasoning behind the adjustments is fully understood. The intention of IAS 39 is that users of financial statements should be given sufficient information to be able to assess the performance of management in respect of this type of transaction, and that it is necessary, therefore, to include the fair value of derivatives.

11.5 Hedging

Hedging establishes a relationship between a hedging instrument and a hedged item or items. It is essentially all about making exceptions to the rules we have been learning about above in respect of where gains and losses on subsequent measurement.

A hedged item is an asset, liability, firm commitment, forecast future transaction or net investment in a foreign operation that (a) exposes the entity to risk of changes in fair value or future cash flows and (b) is designated as being hedged.

A hedging instrument is a designated derivative or (in limited circumstances) a non-derivative financial asset or non-derivative financial liability whose fair value or cash flows are expected to offset changes in the fair value or cash flows of a designated hedged item.

11.5.1 Hedging relationships

Hedging is simply one of management's strategies to reduce risk and volatility in the management of assets and liabilities.

IAS 39 permits hedge accounting with two provisos:

1. The hedging relationship must be formally designated and documented. The formal documentation should include the entity's risk management objective, its strategy in undertaking the hedge, the nature of the hedged item and of the risk being hedged, and the methods the entity will employ in order to assess the effectiveness of the hedge.
2. The hedge must be expected to be highly effective and its effectiveness must be capable of being reliably measured.

The guidance notes to the standard provide more information as to the criteria that must be met for a hedge to be considered highly effective. It can be regarded as highly effective if two conditions are met:

1. At the inception of the hedge and subsequently, there was an expectation that there would be a high level of correlation between the fair value or cash flows of the hedged item and those of the hedging instrument, during the period that the hedge is designated.
2. The actual results of the hedge are within a range of 80–125 per cent. The standard gives the example of a loss on the hedging instrument of CU (Currency Unit) 120, with a gain on the hedged item of CU 100. The offset can be measured either at 120/100 (120 per cent) or 100/120 (83 per cent). In this case the hedge would be regarded as highly effective, provided that condition (1) was also met.

In its original form, IAS 39 prohibited the type of hedging that involves setting a hedging instrument against a group of aggregated hedged items. However, following objections from banks and others, the IASB revisited the issue by issuing an exposure draft, *Fair value hedge accounting for a portfolio hedge of interset rate risk (macro hedging)* in August 2003. These proposals were incorporated into IAS 39 in March 2004, and are effective for accounting periods beginning on the 1 January 2005 and subsequently. This so-called 'portfolio' hedging permits a hedging instrument to be set off against a portfolio containing more than one hedged item.

There are two principal types of hedging relationship. It is important to distinguish between them because they have different effects on the income statement and the reporting of profit or loss.

11.5.2 Fair value hedges

Fair value hedges are those in which the fair value of the item being hedged changes as market prices change. An example of this would be where the entity is due to pay an amount in a foreign currency at a future specified date and has therefore taken out a forward foreign exchange contract to buy the stipulated amount at the future date. Until the contracts mature there will be changes in the fair value of the liability and also the related fair value of the hedging instrument. These do not, however, result in cash flows until the date specified in the future for maturity of the contracts.

Example 11.O

This example was included in the IAS 39 exposure draft to illustrate a fair value hedging arrangement. It illustrates a hedge of exposure to changes in the fair value of an investment in fixed rate debt as a result of changes in interest rates. In year 1 an investor purchases for 100 a debt security that is classified as available for sale. At the end of year 1, the current fair value of the security is 110. The increase of 10 is reported as a gain and the carrying amount of the security is increased to 110. To protect the value of 110, the investor acquires a derivative at the beginning of year 2 with no cost. By the end of year 2, the derivative instrument has a gain of 5 and the debt security has a corresponding decline in fair value. (This is an example of a highly effective hedge, where gains and losses match exactly.)

The accounting entries are as follows:

Year 1		
DR Investment in debt security	100	
CR Cash		100
Recording the purchase of the security		
DR Investment in debt security	10	
CR Equity (via statement of changes in equity)		10

Reflecting the increase in the fair value of the security (note that this is reflected through the statement of changes in equity because the asset is available for sale).

Also, it should be noted that, at this stage, the financial asset is not hedged.

Year 2		
DR Derivative financial asset	5	
CR Gain (to be included in the income statement)		5
Reflecting the increase in the fair value of the derivative		
DR Loss (to be included in the income statement)	5	
CR Investment in debt security		5

Reflecting the decrease in fair value of the debt security.

At the end of year 2, the financial assets subject to the hedging arrangement total 110, the same as at the end of year 1. The only difference is that the financial assets now comprise a derivative asset (at a value of 5) and the investment in debt security (at a value of 105). The effective hedge means that net profit is protected from the effects of changes in value, because the gain on the derivative exactly offsets the loss arising from the decrease in fair value of the debt security.

Gains and losses on available for sale investments are normally recorded through equity, but where a fair value hedge exists the rule is broken, and the gain/loss on the available for sale investment is instead taken to the income statement in the same period as the gain/loss on the derivative that is being used to hedge against the risk of the change in value of the investment.

11.5.3 Cash flow hedges

Cash flow hedges are those in which the cash flows of the item being hedged change as market prices change. The accounting treatment of gains and losses differs from that adopted in respect of fair value hedges. Changes in the fair value of the hedging instrument are initially reported in equity, via the statement of changes in equity. They are then transferred to profit or loss to match the recognition of the offsetting gains or losses on the hedged transaction. This mean that the effect of gains and losses on the hedged transaction is minimised because any gains are matched by losses on the hedging instrument, and vice versa.

Note that a hedge of a net investment in a foreign operation is treated as for a cash flow hedge.

In this case, the rules are different as the gain/loss on the derivative would normally be recorded in the income statement from the date the contract is entered into. The transaction that it is hedging against, however will not be included in the income statement until some future date (the date the transaction will occur). The rules need to be adjusted as this would mean that gain/losses on each item will appear in different accounting periods. As a result the gain/loss on the derivative is held in equity until the transaction occurs and then is released to the income statement to match against the effect of the transaction it is hedging against.

11.5.4 Designation of hedges

Hedging is useful to organisations in helping to mitigate risk. However, the regulation in IAS 39 relating to hedges does allow entities some control over the timing of recognition of losses. In order to avoid manipulation of the reporting of profits and losses, there are some quite stringent rules in the standard about the designation of hedges:

- the hedging relationship has to be designated and the designation must be documented;
- to the extent that a hedging relationship is effective, the offsetting gains and losses on the hedging instrument and the hedged item must be recognised in profit or loss at the same time;
- all hedge ineffectiveness must be recognised immediately in the income statement;
- only items that meet the definitions of assets and liabilities are recognised as such in the statement of financial position.

11.6 IFRS 7 Financial instruments:disclosure

The standard's disclosure requirements are intended to enhance understanding of the significance of financial instruments to an entity's financial position, performance and cash flows. The disclosures should provide users with information that assists them in assessing the extent of risks related to financial statements.

The **disclosure** requirements of IFRS 7 are as follows:

1. Information enabling users to evaluate the significance of financial instruments for the entity's financial position and performance.
2. The carrying amounts of financial assets at fair value through profit or loss, held- to-maturity investments, loans and receivables, available-for-sale financial assets, financial liabilities at fair value through profit or loss and financial liabilities at amortised cost.
3. Information about collateral, both collateral pledged in the form of financial assets, and its holding of collateral.
4. Information about compound financial instruments.
5. Details of any defaults and breaches in respect of loans payable.
6. Information about items of income, expense, gains or losses in respect of financial instruments.
7. Accounting policies relating to financial instruments.
8. Description of fair value hedges, cash flow hedges and hedges of net investments in foreign operations.
9. Disclosure of the fair value of financial assets and financial liabilities where fair value differs from the carrying amount.

Additionally, entities must disclose information about the nature and extent of risks arising from financial instruments, including qualitative descriptions of the exposure to risks and the entity's objectives, policies and procedures for managing the risk and the methods used to measure the risk. Quantitative disclosures are also required.

Risk

Three significant classes of risk are identified in the standard: credit risk, liquidity risk and market risk, but the standard notes that there may be other categories of risk that affect the entity. The following definitions of risk are provided in the standard:

Credit risk: The risk that one party to a financial instrument will cause a financial loss for the other party by failing to discharge an obligation.

Currency risk: The risk that the fair value or future cash flows of a financial instrument will fluctuate because of changes in foreign exchange rates.

Interest rate risk: The risk that the fair value or future cash flows of a financial instrument will fluctuate because of changes in market interest rates.

Liquidity risk: The risk that an entity will encounter difficulty in meeting obligations associated with financial liabilities.

Market risk: The risk that the fair value or future cash flows of a financial instrument will fluctuate because of changes in market prices. Market risk comprises three types of risk: *currency risk, interest rate risk* and *other price risk*.

Other price risk: The risk that the fair value or future cash flows of a financial instrument will fluctuate because of changes in market prices (other than those arising from interest rate risk or currency risk), whether those changes are caused by factors specific to the individual financial instrument or its issuer, or factors affecting all similar financial instruments traded in the market.

Risk management policies and hedging activities. In addition to providing specific information about specific financial balances and transactions, an entity must provide a discussion of the extent to which financial instruments are used, the associated risks and the business purposes served.

Hedging relationships

Disclosure of hedging activities is also required:

Terms, conditions and accounting policies. Information about the nature and extent of financial instruments must be provided. This is to include significant terms and conditions that may affect the amount, timing and certainty of future cash flows, and the accounting policies and methods adopted.

Interest rate risk. For each class of financial assets and financial liabilities, the entity should disclose information about the extent of its exposure to interest rate risk. This is to include information about the dates of maturity, and the effective interest rates applicable to the instruments.

Credit risk. An entity should disclose information about the extent of its exposure to credit risk, including information about significant concentrations of credit risk (e.g., where an entity is exposed to risk in a particular geographical area).

Fair value. Where an entity does not measure a financial asset or financial liability in its statement of financial position at fair value, it should provide sufficient fair value information about financial assets and financial liabilities through supplementary disclosures. Where entities recognise financial instruments at fair value then the methods and assumptions underlying the fair valuation should be disclosed.

11.7 Summary

This chapter of the *Learning System* has covered one of the more complex accounting issues in the syllabus. The following areas of financial instruments have been covered:

- Classification of financial instruments
- Initial recognition and measurement of financial instruments
- Subsequent measurement of financial instruments, including impairment

- Hedging relationships
- Disclosure requirements

Accounting for financial instruments is still in the process of development, and there are likely to be further changes.

Students can expect both computational and discussion-type questions to be set in this area of the syllabus. They are expected to be able to calculate the impact of financial instrument measurement on financial statements in all the aspects explained in the chapter.

Revision Questions 11

Question 1

The directors of QRS, a listed entity, have met to discuss the business's medium-to long-term financing requirements. Several possibilities were discussed, including the issue of more shares using a rights issue. In many respects this would be the most desirable option because the entity is already quite highly geared. However, the directors are aware of several recent cases where rights issues have not been successful because share prices are currently quite low and many investors are averse to any kind of investment in shares. Therefore, the directors have turned their attention to other options. The finance director is on sick leave, and so you, her assistant, have been given the task of responding to the following note from the chief executive:

Now that we have had a chance to discuss possible financing arrangements, the directors are in agreement that we should structure our issue of financial instruments in order to be able to classify them as equity rather than debt. Any increase in the gearing ratio would be unacceptable. Therefore, we have provisionally decided to make two issues of financial instruments as follows:

1. An issue of non-redeemable preference shares to raise $5 million. These shares will carry a fixed interest rate of 6%, and because they are shares they can be classified as equity.
2. An issue of 6% convertible bonds, issued at par value, to raise $6 million. These bonds will carry a fixed date for conversion in 4 years time. Each $100 of debt will be convertible at the holder's option into 120 $1 shares. In our opinion, these bonds can actually be classified as equity immediately, because they are convertible within 5 years on terms that are favourable to the holder.

Please confirm that these instruments will not increase our gearing ratio, should they be issued.

Note: You determine that the market rate available for similar non-convertible bonds is currently 8%.

Requirement

Explain to the directors the accounting treatment, in respect of debt/equity classification, required by *IAS 32 Financial Instruments: Presentation* for each of the proposed issues, advising them on the acceptability of classifying the instruments as equity. Your explanation should be accompanied by calculations where appropriate. **(10 marks)**

Question 2

(a) ABC has the following financial instruments in issue:
On 1 January 20X6, ABC issued 10,000 5% convertible bonds at their par value of $50 each. The bonds will be redeemed on 1 January 20Y1. Each bond is convertible at the option of the holder at any time during the 5 year period. Interest on the bond will be paid annually in arrears.
The prevailing market interest rate at the date of issue was 6%.

Requirement

Calculate the value that should be recorded in respect of the equity element of the hybrid financial instrument be recognised in the financial statements of ABC at the date of issue.

(b) On 1 January 20X6 an entity, ABC, issued a debt instrument with a value of $5,000,000, incurring $150,000 in issue costs. The coupon rate of the debt is 2.5%. It will become repayable on 1 January 20Y6 at a premium of $1,750,000.

Requirement

Calculate the total amount of finance cost associated with the debt instrument.

(10 marks)

Question 3

You are the management accountant of Short. On 1 October 20X3 Short issued 10 million $1 preference shares at par, incurring issue costs of $100,000. The dividend payable on the preference shares was a fixed 4% per annum, payable on 30 September each year in arrears. The preference shares were redeemed on 1 October 20X8 at a price of $1.35 per share. The effective finance cost of the preference shares was 10%. The statement of financial position of the entity as at 30 September 20X8, the day before the redemption of the preference shares, was as follows:

	$
Ordinary share capital (non-redeemable)	100.0
Redeemable preference shares	13.5
Share premium account	25.8
Retained earnings	59.7
	199.0
Total equity	199.0

Requirements

(a) Write a memorandum to your assistant which explains:
- how the total finance cost of the preference shares should be allocated to the income statement over their period of issue;

Your memorandum should refer to the provisions of relevant accounting standards.

(5 marks)

(b) Calculate the finance cost in respect of the preference shares for each of the 5 years ended 30 September 20X8.

(5 marks)
(Total Marks = 10)

Question 4

On 1 January 20X1 A issued 50,000 $100 2% debentures to investors for $55 each. The debentures are redeemable at their par value of $100 in 5 years' time, 31 December 20X5.

The accountant has drafted the financial statements but has omitted to apply IAS 39. The draft income statement and an extract from the balance sheet are as follows:

Income statement

	20X2	*20X1*
	$'000	$'000
Revenue	7,830	6,690
Operating expenses	5,322	5,109
Interest payable	100	100
Profit before taxation	2,408	1,481
Taxation	521	320
Profit for the period	1,887	1,161
Dividends paid	200	200

Statement of financial position (extract)

	20X2	*20X1*
	$'000	$'000
Payable: amounts falling due after 1 year		
2% debenture	2,750	2,750

Requirement

Amend the draft accounts including comparatives to comply with IAS 39. The rate of interest implicit for the debentures is 15.62% per annum.

(10 marks)

Question 5

During its financial year ended 31 December 20X8, CD entered into the following transactions:

1. In August 20X8, CD made an investment in the securities of a listed entity. The directors intend to realise the investment in the first quarter of 20X9 in order to fund the planned refit of the head office.
2. CD lent one of its customers, XY, $1,000,000 at a variable interest rate pegged to average bank lending rates. The loan is scheduled for repayment in 5 years time and CD has provided an undertaking to XY that it will not assign the loan to a third party.
3. CD made some small investments in the securities of some other listed entities. CD does not plan to dispose of these investments in the short term.

Requirements

In accordance with IAS 39 *Financial Instruments: Recognition and Measurement*:

(a) Identify the appropriate classification of these three categories of financial asset and briefly explain the reason for each classification. **(6 marks)**

(b) Explain how the financial assets should be measured in the financial statements of CD at 31 December 20X8. **(4 marks)**

(Total marks = 10)

Question 6

(a) At its year end, 31 March 20X7, entity JBK held 60,000 $1 shares in a listed entity, X. The shares were purchased on 11 February 20X7 at a price of 85¢ per share. The market value of the shares on 31 March 20X7 was 93¢ and the transaction costs associated with the acquisition were $2,000. The investment is categorised as available for sale.

Requirement

Show the journal entries required in respect of both the initial acquisition and its subsequent remeasurement on 31 March 20X7 and show the relevant extract from the statement of comprehensive income and the statement of financial position in respect of this investment. **(6 marks)**

(b) JBK disposed of these shares on 16 May 20X9 for 96¢ per share.

Requirement

Show the journal entries required to record the derecognition of this investment and briefly explain the accounting treatment adopted. **(4 marks)**

(Total marks = 10)

Question 7

XY purchase 100,000 $1 shares in CD for $1.10 during 20X7. The investment was classified on initial recognition as held for trading and transaction costs associated with the purchase totalled $3,000. At the year end 31 December 20X7 the shares were trading at $1.15.

During 20X8 it became apparent that CD was in financial distress and the directors of XY thought it prudent to conduct an impairment review. The review showed that the investment was impaired by $10,000.

Requirement

(a) Prepare the journal entries to record the initial recognition and subsequent measurement of the instrument above and briefly describe the accounting treatment adopted for the year ended 31 December 20X7.

(b) Briefly describe the accounting treatment required in respect of the impairment in the 20X8 accounts and prepare the necessary journal entries. **(10 marks)**

Question 8

CD has an available for sale investment with a carrying value of $130,000 as at the year end date, 31 December 20X6. The value of the investment at 31 December 20X7 is $138,000.

CD was concerned about the value of the shares falling and in order to mitigate this risk it entered into a derivative contract during 20X8 to hedge against the potential effect on the value of the shares of a general downturn in the market. The hedge is 100% effective and the contract has a positive value of $1,800 as at 31 December 20X8. The fall in the value of the available for sale investment was $2,000 as at 31 December 20X8, however $200 of that related to a change in the credit rating of the entity invested in.

Requirement

Briefly describe the treatment of the investments noted above and prepare the required journal entries for the years ended 31 December 20X7 and 20X8. **(10 marks)**

Solutions to Revision Questions

11

Solution 1

In general, under the requirements of *IAS 32 – Financial instruments: presentation* – financial instruments that fulfil the characteristics of a liability should be classified as such. Although preference shares carry the description of 'shares' this does not mean that they can necessarily be classified as equity. In cases where the payment of the 'dividend' is a fixed sum that is normally paid in respect of each accounting period, the instrument is really a long-term liability and must be classified as such.

The convertible bonds would be classified as a compound, or hybrid, instrument by IAS 32; that is, they have characteristics of both debt and equity, and would therefore be presented partly as debt and partly as equity in the statement of financial position. Valuation of the equity element is often difficult. The method required by IAS 32 involves valuation of the liability element using an equivalent market rate of interest for non-convertible bonds, with equity as a residual figure.

Applying this approach to the proposed instrument, the following debt/equity split results:

Present value of the capital element of the bond issue:	$
$6m × 1/(1.08^4)$	4,410,000
Interest at present value:	
($6,000,000 × 6%) × [1/(1.08) + 1/(1.08^2) + 1/(1.08^3) + 1/(1.08^4)]	
= $360,000 × 3.312 (from tables)	1,192,320
Value of liability element	5,602,320
Equity element (balancing figure)	397,680
Total value of instrument	6,000,000

Apart from the relatively small element of the hybrid instrument that can be classified as equity, the two proposed issues will be classified as debt under the provisions of IAS 32. If the directors wish to obtain finance through an issue of financial instruments that can be properly classified as equity, they should reconsider the rights issue proposal.

Solution 2

Bond principal: 10,000 × $50 = 500,000. Annual interest payment = $500,000 × 5% = $25,000.

Present value of principal: $500,000/(1.06)^5 (factor from table = 0.747)	373,500
Present value of interest: $25,000 × cumulative discount factor (from tables = 4.212)	105,300
	478,800
Balancing figure = equity element	21,200
Principal	500,000

The equity element should be held at a value of $21,200.

	$	$
Total amount payable:		
Interest payable: 5,000,000 × 2.5% × 10		1,250,000
Repayment: 5,000,000 + 1,750,000		6,750,000
		8,000,000
Total amount received:		
Issue		5,000,000
Less: issue costs		(150,000)
		4,850,000
Total finance cost		3,150,000

Solution 3

(a)

Memorandum
To: Assistant accountant
From: Management accountant
Date:
Subject: Financial instruments – preference shares

Preference shares are, in substance, similar to a debt instrument. They are issued on the understanding that they will receive a fixed dividend and will be redeemed at a specified amount on an agreed date. It is likely that IAS 32 would require these instruments to be recognised as a financial liability.

In the income statement, the finance charge should be calculated as the effective rate applied to the carrying value of the instrument. However, this charge represents the difference between the net proceeds and the total payments made during the life of the instrument. It will therefore incorporate not only interest charges but also the initial issue expenses, as well as any premiums payable at the end of the instrument's life.

The carrying value of the non-equity shares will increase each year by the difference between the effective interest charge and the dividends paid in cash. At the end of the instrument's life the amount outstanding on the statement of financial position should therefore represent the cash that must be paid to extinguish the full debt at the time.

Signed: Management accountant

(b) Short – finance cost for each of the 5 years to 30 September 20X8

	$'m	$'m
Total payments over the life of the instrument		
10m × $1.35		13.5
Dividends 0.4m × 5 years		2.0
		15.5
Net proceeds		
Proceeds on issue	10.0	
Less issue costs	0.1	
		9.9
Finance charge		5.6

The spreading of the annual finance cost is as follows:

	Opening balance	*Finance charge (10%)*	*Dividend cash flow*	*Closing balance*	
	$'000	$'000	$'000	$'000	
20X4	9,900	990	(400)	10,490	
20X5	10,490	1,049	(400)	11,139	
20X6	11,139	1,114	(400)	11,853	
20X7	11,853	1,185	(400)	12,638	
20X8	12,638	1,262*	(400)	13,500	redeemed
		5,600	2,000		

(*rounding)

Solution 4

You should first show the table for the allocation of interest as follows (with a slight rounding adjustment at the end):

Year	*Balance b/f*	*Interest*	*Cash flow*	*Balance c/f*
	$	$	$	$
20X1	2,750,000	429,550	100,000	3,079,550
20X2	3,079,550	481,026	100,000	3,460,576
20X3	3,460,576	540,542	100,000	3,901,118
20X4	3,901,118	609,355	100,000	4,410,473
20X5	4,410,473	689,527	5,100,000	0

In substance the debentures are issued at a discount and repaid at a premium. This must all be allocated in the finance charge so that users of the financial statements have full information.

The revised income statement and statement of financial position extract will be as follows:

Income statement

	20X2	*20X1*
	$'000	$'000
Revenue	7,830	6,690
Operating expenses	5,322	5,109
Interest payable	481	430
Profit for the period	2,027	1,151
Taxation	521	320
Profit after taxation	1,506	831
Dividends paid	200	200

Statement of financial position (extract)

	20X2	*20X1*
	$'000	$'000
Payable: amounts falling due after 1 year		
2% debenture	3,461	3,080

Solution 5

(a) 1. This is classified as a financial asset at fair value through profit or loss because the directors acquired the securities with the intention of selling them in the short term; they fall into the category of 'held-for-trading'.

2. The loan is classified as a held-to-maturity financial asset. The loan is an unlisted security with determinable payments. The intention to hold the asset until maturity is demonstrated by the undertaking not to assign the loan to a third party.

3. There is no plan to sell these investments in the short term, but they do not appear to fall into the loans and receivables or held-to-maturity classifications either. Financial assets that do not fall into the three other classifications identified by IAS 39 are likely to be classified as available-for-sale.

(b) The standard requires that financial assets held for trading (which are classified as financial assets at fair value through profit or loss, and those available for sale should be measured at fair value (categories 1 and 3 of PX's financial assets). Held-to-maturity financial assets are measured at amortised cost.

Solution 6

(a) IAS 39 requires that the available for sale investment be initially recorded at cost plus transaction costs.

Dr	Available for sale investment	\$53,000
Cr	Bank	\$53,000

Being the initial recording of the investment including transaction costs ((60,000 × \$0.85) + \$2,000)

Subsequent measurement will occur at the year end and available for sale assets are measured at fair value with gains and losses being recorded in equity until derecognition. The shares will be held at \$55,800 (60,000 × 0.93) and the gain of \$2,800 (55,800 − 53,000) will be recorded in equity.

Dr	Available for sale investment	\$2,800
Cr	Other reserves	\$2,800

Being the remeasurement of the available for sale investment

Extracts from the statement of financial position at 31 March 20X7

Assets

Non-current assets

Available for sale investment \$55,800

Equity

Other reserves \$2,800

Extracts from the statement of comprehensive income for the year ended 31 March 20X7

Other comprehensive income

Gain on available for sale asset \$2,800

(b) On disposal the asset will be derecognised and the gain on sale will include the gain in the period (disposal proceeds less carry value) plus the recycled gains that were previously recognised through reserves.

Dr	Bank (60,000 × 0.96)	\$57,600
Cr	Available for sale investment	\$55,800
Cr	Gain on disposal (income statement)	\$1,800
Dr	Other reserves	\$2,800
Cr	Gain on disposal (income statement)	\$2,800

Being the disposal of the shares

Solution 7

(a) The shares are held for trading and so are initially recorded are cost. Transaction costs are not included for investments classed as fair value through profit or loss and so they will be written off to the income statement in the year:

Dr	Held for trading asset	\$110,000
Cr	Bank	\$110,000

Being purchase of held for trading asset

Dr	Expense	\$3,000
Cr	Bank	\$3,000

Being write off of transaction costs

The investment will subsequently be held at fair value and gains and losses from investment held at fair value through profit or loss are recorded in the income statement:

Dr	Held for trading	\$5,000
Cr	Gain in income statement	\$5,000

Being the gain on held for trading investment 100,000 × (\$1.15 − \$1.10)

(b) The impairment should be recorded and the investment should be carried at the impaired value of \$105,000. The impairment loss will be charged to the income statement when it is incurred:

Dr	Impairment loss on financial asset	\$10,000
Cr	Held for trading asset	\$10,000

Being the impairment loss in the year

Solution 8

This is an example of a fair value hedge. CD have entered into a hedging arrangement as it wants to minimise the risk of the value of the AFS investment falling as a result of a fall in value of the share price.

In 20X7 the available for sale asset is recorded as normal with the gain of \$8,000 being recorded in reserves, in accordance with IAS 39:

Dr	Available for sale investment	\$8,000
Cr	Other reserves	\$8,000

This gain of \$8,000 will be shown within other comprehensive income for the year ended 31 December 20X7.

In 20X8 an effective hedge exists to cover any fall in the value of the shares due to general market conditions. The derivative has a positive value and is therefore an asset held at fair value through profit or loss. This hedged item is the AFS but only the effective part of the hedge can be offset in the income statement (we break the rules for AFS gains/losses so that the gain/loss on the hedging instrument matches against the gain/loss on the hedged item). Any effective part or any loss not covered by hedge is recorded according to the normal rules for the available for sale asset, i.e. to reserves. The recording for 20X8 is:

Dr	Financial asset – derivative	$1,800
Cr	Gain on derivative (IS)	$1,800

Being the accounting for the derivative

Dr	Loss on hedged investment	$1,800
Dr	Other reserves	$200
Cr	Available for sale investment	$2,000

Being the accounting for the AFS investment

12 Employee Benefits

Employee Benefits

12

Learning Outcomes

After studying this chapter students should be able to:

- discuss the recognition and valuation issues concerned with pension schemes and the treatment of actuarial deficits and surpluses;
- discuss the recognition and valuation issues concerned with share-based payments.

12.1 Introduction

This chapter will cover the accounting treatment of employee benefits, including pensions and share-based payments. Section 12.2 covers the objective of IAS 19 *Employee Benefits* and introduces the definitions and terms that are specific to pension schemes. Section 12.3 deals with the accounting for defined benefit and defined contribution schemes, including the treatment of actuarial gains and losses. Section 12.4 reviews the amendment to IAS 19. Section 12.5 covers the requirements of IFRS 2 *Share-based payments*.

12.2 IAS 19 *Employee benefits*

The objective of IAS 19 is to prescribe accounting and disclosure in respect of employee benefits. An entity must recognise:

(a) a liability when an employee has provided service in exchange for employee benefits to be paid in the future.
(b) an expense when the entity consumes the economic benefit arising from service provided by an employee in exchange for employee benefits.

Employee benefits include:

(a) short-term benefits such as wages, salaries, holiday pay, bonuses, profit-sharing and benefits;
(b) post-employment benefits such as pensions and post-employment life insurance and medical care;
(c) other long-term benefits such as sabbatical leave and deferred compensation;
(d) termination benefits.

The standard notes that accounting for short-term benefits is generally straightforward; the normal accruals principle applies, and so short-term prepayments and accruals may arise, but discounting and actuarial valuations are not required. The principal area of complexity arises in respect of accounting for post-employment benefits.

Post-employment benefit plans are classified as either defined contribution or defined benefit plans. The standard's definition of defined contribution plans is as follows:

Defined contribution plans are post-employment benefit plans under which an entity pays fixed contributions into a separate entity (a fund) and will have no legal or constructive obligations to pay further contributions if the fund does not hold sufficient assets to pay all employee benefits relating to employee service in the current and prior periods.

Defined benefit plans are all plans not classified as defined contribution plans. Most of the rest of the part of the chapter on IAS 19 relates to accounting for defined benefit plans.

12.2.1 Key definitions

Employee benefits are all forms of consideration given by an entity in exchange for service rendered by employees.

Post-employment benefits are employee benefits which are payable after the completion of employment.

The *present value of a defined benefit obligation* is the present value, without deducting any plan assets, of expected future payments required to settle the obligation resulting from employee service in the current and prior periods.

Current service cost is the increase in the present value of the defined benefit obligation resulting from employee service in the current period.

Interest cost is the increase during a period in the present value of a defined benefit obligation which arises because the benefits are one period closer to settlement.

Plan assets comprise assets held by a long-term employee benefit fund.

Assets held by a long-term employee benefit fund are assets that are held by a fund that is legally separate from the reporting entity, and exists solely to pay or fund employee benefits. Such assets are available only for payment or funding of employee benefits; they are not available for meeting the reporting entity's other obligations and they cannot be returned to the reporting entity.

The *return on plan assets* is interest, dividends and other revenue derived from the plan assets, together with realised and unrealised gains or losses on the plan assets, less any costs of administering the plan and less any tax payable by the plan.

Actuarial gains and losses comprise experience adjustments (the effect of differences between the previous actuarial assumptions and what has actually occurred; these may be gains or losses) and the effect of changes in actuarial assumptions.

Past service cost is the increase in the present value of the defined benefit obligation for employee service in prior periods, resulting in the current period from the introduction of, or changes to, post-employment benefits or other long-term employee benefits. Past service cost may be either positive (where benefits are introduced or improved) or negative (where existing benefits are reduced).

12.3 Accounting for post-employment benefits

12.3.1 Defined contribution plans

When an employee has rendered service to an entity during an accounting period, the entity should recognise that contribution payable to a defined contribution plan in exchange for that service. The receipt of service is thus matched against the amount of contribution paid by the entity in respect of the service. This is the simplest scheme to deal with.

Example 12.A

C operates a defined contribution scheme for all eligible employees. Under the terms of the scheme, C pays 5% of gross salary into the scheme. The payroll cost for the month of October was $450,000.

The pension cost of $22,500 ($450,000 × 5%) will be recorded and paid over to the pension fund. It will normally be included in employee costs in the income statement.

Recorded as:

Dr	Employee costs – pensions	$22,500
Cr	Bank/pension fund liability	$22,500

Being pension costs for October (bank or creditor depending on date it is paid over).

12.3.2 Defined benefit plans

In a typical (funded) defined benefit scheme cash is paid into the scheme's fund by employees themselves, or on their behalf by employers, or both. The assets of the scheme are managed separately from the employer entity, and are invested to produce returns which enhance the value of the fund. The value of the fund is reduced when benefits are paid out. Defined benefit schemes carry the risk that the assets in the scheme will not be sufficient to pay out all the future benefits to employees that are committed under the rules of the scheme. In such cases meeting any shortfall depends upon the resources of the employer entity. As IAS 19 points out: 'the entity is, in substance, underwriting the actuarial and investment risks associated with the plan'.

Periodically, an actuarial valuation is carried out in order to estimate the amount of benefit that employees have earned in return for their service in the current and prior periods. The valuation involves actuarial assumptions about a range of variables such as mortality rates and future increases in salaries. Using such assumptions, the actuary estimates the value of the scheme liability which is then discounted to present value.

The discounted value of the scheme liabilities is compared to the value of the scheme assets, adjusted for any past service cost that may have arisen, and a total amount of actuarial gain or loss is calculated. The application of the IAS 19 rules mean that the actuarial gain or loss may or may not be recognised in the accounting period.

The next subsection of the chapter will examine the accounting in detail.

Defined benefit plan

Accounting for defined benefit plans involves the following steps:

1. Use actuarial techniques to make a reliable estimate of the amount of benefit employees have earned in return for their service in the current period.
2. Discount that benefit to determine the present value of the defined benefit obligation and the current service cost.

Example 12.B

Under the terms of a defined benefit plan, a lump-sum benefit is payable on termination of service equal to 1% of final salary for each year of service. An employee joins on 1.1.20X1 and is paid an annual salary of $10,000. This is assumed to increase at 7% compound each year until the employee leaves. The applicable discount rate is 10%. This particular employee expects to leave on 31.12.20X5. What is the current service cost for 20X3, assuming that there are no changes in actuarial assumptions?

When the employee is due to leave on 31.12.20X5 the expected salary is $\$10{,}000 \times (1.07)^4 =$ $13,108. Each year's service earns an extra lump sum of 1% of final salary so the lump-sum entitlement increases by $131 (1% × $13,108) for each year of service. The current service cost for 20X3 is found by discounting this entitlement by 2 years at the discount rate of 10%, to $108 [$\$131 \div (1.10)^2$].

---

3. The current service cost is charged as an expense in the income statement, together with an interest cost, which is the increase in the present value of liabilities recognised in previous years owing to the fact that they are 1 year closer to payment. The closing liability is then the opening liability plus the interest cost plus the current service cost plus or minus any actuarial differences (see later).

Example 12.C

At the end of 20X2 the employee in the example we are considering would have built up an entitlement to receive $262 (2 × $131) on leaving employment. This would have been shown as a liability of $196 [$\$262 \div (1.10)^3$]. The interest charge for 20 × 3 would be $20 ($196 × 0.10). Therefore the closing liability would be $196 + $20 + $108 (the current service cost for 20X3 we worked out earlier) – a total of $324. This is of course 3 years' entitlement ($131 × 3 = $393) discounted by 10% per annum to its present value at the end of 20X3.

---

4. Determine the fair value of any plan assets. These are assets held by a separate legal entity that are to be used only to settle the employee benefit obligations.
5. The expected rate of return on opening fund assets is recognised as a component of the income statement, effectively reducing the pension cost.
6. Determine the total amount of actuarial gains and losses. Actuarial gains and losses are caused by changes in the actuarial assumptions made regarding the scheme and experience surpluses or deficiencies (the effect of previous actuarial assumptions proving not to be totally accurate).

Example 12.D

The following additional data relates to the benefit plan of which the employee we have been considering is a member for 20X3:

- Present value of the total obligation and fair value of the plan assets at the start of the year = $1,000,000.
- Expected rate of return on plan assets at start of year = 12%.
- Current service cost = $130,000.
- Benefits paid to plan members $150,000.
- Contributions paid into plan $90,000.
- Present value of total obligation at the end of the year = $1,141,000.
- Fair value of plan assets at the end of the year = $1,092,000.

Using the above information we can compute the actuarial gain or loss for the year. This is done in two parts:

Gain or loss on obligation

	$'000
Present value of obligation at start of the year	1,000
Interest cost (10% × $1m 2 10% is the discount rate)	100
Current service cost	130
Benefits paid	(150)
Actuarial loss on obligation – balancing figure	61
Present value of obligation at end of the year	1,141

Gain or loss on assets

	$'000
Fair value of plan assets at start of the year	1,000
Expected return on plan assets (12% × $1m)	120
Contributions	90
Benefits paid	(150)
Actuarial gain on assets – balancing figure	32
Fair value of plan assets at end of the year	1,092

7. The actuarial gains and losses depend on the actuarial assumptions and the experience surpluses or deficiencies. They are not recognised immediately in the income statement. The only time such gains or losses are recognised in the income statement is if, at the beginning of the period, the net cumulative unrecognised gains, actuarial gains and losses exceeded 10 per cent of the greater of:
   - the present value of the obligation before deducting plan assets;
   - the fair value of any plan assets.

   The limit is referred to in the standard as 'the corridor'.

   In those circumstances any excess, divided by the average remaining working lives of the employees participating in the plan, is recognised in the income statement.

   Note, however, that a recent amendment to IAS 19 has introduced a futher option for accounting for actuarial gains and losses (see Section 15.1.3 later in this chapter).

Example 12.E

In the scenario we have been considering, suppose that the average remaining service lives of the employees in the plan is 10 years. At the start of 20X3 the net cumulative unrecognised actuarial gains were $140,000. This means that the amount of actuarial gains and losses recognised in the income statement for 20X3 will be:

- Limits of corridor is $100,000 (10% × $1m – both liability and asset are this figure at the start of the year).
- Excess is $40,000 ($140,000 – $100,000).
- The amount recognised in the income statement in 20X3 is $4,000 $\frac{\$40,000}{10}$.

- And the cumulative unrecognised actuarial gains at the end of 20X3 are $107,000 [$140,000 − $4,000 + $32,000 (gain on assets) − $61,000 (loss on obligation)].
- The corridor at the end of 20X3 is $114,100 [10% × $1,141,000 (the closing obligation)]. Therefore no actuarial gains and losses will be recognised in the income statement in 20X4.

---

8. The statement of financial position shows the net of the following amounts:
   - the present value of the defined benefit obligation;
   - *plus* any unrecognised actuarial gains minus any unrecognised actuarial losses;
   - *less* the fair value of the plan assets.

Example 12.F

In the scenario we have been considering, the net statement of financial position figure for the plan in the financial statements of the contributing entity will be:

	$'000
Present value of pension obligation	1,141
Unrecognised actuarial gains	107
Fair value of plan assets	(1,092)
Net plan liability	156

An evaluation of the IAS 19 requirements for defined benefit plans

The use of actuarial techniques to compute the three ongoing components of the charge to the income statement is a reasonable reflection of the economic exposure facing the contributing companies. However, the treatment of actuarial gains and losses lacks conceptual validity in that it required unrecognised gains to be recognised as residuals in the statement of financial position. Some countries (e.g., the UK) have moved in the direction of immediate recognition of actuarial differences. The IASB intends to undertake a major project on accounting for post-retirement benefits, and it is likely that international accounting practice in this area will be substantially revised. In the meantime, the IASB issued an amendment to IAS 19 in December 2004. An important aspect of this amendment is examined below.

12.4 Amendment to IAS 19 – December 2004

The amendment to IAS 19 published in December 2004 is entitled 'Actuarial gains and losses, group plans and disclosures'. This section of the Learning System will focus upon the amendment to the permitted treatments of actuarial gains and losses. This basis for the conclusions on the amendment observes that actuarial gains and losses are economic events of the period in which they occur. Consequently, the original IAS 19 recommended treatment of such gains and losses (set out in the previous section) is inappropriate in permitting recognition to be deferred or to be spread over several accounting periods. The amendment therefore permits entities to opt for an accounting policy that recognises these gains and losses immediately. Rather than recognising them in the income statement, the amended standard requires that they should be recognised in a statement of changes in equity.

Now with the introduction of the statement of comprehensive income, the gains or losses would be reported within other comprehensive income in the year.

The purpose of recognising and reporting such gains and losses outside the income statement is to protect reported profits from the potentially volatile effects of some very significant items.

In its basis for conclusions, the IASB deals with some of the principal arguments against this amendment. It takes the view that, pending a thorough revision of the standard, which will obviously take some time, it is better to offer an option that allows for more transparent information than that provided by deferred recognition. Also, a drawback of the deferred recognition approach is that it requires recognition of a debit item (where actuarial losses exist) or a credit item (in respect of gains) that do not fulfil the definitions of an asset or a liability.

Some of the principal criticisms of the IASB's approach in respect of this amendment are as follows:

1. It is inherently undesirable to extend the range of options available in an accounting standard. Much of the IASB's improvement project has had the opposite objective of restricting the range of options available. The availability of options impedes comparability.
2. The amendment requires recognition in a separate 'statement of recognised income and expense', requiring an amendment to IAS 1. This may be seen as prejudging issues that should, ideally, be resolved as part of the project on comprehensive income reporting.
3. Conceptually, if such gains and losses are to be recognised, recognition should be within the income statement.
4. This approach diverges from US GAAP, and so runs counter to the prevailing trend of convergence of US and international practice.

However, it should be noted that this potentially very significant amendment to accounting practice is, currently, optional. Entities can, and probably in many cases will, continue with their existing accounting policy. The entities most likely to utilise the amendment are those UK listed entities that have already altered their accounting for post-retirement benefits in accordance with the UK standard FRS 17 (which requires immediate recognition of actuarial gains and losses).

12.5 IFRS 2 *Share-based payment*

Share option schemes are frequently used as a means of rewarding employees. They may also be used as a means of buying-in goods or services from parties outside the entity. Such schemes can become very complicated, especially if the options are dependent in some way on entity or employee performance.

In some cases, share schemes of various types are used as a means of replacing substantial parts of remuneration in the form of regular salary, or indeed as a complete substitute for remuneration. In the case of risky business start-ups (particularly in high-tech industries) employees may agree to work for little or nothing, being rewarded instead either by shares in the entity at start-up (at which point the shares are likely to be worth little or nothing) or by options to purchase shares at a minimal price at some future date. Employees in such cases voluntarily take on a risk, in the hope of material reward in future. The advantage to the start-up entity is obvious: it obtains the advantages of highly skilled labour without having to pay for it. If the business fails, the value of the stock or options will never materialise and the employees bear the opportunity cost of their services which, in the event, have been supplied for no return. If the business prospers the shares gain in value, the options are exercised, and, in some cases, the employees gain huge rewards for the risk they have run.

A simple example, set in the context of an established business, will illustrate the issue.

Example 12.G

Entity A, a listed entity, rewards its senior employees from time to time by granting share options. On 1 January 20X3 it grants each member of a group of senior employees an option on 10,000 shares, at an exercise price of the market value of the shares on 1 January 20X3 ($3.50), the option to be exercised no earlier than 1 January 20X6.

Three years later, on 1 January 20X6 the market value of one share is $4.50. Senior employee B decides to exercise the option. He pays A $35,000 (10,000 shares at $3.50) and receives 10,000 shares in exchange. Employee B has thus gained a benefit with a current value at 1 January 20X6 of $10,000 (current value of shares $4.50 × 10,000 = $45,000 less the $35,000 just paid). Whether or not B chooses to realise his gain immediately by selling the shares at $4.50 each is entirely up to him; henceforth, for as long as he owns the shares, he bears all of the risks and rewards of ownership, just like any other equity shareholder in a listed company.

Accounting for this transaction appears straightforward: $10,000 to be credited to share capital, being the nominal value of shares issued; $25,000 to share premium account; a debit of $35,000 to cash for the amount received from the employee. However, beyond these simple entries there is the question of the $10,000 benefit to the employee, which can be viewed as representing delayed remuneration for his services over the 3-year period. Applying the accruals concept, remuneration should be matched against the revenue which the services of the employee have helped to create. So, in this case, should there not be an additional debit of $10,000 to the income statement over the 3 years in order to reflect the cost of these services? The arguments for and against its inclusion are as follows.

For

- The $10,000 represents remuneration and so should be properly reflected as an expense; the means by which the remuneration is paid is irrelevant.
- If the entity does not fully reflect remuneration for services to employees the performance statement will be incomplete, and users will neither be able to properly assess the stewardship of management nor to make fully informed economic decisions.
- If costs of employment are fully reflected in some entities (because they are paid via regular salaries) and not in others (because rewards are wholly or partly in shares or share options) then the performance statements between companies will not be comparable. (*Remember*: comparability is one of the four key qualitative characteristics of financial statements identified by the IASC in its *Framework*.)

Against

- The $10,000 does not represent an outflow of economic benefits from the entity. The gain arises because of the entity's share price performance, and is receivable by the employee independently of any action by the entity.
- The $10,000 does not represent an expense within the terms employed by the conceptual framework. Losses (which include expenses) 'are decreases in ownership interest not resulting from distributions to owners'. The $10,000 is not a decrease in ownership interest.
- If $10,000 is debited to the entity's income statement, what should happen to the related credit? It is doubtful whether it fulfils the characteristics of either a liability or ownership interest.

12.6 Accounting for share-based payments

12.6.1 Types of share-based payments

The IASB intends that the IFRS should be applied to all share-based payment transactions, and it identifies three principal types:

1. Equity-settled share-based payment transactions. This category would include the transaction in Example 12.G.
2. Cash-settled share-based payment transactions. This is where the provider of services or goods (i.e., in most cases the employee) is rewarded in cash, but the cash value is based upon the price of the entity's shares or other equity instruments.
3. Transactions where one of the parties involved can choose whether the provider of services or goods is rewarded in cash (value based on equity prices) or in shares.

The underlying assumption of the IFRS is that the issue of share options and grants of shares to employees and others creates a financial instrument which must be accounted for.

12.6.2 Recognition of share-based payments

Where payment for goods and services is in the form of shares or share options the transaction should be recognised in the financial statements. There should be a charge to the income statement when the goods or services are consumed. Where the payment is equity-settled (type 1 above) the corresponding credit should be to equity. Where the payment is cash-settled (type 2 above) the corresponding credit should be to liabilities.

12.6.3 Measurement

The transaction should be measured at the fair value of the shares or options issued. Measurement can be *direct*, that is, at the fair value of the goods or services received, or *indirect*, that is, by reference to the fair value of the equity instruments granted. In this latter case, fair value should be measured at the date of grant.

Equity-settled transactions

For equity-settled transactions it is likely that the fair value of the shares will be more easily measured and so the share price of the shares is used to measure the transaction. The fair value used should be the **price at the grant date**.

If the equity instruments **vest immediately** (employees are entitled to the shares immediately and without condition) then it is presumed that the entity has already received the benefit of the services and the full amount is recognised on the grant date.

Example 12.H

GH granted 100 share options to all employees who had been with the entity for the last 12 months. The options had a value of $2.50 at the grant date. 200 employees were eligible.

The share options have been granted in respect of prior services provided by employees. No further conditions must be met and so the full amount will be recorded as an employee cost. The fair value of the service provided cannot be reliably measured, however the fair value of the options granted represents the equivalent value. It is an equity settled transaction so the credit will be to equity (other reserves is probably most appropriate).

Recorded as:

Dr	Staff costs (100 × $2.50 × 200)	$50,000
Cr	Other reserves	$50,000

Being the recording of the equity-settled share-based transaction

If the equity instruments do not vest immediately the company should assume the benefits received will accrue over the vesting period.

Example 12.I

B grants share options to its 1,000 employees in the year to December 20X6. Each employee is entitled to 300 options if they stay employed with B for the next 3 years. At the grant date the options have an estimated value of $2.50.

At the end of 20X6 60 staff had left and another 80 were expected to leave over the next two years.

At the end of 20X7 50 staff had left in the year and another 40 were expected to leave in 20X8.

20 staff left in 20X8.

Let us look at how the associated staff costs would be reflected in the financial statements over the vesting period of 3 years. No estimate is given regarding the fair value of the services provided so we assume the equivalent cost can be based on the fair value of the equity transferred (based on the value at the grant date).

20X6 – estimated eligible employees = 860 (1,000 − 60 − 80)
Total equivalent cost of issuing options = ($2.50 × 860 employees × 300 options) = $645,000
Allocated over the vesting period of 3 years gives a charge of $215,000 ($645,000/3)
Recorded as:

Dr	Staff costs	$215,000
Cr	Other reserves	$215,000

Being the recording of the equity based transaction for 20X6.

20X7 – estimated eligible employees = 850 (1,000 − 60 − 50 − 40)
Total equivalent cost of issuing options = ($2.50 × 850 employees × 300 options) = $637,500.
We want to have recognised two-thirds of this by the end of 20X7 = 425,000
Less the amount recognised in 20X6 = $210,000 ($425,000 − $215,000)
Recorded as:

Dr	Staff costs	$210,000
Cr	Other reserves	$210,000

Being the recording of the equity based transaction for 20X7.

The balance on other reserves is now $425,000.

20X8 – estimated eligible employees = 870 (1,000 − 60 − 50 − 20)
Total equivalent cost of issuing options = ($2.50 × 870 employees × 300 options) = $652,500.
Less the amount recognised over the previous two years = $227,500 ($652,500 − $425,000)
Recorded as:

Dr	Staff costs	$227,500
Cr	Other reserves	$227,500

Being the recording of the equity based transaction for 20X8.

The balance on other reserves is now $652,500.

Cash-settled transactions

Cash-settled equity-based transactions are those where the amount of the goods or services is based on the value of the entity's shares, but the amount is to be paid in cash. The debit is to income statement if for goods/services and the credit is to cash is settled immediately or to liabilities if it is settled at a future date.

As the liability varies with the value of the company's shares it should be remeasured at each statement of financial position date until the date of settlement, with any change going to the income statement.

Example 12.J

100 eligible staff members are entitled to receive payment equivalent to 60% of the increase in value of 1,000 of the entity's shares. During the year to 31 December 20X8 the share price increased from 250 cents to 340 cents. Payment is made on 31 January 20X9.

The amount payable is $54,000 (100 × 1,000 shares × 60% × 0.90) will appear within staff costs and a liability will be shown for the amount due and not yet settled, Recorded as:

Dr	Staff costs	$54,000
Cr	Liability	$54,000

Being the cash-settled transaction.

If the rights to a cash-settled amount vest over a period of time then the cost will be allocated over the vesting period, in a similar way to equity-based transactions. The liability however will be remeasured based on the fair value at the reporting date (as opposed to equity-settled transactions which use the fair value at the grant date and do not remeasure).

Example 12.K

G grants 100 share appreciation rights (SARs) to its 500 employees during 20X7 on the condition that the employees stay with the entity for the next two years. The SARs must be exercised at the start of 20X9.

During 20X7 15 staff leave and another 20 are expected to leave in 20X8.

During 20X8 25 staff leave.

The fair value of the SARs is $10 at 31 December 20X7 and $13 at 31 December 20X8.

The employee cost will be charged over the vesting period of two years. However as this is a cash-settled transaction the liability will be credited and it will be remeasured based on revised fair values until the date of settlement.

20X7 – estimated eligible employees = 465 (500 − 15 − 20)
Total equivalent cost of issuing options = ($10 × 465 employees × 100 SARs) = $465,000.
Allocated over the vesting period of 2 years gives a charge of $232,500 ($465,000/2)
Recorded as:

Dr	Staff costs	$232,500
Cr	Liability	$232,500

Being the recording of the cash-settled transaction for 20X7.

20X8 – estimated eligible employees = 460 (500 − 15 − 25)
Total equivalent cost of issuing options = ($13 × 460 employees × 100 SARs) = $598,000.
Less the amount recognised in 20X7 of $365,500 ($598,000 − $232,500)
Recorded as:

Dr	Staff costs	$365,500
Cr	Liability	$365,500

Being the recording of the cash-settled transaction for 20X8.

12.7 Summary

This chapter looked at the recognition and valuation principles of corporate pension schemes. The accounting treatment adopted for defined contribution schemes and defined benefit schemes, in accordance with IAS 19 *Employee benefits*, was covered, including the calculation and treatment of actuarial gains and losses. Share-based payments were also coverd and the principles laid out in IFRS 2 *Share-based payment* were applied. The treatment of equity-settled and cash-settled transactions were covered.

Revision Questions

Question 1

You are the financial controller of C, a entity which has recently established a pension scheme for its employees. It chose a defined benefit scheme rather than a defined contribution scheme.

C makes payments into the pension scheme on a monthly basis.

C prepare financial statements to 31 December each year.

On 31 December 20X4 the market value of the scheme's assets was $20 million and the present value of the scheme's liability $22 million. Actuarial losses not yet recognised in the income statement amounted to $1.5 million. In 20X5 the following data is relevant:

- current service cost: $2 million,
- unwinding of discount: $1.8 million,
- expected return on pension plan assets: $2.4 million,
- contributions for the year: $1.7 million.

On 31 December 20X5 the market value of the scheme's assets was $21 million and the present value of the scheme's liability $22.5 million.

C's accounting policy is to defer actuarial gains and losses to future periods so far as is permissible under the requirements of IAS 19.

Requirement

Determine the total charge in the income statement for pensions (excluding amounts deducted from employees' gross salaries) and the amounts shown in the statement of financial position in respect of pensions.

Ignore deferred taxation. **(10 marks)**

Question 2

CBA is a listed entity that runs a defined benefit pension scheme on behalf of its employees. In the financial year ended 30 September 20X6 the scheme suffered an actuarial loss of $7.2 million. The entity's directors are aware that the relevant accounting standard, IAS 19 *Employee benefits*, was amended recently. They have asked you, the financial controller, to write a short briefing paper, setting out an outline of the options for accounting for the actuarial loss in accordance with the amended version of the standard.

Requirement

Prepare the briefing paper explaining the options and identifying, as far as possible from the information given, the potential impact on the financial statements of CBA of the two alternative accounting treatments.

(10 marks)

Question 3

On 1 April 20X7, the present value of AB's pension obligation is $1,634,000. The fair value of the pension plan assets is $1,337,000. Unrecognised actuarial losses are $224,000 as at 31 March 20X7. During the year to 31 March 20X8 the current cost if $450,000 and the contributions made totalled $520,000. The expected rate of return on assets was 10% and the interest cost was based on a rate of interest of 12%. The estimated remaining service lives of employees is 10 years. Round figures to the nearest $000.

(a) Calculate the income statement charge in respect of pensions for AB for the year ended 31 March 20X8, assuming that AB adopts the corridor approach under IAS 19.

(6 marks)

(b) Briefly outline the alternative treatment permitted by IAS 19 in respect of actuarial gains and losses and show the extracts from the statement of comprehensive income of AB for the year ended 31 March 20X8, assuming the actuarial loss on pension assets in the year was $85,000 and the actuarial gain on pension obligations was $55,000.

(4 marks)

(Total marks = 10)

Question 4

The following information relates to two share-based transactions that LM entered into in 2006.

(i) LM granted share options to its 200 employees on 1 January 20X6. Each employee will receive 500 share options if they continue to work for LM for the next three years. The fair value of the options at the grant date was $2.00 each.

(ii) LM operates an incentive scheme for its employees which it set up during 2006. under the terms of the scheme the workforce will be offered 80% of the share price increase on 10,000 of the entity's shares. Payment will be made on 31 March 2009. Again the scheme is only open to those who remain employed with LM for the three year period. The fair value of the SARs at the end of each of the three years is:

20X6 – $1.60
20X7 – $1.80
20X8 – $2.10

During 20X6 20 employees left and another 45 were expected to leave over the next two years.

During 20X7 15 employees left and another 20 were expected to leave in 20X8.

During 20X8 10 employees left.

Requirement

Briefly describe the accounting treatment to be adopted for these transactions, in accordance with IFRS 2 *Share-based payment* and calculate the amount to be recorded in the income statement for staff costs in respect of each of the three years.

(10 marks)

Solutions to Revision Questions

Solution 1

The charge to the income statement for 20X5 will be:

	$'000	$'000
Ongoing service cost		2,000
Unwinding of the discount	1,800	
Expected return on pension assets	(2,400)	
		(600)
Net charge to statement		1,400

The 'corridor' for recognition of actuarial losses from prior years is the greater of:

- 10% of the opening market value of the scheme's assets: $20m × 10% = $2m.
- 10% of the opening present value of the scheme's liabilities: $22m × 10% = $2.2m.

It is clear that the unrecognised actuarial losses are less than $2.2 million, so no recognition is appropriate for the current year.

The statement of financial position figures for the end of 20X5 will be:

	$'000	$'000
Market value of plan assets	21,000	
Present value of plan liability	(22,000)	
		(1,000)
Actuarial differences not yet taken to the income statement (see below)		300
So net liability		(700)

Working: *Actuarial differences*

	$'000
Net difference brought forward ($20m–$22m)	(2,000)
Net charge to income statement for the year (see above)	(1,400)
Contributions for the year	1,700
Actuarial difference for the year – to balance	200
Net difference carried forward ($21m–$22.5m)	(1,500)

This means that the end unrecognised actuarial losses at the end of the year are $300,000 ($500,000 − $200,000).

Solution 2

The amended version of IAS 19 permits two possible approaches in accounting for actuarial gains and losses:

1. The first option is the accounting treatment that was required by the original IAS 19. Actuarial gains and losses are not recognised immediately in the income statement except where they exceed certain parameters. Where the parameters in the standard are met, the gain or loss is recognised over the average remaining service lives of the employees. This may be a fairly lengthy period (for example, 10 or 15 years would not be unusual), so, even if the actuarial loss of $7.2 million were to exceed the parameters, the impact on the financial statements is likely to be very small.

   Where this option requires part of the loss to be recognised, it is recognised in the income statement, and so has a direct effect upon reported profit.
2. The standard permits entities to adopt any systematic method that results in faster recognition of actuarial gains and loss than stipulated in the first approach, provided that the same basis is applied to both gains and losses, and that the basis is applied consistently. Thus, entities are able to opt for a policy of recognising the whole of any actuarial gains or losses in the accounting period in which they occur. In CBA's case this would mean recognising the full amount of the $7.2 million loss in the financial year ended 30 September 20X6. In such cases (where actuarial gains and losses are recognised in full as they are incurred), the standard requires that such gains and losses should be recognised in a 'Other Comprehensive Income', within the statement of comprehensive income.

Solution 3

(a) income statement expense for pensions is calculated as follows:

Pension costs	$000
Current service cost	450
Expected return (10% × $1,337,000)	(134)
Interest cost (12% × $1,234,000)	148
Actuarial losses recognised in the period (W1)	9
Income statement expense	473

Working 1

Actuarial losses to be recognised:

Corridor – 10% of the higher or opening plan assets and liabilities = opening liabilities, 10% × $1,337,000 = 133K. Unrecognised actuarial losses brought forward are $224K. The difference of $90,000 will be spread over the remaining service lives of 10 years giving a charge of $9,000 per annum.

(b) IAS 19 permits the actuarial gains/losses to be recognised faster than is achieved using the corridor approach, however to minimise the effect on reported profits the entire gains and losses are recognised in equity and shown in other comprehensive income.

Extracts from statement of comprehensive income for the year end 31 March 20X8.

Income statement

	$000
Staff costs	
Pension cost (as per (a) but without the actuarial loss)	(464)

Other comprehensive income

Actuarial gain on pension obligations	55
Actuarial loss on pension assets	(85)

Solution 4

Transaction (i)

This is an equity-settled share-based payment and under IFRS 2 the fair value of the shares will be used to estimate the fair value of the services provided by employees. The total fair value will be allocated over the vesting period of three years and will be based on the fair value at the grant date and will not be remeasured for subsequent changes in the value of the options. The income statement will be charged and equity will be credited in each of the three years of the vesting period.

20X6 – 500 options × $2 per share × (200 − 20 − 45) = $135,000
The charge for 20X6 is then $135,000/3 = $45,000

20X7 – 500 options × $2 per share × (200 − 20 − 15 − 20) = $145,000
Two-thirds of $145,000 should be recognised to date = $96,667
Less the amount already recognised in 20X6 of $45,000, results in a charge in 20X7 of $51,667.

20X8 – 500 options × $2 per share × (200 − 20 − 15 − 10) = $155,000
Less cumulative total recognised to date of $96,667, results in a charge of $58,333 in 20X8.

Transaction (ii)

This is a cash-settled equity-based transaction. The cost to the income statement will be calculated in a similar way but will take account of the change in the fair value of the SARs. The income statement will be charged with the equivalent expense but as this is cash settled, the credit will be to liability in the statement of financial position.

20X6 – 80% × 10,000 × $1.60 × (200 − 20 − 45) = $1,728,000. Allocated over vesting period of three years:
The charge for 20X6 is then $576,000.

20X7 – 80% × 10,000 × $1.80 × (200 − 20 − 15 − 20) = $2,088,000
Two-thirds of $2,088,000 should be recognised to date = $1,392,000
Less the amount already recognized in 20X6 of $576,000, results in a charge in 20X7 of $816,000.

20X8 – 80% × 10,000 × $2.10 × (200 − 20 − 15 − 10) = $2,604,000
Less cumulative total recognised to date of $1,392,000, results in a charge of $1,212,000 in 20X8.

Financial Reporting in an Environment of Price Changes

Financial Reporting in an Environment of Price Changes

13

LEARNING OUTCOMES

After studying this chapter students should be able to:

- discuss the problems of profit measurement and alternative approaches to asset valuations;
- discuss measures to reduce distortion in financial statements when price levels change.

13.1 Introduction

Historical cost accounting, which has been the accounting system adopted traditionally in the preparation of financial statements, suffers from some significant defects that are especially pronounced in times of changing prices. Where the historical cost system proves to be unsatisfactory, any one of a range of alternative systems could be adopted. This chapter examines some of the alternatives.

This chapter covers the following areas: Section 13.2 examines the defects of the historical cost accounting system. Section 13.3 examines accounting for changing price levels using replacement cost accounting, net realisable value accounting, current cost accounting, current purchasing power accounting and the 'real terms' system of accounting. Section 13.4 addresses the problems of financial reporting in hyperinflationary economies, and the requirements of IAS 29 *Financial Reporting in Hyperinflationary Economies.*

13.2 Defects of historical cost accounting

Historical cost accounting is based upon records of transactions. Transactions such as sales and purchases are recorded at the monetary amount at which goods or services change hands. Once recorded at that amount in the books of the entity, the value remains fixed. Because of these fixed values, historical cost accounting is said to be objective, and up to a point that is true. However, accounting is a process by which raw transaction data is translated into useful and informative statements, a process which, as we have seen, involves often substantial judgement-based adjustments like provisions.

Nevertheless, historical cost accounting has some claim to objectivity. However, it also has significant defects, especially in times of changing prices. Some of these defects are explained below.

- In a time of changing prices reported results in the income statement may be distorted as revenues at current values are matched with costs incurred at an earlier date.
- Cost of sales is likely to be understated in a time of price inflation.
- The valuation of assets in the statement of financial position is at cost *less* accumulated depreciation. The resultant net book values may bear no relationship to the current value of the asset.
- The three points listed above are likely to give rise to faulty estimates of return on capital employed (ROCE). Typically, in a time of rising prices, profits are likely to be overstated and assets understated, relative to current values, thus giving rise to unrealistically rosy measurements of ROCE (see Chapter 14 of this *Learning System* for more information about the calculation of ROCE and other accounting ratios).
- The results of comparison of performance and position statements over time will be unreliable, because amounts are not valued in terms of common units. For example, a business reports revenues of $3 million in 20X5. In 20X0 it reported $2.8 million. The apparent increase of $0.2 million may be more than outweighed by inflationary effects. Even if price inflation has been as low as 3 per cent per annum, once that effect is adjusted it can be seen that revenues in 20X5 are actually lower in real terms than revenues reported in 20X0.
- Borrowings are shown in monetary terms, but in a time of rising prices a gain is actually made (or a loss in times of falling prices) at the expense of the lender as, in real terms, the value of the loan has decreased (in a time of rising prices) or increased (in a time of falling prices).
- Conversely, gains arising from holding assets are not recognised.
- Depreciation writes off the historical cost over time, but, where asset values are low (because based on outdated historical costs), depreciation will be correspondingly lower, so that a realistic charge for asset consumption is not matched against revenue in the performance statements.

These defects result in significant inadequacies in financial statements based on historical cost information for both decision-making and assessment of stewardship. The IASB's *Framework* sets out the objective of financial statements:

> To provide information about the financial position, performance and changes in financial position of an entity that is useful to a wide range of users in making economic decisions.

Historical cost accounting produces statements which are unreliable guides for decision-making, and thus fail to achieve the key qualitative characteristic of relevance.

Inflation is an economic factor of varying importance around the world. During much of the latter part of the twentieth century, most countries in South America experienced very high levels of price inflation. For this reason, accounting for changing price levels has been adopted in various forms in several South American countries, including Brazil and Argentina. During the 1970s, relatively high levels of price inflation were experienced in a number of countries where it had not previously been an important issue. The accountancy professions in the UK, Australia and New Zealand, for example, responded to the problem of inflation by experimenting with the introduction of requirements for price-level adjustments to financial statements. These requirements proved to be almost universally unpopular with business and with accountancy practitioners (although adjustments for changing price levels found favour in some parts of the public sector). The dissent which met attempts by professional bodies in those countries to require reports adjusted for changing price levels was at its height during the early 1980s. This dissent coincided with a reduction in the rate of price-level increases, and by the mid-1980s inflation was no longer the pressing issue that it had been. Mandatory requirements were dropped in favour of, at most, recommended compliance.

The development of international standards on price-level adjustments reflects the pattern of events in the UK, Australia and New Zealand.

The IASC published IAS 6 *Accounting responses to changing prices* in 1977. This standard required entities to present information in their financial statements which described the procedures adopted to reflect the impact of price changes. Where no such procedures were adopted, the entity was required to disclose that fact. The requirements of this standard could not be regarded as onerous, but it was to be replaced by a much more rigorous set of requirements. In 1981, the IASC replaced IAS 6 with IAS 15 *Information reflecting the effects of changing prices*. The standard required a minimum set of disclosures relating to the effects of changing prices for those entities 'whose levels of revenues, profit, assets or employment are significant in the economic environment in which they operate'.

In 1989 the IASC added the following statement to IAS 15:

> The international consensus on the disclosure of information reflecting the effects of changing prices that was anticipated when IAS 15 was issued has not been reached. As a result, the Board of IASC has decided that entities need not disclose the information required by IAS 15 in order that their financial statements conform with International Accounting Standards. However, the Board encourages entities to present such information, and urges those that do to disclose the items required by IAS 15.

IAS 15 was withdrawn in 2003.

The IASB *Framework* document includes a section on 'Concepts of capital and capital maintenance'. It describes two concepts: physical capital maintenance and financial capital maintenance. These are described in detail in the remainder of this chapter.

13.3 Accounting for changing price levels

An important part of the advanced study of accounting and reporting issues is that students should acquire an understanding of the issues and key principles involved in accounting for changing price levels.

In this section we will examine:

- capital and income
- replacement cost (entry value) accounting
- net realisable value (exit value) accounting
- current cost accounting
- current purchasing power accounting
- the 'real terms' system.

13.3.1 Capital and income

The accounting equation represents the relationship between assets, liabilities and capital:

π Assets − Liabilities = Capital

The equation simplifies down to three items the constituents of a statement of financial position, which is prepared periodically, in order to disclose the position of the entity to interested parties. Measurement of assets and liabilities may be problematical. Where 'mixed measurement' or historical cost measurement is adopted the statement of financial position total is highly unlikely to represent a market value for capital. Indeed, the users of the financial statements may be understandably confused by the figure shown for capital. However, the various users are likely to be interested in, at a minimum, maintaining the capital at the previous year's level. Investors and potential investors need to know that their investment has not suffered a major diminution in value as represented by the statement of financial position; creditors are interested in ensuring that there is sufficient asset backing to ensure that their repayment will proceed according to plan.

Conventionally, income is calculated via the income statement; costs are set against revenues and a surplus or deficit emerges. After distribution the surplus or deficit is added to/set against capital in the statement of financial position.

So far in this section we have examined the conventional accountant's view of income and capital. Another way of looking at income and capital is from an economist's viewpoint. Hicks, the economist, defined **income** thus in 1946:

> The purpose of income calculations in practical affairs is to give people an indication of the amount they can consume without impoverishing themselves . . . it would seem that we ought to define a man's income as the maximum value which he can consume during a week, and still expect to be as well off at the end of the week as he was at the beginning.

Applying the 'well-offness' idea to business, the maximum income of a business entity in an accounting period is the amount of the maximum distribution which can be made while ensuring that capital at the end of the period is at least what it was at the beginning. Any distribution in excess of that sum would impoverish the business. This seems fair enough, except that in times of price changes it may be very difficult to ensure that 'well-offness' in a business is the same at the end of a period as at the beginning.

An example will illustrate the effects of changing prices on capital maintenance.

Example 13.A

Entity B starts up in business at 1 January 20X2 with capital, in the form of cash, of $5,000. It spends the whole of the cash immediately on stock which it sells on 31 December for $7,000. No other transactions took place and no expenses were incurred. During the year the retail price index moves from 120 to 140. What is the maximum amount that B can distribute for 20X2 and still remain as well off at the end of the year as at the beginning?

In historical cost accounting terms, the calculation is simple: $7,000 of revenue less $5,000 in cost of sales gives a profit of $2,000. If the maximum $2,000 is distributed to the owners of B, the capital at the end of the year will remain at $5,000, that is exactly the same as it was at the beginning. However, this does not take into account the diminishing real value of money. In order to ensure that the business is as well off in real terms at the end of the year as it was at the beginning, some allowance must be made for the diminution in value of money.

In order to retain the same amount of purchasing power B will require:

$$\$5,000 \times \frac{140}{120} = \$5,833$$

Therefore, looked at in real terms, the maximum amount of the distribution becomes: $7,000 − $5,833 = $1,167, a figure which is substantially less than the $2,000 which would have been available for distribution in historical cost accounting terms.

This example illustrates the danger, in times of rising prices, of making distributions, effectively, out of capital. Over time, the capital of the business entity could be diminished in real terms, but that fact would not be evident from the historical cost accounts.

Capital maintenance, as we noted earlier, is important to users, and, as we have seen, may be difficult to achieve using historical cost accounting in times of changing prices. Formal definitions are given for different types of capital maintenance in CIMA's *Management Accounting: Official Terminology.*

Maintenance of physical capital (i.e., of the operating assets of the business) is defined as:

> The concept that profit is earned only if the physical productive capacity (or operating capability) of the entity (or the resources or funds needed to achieve that capacity) at the end of the period exceeds the physical productive capacity at the beginning of the period, after excluding any distributions to, and contributions from, owners during the period.

Maintenance of financial capital is defined as:

> The concept that profit is earned only if the financial (or money) amount of the net assets at the end of the period exceeds the financial (or money) amount of net assets at the beginning of the period, after excluding any distributions to, and contributions from, owners during the period.

Maintenance of financial capital can be further broken down into 'money financial capital maintenance' and 'real financial capital maintenance'. The former relates to maintaining capital at a value related to historical cost and the latter to capital adjusted for the effects of changing price levels (as in the example above).

Maintenance of operating capital involves ensuring that the business is in no worse position in terms of physical productive capacity at the end of an accounting period than it was at the beginning. Again, an example may assist understanding:

Example 13.B

Entity C starts up in business at 1 January 20X3 with 100 units of inventory which have cost $50 each. The opening inventory valuation is therefore $5,000 represented by capital employed of the same amount. The inventory is sold on the last day of the year for $7,000. At this date it will cost $5,600 to buy in a further 100 identical items of inventory because the price has gone up. What is the maximum amount that C can distribute for 20X2 and still remain as well off at the end of the year as at the beginning?

As in Example 13.A, using historical cost accounting the maximum distribution is $2,000. However, if 'well-offness' in C's case were to be defined in terms of operating capital maintenance, then the entity must ensure that it can operate at the same level. In order to do this it must retain $5,600 to buy 100 units of inventory. The maximum amount of the distribution is therefore $7,000 − $5,600 = $1,400.

13.3.2 Replacement cost (entry value) accounting

We noted earlier that replacement cost may be applied to asset measurement. **Replacement cost** is defined by CIMA's *Official Terminology* as follows:

The price at which identical goods or capital equipment could be purchased at the date of valuation.

Applied to a full set of accounts, in times of rising prices, replacement cost accounting will tend to result in higher asset values than under the historical cost system, and therefore in revaluation surpluses, also known as holding gains.

Example 13.C

Compare the statement of financial positions of K under the historical cost (HC) and replacement cost (RC) conventions.

	HC 20X2 $	*HC* 20X2 $
Non-current assets		
Cost	10,000	14,000
Depreciation	5,000	7,000
	5,000	7,000
Inventories	9,000	10,000
Cash	25,000	25,000
Net assets	39,000	42,000
Opening capital	10,000	10,000
Profit for the period	29,000	32,000
Closing capital	39,000	42,000

It looks at this stage as though profits are higher under the replacement cost method than the historical cost profits. The following reconciliation from historical cost profit to replacement cost profit explains the difference.

	$
Historical cost profit for the period	29,000
Less: extra depreciation required under RC due to the replacement cost of non-current assets	(2,000)
Replacement cost operating profit	27,000
Gain on holding inventories	1,000
Gain on holding non-current assets	4,000
Replacement cost profit for the period	32,000

The gains in value from holding the assets while the replacement cost is increasing (holding gains) must be recognised in the replacement cost profit. The holding gains on inventories are reversed in the next accounting period as the inventories are sold.

Note that the operating profit is lower under the replacement cost convention than under the historical cost convention.

Net current replacement cost

For items of non-current assets the net current replacement cost may be used. It is based on the gross replacement cost, being the replacement cost of the asset as new and the proportion of that asset deemed to be used up.

For example, an asset has a gross current replacement cost, before depreciation, of $40,000 as at 31 December 20X1 and it is assessed to have a 5-year life with nil scrap value. It has been in use for 2 years.

The net current replacement cost will be as follows:

	$
Gross current replacement cost	40,000
Less: accumulated depreciation – 2 years	(16,000)
Net current replacement cost	24,000

Gross replacement cost is usually found using a price index specific to the asset.

Backlog depreciation

The net replacement cost is arrived at after deducting accumulated depreciation on the replacement cost value of the asset. As time passes and replacement cost increases (assuming rising prices) the value of the accumulated depreciation will become out of date and it will also require revaluation to the current replacement value. As Example 13.D shows, where there is an increase in the gross replacement cost of $2,000, to arrive at the correct net replacement cost this increase should be depreciated and netted against the gain.

Example 13.D

An asset with an estimated useful life of 5 years and nil estimated residual value is purchased on 1 January 20X1.

	$
Current cost at 31 December 20X1	10,000
Depreciation for year (5 years, straight line)	2,000
Net replacement cost	8,000
Current cost of same asset at 31 December 20X2	12,000
Depreciation (two years of five, straight line)	4,800
Net replacement cost	7,200
Increase in gross replacement cost: (12,000 – 10,000)	2,000
Less: backlog depreciation: (4,800 – 4,000)	800
Net surplus on revaluation	1,200

An appraisal of replacement cost

Replacement cost accounting, by separating holding gains from operating profits, gives a more meaningful definition of income for the business. The amount that can be distributed or paid in a dividend is clearly identified after providing for the replacement of assets and the continuation of the business, thereby keeping within the true spirit of the prudence concept and maintaining the operating capital of the business.

Furthermore, the statement of financial position gives more relevant information with assets shown at current values.

On the other hand, there can be several drawbacks to using this convention in the preparation of financial statements:

- The values derived for assets can be very subjective. Unlike the historical cost method where the value can be taken directly from the invoice, the replacement cost method will often be based upon estimates by reference to suppliers' lists and government statistics.
- Simply collating the information to prepare replacement cost accounts will be costly. The process may also be time-consuming.
- Assets in the business may not be replaced or a replacement may not be available due to obsolescence or other technological change.

- The basis for the use of replacement cost is to focus on maintaining the operating capital of the business. The investor group, however, is more likely to be interested in maintaining the value of capital in real terms (as affected by the general rate of inflation in the economy at large). The rates of price inflation that affect operating capital may be quite significantly different.

13.3.3 Realisable or exit values

Another way of looking at current values is from the point of view of the realisable values of assets – valuing the statement of financial position on the basis of the selling values of the assets in the business.

This method measures the value of holding the assets by the movement in their selling value from one statement of financial position to the next. Some users of the financial statements may prefer this method as the information is more relevant in that it gives a useful value for the asset – how much it can be sold for, rather than how much it cost. The method of preparing the financial statements is similar to the replacement cost method.

Example 13.E

	HC	*RV*
	20X1	*20X1*
	$	$
Non-current assets	160,000	150,000
Inventories	30,000	60,000
Net assets	190,000	210,000
Share capital	100,000	100,000
Retained profit	90,000	110,000
Shareholders' funds	190,000	210,000

If we analyse the realisable value profit more closely it will give the following results:

	$
Historical cost profit	90,000
Less: additional depreciation	10,000
Operating profits	80,000
Gain on holding inventories	30,000
Realisable value profits	110,000

The information on selling values provided by the realisable value accounts equates to market values and the cash that can be raised by the sale of the asset. This in turn can have advantages for the management of the business as the realisable value approach adopts the principles of opportunity cost, highlighting the current sacrifice of funds employed in the business and returns available elsewhere.

Other users of the financial statements, such as lenders, would find the information relevant in terms of the security of the capital they have loaned to the business. The ultimate liquidation values are the maximum amounts they will receive from the business and so they can assess directly whether their capital is maintained.

In terms of the financial statements the use of realisable values overcomes the problems of depreciation and inventory valuations. These are directly determined by the market and not by arbitrary calculations.

The realisable value method does have several limitations:

- The whole basis for the method is founded on the break-up value of the business and is contrary to the going-concern basis.
- The determination of realisable values in practice may be very difficult. There may be a high degree of subjectivity, particularly where there is a restricted market for the assets.
- In the case of specialised assets, an oil rig for example, their realisable value will be the scrap value. However, the economic value of such an asset may be substantially higher.

13.3.4 Current cost accounting

In valuing assets, current cost accounting (CCA) adopts the principle of *value to the business.* Value to the business is often expressed diagrammatically, as follows:

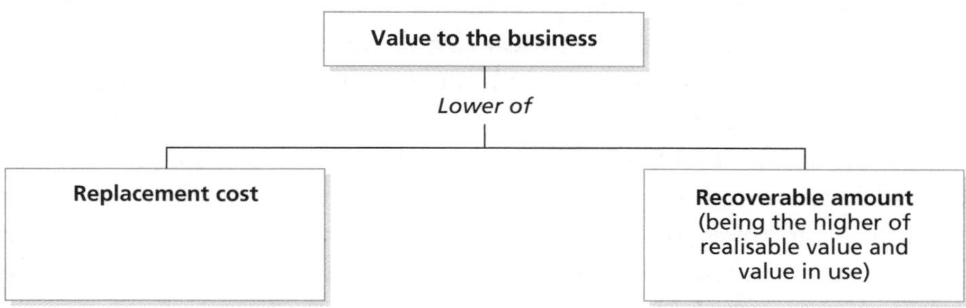

For example, suppose we have a machine that cost $10,000. If we wanted to replace the machine it would cost $12,000; alternatively we could get $11,000 by selling it, or if we keep it, it will generate cash returns discounted to net present value of $15,000. What action should be taken?

First, what are the benefits we can obtain from the machine? Selling it will produce $11,000; keeping it would produce $15,000. Therefore the decision would be to keep the machine. To relate to the diagram it is the higher of realisable value and value in use.

Second, we need to decide whether the asset would remain in the business – do we replace it? In this case we are generating $15,000 in income and costs are $12,000 to replace. Therefore we make a 'profit' by doing so of $3,000 and so the asset would be replaced.

The value to the business of the asset in this case is $12,000.

Consider another alternative: realisable value $15,000, replacement value $16,000, and keeping the asset generates $11,000.

In this case, logically, the decision would be to sell the asset. Selling the asset produces more benefits than keeping it and this in turn is lower than the replacement value so we would not replace the asset as we would make a 'loss'.

The preparation of the financial statements based on value to the business would involve identifying each individual asset and deciding what action would be taken, given the three values available: replacement cost, realisable value and economic value.

In practice replacement cost would be the most likely valuation. Most non-current assets are purchased to be kept in the business; therefore their economic value will normally be higher than the realisable value and so the assets would be replaced. Inventories are bought for resale and if we are making profits the inventories are replaced and so replacement values are again the most relevant.

A similar approach can be applied to liabilities, using the concept of 'relief value' (by contrast to 'deprival value'). Relief value is the lowest amount at which the liability could, hypothetically, be settled.

Statement of financial position assets valuations under CCA may, therefore, be a mix of net realisable values, replacement cost and value in use (economic value).

In the income statement CCA requires the disclosure of a set of four adjustments to historical cost profit:

- *The cost of sales adjustment (COSA).* This adjustment shows the value to the business of the inventories consumed during the year by updating the cost of sales; in practice, this adjustment is usually computed by reference to replacement cost. Usually, entities would use price indices prepared by national statistical services.

- *The depreciation adjustment.* The CCA depreciation charge is the value to the business of the assets consumed during the year. In practice, again, the value is usually computed by reference to replacement cost. The depreciation adjustment is the difference between the CCA depreciation charge and the historical cost depreciation charge.
- *The monetary working capital adjustment (MWCA).* This adjustment takes account of the additional investment required to maintain the monetary working capital of business, recognising that, in a time of rising prices, there may be gains arising from holding trade payables, and losses from holding monetary assets. Monetary working capital comprises trade receivables and trade payables, and the adjustment charges (or credits) the income statement with the increase (or decrease) in the real value of monetary working capital which has arisen between the beginning and the end of the financial year.
- *The gearing adjustment.* Where an entity is financed by a mixture of debt and equity capital, it may be argued that only part of the three adjustments listed above is attributable to equity holders, with the rest attributable to borrowings. The gearing adjustment apportions the total of COSA, depreciation adjustment and MWCA between equity holders and lenders in proportion to their holdings.

As noted earlier, CIMA students will not be required to apply knowledge of any of the systems of accounting for changing price levels to a numerical examination question. However, it is useful to examine some of the features of a set of CCA-adjusted financial statements in order to demonstrate how the concept works out in practice, and how the statements fit together. A simple example is given below.

Example 13.F

Entity E commences trading on 1 January 20X0. Prices are changing rapidly and the chief financial officer decides that he will prepare a set of CCA-adjusted financial statements each year, in order to illustrate the effects of changing price levels for the benefit of other directors. He decides that value to the business can be approximated reasonably well by the use of price indices and he obtains the following indices applicable over the first 2 years of the entity's trading:

	Non-current assets	*Inventories*	*RPI*
1 January 20X0	100	120	100
1 November 20X0	109	131	114
31 December 20X0	110	133	116
Average 20X0	106	127	108
1 November 20X1	122	147	139
31 December 20X1	124	149	142
Average 20X1	116	138	126

Using some of this information he is able to draft a statement of financial position which shows CCA-adjusted values for inventories and non-current assets at 31 December 20X0. This is not a full CCA-adjusted set of accounts, but it establishes an opening position.

Statement of financial positions as at 31 December 20X0

	Historical cost $	*Factor*	*CCA-adjusted* $	*Difference* $
Non-current assets at cost	7,000	110/100	7,700	
Depreciation (at the rate of 10% per annum)	(700)	110/100	(770)	
Net book value	6,300		6,930	630
Inventories (average purchase date: 1 November)	3,000	133/131	3,046	46
Trade receivables	4,200		4,200	
Cash	800		800	
	8,000		8,046	
Total assets	14,300		14,976	
Equity	2,000		2,000	
Accumulated profits	9,500		9,500	
Current cost reserve	–		676	676
	11,500		12,176	
Trade payables	2,800		2,800	
Total equity and liabilities	14,300		14,976	

Note that monetary assets and liabilities are not revalued; they represent amounts receivable, payable or in the bank, and so do not require adjustment.

This set of adjustments establishes a current cost reserve at 31 December 20X0, holding unrealised gains on non-current assets and inventories. In 20X1 it will be possible to prepare a full set of current cost accounts.

At 31 December 20X1, 1 year later, the historical cost statement of financial position of E is as follows:

	Historical cost $
Non-current assets at cost (note)	15,000
Depreciation (at the rate of 10% per annum)	(1,400)
Net book value	13,600
Inventories (average purchase date: 1 November)	3,200
Trade receivables	4,400
Cash	300
	7,900
Total assets	21,500
Equity	2,000
Accumulated profits	15,900
	17,900
Trade payables	3,600
Total equity and liabilities	21,500

The entity's income statement for the year is, in summary, as follows:

	Historical cost $	*Historical cost* $
Revenue		26,700
Cost of sales		
Opening inventories	3,000	
Purchases	18,800	
	21,800	
Less: closing inventories	(3,200)	
		18,600
Gross profit		8,100
Depreciation		(700)
Expenses		(1,000)
Net profit		6,400

Adjustments to current cost income statement

The finance director calculates the following CCA adjustments to HC profit:

- Cost of sales adjustment (COSA) requires a charge of $356 to current cost income,
- The depreciation adjustment requires a charge of $119 to current cost income.
- The monetary working capital adjustment requires a charge of $211 to current cost income.

Note: In this example the value of trade receivables exceeds that of trade payables at both year ends; in a time of rising prices this gives rise to a loss on monetary items and, consequently, a charge to the income statement. However, where trade payables tend to exceed trade receivables in a time of rising prices, there is, effectively, a gain to be made on holding trade payables, and so MWCA would be a credit to current cost income.

E has no borrowings, so there is no gearing adjustment.

Adjustments to current cost statement of financial position

The chief financial officer makes adjustments to the inventories and non-current assets valuations in the statement of financial position, as follows:

- current value of inventories is calculated as $3,244;
- current gross replacement cost of non-current assets is $16,680;
- current value of accumulated depreciation is $1,736.

He uses the indices which are specifically identified for inventories and non-current assets in the table of indices given earlier.

From the above information the chief financial officer prepares the current cost income statement and statement of financial position for E as at 31 December 20X1.

Current cost income statement (extract) for the year ended 31 December 20X1

	$	$
HC operating profit		6,400
Current cost adjustments:		
COSA	356	
Depreciation	119	
MWCA	211	
		686
Current cost operating profit		5,714
Retained profit b/fwd		9,500
Current cost retained profit		15,214

Current cost statement of financial position as at 31 December 20X1

	$	$
Non-current assets		
At gross replacement cost		16,680
Accumulated depreciation		(1,736)
Net replacement cost		14,944
Inventories	3,244	
Trade receivables	4,400	
Cash	300	
		7,944
Total assets		22,888
Equity		2,000
Accumulated profits		15,214
Current cost reserve (bal. figure)		2,074
		19,288
Trade payables		3,600
Total equity and liabilities		22,888

Discussion

CCA calculations are far from straightforward. Examining the results of the calculations we can see that current cost profit is lower than historical cost; this will normally be the case in a time of rising prices. In this example, CC profit is some 11 per cent lower than HC profit. We can perhaps start to appreciate why current cost accounting proved to be so unpopular with preparers. However, it can equally be argued that capital maintenance is important and cannot and should not be ignored by users of financial statements. Current cost accounting provides valuable information about the level of profits which can be distributed while retaining the capital base of the entity. Its restatement of non-monetary assets to current cost has a higher information value than the outdated figures used in historical cost accounting.

Advantages of CCA

- CCA incorporates valuable information into the financial statements which allows users to make informed economic decisions.
- It embodies a concept of capital maintenance which is particularly relevant to industries which are capital intensive in terms of physical assets.
- Appropriate indices are easily obtainable.
- CCA-adjusted statements could provide the basis for a more rational assessment of corporation tax.
- It provides a more prudent statement of profit in times of rising prices than that provided by historical cost accounting.

Disadvantages of CCA

- CCA has been tested in practice and found to be very unpopular with the majority of preparers.
- It is time-consuming and costly to prepare and audit, and it is difficult to assess whether or not these costs are outweighed by the benefits offered by the additional information.
- It is an inappropriate system for service businesses that do not have significant investments in physical capital.
- The selection of appropriate indices introduces an element of subjectivity and judgement.
- It is questionable whether the majority of users would be able to understand CCA statements.
- Essentially CCA is not an inflation accounting system.

13.3.5 Current purchasing power (CPP) accounting

As noted earlier, **CPP accounting** is a system based upon the concept of real capital maintenance. It is defined as follows by CIMA's *Official Terminology*:

> A method of accounting for inflation in which the values of the non-monetary items in the historical cost accounts are adjusted using a general price index to show the change in the general purchasing power of money. The CPP statement of financial position shows the effect of financial capital maintenance.

Example 13.G

We will use the data from Example 13.F, except that only the RPI index numbers are required for CPP accounting. The chief financial officer of E wishes to prepare the financial statements for the second year of the entity's trading using the CPP system, in order to provide a means of comparison with CCA and historical cost.

First of all, the opening statement of financial position as at 1 January 20X1 must be adjusted to current values in order to establish a figure for the opening CPP reserve:

	Historical cost	*Factor*	*CPP-adjusted*	*Difference*
	$		$	
Non-current assets at cost	7,000	116/100	8,120	
Depreciation (at the rate of 10% per annum)	(700)	116/100	(812)	
Net book value	6,300		7,308	1,008
Inventories (average purchase date: 1 November)	3,000	116/114	3,053	53
Trade receivables	4,200		4,200	
Cash	800		800	
	8,000		8,053	
Total assets	14,300		15,361	1,061
Equity	2,000	116/100	2,320	320
Accumulated profits	9,500	Bal. fig	10,241	741
	11,500		12,561	
Trade payables	2,800		2,800	
Total equity and liabilities	14,300		15,361	1,061

Adjustments to the statement of financial position as at 31 December 20X1 result in the following:

E: CPP statement of financial position as at 31 December 20X1

	Historical cost	*Factor*	*CPP-adjusted*
	$		$
Non-current assets at cost	7,000	142/100	9,940
Newly acquired	8,000		8,000
Depreciation (at the rate of 10% per annum)	(1,400)	142/100	(1,988)
Net book value	13,600		15,952
Inventories (average purchase date: 1 November)	3,200	142/139	3,269
Trade receivables	4,400		4,400
Cash	300		300
	7,900		7,969
Total assets	21,500		23,921
Equity	2,000	142/100	2,840
Accumulated profits	15,900	Bal. fig	17,481
	17,900		20,321
Trade payables	3,600		3,600
Total equity and liabilities	21,500		23,921

The income statement for year ended 31 December 20X1 can now be adjusted. Note that items that are assumed to accrue evenly during the year, such as revenue, purchases and expenses, are uplifted from average value to closing value. Depreciation is adjusted to closing value using a base point of the date of purchase of the related non-current assets. Opening and closing inventories are adjusted to year end values using a base point of the assumed average date of purchase 2 months before the year-end.

E: CPP profit and loss account for year ended 31 December 20X1

	Historical cost	*Factor*	*CPP-adjusted*
	$		$
Revenue	26,700	142/126	30,090
Cost of sales			
Opening inventories	3,000	142/114	3,737
Purchases	18,800	142/126	21,187
Closing inventories	(3,200)	142/139	(3,269)
	18,600		21,655
Gross profit	8,100		8,435
Depreciation	(700)	142/100	(994)
Other operating expenses	(1,000)	142/126	(1,127)
Operating profit	6,400		6,314
Loss on short-term monetary items (note)	–		(1,369)
Profit for the year	6,400		4,945

Note

Under the CPP system it is necessary to calculate a gain or loss on holding monetary items, as follows:

	Historical cost	*Factor*	*CPP-adjusted*
	$		$
Opening monetary items (receivables + cash – payables) 4,200 + 800 – 2,800	2,200	142/116	2,693
Revenue	26,700	142/126	30,090
Purchases	(18,800)	142/126	(21,187)
Purchases of non-current assets	(8,000)	142/142	(8,000)
Overheads	(1,000)	142/126	(1,127)
			2,469
Closing monetary items: 4,400 + 300 – 3,600	1,100		(1,100)
Loss on holding monetary items			1,369

Reconciliation of CPP accumulated profits in the statement of financial position as at 31 December 20X1

	$
Opening balance adjusted: $10,241 × 142/116	12,536
CPP profit for the year	4,945
CPP accumulated profits at 31 December 20X1	17,481

Discussion

It is considerably easier in practice to prepare CPP rather than CCA statements. The RPI is easily obtainable, and movements in it are applied in a mechanistic way to the income statement and statement of financial position information. We can see from the income statement above that the CPP profit is substantially lower (by some 23 per cent) than the historical cost figure. The CCA profit was only around 11 per cent lower. Often, in practice, there would be a substantial difference between the three figures: HC, CCA and CPP. The principal reason for the large differences in the E example is that RPI has risen much faster than the non-current assets and inventory indices applicable to the entity. The RPI is an average across the economy as a whole. The prices which mainly affect an entity or an industry may not follow the RPI closely.

Advantages of CPP

- Preparation and audit of CPP statements is not especially costly or time-consuming.
- The method has inherent appeal in that it uses easily obtainable and widely recognised measures of inflation.

- The conceptual basis of CPP is probably easier than that of CCA for the non-specialist user of financial statements to understand.
- In times of rising prices the use of CPP allows for a reasonable measure of capital maintenance.
- The use of the RPI is objective; there is no scope for judgement in the selection of indices as in CCA.

Disadvantages of CPP

- The RPI is based upon average price inflation across the economy. It may bear little relationship to the specific price inflation that affects a particular entity or industry.
- The CPP model is particularly weak as a realistic measure of asset valuation, because it values money rather than assets. This is a very significant objection to its use, especially in the case of entities which employ large amounts of physical capital.
- The application of the CPP model for some entities is as unsatisfactory as historical cost accounting.

13.3.6 The 'real terms' system

As we have seen, both CPP and CCA have significant drawbacks both in practice and theory. The 'real terms' system of accounting for changing price levels is a hybrid system which combines the best features of CPP and CCA. One of the key drawbacks to the CPP system is that assets are presented in terms related to general purchasing power and the resultant 'values' may bear little relationship to the real movement in the value of the asset. The 'real terms' system therefore avoids the problem by retaining CCA valuations for assets. The assets side of the statement of financial position, therefore adopts entirely the CCA system.

However, shareholders do not invest in individual assets and liabilities; their investment is in the entity as a whole. Their concept of capital maintenance is likely to hinge upon the value of their investment in purchasing power terms. The 'real terms' system accommodates this need by calculating and disclosing the amounts needed to maintain the purchasing power of shareholders' funds.

The 'real terms' system serves the useful purpose of clearly comparing the effects of general and specific price inflation. Gains calculated using specific price indices (holding gains) can be compared to the general effects of moving prices. A simple example shows this effect in terms of one asset.

Example 13.H

At 1 January 20X3 an item of inventory costs $150. One year later replacement cost is $230. During the year the RPI has moved from 112 to 127.

	$
Holding gain on one unit of inventory: (230 − 150)	80
Equivalent general terms capital maintenance adjustment: (150 × 127/112) − 150	20
'Real' holding gain on the inventory	60

Essentially 'real terms' accounting adopts CCA but also incorporates CPP valuation of shareholders' funds. The question then arises of how the combination of the two methods articulates to produce a set of accounts. It is, of course, not necessary for CIMA students to be able to prepare a 'real terms' statement, but it will aid understanding to look at an example. The example shows the financial statements for E for the year 20X1, prepared on the 'real terms' basis.

Example 13.1

E: 'real terms' income statement (extracts) for the year ended 31 December 20X1

	$	$
Historical cost profit for the year		6,400
CC adjustments: [note (a)]		
COSA	356	
Depreciation	119	
		(475)
CC retained profit		5,925
Unrealised holding gains in year: [note (b)]	1,187	
Realised holding gains in year: [note (c)]	356	
	1,543	
Less: adjustment to shareholders' funds: [note (d)]	(2,729)	
Net loss in respect of changing prices		(1,186)
Retained 'real' profit		4,739

E: 'real terms' statement of financial position as at 31 December 20X1

	$	$
Non-current assets		14,944
Current assets		
Inventories	3,244	
Trade receivables	4,400	
Cash	300	
		7,944
Total assets		22,888
Equity		2,000
Accumulated profit		
Brought forward	9,500	
Retained 'real' profit for the year	4,739	
		14,239
Financial capital maintenance reserve [note (f)]		3,049
		19,288
Trade payables		3,600
Total equity and liabilities		22,888

Notes

(a) The cost of sales and depreciation adjustments are reported here but MWCA is absorbed in the general price level changes adjusted further down.

(b) Unrealised holding gains are the gains on non-current assets and inventories which have not yet been realised.

(c) COSA is a realised holding gain.

(d) The inflation adjustment to shareholders' funds is the point at which CPP principles enter the financial statements. Opening shareholders' funds are restated in current terms by applying the movement in RPI over the year:

$$(\$12,176 \times 142/116) - 12,176 = \$2,729$$

This will be credited to the real capital maintenance reserve in the statement of financial position, and is debited to the income statement. Deducted from holding gains, it determines how much of the holding gain (which is calculated by reference to specific price movements) remains once the effects of general price inflation have been taken into account. In this instance, we can see that there is nothing left: the holding gains have been more than cancelled out by the eroding of values via general inflation.

(e) Note that the figure for total assets is exactly the same as in the CCA statement of financial position.

(f) Financial capital maintenance reserve includes:

	$
Brought forward 1 January 20X1 (based on RPI applied to opening capital)	320
Current year adjustment [see note (d)]	2,729
	3,049

13.4 Financial reporting in hyperinflationary economies

The examples we examined in Section 13.3 used rates of both specific and general price inflation which seem, relative to current circumstances in many countries, to be wildly exaggerated. In some parts of the world, however, very high rates of price inflation are the norm, as noted earlier.

In times of relatively modest price inflation users of financial statements are usually able to make broadbrush assumptions about the effect that inflation is having upon information they are examining. For example, when comparing 2 years' revenue figures they may mentally adjust the earlier figure in order to estimate the effect of inflation. However, where a very high rate of inflation prevails such approximations are no longer possible.

In 1989 the International Accounting Standards Committee issued IAS 29 *Financial reporting in hyperinflationary economies.*

13.4.1 What is hyperinflation?

IAS 29 identifies the following characteristics of the economic environment of a country which would indicate that hyperinflation is a problem:

- The general population prefers to keep its wealth in non-monetary assets or in a relatively stable foreign currency. Amounts of local currency held are immediately invested to maintain purchasing power.
- The general population regards monetary amounts not in terms of the local currency but in terms of a relatively stable foreign currency. Prices may be quoted in that currency.
- Sales and purchases on credit take place at prices that compensate for the expected loss of purchasing power during the credit period, even if the period is short.
- Interest rates, wages and prices are linked to a price index.
- The cumulative inflation rate over 3 years is approaching, or exceeds, 100 per cent.

13.4.2 Dealing with hyperinflation

The IAS requires that the primary accounting statements of entities reporting in the currency of a hyperinflationary economy should be restated in current terms at the year end date. Corresponding figures for previous periods should also be restated so that all reported figures are expressed in common terms.

The restatement required by the IAS involves the application of a general price index to most non-monetary items and all items in the income statement and is very similar to the CPP system explained earlier in the chapter. The IAS specifically notes, however, that where items in the statement of financial position are stated at current cost they do not need to be further adjusted.

13.5 Summary

> This chapter has dealt with some complex areas of accounting. The chapter looked at the defects of historical cost accounting and the alternative valuation methods available, including replacement cost accounting, net realisable value accounting and current cost accounting. The chapter also considered the problems of financial reporting in hyperinflationary economies.

Students should ensure that they understand the principles involved in all of the alternative methods discussed in the chapter. Questions could include:

- arguments for and against adjusting accounting figures to take account of changing prices levels;
- pros and cons of the different alternative methods;
- discussion about the need for special accounting measures in hyperinflationary conditions;
- knowledge-based questions about features of the different methods of accounting for changing price levels.

Revision Questions

Question 1

Discuss the advantages and disadvantages of using historical cost accounting in preparing financial statements which are presented to shareholders. **(10 marks)**

Question 2

'The recognition and correct treatment of holding gains in entity financial statements are vital for a proper understanding of the position and performance of the business entity.'

Requirements

(a) Explain briefly the significance of the treatment of holding gains for the measurement of business profit. **(4 marks)**

(b) Set out the arguments for and against the recognition of holding gains. **(6 marks)**

(Total marks = 10)

Question 3

DCB is a manufacturing and trading entity with several overseas operations. One of its subsidiaries, GFE, operates in a country which experiences relatively high rates of inflation in its currency, the crown. Most entities operating in that country voluntarily present two versions of their financial statements: one at historical cost, and the other incorporating current cost adjustments. GFE complies with this accepted practice. Extracts from the income cp statement adjusted for current costs for the year ended 30 September 20X5 are as follows:

	Crowns	*Crowns*
	$'000	$'000
Historical cost operating profit		750
Current cost adjustments:		
Cost of sales adjustment	65	
Depreciation adjustment	43	
Loss on net monetary position	16	
		124
Current cost operating profit		626

Requirements

(a) Explain the defects of historical cost accounting in times of increasing prices. **(4 marks)**

(b) Explain how each of the three current cost adjustments in GFE's financial statements contributes to the maintenance of capital. **(6 marks)**

(Total marks = 10)

Question 4

A consolidated historical cost balance sheet gives a realistic valuation for a group. Discuss. **(10 marks)**

Solutions to Revision Questions 13

Solution 1

The advantages of using historical cost accounting in preparing financial statements for presentation to shareholders are as follows:

(a) Historical cost accounts are generally accepted to be understood by users (to a greater or lesser extent). For a reader with no accounting background the concept of cost is one he or she recognises. The use of valuation of certain assets in historical costs (usually properties of some description) does not cause the reader problems as again he or she can relate property values to their everyday experience.
(b) Historical cost accounts are comparatively less expensive to prepare as the information is readily available because the transactions involved have usually already occurred. This reason also makes them easier and cheaper to audit as auditors can verify the information in the accounts.
(c) Despite the criticisms of historical cost accounting, no one has produced a better method that attracts less criticism. The accountancy profession in many countries has made a number of attempts over the last few years to devise an acceptable alternative, but none has met with the approval of preparers and users.

The disadvantages of using historical costs accounting in preparing financial statements for presentation to shareholders are as follows:

(a) In a period of inflation, historical costs are misleading as they do not compare like with like. The following points are relevant:
   (i) Current revenues are matched with costs incurred at an earlier date, so distorting profits and losses for the period.
   (ii) Distributions made out of profits calculated on an historical cost basis may result in a reduction of capital in real terms.
   (iii) The use of historical costs for non-current assets undervalues the actual resources used by the business. Resulting lower depreciation charges in turn distort profit [see (i) above].
   (iv) The result of overstating profits and undervaluing assets is that return on capital employed will be overstated. This will indicate a more efficient use of resources than is actually the case.
   (v) Management's real success or failure in achieving operating results is masked because holding gains or losses attributable to price level changes are not recognised.

(vi) The trend of performance over a period measured by year-to-year comparisons is misleading because no adjustment is made for the changes in the real value of money.

(vii) Historical cost accounts do not recognise the loss that occurs from holding assets of a fixed monetary value (and alternatively the gain that arises from liabilities of the same type).

(b) Historical cost accounts cannot easily be adapted to take account of the effects of rising prices in a period of inflation.

(c) Historical cost accounts which incorporate valuations of assets are often misleading as there is no requirement (except in the case of investment properties), to keep these valuations up to date.

Solution 2

(a) Holding gains are increases in the value of an asset while that asset is owned by a entity. For example, a entity might buy an item of inventory for $100 and then later sell it for $180 when its replacement cost had gone up to $150. The holding gain of $50 is realised at the date of sale; the 'real' profit, or operating gain, on the disposal is $30.

There are several alternative possible accounting treatments for holding gains, both realised and unrealised. Conventional historical cost accounting ignores unrealised holding gains, and includes realised holding gains in the income statement of the period in which the asset is disposed of. Current cost accounting, on the other hand, excludes realised holding gains on the disposals of inventory items by charging a cost of sales adjustment (COSA) against reported profits so that only operating gains are reported as profits.

The significance of the treatment of holding gains is therefore the enormous effect that such treatment will have on reported profits. Although earnings per share is not the only important indicator of financial performance, it is still the most important, and the exclusion of holding gains from earnings will materially depress earnings per share and may thereby reduce the share price.

(b) *Arguments for the recognition of holding gains*

The accruals concept would suggest that gains and losses should be recognised in the period in which they occurred, rather than being deferred. So financial assets would be shown on the statement of financial position at their market value. As a separate issue, prudence might dictate that gains should be credited to reserves rather than to the income statement, but the principle of revaluing investments in the statement of financial position remains valid.

The objective of financial statements is set out in the IASC's *Framework* as being to provide useful information to a wide range of user groups. Surely the current value of assets held is more useful than historical cost.

If holding gains are not recognised year by year, entities experiencing a bad year can flatter their reported profits by deciding to sell assets held for many years which have large unrealised holding gains. Often these assets may be immediately repurchased as a 'bed and breakfast' transaction. The profit generated on this deal does not reflect the genuine economic performance of the entity in that period but under existing accounting practices may be all reported in the year of disposal.

Asset-stripping hostile acquisitive entities will not be able to make money by breaking up target entities whose share prices do not reflect the real value of their underlying assets.

Arguments against the recognition of holding gains

The prudence concept seeks to prevent profits being included in the income statement unless their realisation is reasonably certain. Unrealised holding gains may not be recognised in the income statement.

Subjectivity and uncertainty exist in trying to determine the current value of an asset at the year end date. An advantage of deferring holding gains until the date of disposal is the avoidance of this uncertainty.

If realised holding gains are included in reported profits and distributed out of the business, the entity will not be able to finance the replacement of its assets without raising new funds externally. Operating capital will not be maintained if a policy of maximum distributions is carried on.

✓ Solution 3

(a) In times of increasing prices, historical cost accounting displays the following defects:

(i) Revenues are stated at current values, but they tend to be matched with costs incurred at an earlier date. Therefore, profit is overstated.

(ii) Where historical cost accounting is applied consistently, asset values are stated at cost less accumulated depreciation. Current values of the assets may be considerably in excess of net book value, with the result that the historical cost depreciation charge does not constitute a realistic estimate of the value of the asset consumed.

(iii) By the time monetary liabilities are repayable, the amount of the outflow in current value terms is less than the original inflow. An entity can therefore gain by holding current liabilities, but historical cost accounting does not recognise these gains. The opposite effect is experienced in respect of monetary assets.

(iv) Typically, in a time of rising prices, profits are likely to be overstated, and capital to be understated, thus giving rise to unrealistic measurements of return on capital employed.

(b) The cost of sales adjustment comprises the additional amount of value, over and above value at historical cost, that is consumed at current cost. It represents an additional charge against profits, thus tending to reduce distributable earnings and ensuring that the business conserves the resources that allow it to continue to trade at current levels.

The depreciation adjustment is the difference between the historical cost accounting and current cost depreciation charges. Current cost depreciation is the value of the non-current asset consumption that has taken place during the year. In a time of rising prices it is a more realistic representation of the asset consumption. It tends to reduce distributable profits thus contributing to capital maintenance.

In the case of GFE, there is a loss on net monetary position. As noted earlier in part (a) holding monetary liabilities in times of rising prices tends to give rise to gains, whereas holding monetary assets produces losses. GFE appears, therefore, to have an excess of monetary assets over monetary liabilities, as the net effect is a loss.

The recognition of this loss produces a more realistic estimation of distributable profit, and thus contributes to capital maintenance.

Solution 4

No balance sheet drafted according to the historical cost convention can give a realistic valuation of a business. Historical costs represent the price level when an asset was originally acquired, and after a period of inflation they significantly understate the value of assets. Unless assets are revalued to reflect their current values, holding gains which have accrued since their purchase will not be disclosed. The balance sheet is not intended as a valuation device for a business since it discloses only the book value, or carrying value, of assets and liabilities. Certain significant assets will be excluded because, under the monetary measurement convention, they cannot be accurately recorded.

Such items as managerial efficiency, good labour relations, know-how, and so on, from which the entity may earn profit, are nevertheless not disclosed on the balance sheet. If individual assets such as machinery, vehicles, stock and cash are added together in a business, the value of the combination will exceed the aggregate value of the individual items. This extra value is sometimes expressed in a balance sheet as the goodwill of the entity. Goodwill is accounted for in consolidated accounts as the surplus of the price paid for a subsidiary above the fair value of the assets acquired. Current moves to include the cost of purchased 'brand names' in the balance sheet bring a further note of inconsistency because group brands built-up over time are not valued and disclosed as assets.

In a consolidated balance sheet the assets of the subsidiary and holding entities are aggregated together but this total of assets may not belong to group shareholders because a non-controlling interest of non-group shareholders in subsidiary entities has an ownership right to a significant proportion of the group assets. This non-controlling interest is calculated and disclosed on the group balance sheet. Under the equity method, the group's interest in an associated entity is shown as the original cost paid for the investment plus the group's share of retained post-acquisition profits. This is a convenient book-keeping method to account for a non-controlling, but significant, interest in another entity, but it cannot show the true value of the investment. Under the acquisition method of accounting, when a subsidiary is purchased by a group the assets of that entity are brought into the group accounts at 'fair value'.

The measurement of a realistic value for a group of entities is dependent upon a number of factors which are in no way connected with the consolidated balance sheet. Value depends on the future profitability to be earned by the group and, since this is an estimate, cannot form part of an audited balance sheet. The value of the group can be expressed as the stock exchange price of the shares multiplied by the number of shares in issue, but even this amount is based on the market price for the purchase of a small holding of the shares and not a controlling interest of the group as a whole. Consequently when a takeover bid is made, the ultimate value of the group thus disclosed may exceed the stock exchange value and bear no relation whatsoever to the amount of net assets as disclosed by the consolidated historical cost balance sheet.

14

Interpretation of Accounting Ratios

Interpretation of Accounting Ratios

14

LEARNING OUTCOME

After studying this chapter students should be able to:

- interpret a full range of accounting ratios.

14.1 Introduction

This chapter covers the calculation and interpretation of various accounting ratios. Section 14.2 focuses on identification of the user and understanding the business. Sections 14.3 to 14.5 cover ratios that you will be familiar with, including ratios on performance, liquidity, and capital structure. Section 14.6 looks specifically at investors' ratios and finally Section 14.7 looks at how to use relevant ratios when analysing the statement of cash flows.

14.2 Interpretation and analysis

The IASB *Framework* states:

> The objective of financial statements is to provide information … that is useful to a wide range of users in making economic decisions.

Interpretation and analysis of the financial statements is the process of arranging, examining and comparing the results in order that users are equipped to make such economic decisions.

The interpretation process is assisted by adopting an analytical framework. The main components of an appropriate framework are:

- identification of the user of the analysis;
- an understanding of the nature of the business, industry and organisation;

- identification of relevant sources of data for analysis;
- numerical analysis of the data available;
- interpretation of the results of the analysis;
- writing the report detailing the analysis of the results and recommendations.

14.2.1 Identification of the user of the analysis

There is a wide range of user groups that may be interested in an entity's financial statements. Historically, of course, financial statements have been prepared for the benefit of the investor group. However, those interested in the statements extend far beyond existing investors.

A major creditor of an entity, such as a bank which has provided material amounts of long-term finance, may commission specific financial reports, in fact it may be a condition of continuing financial backing that the entity prepares, say, quarterly statements to the bank's specifications. Most users, however, are not in a position to command such privileges.

Although the various user groups will almost invariably be using general-purpose financial reports, their needs may vary. It is important that any analysis and interpretation exercise is oriented towards the needs of the particular user who requires a report.

Examination questions will usually identify the type of user for whom a report is being prepared, so it is important to recognise the differences between users and their needs.

Present and potential investors

Both present and potential investors are interested in information that is useful in making buy/sell/hold decisions. Will the entity be able to generate cash in the future? How risky is the investment? Does its financial performance exceed that of other potential investee entities? How much is the investment likely to yield in capital growth and/or dividend? Analysis of the financial statements can help to answer these questions. There is a range of ratios of particular interest to the investor group; these are examined in detail later in the chapter in Section 14.6. In addition, return on capital employed (ROCE) and related performance and asset management ratios are likely to be of interest to this group of users.

Lenders and potential lenders

Lenders are principally interested in assessing whether or not the loans that they have made are likely to be repaid, and whether or not the related interest charge will be paid in full and on time. Potential lenders require analysis of financial statements in order to assist them in deciding whether or not to lend. Lender groups are likely to be particularly interested in ratios such as interest cover and gearing, and will be interested in the nature and longevity of other categories of loan to the entity.

Suppliers and other creditors

This group is interested in information that helps them to decide whether or not to supply goods or services to an entity. Availability of cash will be of particular interest, together with such evidence as is available in general-purpose financial statements about the entity's record in paying its creditors on time. Working capital ratios, and the working capital cycle, may be appropriate calculations to undertake when analysing financial statements for the benefit of this class of user.

Employees

In large organisations employees are likely to be particularly interested in one part of the entity's operations. They may, therefore, find segmental information to be useful. More generally, they need to be able to assess the stability and performance of the entity in order to gauge how reliable it is likely to be as a source of employment in the longer term. Employees are likely to be interested in disclosures about retirement benefits and remuneration.

Customers

Customers may be in a vulnerable position if there are few potential suppliers in a market for goods. They may therefore be interested in assessing the risks which threaten their supplier. Potentially they may be interested in takeover opportunities in order to ensure the continuing supply of a particular raw material.

Governments and their agencies

The governmental group is in a position to require special-purpose reports. Tax computations would fall into this category. However, general-purpose reports may also be of use, for example in gathering statistics on particular industries.

The general public

Members of the public may have special interests in the activities of certain entities, especially where, say, an individual entity dominates the local employment market. Pressure groups and their members would also fall under the umbrella category of 'general public', and their needs will vary according to their special interest. Environmental issues are of increasing concern to many people, and it is likely that pressure groups will take a particular interest in firms that are perceived as polluters. Analysis of the financial statements for this type of user would tend to focus on any additional voluntary disclosures made about the entity's environmental policies, on provisions and contingent liabilities related to environmental damage, and on capital investment (e.g., investment in new plant).

14.2.2 Understanding the business

It is often thought that financial analysis involves the direct application of a routine set of numerical calculations to a set of published accounts. This is only one part of the task. In order to interpret those calculations it is important to understand the relationships between the data and the underlying reasons, economic and other, that account for the business's current position.

The history of the business underlies the current position and future outlook. Furthermore, the owners and their individual characteristics will influence factors such as the level of risk in the business and dividend policy. Knowledge of the quality, qualifications and experience of management will assist in evaluating the performance and position of the business.

Financial analysis requires an understanding of the products, services and operating characteristics of the business. This will assist in understanding data such as turnover, profitability, inventories and working capital.

The business operates within an industry consisting of businesses with similar operating characteristics. If the analysis requires comparison of the business with the industry norms, it is important to identify the key characteristics of the industry and to establish benchmarks such as gross profit ratios, receivables collection days, etc.

14.2.3 Identifying relevant sources of data

In practice, the analyst needs to consider carefully the possible sources of information available about an entity. Perhaps the most obvious source is the wealth of financial and non-financial information contained in the entity's annual report. In addition to all the information that statute law and accounting standards require to be included in the annual report, there may be further voluntary disclosures that will be helpful to the analyst. Examples of such voluntary disclosures include supplementary information about an entity's environmental impact, employment reports, graphs, pie charts and ratio calculations. In some jurisdictions, interim financial reports are also available. Listed companies in the USA report quarterly, but in the UK, for example, listed companies (with a very small number of exceptions) report every 6 months.

There are likely to be further useful sources of information available to the analyst, especially in the case of larger, listed, companies. Specialist agencies collect and analyse data about industry sectors from which it may be possible (often at a price) to obtain, say, average return on capital employed figures for a sector. Brokers' reports may contain information about the prospects for the entity, together with predictions about certain key ratios such as earnings per share. Because this information has a value it is usually available to the broker's clients only, at least initially. However, some listed entities have started to make this information available, after a certain lapse of time, on their websites. It is always worth examining the website of an entity in case it contains some additional voluntary disclosures that may be useful in the analysis.

In the *Financial Management* examination it will not be possible, because of time restrictions, to carry out an analysis in great depth, and there are obvious limitations on the amount of information that can be provided in an examination question. The information provided for analysis in a question is likely to include one or more of the following:

- income statement data for one or more years;
- cash flow data for one or more years;
- industry wide ratios and benchmarks;
- statement of financial position data for one or more years;
- budget data, and variance analysis;
- data regarding a competitor, potential subsidiary or customer applying for credit.

Working with this information and with any descriptive background provided in the question, we need to gain an understanding of the business and the relationships between the data. Where information in the form of extracts from the financial statements is given, it is often possible (and is often specifically required by the requirements of the question) to calculate a set of financial ratios as the basis for further analysis and comment. The rest of this chapter examines numerical data analysis in the form of the most frequently used accounting ratios.

14.3 Performance ratios

14.3.1 Profitability ratios

Revenue

When analysing the performance of an entity, a useful starting point is the examination of revenue. Revenue is important in both absolute and relative terms. Increases or decreases in revenue may be attributable to changes in selling prices or sales volumes or a combination of the two factors.

Problems can arise in making a valid interpretation of movements in revenue. For example:

- Accounting policies on revenue recognition may vary between businesses. There may be inconsistencies between accounting periods, especially where the business derives some or all of its revenue from long-term contracts.
- Inflation may account for some of the increase in price.
- A detailed breakdown of revenue for the business may not be available. To some extent IFRS 8 *Operating Segments* (see Chapter 16 of this *Learning System* for more details) stipulates revenue details for different segments of the business. However, there are, as we shall see, problems in using segmental data, in that, for example, segments may not be consistently defined.

Understanding the reasons for movements in revenue may help to explain movements in costs such as cost of sales, advertising, selling and distribution costs and telephone charges. If revenue increases, then a similar increase in these revenue-related costs could be expected. Conversely, an increase in, say, marketing and advertising expenditure might help to explain an increase in revenue.

Profitability

Several profit figures are identified in a typical income statement. Each may be used to evaluate the profitability of the business.

Gross profit margin

The CIMA *Official Terminology* definition of gross profit percentage is:

$$\frac{(\text{Sales} - \text{cost of sales})}{\text{Sales for the period}} \times 100$$

This ratio might be expected to be more or less constant from 1 year to the next within a business. Even if there is an increase in direct costs, an efficient business could be expected to pass on the increases in the form of increased sales prices. However, this may not be the case in practice.

The gross profit margin requires a detailed breakdown in order to gain an understanding of variations. Ideally, the analyst requires information relating to opening and closing inventories, purchases, direct wages and overheads. Further information as to the following items would be required in order to evaluate gross profit margin fully:

- breakdown by product, geographical area or other segment;
- inventory valuation policies;
- overhead allocation methods;
- purchasing details such as bulk discounts, purchasing errors, wastage or theft;
- selling prices of different products over the period.

Obviously, much of this information is not available from a business's annual report. Some businesses do not even report gross profits.

Operating profit margin

$$\frac{\text{Operating profit}}{\text{Revenue}} \times 100$$

The operating profit margin is the trading or operating profit in relation to revenue, expressed as a percentage.

Operating profit is the profit from the trading activities of the business; it comprises profits after operating costs, but before finance costs and tax, and before investment income. Note that IAS 1 revised does not encourage the reporting of operating profit as a separate line item, although there is nothing to prevent entities providing additional information. It is likely, though that in many cases it will not be possible to calculate operating profit margin. Further analysis might include measuring operating costs as a percentage of revenue, and comparing to benchmarks, budgets, previous years or industry averages. For example:

$$\frac{\text{Administration costs}}{\text{Revenue}} \times 100$$

$$\frac{\text{Telephone costs}}{\text{Revenue}} \times 100$$

$$\frac{\text{Advertising costs}}{\text{Revenue}} \times 100$$

Net profit margin

Net profit margin expresses the relationship between net profit and sales. Net profit for this purpose would be profit after deduction of finance cost. It may be calculated on either pre-tax or post-tax profit.

$$\frac{\text{Net profit}}{\text{Revenue}} \times 100$$

Where comparing net profit year on year, it is important to allow for any exceptional charges or credits. Also, it would be sensible to take into account any large adjustments in respect of under- or over-provided tax provisions.

EBITDA

EBITDA is an acronym for earnings before interest, tax, depreciation and amortisation. In recent years many large entities have adopted EBITDA as a key measure of financial performance. Sceptics suggest that they do this in order to publicise a higher measure of earnings than profit from operations (this type of measurement is sometimes cynically referred to as EBB – earnings before the bad bits).

However, it does make some sense to measure EBITDA, provided that the user fully understands what is included and what is left out. Depreciation and amortisation are accounting adjustments, not representing cash flows, that are determined by management. It can therefore be argued that excluding these items in assessing earnings eliminates a major area where management bias can operate. Unfortunately, EBITDA is consequently often misunderstood as being a measurement of cash flow, which of course it is not. Even though two categories of non-cash adjustment are eliminated, financial statements are prepared on an accruals basis. EBITDA makes no adjustments in respect of accruals or working capital movements, and so is emphatically not a cash flow measurement.

14.3.2 Activity ratios

A further, related, set of ratios can be calculated that indicate the efficiency of usage of the entity's assets in producing revenue and profits.

Asset turnover

$$\frac{\text{Revenue}}{\text{Total assets}}$$

This calculation is usually expressed as a simple ratio, rather than as a percentage. It shows how much revenue is produced per dollar of investment in fixed assets.

The overall ratio can be further broken down to show revenue in relation to other categories of asset. For example, a useful ratio in certain contexts is:

$$\frac{\text{Revenue}}{\text{Non-current assets, excluding investments}}$$

This ratio shows the productivity of non-current assets in generating sales. It should be noted that this ratio is not always useful or informative. Where a business is using assets that are nearing the end of their useful lives, having been subject to annual depreciation charges over a relatively long period, the ratio is likely to be rather high. Similarly, where a business uses the historical cost convention, unmodified by revaluation, asset values are also likely to be relatively low, an effect which is more intrusive as the assets age. Also, in labour-intensive businesses, where the non-current asset base is low, the ratio tends to lack significance.

Note that, where possible, the average asset figure over the year should be used in the denominator of the fraction. This is likely to give a more consistent and representative result. External users of annual reports do not have access to monthly information with which to calculate an average, but opening and closing figures often give a reasonable approximation.

Inventory turnover

Conventionally, inventory turnover is expressed in terms of cost of sales, rather than of revenue. If cost of sales is not available, perhaps because the entity does not have a policy of disclosing gross profit, revenue could be used. Provided it is used consistently when making comparisons, the ratio will have some information content. However, where the information is available, cost of sales is to be preferred. The inventory turnover ratio indicates the liquidity of inventories. The higher the ratio, the more quickly inventory is being sold:

$$\frac{\text{Cost of sales}}{\text{Average inventory}}$$

Application of this formula produces a figure which shows the number of times, on average, that inventory has turned over during the year. If only a closing figure is available for inventory, then that can be used. However, the result must be treated with some caution, as the closing figure may be unrepresentative.

The ratio can be inverted to give the number of days, weeks or months that inventory, on average, has remained in the warehouse:

$$\frac{\text{Average inventory}}{\text{Cost of sales}} \times 365 \text{ days (or 52 weeks, or 12 months)}$$

14.3.3 Return on capital ratios

Return on capital employed

Return on capital employed (ROCE) is a measurement that is frequently used in the analysis of financial statements. This shows the overall performance of the business, expressed as a percentage return on the total investment. It measures management's efficiency in generating profits from the resources available.

Return on capital employed is expressed as a percentage, and is calculated as follows:

$$\frac{\text{Profit}}{\text{Capital employed}} \times 100$$

For the purposes of the ROCE measurement, capital employed includes the following:

Issued share capital
+ Reserves
+ Preference shares
+ Non-controlling interests
+ Loan capital
+ Provisions (including provisions for tax)
+ Bank overdraft
− Investments

It is important in this type of calculation that the numerator and denominator should be consistent. Therefore, in calculating ROCE, the numerator should include profit before any deductions for finance cost. If capital employed includes a bank overdraft, the profit figure used in the calculation should exclude interest paid and payable on the overdraft.

Return on assets

Return on assets (ROA) involves a similar calculation to ROCE, but the denominator represents total assets (i.e., the statement of financial position total). Where a business has a policy of regular revaluation of assets, both ROCE and ROA are likely to provide a better measure of economic performance.

ROA, which is expressed as a percentage, is calculated as follows:

$$\frac{\text{Operating profit}}{\text{Total assets}} \times 100$$

Return on assets: relationship with other ratios

ROA can be broken down into two component ratios that have already been introduced: operating profit margin and asset turnover ratio.

Operating profit margin × asset turnover = Return on assets

The relationship becomes clear when we put the ratio calculations into the formula:

$$\frac{\text{Operating profit}}{\text{Revenue}} \times \frac{\text{Revenue}}{\text{Assets}} = \frac{\text{Operating profit}}{\text{Assets}}$$

Return on shareholders' funds

Sometimes it can be useful to calculate return from the shareholders' point of view. The formula for the ratio is:

$$\frac{\text{Profits attributable to shareholders}}{\text{Shareholders' funds}}$$

Profits attributable to shareholders comprises profits after tax, non-controlling interest and non-equity appropriations (such as preference dividends). Shareholders' funds comprise equity share capital and reserves.

14.4 Liquidity ratios

14.4.1 Working capital analysis

The profitability and activity ratios indicate how the business is performing. It is important to supplement this review with an examination of the effects of the performance on the liquidity and cash position of the business.

The bank balance

The analysis of the liquidity of an entity may commence with a review of the actual bank balance in absolute terms. Has the bank balance increased or decreased significantly? It could be that the overdraft is near to its permitted limit or that high cash resources indicate a good takeover prospect.

Short-term liquidity

The liquidity of the business is measured by examining the relationships between current assets and current liabilities. To what extent is the business able to meet its current liabilities as they fall due?

Two common ratios are used to answer this question: the current ratio and the quick ratio:

$$\text{Current ratio} = \frac{\text{Current assets}}{\text{Current liabilities}}$$

$$\text{Quick ratio} = \frac{\text{Current assets less inventory}}{\text{Current liabilities}}$$

The quick ratio recognises that the time taken to convert inventory into cash in many businesses is significantly longer than other current assets and so gives a more conservative view of liquidity. However, it is important to select ratios suitable for the circumstances of the business. If inventory is an insignificant amount (as it would be, for example, in most service businesses), there is little point in calculating the quick ratio.

There is no standard number that should be expected in these calculations; it should depend on the industry and should be linked to other areas of the analysis. The higher the ratio, the more liquid the business, but high liquidity can itself be a problem. It may mean that the business is unable to utilise cash effectively by investing it profitably.

The immediate liquidity of a business can be defined using the cash balance itself:

$$\frac{\text{Cash}}{\text{Current liabilities}}$$

The working capital cycle

The length of the working capital cycle can assist in determining the immediate effects of the financial position on the bank balance.

The working capital cycle comprises cash, receivables, inventory and payables. The business uses cash to buy inventory. Additional inventory may be purchased on credit.

Inventories are sold and become receivables. Receivables pay and then the business has cash available to repay payables or buy further inventory.

The length of this cycle is determined using ratios of inventory turnover, receivables days and payables days.

Earlier, we examined the calculation of inventory turnover in terms of days, weeks or months. The same type of calculation is used for both receivables and short-term payables:

Receivables days

The number of days it takes for the average customer to pay may be measured as follows:

$$\frac{\text{Average receivables}}{\text{Credit sales}} \times 365 \text{ days (or 52 weeks) (or 12 months)}$$

A retail or cash-based business may have zero or very low receivables days. Note that, where a business sells for both cash and on credit, it will be necessary to split revenue into the two types.

Payables days

The length of time taken to settle payables may be measured as follows:

$$\frac{\text{Average payables}}{\text{Credit purchases}} \times 365 \text{ days (or 52 weeks) (or 12 months)}$$

Current payables comprise a form of finance which is free, or almost free. However, there may be costs in terms of loss of prompt payment discount, and loss of supplier goodwill where excessive time is taken to pay. Efficiency is measured relative to industry norms, receivables days and supplier terms.

In the ratios above, if figures are not available for credit sales and credit purchases (as may well be the case if the data source is a set of published accounts) an approximation may be obtained by using total revenue and cost of sales respectively, but the results of such ratio calculations must be treated with caution.

The total length of the working capital cycle is the inventory turnover days plus the receivables days less the payables days, which approximates to the total time it takes to purchase the inventory, sell the inventory and receive cash.

Example 14.A

X: statement of financial position (extract)

	20X2	*20X1*
	$'000	$'000
Inventories	790	650
Trade receivables	503	535
Financial assets	86	75
Cash	113	–
	1,492	1,260
Current liabilities*	773	751
Net current assets	719	509

*Current liabilities analysed as follows:

	20X2	*20X1*
	$'000	$'000
Trade payables	520	443
Income tax	139	164
Other payables	114	108
Bank overdraft	–	36
	773	751

X: income statement (extract)

	20X2	*20X1*
	$'000	$'000
Revenue	3,559	3,343
Cost of sales*	(2,420)	(2,240)
Gross profit	1,139	1,103

*Cost of sales is analysed as follows:

	20X2	*20X1*
	$'000	$'000
Opening inventory	650	630
Add: purchases	2,560	2,260
Less: closing inventory	(790)	(650)
Cost of sales	2,420	2,240

In both 20X1 and 20X2 credit sales comprise 83% of total revenue. Calculate the working capital cycle for each of 20X2 and 20X1 for X.

Solution

The components of the working capital cycle are:

Inventories

$$\frac{\text{Average inventories}}{\text{Cost of sales}} \times 365 \text{ days}$$

$$20X1: \frac{(650 + 630)/2}{2,240} \times 365 \text{ days} = 104 \text{ days}$$

$$20X2: \frac{(790 + 650)/2}{2,420} \times 365 \text{ days} = 109 \text{ days}$$

Trade receivables

$$\frac{\text{Trade receivables}}{\text{Credit sales}} \times 365 \text{ days}$$

$$20X1: \frac{535}{3,343 \times 0.83} \times 365 \text{ days} = 70 \text{ days}$$

$$20X2: \frac{503}{3,559 \times 0.83} \times 365 \text{ days} = 62 \text{ days}$$

Trade payables

$$\frac{\text{Trade payables}}{\text{Credit purchases}} \times 365 \text{ days}$$

$$20X1: \frac{443}{2,260} \times 365 \text{ days} = 71 \text{ days}$$

$$20X2: \frac{520}{2,560} \times 365 \text{ days} = 74 \text{ days}$$

Working capital cycle

	20X2	*20X1*
Inventories days	109	104
+ Trade receivables days	62	70
− Trade payables days	(74)	(71)
Total	97	103

The working capital cycle has shortened in 20X2. Although inventories are, on average, spending an extra 5 days on the premises, collection from receivables has improved in 20X2 and X is taking an extra 3 days on average to meet its payables. It is very difficult to make a judgement, in absolute terms, about this length of working capital cycle. Much depends upon the nature of the industry, the type of inventories held and acceptable patterns of payment. If we had access to some industry averages for the working capital cycle we would be able to comment more confidently.

14.5 Analysis of capital structure

The gearing (or leverage) ratio is an important measure of risk. It is important to analyse, particularly for users such as shareholders and creditors, the ability to satisfy debts falling due after 1 year. There are two elements to consider: repayment of capital and payment of interest.

The assessment of an entity's gearing risk can be identified from two areas. The statement of financial position shows the current liquidity and capital structure of the business, that is the short-term liquidity and the level of fixed prior charge capital. The income statement shows the profitability of the business generally, indicating its ability to generate cash, some of which may be available to repay debt.

The capital structure of the business provides information about the relative risk that is accepted by shareholders and creditors. As long-term debt increases relative to shareholders' funds then more risk is assumed by long-term creditors and so they would require higher rewards, thereby decreasing resources available for the shareholders. As risk increases, creditors require higher interest in order to compensate for the higher risk.

However, the use of debt by management in their capital structure can assist in increasing profits available to shareholders. Cash received into the business from lenders will be used to generate revenue and profits. As interest costs are fixed, any profits generated in excess of the interest costs will accrue to the shareholders. There is, however, a negative side to the use of debt in the business. If the cash from the debt does not raise sufficient profits then the fixed interest cost must be paid first and so profits available to shareholders are decreased, and may be extinguished completely.

14.5.1 Measuring the performance effects of capital structures

Although the use of debt may generate higher profits for shareholders there is a limit to its use. This may be gauged from the income statement by focusing on the profitability and interest repayments in the interest cover ratio:

$$\frac{\text{Profit before interest and tax}}{\text{Interest expense}}$$

This ratio indicates the number of times profits will cover the interest charge; the higher the ratio, the better.

14.5.2 Measuring statement of financial position gearing

The gearing ratio can be calculated using either of the following:

$$\frac{\text{Total long-term debt}}{\text{Shareholders' funds}} \times 100$$

Or:

$$\frac{\text{Total long-term debt}}{\text{Shareholders' funds} + \text{long term debt}} \times 100$$

Long-term debt includes debentures, mortgages and other long-term debt, including preference shares. Any bank overdraft would be included to the extent that it is actually a source of long-term finance. Shareholders' funds comprises equity share capital and reserves.

Another useful ratio is the ratio of long-term debt to total assets, which is calculated as follows:

$$\frac{\text{Total long-term debt}}{\text{Total assets}} \times 100$$

This can provide very useful information for creditors as it measures the availability of assets in the business in relation to the total debt.

14.6 Valuation ratios and analysis for the investor

The analytical process for investment purposes will utilise the ratios identified in the above sections. These ratios may be supplemented by further ratios specifically for investors. The use of the market price of equity is an important component of this type of analysis.

14.6.1 Price/earnings ratio

A common benchmark for investors analysing different companies is the use of the price/earnings (P/E) ratio:

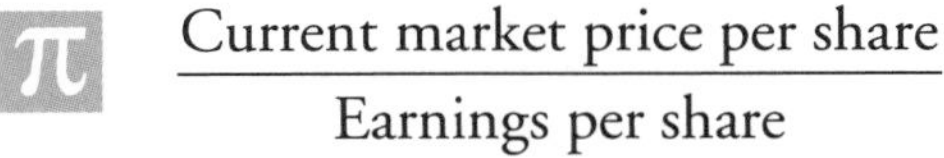

$$\frac{\text{Current market price per share}}{\text{Earnings per share}}$$

Earnings per share is basically the earnings available for distribution divided by the number of ordinary shares in issue. The calculation of earnings per share is covered in detail in Chapter 15 of this *Learning System.*

The P/E ratio calculation produces a number which can be useful for assessing the relative risk of an investment.

Example 14.B

	V	W
Current market price per share	396¢	288¢
Most recent earnings per share	13.4¢	35.6¢
P/E ratio	29.6	8.1

W has much higher earnings per share than V, but the price of one share in W is lower than one share in V, giving rise to two very different P/E ratios. Generally, the lower the P/E ratio the greater the indication of risk for the investor.

The rational expectations of buyers and sellers in the stock market tend to be incorporated in the price of the share. The P/E ratios of these entities tend to suggest that the market considers investment in W to be riskier than investment in V.

There may be reasons to account for this difference, for example:

- The numerator of the fraction is current (an up-to-date market price can be obtained easily during the market's opening hours), but the EPS figure is the latest available which, for a listed entity in many markets, can be up to 6 months old. The EPS of either entity may therefore be quite significantly out of date.
- W may have issued a profits warning, or might have suffered adverse events, such as, for example, the loss of a major contract or the resignation of a key director. These events may have depressed the share price.
- W may be in a sector which is unfashionable or relatively undervalued.
- W may have had a difficult recent history with a volatile pattern of earnings. On the whole, markets prefer companies with a smooth profit record.

As usual, the process of analysis leads to demands for more information. A better picture could be obtained of V and W if share price graphs for the last year, for example, were available, so that the analyst could see whether the share prices quoted above are near to average or not.

14.6.2 Dividend-related ratios

Growth potential and the ability to generate future wealth in the business may depend on the amount of profits retained. This relationship may be measured using the profit retention ratio:

$$\frac{\text{Profit after dividends}}{\text{Profit before dividends}} \times 100$$

The higher the proportion of earnings retained, the higher the growth potential. Cash is retained in the business for growth as opposed to being paid to shareholders.

$$\frac{\text{Cash dividend per share}}{\text{Earnings per share}} \times 100$$

When analysing financial statements from an investor's point of view it is important to identify the objectives of the investor. Does the investor require high capital growth, usually associated with high risk, or a lower risk fixed dividend payment and low capital growth?

Dividend yield will indicate the return on capital investment, relative to market price:

$$\frac{\text{Dividend per share}}{\text{Market price per share}} \times 100$$

Dividend cover measures the ability of the entity to maintain the existing level of dividend and is used in conjunction with the dividend yield:

$$\frac{\text{Earnings per share}}{\text{Dividends per share}}$$

The higher the dividend cover, the more likely it is that the dividend yield can be maintained.

14.6.3 Statement of financial position ratios

The statement of financial position may be used in computing ratios of particular interest to the investor. The book value per share indicates the asset backing of the investment:

$$\frac{\text{Shareholders' funds}}{\text{No. of equity shares in issue at the balance sheet date}}$$

However, this must be interpreted with care:

1. Assets in the statement of financial position may be measured on historical cost values. Other valuations of assets may be more informative.
2. The ratio may be irrelevant in service-based businesses where the major asset is the quality of staff and other intangibles which may not be included in the statement of financial position.

The book value per share may be compared to the market value per share to determine the market's evaluation of the business.

Example 14.C

This example will be used to illustrate the calculation of most of the accounting ratios illustrated so far in this chapter.

The income statement of PX for the year ended 31 December 20X4 and its statement of financial position at that date are as follows:

Income statement

	$m	$m
Revenue		1,845
Cost of sales		(758)
Gross profit		1,087
Distribution costs	(136)	
Administrative expenses	(61)	
		(197)
Profit from operations		890
Finance cost		(104)
		786
Income tax expense		(69)
Profit for the period		717

Statement of financial position

	$m	$m
Assets		
Non-current assets		
Property, plant and equipment		4,002
Current assets		
Inventories	42	
Trade receivables	180	
Cash and cash equivalents	113	
		335
Total assets		4,337
Equity and Liabilities		
Issued capital ($1 shares)	600	
Retained earnings	1,132	
		1,732
Non-current liabilities		
Interest-bearing borrowings	2,022	
Deferred tax	291	
		2,313
Current liabilities		292
Total equity and liabilities		4,337

Note 1: The market price of one share of PX at 31 December 20 × 4 was \$ 10.22.
Note 2: Earnings per share is calculated as \$717m/600m = 1 19.5¢
Note 3: All sales are made on credit
Note 4: Purchases on credit in the year were \$527 million and trade payables at 31 December 20 × 4 was \$61 million
Note 5: The dividend for the year was \$400 million.

Performance: profitability ratios
Gross profit margin:

$$\frac{\text{Gross profit}}{\text{Revenue}} \times 100 = \frac{1{,}087}{1{,}845} \times 100 = 58.9\%$$

Operating profit margin:

$$\frac{\text{Operating profit}}{\text{Revenue}} \times 100 = \frac{890}{1{,}845} \times 100 = 48.2\%$$

Net profit margin

$$\frac{\text{Net profit}}{\text{Revenue}} \times 100 = \frac{717}{1{,}845} \times 100 = 38.9\%$$

Performance: activity ratios
Asset turnover:

$$\frac{\text{Revenue}}{\text{Total assets}} = \frac{1{,}845}{4{,}337} = 0.42$$

(This means that for every \$1 invested in assets, the business has produced \$0.42 in revenue)

Non-current asset turnover:

$$\frac{\text{Revenue}}{\text{Non-current assets}} = \frac{1{,}845}{4{,}002} = 0.46$$

Inventory turnover:

$$\frac{\text{Cost of sales}}{\text{Average inventory}} = \frac{758}{42} = 18 \text{ times}$$

$$\frac{\text{Average inventory}}{\text{Cost of sales}} \times 365 = \frac{42}{758} \times 365 = 20.2 \text{ days}$$

(Note that in this case the opening inventory figure is not available and we cannot, therefore, calculate an average, so closing inventory has been used.)

Performance: return on capital ratios
Return on capital employed:

$$\frac{\text{Profit}}{\text{Capital employed}} \times 100 = \frac{890}{4{,}337 - 292^*} \times 100 = 22\%$$

*Capital employed is calculated as issued capital + accumulated profits + interest-bearing borrowings + deferred tax provision, that is, total assets less current liabilities. If a breakdown of current liabilities were available, any bank overdraft could also be included.

Return on assets

$$\frac{\text{Operating Profit}}{\text{Total assets}} \times 100 = \frac{890}{4{,}337} \times 100 = 20.5\%$$

To demonstrate the relationship with other ratios, return on assets can be broken down as follows:
Operating profit margin × asset turnover = return on assets
From the calculations above:

$$48.2\% \times 0.42 = 20.5\%$$

Liquidity ratios: short term liquidity

Current ratio:

$$\frac{\text{Current assets}}{\text{Current liabilities}} = \frac{335}{292} = 1.15{:}1$$

Quick ratio:

$$\frac{\text{Current assets less inventory}}{\text{Current liabilities}} = \frac{335 - 42}{292} = 1.0{:}1$$

Note that these ratios are usually expressed as shown above, that is, as a figure compared to 1.
Immediate liquidity ratio:

$$\frac{\text{Cash}}{\text{Current liabilities}} = \frac{113}{292} = 0.37{:}1$$

Liquidity ratios: the working capital cycle

Trade receivables days:

$$\frac{\text{Average receivables}}{\text{Credit sales}} \times 365 = \frac{180}{1{,}845} \times 365 = 35.6 \text{ days}$$

Trade payables days:

$$\frac{\text{Average payables}}{\text{Credit purchases}} \times 365 = \frac{61}{527} \times 365 = 42.2 \text{ days}$$

Note that, because of limited information, closing receivables and payables have been used instead of average figures. Working capital cycle:

Inventories days	20.2
+ Receivables days	35.6
− Trade payables days	(42.2)
	13.6

Analysis of capital structure: performance effects

Interest cover:

$$\frac{\text{Profit before interest and tax}}{\text{Interest expense}} = \frac{890}{104} = 8.6 \text{ times}$$

Analysis of capital structure: gearing

Gearing ratio (debt to equity):

$$\frac{\text{Total long-term debt}}{\text{Shareholders' funds}} \times 100 = \frac{2,022}{1,732} \times 100 = 116.7\%$$

Debt to total assets ratio:

$$\frac{\text{Total long-term debt}}{\text{Total assets}} \times 100 = \frac{2,022}{4,337} \times 100 = 46.6\%$$

Investor ratios

Price/earnings ratio:

$$\frac{\text{Current market price per share}}{\text{Earnings per share}} = \frac{1,022¢}{119.5¢} = 8.6$$

Profit retention ratio:

$$\frac{\text{Profit after dividends}}{\text{Profit before dividends}} \times 100 = \frac{317}{717} \times 100 = 44.2\%$$

Dividend payout rate:

$$\frac{\text{Cash dividend per share}}{\text{Earnings per share}} \times 100 = \frac{66.7¢}{119.5¢} \times 100 = 55.8\%$$

Dividend yield:

$$\frac{\text{Dividend per share}}{\text{Market price per share}} \times 100 = \frac{66.7¢}{1,022¢} \times 100 = 6.5\%$$

Dividend cover:

$$\frac{\text{Earnings per share}}{\text{Dividends per share}} = \frac{119.5¢}{66.7¢} = 1.79 \text{ times}$$

Book value per share

$$\frac{\text{Shareholders' funds}}{\text{No. of equity shares in issue at the balance sheet date}} = \frac{1,732}{600} = \$2.89$$

14.7 Analysing the cash flow statement

The cash flow of an entity is regarded by many users as being of primary importance in understanding the operations of the business. After all, a business that cannot generate sufficient cash will, sooner or later, fail. The cash flow statement provides valuable information for the analysis of a business's operations and position. Students should note that the analysis of cash flow statements is examinable in *Financial Management.*

IAS 7 requires that all entities include a cash flow statement as an integral part of the financial statements. Chapter 6 of this *Learning System* explained in detail how to prepare a cash flow statement for a group of companies, and so the techniques of preparation will not be explained further in this chapter. It should be remembered that the IAS 7 cash flow statement categorises cash flow under three principal headings: cash flows from operating activities, investing activities and financing activities. As well as comparing these totals from year to year, various useful ratios can also be calculated. These will be illustrated using the example of a relatively simple, single entity, business operation.

Example 14.D

BC is an entity trading in high specification computer equipment. Its income statement and cash flow statement for the year ended 31 March 20X6 and its statement of financial position at that date are presented below:

Income statement

	$'000	$'000
Revenue		896
Cost of sales		(554)
Gross profit		342
Distribution costs	76	
Administrative expenses	142	
		(218)
Profit from operations		124
Finance cost		(3)
		121
Income tax expense		(32)
Profit for the period		89

Note: the dividend for the year was $30,000.

Statement of financial position

	$'000	$'000
Assets		
Non-current assets		
Property, plant and equipment		174
Current assets		
Inventories	79	
Trade receivables	96	
Cash and cash equivalents	–	
		175
Total assets		349
Equity And Liabilities		
Capital and reserves		
Issued capital ($1 shares)	40	
Retained earnings	165	205
Non-current liabilities		
Deferred tax		26
Current liabilities (including bank overdraft of $33,000)		118
Total equity and liabilities		349

Statement of cash flows

	$'000	$'000
Cash flows from operating activities		124
Adjustments for:		
Depreciation		14
Operating profit before working capital changes		138
Increase in inventories	(43)	
Increase in trade receivables	(61)	
Increase in trade payables	41	
		(63)
Cash generated from operations		75
Interest paid		(3)
Income taxes paid		(15)
Net cash from operating activities		57
Cash flows from investing activities		
Purchase of property, plant and equipment	(94)	
Proceeds from sale of equipment	4	
Net cash used in investing activities		(90)
Cash flows from financing activities		
Dividends paid		(24)
Net decrease in cash and cash equivalents		(57)
Cash and cash equivalents at the beginning of the period		24
Cash and cash equivalents at the end of the period		(33)

Certain important features are evident from only a brief scrutiny. The business started the year with $24,000 in the bank, but ends with an overdraft of $33,000. This is despite generating a positive operating profit. We can also easily see that there has been a substantial investment in working capital, financed partly by an increase in trade payables. Equally, it is clear that the business has made a large investment in property, plant and equipment, although it has not obtained long-term financing for this.

Useful ratios which can be calculated include the following:

Return on capital employed: cash

$$\frac{\text{Cash generated from operations}}{\text{Capital employed}} \times 100$$

$$\frac{75}{205 + 26 + 33} \times 100 = 28.4\%$$

Note that the overdraft is included as part of capital employed in this calculation. Also, the deferred tax provision is included. We could also include the current tax provision, but it is not identified in the information given. For many external users, cash is a more significant indicator than profit, and this ratio should be calculated where the information is available.

Cash generated from operations to total debt

$$\frac{\text{Cash generated from operations}}{\text{Total long-term borrowings}}$$

This gives on indication of an entity's ability to meet its long-term obligations. The inverse ratio can also be calculated:

$$\frac{\text{Total long-term borrowings}}{\text{Cash generated from operations}}$$

This provides an indication of how many years it would take to repay the long-term borrowings if all of the cash generated from operations were to be used for this purpose.

We cannot calculate these ratios for BC because the business has no long-term borrowings.

Net cash from operating activities to capital expenditure

This is calculated as follows:

$$\frac{\text{Net cash from operating activities}}{\text{Net capital expenditure}} \times 100$$

In the case of BC:

$$\frac{57}{90} \times 100 = 63.3\%$$

This gives some idea of the extent to which the business can finance its capital expenditure out of cash flows from operating activities. If it cannot meet its capital expenditure from this source, then some kind of longer-term financing is likely to be required. However, this ratio could be misleading unless calculated and compared for several years. In the case of BC the current level of capital expenditure may not be typical. The business appears to be expanding fast (judging by the greatly increased levels of investment in working capital), and it may be that levels of operating profit and cash flow have yet to catch up with the investment.

14.8 Using ratios in the exam

When answering a *Financial Management* question it is important to be able to calculate ratios with a fair degree of accuracy from the information provided. However, students should bear in mind the following points:

- Only a proportion of the marks will be awarded for calculation, and this proportion may be relatively small. Generally, the majority of the marks will be awarded for the analysis and interpretation of data given in the question. Therefore, it is important not to get too absorbed in the calculations themselves; they are a means to an end. This chapter has been an introduction to the calculations; the next following two chapters will provide much more detailed guidance as to the interpretation and analysis of financial statements.
- Where a question asks for calculation of, say, 'relevant ratios', it is best to be fairly selective. Calculating the full range of ratios, as given in this chapter, may be inappropriate for the circumstances of the question. Time can be wasted in calculating ratios that are really not very useful.

- Some ratios may be of limited use, or may even be misleading in the context of service businesses. For example, care should be taken in respect of return on capital ratios in businesses with a low level of conventional non-current assets but a high level of unrecognised intellectual capital 'assets'.
- It is usually appropriate to round to no more than one or two decimal places.

Exam candidates should always read recent Post-Examination Guides (PEGs). The analysis learning outcomes for F2 are similar to those of its predecessor, P8 and so many of the comments about the analysis and interpretation of financial statement are valid. The PEG following the November 2006 examination made the following comments about analysis and interpretation questions:

> While the general standard of analysis and interpretation has tended to improve since the first sitting of the Paper 8, many candidates produce very poor answers. One of the markers submitted the following comment: 'Some candidates displayed an inability to calculate basic ratios. The problem with ROCE persists but asset turnover was also a problem. They appear to have a lack of understanding of what they are trying to do and seem to calculate and interpret on a formulaic approach rather than demonstrating that they can apply ratio analysis as a useful tool. They do not appear to really understand what ratios can tell them and what they cannot. There seems to be a rote-learning approach as opposed to full understanding of the uses and limitations of ratio analysis.'

Please note and act upon the above!

14.9 Summary

This chapter has examined part of one learning outcome: to interpret a full range of accounting ratios. In order to interpret ratios we must appreciate how they are calculated and understand the figures behind the ratios and what the ratios can tell us about the business activities. More detailed analysis is developed in the forthcoming chapters. Calculation of accounting ratios is a key analytic toll, but it is just a means to an end. The important part is to be able to analyse the information and draw conclusions about the entity's performance and position.

Revision Questions 14

The first two questions are not of exam standard, they are included so as to allow students to practice the calculations of ratios. The calculation of ratios is usually an integral part of a question requiring interpretation of financial statements (covered in more depth in the next chapter). The third question is of exam standard and can be answered using the knowledge gained from studying this chapter.

Question 1

The following balances were extracted from the books of B, a listed entity, at 30 April 20X8:

	$m
Sales (all on credit)	300
Cost of sales	200
Gross profit	100
Closing inventory	15
Trade receivables	36
Trade payables	28

(a) Calculate the receivables days for B for the year ended 30 April 20X8.
(b) Calculate the working capital cycle for B for the year ended 30 April 20X8.

Tutorial note: a figure for purchases is not available, so use cost of sales instead. This gives a less reliable result, but in practice, a purchases figure is often not disclosed.

B has 100,000,000 issued ordinary shares with a par value of 20¢ each. There were no movements of issued share capital during the year. B had the following results for the year ended 30 April 20X8:

	$m
Profit before tax	50
Income tax expense	10
Profit for the year	40

The dividend for the year was $20 million

The quoted price of B shares on 30 April 20X8 was $1.50.

(c) Calculate the P/E ratio of B at 30 April 20X8.

(5 marks)

Question 2

The income statement, statement of changes in equity and cash flow statement for DE for the year ended 31 March 20X2 and its statement of financial position at that date are given below:

Income statement

	$'000	$'000
Revenue		3,920
Cost of sales		(2,743)
Gross profit		1,177
Distribution costs	(184)	
Administrative expenses	(308)	
		(492)
Profit from operations		685
Income from investments	31	
Finance cost	(191)	
		(160)
Profit before tax		525
Income tax expense		(110)
		415

Summarised statement of changes in equity

	$'000
Equity at start of year	1,586
Revaluation	989
Profit for the period	415
Dividends paid	(320)
Share issue	1,575
Equity at end of year	4,245

Statement of financial position

	$'000	$'000
Assets		
Non-current assets		
Intangible assets	550	
Tangible assets	3,260	
Investments	400	
		4,210
Current assets		
Inventories	515	
Trade receivables	1,000	
Investments	315	
Bank	650	
		2,480
Total assets		6,690
Equity And Liabilities		
Capital and reserves		
Issued capital ($1 shares)	325	
Share premium	2,300	
Revaluation reserve	1,339	
Retained earnings	281	
		4,245
Non-current liabilities		
10% loan notes 2003/2006		251

Current liabilities		
Trade payables	784	
Other payables	460	
Bank loans and overdrafts	950	
		2,194
Total equity and liabilities		6,690

Cash flow statement

	$'000	$'000
Cash flows from operating activities		
Profit from operations		685
Adjustments for:		
Depreciation		480
Operating profit before working capital changes		1,165
Increase in inventories	(155)	
Increase in trade receivables	(50)	
Increase in trade and other payables	158	
		(47)
Cash generated from operations		1,118
Interest paid		(191)
Income taxes paid		(71)
Net cash from operating activities		856
Cash flows from investing activities		
Purchase of non-current assets and investment	(1,556)	
Interest received	31	
Net cash used in investing activities		(1,525)
Cash flows from financing activities		
Proceeds from issuance of share capital	1,575	
Repayment of long-term borrowings	(728)	
Dividends paid	(320)	
		527
Net decrease in cash and cash equivalents		(142)
Cash and cash equivalents at the beginning of the period		(158)
Cash and cash equivalents at the end of the period		(300)

Note

1. all sales are on credit;
2. purchases for the year were $2,555,000;
3. earnings per share for the year is 180¢;
4. the current market price of one share at 31 March 20X2 is $15.76;
5. dividend per share is 98.5¢.

Requirement

Calculate as many accounting ratios as possible from the information provided.

Question 3

BSP, a listed entity, supplies, installs and maintains burglar alarm systems for business clients. As a response to increased competition and falling margins in the burglar alarm market, the entity's directors decided, towards the end of 20X5, to extend its operations into the provision of fire alarm and sprinkler systems. A training programme for staff was undertaken in the early months of 20X6 at a cost of around $200,000. An aggressive marketing campaign, costing $250,000, was launched at the same time. Both costs were incurred and settled before the 31 March 20X6 year end. BSP commenced its new operation with effect from the beginning of its financial year on 1 April 20X6.

BSP's cash resources were at a low level in early 20X6, so, in order to finance the costs of the new operation and the necessary increase in working capital to fund the new operations, BSP made a new issue of shares. The issue took place in May 20X6. During March 20X7, BSP disposed of its two overseas subsidiaries in order to concentrate on operations in its home market. Both were profitable businesses and therefore sold for an amount substantially in excess of carrying value. Therese subsidiaries accounted for almost 10% of group sales during the 20X6/20X7 financial year.

As the finance director's assistant you have been responsible for the preparation of the draft financial statements, which have been circulated to the directors in advance of a board meeting to be held later this week.

The marketing director, who as appointed in June 20X6, has sent you the following e-mail:

'When I did my university course in marketing I studied a module in finance and accounting, which covered the analysis of financial statements. Unfortunately, it was a long time ago, and I've forgotten quite a lot about it.

I'm puzzled by the statement of cash flows, in particular. The income statement shows a loss, which is obviously bad news, especially as the budget showed a profit for the year. However, the cash resources of the business have actually increased by quite a large amount between March 20X6 and March 20X7. It is said that "cash is king", So I'm assuming that the poor profitability is a short-term problem while the new operation settles down.

As you know, we almost managed to achieve our sales targets in both the fire and burglar alarm sectors for the year, (although of course we did have to offer some customers special discounts and extended credit as inducements). I'm assuming, therefore, that the lack of profitability is a problem of cost control.

It would be really helpful if you could provide me with a brief report, in advance of this week's meeting, which tells me what this statement of cash flows means. You could include ratios, provided that you show how they are calculated.'

The consolidated statement of cash flows for the year ended 31 March 20X7 (with comparative figures for 20X6) is as follows:

BSP: Consolidated statement of cash flows for the year ended 31 March 20X7

	20X7	*20X7*	*20X6*	*20X6*
	$000	$000	$000	$000
Cash flows from operating activities				
(Loss)/profit before tax	(453)		306	
Adjustments for:				
Depreciation	98		75	
Foreign exchange loss	22		37	
Profit on sale of investments	(667)		–	
Interest expense	161		45	
		(839)		463
Increase in inventories		(227)		(65)
Increase in receivables		(242)		(36)
Increase in payables		62		12
Cash (outflow)/inflow from operations		(1,246)		374
Interest paid		(157)		(42)

Tax paid		(38)		(55)
Net cash (outflow)/inflow from operating activities		(1,441)		277
Cash flows from investing activities				
Proceeds from sale of investments	2,320		–	
Purchase of property, plant and equipment	(661)		(425)	
Income from associates	23		26	
Net cash inflow/(outflow) from financing activities		1,682		(399)
Cash flows from financing activities				
Proceeds from issue of share capital	850		–	
Dividends paid	–		(200)	
Net cash inflow/(outflow) from financing activities		850		(200)
Net increase/(decrease) in cash		1,091		(322)
Cash at start of period		27		349
Cash at end of period		1,118		27

Additional information:
Revenue in the 20X5/X6 financial year was $12.11 million. In the 20X6/X7 financial year, total revenue was $12.32 million, $10.93 million of which arose in respect of the sale of burglar alarms.

Inventories at the start of the 20X5/X6 financial year were $591,000, and receivables were $1,578,000. There was no increase in long-term borrowings throughout the two year period covered by the cash flow statement above.

Requirement

Analyse and interpret the information given, and produce a report to the marketing director. The report should explain the difference between cash and profit, and should discuss the business's profitability and working capital position. It should also discuss, to the extent possible from the information given, the prospects for BSP's future. **(25 marks)**

Solutions to Revision Questions

Solution 1

(a) $\dfrac{\text{Trade receivables}}{\text{Sales}} \times 365 = \dfrac{36}{300} \times 365 = 43.8 \text{ days}$

(b) Working capital cycle:

$$\dfrac{\text{Trade receivables}}{\text{Sales}} \times 365 = \dfrac{36}{300} \times 365 = 43.8 \text{ days}$$

$$\dfrac{\text{Trade payables}}{\text{Cost of sales}} \times 365 = \dfrac{28}{200} \times 365 = (51.1 \text{ days})$$

$$\dfrac{\text{Inventory}}{\text{Cost of sales}} \times 365 = \dfrac{15}{200} \times 365 = 27.4 \text{ days}$$

Working capital cycle 20.1 days

(c) $\text{Earnings per share} = \dfrac{\text{profit for the year available to ordinary shareholders}}{\text{number of ordinary shares in issue}}$

$$= \dfrac{\$40,000,000}{100,000,000} = 40¢ \text{ per share}$$

$\text{P/E ratio is} = \dfrac{150¢}{40¢} = 3.75$

Solution 2

Performance: profitability ratios

Gross profit margin:

$$\dfrac{\text{Gross profit}}{\text{Revenue}} \times 100 = \dfrac{1,177}{3,920} \times 100 = 30\%$$

Operating profit margin:

$$\frac{\text{Operating profit}}{\text{Revenue}} \times 100 = \frac{685}{3{,}920} \times 100 = 17.5\%$$

Net profit margin:

$$\frac{\text{Net profit}}{\text{Revenue}} \times 100 = \frac{415}{3{,}920} \times 100 = 10.6\%$$

Performance: activity ratios
Asset turnover:

$$\frac{\text{Revenue}}{\text{Total assets}} = \frac{3{,}920}{6{,}690} = 0.59$$

Non-current asset turnover:

$$\frac{\text{Revenue}}{\text{Non-current assets}} = \frac{3{,}920}{4{,}210} = 0.93$$

Inventory turnover:
Note that in this case it is possible to derive opening inventory by using information in the cash flow statement. Closing inventory was \$515,000, an increase of \$155,000 over the previous year end. Opening inventory was, therefore, \$360,000, so the average figure for the year is:

$$\frac{\$515{,}000 + 360{,}000}{2} = \$437{,}500$$

$$\frac{\text{Cost of sales}}{\text{Average inventory}} = \frac{2{,}743}{437.5} = 6.3 \text{ times}$$

$$\frac{\text{Average inventory}}{\text{Cost of sales}} \times 365 = \frac{437.5}{2{,}743} \times 365 = 58.2 \text{ days}$$

Performance: return on capital ratios
Return on capital employed:

$$\frac{\text{Profit}}{\text{Capital employed*}} \times 100 = \frac{685}{4{,}245 + 251 + 950} \times 100 = 12.5\%$$

*Capital employed is calculated as issued capital + retained earnings + interest-bearing borrowings + overdraft.
Return on assets:

$$\frac{\text{Operating Profit}}{\text{Total assets}} \times 100 = \frac{685}{6{,}690} \times 100 = 10.2\%$$

Liquidity ratios: short term liquidity
Current ratio:

$$\frac{\text{Current assets}}{\text{Current liabilities}} = \frac{2{,}480}{2{,}194} = 1.13{:}1$$

Quick ratio:

$$\frac{\text{Current assets less inventory}}{\text{Current liabilities}} = \frac{2,480 - 515}{2,194} = 0.90{:}1$$

Liquidity ratios: the working capital cycle
Trade receivables days:
As for inventory, we can calculate an opening figure for receivables, so it is possible to work out average receivables. Opening receivables was: \$1,000,000 − 50,000 = 950,000. The average for the year is \$975,000.

$$\frac{\text{Average receivables}}{\text{Credit sales}} \times 365 = \frac{975}{3,920} \times 365 = 90.8 \text{ days}$$

Trade payables days:

$$\frac{\text{Closing trade payables}}{\text{Credit sales}} \times 365 = \frac{784}{2,555} \times 365 = 112 \text{ days}$$

Working capital cycle:

Inventories days	58.2
+ Receivables days	90.8
− Trade payables days	(112.0)
	37.0

Analysis of capital structure: performance effects
Interest cover:

$$\frac{\text{Profit before interest and tax}}{\text{Interest expense}} = \frac{685 + 31}{191} = 3.75 \text{ times}$$

Analysis of capital structure: statement of financial position gearing
Gearing ratio:

$$\frac{\text{Total long-term debt}}{\text{Shareholders' funds}} \times 100 = \frac{251}{4,245} \times 100 = 5.9\%$$

Debt to total assets ratio:

$$\frac{\text{Total long-term debt}}{\text{Total assets}} \times 100 = \frac{251}{6,690} \times 100 = 3.7\%$$

Investor ratios
Price/earnings ratio:

$$\frac{\text{Current market price per share}}{\text{Earnings per share}} = \frac{1,576¢}{180¢} = 8.7$$

Profit retention ratio:

$$\frac{\text{Profit after dividends}}{\text{Profit before dividends}} \times 100 = \frac{415 - 320}{415} \times 100 = 22.9\%$$

Dividend payout rate:

$$\frac{\text{Cash dividend per share}}{\text{Earnings per share}} \times 100 = \frac{98.5¢}{180¢} \times 100 = 54.7\%$$

Dividend yield:

$$\frac{\text{Dividend per share}}{\text{Market price per share}} \times 100 = \frac{98.5¢}{1{,}576¢} \times 100 = 6.3\%$$

Dividend cover:

$$\frac{\text{Earnings per share}}{\text{Dividends per share}} = \frac{180¢}{98.5¢} = 1.82 \text{ times}$$

Statement of financial position ratio: book value per share

$$\frac{\text{Shareholders' funds}}{\text{No. of equity shares in issue at the balance sheet date}} = \frac{4{,}245}{325} = \$13.06$$

Return on capital employed: cash

$$\frac{\text{Cash generated from operations}}{\text{Capital employed}} \times 100 = \frac{1{,}118}{5{,}446^*} \times 100 = 20.5\%$$

* Same as used in the ROCE calculation earlier.

Cash generated from operations to total debt

$$\frac{\text{Cash generated from operations}}{\text{Total debt}} = \frac{1{,}118}{251} = 4.5$$

Net cash from operating activities to capital expenditure:

$$\frac{\text{Net cash from operating activities}}{\text{Net capital expenditure}} \times 100 = \frac{856}{1{,}556} \times 100 = 55\%$$

Solution 3

To: Marketing Director of BSP

From: Assistant to Finance Director

Report on draft statement of cash flows for the financial year ended 31 March 20X7

Note: The appendix to this report contains some ratio and other relevant calculations.

1. The difference between cash and profit

Because of the use of the accruals basis in financial accounting, it is often the case that profit or loss differs significantly from the cash flows arising during an accounting period. This is not necessarily a problem, unless significant cash shortages affect the viability of the business, but it does mean that the statement of cash flows should be interpreted with some caution. An apparently healthy cash balance can disguise underlying problems.

In the case of BSP's statement of cash flows, there is, indeed, a significant amount of cash at 31 March 20X7. However, upon closer examination, it can be seen that the cash inflows have arisen from investing and financing activities, rather than from operating activities which produced negative cash flows. A total of $3,170,000 (i.e. $2,320,000 from the sale of the subsidiaries and $850,000 from the issue of share capital) was received in cash during the year. While some of this (approximately one-third) remained in the statement of financial position at 31 March 20X7, most of it had been absorbed by the major cash outflow from operations and the acquisition of property, plant and equipment.

2. Profit and loss

BSP's profit before tax has declined sharply between 20X6 and 20X7. The decline is even more marked if unusual items are taken into account. Towards the end of the 20X6 financial year, the business incurred $450,000 in costs of training and marketing associated with the new product line. Profit before these items was $756,000. The loss before tax in the year ended 31 March 20X7 was mitigated substantially by the profit on disposal of the foreign subsidiaries. If this profit is excluded, the loss from operations is $1,120,000. Using these adjusted figures, net profitability (measured on a pre-tax basis) was 6.2% in the 20X6 financial year, whereas the loss in 20X7 represented 9.1% of revenue.

1. Working capital

The operating section of the statement of cash flows includes adjustments for increases and decreases in working capital. Both inventories and receivables increased by a substantial amount in the year ended 31 March 20X7. Inventories increased by 10.9% in 20X6 and by 34.6% in 20X7. Some increase in inventories is consistent with the move into a new area of operations, but the increase of 34.6% does appear very high.

Receivables have also increased substantially, by 15% between 20X6 and 20X7. The overall revenue figure has increased very little. The receivables figure at 31 March 20X7 does not include any amounts relating to the two subsidiaries disposed of. The revenue figure for the year has therefore been reduced to 90% of the total, to exclude the revenues relating to these subsidiaries. Using these two figures, receivables days at the year end is approximately 61 days. Receivables days at the previous year end was about 49 days. (It should be noted that these two figures are not directly comparable because the 20X6 revenue and receivables figures include the two subsidiaries.) The policy of offering extended credit as an inducement to customers may very well have paid off in terms of additional sales, but there are some drawbacks.

Compared to inventories and receivables, the movements in the 2 years in payables are relatively minor. In both 20X6 and 20X7 there are increases which offset the outflows on other working capital items.

2. Prospects for the future

Although sales targets for the 20X7 financial year were almost met, the decline in profitability does, as you suggest, indicate that there is a problem in controlling costs. However, it cannot necessarily be assumed that this is a short-term problem while the new operation settles down; careful cost control will be required if the business, overall, is to return to profitability. Offering discounts in order to attract new business may be effective in increasing revenue, but this practice tends to reduce profitability.

Because the sale of the subsidiaries took place so recently, the revenue figures for 20X7 are not affected. However, these two subsidiaries have accounted for around 10% of the sales, and have been consistently profitable. Therefore, unless there is an improvement in sales and profitability in the remaining group businesses, the 20X8 performance is likely to be even worse than in 20X7. The effect may be mitigated to some extent by lower interest charges. These rose substantially in 20X7, compared to 20X6, but the large cash balance in hand at the beginning of the new financial year should ensure that, for some months at least, there will be no short-term borrowings and hence, no interest payments.

The breakdown of the revenue figure shows that there has been a sharp decline in the sales relating to burglar alarms; sales in 20X7 were only 90.3% of sales in 20X6. The shortfall has been made up by sales of fire alarm systems, which tends to justify the change in business strategy. However, if tough conditions continue in the burglar alarm market, revenues from this source may continue to fall.

A final point relates to dividend. A dividend of $200,000 was paid in the 20X6 financial year, but there was no dividend in 20X7. Shareholders made a substantial contribution in the form of new capital in 20X7; while they may be content to wait for a return while the new line of business is getting established, they may become impatient if no dividend is forthcoming in 20X8.

3. Conclusion

In conclusion, the statement of cash flows serves to emphasise some worrying trends in the business. The cash balance available at 31 March 20X7 will rapidly disappear unless the losses can be reversed. Working capital management and cost control must be improved. This statement of cash flows shows the more positive side of disposing of two profitable subsidiaries; the negative aspects are likely to make an impact on the 20X8 and subsequent statement of cash flows.

APPENDIX: Calculations

1. (Loss)/profit before tax as a percentage of revenue

20X7	*20X6*
(453)/12,320 × 100 = (3.7%)	306/12,110 × 100 = 2.5%

2. (Loss)/profit before tax as a percentage of revenue – after adjustment for unusual items

20X6: calculate profit before deduction of unusual items: $306 + 200 + 250 = $756
20X7: calculate loss before setting off profit on disposal of subsidiaries: $(453) + (667) = (1,120)

20X7	*20X6*
(1,120)/12,320 × 100 = (9.1%)	756/12,110 × 100 = 6.2%

3. Inventory movement

	$	*Increase year on year %*
At 1 April 20X5	591,000	
At 31 March 20X6 (591 + 65)	656,000	10.9%
At 31 March 20X7 (656 + 227)	883,000	34.6%

4. Receivables movement

	$	*Increase year on year %*
At 1 April 20X5	1,578,000	
At 31 March 20X6 (1,578 + 36)	1,614,000	2.3%
At 31 March 20X7 (1,614 + 242)	1,856,000	15%

Receivables days (using year end figures):

20X7	*20X6*
1,856/(12,320 × 90%) × 365 = 61.1 days	1,614/12,110 × 365 = 48.6 days

Earnings Per Share

Earnings Per Share

15

Learning Outcome

After studying this chapter students should be able to:

- interpret a full range of accounting ratios.

This chapter completes the work begun in Chapter 14 on how to calculate accounting ratios.

15.1 Introduction

This chapter is devoted to the study of a single accounting ratio. This may at first seem a little odd, given that a very large number of accounting ratios were covered in Chapter 14. However, earnings per share is regarded as particularly important. Investors and others who are looking for headline measurements of a entity's performance will often look first (and perhaps last) to the eps figure. It has additional significance in that it forms the denominator of the price/earnings ratio, a measurement that is regarded as being of great significance for listed entities.

The status accorded to earnings per share leads to it being dealt with as a special case in accounting standards. There are no regulations about the calculation of any of the other accounting ratios. Earnings per share, on the other hand, has its own accounting standard (IAS 33) which sets out rules relating to its consistent calculation and presentation.

This chapter covers the following areas:

Section 15.2: IAS 33 *Earnings per share* – some basic definitions.
Section 15.3: Basic earnings per share, including adjustments for changes in number of shares in issue during the year (rights issues and bonus issues).
Section 15.4: Diluted earnings per share, including adjustments in respect of convertible financial instruments, share warrants and options, and dilutive potential ordinary shares.

15.2 IAS 33 *Earnings per share*

The EPS of an entity whose shares are publicly traded is regarded as a very important measure of performance. It is therefore important that EPS should be reported on a standard basis for all relevant companies. IAS 33 lays down clear and generally accepted definitions and procedures for calculating EPS and applies to all entities whose ordinary shares or potential ordinary shares are publicly traded. The basic principle of EPS is to obtain a consistent and comparable ratio for measuring earnings.

Definitions

> *Net profit attributable to ordinary shareholders.* Consolidated profit or loss for the year after tax, minority interests and appropriations in respect of non-equity shares. The shares of net profit of associates and joint ventures are included.

> *Weighted average number of ordinary shares.* IAS 33 defines an ordinary share thus: 'An ordinary share is an equity instrument that is subordinate to all other classes of equity instruments.' The weighted average number of ordinary shares reflects the issues and repurchases of shares during the year. The weighting of the average is on a time basis.

Example 15.A

A's year end is 31 December. The following transactions in shares took place during the year ended 31 December 20X1:

1 January ordinary shares in issue	1,000,000
1 April 100,000 shares issued	100,000
1 May 200,000 shares issued	200,000
1 Dec 10,000 shares repurchased	(10,000)
As at 31 December	1,290,000

The weighted average number of shares is:

1 Jan–31 Mar: 1,000,000 × 3/12	250,000
1 April–30 Apr: 1,100,000 × 1/12	91,667
1 May–30 Nov: 1,300,000 × 7/12	758,333
1 Dec–31 Dec: 1,290,000 × 1/12	107,500
Weighted average number of shares	1,207,500

Shares are included in the weighted average number of shares from the date the consideration is receivable:

- when cash is receivable, where shares are issued in exchange for cash;
- at the date of payment of dividend, when dividends are reinvested as shares;
- when interest ceases to accrue, for convertible debt and other financial instruments;
- at the date of acquisition, when shares are issued for consideration in the acquisition of another entity.

15.3 Basic earnings per share

EPS can be a relatively straightforward ratio to calculate. However here are some complications that may arise in practice.

Problems in arriving at the number of equity shares in issue

Arriving at the number of equity shares in issue can present a problem if there is an issue of shares during the year.

The following situations may arise:

- issue at full market price;
- bonus issue (also known as capitalisation issue or scrip issue);
- share exchange;
- rights issue.

The key to understanding the calculations is to assess whether the change in share capital has increased the earnings potential of the entity.

15.3.1 Issue at full market price

Where there is an issue at full market price, cash or other assets will flow into the entity – these will then generate earnings. In order to reflect this in the calculations, the earnings are apportioned over the average number of shares in issue and ranking for dividend during the period weighted on a time basis.

Example 15.B

A had four million ordinary shares in issue and ranking for dividend at 1 January 20X1. On 30 September, one million further shares were issued. Earnings for the year ended 31 December 20X1 were $500,000.

The number of shares would be time apportioned as follows:

1 Jan–30 Sep: 4,000,000 × 9/12	3,000,000
30 Sept–31 Dec: 5,000,000 × 3/12	1,250,000
Weighted average number of shares	4,250,000
Earnings per share are 500,000/4,250,000	11.8¢

15.3.2 Bonus issue

In a bonus issue, no fresh capital enters the business and no further earnings are generated. The effect is merely to revise the number of shares in issue. We therefore use the number of shares ranking for dividend after the bonus issue. This can be done by multiplying the original share capital by the bonus factor. If the bonus issue is a 1 for 4, the bonus factor is 5/4. This is irrespective of the date when the bonus issue was made.

The corresponding figures for all earlier periods are recalculated to include the bonus issue. This can be done by multiplying the corresponding EPS by the reciprocal of the bonus factor.

Example 15.C

B has four million ordinary shares in issue at 1 January 20X1. On 30 September the entity made a bonus issue of 1 for 4. Earnings for the year ended 31 December 20X1 were $500,000. The EPS for 20X0 was 9 cents per share.

The number of shares would be:

$$4{,}000{,}000 \times \frac{5}{4} = 5{,}000{,}000$$

$$\text{EPS would be } \frac{500{,}000}{5{,}000{,}000} = 10¢ \text{ per share}$$

The EPS for the previous year's comparative is restated using the bonus fraction:

$$\text{20X0 EPS} = 9¢ \times \frac{4}{5} = 7.2¢ \text{ per share}$$

Share exchange

Where shares (ranking for dividend) or loan stock have been issued during the year in consideration for shares in a new subsidiary, they are included in the weighting calculation as of the date on which the acquisition is recognised.

In the calculation of EPS, this is treated as an issue at full market price.

15.3.3 Rights issue

A rights issue is an issue to existing shareholders, made at a price below current market price, to encourage shareholders to take up the shares. Cash is received into the entity to generate income, but not as much as an issue at full market price. Therefore a rights issue is a combination of an issue at full market price and a bonus issue.

The calculation will have to reflect the bonus element of the rights issue; this is done by calculating the bonus fraction as follows:

$$\text{Bonus fraction} = \frac{\text{Fair value before the exercise of rights}}{\text{Theoretical ex-rights price}}$$

The numerator of the bonus fraction can be obtained from the share prices or is given in the examination question. The denominator is calculated as the theoretical value of the shares after the issue.

The bonus fraction is applied, as with a bonus issue, to all periods and will affect the number of shares prior to the issue and the corresponding year's EPS.

The other element of the rights issue, the issue at full market price, is reflected by calculating the weighted average number of shares on a time basis.

Example 15.D

C had four million ordinary shares in issue and ranking for dividend at 1 January 20X1. On 30 September, a rights issue of 1 for 4 at 50 cents per share was made. The market price of the shares prior to the issue was $ 1 per share. Earnings for the year ended 31 December 20X1 were $500,000. The EPS for 20X0 was 9 cents per share.

1. Calculate the price of the shares after the rights issue, the theoretical ex-rights price*:

		$
If a shareholder had four shares at $1 per share	=	4.00
They would be entitled to a further one share at 50¢ per share	=	0.50
Holding after the rights issue five shares (at 90¢)		4.50

* *Note:* This ex-rights price is theoretical. It may not be (and probably will not be) the same as the market price of the shares immediately after the rights issue.

2. The bonus fraction would be:

$$\text{Bonus fraction} = \frac{\text{Fair value before the exercise of rights}}{\text{Theoretical ex-rights price}}$$

3. Calculate the weighted average number of shares:

1 Jan–30 Sep: (4,000,000 × 100/90) × 9/12	3,333,333
30 Sept–31 Dec: 5,000,000 × 3/12	1,250,000
Weighted average number of shares	4,583,333

4. Calculate EPS:

$$\frac{500{,}000}{4{,}583{,}333} = 10.9¢$$

5. The EPS for the prior year comparative is restated using the inverse of the bonus fraction:

$$\text{20X0 EPS} = 9¢ \times \frac{9}{10} = 8.1¢ \text{ per share}$$

15.3.4 Other relevant points

Changes in ordinary shares without any corresponding changes in resources

The bonus issue example discussed above required that the ratio reflects a change in ordinary shares; the increase is due to the bonus, while profits are not affected as no new resources were introduced into the entity following the issue. Therefore the EPS ratio is amended for all periods disclosed in the financial statements.

Another example is the *scrip dividend.* A entity may offer to its shareholders the choice of receiving further fully paid-up shares in the entity as an alternative to receiving a cash dividend.

One interpretation is that the dividend forgone represents payment for the shares. This would mean that there is a change in resources and so no restatement of previous periods is necessary.

Alternatively, it may be interpreted that the market value of the shares received is greater than the dividend value. In this instance a bonus element is identified and should be applied to prior periods. This is then like a rights issue.

Special dividends

An entity may declare a special dividend (usually very large) and will then consolidate its ordinary shares.

The two transactions need to be viewed as a whole. The consolidation of shares will reduce the number of shares. In this case there is an outflow of resources, being the special dividend, which indicates that prior periods need not be affected. There is no bonus element to be calculated and applied to prior periods.

Example 15.E

N's reported earnings for the year ended 31 March 20X4 were $3 million. On 1 December 20X3 the directors decided to declare a special dividend of $ 1,500,000. The 1,000,000 $1 ordinary shares would be consolidated on a 2:1 basis. One new share would be issued for every two old shares held. The basic earnings per share for the year ended 31 March 20X3 was 200 cents per share.

Calculate the basic earnings per share year ended 31 March 20X4 with comparatives.

Solution

The reduction in shares is compensated by the special dividend. There is an outflow of resources from N and so the EPS is calculated using a weighted average number of shares and the comparative is not affected.

1 April 20X3 to 30 November 20X3	1,000,000 × 8/12	666,667
1 December 20X3 to 31 March 20X4	500,000 × 4/12	166,667
Total weighted average number of shares		833,334

20X4 Basic EPS (3m/833,334)	360¢
20X3 Basic EPS no change	200¢

15.4 Diluted earnings per share

An entity may have in issue at the year end date a number of financial instruments that give rights to ordinary shares at a future date. These are referred to as potential ordinary shares in IAS 33. Examples of potential ordinary shares are:

- convertible debt or equity instruments;
- share warrants and options;
- rights granted under employee share schemes;
- contingently issuable shares, where the ordinary shares are issued upon completion of some contractual agreement.

When the obligations are realised the number of ordinary shares will increase, therefore lowering the earnings per share. This is said to have a potential dilutive effect on EPS. Earnings can be affected in some cases and the diluted EPS is calculated using an adjusted profits figure.

In order that users are informed of the potential 'dilution' of their earnings, IAS 33 requires that a diluted EPS is calculated.

The diluted EPS ratio is:

$$\frac{\text{Earnings per basic EPS} + \text{Adustment for dilutive potential ordinary shares}}{\text{Number of shares per basic EPS} + \text{Adjustment for dilutive potential ordinary shares}}$$

Potential ordinary shares are deemed to be converted to ordinary shares at the start of the period. Where the potential ordinary shares are issued during the period, they are taken from the date of issue of the financial instrument.

We shall look at the effect of each type of financial instrument. It is included in the diluted EPS only if the effect of the conversion to ordinary shares is dilutive. Dilution is where the conversion decreases EPS or increases the loss per share.

15.4.1 Convertible financial instruments

Where an entity has in issue at the year end date convertible loan stock or convertible preference shares they will affect the ratio as follows:

- *Profits*
  - There will be a saving of interest. Interest is a tax-deductible expense and so the post-tax effects will be brought into the adjusted profits.
  - There will be a saving of preference dividend. There are no associated tax effects here.
- *The number of shares will increase*. Where there is a choice of dates for conversion, IAS 33 assumes the most advantageous conversion rate or exercise price from the standpoint of the holder that is still available.

Example 15.F

Throughout the year ended 31 December 20X3 A had in issue $2,000,000 10% convertible loan stock. The terms of conversion for every $100 of loan stock are as follows:

31 December 20X3	122 ordinary shares
31 December 20X4	120 ordinary shares
31 December 20X5	110 ordinary shares

Profits attributable to ordinary shareholders for the year amounted to $25,000,000.
The weighted average number of shares in issue during the year was 100,000,000.
A paid tax at 33%.

1. *Adjust profits.*

	$	$
Earnings		25,000,000
Add net interest saved		
Interest (2m × 10%)	200,000	
Taxation (200,000 × 33%)	(66,000)	
		134,000
Fully diluted earnings		25,134,000

2. *Adjust number of shares.* The maximum number of shares that convertible loan stockholders could take up is 120 on 31 December 20X4. The 122 ordinary shares available at 31 December 20X3 would have already been taken up and so the next available time is the following year (120 shares available).

Weighted average number of shares in issue	100,000,000
Dilution (2,000,000 × 120/100)	2,400,000
Fully diluted number of shares	102,400,000
Fully diluted EPS	24.5¢

15.4.2 Share warrants and options

A share option or warrant gives the holder the right to purchase or subscribe for ordinary shares. This would involve an inflow of resources or monies into the entity and so potentially can increase profits. For the purpose of computing diluted EPS, IAS 33 requires that the assumed proceeds from these shares should be considered to have been received from the issue of shares at fair value. The difference between the number of shares that would have been issued at fair value and the number of shares actually issued is treated as an issue of ordinary shares for no consideration.

Example 15.G

B has in issue options to subscribe for 1,000,000 $1 ordinary shares at $4 per share. The average fair value of one share during the year was $6 per share.

Profits attributable to ordinary shareholders amounted to $25,000,000.
The weighted average number of shares in issue during the year was 100,000,000.

When the transaction is analysed carefully there are two elements to the issue of options:

1. an amount of shares at fair market value;
2. the remainder for no consideration.

Basic EPS = 25,000,000 ÷ 100,000,000 = 25¢

Diluted EPS:

Increase in number of shares	1,000,000
Number of shares that would have been issued at fair value (1,000,000 × \$4) ÷ \$6	(666,667)
Shares issued for no consideration	333,333

Diluted EPS = 25,000,000 ÷ (100,000,000 + 333,333) = 24.9¢

15.4.3 Dilutive potential ordinary shares

It is, of course, possible that potential ordinary shares as above could increase EPS. IAS 33 requires that the fully diluted EPS is adjusted only for those instruments that cause a dilutive effect, that is, they decrease EPS or increase loss per share.

IAS 33 requires that the calculation for the inclusion of potential ordinary shares is done by reference to net profit from continuing operations. There is also an ordering of potential ordinary shares according to their effect on the dilution of EPS from most to least dilution.

Example 15.H

A has the following data:

Profits attributable to ordinary shareholders	\$25,000,000
Net profit attributable to discontinuing operations	\$5,000,000
The weighted average number of shares in issue during the year	100,000,000
Average fair value per share	\$6
Tax rate 33%	

Potential ordinary shares as follows:

1. Options to subscribe for 1,000,000 \$1 ordinary shares at \$4 per share.
2. \$10,000,000 2% convertible bonds, the conversion terms being 500 ordinary shares per \$1,000 bond.
3. 500,000 convertible preference shares. The dividend is \$5 per share and the conversion terms are one ordinary share for one convertible preference share.

As before, we calculate the effects of the potential shares on the EPS calculation using the profits from continuing operations. This is done by order of dilution which may be found by calculating the earnings per incremental share.

Options would not increase earnings but shares increase as above by the amount of shares deemed to be issued at no consideration, that is, [1,000,000 − (1,000,000 × \$4) ÷ \$6] 333,333 shares. Therefore, no earnings per incremental share.

Two per cent convertible bonds would save interest net of tax of [10,000,000 × 2% × (1 − 0.33)] \$134,000 and would increase the number of shares by 5,000,000. The incremental earnings per share would be (134,000 ÷ 5,000,000) 2.68 cents.

Convertible preference shares increase earnings by \$2,500,000 and increase shares by 500,000, the incremental earnings per share being (2,500,000 ÷ 500,000) \$5.

The order of dilution is therefore:

1. options;
2. 2% convertible bonds;
3. convertible preference shares.

	Net profit attributable to continuing operations $	*Ordinary shares*	*Per share* ¢
Basic	20,000,000	100,000,000	20.00
Options	–	333,333	
	20,000,000	100,333,333	19.90
2% convertible bonds interest saved	134,000	5,000,000	
	20,134,000	105,333,333	19.11
Convertible preference shares	2,500,000	500,000	
	22,634,000	105,833,333	21.40

In this example the convertible preference shares increase the diluted EPS and so are eventually excluded from the calculation disclosed in the financial statements.

Final disclosure:

Basic EPS = 25,000,000 ÷ 100,000,000 = 25¢
Diluted EPS = (25,000,000 + 134,000) ÷ 105,333,333 = 23.9¢

Note that the distinction between continuing and discontinuing profits is required only for the purpose of the dilution effect calculation, and the full profit figure attributable to ordinary shareholders (i.e., $25 million) is used.

15.4.4 Disclosure requirements

The basic and diluted earnings per share should be shown on the face of the income statement.

The calculation of the weighted average number of shares should be disclosed. The number of shares used in the diluted EPS should be reconciled to the weighted average number of shares in the basic EPS.

The profit attributable to ordinary shareholders should be reconciled to the net profit or loss for the period.

IAS 33 requires that any historical data in the financial statements should be consistent with the calculations of EPS, and any restatements incorporated into the historical summary. Furthermore, IAS 33 requires that the same rules are applied to any per share calculation, for example, net assets per share, dividend per share.

15.5 Summary

This chapter covered earnings per share which is unique amongst accounting ratios in having an accounting standard devoted to it, and it therefore requires additional care in calculation. The basic calculation of earnings per share is straightforward, but as we have seen in this chapter, it can be complicated, for example, by the issue of new financial instruments during the year, and by the existence of potentially dilutive financial instruments.

Revision Questions 15

Question 1

BAQ is a listed entity with a financial year end of 31 March. At 31 March 20X7, it had 8,000,000 ordinary shares in issue.

The directors of BAQ wish to expand the business's operations by acquiring competitor entities. They intend to make no more than one acquisition in any financial year.

The directors are about to meet to discuss two possible acquisitions. Their principal criterion for the decision is the likely effect of the acquisition on group earnings per share.

Details of the possible acquisitions are as follows:

1. *Acquisition of CBR*
   - 100% of the share capital of CBR could be acquired on 1 October 20X7 for a new issue of shares in BAQ;
   - CBR has 400,000 ordinary shares in issue;
   - Four CBR shares would be exchanged for three new shares in BAQ;
   - CBR's profit after tax for the year ended 31 March 20X7 was $625,000 and the entity's directors are projecting a 10% increase in this figure for the year ending 31 March 20X8.
2. *Acquisition of DCS*
   - 80% of the share capital of DCS could be acquired on 1 October 20X7 for a cash payment of $10.00 per share;
   - DCS has 1,00,000 ordinary shares in issue;
   - The cash would be raised by a rights issue to BAQ's existing shareholders. For the purposes of evaluation it can be assumed that the rights issue would take place on 1 October 20X7, that it would be fully taken up, that the market value of one share in BAQ on that date would be $5.36, and that the terms of the rights issue would be one new share for every five BAQ shares held at a rights price of $5.00;
   - DCS's projected profit after tax for the year ending 31 March 20X8 is $860,000.

BAQ's profit after tax for the year ended 31 March 20X8 is projected to be $4.2 million. No changes in BAQ's share capital are likely to take place, except in respect of the possible acquisitions described above.

Requirements

Calculate the group earnings per share that could be expected for the year ending 31 March 20X8 in respect of each of the acquisition scenarios outlined above. **(10 marks)**

Question 2

On 1 February 20X4, CB, a listed entity, had 3,000,000 ordinary shares in issue. On 1 March 20X4, CB made a rights issue of 1 for 4 at $6.50 per share. The issue was completely taken up by the shareholders.

Extracts from CB's financial statements for the year ended 31 January 20X5 are presented below:

CB: Extracts from income statement for the year ended 31 January 20X5

	CB
	$'000
Operating profit	1,380
Interest payable	(400)
Profit before tax	980
Income tax	(255)
Profit for the period	725

CB: Extracts from summarised statement of changes in equity for the year ended 31 January 20X5

	CB
	$'000
Balance as at 1 February 20X4	7,860
Issue of share capital	4,875
Surplus on revaluation of properties	900
Profit for the period	725
Ordinary dividends	(300)
Balance as at 31 January 20X5	14,060

Just before the rights issue, CB's share price was $7.50, rising to $8.25 immediately afterwards. The share price at close of business on 31 January 20X5 was $6.25.

At the beginning of February 20X5 the average price earnings (P/E) ratio in CB's business sector was 28.4, and the P/E of its principal competitor was 42.5.

Requirements

(a) Calculate the earnings per share for CB for the year ended 31 January 20X5, and its P/E ratio at that date. **(6 marks)**

(b) Explain the significance of P/E ratios to investors, and compare CB's P/E ratio relative to those of its competitor and industry sector. **(4 marks)**

(Total marks = 10)

Question 3

Earnings per share (EPS) is generally regarded as a key accounting ratio for use by investors and others. Like all accounting ratios, however, it has its limitations. You have been asked to make a brief presentation to CIMA students on the topic.

Requirements

(a) Explain why EPS is regarded as so important that the IASB has issued an accounting standard on its calculation; **(2 marks)**

(b) Explain the general limitations of the EPS accounting ratio and its specific limitations for investors who are comparing the performance of different entities. **(8 marks)**

(Total marks = 10)

Question 4

(a) GHJ, a listed entity, has 1,000,000 ordinary shares in issue throughout 20X8. The profits after tax for the period total $800,000. The entity has two convertible financial instruments in issue:

- $500,000 10% loan stock, each $1,000 of stock having the right to convert into 2,000 ordinary shares.
- 400,000 convertible $1 non-equity shares, paying a dividend of 10p per share. Each preference share is convertible to 2 ordinary shares.

Requirement

Calculate the basic and diluted earnings per share for GHJ assuming a tax rate of 30%. **(6 marks)**

(b) ACD, another listed entity, has earnings per share in 20X7 of 25 cents per share. ACD has 4,000,000 ordinary shares in issue throughout 20X7. In 20X8 1,500,000 ordinary shares were issued by way of a capitalisation (bonus) issue. The profits after tax for the year were $1,200,000.

Requirement

Calculate the EPS for 20X8 and the restated eps for 20X7 that will be included in the 20X8 financial statements. **(4 marks)**

(Total marks = 10)

Solutions to Revision Questions

Solution 1

1. *CBR acquisition*

	$
BAQ's projected earnings	4,200,000
CBR's projected earnings – 6 months	
\$625,000 × 110% × 6/12	343,750
Projected group earnings for year ending 31 March 20X8	4,543,750

Weighted average of shares in issue:

1.4.X7 – 30.0.X7 6/12 × 8,000,000	4,000,000
1.10.X7 – 31.3.X8 {[¾ × (200,000/50¢)] + 8,000,000} × 6/12	4,150,000
	8,150,000

Projected group earnings per share if CBR acquisition takes place:

$$\frac{\$4{,}543{,}750}{8{,}150{,}000} = 55.8¢$$

2. *DCS acquisition*

Working 1: theoretical ex-rights price

5 × \$5.36	26.80
1 × \$5.00	5.00
	31.80

TERP = \$31.80/6 = \$5.30
Bonus fraction = \$5.36/5.30

Working 2: number of BAQ shares in issue after 1 October 20X7

(1/5 × 8,000,000) + 8,000,000 = 9,600,000

	$
BAQ's projected earnings	4,200,000
DCS's projected earnings – group share	
for 6 months \$860,000 × 80% × 6/12	344,000
Projected group earnings for year ending 31 March 20X8	4,544,000

Weighted average of shares in issue:

		$
1.4.X7 – 30.9.X7 (W1)	6/12 × 8,000,000 × 5.36/5.30	4,045,283
1.10.X7 – 31.3.X8	6/12 × 9,600,000 (W2)	4,800,000
		8,845,283

Projected group earnings per share if DCS acquisition takes place:

$$\frac{\$4{,}544{,}000}{8{,}845{,}283} = 51.4¢$$

Solution 2

(a)

Workings

1. *Calculate theoretical ex-rights price*

	$
4 shares × $7.50	30.00
1 share × $6.50	6.50
Theoretical value of holding of 5 shares	36.50
Theoretical ex-rights price of 1 share after rights issue: $36.50/5	7.30

2. *Calculate bonus fraction*

$$\frac{\text{Fair value of one share before rights issue}}{\text{Theoretical ex-rights price of one share (W1)}} = \frac{7.50}{7.30}$$

3. *Weighted average number of shares in issue in the year to 31 January 20X5*

	Number of shares
1 February–1 March 20X4: 3,000,000 × 7.50/7.30 × 1/12	256,849
1 March 20X4–31 January 20X5: 3,750,000 × 11/12	3,437,500
	3,694,349

$$\text{Earnings per share} = \frac{\$725{,}000}{3{,}694{,}349} = 19.6¢$$

$$\text{P/E ratio} = \frac{625}{19.6} = 31.9$$

(b)

The price earnings ratio is a measure of how the stock market views the shares of an entity. A relatively high P/E usually suggests that the shares are regarded as a safe investment. Lower P/Es suggest risk and volatility. However, it is unsafe to generalise too much. Where a listed entity has become a highly fashionable investment for some reason (for example, technology shares have in the past been regarded in this way from time to time) its high P/E ratio may help to mask fundamental weaknesses.

CB's P/E is a little above the sector average indicating that it is probably regarded as a slightly less risky investment within its sector. Its competitor has a substantially higher

P/E, which, on the face of it, would suggest that it is regarded as a very sound investment, and that its shares are currently preferred by the market compared to those of CB.

Solution 3

Notes on earnings per share

(a) eps is of particular importance because it is one of the component parts of the price/earnings (P/E) ratio. P/E is used by investors to help them identify the relative riskiness of investments, and investments that are over-valued or under-valued by the stock market. Also, eps is accorded great importance by investors, analysts and others as a key measurement of performance and as a basis for making decisions. It is principally for these reasons that some accounting standard setters, amongst them the IASB, have produced accounting standards regulating its calculation.

(b) The principal general weaknesses of eps include the following:
- eps is based on accounting figures, and can only be as reliable as those figures. Accounting figures may be subject to manipulation by using creative accounting techniques. Even where no malicious manipulation is intended, the figures are often imprecise because they involve the use of estimation.
- eps is essentially a backward looking measure because it is based on accounting figures reporting on transactions and events that have already taken place. It is of limited use for predictive purposes, although, perhaps inevitably, it is used as an indicator of future performance.
- eps, like all other accounting information published in the annual report of a business, is soon out of date. The P/E ratio calculation uses an up to date price figure, but where the price has been affected significantly by events after the year end date, the mixing of a current price with an old earnings figure may be, essentially, meaningless.

The specific weaknesses of eps for the purposes of making comparisons include the following:
- The number of shares in issue is rarely comparable between entities.
- In some instances, accounting standards permit a choice of accounting treatments. It is quite likely, therefore, that entities being compared with each other, use different policies and or bases for preparation of the financial statements. Where such policies and bases impact upon the profit figure, as will usually be the case, eps figures are not strictly comparable.
- The problem of comparability is made worse where the entities being compared are subject to different sets of accounting standards.

  eps is calculated on the basis of after tax figures. Where entities are subject to significantly differing rates of taxation because they are based in different countries, the comparison is unrealistic.

Solution 4

(a) Calculation of basic earnings per share

Profit after tax	$800,000
Weighted average number of shares outstanding	1,000,000
Basic eps	80 cents

Calculation of diluted earnings per share

Profit (working 1)	$875,000
Weighted average number of shares outstanding (working 2)	2,800,000
Fully diluted eps	31.25 cents

Calculation of profit for diluted earnings per share

	$
Profit as per basic eps	1,200,000
Plus post-tax saving on 10% loan stock (10% × $500,000 × 70%)	35,000
Plus saving on preference dividend (10% dividend × $400,000)	40,000
Profit for diluted eps	875,000

Calculation of number of shares for diluted earnings per share

Shares for basic eps	1,000,000
Plus conversion of loan stock ($500,000 × 2,000/1,000)	1,000,000
Plus conversion of preference shares ($400,000 × 2)	800,000
Number of shares for diluted eps	2,800,000

Note that the most dilutive outcome is given and in one calculation

(b) GHJ's Basic eps for 20X8 is $1,200,000/(4,000,000 1 1,500,000) 5 20 cents (note the basic eps is calculated including the bonus issue in the period – this is not time weighted – it brings no new resources and therefore is treated as if the shares were in issue from the earliest reporting date).

The comparative figure for 20X7 eps is restated to:
25 cents × 4,000,000 shares = earnings in the year of $1,000,000
Restated eps = $1,000,000/6,000,000 = 16.7 cents
Or calculated as 25 cents × 4,000,000/6,000,000 = 16.7 cents

16

Interpretation of Financial Statements

Interpretation of Financial Statements 16

Learning Outcomes

After studying this chapter students should be able to:

- Interpret a full range of accounting ratios;
- analyse financial statements in the context of information provided in the accounts and corporate report;
- evaluate performance and position based on analysis of financial statements;
- discuss segemental analysis, with inter-firm and international comparisons taking account of possible aggressive or unusual accounting policies and pressures on ethical behaviour;
- discuss the results of an analysis of financial statements and its limitations.

16.1 Introduction

This chapter extends the range of techniques covered by Chapter 14 in looking at horizontal, vertical and common size analysis in Section 16.2. Section 16.3 examines the provisions of IFRS 8 *Operating Segments.* Section 16.4 examines the limitations that are inherent in financial statements themselves. Section 16.5 looks at a closely related issue: the limits to the use of ratio analysis in practice. Section 16.6 is concerned with the need to be aware of aggressive or unusual accounting policies that may be employed by preparers in some circumstances to alter the appearance of the financial statements: the problem of creative accounting. Section 16.7 examines some of the particular problems associated with the reporting of financial obligations.

16.2 Horizontal, vertical and common size analysis

16.2.1 Horizontal analysis

Where at least 2 years' worth of information is available, it is possible to conduct a horizontal analysis of the figures. This involves tracking and explaining, as far as possible, the changes between the two sets of figures, for example, making an observation that sales have increased by more than the rate of inflation applicable to the industry.

Where several years' information is available it is possible to conduct an analysis of trends over time. Some entities provide 5- or 10-year summaries of the key figures in their financial statements and where this information is available a trend analysis can offer some interesting insights into the development of the business. The following example illustrates the technique:

Example 16.A

XY produces a 5-year summary in its annual financial statements. The financial statements for the year ended 31 March 20X7 show the following key figures extracted from the income statement:

	20X7	*20X6*	*20X5*	*20X4*	*20X3*
	$m	$m	$m	$m	$m
Revenue	2,619.7	2,381.4	2,371.5	2,347.7	2,522.9
Operating profit	324.5	298.6	277.7	334.6	372.4
Interest costs	102.6	74.4	73.0	62.1	21.0

The annual report details make it clear that sales of XY's principal product is under threat from new entrants to the market. Heavy investment in intangible assets has been required in order to maintain market share.

Before rushing into calculations it is always sensible to start with a brief scrutiny of the figures to establish a factual base on which to build the analysis. From the limited set of figures given above, we can see that revenue has increased each year since 20X4, but that the 20X4 figure represented quite a significant drop on the figure reported in 20X3. Operating profit reached a low point in 20X5 but has picked up since, although it is still not at 20X3/4 levels. This suggests that the business's margins have been squeezed, probably by competition, and/or that it is struggling to maintain control over costs. Interest costs have increased, with big increases between 20X3/4 and between 20X6/7.

It is quite possible to discern all of these points from the data without touching a calculator, and the analysis above could form quite a reasonable introductory paragraph to a report to an investor.

A few calculations will help to extend the analysis further. We can calculate the percentage rate of increase/decrease over the years, as follows:

Annual percentage increases/(decreases) in a range of key figures for XY – 20X3 to 20X7

	20X7	20X6	20X5	20X4
	%	%	%	%
Revenue	10.0	0.4	1.0	(6.9)
Operating profit	8.7	7.5	(17.0)	(10.0)
Interest cost	37.9	1.9	17.6	295.7

The horizontal analysis reinforces the point that revenue dropped significantly between 20X3 and 20X4, and that it has finally started to make a significant recovery in 20X7. The increase in 20X7 may be related directly to additional investment financed by borrowing. Operating profit performance overall looks even worse than sales performance. The figures appear to support the message picked up from elsewhere in the annual report, that the business faces a difficult competitive environment, and that it has had to invest quite heavily to maintain market share.

So, provided with 15 different figures in three categories of income statement item, we have been able to identify some quite important trends, and we have the makings of a credible report on the business for an interested party. Of course, a limited range of figures like this does not tell us everything we need to know.

Questions prompted by the analysis might include the following:

- How much has been borrowed, and what are the terms (e.g., interest rates, security provided, repayment conditions)?
- What is the nature of the investment in non-current assets? What kind of intangibles has the business invested in?
- Is there some information about costs that will allow us to see if the business has lost control over certain categories?
- Is the business performing better in some markets than in others?

The financial statements should provide some information on all of these matters. Whether or not it's sufficient information to provide comprehensive answers is another matter.
There are some problems with horizontal analysis that should be borne in mind:

- Lack of comparability because of changes in the business. Many large businesses choose to grow through acquisitions. Where there is a significant degree of mergers and acquisition activity, it can be difficult to identify true underlying trends.
- Lack of comparability because of accounting policy changes and changes in financial reporting standards. Sometimes, when presenting several years' worth of data, businesses will adjust the figures so that they are all presented in accordance with its current accounting policies and currently valid financial reporting standards. This is, obviously, helpful to the analyst. However, notes should be read very carefully to see whether or not such adjustments have been made.
- Failure to take the effects of changing price levels into account. Usually, no adjustment is made, year on year, to take changing price levels into account. However, even at a low rate of inflation in the economy, the effects of price changes can be quite substantial over several years. In the example of XY above, it is quite likely that the very small increases in revenue in 20X5 and 20X6 were decreases in real terms, if price inflation were taken into account.

16.2.2 Vertical analysis

Vertical analysis is a simple, but potentially effective technique, that involves expressing each figure in a primary financial statement as a percentage of one key figure.

Example 16.B

BB has the following summarised income statement for 20X5:

	20X5
	$'000
Revenue	1,377
Cost of sales	(897)
Gross profit	480
Distribution costs	(247)
Administration expenses	(152)
Profit before tax	81

Taking the key figure of revenue as 100%, the statement can be vertically analysed as follows:

	20X5	*20X5*
	$'000	%
Revenue	1,377	100
Cost of sales	(897)	(65)
Gross profit	480	35
Distribution costs	(247)	(18)
Administration expenses	(152)	(11)
Profit before tax	81	6

On its own this analysis is not perhaps very helpful: it requires some kind of comparison which will attribute meaning. If the data is available we can extend it over several periods in the form of common size analysis. Note that it is usual to express figures in the income statement in relation to sales. Statement of financial position figures would normally be expressed in relation to total assets.

16.2.3 Common size analysis

Common size analysis extends across several periods. Vertical common size analysis involves the type of calculation shown in Example 16.B but for the data from several accounting periods.

It is also possible to use a horizontal approach to common size analysis: a particular year is recognised as the base year and each component is assigned a value of 100 per cent. The amount of the component for each subsequent year is expressed as a percentage of the base year.

Example 16.C

Extending the example of BB above: the following data is provided for the years 20X2 to 20X5:

BB: income statements

	20X5	*20X4*	*20X3*	*20X2*
	$'000	$'000	$'000	$'000
Revenue	1,377	1,269	1,109	1,100
Cost of sales	(897)	(844)	(789)	(750)
Gross profit	480	425	320	350
Distribution costs	(247)	(225)	(210)	(199)
Administration expenses	(152)	(103)	(85)	(100)
Profit before tax	81	97	25	51

The income statement data can be common-sized vertically in relation to sales as follows:

	20X5	*20X4*	*20X3*	*20X2*
	%	%	%	%
Revenue	100	100	100	100
Cost of sales	(65)	(67)	(71)	(68)
Gross profit	35	33	29	32
Distribution costs	(18)	(18)	(19)	(18)
Administration expenses	(11)	(8)	(8)	(9)
Profit before tax	6	7	2	5

Some of the income statement data can be common-sized horizontally using 20X2 as a base year:

	20X5	*20X4*	*20X3*	*20X2*
	%	%	%	%
Revenue	125	115	100	100
Profit before tax	159	190	49	100

From this limited analysis we have an overall view and we can see that sales have increased by 25% over the period but that profits have fluctuated. The vertical common size analysis shows that gross profit margin has increased, distribution costs have remained more or less the same in relation to sales revenue, and that there has been a sharp increase in administration expenses in the most recent year. We can now investigate further using other techniques.

BB's statement of financial position data for the same accounting periods is as follows:

BB: Statements of financial position

	20X5	20X4	20X3	20X2
	$'000	$'000	$'000	$'000
Non-current assets				
Buildings	756	744	732	720
Plant	452	460	430	410
Other	69	38	30	–
	1,277	1,242	1,192	1,130
Current assets				
Inventory	267	262	296	309
Receivables	174	167	145	130
Cash	102	82	107	160
Total assets	1,820	1,753	1,740	1,729
Share capital	100	100	100	100
Retained earnings	1,492	1,440	1,420	1,383
	1,592	1,540	1,520	1,483
Current liabilities	228	213	220	246
	1,820	1,753	1,740	1,729

BB's statement of financial position can be common-sized vertically in relation to total assets as follows:

	20X5	*20X4*	*20X3*	*20X2*
	%	%	%	%
Non-current assets				
Buildings	41	42	42	42
Plant	25	26	25	24
Other	4	2	2	–
Current assets				
Inventory	15	15	17	18
Receivables	9	10	8	7
Cash	6	5	6	9
Total assets	100	100	100	100

Some of the statement of financial position data can be common-sized horizontally, using 20X2 as a base year:

	20X5	*20X4*	*20X3*	*20X2*
	%	%	%	%
Plant	110	112	105	100
Inventory	86	85	96	100
Total assets	105	101	101	100

From this limited analysis we can see that, while total assets have increased only slowly over the period, there have been larger fluctuations in inventory value (which has fallen) and plant (which has increased at a faster rate than total assets).

The common-size data forms a basis for further analysis, which is likely to incorporate some of the ratio calculations explained in Chapter 14.

16.3 Segment analysis

Many business organisations have developed into very large multinational corporations whose economic significance is substantial. As we have seen in the early chapters of this *Learning System*, groups of companies produce consolidated financial statements. These draw together the results of business that may be engaged in quite disparate activities. The advantage of such statements is that they allow the user to appreciate the financial results and position of the group as a whole. However, in the process of consolidation a great deal of detail is lost that would potentially be of great assistance to users.

Users of financial statements need sufficient information to allow them to understand how the individual segments of the business contribute to its overall performance and financial position.

16.3.1 IFRS 8 *Operating Segments*

This financial reporting standard was issued in November 2006, and was effective in respect of accounting periods beginning on or after 1 January 2008. The new IFRS replaced the existing standard IAS 14 *Segment Reporting.* The principal reason for issuing a new standard in this area was to achieve convergence with US GAAP. In this instance convergence was achieved by adopting many aspects of US SFAS 131 *Disclosures about Segments of an Enterprise and Related Information*. IFRS 8 has been subject to a degree of criticism in some quarters (and especially within the European Union) because the IASB is seen as having uncritically adopted US regulation, and also because there are, it is argued, flaws in the new standard. These will be identified and discussed below.

The principal requirements of IFRS 8 are as follows:

Scope

The scope of IFRS 8 is limited to those entities whose debt or equity instruments are traded on a public market.

Definition of an operating segment

Quoting directly from the standard:

'An operating segment is a component of an entity:

(a) that engages in business activities from which it may earn revenues and incur expenses (including revenue and expenses relating to transactions with other components of the same entity),
(b) whose operating results are regularly reviewed by the entity's chief operating decision maker to make decisions about resources to be allocated to the segment and assess its performance, and
(c) for which discrete financial information is available.'

This description therefore excludes those parts of a business that do not engage directly in business activities, such as head office functions. However, it does include business segments whose activities are principally concerned with trading intra-group.

One of the criticisms of IFRS 8 is that it allows an entity's managers to determine what is a reportable segment. Managers therefore are potentially able to conceal information by judicious selection of segments. A further, related, criticism is that comparability of segment information between businesses suffers because segment identification is likely to differ between businesses. However, it should be recognised that comparability between businesses is often problematic, and users should in any case be very cautious when comparing entities even if they appear, superficially, to be quite similar in their operations.

Criteria for reporting segment results

IFRS 8 sets quantitative thresholds for reporting. Entities should report information about an operating segment that meets any one of three quantitative thresholds:

1. Segment reported revenue (including both intra-group and external sales) exceeds 10% of the combined revenue of all operating segments.
2. Segment profit or loss is 10% of the greater of (i) the combined reported profit of all operating segments that did not report a loss; and (ii) the combined reported loss of all operating segments that reported a loss.
3. Segment assets exceed 10% of the combined assets of all operating segments.

The revenue of the disclosed operating segments that meet the criteria should equal at least 75% of total revenue of the entity. If this threshold is not met, additional operating segments should be disclosed until at least 75% of reported revenue is included in operating segments.

Reporting of comparatives

As with other financial information included in the annual report of an entity, segment disclosures should include comparatives for the previous year. It is possible that an operating segment could meet the reporting criteria in 1 year but not in another. Where a segment ceases to meet the reporting criteria information about it should continue to be disclosed provided that management judge it to be of continuing significance. Conversely, where a segment is newly identified and reported because it meets the reporting criteria for the first time, the previous year's comparatives should be reported for it, even though the segment was not significant in the prior period.

Disclosure requirements

General information about operating segments must be disclosed as follows:

1. The factors used to identify the reportable segments, including the basis on which they have been identified – for example, geographical areas, types of product or service.
2. The types of product or services from which each reportable segment derives its revenues.

The entity must disclose for each segment measures of profit or loss AND total assets. The extent of other disclosures depends to some extent on the nature and content of information that is reviewed by the 'chief operating decision maker' (probably the CEO or equivalent). A measure of liabilities must be disclosed for each segment if that information is regularly made available to the chief operating decision maker. If the following information is regularly reviewed by the chief operating decision maker it must be disclosed:

- Revenues from external customers
- Revenues from transactions with other operating segments
- Interest revenue
- Interest expense
- Depreciation and amortisation
- Material items of income and expense
- Interests in profit or loss of associates and joint ventures
- Income tax expense or income

- Material non-cash items other than depreciation or amortisation
- The amount of investment in associates and joint ventures
- The amounts of additions to non-current assets (with some exclusions).

Reconciliations

Reconciliations are required to be disclosed as follows:

The total of the reportable segments' revenues to the entity's revenue
The total of the reportable segments' profits or losses to the entities profit or loss before tax and discontinued operations
The total of the reportable segments' assets to the entity's assets
The total of the reportable segments' liabilities to the entity's liabilities (if reported)
The total of the reportable segments' amounts in respect of every other reportable item of information.

Information about products and services

In addition to the information requirements set out above, an entity must make the following disclosures (unless these are already made via the disclosures described above):

Information about products and services: the revenues from external customers for each product and service, or similar groups of products and services.

Information about geographical areas:

1. Revenues from external customers attributable to the entity's country of domicile and the total of revenues attributable to all foreign countries.
2. Non-current assets located in the entity's country of domicile and the total of non-current assets located in all foreign countries.

Information about major customers:

If revenues in respect of a single customer amount to 10% or more of total revenues this should be disclosed (there is no requirement to disclose the name of the customer).
In respect of information about products, services and geographical areas, the disclosure requirement is waived if the cost to develop the information would be 'excessive'.

16.3.2 Operating segments – discussion

The disclosures required by IFRS 8 for a large multinational group of entities could be very extensive indeed. However, the nature and extent of the disclosure is, at least in part, determined by the entity's own internal reporting and decision-making processes because of the stipulation, applicable to many of the disclosure items, that information is to be disclosed only if it is made available to the chief operating decision maker. This means that disclosures are unlikely to be directly comparable between entities. However, IFRS 8 is designed to allow users to see the type and categories of information that are used at the highest levels in the entity for decision-making. There is the further advantage that disclosure, while in many cases extensive, should not be excessively costly because it is based upon information reported and used within the business.

16.4 The limitations of financial reporting information

The objective of financial statements is set out in the IASB's *Framework for the Preparation and Presentation of Financial Statements,* published in July 1989:

The objective of financial statements is to provide information about the financial position, performance and changes in financial position of an enterprise that is useful to a wide range of users in making economic decisions.

A rather substantial limitation of financial statements, is, however, stated in the following paragraph:

Financial statements prepared for this purpose meet the common needs of most users. However, financial statements do not provide all the information that users may need to make economic decisions since they largely portray the financial effects of past events and do not necessarily provide non-financial information.

In summary, it appears that although financial statements may well be useful to a wide range of users, their usefulness is somewhat limited. The principal drawback is the fact that financial statements are oriented towards events that have already taken place. However, there are other significant limitations in the value of the information contained in a set of financial statements. These can be summarised under the following principal headings.

Timeliness

By the time financial statements are received by users, 2 or 3 months or longer may have elapsed since the year end date. The earliest of the transactions that contribute to the income and expense items accumulated in the income statement will have taken place probably 15 or more months previously.

In some jurisdiction there may be a requirement for large, listed, entities to produce half-yearly or even quarterly financial statements. Where these are available, the timeliness problem is somewhat diminished. However, the information contained in such statements may be limited in comparison to that produced in the annual report. For example, quarterly statements may include only an income statement without a statement of financial position or statement of changes in equity. Also, it is possible that they will have not been subject to verification is the form of audit.

Comparability

1. Comparisons over time between the financial statements of the same entity may prove to be invalid, or only partially valid, because significant changes have taken place in the business. The disclosure provisions of IFRS 5 *Non-current Assets Held for Sale and Discontinued Operations* may assist the analyst in respect of this particular category of change. However, it may not be possible to discern the effect of other significant changes. For example, a business that makes an investment in a new non-current item, say a major addition to its production facilities coupled with a significant increase in working capital, is not obliged to disclose any information about how well or badly the new investment has performed. The analyst may, for example, be able to see that the entity's profitability overall has decreased, but the explanations could be as follows:

- The investment has proved to be very successful, but its success is offset by the rapidly declining profitability of other parts of the business's productive capacity. As these elements are gradually replaced over the next 2 or 3 years, profitability is likely to increase overall.
- The investment has proved to be less successful than expected and is producing no better a return than the worn-out machinery it replaced.
- Although productive capacity has increased, the quality of goods overall has declined, and the business has not been able to maintain its margins.

   Financial statements simply do not provide sufficient information to permit the analyst to see these finer points of detail.

2. Comparability over time is often threatened by the effects of price inflation. This can, paradoxically, be particularly insidious where the general rate of inflation in the economy is comparatively low because analysts and others are not conscious of the effect. For example, suppose that the rate of price inflation applicable to a particular entity has been around 2.5 per cent per year over a 5-year period. Sales in 20X3 were reported at \$100,000. A directly comparable level of sales in 20X4 would be \$102,500 (\$100,000 × 1.025). Therefore, sales in 20X4 would have to have increased to more than \$102,500 before any real increase could be claimed. However, the analyst, seeing the two figures alongside each other on the income statement, and knowing that inflation is running at a low level, may very well not take this factor into account.
3. Changes in accounting policy and accounting practices may affect comparability over time in the same entity. Also, when comparing the financial statements of two or more entities, it is really quite likely that there will be some differences in accounting policy and/or practice between them. The type of differences which make comparisons difficult include the following:
   - Different approaches to valuation of non-current assets, as permitted under IAS 16 *Property, Plant and Equipment*. An entity that revalues its non-current assets on a regular basis, as permitted by that standard, is likely to have higher carrying values for its assets than an entity that carries non-current assets at depreciated historical cost. Also, the depreciation charges of the revaluing entity are likely to be higher. The two entities are therefore not strictly comparable.
   - A different approach to the classification of expenses in the income statement. At the margins it is not always easy to decide whether or not expenses should be classified as part of cost of sales. Different entities may vary in their treatment of some expenses, and so may produce variations between them in gross profit margin.
   - More or less conservative approaches to judgements about the impairment of assets. Impairment review inevitably involves some degree of estimation.

   Only the first of these three items relates to, strictly speaking, an accounting policy difference. The other two relate to variations in respect of judgemental issues. Where there is a difference in formal accounting policies adopted, it is, at least, possible to discern this from the financial statements and to make some kind of adjustment to achieve comparability. However, judgemental matters are almost impossible to adjust for.
4. Businesses may appear to be comparable in that they operate in the same business sector. However, each business has unique features, and a particular business may not be

strictly comparable with any other. Segment disclosure does allow for a more required approach to comparisons, although as we have seen:

- Not all entities are required by the accounting standard to make segment disclosures.
- Identifying segments is, necessarily, a judgmental matter. It is quite possible that one entity would identify a particular part of its business as a reportable segment, whereas another would not make the same judgement.

5. Financial statements are prepared to a particular date annually. The annual financial statements of an entity with a year end of 31 December are not strictly comparable with those of an entity with a June year end. The difference is only 6 months, but significant events may have occurred in the industry or the economy as a whole that affect the statements prepared to the later date but not those prepared to the earlier date.
6. It may be inappropriate to compare two companies of very different sizes, or to compare a listed with a non-listed entity. A large entity may be able to take advantage of economies of scale that are unavailable to the small entity, but that is not to say that the smaller entity is inefficient. It may, relatively speaking, be a better manager of the resources available to it. Conversely, a smaller entity may be able to react more rapidly to changes in economic conditions, because it can be easier to effect radical change in that environment.

   Listed entities are subject to a great deal of additional regulation and their activities are far more likely than those of an unlisted entity to attract media coverage. Their share prices are widely advertised and are sensitive to alterations in market perceptions. It can be less acceptable for a listed entity to take risks or any course of action that might affect a regular flow of dividends to shareholders. By contrast, an unlisted entity whose shares are held by a limited number of people may be able to make investment decisions that result in a curtailment of dividends in the short term in exchange for projected higher returns in the long-term. So, operational flexibility varies between companies, and this may mean that their financial statements are not really comparable, or at least, that comparisons must be treated with caution.

Verification

Although regulations relating to audit vary from one country to another, it is likely that, in most jurisdictions, the financial statements of larger entities are audited. However, smaller entities' financial statements may not be subject to audit, and so the analyst has no external report on their validity or the fairness of their presentation.

International issues

Where the financial statements of entities based in different countries are being compared, there may be further sources of difference in addition to those already covered in this section.

1. The entities may be subject to differing tax regimes.
2. The financial statements may be based on different legal and regulatory systems. For example, traditionally, German, French and Spanish financial statements have been prepared in accordance with tax regulation (so, e.g. the depreciation allowances provided for in the financial statements are exactly those allowable for tax purposes). The preparation of British and Irish financial statements, by contrast, is focused much more

upon the objective of achieving a true and fair view, and the link between accounts for tax purposes and accounts for filing and presentation purposes has been relatively weak.

3. The relative strength and weaknesses of a national economy, and of the exchange rate relating to its national currency, may produce cyclical differences in the profitability of business entities. These effects may have the result of reducing comparability of the financial statements of two businesses located in different countries.

Provision of non-financial information

It was noted earlier in this section: '... financial statements do not provide all the information that users may need to make economic decisions since they largely portray the financial effects of past events and do not necessarily provide non-financial information.' (the IASB's *Framework for the Preparation and Presentation of Financial Statements*). Major listed entities have tended, in recent years, to provide more non-financial information in their financial statements, and it is increasingly common to find disclosures relating to, for example, environmental issues. However, there is a dearth of regulation relating to non-financial disclosure, and users cannot rely on finding a consistent level of high quality information in annual reports.

16.5 Limitations of ratio analysis

Ratio analysis is dependent upon the range and quality of quantitative information available in entities' financial statements. If the quality of information is restricted in one or more of the ways described in Section 16.2, any ratios calculated using the information are likely to be of limited assistance. For example, an accounting ratio that can be very misleading is return on capital employed. The following example illustrates the danger of drawing inappropriate conclusions from accounting information.

Example

Two entities, A and B, operate in the same industry sector and have a similar scale of operations. Their profit, capital employed and ROCE figures are as follows for the year ended 31 December 20X3:

	A	*B*
	$	*$*
Profit	260,000	310,000
Capital employed	1,820,000	1,360,000
ROCE%	14.3%	22.8%

On the face of it, B appears to produce a ROCE figure far in excess of A. However, our view of the comparison might change if we were informed that A has a policy of revaluing non-current assets, whereas B does not. B's capital employed is lower for this reason, but its profits are also higher because it deducts relatively lower depreciation figures in its income statement.

Additional limitations of ratio analysis include the following:

Calculation method

As we have seen in preceding chapters the only accounting ratio to have a prescribed method of calculation is earnings per share which is regulated through IAS 33 *Earnings per share*. In respect of some of the other accounting ratios, there may be more than one, quite valid, method of calculation. In Section 14.5.2, for example, we encountered two perfectly valid approaches to the calculation of gearing. When making comparisons between financial statements it is important to ensure that the same method of calculation is used consistently, otherwise the comparison will not be valid.

Reliability

As we saw in Chapter 14, many ratios are calculated using average figures. Often the average is based on only two figures: the opening and closing. However, these may not be representative of a true average figure, and so any ratios calculated on the basis of such a figure will be unreliable. This effect is noticeable in businesses with seasonal operations. For example, suppose that an artificial Christmas tree business starts building up its stock from a low point at the beginning of February, gradually accumulating stock to build up to a maximum level at the beginning of November. Eighty-five per cent of its annual sales total is made in November and December. If the business has an accounting year end of 31 January (which would make sense as there's not much going on at the time of year), stock levels will be at their lowest level. (Opening stock + closing stock)/2 will certainly produce an average stock figure but it will not be representative of the business's level of activity.

The idea of the norm

Sometimes textbooks and lecturers attempt to set norms for ratios: for example, that current ratio should ideally be around 2, or 1.5 or 2.5. However, setting norms is both unrealistic and unhelpful. Some types of successful business can, and do, operate successfully with a substantial excess of current liabilities over current assets. Such businesses typically sell for cash, so don't have receivables, turn over their stock very quickly (perhaps because it's perishable) but manage to take the maximum amounts of credit from their suppliers.

Inappropriate use of ratios

Not all ratios are useful or applicable in all business situations, and the analyst must take care over the selection of ratios to use. For example, a business may have a mixture of cash and credit sales, but it would normally not be possible to distinguish between them armed only with the information included in the annual financial statements. However, seeing a line for revenue and a line for receivables, the analyst (or student) might assume that it was therefore sensible to work out the number of days sales represented by receivables. In fact, though, the ratio would be meaningless, and the analyst could be seriously misled by it.

Limited usefulness of ratios

Mostly, the calculation and analysis of ratios simply leads to more questions, and these cannot necessarily be answered where information is limited. Ratios, and more importantly, their analysis may contribute to an understanding of a entity's business operations, but quite often they simply lead to more questions.

A related point is that stand-alone ratios are generally of very limited use. The analyst may be able to calculate that a business's gross profit percentage is 14.3 per cent for a particular year. In isolation, that piece of information is really quite useless. It's reassuring to know that the business has actually made a positive gross profit, but without comparators, it's hard to say much more than that.

16.6 Creative accounting

'Creative accounting' goes by many names. In the USA it is more commonly referred to as 'earnings management' or 'aggressive accounting'. 'Creative accounting' is probably the most widely used term in the UK and Europe, but the term 'window dressing' may also be found. In this chapter the term 'creative accounting' will be used.

Defining the nature and scope of creative accounting is not a straightforward matter. On a very broad level, it is possible to argue that all accounting is creative, because it involves a series of choices about policies, about what should be included and so on. Financial reports present only a partial view of the business they represent (e.g. internally generated goodwill is not capitalised and human resource assets do not figure in the statement of financial position). Despite the best efforts of accounting regulators there remains wide scope for the use of judgement in matters such as the determination of useful lives of assets and provisions for doubtful debts.

Creativity may be a natural element in the development of accounting. Accountants may need to be creative where, for example, there is no prescribed accounting treatment for a transaction. This need arose more frequently at times in the past when accounting regulation was sketchy or non-existent. Creativity in this context may positively enhance and assist the development of accounting. However, these days, the term 'creative accounting' is more commonly used in a way which suggests that it involves a rather suspect, shady approach to accounting. It carries connotations of manipulation of figures, deliberate structuring of series of transactions and exploitation of loopholes in the rules.

Is creative accounting wrong? It can be very difficult to draw a distinction between aggressive use of the options offered by regulation, creative accounting and fraud. Some years ago, Alun Jones of the securities firm UBS Phillips & Drew employed the analogy of a slippery slope in categorising various approaches to accounting. There are six stages on the slippery slope:

1. conservative accounting
2. less conservative accounting
3. low quality profits
4. wishful thinking
5. creative or misleading accounting
6. fraud.

In this analysis creative accounting is next door to outright fraud. Accounting and securities regulation has become more stringent in recent years, and prosecutions for fraud involving accounting manipulation have become more common, especially in the United States.

16.6.1 Methods employed by creative accountants

Financial statements can be manipulated in many ways, some more acceptable than others. Methods include the following:

Altering the timing of transactions

For example, the despatch of sales orders could be hurried up or delayed just before the year end to either increase or decrease sales for the reporting period. Other examples include delaying sales of non-current assets and the timing of research and development expenditure. If an entity needs to improve its results it may decide upon a lower level of research and development activity in the short term in order to reduce costs. Delaying the replacement of worn-out assets falls into the same category. Some people would regard this type of 'manipulation' as falling outside of the definition of creative accounting.

Artificial smoothing

This approach involves the exploitation of the elements of choice that exist in accounting regulation. Although the IASB has worked hard to reduce the number of allowed alternative treatments, there remains some scope for artificial adjustments in respect of, for example, the choice of inventory valuation method, the estimated useful lives of non-current assets and the choice between valuation of non-current assets at revalued amounts or depreciated historical cost that is permitted by IAS 16 *Property, Plant and Equipment* and IAS 40 *Investment Property.* A change in accounting policy would, of course, have to be noted in the year in which it occurs, but its effects are not so easily discernible after that first year.

The use of provisions has been exploited in the past as a way in which to manage reported earnings. The judicious creation and then subsequent release of provisions has been a very effective way of ensuring that reported profits showed a consistent picture of growth. However, by issuing IAS 37 *Provisions, Contingent Liabilities and Contingent Assets,* the IASB effectively put a stop to many of the abuses of provisions that had taken place previously.

Classification

One of the grey areas that persists in accounting is the classification of debit items as either expenses of the current year or as non-current assets. If items are classified as non-current assets they do not impact (unless they are depreciated) on the reported income for the period. One of the most celebrated cases of mis-classification in recent years occurred in the US long-distance phone company WorldCom. Over a 3-year period the business improperly reported $3.8 billion of expenses as non-current assets, thus providing a considerable boost to reported earnings. The company is also reported as having manipulated provisions in order to increase reported earnings. In this particular case, the scale of the irregularities has been such that senior officers are currently being prosecuted for fraud.

Other areas of the financial statements which provide opportunities for creative accounting via classification include the categorisation of expenses and income as exceptional or extraordinary items, and the decisions about classification as reportable segments where the entity is required to undertake segment reporting.

Exclusion of liabilities

Under-reporting liabilities in the statement of financial position can help to improve accounting ratios. For example, the calculation of gearing would be affected. Also, total capital employed would be reduced, so that return on total capital employed would appear to be higher. Entities have sometimes been able to take advantage of loopholes in accounting regulation to arrange off-balance sheet financing in the form of subsidiary undertakings that are technically excluded from consolidation. Generally, regulation has been tightened to make this more difficult, but as shown by the recent celebrated Enron case (where so-called Special Purpose Entities were set up to provide finance to the business; these SPEs were, however, excluded from the group accounts, so that their liabilities did not impact on the business) off-balance sheet finance remains a possibility.

Recognition of revenue

Aggressive accounting often exploits relatively tax revenue recognition rules. Some examples of inappropriate revenue recognition include:

- recognising revenue from sales that are made conditionally (i.e. where the purchaser has the right to return the goods for an extended period, or where experience shows that returns are likely);
- failing to apportion subscription revenue over the appropriate accounting periods but instead recognising it immediately;
- recognising revenue on goods shipped to agents employed by the entity;
- recognising the full amount of revenue when only partial shipments of goods have been made.

Managing market expectations

This final category of manipulation has nothing to do with massaging an entity's figures, but it does involve the way the entity presents itself to the world. Reporting by listed entities, especially in the US market, is driven very much by analysts' expectations. It may be easier to massage their expectations rather than to improve the reported results by use of creative accounting techniques. Directors of listed entities meet analysts in briefing meetings where they have the opportunity to influence analysts' expectations by forecasting fairly poor figures. When the entity then proceeds to turn in a better result than expected, the market's view of the shares may be enhanced. This is a psychological game of bluffing which may backfire on the reporting entity if analysts become aware of what it is doing.

16.6.2 The motivation to use creative accounting

Various research studies have examined the issue of managerial motivation to use creative accounting. The following have been identified as significant factors:

Tax avoidance. If income can be understated or expenses overstated, then it may be possible to avoid tax.

Increasing shareholder confidence. Creative accounting can be used to ensure an appropriate level of profits over a long period. Ideally, this would show a steady upward trajectory without nasty surprises for the shareholders, and so would help to avoid volatility in share prices, and would make it easier to raise further capital via share issues.

Personal gain. Where managerial bonuses are linked to profitability, there is a clear motivation for managers to ensure that profits hit the necessary threshold to trigger a bonus payment.

Indirect personal gain. There is a market in managerial expertise, in which demand often appears to outstrip supply. A manager's personal reputation in the marketplace will almost certainly be enhanced by association with entities that have strong earnings records. So, although the pay-off may not be either immediate or obvious, there is likely over the longer term to be a reward in terms of enhanced reputation and consequent higher earning power.

Following the pack. If managers perceive that every other entity in their sector is adopting creative accounting practices, they may feel obliged to do the same.

Meeting covenants. Sometimes, lenders insist on special covenant arrangements as a condition of making a loan: for example, they may stipulate that an entity's current ratio should not fall below 1.5:1, or that gearing never exceeds 35 per cent. In such cases, if the entity cannot meet those covenants that it has agreed to, the lender may be able to insist upon immediate repayment, or to put the entity into liquidation. Where an entity is in danger of failing to meet its covenants, there is an obvious incentive for managers (especially if they genuinely feel that the difficulty is short-term in nature) to massage the figures so that the covenant is, apparently, met.

16.7 Special problems in analysing financial obligations

It was noted in the previous section that one possible method of creative accounting is to under-report liabilities. If liabilities are not reported, investors and other users of financial statements may be seriously misled. The analysis of financial obligations may be complicated by the existence of creative accounting techniques designed to keep obligations off the statement of financial position, but there are other problems that do not necessarily fall into the category of creative accounting.

Some of these problems are briefly discussed below.

Interpretation of redeemable debt

Debt may be redeemable at the option of the entity or of the holder. Sometimes it will carry a range of dates. For example, a security may be described as '10 per cent redeemable loan notes 2008/2012'. The analyst must be aware of such securities as their redemption could prove difficult if the business is short of liquid funds and/or is already highly geared. Where a date range is shown, it is probably most prudent to assume that the business will be obliged to redeem at the earliest possible date.

Contingencies

The accounting treatment of contingencies is covered by IAS 37 *Provisions, Contingent Liabilities and Contingent Assets.* Students should recall that a provision is recognised when:

(a) an entity has a present obligation (legal or constructive) as a result of a past event;
(b) it is probable that an outflow of resources embodying economic benefits will be required to settle the obligation;
(c) a reliable estimate can be made of the amount of the obligation.

'Probable' means more likely than not; that is, there is a greater than 50 per cent probability of the obligation requiring settlement. If the probability is below 50 per cent but is not regarded as remote, then the potential obligation is noted as a contingent liability. It should be clear that much hinges on the probability estimate. It is quite possible that substantial potential obligations could be included as contingent liabilities on the basis that they have, say, a 40 per cent probability of occurrence. The analyst must read the notes to the financial statements carefully so as to be aware of the existence of contingencies. Where an item is noted as a contingent liability together with a note of the estimated financial impact, it may be useful to calculate the impact on the entity's liquidity and to work out accounting ratios both with and without the item.

Earn-out arrangements

Earn-out arrangements are a special type of contingency that may arise upon the acquisition of a group undertaking.

Example

During its financial year ended 31 December 20X4, CY acquired 80% of the issued share capital of DZ for $3.2 million. An earn-out arrangement was written into the contract whereby if total audited profit before distributions for the two full financial years ending 31 December 20X6 were to exceed $600,000, CY would be obliged to pay an additional $0.4 million to the shareholders from whom it purchased the DZ shares.

How should CY account for this potential obligation in its financial statements for the year ended 31 December 20X5?

The potential obligation should be accounted for in accordance with IAS 37. There is a legal obligation arising from a past event, and the extent of the obligation can be measured reliably. The only point at issue is whether or not the outflow of funds associated with the obligation can be regarded as probable or not. If it is probable (and a reasonable probability estimate is feasible given that DZ's results will be available) then a provision will be made in the financial statements of the group or the year ended 31 December 20X5. If the outflow is not probable it is likely to be disclosed as a contingency.

As in the case of other contingent liabilities, the analyst must read the financial statements throughly, so as to be aware of all noted contingencies. If the obligation is not already recognised it may be worth examining the effect of the earn-out payment on the group's cash flow and statement of financial position ratios.

16.8 Summary

This chapter has completes the coverage of the learning outcomes associated with the financial analysis section of the learning system. Once this chapter has been fully absorbed and the end of chapter questions have been practiced, students should be able to analyse financial statements in the context of information provided in the accounts and corporate report to comment on an entity's performance and position.

The chapter has extended the ranges of knowledge about analysis techniques and the disclosure of segment information.

Note to students:

It cannot be emphasised too frequently, that the way to acquire the skills of a financial analyst is to keep on practising. Students should obtain a range of annual reports of entities reporting under IFRS, in order to exercise their ability to analyse and interpret financial information. This can be quite hard work, especially at first, but it is worth persevering. A high level of ability in analysing financial information is to be expected of a CIMA qualified accountant.

Students should find that, with the appropriate level of practice they are able to prepare a concise report on the results of their analysis. There are additional notes on how to practice these types of questions in the section entitled preparing for the examination.

Note that question 1 at the end of this chapter is an example of a type of question that could be set in F2: it combines elements of two different syllabus areas, in this case financial analysis and accounting for groups of companies.

Revision Questions 16

Question 1

A friend of yours has recently been left a portfolio of investments by a relative. The portfolio includes 150 shares in SDB, a listed entity that designs, manufactures and supplies houses in kit form for export to developing countries. Having recently received the financial statements of the entity for the financial year ended 31 July 20X6, your friend, who has some basic knowledge of accounting, has asked you to clarify certain points for him, and to provide him with a brief report on the position of the business.

The income statement, statement of changes in equity, and statement of financial position, together with comparatives are as follows:

SDB: Consolidated income statement for the year ended 31 July 20X6

	20X6	*20X5*
	$'000	$'000
Revenue	25,200	25,300
Cost of sales	18,400	18,000
Gross profit	6,800	7,300
Distribution costs	970	1,030
Administrative expenses	1,750	1,720
Finance costs	1,220	1,140
Share of losses of joint venture	1,670	–
Profit before tax	1,190	3,410
Income tax expense	250	780
Profit for the period	940	2,630
Attributable to:		
Equity holders of the parent	810	2,230
Non-controlling interest	130	400
	940	2,630

SDB: Consolidated statement of changes in equity for the year ended 31 July 20X6

	Share capital $'000	*Other reserves* $'000	*Retained earnings* $'000	*Minority interest* $'000	*Total equity* $'000
Balance at 1 August 20X5	4,000	–	18,600	540	23,140
Profit for the period			810	130	940
Dividends			(2,470)	(330)	(2,800)
Issue of share capital	1,600	2,000			3,600
Balance at 31 July 20X6	5,600	2,000	16,940	340	24,880

SDB: Consolidated statement of financial position as at 31 July 20X6

	20X6 $'000	$'000	*20X5* $'000	$'000
ASSETS				
Non-current assets:				
Property, plant and equipment	19,900		17,200	
Investment in joint venture	7,500		–	
		27,400		17,200
Current assets:				
Inventories	8,300		6,900	
Trade receivables	4,700		4,100	
Cash	3,100		13,000	
		16,100		24,000
		43,500		41,200
EQUITY AND LIABILITIES				
Equity attributable to shareholders of the parent:				
Called up share capital ($1 shares)	5,600		4,000	
Retained earnings	16,940		18,600	
Other reserves	2,000		–	
		24,540		22,600
Non-controlling interest		340		540
Total equity		24,880		23,140
Non-current liabilities:				
Long-term loans		13,600		13,000
Current liabilities:				
Trade payables	4,770		4,280	
Income tax	250		780	
		5,020		5,060
		43,500		41,200

Your friend's queries are as follows:

1. 'I've looked up IAS 31 *Interests in joint ventures,* which mentions proportionate consolidation and equity accounting as possible methods of accounting for joint ventures. I've not previously encountered joint ventures, or proportionate consolidation. Can you explain how IAS 31 affects these financial statements?
2. The long-term loans are described in a note as redeemable loan notes 20X8–10. What does this mean, and what are the implications for SDB's position?

3. There is a note about a contingent liability of $10 million. Apparently, one of the models of house kit supplied by SDB has a tendency to collapse in adverse weather conditions, and $10 million is the amount claimed by litigants in a case that is due to be heard within the next 18 months. SDB's directors think it's possible that the entity will have to pay out. This seems a very large amount of money. How likely is it that the entity will have to pay out, and how bad would the effect be?
4. I can see that the business's profitability has suffered during the year, but if anything, I'm more concerned about the fact that the cash balance has fallen by more than $9 million. I'd very much like to have your opinion on the business's position.'

Requirements

Write a report to your friend that:

(a) Explains the concept of a jointly controlled entity and the possible approaches to accounting for it, identifying possible reasons for the selection of accounting method by SDB. **(9 marks)**

(b) Analyses the financial statements of SDB, focusing as requested upon the business's position, and including references to the queries about the redeemable loan notes and the contingent liability. **(16 marks)**

(Total marks = 25)

Question 2

AXZ is a rapidly expanding entity that manufactures and distributes hair care and other beauty products. Its directors are currently considering expansion into foreign countries by means of acquisitions of similar entities. Two acquisition possibilities are to be considered at the next board meeting: DCB, an entity operating in Lowland, and GFE which operates in Highland. The targets are of similar size, and operate within similar economic parameters and the same currency, although their tax regimes differ substantially. Neither entity is listed. Neither Lowland nor Highland require unlisted entities to comply with IFRS, and consequently both entities comply with local GAAP. Local GAAP in both countries is in most respects similar to IFRS but there are some differences which must be taken into account when making comparisons between financial statements produced in the two countries. AXZ is listed, and complies with IFRS.

The directors of both DCB and GFE have co-operated fully in providing detailed information about their businesses. Provided that a reasonable price is offered for the shares, takeover is unlikely to be resisted by either entity. AXZ can afford to fund one acquisition but not both.

The most recent income statements of the three entities are provided below, together with some relevant statement of financial position totals.

Income statements for the year ended 30 September 20X6

	AXZ	*DCB*	*GFE*
	$'000	$'000	$'000
Revenue	8,300	1,900	2,200
Cost of sales	5,600	1,300	1,400
Gross profit	2,700	600	800
Distribution costs	252	60	65
Administrative expenses	882	180	250
Finance costs	105	25	65
Profit before tax	1,461	335	420
Income tax expense	366	134	105
Profit for the period	1,095	201	315

Extracts from statements of financial position as at 30 September 20X6

Total equity	4,820	1,350	1,931
Non-current liabilities (borrowings)	1,500	500	650
Non-current assets	9,950	1,680	2,400

Notes

1. It is customary for entities complying with local GAAP in Lowland to adopt the rates of depreciation used by the tax authorities. Tax depreciation is calculated on the straight-line basis in all cases, at a rate of 12.5% each year on all non-current assets. DCB's non-current assets have been held, on average, for three years, and none are fully depreciated. The age profile of non-current assets held by AXZ and GFE is very sim ilar, but both entities charge an average of 10% straight line depreciation each year. In order to be able to appraise the potential investments using comparable data, the directors of AXZ intend to use figures adjusted by applying a 10% depreciation rate to the non-current assets of DCB.

   All depreciation in all three entities has been charged to cost of sales.
2. Accounting for financial instruments is similar under Lowland GAAP and IFRS. However, Highland's GAAP takes a less prescriptive approach. GFE has $100,000 of 5% non-participating shares included in equity. Under IFRS, these shares would be classified as long-term liabilities. The 5% fixed charge on these shares has been reflected in the statement of changes in equity; under IFRS it would be shown as part of finance costs. This charge would not, however, be allowable against income tax in Highland.
3. The directors of AXZ plan to finance the acquisition through a combination of equity and debt that will be similar, proportionately, to the existing capital structure. When assessing possible takeover targets the following accounting ratios are of especial interest:

   Gross profit margin
   Profit before tax as a percentage of revenue
   Return on equity
   Return on total capital employed
   Non-current asset turnover
   Gearing (long-term debt as a percentage of equity)

Their policy is to consider targets for takeover only if the above ratios for the combined group would not be adversely affected to any material extent.

Requirements

(a) Calculate and tabulate the key ratios both before and after taking into account the information in notes 1 and 2 above. **(15 marks)**

(b) Analyse, interpret and prepare a concise report for the directors of AXZ upon the financial statement information provided for the three entities, together with the ratios provided in the table prepared in part (a). (You should calculate any additional ratios that are likely to be useful to the directors in making their decision). **(10 marks)**

(Total marks = 25)

Question 3

You are the assistant to the finance director (FD) of OPQ, a well-known retailer of music, video and games products. The entity's profit margins are under increasing pressure because of the entry of on-line retailers into the market. As part of their response to this challenge, OPQ's directors have decided to invest in entities in the supply chain of their most popular products. They are currently considering the acquisition of the business that supplies some of their best-selling computer games, PJ Gamewriters (PJ). The FD has asked you, as a preliminary step, to examine the most recent financial statements of the entity.

PJ was established in 20W9 by twin brothers, Paul and James, who had recently graduated in computing. Their first business success was a simulated empire building game; this has continued to bring in a large proportion of their revenue. However, they have also been successful in a range of other games types such as combat simulations, golf and football management games. The business has grown rapidly from year to year, and by 20X5 it employed ten full-time games writers. Manufacture and distribution of the software in various formats is outsourced, and the business operates from office premises in a city centre. PJ bought the freehold of the office premises in 2002, and its estimated market value is now $900,000, nearly $350,000 in excess of the price paid in 2002. Apart from the freehold building, the business owns few non-current assets.

The equity shares in PJ are owned principally by Paul, James and their parents, who provided the initial start-up capital. Paul and James are the sole directors of the business. A small proportion of the shares (approximately 8%) is owned by five of the senior software writers. PJ is now up for sale as the principal shareholders wish to realise the bulk of their investment in order to pursue other business interests. It is likely that about 90% of the shares will be for sale. The copyrights of the games are owned by PJ, but no value is attributed to them in the financial statements.

PJ's income statement and summarised statement of changes in equity for the year ended 31 July 20X5, and a statement of financial position at that date (all with comparatives) are as follows:

PJ: Income statement for the year ended 31 July 20X5

	20X5	*20X4*
	$'000	$'000
Revenue	2,793	2,208
Cost of sales (see note)	(1,270)	(1,040)
Gross profit	1,523	1,168
Operating expenses	(415)	(310)
Profit from operations	1,108	858
Interest receivable	7	2
Profit before tax	1,115	860
Income tax expense	(331)	(290)
Profit for the period	784	570

Note: Cost of sales comprises the following:

	20X5	*20X4*
	$'000	$'000
Games writers' employment costs	700	550
Production costs	215	160
Directors' remuneration	200	200
Other costs	155	130
	1,270	1,040

PJ: Summarised statement of changes in equity for the year ended 31 July 20X5

	20X5	*20X4*
	$'000	$'000
Opening balance	703	483
Profit for period	784	570
Dividends	(500)	(350)
Closing balance	987	703

PJ: Statement of financial position at 31 July 20X5

	20X5		*20X4*	
	$'000	$'000	$'000	$'000
Non-current assets				
Property, plant and equipment		610		620
Current assets				
Inventories	68		59	
Trade receivables	460		324	
Cash	216		20	
		744		403
		1,354		1,023
Equity				
Share capital	60		60	
Retained earnings	927		643	
		987		703
Current liabilities				
Trade and other payables	36		30	
Income tax	331		290	
		367		320
		1,354		1,023

Requirements

(a) Prepare a report commenting upon the financial performance and position of PJ Games writers, calculating and interpreting any relevant accounting ratios. **(17 marks)**

(b) Explain the limitations of your analysis, identifying any supplementary items of information that would be useful. **(8 marks)**

(Total marks = 25)

Question 4

You are the accountant of Acquirer. Your entity has the strategy of growth by acquisition and your directors have identified an entity, Target, which they wish to investigate with a view to launching a takeover bid. Your directors consider that the directors of Target will contest any bid and will not be very co-operative in providing background information on the entity. Therefore, relevant financial information is likely to be restricted to the publicly available financial statements.

Your directors have asked you to compute key financial ratios from the latest financial statements of Target (for the year ended 30 November 20X2) and compare the ratios with those for other entities in a similar sector. Accordingly, you have selected ten broadly similar entities and have presented the directors with the following calculations:

Ratio	*Basis of calculation*	*Ratio for target*	*Spread of ratios for comparative entities* Highest	Average	Lowest
Gross profit margin	Gross profit / Revenue	42%	44%	38%	33%
Operating profit margin	Profit from operations / Revenue	29%	37%	30%	26%
Return on total capital	Profit from operations / Total capital	73%	92.5%	69%	52%
Interest cover	Profit from operations / Finance cost	1.8 times	3.2 times	2.5 times	1.6 times
Gearing	Debt capital / Total capital	52%	56%	40%	28%
Dividend cover	Profit after tax / Divident	5.2 times	5 times	4 times	3 times
Turnover of inventory	Cost of sales / Closing inventory	4.4 times	4.5 times	4 times	3.2 times
Receivables days	Trade receivables / 1 day's sales revenue	51 days	81 days	62 days	49 days

Requirements

(a) Using the ratios provided, write a report that compares the financial performance and position of Target to the other entities in the survey. Where an issue arises that reflects particularly favourably or unfavourably on Target, you should assess its relevance to a potential acquirer. **(16 marks)**

(b) Identify any reservations you have regarding the extent to which the ratios provided can contribute to an acquisition decision by the directors of Acquirer. You should highlight the extent to which the financial statements themselves might help you to overcome the reservations you have identified. **(9 marks)**

(Total marks = 25)

Question 5

DM, a listed entity, has just published its financial statements for the year ended 31 December 20X4. DM operates a chain of 42 supermarkets in one of the six major provinces of its country of operation. During 20X4 there has been speculation in the financial press that the entity was likely to be a takeover target for one of the larger national chains of supermarkets that is currently under-represented in DM's province. A recent newspaper report has suggested that DM's directors are unlikely to resist a takeover. The six board members are all nearing retirement, and all own significant minority shareholdings in the business.

You have been approached by a private shareholder in DM. She is concerned that the directors have a conflict of interests and that the financial statements for 20X4 may have been manipulated.

The income statement and summarised statement of changes in equity of DM, with comparatives, for the year ended 31 December 20X4, and a statement of financial position, with comparatives, at that date are as follows:

DM: Income statement for the year ended 31 December 20X4

	20X4	*20X3*
	$m	$m
Revenue, net of sales tax	1,255	1,220
Cost of sales	(1,177)	(1,145)
Gross profit	78	75
Operating expenses	(21)	(29)
Profit from operations	57	46
Finance cost	(10)	(10)
Profit before tax	47	36
Income tax expense	(14)	(13)
Profit for the period	33	23

DM: Summarised statement of changes in equity for the year ended 31 December 20X4

	20X4	*20X3*
	$m	$m
Opening balance	276	261
Profit for period	33	23
Dividends	(8)	(8)
Closing balance	301	276

DM: Statement of financial position as at 31 December 20X4

	20X4		*20X3*	
	$m	$m	$m	$m
Non-current assets				
Property, plant and equipment	580		575	
Goodwill	100		100	
		680		675
Current assets				
Inventories	47		46	
Trade receivables	12		13	
Cash	46		12	
		105		71
		785		746
Issued capital and reserves				
Share capital	150		150	
Retained earnings	151		126	
		301		276
Non-current liabilities				
Interest-bearing borrowings	142		140	
Deferred tax	25		21	
		167		161
Current liabilities				
Trade and other payables	297		273	
Short-term borrowings	20		36	
		317		309
		785		746

Notes

1. DM's directors have undertaken a reassessment of the useful lives of non-current tangible assets during the year. In most cases, they estimate that the useful lives have increased and the depreciation charges in 20X4 have been adjusted accordingly.
2. Six new stores have been opened during 20X4, bringing the total to 42.
3. Four key ratios for the supermarket sector (based on the latest available financial statements of twelve listed entities in the sector) are as follows:
   (i) Annual sales per store: $27.6 million
   (ii) Gross profit margin: 5.9%
   (iii) Net profit margin: 3.9%
   (iv) Non-current asset turnover (including both tangible and intangible non-current assets): 1.93

Requirements

(a) Prepare a report, addressed to the investor, analysing the performance and position of DM based on the financial statements and supplementary information provided above. The report should also include comparisons with the key sector ratios, and it should address the investor's concerns about the possible manipulation of the 20X4 financial statements. **(20 marks)**

(b) Explain the limitations of the use of sector comparatives in financial analysis. **(5 marks)**

(Total marks = 25)

Solutions to Revision Questions 16

Solution 1

Report on the financial statements of SDB for the year ended 31 July 20X6

Requirements

(a) Joint ventures, according to IAS 31, fall into three principal categories: jointly controlled assets, operations and entities. Joint control arises where decisions must be made unanimously between the controlling parties, and no one party is dominant. It appears that during the year, SDB has invested in a jointly controlled entity. A jointly controlled entity is a venture involving the establishment of an entity in which each venturer has an interest. The entity could be, for example, a partnership or a limited liability corporation. IAS 31 prefers the adoption of the proportionate consolidation method: this involves combining the entity's share of assets, liabilities, income and expenses with its own assets, liabilities and so on. However, it also permits the use of the equity method which involves recognising the investment (at cost plus share of any subsequent profits less amounts distributed) on one line in the statement of financial position, with a one line entry in the income statement showing the share of profits in the joint venture for the period. The proportionate consolidation method has the advantage that it results in financial statements that show the assets, liabilities and profits over which the entity has either control or joint control.

IAS 31 permits the use of equity accounting because it recognises the argument that joint control is not the same as control. In SDB's case, its directors may feel that they exert significant influence rather than joint control. However, it is also possible that the directors wish to avoid augmenting, for example, liabilities by including those under joint control because it would provide a less positive view of the entity. (Note: where equity accounting is adopted, IAS 31 requires extensive disclosure by note of the amounts of assets and liabilities in the joint venture. Therefore, it should be possible to adjust the statement of financial position figures to an approximation of proportionate consolidation.)

(b) The position of the business has deteriorated in some respects between 20X5 and 20X6. As you pointed out, the cash balance has declined by almost $9 million. This is not necessarily a problem, of course: cash that is not needed in the working capital cycle should be used for investment in profitable opportunities. There appears to have been some investment in property, plant and equipment (the net book value has increased by $2.7 million – 15.7%), but the principal investment has been in the joint venture. The income statement shows that this investment has resulted in substantial losses so far, but it is possible that the venture will show improved results in its second year of operation. Overall, however, it is clear that profitability is reduced, and if this reduction continues into the longer term it will have an effect upon the business's position and level of risk. The non-current asset turnover ratio has worsened, indicating that the new investment in property, plant and equipment has not yet paid off in terms of higher revenues.

Another substantial outgoing during the year was the payment of a dividend. This was in excess of the profit for the period for the year ended 31 July 20X5, and it is likely to be difficult for the business to sustain a dividend at that level unless profitability improves significantly.

Working capital management has declined in effectiveness. Both inventory and receivables turnover are high in absolute terms and have worsened significantly during the year. Inventory, on average, spends nearly 165 days or 5.5 months on the premises. There may be operational reasons for this, but it could also suggest that management is not in full control of the current assets. While the current and quick ratio suggest no immediate problems, both have declined substantially in the year.

The description attached to the loan notes shows that they are payable between the years 20X8 and 20Y0. It is quite possible that the directors plan to replace them with other long-term loans. However, if the fall in profitability and the deterioration in working capital management were to continue, a lender might require higher interest rates to reflect increased risk. The interest rates on the current loan appear to be around 9%. Interest cover is not a problem at the moment, but, again, this ratio has declined over the year because of the reduction in profitability.

The contingent liability is, indeed, worrying. Such liabilities would be recognised (that is, would appear in the statement of financial position) only where the assessment of probability of adverse outcome exceeded 50%. The fact that the contingent liability is noted means that the probability of an adverse outcome is assessed at less than 50%. If the full amount of $10 million were to be payable the outlook for the business could be very poor. If a major product failure were to be proven, it is likely to have a very bad effect on sales of similar products, and could even result in the closure of the business. Even if other product sales are not affected, the business would be left with the problem of how to find the very large sum required. It is not immediately clear how this could be done, especially as the outcome of the case may very well coincide with the redemption of loan notes.

Conclusion

While the business is currently solvent, and, indeed, has a positive cash balance of $3.1 million, the position in the slightly longer term could become very much worse. The product liability case represents a severe threat to the business. Most indicators already show a worsening position, and the directors need to address, as a matter of urgency, the disappointing joint venture results, the general decline in profitability and the poor working capital management.

Appendix

	20X6	20X5
Inventory turnover	8,300/18,400 × 365 = 164.6 days	6,900/18,000 × 365 = 139.9 days
Receivables turnover	4,700/25,200 × 365 = 68.1 days	4,100/25,300 × 365 = 59.1 days
Current ratio	16,100/5,020 = 3.2	24,000/5,060 = 4.7
Quick ratio	(16,100 − 8,300)/5,020 = 1.6	(24,000 − 6,900)/5,060 = 3.4
Gearing	13,600/24,880 × 100 = 54.7%	13,000/23,140 × 100 = 56.2%
Asset turnover	25,200/19,900 = 1.27	25,300/17,200 = 1.47
Interest cover	(6,800 − 970 − 1,750)/1,220 = 3.3	(7,300 − 1,030 − 1,720)/1,140 = 4.0

Solution 2

Requirements

(a)

Table: key ratios before and after adjustment for GAAP differences

	AXZ	DCB		GFE	
		Before adjusting	*After adjusting*	*Before adjusting*	*After adjusting*
Gross profit margin	32.5%	31.6%	35.1%	36.4%	Unchanged
PBT/Sales %	17.6%	17.6%	21.2%	19.1%	18.9%
Return on equity	30.3%	24.8%	25.9%	21.8%	22.6%
ROTCE	24.7%	19.5%	20.8%	18.8%	18.8%
NCA turnover	0.83	1.13	1.0	0.92	Unchanged
Gearing	31.1%	37.0%	32.2%	33.7%	40.1%

Workings

(W1) *Ratios before adjustment*

	AXZ	DCB	GFE
Gross profit margin	2,700/8,300 × 100 = 32.5%	600/1,900 × 100 = 31.6%	800/2,200 × 100 = 36.4%
PBT/Sales %	1,461/8,300 × 100 = 17.6%	335/1,900 × 100 = 17.6%	420/2,200 × 100 = 19.1%
ROE	1,461/4,820 × 100 = 30.3%	335/1,350 × 100 = 24.8%	420/1,931 × 100 = 21.8%
ROTCE	(1,461 + 105)/(4,820 + 1,500) × 100 = 24.7%	(335 + 25)/(1,350 + 500) × 100 = 19.5%	(420 + 65)/(1,931 + 650) × 100 = 18.8%
NCA turnover	8,300/9,950 = 0.83	1,900/1,680 = 1.13	2,200/2,400 = 0.92
Gearing	1,500/4,820 × 100 = 31.1%	500/1,350 × 100 = 37.0%	650/1,931 × 100 = 33.7%

(W2) *Adjustments to DCB's depreciation and non-current assets*

Non-current assets at net book value = \$1,680,000, after an average 3 years' depreciation out of an 8 year estimated life. NBV = 5/8 × cost, so cost = \$1,680,000 × 8/5 = \$2,688,000. Annual depreciation charges on this basis = \$2,688,000 × 12.5% = \$336,000.

If a rate of 10% SL depreciation is applied, net book value would be as follows:

\$2,688,000 × 7/10 = \$1,881,600. Annual depreciation charges on this basis = \$2,688,000 × 10% = \$268,800.

NBV would increase by \$1,881,600 − \$1,680,000 = \$201,600
Equity would increase to \$1,551,600 (\$1,350,000 + \$201,600)

Cost of sales would decrease by the difference in depreciation charges: \$1,300,000 − \$336,000 + \$268,800 = \$1,232,800.
Gross profit would be: \$1,900,000 − \$1,232,800 = \$667,200.
Profit before tax would be \$667,200 − \$60,000 − \$180,000 − \$25,000 = \$402,200

(W3) *Revised ratio calculations for DCB*

	DCB
Gross profit margin	667.2/1,900 × 100 = 35.1%
PBT/Sales %	402.2/1,900 × 100 = 21.2%
ROE	402.2/1,551.6 × 100 = 25.9%
ROTCE	(402.2 + 25)/(1,551.6 + 500) × 100 = 20.8%
NCA turnover	1,900/1,881.6 = 1.0
Gearing	500/1,551.6 × 100 = 32.2%

(W4) *Adjustments in respect of reclassification of GFE's financial instrument*

Equity reduces from \$1,931,000 to \$1,831,000
Non-current liabilities increase from \$650,000 to \$750,000
Finance costs increase from \$65,000 to \$75,000
Profit before tax decreases from \$420,000 to \$415,000.

(W5) *Revised ratio calculations for GFE*

	GFE
Gross profit margin	Remains the same
PBT/Sales %	415/2,200 × 100 = 18.9%
ROE	415/1,831 × 100 = 22.6%
ROTCE	(415 + 70)/(1,831 + 750) × 100 = 18.8%
NCA turnover	Remains the same
Gearing	750/1,831 = 40.1%

(b)

Report on financial statement information for AXZ, DCB and GFE: financial year ended 30 September 20X6

Before any adjustment is made in respect of depreciation, DCB's ratios indicate a poorer performance and position than GFE in several important respects: gross margin, profit before tax as a percentage of sales and gearing are all worse than GFE's, and all ratios, with the exception of non-current asset turnover are worse than AXZ's.

After adjustment, however, DCB's ratios are much improved, especially once adjustments in respect of GFE's financial instruments are made. The adjusted figures show that both DCB and GFE produce significantly better profit margins than AXZ. DCB's profit before tax as a percentage of sales and return on equity are both superior to those of the other entities. Non-current asset turnover in DCB has reduced following the increase in net book value because of the depreciation adjustment. However, it is still better than the equivalent for the other entities. DCB's gearing percentage is similar to that of AXZ; both are lower than GFE's which is significantly higher following the reclassification of some of the equity to debt. Interest cover (see appendix) would not give cause for concern in any of the entities, but GFE's is significantly lower than in the other two entities.

On most of the key ratios, DCB appears to be the preferable acquisition target. Return on equity and return on total capital employed are both lower, and gearing is slightly higher than in AXZ. However, the effect overall on the new group's ratios might not be regarded as material. On the other hand, even where the ratios are more advantageous, the overall effect on group ratios might not make much of a difference. For example, if AXZ and DCB were to combine, total profit before tax would be $1,461,000 + 402,200 = $1,863,200, all other things being equal. Total sales would be $8,300,000 + $1,900,000 = $10,200,000. The group profit as a percentage of sales figure would be $1,863.2/10,200 × 100 = 18.3%. This is only 0.7% higher than AXZ's existing figure.

Further investigation would be needed before making a final decision. DCB has followed the tax treatment in depreciating its non-current assets; however, it is possible that an average asset life of eight years actually represents a better assessment of DCB's own asset base. Also, it is worth noting that DCB does appear to be subject to a significantly higher rate of income tax than the other two entities (see appendix). This perception requires further investigation, and detailed tax advice should be obtained before the directors of AXZ make their decision.

Appendix

Additional ratio calculations

	AXZ	DCB	GFE
Income tax expense as a percentage of profit before tax	336/1,461 × 100 = 23.0%	134/335 × 100 = 40%	105/415 × 100 = 25.3%
Interest cover	(2,700 − 252 − 822)/105 = 15.5	(667.2 − 50 − 180)/25 = 17.5	(800 − 65 − 250)/70 = 6.9

Solution 3

(a) **Report**

To: The Finance Director
From: Assistant
Subject: PJ Gamewriters

PJ Game writers is a very successful business. Between 20X4 and 20X5 its revenue increased by 26.5% and its gross profit by 30.4%. However, unusually, cost of sales includes directors' remuneration, presumably because the directors are directly involved in games writing. If director's remuneration is excluded from the analysis, gross profit restated increased by 26.0%, that is, very much in line with the revenue increase.

Games writers' employment costs comprise a significant part of cost of sales (55.1% – 20X4: 52.9%). If the business were to be taken over by OPQ this expense might change if new writers were brought in to replace Paul and James. Production costs have increased to 17% of cost of sales (20X4: 15.4%). These costs are outsourced, and it may be worth considering whether it is cost effective to continue such arrangements. Distribution costs are, presumably, included within cost of sales, probably under the category 'other costs'.

Operating expenses have increased by 33.9% between 20X4 and 20X5, that is, at a faster rate than revenue. Given that some of these expenses might be expected to be fixed, this rate of increase would require further information and explanation. Despite this increase, net profit margin has increased slightly, helped by an increase in interest receivable.

Turning to the statement of financial position, the position appears healthy. No cash flow statement is provided, but nevertheless, it is clear that the business generates substantial amounts of cash. During the 20X4-5 financial year, PJ managed to pay substantial amounts of dividend, directors' remuneration and income tax, while increasing its cash balance by almost $200,000. The current ratio has improved by a large margin from 1.26:1 at the 20X4 year end to 2.03:1. There is little change to inventories which, in any case, constitute a relatively minor element in current assets, but trade receivables has increased sharply, representing 60.1 days of sales (20X4: 53.6 days). It might be possible to make a significant improvement in this collection period.

Return on equity is very substantial in both years. However, this ratio should be treated with caution. Equity has been increased by $350,000 for the purposes of the calculation in both years so as to produce a more realistic result. The figure of $350,000 is strictly applicable only in 20X5, however, and the equivalent figure in 20X4 might well have been lower. It should also be appreciated that a higher asset valuation would give rise to additional depreciation charges which would reduce profits. In addition it is worth noting that the value of equity would almost certainly be substantially higher if the intangible asset of software copyrights were to be included.

Conclusion

PJ has expanded significantly whilst managing to maintain its margins and a sound financial position. The business is cash rich and has needed no external financing. It appears to be a good prospect for acquisition and further detailed investigation is recommended.

Appendix: calculations

1. Cost of sales analysis

	20X5 $'000	*% of total*	*20X4* $'000	*% of total*
Games writers' employment costs	700	55.1	550	52.9
Production costs	215	17.0	160	15.4
Directors' remuneration	200	15.7	200	19.2
Other costs	155	12.2	130	12.5
	1,270	100.0	1,040	100.0

2. Gross profit margin (excluding directors' remuneration from cost of sales)

	20X5	*20X4*
	$'000	$'000
Gross profit (as stated)	1,523	1,168
Add: directors' remuneration	200	200
Gross profit restated	1,723	1,368
Gross profit margin	1,723/2,793 × 100 = 61.7%	1,368/2,208 × 100 = 62.0%

3. Operating expenses as a percentage of revenue

20X5: 415/2,793 × 100 = 14.9%
20X4: 310/2,208 × 100 = 14.0%

4. Net profit margin (excluding directors' remuneration from profit)

	20X5	*20X4*
	$'000	$'000
Net profit (as stated)	784	570
Add: directors' remuneration	200	200
Net profit restated	984	770
Net profit margin	984/2,793 × 100 = 35.2%	770/2,208 × 100 = 34.9%

5. Current ratio

20X5: 744:367 = 2.03:1
20X4: 403:320 = 1.26:1

6. Trade receivables collection period

$$20X5 \quad \frac{460}{2,793} \times 365 = 60.1 \text{ days}$$

$$20X4 \quad \frac{324}{2,208} \times 365 = 53.6 \text{ days}$$

7. Return on equity (including potential revaluation of $350,000)

$$20X5 \quad \frac{1,115}{987 + 350} \times 100 = 83.4\%$$

$$20X4 \quad \frac{860}{703 + 350} \times 100 = 81.7\%$$

Directors' remuneration may not be relevant to the analysis here. ROE excluding directors' remuneration is:

$$20X5 \quad \frac{1,115 + 200}{987 + 350} \times 100 = 98.4\%$$

$$20X4 \quad \frac{860 + 200}{703 + 350} \times 100 = 100.7\%$$

(b) Financial analysis is almost always hampered by limitations. In the case of PJ there are some specific limitations in respect of the scope of the information reported in the annual financial statements. The value of the software titles generated during the life of the business is likely to be a substantial sum. As noted in part (a) it is not possible to calculate a realistic return on equity figure without this information. If OPQ is going to enter into serious negotiations to purchase PJ, the value of the copyrights should be established at an early stage. A further limitation is that financial statements place no value on the human assets employed within the business. However, where a business like PJ is to be taken over, such elements should, in any event, be downplayed. Paul and James will, presumably, leave the business, and it may not be possible to retain the services of all of the software writers.

A more detailed breakdown of certain elements in the income statement would be helpful in analysing the performance of the business. Within cost of sales 'other costs' constitute a significant item in both years, and the nature of operating expenses is obscure.

There are general limitations to the value of financial statements to the analyst. Some of the limitations relevant to PJ include the following:

(i) Financial statements are prepared for the common needs of most users. Where they are being used to assist in making a specific decision (such as whether or not to invest in an entity, as in this case) the information they contain is likely to be found wanting.

(ii) Timeliness is often a problem. PJ's financial statements have apparently been prepared within a quite reasonable timeframe. However, this is clearly a business experiencing rapid growth, and it is likely that more current information will be needed, perhaps in the form of management accounts, in order to make an informed decision.

(iii) It is usually helpful to have a more complete picture than that provided by a single set of financial statements. Also, it is important to obtain a full set of notes to the financial statements as these often contain useful information. In the case of PJ, complete sets of the financial statements since the business was founded would be helpful.

Solution 4

(a)

Report on the ratios and their implications

To: The board of directors of Acquirer
From: An accountant
Subject: Proposed acquisition of Target
Date: 19 November 20X3

Following our earlier discussions, I have computed key ratios for Target and some similar entities. These are attached as an appendix to this report.

It is notable that the gross profit margin of Target is towards the upper end of the range of comparison, while the net margin is towards the lower end. The relatively high gross margin could be due to a sales mix of relatively more profitable products or, alternatively, because of a tighter than average control of manufacturing costs. Given apparent problems in controlling other operating expenses (see below) a different sales mix is perhaps the most likely explanation.

The superior performance at gross margin level is largely negated by an apparently extremely poor control of other operating expenses. These seem to be running at around 13% of revenue as against 7 or 8% for the entities in the sample. It may be that the costs are being incurred to finance future growth and cannot be capitalised under existing accounting standards. However, they could equally be due to inherent inefficiencies and this issue will certainly require further investigation before proceeding further.

Return on capital is slightly higher than the average for the sample and given that net profit margin is towards the lower end, this implies a ratio of revenue to capital that is towards the upper end of the range revealed by the sample. This is quite encouraging as capital investment does appear to produce strong revenue streams provide costs can be controlled.

Interest cover is towards the lower end of the range of comparison and gearing is towards the upper end. There is a good chance these two issues are linked as other things being equal you would expect interest cover to vary in inverse proportion to gearing. The level of gearing may not be a key factor in an acquisition decision as we may well wish to refinance the entity if it becomes a subsidiary.

Dividend cover is relatively high compared with other entities in the sample. This could be due to strategic decision by current management to retain a greater proportion of profits, but it could equally well be indicative of a strain on liquidity and this issue would require further investigation. However, the level of past divided payout will not necessarily be a key future issue since, if Target becomes our subsidiary, we will be in a position to determine divided levels within legal constraints.

Both inventory turnover and receivables days are towards the higher end of the performance range. This is a good sign which might have been expected given the relatively high turnover of capital that Target seems to enjoy.

I hope you find this report useful. Please do not hesitate to contract me if you have any queries regarding its contents.

Yours sincerely
Accountant

(b)

Limitations of the ratios

One key factor is the appropriateness of the sample as a basis for comparison with Target. It is inevitably subjective to identify 10 entities that are valid for this purpose. It is rare to find two entities with exactly the same operating environments and there may well have been a number of other equally valid samples of 10 entities that would have produced different ratios and therefore a different interpretation.

Another issue is the extent to which conventional ratios are computed from the results of a single accounting period. Different entities have different year ends and in the case of Target the most recently available financial statements are nearly a year old. The latest available financial statements could be for a period that is not typical of the trend of performance over a longer period due to unusual or non-recurring items. There is also the inherent problem of computing a ratio such as return on capital, where a performance figure, like profit, is expressed as a ratio or percentage of a position figure like capital.

A further key factor to bear in mind is that, despite the existence of an increasingly complex regulatory framework, entities still have considerable discretion in the manner that the financial statements are prepared and presented given the significant amount of judgement that is involved in selecting accounting policies.

A final factor to bear in mind is that financial ratios inevitably focus on historical financial aspects. Many useful performance indicators are non-financial in nature. It is possible to compute non-financial ratios, but these are often difficult to compare between entities given the voluntary nature of much non-financial information that is currently disclosed. It is also questionable as to how much historical financial data can contribute to a future acquisition decision.

The financial statements themselves would be of some assistance in overcoming the defects mentioned in this report. They would provide information on the key accounting policies followed by the entity and would provide separate disclosure of non-recurring items. They may well also provide a degree of non-financial information and some predictions about the future prospects of the entity. However, as stated earlier, this information is unlikely to be as highly regulated as the historical financial data and so its reliability may be questioned.

Solution 5

(a)

Report to Investor on DM

Date: May 20X5

Note: The ratio calculations referred to in the report can be found in the Appendix. In 20X4 DM has expanded rapidly, increasing the number of its stores from 36 to 42. The annual sales figure per store has fallen substantially since 20X3; however, this may be because the new stores have been open for only part of the year. Even so, DM's annual sales per store is significantly higher than the sector average. However, it may simply have larger stores than average.

Gross profit margin has increased slightly, but the increase in operating profit margin is substantial. Operating expenses have actually fallen by over 27% in the year. The expenses may have been affected by the lengthening of most non-current asset lives, and the consequent decrease in depreciation charges.

The review of depreciation has resulted in higher profits and it is certainly possible that the directors have deliberately manipulated the results. Also, the significant decrease in operating expenses may indicate that some items of expenditure have been classified as capital rather than revenue in nature. This method of creative accounting can be quite difficult to confirm using the information available in a set of financial statements. Nevertheless, it would be sensible to conduct further comparisons using information in the notes to the financial statements.

Net profit margin is significantly lower in both years than the sector average, despite higher than average gross profit margin. It is noticeable, however, that the net profit margin has increased from 1.9% to 2.6% in the year, and this could, for reasons already given, be a result of deliberate manipulation.

The current ratio in both years is low. It appears that suppliers are being squeezed for credit. The cash level is higher in 20X4 than in 20X3. It appears from the statement of financial position that suppliers may be providing even longer credit than usual. Trade and other payables have increased by over 8%, whereas the increase in cost of sales is only 2.8%. Gearing does not appear to give cause for concern.

Despite several new store openings the level of property, plant and equipment remains almost the same. It may be that the majority of the investment in new stores was made during 20X3. Non-current asset turnover has improved although it has not quite reached the sector level.

Summary

DM is a profitable and rapidly expanding entity. Its margins compare reasonably well with the sector average although net profit margin is relatively poor. It is possible that the entity's directors have deliberately manipulated the financial statements in order to produce better results in the hope of affecting the offer price in a takeover bid. They do stand to benefit personally and may be keen to sell the company in order to realise a lump sum upon retirement. However, it is not possible to state conclusively that the financial statements have been manipulated. Further investigation would be required, especially, if sufficient information is available, to ascertain the reasons for the fall in operating expenses.

APPENDIX: ratio calculations

Ratio	*20X4*		*20X3*		*Sector comparative*
Gross profit	78/1,255 × 100	6.2%	75/1,220 × 100	6.1%	5.9%
Operating profit margin	57/1,255 × 100	4.5%	46/1,220 × 100	3.8%	N/A
No of stores		42		36	N/A
Annual sales per store	1,255/42	$29.9 m	1,220/36	$33.9 m	$27.6 m
Net profit margin	33/1,255 × 100	2.6%	23/1,220 × 100	1.9%	3.9%
Non-current asset turnover	1,255/680	1.85	1,220/675	1.81	1.93
Current ratio	105/317	0.33:1	71/309	0.23:1	N/A
Gearing (debt/equity)	142/301 × 100	47.2%	140/276 × 100	50.7%	N/A

Note: (a) The gearing calculation could also include short-term borrowings as part of debt capital.

(b) Sector comparatives often provide useful information for the analyst, but should be treated with some caution for the following reasons:

- The comparatives are usually, as in this case, based on an average of entities. Averages can be skewed by one or two atypical cases.
- No two entities are completely alike. For example, DM trades in only one of six provinces in its country. Economic conditions may vary between provinces, and so it may not be valid to compare DM using averages based on entities operating in other provinces.
- Although international standard setters have attempted to reduce the range of accounting choices available, there remain, quite legitimately, areas of accounting policy difference between entities.
- There are different ways of calculating some of the common accounting ratios. The analyst must be sure that the method of calculation is consistent.
- Information published for the sector may not contain all the ratios that the analyst would ideally require. For example, in this case, it would be useful to know the average gearing and current ratios.

Scope of External Reporting

Scope of External Reporting

17

Learning Outcomes

After studying this chapter students should be able to:

- describe pressures for extending the scope and quality of external reports to include prospective and non-financial matters, and narrative reporting generally;
- explain how financial information concerning the interaction of a business with society and the natural environment can be communicated in the published accounts;
- discuss social and environmental issues which are likely to be most important to stakeholders in an organisation;
- explain the process of measuring, recording and disclosing the effects of exchanges between a business and society – human resource accounting.

17.1 Introduction

This chapter covers discusses the current pressures that exist to extend the scope and quality of annual reports. 17.2 includes discussion of user needs in the context of a increased volume of reporting, the need for forecast information, the effect of accounting scandals and the move towards corporate social reporting. Section 17.3 covers the IASB moves to extend narrative reporting, with the management commentary. The section also looks at the example set in the UK with the Operating and Financial Review (OFR) and the Business Review and looks at their current status. Section 17.4 examines social accounting and reporting as a general introduction to later sections in the chapter. Section 17.5 looks at accounting for the impacts of the entity on the natural environment. Section 17.6 examines various aspects of human resource accounting, including intellectual capital reporting, and human asset accounting. Section 17.7 looks at the Global Reporting Initiative.

17.2 The pressure to extend external reporting

The annual reports of entities have never been more complex and comprehensive. Despite, or perhaps partly because of, the growth in disclosure that has taken place in recent years, there seems to be an increasing need for different approaches to disclosure of information. Part of the problem lies in a fundamental inconsistency between the overall objective of financial statements and the type of information that has traditionally been provided. The IASB's Framework states that the objective of financial statements is 'to provide information about the financial position, performance and changes in financial position of an entity that is useful to a wide range of users in making economic decisions'. However, financial statements, by their very nature, tend to be backward looking in that they report on transactions that have already taken place. In order to be able to make economic decisions, users may feel that they need information that has an orientation towards the future. This may be provided to a limited extent by the historical information reported in the financial statements: for example, a business that has always turned in a steady profit may perhaps be relied upon to do so again in the future.

17.2.1 Inclusion of forecasts in annual reports

Ideally, perhaps, users would like to see the inclusion of quantified forecast information as part of the annual report. However, the provision of such information is likely to be unacceptable to the management of commercial entities. If a business were to include an optimistic forecast which was not subsequently met, the financial market's perception is likely to be that management is incompetent. There might very well be an adverse effect on the share price, which would hardly be of benefit to shareholders. If, on the other hand, the forecast were too pessimistic, the outcome, in this case too, might be an adverse effect on the share price, resulting in an undervaluation of the business. The sensitivity of share prices to such events is suggested by the fact that there is often an adverse reaction in the financial market where a listed entity's preliminary announcement does not meet analysts' expectations.

Two other potentially sound reasons for not including forecasts are cost and confidentiality. The provision of the already complex level of disclosures in annual reports is expensive and the inclusion of forecast information would be likely to significantly increase costs. Also, the managers of commercial entities are likely to be very reluctant to disclose commercially sensitive, quantified, information about future plans.

17.2.2 The effect of accounting scandals

Whenever there is a major accounting scandal, the usual response of regulatory authorities is to increase regulation resulting in increased levels of disclosure. For example, the Enron case in the United States has resulted in a fundamental reappraisal of regulation, and has been largely responsible for the promulgation of the Sarbanes–Oxley Act which significantly increases regulation of financial reporting and auditing. Increased regulation usually results in increased quantities of disclosure.

A related effect is that over the last decade or so, there has been an increased demand for listed entities to demonstrate good corporate governance. Although there has not, as yet, been a unified international response to this demand, many countries have taken measures to improve corporate governance via legislation or the implementation of voluntary codes of conduct. The improvements are often accompanied by increased levels of disclosure.

17.2.3 Corporate social responsibility

The original model of the corporation envisaged a relationship that subsisted principally between the entity, its management and its owners. The separation between owners and managers resulted in some tension, but this could be at least partially addressed by financial reporting and by the imposition of external audit requirements. However, throughout the latter half of the twentieth century this model looked increasingly old-fashioned. Although some authorities continued to maintain that a corporate entity should be responsible only for increasing shareholder wealth, the idea took hold that corporate entities have 'stakeholders', a much more broadly based group of interested parties, and that they bear responsibilities towards those stakeholders.

Milton Friedman, the economist, is famous for, amongst other things, asserting the values of the old model of the corporation. In an article in 1970 ('The social responsibility of business to increase its profits', *The New York Times Magazine*), he argued as follows:

> What does it mean to say that the corporate executive has a 'social responsibility' in his capacity as a businessman? If this statement is not pure rhetoric, it must mean that he is to act in some way that is not in the interest of his employers [the shareholders]. ... Insofar as his actions in accord with his 'social responsibility' reduce returns to stockholders, he is spending their money ...

The counter-arguments to Friedman's view include the following points:

- Modern corporations are so powerful that they are able to influence every aspect of community life. Power must, in a just society, be accompanied by responsibility.
- The community bears the hidden cost of many corporate activities. For example, if businesses pollute the environment they do not, unless there is some legal constraint, have to bear the cost of cleaning up. This is borne through public expenditure and is financed by general taxation. The public therefore has some right to hold corporations accountable.
- The corporate business is a legal person, but in fact this is a convenient fiction. Businesses should not be able to hide behind this fiction in order to avoid the consequences of decisions made by managers (who, obviously, are real people).
- The old-fashioned view of the corporation is too simplistic to operate successfully in a complex modern society.

17.2.4 Demands for more information

The pressure to extend the scope of reporting results in demands by stakeholders for the following types of information:

1. a general increase in narrative in financial statement;
2. an increase in the depth of commentary provided by management on both the past performance of the business and its prospects for the future;
3. more, better quality, and more consistent reporting on environmental and social issues.

In the remainder of this chapter we will look at some of the ways in which entities can, and sometimes do, provide more information to their stakeholders.

17.3 Increasing the scope of reporting

In October 2005, the IASB issued a discussion paper on 'Management commentary' (this is a term synonymous with 'Operating and financial review' in the UK or 'Management discussion and analysis' which is the term commonly used in the USA).

The likely objective of the management commentary is to assist current and potential investors in assessing the strategies adopted by the entity and the potential for achieving these strategies. The management would set out their analysis of the business, which supplements and complements the financial statements but taking account of likely future activities. It would be intended that the management commentary be comprehensive, focusing on matters that are relevant to investors and should be understandable, neutral and balanced, comparable and reliable.

Initial indications are that the management commentary would not be included in IFRS but would have a voluntary but best practice status. The terms 'neutral' and 'balanced' are obviously less onerous than achieving fair presentation, which is what the auditor is charged with ensuring. The issue of verifiability of the information that is included in the management commentary will be a difficult one as much of what is likely to be covered will be forward looking and so not necessarily verifiable. It is intended to be 'through the management's eyes' and so the term 'balanced' is used to reflect the fact that the commentary is unlikely to avoid some element of bias as the management is likely to have a positive outlook on their strategies.

The current status of this, and all its other projects, may be determined by accessing the IASB's website (www.iasb.org). At the time of updating this *Learning System* the IASB is planning to issue an exposure draft in the second quarter of 2009.

In order to appreciate the content that is likely to form such a report, it is useful to look at what has been introduced in the UK, namely the Operating and Financial Review and the Business Review.

17.3.1 The Operating and Financial Review

In 1993, the Accounting Standards Board (ASB) in the UK issued a statement on a form of disclosure known as the Operating and Financial Review (OFR). An OFR is intended to set out the directors' analysis of the business, so as to provide both an historical *and* a prospective analysis of the business as seen by senior management. The inclusion of such a review as part of entities' annual reports was not mandatory. However, the Company Law Review in the UK proposed that all UK companies over a certain size should publish an OFR, and in 2005 a statutory instrument (a statutory instrument is an amending piece of government legislation – in this case amending existing companies' legislation in the form of the Companies Act 1985) was published that would require listed companies to publish an OFR.

The statutory instrument was supported by detailed guidance in the form of Reporting Standard 1 *Operating and financial review* (RS1), which was issued by the ASB in May 2005. However, in November 2005 the Chancellor of the Exchequer, Gordon Brown, made a surprise announcement that the statutory instrument would be withdrawn as part of an effort to cut down on red tape affecting UK businesses. The ASB in consequence converted its RS1 in January 2006 into a Reporting Statement of Best Practice (recently updated to reflect changes in companies' legislation in the Companies Act 2006) which altered its status from a standard with mandatory application. The key points from this statement are summarised in the section below.

Many listed companies in the UK choose to disclose the OFR information on a voluntary basis, notwithstanding the withdrawal of the change to the law.

17.3.2 The Business Review

The Companies Act 2006 introduced additional requirements in the Business Review that were brought into force for financial years beginning on or after 1 October 2007.

The Business Review has a statutory purpose, which is to inform the shareholders and help them assess how the directors have performed their duties to promote the success of the company.

The Act also requires quoted companies to provide additional disclosures in their Business Review to the extent necessary for an understanding of the development, performance and position of the business. The additional disclosures include:

- The main trends and factors likely to affect future developments and activities
- Information about employees, environmental matters and social and community issues
- Information about contractual arrangements that are central to the company's activities.

All of these provisions were originally introduced in the OFR.

17.3.3 OFR: the ASB's reporting statement of best practice

The ASB specifies that an OFR should be a balanced and comprehensive analysis, consistent with the size and complexity of the business, of:

(a) the development and performance of the entity during the financial year;
(b) the position of the entity at the end of the year;
(c) the main trends and factors underlying the development, performance and position of the business of the entity during the financial year; and
(d) the main trends and factors which are likely to affect the entity's future development, performance and position.

The OFR should be prepared so as to assist members (i.e., shareholders) to assess the strategies adopted by the entity and the potential for those strategies to succeed. It is thus capable, potentially, of addressing some of the traditional limitations of financial statements, in that it specifically examines future business developments.

The ASB sets out the following principles for the preparation of an OFR:

The OFR shall:

(a) set out an analysis of the business through the eyes of the board of directors;
(b) focus on matters that are relevant to the interests of members (i.e., shareholders);
(c) have a forward-looking orientation, identifying those trends and factors relevant to the members' assessment of the current and future performance of the business and the progress towards the achievement of long-term business objectives;
(d) complement, as well as supplement, the financial statements in order to enhance the overall corporate disclosure;
(e) be comprehensive and understandable;
(f) be balanced and neutral, dealing even-handedly both with good and bad aspects;
(g) be comparable over time.

The principal disclosure requirements are as follows:

(a) the nature of the business, including a description of the market, competitive and regulatory environment in which the entity operates, and the entity's objectives and strategies;
(b) the development and performance of the business, both in the financial year under review and in the future;

(c) the resources, principal risks and uncertainties, and relationships that may affect the entity's long-term value;
(d) the position of the business including a description of the capital structure, treasury policies and objectives and liquidity of the entity, both in the financial year under review and the future.

Some more specific requirements relating to particular matters are added to this broad, general description of disclosures. The statement specifies that information should be included about:

(a) environmental matters (including the impact of the business on the environment);
(b) the entity's employees;
(c) social and community issues;
(d) persons with whom the entity has contractual or other arrangements which are essential to the business of the entity;
(e) receipts from, and returns to, members of the entity in respect of shares held by them; and
(f) all other matters directors consider to be relevant.

It can be seen, therefore, that a mandatory OFR would have added very materially to the disclosures of many listed businesses, and that some aspects of the disclosures (notably the environmental and social aspects) would have represented a major development in disclosure for many businesses

Advantages and drawbacks of the OFR

The advantages of including an OFR as part of the annual report are as follows:

- Such a statement is a useful summary of information that can be found in a more complex form elsewhere in the financial statements.
- It may provide genuinely useful statements of management's intended business strategy, and sufficient information to be able to assess the relative success of business strategies to date.
- It may be more likely to be read and absorbed than some other parts of the annual report.

There are, however, some potential drawbacks:

- Users may rely too heavily on the OFR, and may read it in preference to a thorough examination of the detailed figures.
- Even though there is a basic template for the OFR, these statements may vary significantly in practice and may not be readily comparable.
- OFRs currently (both in the UK and elsewhere) have the status of voluntary disclosures and so they suffer from all the general drawbacks of voluntary disclosure (e.g., they may not be prepared on an entirely consistent basis, bad news may be underplayed and so on).

17.3.4 International developments

Many entities outside the UK voluntarily include an OFR as part of their annual report.

Example 17.A

Novartis is a major multinational pharmaceuticals entity based in Switzerland. Its financial statements are prepared in accordance with IFRS, but it also includes an OFR statement in its annual report. In its 2007 annual report, the OFR runs to 31 pages. It can be accessed at the Novartis website (www.novartis.com). The content of this OFR can be summarised as follows:

Factors affecting results. This section includes commentary on competitive conditions, identification of new products and exchange rate exposures.
Critical accounting policies and estimates. This includes comments on revenue, impairment, derivative financial instruments, investments in associates, pension costs and provisions.
Results of operations. This section occupies several pages, commenting on growth, the success of product lines and income and expenses.

Several pages in the OFR contain quantitative information in the form of condensed financial statements, or expanded information about income statement and statement of financial position items. However, the OFR is dominated by narrative.

17.4 Social accounting and reporting

Reporting of non-financial issues is not a new concept. Accounting theorists for many years now have questioned the role of financial reports. Traditionally, such reports have communicated financial information resulting from transactions (denominated in money values) entered into by the firm. Such transactions relate primarily to the exchange of goods and services; they exclude recognition of human capital and the effect of the entity on the social and natural environment.

Society can be seen as a set of sub-systems with which the entity interacts. Interaction with the economic sub-system is generally fairly fully reported. However, traditional financial reports have not dealt with interactions with the following sub-systems:

1. *The natural environment. A* business uses physical resources such as coal, gas, water, air but the full cost of this usage is not reflected in the financial statements. Firms may have adverse impacts on the environment, but until recently, these effects were not recognised at all in the financial statements.
2. *The sociological environment.* The way in which firms attract human resources, and the use of those resources, has an impact on society. For example, a decision to close a large division will have an adverse impact on local society. On a global level, certain groups of consumers are likely to express preferences against those firms that exploit child labour in developing countries.

Social accounting and reporting covers both financial and non-financial aspects of reporting. It is potentially very wide-ranging in its coverage, and might encompass such matters as:

- reporting on the environmental impacts of an entity's policies;
- measuring and reporting the expected value of future obligations related to rectification of environmental damage;
- measuring and reporting on the value of human assets in an entity;
- reporting policies and measurements relating to the workforce, for example, the policy on employment of disabled people, and statistics reporting on the numbers of disabled staff employed;

- reporting on an entity's intellectual capital;
- reports on an entity's policies on ethical issues.

Note that this is not a complete list of potential social reporting issues. In this chapter we will examine two principal strands in social reporting: first, measuring and reporting the impacts of an entity's activities on the natural environment, and second, measuring, reporting and disclosing the effects of exchanges between a business and society in the form of human resources. Finally, we will look at an important current development in the field of social reporting: the Global Reporting Initiative.

17.5 Accounting for the impacts of the entity on the natural environment

Environmental accounting is an umbrella term that covers many different aspects of reporting. We can distinguish, broadly, between two aspects:

1. accounting for, and disclosing, financial information relating to the interaction of the entity with its environment;
2. providing non-financial disclosures that assist the user in determining, for example, the nature of the entity's commitment to sound environmental practice, its record on sustainable development and so on.

17.5.1 Measuring and reporting financial information relating to the environment

There is an increasing trend towards holding businesses to account for their activities in relation to environmental damage. For example, the Kyoto accord commits governments around the world to significant reductions in greenhouse gas emissions. The business sector in many countries is currently being targeted by governments to meet emissions reduction targets. These have impacts on many aspects of measurement, reporting and disclosure, and some of the principal areas are described below.

Taxation-related matters

Taxation measures relating to the environment are becoming increasingly common. In the UK, for example, some or all of the following may affect organisations:

1. *Climate change levy*: This may have the effect of encouraging businesses to improve energy efficiency and to reduce emissions of carbon dioxide.
2. *Landfill tax*: A landfill tax was introduced in 1996. This may have significant financial impacts on the profitability of those businesses that dispose of large volumes of waste.
3. *Capital allowances*: For example, there are currently 100 per cent first year allowances for capital expenditure on natural gas refuelling infrastructure.

Accounting for additional costs related to the environment

Significant costs may be incurred by, for example, house-builders who build on brownfield land that has previously been contaminated. Highly restrictive planning policies limit the use of greenfield sites for building, and so in very densely populated areas (such as England) significant decontamination activity may be required before land can be built on.

Increasingly stringent laws may involve business entities in incurring additional costs in respect of environmental damage they have caused. Where sites are polluted by, for example, mining activities, local legislation is increasingly likely to require reinstatement.

Environmental provisions

Sometimes anticipated costs related to environmental damage require provisions. Provisions required in respect of environmental costs are no different from any other provisions, in that they must follow the requirements of IAS 37 *Provisions, contingent liabilities and contingent assets*. Students should remember the recognition rules in respect of provisions.

A provision should be recognised when:

(a) an entity has a present obligation (legal or constructive) as a result of a past event;
(b) it is probable that an outflow of resources embodying economic benefits will be required to settle the obligation;
(c) a reliable estimate can be made of the amount of the obligation.

The issue of recognition of related non-current assets may occur in respect of environmental provisions, as illustrated in the following example.

Example 17.B

B has commissioned an oil rig. The rig has an estimated useful life of 8 years, and initial commissioning costs are $80 million, all of which are incurred shortly before the year ending 31 December 20X0. B adopts a policy of straight-line depreciation and is assuming a residual value of nil in respect of the oil rig asset. Depreciation will be charged for the first time in the year ending 31 December 20X1. B is obliged to recognise decommissioning and environmental restitution costs totalling $10 million which will occur at the end of the 8-year period. These costs are unavoidable. However, the provision carries with it a related asset, in that the oil rig gives rise to future benefits in the form of access to valuable oil resources which will be exploited over the 8-year life of the rig. The appropriate rate of discount is 10% per year.

The amount of the provision required is $10 million, on the basis of estimated future prices 8 years from now. How will the above transactions be reflected in the entity's statement of financial position at 31 December 20X0 and 31 December 20X1?

Solution

The discounted NPV of the provision at 31 December 20X0 is $4,670,000 ($10m × discount factor from tables of 0.467).

At 31 December 20X0 extracts from B's statement of financial position show the following:

	$
Non-current assets at cost	84,670,000
Provisions for liabilities and charges	
Provisions for decommissioning and environmental restitution costs	4,670,000

Both the original cost of the asset ($80 million) and the discounted decommissioning and environmental costs have been capitalised. At this point the effect on the income statement is nil.

One year later, the provision is remeasured to take account of the change in the time value of money (assuming that the original estimate of $10 million of costs is still valid). The appropriate discount factor is 0.512, giving a balance on the provision account of $5,120,000. The increase of $450,000 will be charged to the income statement as part of financing charges. It is sometimes referred to as 'the unwinding of the finance charge'. In 20X1, the first full year of operation of the oil rig, depreciation will be charged for the first time.

At 31 December 20X1, extracts from B's statement of financial position show the following:

	$
Non-current assets at cost	84,670,000
Less: accumulated depreciation (1/8)	10,583,750
Net book value	74,086,250
Provisions for liabilities and charges	
Provision for decommmissioning and environmental restitution costs	5,120,000

The income statement will include the depreciation charge for the year ($10,583,750) and the unwinding of the finance charge of $450,000.

Contingent environmental liabilities

Many industries are now facing a broad range of potential environmental liabilities. Where those liabilities fit the definition of a provision, they must, of course, be recognised in the financial statements. Some potential liabilities may not, however, meet the recognition criteria, but should nevertheless be noted as contingent liabilities.

17.5.2 Non-financial disclosures

The annual report of an entity is traditionally a vehicle for presenting financial information. However, in recent times, it has also become the medium through which an often large amount of voluntary disclosure is made to stakeholders. Many of the voluntary disclosures include environmental information. This may be no more than a few additional paragraphs on the entity's policy in respect of, say, waste disposal. However, many entities, especially those engaged in environmentally sensitive operations, make very extensive disclosures. These are often narrative in nature, but they may also contain detailed quantitative data about, for example, emissions. A very thorough example of this type of disclosure is that of the Royal Dutch/Shell business. Each year since 1997, the business has published a separate report with the purpose of illustrating the group's contribution to sustainable development. The report is published in full on the group's website at www.shell.com. At the time of updating this *Learning System* (February 2008) the 2006 *Shell Sustainability* Report was available on the website. It is extensive, including a lot of information about the group's policies and activities, and it also contains some hard data in the form of quantitative measurements of, for example:

- carbon dioxide
- methane
- other Kyoto greenhouse gases
- oil spills
- hazardous and non-hazardous waste.

Several years of comparatives are provided.

However, although the standard and volume of environmental disclosure has undoubtedly increased in recent years, the current situation is not wholly satisfactory. Problems include the following:

- Not all entities report environmental information. Some entities may report only when it suits them to do so, and even where there is annual reporting, there is no guarantee of consistency in approach.
- As the disclosures are still of a voluntary nature, there is a danger that the information is unreliable. Although environmental audit exists, there is no compulsory requirement

to have environmental statements audited, unless the disclosures fall under the remit of the financial auditor (as would be the case, for example, where provisions were made or contingent liabilities were disclosed).

- The importance of disclosure varies from one industry to another. Heavily polluting industries may be suspected of putting a positive spin on their environmental disclosures. There is, in any case, often a suspicion that such disclosures are made more for public relations reasons than with the aim of genuinely assisting stakeholders.

17.6 Accounting for, and reporting on, human resource issues

Social reporting could take many forms. It could include a 'social income statement' which would report social costs and benefits to different areas of society, and a social statement of financial position disclosing human assets, organisational assets, and the use of public goods, and of financial and physical assets.

One of the most important documents to be produced on the subject was *The Corporate Report,* published in the UK in 1975. This was, both for its time and ours, a radical document that advocated not only the publication of financial statements, but also of supplementary reports to serve the needs of users other than the investor group. Supplementary reports would include:

1. *Statement of corporate objectives.* The statement could take many forms, but would include objectives relating to all stakeholders.
2. *Employment report.* This would give information about the number of employees, wage rates and training.
3. *Statement of future prospects.* Although *The Corporate Report* acknowledged the difficulty of reporting about future prospects, this would provide welcome information to all types of stakeholder.
4. *Value-added reports.* This would show the development of resources throughout the entity, demonstrating the interdependency of all parties (employee, government and the providers of capital). A typical value-added statement would show a split of 'value added' between the various providers of resources to the business:

ABC Group: value-added statement for the year ended 31 December 20X1

	$
Revenue	X
Less: bought-in materials and services	(X)
Value added	X
Applied to	
Employees	
Wages, pensions and other benefits	X
Government	
Corporation tax	X
Providers of capital	
Interest on loans	X
Dividends	X
Retained by the company for future growth and	
Capital expenditure	
Depreciation	X
Retained earnings	X
Total allocated funds	X

The provision of such information would be costly. There would be a need for independent review or audit, further adding to the cost. The incorporation of this additional information in the annual report would before truly widespread only if encapsulated in regulation.

17.6.1 Disclosures in respect of social issues

Many entities, especially larger listed entities, now include some elements of disclosure relating to social issues and human resources. As in the case of environmental reporting, this may be largely narrative in nature, but it is sometimes appended with quantitative disclosures. Taking the Shell Report as an example, the following are amongst the quantitative social disclosures made in 2006:

- fatalities
- lost time injury frequency
- reportable occupational illness frequency
- numbers of security personnel
- gender diversity
- child labour
- union membership.

17.6.2 Intellectual capital reporting

The definition of 'intellectual capital' (CIMA's *Official Terminology*) is as follows:

> Knowledge which can be used to create value. Intellectual capital includes (i) *human resources*: The collective skills, experience and knowledge of employees; (ii) *intellectual assets*: Knowledge which is defined and codified such as a drawing, computer program or collection of data; and (iii) *intellectual property*: Intellectual assets which can be legally protected, such as patents or copyrights.

Interest in intellectual capital has grown in recent years, as economic activity has become more oriented towards service and knowledge based industries, by contrast with the old industrial model of industries which employed large amounts of physical capital. Entities in many major industrial sectors these days rely upon human capital to generate wealth. Where physical capital in the form of non-current tangible assets is negligible in size, entities may produce statement of financial position that show very low levels of net worth. At the same time their market capitalisation may be many times greater than book value. This can often be explained in part by out of date valuations for items such as land and buildings, but the more frequently encountered hypothesis is that the gap represents intangible assets in the form of intellectual capital.

Many entities nowadays are taking up the challenge to report their intellectual capital. Such reporting undoubtedly does represent a challenge because intellectual capital is such a nebulous concept. The Swedish insurance company, Skandia, was one of the first companies to attempt comprehensive reporting of intellectual capital. One of the readings at the end of this chapter, 'Intellectual assets: the new frontier' by Peter Atrill, charts the development of intellectual capital reporting, setting out the key features of the Skandia approach. A more recent initiative is the Meritum Project, financed by the European Union between 1998 and 2001, which brings together academics and professionals from different countries to create a guide for companies interested in implementing intellectual capital management systems. (More information on the Meritum project can be found at www.eu-know.net/tools.)

During 2003 the UK government established a taskforce on human capital management reporting, led by Denise Kingsmill. The taskforce reported in November 2003, and the full report can be downloaded from www.accountingforpeople.gov.uk. The readings at the end of this chapter include an account by Lesley Bolton of the setting up and objectives of the taskforce.

17.6.3 Human asset accounting

One possible approach to intellectual capital reporting would be to attempt to identify the intangible components of the very large gap that exists between market capitalisation and book value in many 'people' businesses. The possibility of measuring and recognising a value for the workforce as part of the non-current assets of a business has been recognised in theory for the last 30 or 40 years. However, there are many barriers to adopting this approach. The IASB in its *Framework for the Preparation and Presentation of Financial Statements* defines an asset thus:

> An asset is a resource controlled by the entity as a result of past events and from which future economic benefits are expected to flow to the entity.

Although it is certainly realistic to expect that human assets in the form of employees will generate economic benefits in the future, a significant problem arises in respect of control. Non-current assets are legally owned or are under the control of the entity as the result of a binding agreement (such as a lease). However, it is hard to see how, unless in conditions of slavery, human assets can be controlled in that way. It is customary to control even the most creative of employees in some way, but that control does not operate for 24 hours a day, and is, in any case, short-term. By giving and serving out notice, an employee can soon be free of the partial control that is exerted by the employer.

A further problem relates to reliable measurement. This was identified by the most recent exposure draft to amend IAS 38 *Intangible Assets.* The draft discussed the possibility of recognising the workforce as an asset. It stated: 'an entity usually has insufficient control over the expected future economic benefits arising from a team of skilled staff and from training to conclude that these items meet the definition of an asset'. It goes on the state that, even if control over the future economic benefits could be demonstrated, and even if it could be demonstrated that the workforce could meet the criteria for identification as an intangible asset, it is highly unlikely that the fair value of the workforce and related intellectual capital could be measured reliably. Therefore, the exposure draft specifically prohibited recognition of an assembled workforce as a separately intangible asset.

If the value of the workforce were to be measured, how could it be achieved? Cost-based methods are a possibility. Currently, remuneration and training costs are treated as income statement deductions. However, looked at in a different way, they could be considered as investments in the workforce, and could be capitalised as part of intangible assets. Another possibility would be a valuation based approach, which could, for example, discount a future expected cash outflow on salaries to net present value.

17.7 The Global Reporting Initiative

The Global Reporting Initiative (GRI) was launched in 1997 as a joint initiative of the US non-governmental organisation, the Coalition for Environmentally Responsible Economies (CERES) and the United Nations Environment Programme. The GRI's goal was to enhance the quality, rigour and utility of sustainability reporting. In June 2000 the GRI issued its first set of reporting guidelines. These were replaced, in 2002, by a new set of guidelines, and have now been replaced by version 3.

The new guidelines are available (at the time of writing) on the organisation's website at www.globalreporting.org. The guidelines are for voluntary use.

The GRI's intention is that reporting on economic, environmental and social performance by organisations becomes as routine and comparable as financial reporting. To this end it has created a Sustainability Reporting Framework, some details of which are given below.

The Framework sets out a series of key stages that are involved in the sustainability reporting process:

- defining report content
- defining report quality
- setting the report boundary
- profile
- disclosure on management approach
- performance indicators
- Sector supplements.

The 'Profile' stage identifies the base content that should appear in a sustainability report, which can be briefly summarized as follows:

1. *Strategy and analysis*

This section provides a strategic view of the organization's relationship to sustainability. It should include a statement from the most senior decision-maker in the organisation (typically, the CEO in a commercial organisation) which should present the overall vision and strategy of the organisation in relation to sustainability. The report should then describe the key impacts, risks and opportunities in relation to sustainability.

2. *Organisation profile*

This section should provide information on the principal brands, products and services offered, the countries in which the organisation operates, markets service, scale of the organisation (e.g., number of employees, capitalisation) and any significant changes during the reporting period.

3. *Report profile*

This section should include information on the process for defining report content (e.g., how materiality has been defined), the boundary of the report, the basis for reporting on joint ventures, subsidiaries and other related organisations, data measurement techniques, and the policy and current practice for seeking assurance on the report.

4. *Governance*

The report should describe under this heading the entity's governance arrangements, including the mandate and composition of boards and committees, processes in place to avoid conflicts of interest, internally developed statements of mission, values, codes of conduct, and stakeholder engagement.

The disclosure on management approach should report on the following aspects:

1. **Economic**: Performance, market presence and indirect economic aspects, goals, policies, and any other relevant contextual information.
2. **Environmental**: A concise disclosure should be provided on materials, energy, water, biodiversity, emissions, effluent and waste, products and services, compliance, transport and any other relevant items. Details should also be provided of policies, goals and performance.
3. **Social**: This area of the report should report under the headings of Labour Practices and Decent Work, Human Rights and Society. For each of these the report should discuss goals and performance, policies, organisational responsibility, training and awareness, monitoring and any other relevant contextual information.

Extensive guidance is also offered in respect of the choice of performance indicators.

The GRI website now contains a database of reports prepared by organizations. For example, go to the website and access the Cadbury Schweppes' Corporate and Social Responsibility Report.

This section of the chapter provides only a brief outline of the GRI reporting guidelines. As the GRI has developed, the website has expanded and it now contains a very sizeable and useful resource.

17.8 Summary

This chapter has examined the pressures that currently exist to extend the scope of reporting by business entities, including a review of some of the reasons for the movement towards corporate social reporting.

The Operating and Financial Review is a potentially very useful development that is gradually being extended from its origins in the UK and is now used by several international businesses, including some that report under international standards.

The chapter proceeded to examine the broad context of social accounting and reporting before going on to describe in some detail the features of environmental reporting. The section on accounting for human resources considered *The Corporate Report* and the various statements that it recommended, and then considered some issues in relation to social reporting, intellectual capital reporting and human asset accounting.

Finally, the last section in the chapter examined the guidelines produced by the Global Reporting Initiative, outlining the nature of the recommended disclosures.

Students should note the dynamic nature of all of the topics covered in this chapter. They should try to keep up to date with the latest developments in these areas by consulting the recommended websites and by observing recent developments via the annual reports of businesses, especially those that report internationally.

Examination questions will certainly be set that relate to the areas covered here. These could take various forms, including the following:

- Discussion questions relating to the need for social reporting in its various forms. Some awareness of current developments would often be expected.
- Questions involving analysis of financial and/or non-financial statements. These might include some commentary on, for example, the usefulness of statements prepared using the GRI guidelines.

Bibliography

This chapter contains several references to useful websites. These are collected here:
Global Reporting Initiative: www.globalreporting.org

Novartis: www.novartis.com (for an example of a group reporting under international standards that also provides an Operating and Financial Review)

Royal Dutch/Shell: www.shell.com (for an example of a group providing a comprehensive environmental and social report)

Kingsmill taskforce: go to www.berr.gov.uk then search for 'accounting for people'.

Meritum project: for subsequent developments and research resources go to ww.som.cranfield.ac.uk and search for 'Meritum' or 'intangible assets'.

Readings 17

Index fingers bad behaviour

Liz Fisher, *Accountancy,* May 2003, p 58–60. © Liz Fisher. Reprinted with the kind permission of the author.

'Our motives, of course, may be misconstrued by a cynical world.' It was less than half an hour into one of the largest conferences on corporate responsibility the UK has ever seen, and the words in almost everyone's mind had been spoken. None of the 300 or so delegates seemed particularly surprised. When you are part of a group of large organisations that are committed to telling the world as loudly as possible that you are the good guys, you should expect a degree of cynicism.

Evidence of bad behaviour

It took a couple of years of successive and violent protests at World Trade Organisation summits for large corporations to realise that they were seen as the sharp end of the 'cancer' of capitalism. The reasons for this are many and complicated and encompass both fact and perception. A succession of local and global accidents and incidents – Bhopal, Exxon Valdez, deforestation, the ozone layer, child labour, Twyford Down – built up into an irrefutable pile of evidence against large corporations. The proliferation of fast-food and coffee chains on our high streets, often replacing the local stores that had been put out of business when consumers chose the out-of-town supermarket experience, added to the view of large corporations as the enemy of old-fashioned values. But Hollywood, too, made its own unique contribution in the form of 'David and Goliath' stories such as *Erin Brokovich* and pantomime corporate super-villains such as Jonathan Price in *Tomorrow Never Dies.* The end result is that business executives are now considered some of the most untrustworthy people in the developed world – which must be a great relief to estate agents and second-hand car salesman everywhere.

To suggest that the emergence of corporate social responsibility (CSR) is the direct result of the damage caused to the reputation of large organisations is cynical in itself. But there is more than a grain of truth in the statement. Companies have recognised that the bad publicity caused by environmental and social issues can affect their reputation and even their financial performance. It is no accident that the largest oil producers in the world published some of the most comprehensive and glossy environmental and social reports.

The first index of corporate responsibility

The main aim of the London conference in March was to launch the first Corporate Responsibility Index, produced and published by Business in the Community (BITC), a charity with 700 member companies across the globe. BITC's mantra is that its members 'commit to action and to the continual improvement of their company's impact on society.' In particular, the BITC's members 'integrate responsible business practice throughout their business, impact through collaborative action to tackle disadvantage, and inspire, innovate and lead by sharing learning and experience'.

Socially responsible efforts, though, are difficult to quantify and this has been a handicap of the BITC's since its inception. The Corporate Responsibility Index represents its answer to the – a tangible measure of how companies are tackling corporate responsibility (see box).

It is hoped that the index will also persuade more companies to consider corporate responsibility in the future. The way corporate responsibility in general and the index in particular is sold to companies, though, is rather striking. Environmental and social issues were a feature of the 'caring, sharing' 1990s and it is perhaps a reflection of the tougher economic times that this decade is more about the measurement and communication of companies' environment and social performance.

The emphasis during the conference was firmly on the economic arguments of corporate responsibility. Stephen Timms, minister for corporate social responsibility, summed up the theme in saying that 'companies in the UK are beginning to understand the business benefits of socially responsible behaviour'. Patrick Mallon of BITC echoed this sentiment: 'Senior business leaders realise more than ever that responsible business practice enhances competitiveness – if it is integrated throughout the organisation,' he said. Successive speakers at the conference repeated the theory that the way to get senior management interested in social responsibility was to emphasise the economic and business benefits. Do it because it is good for business, in other words, not because it is good for the world.

Avoiding corporate spin

This is probably a sensible approach in the sense that it is language that corporations understand. But it does little to resolve one of corporate responsibility's major handicaps – the impression that it is nothing more than corporate spin, or 'greenwash', as some environmentalists have labelled it. It is easy to be cynical when McDonald's announces as part of its corporate responsibility programme 'World Children's Day', when the doors of 100 of its restaurants are thrown open in order to raise money for children in need. True, almost $20 million (£12.9 million) was raised for children's charities but with so much of McDonald's marketing aimed at a younger audience, amid so much concern over the dietary habits of children thanks to fast food outlets such as McDonalds, should the company be surprised at cynicism?

Supporters of corporate responsibility argue that any step towards more socially responsible behaviour has to be welcomed, whatever the motives. The index, though, does serve to highlight a number of difficulties with corporate responsibility in general. It concentrates, for instance, on the reporting of social and environmental issues and the extent to which the policies and systems are embedded within an organisation. Some of the companies in the highest quintiles of the index are, by their nature, some of those that can potentially cause great damage to the environment, while a number of media groups and companies from other seemingly benign sectors fall into the lower quintile. The fact that the largest oil companies publish comprehensive environmental and social reports does not alter the fact that drilling for oil, however 'sensitively' it is done, damages the planet and burning oil products damages the atmosphere. The fact that you are honest about something does not make it right. This presents environmental campaigners with a dilemma – social and environmental reporting must be encouraged, as must the indexes that could highlight the companies that are more reluctant to buy on to corporate responsibility issues. But that could leave the impression that talking about it is enough.

The ultimate aim of the index, according to BITC, was to present a figure that analysts and the general public can 'kick the tyres of' – in other words, to provide some sort of tangible evidence that companies were attempting to tackle the issues. There is also the underlying suggestion that the index may prompt more companies to tackle environmental and social reporting in a more enthusiastic manner. There is some evidence that this index and other voluntary initiatives such as the FTSE4Good 'ethical' stock market index are proving more effective than previous attempts at persuasion. Fifty-three of the FTSE 100 took part in the BITC's survey this year, although generally the UK's record on environmental and social reporting is still poor.

Farcical or sour grapes?

That said, it was perhaps predictable that reporting of the BITC's Corporate Responsibility Index should concentrate on the top and bottom quartiles, or the 'good and bad' at socially responsible reporting. There was some consternation among speakers at the BITC's conference that the survey should be reduced to such simple terms, with one speaker saying that the reporting had 'done BITC a disservice'. Companies features in the lower quintiles of the index were also unhappy. Reuters told the *Financial Times* that the index was 'meaningless' because it did not reflect the company's own personal form of responsible efforts. 'To assess us in terms of global warming and solid waste is a waste of time and farcical,' director of corporate communications Simon Walker told the newspaper.

The publicity generated by the first index suggests that it has the potential to become a force for good in that it will ensourage companies and investors to look at environmental and social issues. But realistically, the index represents only the tip of a growing iceberg. The number of ethical funds and investors has increased over recent years but, in general, the City remains largely disinterested in social and environmental issues. A delegate at the BITC's conference pointed out that he was 'yet to see a sales-side report that has focused on corporate social responsibility'.

Analysts counter that if a company has a CSR policy that is making a difference, they need to be told about it. But, ethical investors aside, analysts are looking for financial results and if campaigners wish to concentrate on the economic case for corporate responsibility, there is little solid evidence as yet to support them. A bad environmental record can damage a company's brand and reputation but there is little evidence to suggest that responsible actions result in a healtheir bottom line – neither, the FTSE4Good index nor the Dow Jones Sustainability Index has outperformed their respective markets.

The ultimate problem is that stockmarkets – and business in general – work on the short-term view. Analysts work on short-term information and companies and executives are rewarded for short-term performance. Environmental campaigners necessarily take the long-term view. In 100 years' time, circumstances may force their views to converge – but at what cost?

The Corporate Responsibility Index

The Corporate Responsibility Index is described as 'the first authoritative, voluntary benchmark of responsible business practice' and measures 'how companies integrate responsible practices throughout their organisation in four key impact areas: environment, marketplace, workplace and community'. Unfortunately, it is as complicated as it sounds and it is difficult to glean clear information from the results. Companies are given an overall score achieved for strategy, integration, management practice on community, environment, marketplace and workplace, as well as their performance in their choice of five out of seven 'impact' areas (from product safety to global warming). The companies are also ranked according to how well they are managing their corporate responsibility: 'A' if they are measuring and reporting progress, 'B' if they move beyond a basic commitment and 'C if they are beginning to measure progress. The companies were then presented alphabetically in 'quintiles', according to their score.

Top quintile	*Bottom quintile*
3m	3I Group
AstraZeneca	Amersham
Aviva	British Sky Broadcasting
BAA	Brixton
BP	Capita Group
BT Group	Croda International
Carillion	De la Rue
Dow Chemical Company	Expro International
ISIS	Geest
J Sainsbury	GWR Group
Marks & Spencer	International Power
MmO2	Meggitt
National Grid Transco	Mersey Docks & Harbour Co
Rio Tinto	Reuters Group
Safeway	RMC Group
Scottish Power	Taylor Woodrow
Shell International	Trinity Mirror
Tesco	United Business Media
Unilever	WH Smith Group
Waste Recycling Group	WPP Group

Intellectual assets: the new frontier

Dr Peter Atrill, *ACCA Students' Newsletter,* December 1998. Reprinted with the kind permission of the author.

Many readers will probably not remember the mid-1970s. For fashion conscious young men, it was the time to be wearing tank tops, flared trousers and cuban-heel boots. However, it was also around this period that the economic environment started to change in a fundamental way. The mid-1970s will probably be remembered, not so much for its contribution to fashion, but as a turning point in the world economy. Since this period we have entered a new economic era.

The period from the industrial revolution up to the mid-1970s is now described as the Industrial Age. During this age, the economic environment was relatively stable and many companies obtained competitive advantage over their rivals through the use of technology. They made large investments in physical assets, such as plant and equipment, which provided the capability to mass produce standard products. Accounting techniques such as ratios, budgeting and standard costing were developed during this Industrial Age to manage the production process more efficiently.

However, since the mid-1970s, the world economy has change dramatically. Deregulation, greater competition, rapidly changing technology and the growing sophistication of information systems have resulted in a much less stable environment within which companies must operate.

This new economic era is often described as the Information Age and it demands from companies fresh thinking about how to keep ahead of their rivals. It has been argued that, increasingly, competitive advantage will be gained through exploiting the information technology fully, through developing innovative products and through generating strong customer loyalty.

The demands of the Information Age mean that companies must reconsider their priorities. Knowledge has become the critical factor in achieving success. The successful companies will be those which exploit the knowledge and abilities of its employees most effectively. Knowledge is the 'invisible' asset which will produce the innovative products, high quality service and satisfied customers necessary for success. Companies must, therefore, give priority to developing and managing the knowledge of its employees in order to create value. The growing importance of knowledge means that physical assets, such as plant and equipment, will play a less decisive role in determining success. We can see already that for companies engaged in business services, pharmaceuticals and information technology, physical assets already play a minor role. The Chief Executive of Merck has said:

> A low value product can be made by anyone anywhere. When you have knowledge no one else has access to – that's dynamite. We guard our research even more carefully than our financial assets.[1]

Accounting and economic change

The changes in the economy described above have important implications for accounting. Traditional accounting was developed during the Industrial Age. It records transactions with external parties, such as the purchase and sale of goods and services, and it is these external transactions which generate a price, or value, and which, in turn, provide the basis for financial reporting. Whilst traditional accounting may have served companies well during the Industrial Age, its limitations have become more apparent in the Information Age. We have seen that knowledge is now the key to success and that it is those companies which invest effectively in managing and developing the knowledge of its employees, and in developing relationships with customers, which will succeed. However, the investment in, and condition of, these 'intellectual assets' is not revealed by traditional accounting methods. It cannot tell us whether the knowledge base of the company or the strength of customer loyalty is increasing or decreasing. Thus, it is difficult to assess the current health of the company or its capacity to survive and prosper in the future.

This kind of argument, however, is not really new. Those of us who are old enough to have worn the flared trousers and tank tops referred to earlier may remember that a topic called 'human asset accounting' emerged during the early 1970s and then sank without trace a few years later.

Human asset accounting aimed to raise awareness of the value of a company's human resources by attempting to place a value on its employees and by including this value in the statement of financial position of the company. Although human asset accounting aroused some interest, the time for such an idea was not right. In the early 1970s, most companies were still enjoying a comfortable existence and the 'winds of change' had not yet ushered in the new order. At this time, the rhetoric of company chairmen concerning the vital importance of harnessing the knowledge and capabilities of employees to obtain competitive advantage had yet to become reality. This meant there was little incentive to adopt new and radical forms of financial reporting. Furthermore, the rather conservative accounting profession displayed little interest in such fanciful notions and, anyway, had more pressing problems to resolve.

Since the early 1970s, however, we have seen a growing recognition, from both inside and outside the profession, of the need to expand the boundaries of accounting. Accounting is under increasing threat from various quarters and will only survive if it embraces new concepts and measurement models. If accounting is to be relevant to companies in the Information Age it must recognise the growing importance of the 'intellectual assets' which reflect the knowledge held within a company and find ways of describing their characteristics which decision makers will find useful.

Types of intellectual assets

Intellectual assets (or 'intellectual capital' as they are sometimes called) can be categorised in various ways. One approach is to divide intellectual assets into three main types as follows:

1. *External assets* (*capital*). These include the reputation of brands and franchises and the strength of customer relationships.
2. *Internal assets* (*capital*). These include patents, trademarks and information held in customer databases.
3. *Competencies.* These reflect the capabilities and skills of individuals.[2]

We can see that the term 'intellectual assets' is much broader in its scope than human asset accounting which preceded it. Although it embraces human assets (under competencies), it recognises that the knowledge and skills of individuals is not the only source of competitive advantage. According to Hope and Hope,[2] human assets are the mainspring of new ideas and innovation but it will be the other forms of intellectual assets which provide the systems and channels to ensure that value is created. In Figure 1, further examples of each type of intellectual asset are provided.

External asset	**Internal assets**	**Competencies**
Brands	*Intellectual property*	*People competencies*
Product brands	Patents	Professional experience
Service brands	Copyright	Levels of education and skills
Corporate brands	Trademarks and design rights	Training methods
	Trade secrets and know-how	Management education
Customers	*Infrastructure*	*Learning capability*
Individual customers	Processes	Knowledge sharing
Sales channels	IT systems and databases	Communities of practice
Distribution channels	Communication systems	Problem-solving capabilities
	Operating models	
	Financial structure	
Contracts	*Culture*	*Management capability*
Franchise agreements	Management philosophy	Entrepreneurship
License agreements	Recognition and rewards	Leadership
Other favourable contracts	Management structure	Growth record

Figure 1 Some elements of 'intellectual assets'

We can see that some of the intellectual assets (e.g., intellectual property and contracts) can fall within the conventional boundaries of accounting as an external transaction will have arisen. However, these items may represent only the 'tip of the iceberg'. The 'invisible' intellectual assets can often account for a much larger proportion of the value of a business.

Measuring intellectual assets

Value based approach. The challenge facing accountants is how to measure intellectual assets. One approach is to employ existing value based measures. It has been suggested that intellectual assets, when taken as a whole, is reflected in the difference between the market value of a company and the statement of financial position value of its net assets. In many cases, the market value of a company is considerably higher than the statement of financial position figures. In the case of BP plc, for example, the market value is almost four times higher than the book values. However, there are problems with using this approach. The difference between the market value of the business and the book values of assets cannot be wholly ascribed to intellectual assets. Accounting assets, such as freehold land, may be shown at a figure in the statement of financial position which is well below their current market values. Another problem is that share prices may fluctuate from day-to-day and so may prove unreliable when assessing changes in intellectual assets over the short term.

It has been suggested that this market based approach could be more useful if, instead of taking the absolute measure of the difference between market values and statement of financial position values, we take the ratio between the two. In this way, comparisons between similar companies and across time periods would be more meaningful. Although this suggestion may be helpful, the information derived will still only provide an overall measure of intellectual assets. The separate elements of intellectual assets are not measured. What managers will often need for decision making purposes is a breakdown of the condition of, and changes in, particular types of intellectual assets held. This separability problem places real limitations on value based measures. They are likely to be of most benefit to managers when taken together with a range of other monetary and non-monetary measures.

Skandia approach

Skandia AFS is a large Swedish financial services group which recognised the significance of the gap between the market value of the business and its book value. This led Skandia to develop ways of reporting the 'hidden' intellectual assets of the business. In a supplement to the company's 1994 annual report, the first attempt was made to describe the invisible assets of the business. It was argued:

> A clearer and more balanced reporting of Skandia not only makes it easier for the world around us to value our operations, it also gives us more effective instruments to better manage and develop our hidden values. And the more tangible we can make our hidden values, the better for all of us.[3]

Skandia has developed a model which it refers to as the Skandia Navigator. The model reflects the four key dimensions of the business and identifies the critical success factors relating to each dimension. These critical success factors are quantified in order to measure changes overtime. The Skandia Navigator is shown in Figure 2.

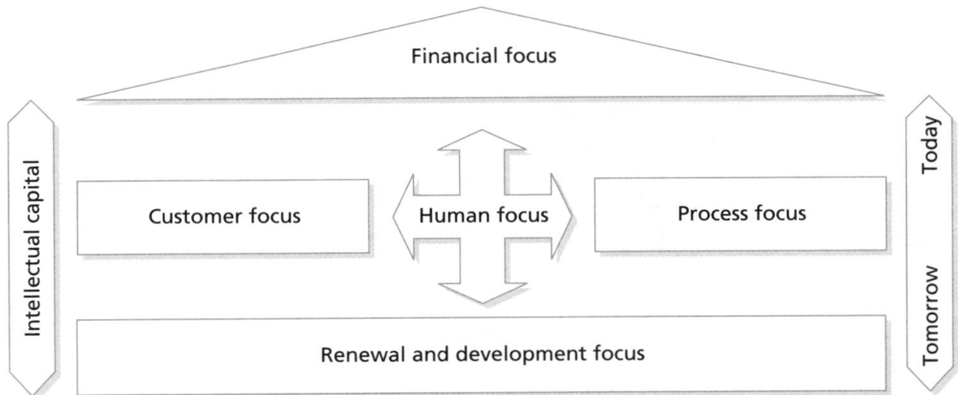

Figure 2 The Skandia Navigator.[3] Skandia life assurance company limited, company report and accounts, 1994

To provide an example of the kind of measures used by the group let us consider the renewal and development focus of one of its subsidiaries, SkandiaBanken Fonder, which operates a fund management business. The key measures reflecting the critical success factors were:

- competence development expense per employee;
- employee satisfaction index (scale 1–5);
- marketing expenses/managed assets;
- marketing expense per customer.

The critical success factors will differ between businesses and must be derived through an analysis of business processes and operations.

The Skandia Navigator is an interesting approach which is closely related to the balanced scorecard approach developed by Robert Kaplan and David Norton.[4]

Intellectual capital (IC) index approach

The IC index approach attempts to provide a measure of the efficiency of intellectual assets which can be related to traditional accounting measures of efficiency. The approach recognises that a company must be efficient in transforming financial resources into intellectual assets and then, in turn, transforming its intellectual assets into financial value for shareholders.

The IC-index approach attempts to consolidate different measures for intellectual assets. To achieve this, the key measures of success must first be identified and then weighted according to their importance in order to provide a single, summary index. The choice of measures and choice of weights will again be specific to the company. In the example below, four key dimensions of the intellectual assets of a business, relationship, innovation, human and infrastructure, have been combined to obtain an IC-index score (see Figure 3).

An IC-index can be developed for each business segment as well as for the company as a whole. It is designed to be a lead indicator of changes in financial performance. Thus, a fall in the index should provide an early-warning signal of a deterioration in the financial health of the business.

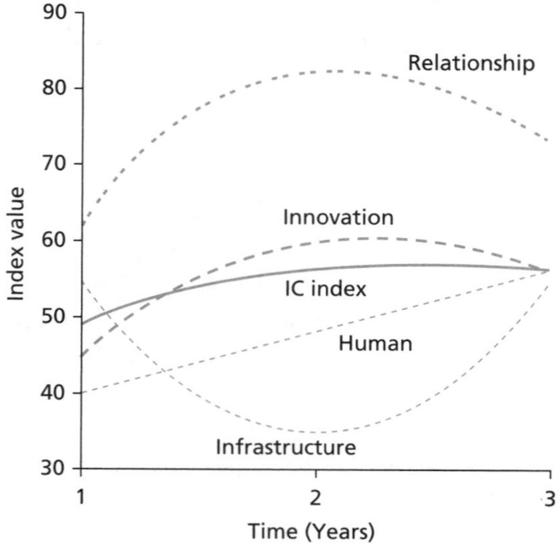

Figure 3 An example of an IC-index[5]

Summary

We have seen that, in the Information Age, knowledge has become the key to achieving competitive advantage. Successful companies will be those who can develop and manage their knowledge base effectively. In order to do this, suitable measures must be developed to provide managers with the guidance they need. This issue will take on increasing importance in future years. The value of intellectual assets will continue to rise and will represent an increasing proportion of the value of most companies. The challenge facing accountants is to contribute towards the development of intellectual asset measures. Unless we face this challenge, accountancy will become less relevant to business. Indeed, it could become as irrelevant as the tank tops and flared trousers of the mid-1970s have now become.

References

1. Stewart, T. A. (1997) *Intellectual Capital: The New Wealth of Organizations*. Nicholas Brealey Publishing.
2. Hope, J. and Hope, T. (1997) *Competing in the Third Wave*. Harvard Business School Press.
3. Skandia, 'Visualizing Intellectual Capital in Skandia', Supplement to Skandia's 1994 Annual Report.
4. Kaplan, R. and Norton, D. (1996) *The Balanced Scorecard*. Harvard Business School Press.
5. Roos, J., Roos, G., Dragonetti, N., and Edvinsson, L. (1997) *Intellectual Capital: Navigating in the New Business Landscape*. Macmillan Press.

Mental Arithmetic

Tony Wall, *Financial Management*, December/January 2002/03

Financial accounting professionals have spent the past decade debating how companies should report their intellectual capital (IC). Some people argue that many more of these intangible assets – beyond those associated with intellectual property such as patents – should appear on the statement of financial position, because without them shareholders aren't aware of all the elements that contribute to the overall market value of their company.

The main argument against their inclusion is that no universally acceptable method of measuring them has yet been determined. Until such an agreement is reached, these assets – generally categorised as human capital, customer capital or organisational capital (*seepanel 1, below*) – could appear at randomly selected valuations, thereby distorting the picture for investors.

1 THE KEY COMPONENTS OF INTELLECTUAL CAPITAL

Human capital	**Customer capital**	**Organisational capital**
Knowledge	Customer relationships	Patents
Skills	Customer retention	Research and development
Expertise	Customer satisfaction	Copyrights
Motivation	Favourable contracts	Trademarks
Innovation	Reputation	Licences
Entrepreneurial spirit	Brand image	Processes
Leadership qualities	Sales channels	Best practices
Employee satisfaction	Distribution channels	Databases
Employee turnover	Supplier relationships	IT systems
Vocational qualifications	Business collaborations	Networking systems
Education	Franchising agreements	Management philosophy
Training	Market intelligence	Corporate culture

Other people see the debate as far too narrow and feel that a lot of work can be done on the strategic management of IC to increase the value of any company.

IC therefore cannot be ignored and, while financial accountants may have to wait for regulatory guidance before these assets can appear on the statement of financial position, it doesn't mean that the annual report can't be used as a medium for communicating how an organisation's IC is adding value. In Scandinavia – particularly Sweden – shareholders already receive a great deal of information about IC, although the reporting of such assets is more piecemeal in the rest of the developed world.

In order to gather the relevant information, financial accountants will have to rely on management accountants to capture, measure and value these assets, and to monitor any changes on a yearly basis. This, of course, will require a robust accounting system.

Although several generic frameworks for this exist, the suggested measurements will have to be adjusted to fit an organisation's particular circumstances. Proxy measurements are seen as better than no measurements at all, and there are many that can be made – for example, tracking your company's investment in training and seeing whether employee turnover decreases or productivity increases as a result of that training.

In order to see how companies in Ireland (both Northern Ireland and the Republic) have been dealing with IC, the University of Ulster conducted a survey last year. Its main aim was to see what stage they had reached when it came to measuring IC. A mixture of traditional manufacturing firms and new-economy companies – that is, those in telecoms, software, etc. – were used for the survey.

Part of the questionnaire asked the companies to rank certain elements of IC in order of importance (*see panel 2, below*). It's notable that the three most highly ranked elements represented each of the three categories of IC. These were software (organisational capital), customer satisfaction (customer capital) and workforce expertise (human capital).

2	*THE HIGHEST-RANKED ELEMENTS*
1	Software
2	Customer satisfaction
3	Workforce expertise
4	Brands
5	Market intelligence
6	R&D know-how
7	Mailing/phone lists
8	Distribution networks
9	Design rights
10	Licences
11	The Internet
12	Consultancy/advice
13	Manufacturing processes
14	Patents
15	Royalties

The questionnaire also attempted to determine which elements of the three categories of IC were already being measured. The most measured elements of human capital were concerned with employee loyalty – that is, length of service and staff turnover, which were both measured by more than two-thirds of the respondents. Perhaps surprisingly, the next most popular measure concerned the number of employees with professional qualifications. Although this might seem less crucial than other elements, the large proportion of respondents measuring it is probably explained by the simple fact that the information is easy to find.

Two elements that were measured by a surprisingly small number of companies were value added per employee and new ideas generated. The first finding can possibly be explained by the problems of developing an accurate method beyond simple ratio measurements such as turnover divided by the number of employees. On the other hand, there is nothing new about staff suggestion schemes. You would assume that, if a company were to have such a scheme, it would assess how well it was working.

As with some of the human capital measures, companies were not examining certain important aspects of customer capital. For example, it's hard to believe that some businesses still aren't taking note of the number of customers they have. It is also surprising that, although many respondents said customer satisfaction was important, not all of them were actually measuring it. At the same time, almost 90 per cent of the respondents were keeping track of the number of customer complaints they were receiving.

Relatively few were measuring the effectiveness of advertising campaigns, which is precisely the sort of thing that should be measured, or there is a danger that crucial marketing initiatives will be dropped during times of financial hardship.

Out of the three IC categories, organisational capital was the one that companies measured the least. Only two elements were measured by more than half of the respondents and these were both expense items: expenditure on research and development and IT spending as a percentage of administrative costs. It could be argued that these are the simplest elements to measure, because both figures would be gathered as part of the process of drafting the financial statement.

Although some companies measured the value of new ideas generated by members of staff, not all of them kept track of how many of these were actually implemented. You would expect this to be done – if for no other reason than to provide feedback to employees.

Another point of interest was the number of companies that were failing to follow up on their employee and customer satisfaction surveys. Two-thirds of the respondents were measuring employee and customer satisfaction, but fewer-than a third were monitoring any changes resulting from the feedback.

One of the most important aims of the research was to ascertain which formal systems the companies were using to evaluate their IC, having measured the various elements. Just over a third of the respondents were using no system at all. The most popular method was the balanced scorecard, which was being used by 28 percent of our sample.

Although the remaining companies listed a variety of methods by which they measured their IC – for example, key performance indicator systems, employee opinion surveys and value-chain analysis – follow-up interviews revealed that these were generally measurement systems that focused on one particular matter, such as recruitment or procurement, and were not covering all aspects of IC. Apart from those using the balanced scorecard, only one organisation seemed to be using a comprehensive measurement system, which it called a business benefit scorecard.

There is no doubt that Irish companies are highly aware of IC – most of them are already measuring certain elements of human, customer and organisational capital. But it appears that this may be occurring as part of their normal working practices and not co-ordinated within a single IC programme. The main problem seems to be that much of the work on IC is being done in isolation and is not part of on overall strategy.

Our analysis of the companies' responses indicates that there is a lack of a defined link between a working practice, the capture of information on this practice and any evaluation of it alongside data gathered from other parts of the organisation. Furthermore, although nearly all of the companies we surveyed were familiar with the term IC, only a tiny proportion of them had people dedicated to working with it. Ireland is therefore typical of most developed nations when it comes to IC. Apart from in Scandinavia and North America, little pioneering work is being done in this area and a 'wait and see' strategy seems to be in place.

Accounting for people

Lesley Bolton, *Accountancy,* May 2003

Back in the 1980s, during the IT revolution, a constant chorus went up for businesses to recognise the strategic importance of computing at board level. Today a new government taskforce is looking at way to elevate 'human capital management' to the top of the transparency agenda and is examining how organisations can measure the quality and effectiveness of the way they manage people and how this can be reflected in the annual report.

The taskforce, which is due to present its final report in the autumn, is being led by deputy Competition Commission chairman Denise Kingsmill. Its formation follows one of the recommendations in the 2001 *Kingsmill Review into Women's Pay and Development,* although its remit covers far more than gender issues.

'You don't measure the people element in the same way that you're accustomed to measuring how many widgets you've got or how many contracts you've signed. In our enquiry we're not looking to develop metrics in a formal way to put people in the statement of financial position, because that would be the wrong approach,' says Kingsmill, harking back to the 1970s, when theorists dabbled with 'human asset accounting'.

Indeed, the method of measurement is crucial if human capital is to be usefully included on the annual report. As PricewaterhouseCoopers UK board partner and taskforce member Ed Smith puts it: 'Unless you convince people of the measurement and recognition criteria, then you will have difficulty pushing it into an external environment. I start with the business case inside an organisation. How far are companies themselves really focusing on the management of people – recruitment, retention and development – and how do they measure that at board level?'

Best practice

The taskforce's main objective is to create best practice guidance for organisations on how they can meaningfully account for 'human capital assets' – as opposed to regarding them as 'costs'. Its first job is to review existing studies and seek expert evidence from key sectors, including the corporate sector, the investment management community and academic research. 'We want all sides of the story,' say Smith. 'We're interested in hearing from cynics as well as the enthusiasts.'

Both Kingsmill and Smith emphasise that the focus is on performance indicators, which will include 'fairness of employment' and 'employee satisfaction.'

'It's very important to keep this as a performance issue, as something which says 'this is an indicator of good performance' as opposed to it being a nice add-on. We wouldn't want to slag off any environmental reporting for instance, but we see this not as an optional extra but as absolutely key to the performance of an organisation, particularly in times of full employment where there is a great deal of competition for the best people, and where retaining people is important. In the past, people management has been confined to car policies and redundancy packages and the like rather than being part of the organisation's strategic objectives,' says Kingsmill.

'What gets me about glossy company reports is that you flick through the pages of smiling, happy people, then you look at the text and there's nothing about them. You get pages and pages about the remuneration of a company's top team, but it tells you nothing about the company's performance. If you were a potential investor that report would give you no clue as to whether that was a company worth investing in. If there was information about how the company recruited, developed and grew their human capital, then that might be an indicator of future performance,' she adds.

The taskforce may well find the climate right for encouraging companies to take employment practices seriously. The ICAEW has already issued a policy briefing, *Valuing Human Capital*, under which it says that 'cultivating and measuring this 'great intangible' is one of the next big challenges for UK business if the UK is to remain at the forefront of the new economy.' The subject is now the mandate of the institute's dedicated thinktank, the Centre for Business Performance. 'We believe there needs to be a dedicated government drive to help businesses and investors understand how human capital builds long-term corporate value and improves UK competitiveness.'

Not only that, but a new management book, *Going Off the Rails*, by John Plender, and reviewed in *Accountancy* (April, p.21) has as its central argument that we are in the midst of 'the transition to an economy in which human and social capital are of far greater importance than physical capital'.

Directors take note.

Revision Questions

17

Question 1

You are the assistant to the finance director of MNO, a medium-sized listed entity that complies with IFRS. One of MNO's directors has proposed the publication of an Operating and Financial Review (OFR) as part of the annual financial statements. Most of the directors know very little about the OFR, and the finance director has asked you to produce a short briefing paper on the topic for their benefit.

Requirements

Write the briefing paper, which should discuss the following issues:

- any relevant regulatory requirements for an OFR;
- the purpose and, in outline, the typical content of an OFR;
- the advantages and drawbacks of publishing an OFR from the entity's point of view.

(10 marks)

Question 2

In many industries there is a large gap between the market capitalisation of listed entities and the statement of financial position value of their net assets. Some commentators have suggested that the gap comprises unrecognised intangible assets in the form of intellectual capital obtained through the employment of human resources, and that these assets should be capitalised.

Requirement

Identify the principal arguments for and against the proposal to capitalise intellectual capital.

(10 marks)

Question 3

It is becoming increasingly common for listed entities to provide non-financial disclosures intended to inform stakeholders about the business's environmental policies, impacts and practices. Supporters of such voluntary disclosures argue that stakeholders have a right to be informed above environmental issues in this way. However, there are also arguments against this type of disclosure.

Requirement

Identify and explain the principal arguments against *against* voluntary disclosures by business of their environmental policies, impacts and practices. **(10 marks)**

Question 4

The first part of this question relates to the analysis of financial statements. Students may find it useful to review Chapters 16–19 of the Learning System before attempting the question.

FW is a listed entity involved in the business of oil exploration, drilling and refining in three neighbouring countries, Aye, Bee and Cee. The business has been consistently profitable, creating high returns for its international shareholders. In recent years, however, there has been an increase in environmental lobbying in FW's three countries of operation. Two years ago, an environmental group based in Cee started lobbying the government to take action against FW for alleged destruction of valuable wildlife habitats in Cee's protected wetlands and the displacement of the local population. At the time, the directors of FW took legal advice on the basis of which they assessed the risk of liability at less than 50%. A contingent liability of $500 million was noted in the financial statements to cover possible legal costs, compensation to displaced persons and reinstatement of the habitats, as well as fines.

FW is currently preparing its financial statements for the year ended 28 February 20X5. Recent advice from the entity's legal advisers has assessed that the risk of a successful action against FW has increased, and must now be regarded as more likely than not to occur. The board of directors has met to discuss the issue. They accept that a provision of $500 million is required, but would like to be informed of the effects of the adjustment on certain key ratios that the entity headlines in its annual report. All of the directors are concerned about the potentially adverse effect on the share price, as FW is actively engaged in a takeover bid that would involve a substantial share exchange. Also, they feel that the public's image of the entity is likely to be damaged. The chief executive makes the following suggestion:

> 'Many oil businesses nowadays publish an environmental and social report, and I think it may be time for us to do so. It would give us the opportunity to set the record straight about what we do to reduce pollution, and could help to deflect some of the public attention from us over this law suit. In any case it would be a good public relations opportunity; we can use it to tell people about our equal opportunities programme. I was reading about something called the Global Reporting Initiative (GRI) the other day. I don't know much about it, but it might give us some help in structuring a report that will get the right message across. We could probably pull something together to go out with this year's annual report'.

The draft financial statements for the year ended 28 February 20X5 include the following information relevant for the calculation of key ratios. All figures are before taking into account the $500 million provision. The provision will be charged to operating expenses.

	$m
Net assets (before long-term loans) at 1 March 20X4	9,016
Net assets (before long-term loans) at 28 February 20X5	10,066
Long-term loans at 28 February 20X5	4,410
Share capital + reserves at 1 March 20X4	4,954
Share capital + reserves at 28 February 20X5	5,656
Revenue	20,392
Operating profit	2,080

Profit before tax	1,670
Profit for the period	1,002

The number of ordinary shares in issue throughout the years ended 29 February 20X4 and 28 February 20X5 were 6,000 million shares of 25 cents each.

FW's key financial ratios for the 20X4 financial year (calculated using the financial statements for the year ended 29 February 20X4) were:

- Return on capital employed (using average capital employed): 24.7%
- Return on assets (operating profit as a percentage of average net assets): 17.7%
- Gearing (debt as a percentage of equity): 82%
- Operating profit margin: 10.1%
- Earnings per share: 12.2 cents per share

Requirements

In your position as assistant to FW's Chief Financial Officer produce a briefing paper that:

(a) Analyses and interprets the effects of making the environmental provision on FW's key financial ratios. You should take into account the possible effects on the public perception of FW. **(12 marks)**

(b) Identifies the advantages and disadvantages to FW of adopting the chief executive's proposal to publish an environmental and social report. **(7 marks)**

(c) Describes the three principal sustainability dimensions covered by the GRI's framework of performance indicators. **(6 marks)**

(Total marks = 25)

? Question 5

> ! This question relates in part to the analysis of financial statements. Students may find it useful to review Chapters 14–16 of this *Learning System* before attempting this revision question.

Recycle is a listed company which recycles toxic chemical waste products. The waste products are sent to Recycle from all around the world. You are an accountant (not employed by Recycle) who is accustomed to providing advice concerning the performance of companies, based on the data available from their published financial statements. Extracts from the financial statements of Recycle for the 2 years ended 30 September 20X7 are given below.

Recycle: income statements for the year ended 30 September

	20X7	*20X6*
	$m	$m
Revenue	3,000	2,800
Cost of sales	(1,600)	(1,300)
Gross profit	1,400	1,500
Other operating expenses	(800)	(600)
Finance costs	(200)	(100)
Profit before income tax	400	800
Income tax	(150)	(250)
Profit for the period	250	550

Recycle: statement of financial position as at 30 September

	20X7		20X6	
	$m	$m	$m	$m
Assets				
Tangible non-current assets		4,100		3,800
Current assets				
Inventories	500		350	
Trade receivables	1,000		800	
Cash in hand	50		50	
		1,550		1,200
Total assets		5,650		5,000
Equity and Liabilities				
Capital and reserves				
Called-up share capital ($1 shares)		2,000		2,000
Retained earnings		950		900
		2950		2900
Non-current liabilities				
Interest-bearing borrowings		1,000		1,000
Current liabilities				
Trade payables	600		600	
Taxation payable	150		250	
Proposed dividend	200		200	
Bank overdraft	750		50	
		1,700		1,100
Total equity and liabilities		5,560		5,000

Proposed dividend is $200 million (20X6: $200 million).

You ascertain that depreciation of tangible non-current assets for the year ended 30 September 20X7 was $1,200 million. Disposals of non-current assets during the year ended 30 September 20X7 were negligible.

You are approached by two individuals:

1. A is a private investor who is considering purchasing shares in Recycle. A considers that Recycle has performed well in 20X7 compared with 20X6 because revenue has risen and the dividend to shareholders has been maintained.
2. B is resident in the area immediately surrounding the premises of Recycle and is interested in the contribution made by Recycle to the general well-being of the community. B is also concerned about the potential environmental effect of the recycling of chemi cal waste. B is uncertain how the published financial statements of Recycle might be of assistance in addressing social and environmental matters.

Requirements

(a) Write a report to A which analyses the financial performance of Recycle over the 2 years ended 30 September 20X7.

Assume that inflation is negligible.

Your report should refer specifically to the observations made by A concerning the performance of Recycle. **(20 marks)**

(b) Briefly discuss whether published financial statements satisfy the information needs of B.

You should consider published financial statements *in general,* not just the extracts which are provided in this question. **(5 marks)**

(Total marks = 25)

Question 6

You are the management accountant of Clean, an entity listed in a country that permits entities to publish financial statements in accordance with IFRS. Clean is considering seeking a listing on a US stock exchange in the near future. Your Chief Executive Officer takes a keen interest in financial reporting but he is not a professionally qualified accountant. He has recently sent you a memorandum that raises the following issue:

My political contacts tell me that government ministers are very interested in extending the practice of environmental reporting. What exactly does 'environmental reporting' mean, and to what extent is it mandatory? Why does there seem to be a trend towards greater environmental reporting? You don't need to go into massive detail, just give me an outline of what is involved.

Requirements

Draft a reply that deals with this issue. You should refer to the provisions of IFRS, and any other relevant documents where you consider them to be of assistance in supporting your reply. **(10 marks)**

Question 7

You are the Management Accountant of Clean, an entity listed in a country that permits entities to publish financial statements in accordance with IFRS. Your Chief Executive Officer takes a keen interest in financial reporting but he is nto a professionally qualified accountant. He has recently sent you a memorandum that includes the following query.

One of the phrases I often hear is 'our employees are our most important asset'. I largely agree with this sentiment, but if it is true, then surely this should be reflected in some way on the statement of financial position. I do not recall seeing such an asset in previous statement of financial position and would be most grateful for your advice.

Requirement

Draft a reply to the Chief Executive Officer's query. You should refer to the provisions of IFRS and any other relevant documents. **(10 marks)**

Solutions to Revision Questions

17

Solution 1

Briefing paper to the directors of MNO

The Operating and Financial Review

Many international entities are choosing to expand the scope of their reporting in the form of an Operating and Financial Review (OFR). There is currency no formal regulatory requirement to publish such a review. Any such publication would constitute a set of voluntary disclosures.

The principal source of guidance on the purpose and content of an OFR is the UK Accounting Standards Board (ASB) *Reporting Statement of Best Practice* which was issued in January 2006. However, this statement has no international application, except as a source of general guidance. In October 2005, the IASB issued a discussion paper on 'Management Commentary'. The topic is on the IASB's research agenda, and an Exposure Draft is expected during 2008.

The purpose of an OFR is to assist users, principally investors, in making a forward-looking assessment of the performance of the business by setting out management's analysis and discussion of the principal factors underlying the entity's performance and financial position.

Typically, an OFR would comprise some or all of the following:

- description of the business and its objectives;
- management's strategy for achieving the objectives;
- review of operations;
- commentary on the strengths and resources of the business;
- commentary about such issues as human capital, research and development activities, development of new products and services;
- financial review with discussion of treasury management, cash inflows and outflows and current liquidity levels.

The publication of such a statement would have the following advantages for MNO:

- It could be helpful in promoting the entity as progressive and as eager to communicate as fully as possible with investors.
- It could be a genuinely helpful medium of communicating the entity's plans and management's outlook on the future.

- If the IASB were to introduce a compulsory requirement for management commentary by listed entities, MNO would already have established the necessary reporting systems and practices.

However, there could be some drawbacks:

- If an OFR is to be genuinely helpful to investors, it will require a considerable input of senior management time. This could be costly, and it may be that the benefits of publishing an OFR would not outweigh the costs.
- There is a risk in publishing this type of statement that investors will read it in preference to the financial statements, and that they may therefore fail to read important information.

Solution 2

The principal arguments for the proposal are as follows:

1. Those organisations that depend upon human resources, know-how and intellectual capabilities to generate revenue, often have a relatively low level of traditional capital investment. The statement of financial position of such businesses does not reflect the true value of the capital used in revenue generation: indeed, as noted in the question, the gap between market capitalisation and the book value of net assets may be very substantial. The mismatch between statement of financial position and revenue generation could be addressed by recognising a wider range of intangible assets, including intellectual capital.
2. At present, financial statements fail to provide sufficient information to permit interested parties to assess the full range of resources available to the organisation. Their information content suffers because of low levels of intangible asset recognition.
3. It is also argued that the recognition of intellectual capital would encourage better management of human resources because it would make visible resources that have tended to be hidden and under-valued.

The principal arguments against the proposal are as follows:

1. The recognition of intellectual capital would present problems in that it does not fulfil all aspects of the definition of an asset. The Framework defines an asset as: '… a resource controlled by an entity as a result of past events and from which future economic benefits are expected to flow'. The problem lies in the area of control: human resources cannot be fully controlled, because staff are free to leave their employment whenever they wish.
2. The measurement of intellectual capital would present many practical difficulties. It is unlikely that the fair value of a group of employees could ever be measured m reliably.
3. Recognition and measurement of such intangible factors as know-how and skills would allow for considerable latitude in practice, and it would be possible for the unscrupulous to exploit the element of judgement involved in making valuations in order to manipulate their financial statements.

Solution 3

Arguments against voluntary disclosures by businesses in respect of their environmental policies, impacts and practices might include the following principal points:

The traditional view of the corporation is that it exists solely to increase shareholder wealth. In this view business executives have no responsibility to broaden the scope or nature of their reporting as doing so reduces returns to shareholders (because there is a cost associated with additional reporting).

From a public policy perspective, if governments wish corporations and similar entities to bear the responsibility for their environmental impacts, they should legislate accordingly. In the absence of such legislation, however, businesses bear no responsibility for environmental impacts, and in consequence there is no reporting responsibility either.

Voluntary disclosures of any type are of limited usefulness because they are not readily comparable with those of other entities. Therefore, it is likely that the costs of producing such disclosures outweigh the benefits to stakeholders.

The audit of voluntary disclosures is not regulated. Even where such disclosures are audited, the scope of the audit may be relatively limited, and moreover, its scope may not be clearly laid out in the voluntary report. Voluntary reports are not necessarily, therefore, reliable from a stakeholder's point of view.

Especially where voluntary disclosures are included as part of the annual report package, there is a risk of information overload: stakeholders are less able to identify in a very lengthy report the information that is relevant and useful to them.

Voluntary disclosures by business organisations, because they are at best lightly regulated, may be treated by the organisation in a cynical fashion as public relations opportunities. The view of the business's activities could very well be biased, but it would be quite difficult for most stakeholders to detect such bias.

It is questionable whether voluntary disclosures about environmental policies, impacts and practices would meet the qualitative characteristics of useful information set out in the IASB's Framework. The key characteristics are: understandability, reliability, relevance and comparability. Voluntary environmental disclosures might well fail to meet any of these characteristics and, if this is the case, it is highly questionable whether or not they merit publication.

Solution 4

Briefing paper for the attention of the directors of FW
From: Assistant to CFO

(a) The appendix to this paper demonstrates the effect on our key financial ratios of making the provision of $500 million for environmental costs. The effect is substantial and is likely to make a difference to the public and market perception of the business.

The ratios before taking into account any adjustment for the provision all show significant improvements in performance during 20X5, demonstrating the strength of the business fundamentals. There is, however, a dramatic change once the provision is accounted for: compared to performance in 20X4, the post-adjustment return on equity figure has fallen by just under 2 per cent. Gearing, post-adjustment, is higher than in 20X4. Although these are both adverse effects, the 20X5 and 20X4 numbers do not differ greatly from each other. Similarly, return on assets is lower, post-adjustment, but not by very much. Unfortunately, the effect on operating profit margin is much more noticeable. After adjusting for the provision, the ratio falls to 7.7 per cent, substantially lower than the 20X4 figure. Earnings per share is also very badly affected; the ratio, post-adjustment, drops to 8.3 cents.

The effect on public perception of our business is likely to be mostly adverse, especially once the key figure of earnings per share is absorbed by the market. However, the inclusion of the provision may prove advantageous in some respects in that we will be seen to be acting promptly and responsibly in making a provision for liabilities that have now become probable. The income statement still shows a respectable profit after all the bad news has been fully reflected and analysts may prefer to see the worst case position.

Appendix

Key financial ratios table

Ratio	*20X5 ratio before provision*	*20X5 ratio after provision*	*20X4 ratio*
Return on equity	31.5%	23.1%	24.7%
Return on assets	21.8%	17.0%	17.7%
Gearing	78.0%	85.5%	82.0%
Operating profit margin	10.2%	7.7%	10.1%
Earnings per share	16.7¢	8.3¢	12.2¢

Workings

1. *Basis of ratio calculation*

Return on equity: $\dfrac{\text{Profit before tax}}{\text{Average share capital}}$ + reserves

Return on assets $\dfrac{\text{Operating profit}}{\text{Average net assets}}$

Gearing $\dfrac{\text{Debt}}{\text{Equity}}$

Operating profit margin $\dfrac{\text{Operating profit}}{\text{Revenue}}$

Earnings per share $\dfrac{\text{Profit for the year}}{\text{Number of shares in issue}}$

2. *Adjusting for the provision (all figures in \$ millions)*

Profit before tax: \$1,670 − 500 = 1,170
Closing share capital + reserves: \$5,656 − 500 = 5,156
Closing net assets: \$10,066 − 500 = 9,566
Operating profit: \$2,080 − 500 = 1,580
Profit for the period: \$1,002 − 500 = 502

3. *Ratio calculations*

		Ratio before provision		*Ratio after provision*
Return on equity	$\frac{1,670}{(4,954+5,656)/2} \times 100$	31.5%	$\frac{1,170}{(4,954+5,156)/2} + 100$	23.1%
Return on assets	$\frac{2,080}{(9,016+10,066)/2} \times 100$	21.8%	$\frac{1,580}{(9,016+9,566)/2} \times 100$	17.0%
Gearing	$\frac{4,410}{5,656} \times 100$	78.0%	$\frac{4,410}{5,156} \times 100$	85.5%
Operating profit margin	$\frac{2,080}{20,392} \times 100$	10.2%	$\frac{1,580}{20,392} \times 100$	7.7%
Earnings per share	$\frac{1,002}{6,000} \times 100$	16.7¢	$\frac{502}{6,000} \times 100$	8.3¢

(b) Entities have moved towards meeting stakeholder demands for additional reporting, especially in respect of social and environmental issues. By producing such a report FW would indicate its willingness to respond to the pressure for a wider scope in reporting, and to be a good 'corporate citizen'. If we genuinely feel that there are corporate achievements in respect of social and environmental activity that are currently insufficiently publicised, a regular annual report on these aspects could be helpful and would perhaps enhance FW's reputation.

However, the publication of a social and environmental report is not a risk-free endeavour. If the report is too obviously a public relations document, it may arouse suspicion that we are indeed trying to 'deflect attention' from other matters.

The production of a high-quality report is not a trivial matter and it seems unlikely that it could be 'pulled together' very quickly. We are likely to incur substantial costs in producing a good report. Because there are no regulatory constraints on the content of such reports, businesses are able to be selective in their reporting (although it should be noted that the GRI does provide rigorous guidelines). However, having reported a piece of information on one occasion, we will set up an expectation that it will report a valid comparative in the future. This may be inconvenient where the indicator worsens.

Finally, the publication of a report may not produce the anticipated positive reputational effects. It may suffer in comparison with similar reports from our competitors.

(c) The three principal sustainability dimensions are:

1. *Economic*: To include performance ratios related to the direct economic impacts of the entity on, for example, customers and suppliers.
2. *Environmental*: To include performance ratios related to environmental impacts in such areas as biodiversity, emissions, effluents and waste.
3. *Social*: To include performance ratios related to labour practices, human rights and product responsibility.

Solution 5

(a) **Report**

To: A
From: Reporting accountant
Date:
Re: The financial performance of Recycle (R)

The revenue of R has increased by 7.1% during the year, but over the same period its gross profit has fallen by 6.6%, from a gross profit ratio of 53.6% to one of 46.6%. During this period, operating expenses have increased by 33.3% and finance costs have doubled. These circumstances have had the effect of halving net profit before income tax, from a rate against sales of 28.5% to one of 13.3%. While income tax is lower, the effect of maintaining the dividend on reduced profits is to limit the retained profits available to finance investment. Dividend cover has fallen from 2.75 times to 1.25 times.

As profits have fallen there is evidence of expansion, as tangible non-current assets have increased by $1,500 million [i.e., $4,100 m − ($3,800 m − $1,200 m)], inventories by $150 million and trade receivables by $200 million. This investment has been financed by an increased overdraft of $700 million, depreciation $1,200 million, and retained profits $50 million, less reduced credit for unpaid tax $100 million. It is imprudent to finance non-current asset purchases from short-term overdraft finance.

There is clear evidence of poor management of working capital, which has deteriorated from a positive to a negative figure this year. The current ratio shows 0.91:1 for 20X7 as against 1.09:1 last year, and the quick ratio 0.62:1 this year against 0.77:1 last. This situation has been caused by the increase in the inventory-holding period (from 98 days to 114), and the receivables payment period (from 104 days to 122), largely financed by the increased overdraft. Creditors and the bank must be concerned by these items.

The gearing ratio shows little change at about 25%, but the debt:equity ratio has deteriorated from 0.72:1 to 0.92:1, and the interest cover is now only 3 times, against 9 times last year. This could presage difficulties in raising long-term funds to refinance loan payments in 20X9. Unless receivables can be collected faster and inventories controlled there may not be sufficient future cash flow to pay creditors, tax, dividends and the bank.

Signed: Reporting accountant

(b) The contribution made by published financial statements to satisfy the information needs of B, by addressing social and environmental matters, is disappointing. Such information contained in the corporate report is usually in the unaudited public relations section and not part of the financial statements.

GAAP offers little in the way of rules to ensure the disclosure of social or environmental information, other than figures for charitable donations and a crude analysis of the labour force, and details of the employment of disabled persons. It is very much left up to companies to decide what to disclose and how to disclose it. In the case of a material amount to clean up an environmental disaster, this would be noted as an exceptional item or as a provision for a future liability if a legal obligation existed.

Solution 6

As its name suggests, environmental reporting refers to the inclusion in the annual financial report of the actions of entities to maintain and enhance the environment. There are no detailed requirements for environmental reporting contained within international accounting standards. However, IAS 37 *Provisions, contingent liabilities and contingent assets* requires the reporting of certain environmental liabilities. Many jurisdictions are encouraging entities to provide environmental reports on a voluntary basis, and it is becoming increasingly common for listed entities to provide one. There appears to be a clear trend towards making such reports mandatory as the scope of stakeholder reporting widens. Reasons for the increasing incidence of environmental reports include:

- A greater acceptance that the financial report should contain information to appeal to a wide range of stakeholders, rather than merely to the arguably narrow interests of the equity investor group.
- An increasing perception that an annual report is a public relations document that needs to report the extent to which the entity is a good 'corporate citizen'.

Solution 7

It is very unusual for a company to include its employees as assets in its statement of financial position. There are essentially two main reasons for this:

1. Assets are defined by the IASB in its *Framework for the Preparation and Presentation of Financial Statements* as 'a resource controlled by the entity as a result of past transactions and events and from which future economic benefits are expected to flow to the entity'. It is questionable whether an employee could be regarded as satisfying this definition. It could be argued that, in practice, no contract of employment can *force* an individual to work so as to provide future benefits to the employer. Therefore, the essential features of the definition do not appear to be satisfied in this context.
2. Even if an employee can be regarded as an asset of an entity, that asset can only be recognised if it can be measured at a monetary amount with sufficient reliability. This means ascribing a cost or value to the employee. In most cases (although there are certain exceptions) no up-front payment is made in consideration of future services, so no valid cost exists. It would be theoretically possible to arrive at a value for an employee by capitalising the present value of future economic benefits but this exercise would be fraught with uncertainty. Even if such a value were to be computed, and the asset duly included on the statement of financial position, the question of period of write off would arise.

The exposure draft proposing changes to IAS 38 *Intangible Assets* considered, but rejected, the possibility of requiring recognition and measurement of the workforce and its related intellectual capital.

To summarise, the practial problems of accounting for human resources as assets probably outweigh the potential benefits.

18

International Issues in Financial Reporting

International Issues in Financial Reporting

18

Learning Outcome

After studying this chapter, students should be able to:

- discuss major differences between IFRS and US GAAP and the measures designed to contribute towards their convergence.

18.1 Introduction

This chapter covers the area of international convergence Section 18.2 introduces the developments in this area and the progress that has been achieved, together with some background information on recent developments in international reporting.

Section 18.3 – includes a discussion of recent developments in convergence between IFRS and US GAAP, and the significant differences that remain between international and US standards.

18.2 International convergence in financial reporting

First, it is worth considering why international convergence is considered to be of such importance. Entities have many reasons for engaging in international commerce. The potential for profits can be significantly expanded by seeking new markets overseas. The cost of labour across the world varies enormously, and entities may be able to obtain a competitive advantage by manufacturing a product in a foreign country where labour is flexible and cheap. Multinational entities attempt to minimise their risks and maximise their potential markets by operating in many countries across the globe.

The increase in international trade and commerce that has taken place in recent years often requires entities to seek additional resources in the form of capital to finance their international operations. Many multinational entities are quoted on more than one national stock exchange in order to obtain capital from a broad base. Financial reports play an important role in informing the decisions of investors and potential investors. However, financial reporting has differed widely in the past from one country to another, and it has been difficult to make valid comparisons between financial statements prepared in different countries. Major differences in national regulatory and political systems have resulted in divergent sets of accounting regulations. Taxation policy and practice have contributed, in many cases significantly, to differences in accounting practice. The advent of international financial reporting standards is having a significant influence in diminishing the importance of such differences in practice, and in contributing to improved transparency in capital markets.

18.2.1 Recent history of international standard-setting

An international accounting standards board has been in existence in 1973, but the impetus for international harmonisation has gathered pace over the last 15 or 20 years. The International Accounting Standards Committee (IASC) was formed in 1973 with the objective of promoting convergence of the accounting principles that are used by businesses and other organisations for financial reporting. The objectives originally set out by the IASC were as follows:

- to formulate and publish in the public interest accounting standards to be observed in the presentation of financial statements and to promote their worldwide acceptance and observance;
- to work generally for the improvement and harmonisation of regulations, accounting standards and procedures relating to the presentation of financial statements.

The IASC lacked the kind of formal authority that is lent by backing under a national legal system, and so its objectives were necessarily quite general in nature. Compliance with its standards could not be enforced, and so instead was 'promoted'. The objective of standardisation of accounting practice internationally would have been unrealistic at the time, and so a more general thrust towards 'harmonisation' was encouraged. More recently, the emphasis in international accounting has changed from the promotion of 'harmonisation' towards 'convergence'. Harmonisation is a process or set of processes by which differences in financial reporting between countries can be reduced. Harmonisation does not aim for complete uniformity in practice, but rather at the minimisation of differences over time. Convergence, on the other hand, implies a much closer drawing together of accounting practices in different jurisdictions.

The work of the IASC was given significant additional relevance during the 1990s because of the international securities regulator, IOSCO (the International Organization of Securities Commissions). IOSCO was formed in 1983 as a representative body of securities regulators and stock exchanges. Its own legitimacy was assured when the most influential body of all, the USA's Securities and Exchange Commission (SEC), joined it in 1986/7. IOSCO became instrumental in augmenting the authority of international standards when, in 1995, it agreed to adopt a 'core' set of thirty international accounting standards as binding upon its members in respect of cross-border listings, provided that the standards reached a certain quality threshold. The IASC was required to have the 'core' standards in place by the end of 1998, a deadline which it only just succeeded in achieving. In May 2000, IOSCO concluded its deliberations by endorsing the 30 'core' standards.

The work done by the IASC towards the 'core' standards project tended to emphasise its own limitations as an underfunded and somewhat unwieldy organisation. Reform was initiated during the 1990s and came to fruition as a new organisational structure was put in place between 1999 and 2001. The International Accounting Standards Board (IASB) has, since 2001, assiduously followed its demanding program of work, under the chairmanship of Sir David Tweedie. The IASB's objectives are:

(a) to develop, in the public interest, a single set of high-quality, understandable and enforceable global accounting standards that require high-quality, transparent and comparable information in financial statements and other financial reporting to help participants in the world's capital markets and other users make economic decisions;
(b) to promote the use and rigorous application of those standards;
(c) to bring about convergence of national accounting standards and international financial reporting standards to high-quality solutions.

18.2.2 The IASB's progress towards its objectives

There have been major developments in international accounting in recent years, most of which have tended to endorse the authority and scope of the international standards project. (The fact that CIMA examines financial reporting issues only in terms of IFRS exemplifies the point.) Many countries have already adopted IFRS either partially or fully. A very important endorsement of the international standards was made when the European Union decided to required listed entities throughout Europe to prepare consolidated financial statements in accordance with IFRSs by 2005.

There seems little doubt that IFRS are well on the way towards global acceptance. This is not to say that the process has been trouble-free. For example, the European Union requires an endorsement process for the acceptance of international standards. Whilst most of the international standards have been endorsed without significant problems (by the endorsing body, EFRAG), IAS 39 *Financial Instruments: Recognition and Measurement* proved to be an area of significant controversy, and it was not adopted in full in the first instance. Also, there is still a very large amount of work to be done to achieve convergence, and the process is unlikely to be substantially complete for many years yet.

Also, adoption of IFRS by many countries is incomplete. In Europe, for example, IFRSs are mandatory only for the consolidated financial statements of listed companies, and are optional for unlisted companies. National accounting standards regimes remain in many countries. While the national standard setters of some countries, such as the UK, are producing new standards that bring national practice into convergence with IFRS, this is not universally the case. Even where national and international practices are similar, important differences may remain. A further potential problem remains in respect of the extent of compliance with IFRS. Having no compliance mechanism of its own, the international standard setter relies upon national regulatory mechanisms to ensure enforcement of the standards. This may not be a uniformly successful process. Also, subtle differences in adoption and application may persist, even in financial statements that appear to be fully comparable with each other. An article by Professor Parker is included in the readings at the end of the chapter, exploring some of the problems of convergence.

18.3 Convergence between IFRSs and US GAAP

18.3.1 US GAAP – background

The SEC plays an important role in the accounting regulatory framework in the USA. It is an independent government agency, with a full-time staff of over 2,500, whose responsibility it is to oversee the activities of entities listed on Stock Exchanges in the US – some 12,000 entities. The SEC is authorised to issue accounting standards, but in practice it has always ceded this responsibility to private-sector accounting standard setters. Since 1973 the US standard setter has been the Financial Accounting Standards Board (FASB); during its lifetime it has issued many standards. US standards tend to be very detailed and to follow a 'rule-book' approach.

Although the SEC does not issue standards, it has a host of stringent disclosure requirements. Taken together the SEC requirements and the financial accounting standards issued by FASB contribute to the most tightly regulated and controlled capital market in the world. It was never likely that the US would simply adopt international accounting standards, and, indeed, in the 1990s the possibility of significant convergence between the two seemed fairly remote. However, in the early years of this century several factors combined to make convergence between the two both desirable and possible. The authority of the international standard setter was greatly increased by the IOSCO endorsement, the adoption by the EU and by its new constitution. In the US the stock market bubble came to an abrupt end, and the confidence of market participants was severely shaken by a series of major accounting scandals. The most significant of these in terms of economic significance was probably WorldCom, but it was Enron that really undermined confidence in the US regulatory system. Suddenly, it seemed distinctly possible that the rule-book approach to accounting regulation might not be the most effective.

In September 2002, IASB and FASB agreed to undertake a convergence project with the objective of reducing differences between IFRS and US GAAP. The full text of the so-called 'Norwalk agreement' between the two bodies is given below:

At their joint meeting in Norwalk, Connecticut, USA on September 18, 2002, the Financial Accounting Standards Board (FASB) and the International Accounting Standards Board (IASB) each acknowledged their commitment to the development of high-quality, compatible accounting standards that could be used for both domestic and cross-border financial reporting. At that meeting, both the FASB and IASB pledged to use their best efforts to (a) make their existing financial reporting standards fully compatible as soon as is practicable and (b) to coordinate their future work programs to ensure that once achieved, compatibility is maintained.

To achieve compatibility, the FASB and IASB (together, the 'Boards') agree, as a matter of high priority, to:

(a) *undertake a short-term project aimed at removing a variety of individual differences between US GAAP and International Financial Reporting Standards (IFRSs, which include International Accounting Standards, IASs);*

(b) *remove other differences between IFRSs and US GAAP that will remain at January 1, 2005, through coordination of their future work programs; that is, through the mutual undertaking of discrete, substantial projects which both boards would address concurrently;*
(c) *continue progress on the joint projects that they are currently undertaking;*
(d) *encourage their respective interpretative bodies to coordinate their activities.*

The Boards agree to commit the necessary resources to complete such a major undertaking.

The Boards agree to quickly commence deliberating differences identified for resolution in the short-term project with the objective of achieving compatibility by identifying common, high-quality solutions. Both Boards also agree to use their best efforts to issue an exposure draft of proposed changes to US GAAP or IFRSs that reflect common solutions to some, and perhaps all, of the differences identified for inclusion in the short-term project during 2003.

As part of the process, the IASB will actively consult with and seek the support of other national standard setters and will present proposals to standard setters with an official liaison relationship with the IASB, as soon as is practical.

The Boards note that the intended implementation of IASB's IFRSs in several jurisdictions on or before January 1, 2005 require that attention be paid to the timing of the effective dates of new or amended reporting requirements. The Board's proposed strategies will be implemented with that timing in mind.

18.3.2 Progress towards convergence

The IASB and FASB have lost no time in pursuing their convergence programme. The fruits of it to date include the following:

- An extensively revised version of IFRS 3 *Business Combinations* issued in January 2008.
- The standard on segment reporting (IFRS 8 *Operating segments*) issued in November 2006 (see Chapter 17 of this *Learning System*).
- IFRS 5 *Non-current Assets Held for Sale and Discontinued Operations*.
- An extensively revised version of IAS 1 *Presentation of Financial Statements*, issued in September 2007.

As well as the projects currently under way which have reached the exposure draft stage (business combinations, non-financial liabilities and segment reporting), there are several other active projects:

Short-term convergence projects

- IAS 12 income taxes
- impairment.

Long-term projects

- revenue recognition
- the conceptual framework
- post-retirement benefits.

The biggest step so far was taken by SEC in December 2007 when it removed the need for companies listing in the US and preparing their financial statements in accordance with IFRS, to prepare a reconciliation to US GAAP. The removal of this requirement was seen as the most significant step towards full convergence.

Despite all this activity, many significant differences remain between IFRS and US GAAP. These are the subject of the following section.

18.3.3 Remaining differences between US GAAP and IFRS

The set of differences between the two sets of regulations changes frequently with the issue of new standards. Significant recent changes have included the issue of IFRS 8 *Operating Segments*, and the updated versions of IFRS 3, IAS 27 and IAS 1. All of these have significantly reduced differences between US GAAP and IFRS.

This means that any list of differences is soon out of date, and all such lists should be treated with caution. Nevertheless, the list provided by, for example, the accounting firm PricewaterhouseCoopers is helpful. It was last updated (at the time of the update of this Learning System) in August 2007, and is available at www.pwc.com.

The table below summarises some of the significant remaining differences:

Issue	IFRS	US GAAP
General approach	Broadly, principles-based	Broadly, rule-based
Comparative information	One year of comparative information is required	No specific requirement, but SEC rules required 3 years of comparative information (2 years for the statement of financial position)
Extraordinary items	Prohibited	Defined as being both infrequent and unusual, and are rare
Jointly controlled entities	Both proportionate consolidation and equity method are permitted	Equity method is required except in certain circumstances
Revenue recognition	IAS 18 contains general principles only	While principles are similar to IFRS, there is extensive industry-specific guidance
Development costs	Are capitalised and amortised when specific criteria are met	Development costs are expensed as incurred
Property, plant and equipment	Either cost or revaluation bases are permitted	Historical cost is used; revaluation is not permitted
Inventories	Use of LIFO is not permitted	Use of LIFO is permitted
Investment property	Measured at fair value or depreciated cost	Depreciated historical cost is the only permitted measurement

Detailed knowledge of the differences is not required for F2 *Financial Management*. However, it is expected that candidates will be able to identify some of the principal differences that still exist between IFRS and US GAAP. Questions are quite frequently set in this area, and are often badly handled by candidates.

18.4 Summary

This chapter has examined a range of issues relating to international financial reporting. Section 18.2 examined the important issue of international convergence in financial reporting. Three relevant readings are appended at the end of this chapter which will help to consolidate knowledge of this important topic. Section 21.3 examined the special case of convergence between IFRS and US GAAP, providing a list of some of the important differences that remaining, as well as a discussion of the substantial progress towards convergence that has been made in a short period of time.

Students should note that the position changes rapidly. They can keep up to date by referring to the IASB website (at www.iasb.org). FASB's website is excellent and comprehensive (www.fasb.org).

Examination questions can be expected relating to the areas covered in this chapter. One possibility is to present a financial statement (or statements) prepared under international standards and to require comment on/calculation of the differences if the statement were presented under US GAAP (or vice-versa). Questions requiring discussion of the issues are also likely to occur from time to time. Students who prove themselves to be knowledgeable about current/recent developments are likely to be at a distinct advantage.

Readings 18

Have IFRSs conquered the world?

Bob Parker, *Accountancy*, November 2005.

It's far from a foregone conclusion, argues Bob Parker

'Learning International Financial Reporting Standards (IFRSs) is a chore for us accountants in the UK but once we have mastered them, then not only do we know the rules of British accounting we also know the rules throughout the world.' How true is this? Have IFRSs really conquered the world?

Certainly they seem at first sight to have conquered the two parts of the world to which the UK has the greatest political attachment: the EU and the Commonwealth. From 1 January 2005 (or at the latest from 1 January 2007), the consolidated financial statements of listed companies within all 25 members of the EU are required to comply with all International Accounting Standards and IFRSs approved by the European Commission (EC). Leading members of the Commonwealth such as Australia, South Africa, New Zealand and Singapore all claim to have adopted international standards. Canada has pledged convergence by 2011.

Not the only game in town

But there is the great exception: the US is not giving up US GAAP. IFRSs are not the only game in town. The US Financial Accounting Standards Board is the best-funded in the world, and the Securities and Exchange Commission (SEC) the strictest enforcer of accounting standards. Nevertheless, strenuous efforts are being made to bring IFRS and US GAAP closer together. There has been a 'race to the top' as international and US standard-setters have competed to produce standards acceptable to stock exchanges and government regulatory bodies. International standards have appealed to the EC not only because they are not US GAAP but also because they are not all that different from US GAAP.

However, within the EU, harmonisation is not as great as it might appear to be. The UK is exceptional in its strong support of the concept of international standards. This should not surprise us. British accountants were active in the formation and development of the International Accounting Standards Committee from 1973 onwards. International standards have been much more influenced by UK accounting rules and practices than by continental European ones and thus the adjustment we have to make is much less.

Since IFRSs are mandatory within the EU only for the consolidated statements of listed companies, the great majority of German and French companies will not be applying international standards. In particular, the subsidiaries of German and French parent companies will be using local GAAP. Adjustments will of course be made during the consolidation process, but many local features (for example, the way depreciation is calculated) are likely to remain.

Casting doubts

One may also be permitted to have doubts about the extent to which IFRSs will be complied with in practice. For several years now several large companies in Germany and France have purported to be applying International Accounting Standards or US GAAP in their consolidated statements, but research has shown less than complete compliance and a tendency to pick and choose. The monitoring and enforcement of accounting standards is strongest in the US and the UK but noticeably weak in Germany. Germany has recently set up institutions based on both the US SEC and the UK Financial Reporting Review Panel. It remains to be seen how successful they will be.

Finally, there has been an understandable reluctance for national standard-setters and government authorities to accept international standards which they see as against their own interests, especially if major companies lobby against them. Commonwealth countries other than the UK are converging with international standards rather than adopting them. Close scrutiny of what is happening in Australia, for example, suggests convergence rather than adoption, with portions of standards omitted or amended.

So, have IFRSs conquered the world? Not quite, but the achievements of the IASC/B are surely greater than its founders in 1973 dared to hope.

Financial Analysis

The Examiner, Financial Management, December/January 2007/2008

The content of the following article is relevant to the F2 exam as the related learning outcome is the same for F2 as it was for P8.

Candidates have tended to struggle with questions on US GAAP versus IFRS. **The examiner for paper P8** offers her guidance on the topic.

The P8 learning outcome 'identify major differences between IFRS and US GAAP' has been tested twice so far. The November 2005 paper asked candidates to cite examples of the two systems' differences and similarities, while a question in May 2007 asked for a brief paper describing the progress of the convergence project. These questions were answered badly in most cases – many candidates didn't even attempt an answer.

The biggest weakness was a sheer lack of knowledge. Some candidates were unaware that convergence was occurring at all. In May 2007 they were asked to describe how it was progressing, giving examples. Many did the opposite by listing the continuing differences between IFRS and US GAAP. Others repeated the few relevant points that they did know in different guises – also a waste of valuable exam time.

The use of the verb 'identify' in the learning outcome means that the outcome is pitched at the level of 'comprehension' in CIMA's hierarchy of learning objectives. This is a relatively low level, which means that advanced analytic and evaluative skills are not required to tackle questions in this area. So, although the differences between the sets of regulations are often extremely complex, for the purposes of P8 it's necessary only to know the key issues.

At a meeting in Norwalk, Connecticut, in 2002 the International Accounting Standards Board (IASB) and the US Financial Accounting Standards Board (FASB) agreed to start the convergence project. The Norwalk agreement set out their plan to reduce the differences between IFRS and US GAAP. Today, a list of standards, exposure drafts and discussion papers bears witness to their progress. Some May 2007 P8 candidates could name a few of their joint projects, but many could not.

Despite all this work, there are still many differences that are likely to last. The one that everyone seems to know is that the use of LIFO as an inventory valuation method is permitted under US GAAP but not under IFRS. Some others were described in a Study notes article in the June 2007 issue of *FM*.*

Currently, foreign issuers listed on the US markets must submit a reconciliation of their financial statements with US GAAP to the US Securities and Exchange Commission (SEC). But the SEC recently proposed dropping this rule, so it's likely that filing a reconciliation will no longer be required by 2009. Even more striking is an SEC proposal, now out for comment in the form of a 'concept release', to allow US companies to file statements using IFRS rather than US GAAP. It's unlikely that many of them would take advantage of this change, but the fact that it's being discussed at all indicates how much more acceptable IFRS has become in the US.

Chapter 18.3 of the *Financial Analysis CIMA Learning System* (*now Chapter 18.3 of the* F2 *CIMA learning system*) covers the background to convergence, the Norwalk agreement, current developments and the key remaining differences. For the 2008 exams, any changes made up to and including December 1, 2007 are examinable. So, as long as you use the latest edition of the learning system, you shouldn't have a problem. For those students who wish to impress the examiner with the depth of their knowledge – and the examiner will be impressed – several other information sources can be consulted.

The following web sites are useful:

- The International Accounting Standards Board: www.iasb.org.
- The Financial Accounting Standards Board: www.fasb.org.
- The US Securities and Exchange Commission: www.sec.gov.
- Deloitte, which produces comprehensive updates: www.iasplus.com.
- PricewaterhouseCoopers, which has published a booklet entitled 'Similarities and differences – a comparison of IFRS and US GAAP': http://snipurl.com/1t01q.

Once they have gained an outline knowledge of the key issues, candidates should aim to improve this by keeping their eyes open for news of developments and consulting some of the above sources.

The May 2007 post-exam guide included the following observation: 'Candidates should be aware (but, on the evidence of this paper, are mostly not aware) that this is not a trivial or marginal topic. On the contrary, it could be argued that the issue of US GAAP/IFRS convergence is the most important contemporary issue in financial reporting.'

The question of whether or not the learning outcome is likely to be examined again in the foreseeable future should, therefore, be relatively easy to answer.

* One of the differences identified in that article is no longer valid: changes in accounting policy under US Gaap are now handled in the same way as they are under IAS8 – that is, there is a requirement to make a full prior period restatement. (Thanks to Malcolm Greenbaum of BPP Professional Education for highlighting this development.)

Revision Questions 18

Question 1

You are the management accountant of X, an entity with a number of subsidiaries located in Europe and the United States of America (USA). One of these subsidiaries is US Inc., a entity incorporated in the USA. You are looking at the differences between the accounting treatment used in the accounts of US Inc. and X, which prepares financial statements in accordance with IAS.

The financial statements of US Inc. (drawn up in US dollars) are prepared in accordance with generally accepted accounting practice (GAAP) prevailing in the USA. The draft financial statements of US Inc. for the year to 31 December 20X5 showed a profit before taxation of $25 million. You are given the following information regarding US Inc.:

(i) During 20X4, US Inc. completed a development project, incurring costs of $20 million. US Inc. has no other development projects. The project was expected to generate cost savings of at least $5 million per annum for 5 years from the end of 20X4. All necessary market testing was carried out in 20X4 and the anticipated savings did in fact materialise in 20X5 and are expected to continue through until the end of 20X9. The costs of $20 million were written off in the income statement of US Inc. in 20X4 in accordance with GAAP in the USA. In the consolidated financial statements, X capitalises development expenditure whenever required by IAS 38.

(ii) The financial statements of US Inc. carry stocks at cost determined according to the last in, first out (LIFO) basis of valuation. However, stock values are also computed and reported to X using the first in, first out (FIFO) basis of valuation. X uses the FIFO method of stock valuation in its own (and in its consolidated) accounts. Relevant figures for US Inc. for 20X5 are given below:

	Valuation of stocks of US Inc. under:	
	LIFO	*FIFO*
Date	$m	$m
1 January 20X5	41	44
31 December 20X5	55	65

Requirement

Prepare a schedule in US dollars, which reconciles the profit before taxation of US Inc. as computed for its own draft financial statements with the profit before taxation which will be used for incorporation into the consolidated financial statements of X. Explain clearly the reasons for the adjustments. **(10 marks)**

Question 2

At a recent staff seminar on accounting standards, a senior member of your firm's accounting staff made the following observation:

'International standards have now been adopted in many countries across the world. Unfortunately, though, they can never be truly international because US GAAP will continue to dominate accounting in the USA and therefore in many multinational businesses.'

Requirement

Explain the rationale for this observation, illustrating your explanation with examples of significant differences and similarities between US GAAP and international accounting standards. **(10 marks)**

Solutions to Revision Questions

Solution 1

Reconciliation of US to IAS

	\$m
Profit of US Inc computed according to American GAAP	25
1. Development costs – share charged against profit	(4)
2. Stock valuation – reduction in cost of sales under FIFO	7
Profit of US Inc to be incorporated into X group accounts	28

- IAS 38 requires development costs to be capitalised and spread over the life of the development, whereas in the US a more conservative rule prevails and such costs are written off against profits when they are incurred. The project is expected to last 5 years and therefore the profits would be reduced by (\$20 m/5 years) = \$4 m amortisation of development costs.
- Group policy is to value stock using FIFO.

Solution 2

IFRS have, indeed, been adopted in many countries across the world: for example, compliance with them is compulsory in companies listed on a Stock Exchange within the European Union, and their adoption in Australia and New Zealand is well underway.

Nevertheless, it is certainly the case that accounting in accordance with international standards continues to differ from US GAAP in many respects. To this extent, the observation by the senior staff member has some validity. An example of an important difference is: *Valuation*. International accounting practice allows the option to value property, plant and equipment at either depreciated cost or fair value. US GAAP is more restrictive in this respect and reporting at depreciated cost is much more prevalent.

On the other hand, convergence between US and international practice is becoming increasingly common. For example, a significant area of difference in the past has been that of business combinations: it was common in the US until recently to account for many business combinations as pooling of interests. While international practice did not outlaw pooling of interests, its use was far less common. However, developments in US and international standards have now resulted in a position where pooling of interests accounting is no longer available.

The senior staff member does not mention the 'Norwalk agreement', which established a formal convergence project between the IASB and its US counterpart, the Financial Accounting Standards Board (FASB). Under the terms of this agreement, the IASB and FASB agreed to work together to remove differences between their respective sets of standards, and to co-ordinate their future programmes of work. The agreement has already resulted in a narrowing of differences: for example, IFRS 5 *Disposal of Non-Current Assets and Presentation of Discontinued Operations* brings international practice into line with US GAAP. Major recent developments include the issue of the IAS 1 (revised) *Presentation of Financial Statements* which brings international and US practice much more closely into line with each other.

There is a great deal of work to be done before US GAAP and international practice can be described as 'convergent'. However, much has already been achieved in a short time. The view expressed by the senior staff member would have been widely regarded as valid until very recently, but it has been overtaken by events. The convergence project has undoubtedly been given additional impetus by the recent, spectacular, corporate and accounting failures in the US. These have resulted in a period of introspection and self-criticism amongst US regulators and in a push towards significant improvement in financial reporting. Traditionally, the US approach to accounting regulation has been 'rules-based'; this has resulted in the production of very lengthy, detailed accounting standards. By contrast, international accounting standards have tended to be 'principles-based'. For example, instead of having a very detailed international standard addressing substance over form, international accounting practice relies much more upon promulgation and acceptance of the general principle of substance over form. The recent US accounting scandals have led to a great deal of criticism of the 'rules-based' approach and greater acceptance of the value of the 'principles-based' approach. On the other hand, international regulation appears to be moving to some extent in the opposite direction, as international standards become lengthier and more prescriptive (e.g.: IAS 39 *Financial Instruments: Recognition and Measurement*). Therefore, it seems likely that US and international regulators will find it easier to occupy common ground in their approach to standard setting.

Solution 3

The convergence project: progress to date

Traditionally, the US has adopted a 'rule-book' approach to financial reporting standard setting, whereas the approach taken by the IASB, and its predecessor body, has been to encourage adherence to principles. This fundamental difference in approach made it appear, for a long time, as though the US would never accept international standards. However, the rule-book approach was found wanting in a series of financial scandals in the US in the late 1990s and early years of the 21st century. The climate was therefore amenable to a change in approach which would make convergence possible between US and international financial reporting standards.

In September 2002 the US standard setter (Financial Accounting Standards Board – FASB) and the IASB agreed to undertake a project which would have the objective of converging their accounting practices, reducing the number of differences between US GAAP and IFRS. This agreement (the 'Norwalk agreement') committed the parties to making their existing standards fully compatible as soon as practicable, and to co-ordinating their future work programmes. In order to address the first commitment, a short-term project was undertaken to remove some of the differences between existing standards. The second commitment was to be met by collaborating on the development of standards.

A memorandum of understanding between FASB and the IASB sets out a 'Roadmap of Convergence between IFRS and US GAAP 2006-8'. This is aimed at removing the need for a reconciliation to US GAAP requirement for those companies that use IFRS and are registered in the USA.

Progress to date has been impressive. Projects undertaken jointly between FASB and IASB have produced the following:

- IFRS 5 *Non-current Assets Held for Sale and Discontinued Operations*
- IFRS 3 *Business combinations*
- IFRS 8 *Operating Segments*
- IAS 1 *Presentation of Financial Statements: a revised presentation*

There are several on-going projects that will run into the longer-term. For example, the amendment to IAS 1 noted above represents just a first phase in a larger project on financial statement presentation. Subsequent phases will address fundamental issues in presenting information and the issue of interim reporting.

Other longer-term projects include convergence of the conceptual frameworks and revenue recognition.

Finally, despite the high level of activity on convergence, it should be noted that many significant differences remain between US GAAP and IFRS.

Preparing for the Examination

Preparing for the Examination

This chapter is intended for use when you are ready to start revising for your examination. It contains:

- a summary of useful revision techniques;
- details of the format of the examination.

Revision technique

Planning

The first thing to say about revision is that it is an addition to your initial studies, not a substitute for them. In other words, don't coast along early in your course in the hope of catching up during the revision phase. On the contrary, you should be studying and revising concurrently from the outset. At the end of each week, and at the end of each month, get into the habit of summarising the material you have covered to refresh your memory of it.

As with your initial studies, planning is important to maximise the value of your revision work. You need to balance the demands of study, professional work, family life and other commitments. To make this work, you will need to think carefully about how to make best use of your time.

Begin as before by comparing the estimated hours you will need to devote to revision with the hours available to you in the weeks leading up to the examination. Prepare a written schedule setting out the areas you intend to cover during particular weeks, and break that down further into topics for each day's revision. To help focus on the key areas try to establish:

- which areas you are weakest on, so that you can concentrate on the topics where effort is particularly needed;
- which areas are especially significant for the examination – the topics that are tested frequently.

Don't forget the need for relaxation, and for family commitments. Sustained intellectual effort is only possible for limited periods, and must be broken up at intervals by lighter activities. And don't continue your revision timetable right up to the moment when you enter the exam hall: you should aim to stop work a day or even 2 days before the exam. Beyond this point the most you should attempt is an occasional brief look at your notes to refresh your memory.

Getting down to work

By the time you begin your revision you should already have settled into a fixed work pattern: a regular time of day for doing the work, a particular location where you sit, particular equipment that you assemble before you begin and so on. If this is not already a matter of routine for you, think carefully about it now in the last vital weeks before the exam.

You should have notes summarising the main points of each topic you have covered. Begin each session by reading through the relevant notes and trying to commit the important points to memory.

Usually this will be just your starting point. Unless the area is one where you already feel very confident, you will need to track back from your notes to the relevant chapter(s) in the *Learning System.* This will refresh your memory on points not covered by your notes and fill in the detail that inevitably gets lost in the process of summarisation.

When you think you have understood and memorised the main principles and techniques, attempt an exam-standard question. At this stage of your studies you should normally be expecting to complete such questions in something close to the actual time allocation allowed in the exam. After completing your effort, check the solution provided and add to your notes any extra points it reveals.

Tips for the final revision phase

As the exam looms closer, consider the following list of techniques and make use of those that work for you:

- Summarise your notes into more concise form, perhaps on index cards that you can carry with you for revision on the way into work.
- Go through your notes with a highlighter pen, marking key concepts and definitions.
- Summarise the main points in a key area by producing a wordlist, mind map or other mnemonic device.
- On areas that you find difficult, rework questions that you have already attempted, and compare your answers in detail with those provided in the *Learning System.*
- Rework questions you attempted earlier in your studies with a view to producing more 'polished' answers (better layout and presentation earn marks in the exam) and to completing them within the time limits.
- Stay alert for practical examples, incidents, situations and events that illustrate the material you are studying. If you can refer in the exam to real-life topical illustrations you will impress the examiner and earn extra marks.

The format of the examination

Structure of the paper

The examination paper for *Financial Management* has two sections:

1. Section A will be a compulsory section for 50 marks, containing five 10 marks questions.
2. Section B will be a compulsory section for 50 marks, containing two questions of 25 marks each, or one case study style question for 50 marks.

Any changes in the structure of the examination or in the format of questions will be indicated well in advance in the appropriate CIMA journals.

How to tackle the examination

There are a number of general points that are relevant to sitting the *Financial Management* examination.

- *Examination pressure.* We have all sat examinations at some point in our lives. They are unusual situations; the body and mind can behave in strange and sometimes uncontrollable ways. You need to be able to overcome this examination room pressure in order to deliver and show the examiner that you are worthy of passing the examination.

  You will need plenty of practice of questions under time constraints, and should practise 'mock' examinations. It is also important to have a rest and proper sleep the night before the exam.
- *Timing.* A common mistake made by students is the failure to allocate time properly. While it is easy to become engrossed in a complex numerical question, it is imperative that time available for the whole examination is allocated between the different questions.

  Reading time of 20 minutes is allocated to F2 and during this time you may study the exam paper and make annotations on the exam paper, but are prohibited from writing on your answer paper until instructed to do so by the exam invigilator. It is important to use this time effectively. When practising the mock exam questions, allow yourself the 20 minutes reading time and decide how best to use it prior to the exam.

  You have 1.8 minutes per mark and should allocate time to questions on this basis. Most marks are obtained within the time allocation and the question should be left when this time has run out. Excessive time applied to a question will almost certainly produce a diminishing return in terms of marks awarded. Any time savings achieved on questions may be used to return to the unfinished questions at the end.

  It is essential to answer all the questions required, if you are to stand a reasonable chance of passing.

  The manner in which you tackle questions is important. Attempting the question you know best first is advisable. In sections of the examination which involve little choice you must select the questions that best reflects your abilities, but not waste time deciding which questions these are.
- *Planning.* In order to overcome examination pressure and time pressure, it is a good idea to train yourself to plan answers before writing. You should prepare across the full syllabus and not rely on 'question-spotting'.
- *Understanding the questions.* Students sometimes fail because they give a good answer to the 'wrong' question.

It is essential that you read the question carefully to ensure a full understanding of what is required.

Time should not be wasted in a detailed reading of a lengthy practical question. You should become practised at scanning these questions to extract the fundamental background, the structure involved and the detailed requirements.

You should first look at the requirements of the question. Second, gain an appreciation of any complications caused by structure, organisation or circumstances. Third, discover any major factors which will require a modified approach to the question.

Do not just write everything you know about a subject; this may cause you to overrun on time for that question and will give the impression to the marker that you don't fully understand the question and the key issues. And if there are marks for the format (there are not normally any more than 2 marks attributed to format in this exam) of your answer, make sure you comply with the instructions – report format or memorandum, for example.

- *Working calculations.* Whatever the form of the question, all calculations and adjustments should be written out carefully. Credit is given in examinations for workings, even where you may have inserted the wrong figure in the final answer.
- *Presentation.* A high standard of presentation is an essential quality of a professional accountant. This applies not only to clarity and neatness in both the solutions and workings, but to presentation of answers in accordance with generally accepted accounting practice, for example, formats followed in accordance with IAS 1 (revised) and IAS 7, and the absence of abbreviations in statements of financial position and income statements.
- *Quality of English.* Frequent comment is made by examiners about the poor standards of written English. All that is required is care with the written parts of the examination. Some forethought and planning of answers will reap benefits in clarity of writing.

  Examiners have often stressed that students should avoid contentious remarks such as 'obviously'. These words should be used very carefully. If something is obvious, why state it? This does not mean to say that an answer should not include the obvious, but it is better not to say that it is! In any case, very often what actually follows the word 'obviously' is far from so. Another example is the report which ends with a phrase along the lines of 'I hope that this has clarified the situation', or 'Do not hesitate to contact me if you require further clarification'. Avoid these terms, as all too often they indicate muddled thinking.

Revision Questions

Section A

The following questions are those that reflect exam standard questions worth 10 marks. These cover all 4 sections of the syllabus and combine numerical and narrative components.

Question 1

(a) Pot owns all the share capital of Noodle. The following information is extracted from the individual statements of financial position of the two entities on 31 December 20Y0:

	Pot	*Noodle*
	$	$
Current assets	400,000	350,000
Current liabilities	250,000	100,000

The receivables of Pot include $40,000 receivable from Noodle, while the payables of Noodle include $25,000 payable to Pot. The difference is accounted for by cash in transit.

Requirement
If there are no other intra-group balances, what is the value of the net current assets in the consolidated statement of financial position of Pot? **(3 marks)**

(b) Peter owns 75% of the issued capital of Paul. The investment was made when the retained earnings of Paul were $100,000. The draft statements of financial position of the two entities at 31 December 20X0 showed the following balances:

	Peter	*Paul*
	$'000	$'000
Share capital ($1 shares)	250	160
Retained earnings	200	180
	450	340

On 31 December 20X0 Peter and Paul paid dividends of $40,000 and $20,000 respectively. Neither entity has made any entry in its financial statements in respect of either dividend.

Requirement
Calculate the balance on the consolidated retained earnings of Peter after accounting for both dividends (ignore goodwill on consolidation)? **(3 marks)**

(c) BJS, a listed entity, had a weighted average of 27,000 shares in issue in its financial year ended 31 August 20X6. It was also financed throughout the year by an issue of convertible loan stock with a par value of $50,000. The loan stock is convertible at the option of the holders at the rate of 12 new ordinary shares for every $100 of loan stock at par value. The finance cost recognised in BJS's income statement for the year ended 31 August 20X6 in respect of the loan stock was $6,000. The tax rate applicable to BJS was 30% during the financial year. The profit attributable to ordinary shareholders for the year ended 31 August 20X6 was $100,000.

Requirement

Calculate earnings per share, and diluted earnings per share for BJS for the year ended 31 August 20X6. **(4 marks)**

(Total marks = 10)

Question 2

(a) Abbott purchased 20 million of the 25 million issued $1 ordinary shares in Costello on 31 December 20X4, when the reserves of Costello showed a balance of $25 million and the net assets were $50 million. The cost of the purchase was $62 million. It is group policy to value non-controlling interest at acquisition at fair value. The fair value of the non-controlling interest of Costello was $6.5 million at the acquisition date. For the purposes of the consolidation the following matters may be relevant:

- At 31 December 20X4 there was a contingency in existence that resulted in a gain of $5 million to Costello on 31 March 20X5.
- At 31 December 20X4 the property, plant and equipment of Costello had a fair value that was $10 million in excess of its carrying value in the financial statements of Costello.
- At 31 December 20X4 Costello sold a branded product. The directors of Abbott considered that this brand name was worth around $7.5 million but the brand name has no readily ascertainable market value.

Requirement

Explain how the investment in Costello should be accounted for in the consolidated financial statements of Abbott and calculate the goodwill on consolidation of Costello that will appear in the consolidated statement of financial position of Abbott at 31 December 20X4? **(6 marks)**

(b) The statements of financial position of the two entities at 31 December 20X8 showed the following:

	Abbott	*Costello*
	$'000	$'000
Ordinary share capital	50,000	25,000
Retained earnings	60,000	35,000
	110,000	60,000

- The property, plant and equipment of Costello that was included in its statement of financial position at 31 December 20X4 (the date of acquisition) had an estimated future economic life of 10 at 31 December 20X4. None had been sold or scrapped by 31 December 20X8.

Requirement
Calculate the consolidated retained earnings balance of Abbott at 31 December 20X8?

(4 marks)
(Total marks = 10)

Question 3

(a) Tea owns 75% of the ordinary share capital of Cup. Cup supplies goods to Tea at a profit margin of 20% on sales. In the year to 31 December 20W9 the total supplies of goods from Cup to Tea were \$6 million. At 31 December 20W9 the inventory of Tea included \$1,200,000 in respect of goods purchased from Cup.

Requirement
Explain what adjustment is required to consolidated revenue in respect of the intra-group sales during 20W9? **(3 marks)**

(b) The inventory of Tea at 31 December 20W8 included \$750,000 in respect of goods purchased from Cup under the same terms as described in (a) above.

Requirement
Explain what adjustment is required to the consolidated gross profit in respect of the intra-group sales for the year ended 31 December 20W9? **(3 marks)**

(c) At 31 December 20W9 the reserves of Tea and Cup were \$6 million and \$4 million respectively. Cup is the only subsidiary of Tea and it has been a subsidiary since incorporation.

Requirement
Calculate the consolidated reserves of Tea at 31 December 20X9? **(4 marks)**
(Total marks = 10)

Question 4

The following summary statements of financial position relate to Frank, Frank's subsidiary Dean and Dean's subsidiary Sammy, at 31 December 20X0:

	Frank	*Dean*	*Sammy*
	\$'000	\$'000	\$'000
Investment in subsidiary	32,000	24,300	
Other net assets	40,000	30,000	45,000
	72,000	54,300	45,000
Ordinary shares of \$1	30,000	30,000	20,000
Retained earnings	42,000	24,300	25,000
	72,000	54,300	45,000

- On 31 December 20W5 Frank purchased 20 million shares in Dean, when the retained earnings of Dean stood at \$22 million and the retained earnings of Sammy stood at \$12 million.
- On 31 December 20W4 Dean purchased 12 million shares in Sammy, when the retained earnings of Sammy stood at \$10.5 million.
- The group's policy is to value non-controlling interest at the acquisition date at the proportionate share of the fair value of the subsidiary's identifiable net assets.

Requirement

Prepare the consolidated statement of financial position for the Frank group as at 31 December 20X0. **(10 marks)**

Question 5

(a) Extracts from the consolidated financial statements of Spender show the following regarding non-controlling interests:

- Opening non-controlling interests in the statement of financial position were $50 million.
- Closing non-controlling interests in the statement of financial position were $80 million.
- The charge in the consolidated income statement in respect of non-controlling interests was $25 million.
- During the year Spender acquired 80% of the ordinary shares of a new subsidiary, Jacked, that had net assets of $100 million at the date of acquisition.
- There were no unpaid dividends to minority shareholders at the beginning or end of the year.
- The group's policy is to value non-controlling interest at the acquisition date at the proportionate share of the fair value of the subsidiary's identifiable net assets.

Requirement

Calculate the amount that will be shown in the consolidated cash flow statement as payments to the non-controlling interest in the year and explain where this figure would be included? **(4 marks)**

(b) The cost of the acquisition in Jacked, referred to in (a) was $140 million and it was financed as follows:
  - a cash payment of $20 million;
  - loan notes of $50 million in Spender issued at par;
  - 20 million $1 shares in Spender issued when the market value of the shares was $3.50 per share;
  - the acquired subsidiary had net bank overdrafts of $10 million at the date of acquisition.

Requirement

Calculate the amount that will be shown as the acquisition cost of Jacked in the consolidated cash flow statement of Spender and explain where this figure would be included? **(3 marks)**

(c) The opening balance on non-current assets of Spender totalled $10 million. The closing balance was $14 million. The depreciation charge for the period was $2.6 million and the non-current assets of Jacked at the date of acquisition totalled $3 million. There were no disposals or revaluations in the period.

Requirement

Calculate the amount that would be included as purchase of non-current assets in the consolidated cash flow statement of Spender and explain where this cash flow would be included. **(3 marks)**

(Total marks = 10)

Question 6

You are the management accountant of XYZ, a company with several subsidiaries.

The financial statements for the year ended 30 June 20X6 are currently being finalised and are due to be published and filed in January 20X7.

Your assistant has a good knowledge of basic accounting techniques but knows little of the provisions of accounting standards. Accordingly, it is the practice within your organisation for your assistant to prepare a first draft of the basic financial statements and a summary of transactions which require your attention, highlighting a recommendation of the appropriate accounting treatment for each transaction.

Requirements

Draft a reply to your assistant which evaluates the correctness, or otherwise, of the proposed treatment for *each* transaction and suggests any changes you consider appropriate.

If you consider the recommended treatment to be incorrect, your advice should include a statement of, *and* reasoning *for*, what you consider to be the correct treatment.

In *each* case, your answer should refer to relevant provisions of IFRS.

The transactions highlighted by your assistant are as follows:

(a) XYZ has a subsidiary, GHI, in which it owns 80% of the issued ordinary share capital. On 1 June 20X6, GHI sold goods to XYZ having an invoiced price of $50 million. These goods (which cost GHI $40 million to manufacture) were included in the inventory of XYZ at 30 June 20X6. Your assistant proposes to eliminate unrealised profit of $8 million from inventory and consolidated reserves, on the basis that the total unrealised profit of $10 million was made by a subsidiary in which XYZ has an 80% interest. **(5 marks)**

(b) For a number of years XYZ has been selling a product called 'Timid' which is a superior brand of washing powder. This product was developed by the company and has now become a household name and has captured a substantial share of the market. Your assistant has heard members of the board express the view that the value of the Timid brand name 'must be worth at least $40 million' and proposes to bring an intangible asset of $40 million into the financial statements by debiting intangible non-current assets and crediting reserves. **(5 marks)**

(Total marks = 10)

Question 7

Textures manufactures artificial limbs. Its financial year end is 30 November 20X6. It manufactures in the United Kingdom and exports more than 60% of its output. It has several foreign subsidiary companies.

It has developed a number of arrangements to support its export sales. These include agreements with Pills, Eduaid, Bracos and Computer Control. Information on the agreements is as follows.

1. *Agreement with Pills*. An agreement was made in 20X2 with Pills, a pharmaceutical company, to jointly establish on a 50:50 basis Textures & Pills Joint Venture. Both Textures and Pills guarantee to meet liabilities if the other party fails to meet its share of the costs and risks.

Accounts prepared for Texture & Pills Joint Venture for the year ended 30 November 20X6 showed the following:

	$'000
Non-current assets	
Premises	300
Current assets	
Bank and cash	30
	330
Capital	
As at 1 December 20X5	
Textures	211
Pills	211
	422
Less expenses	92
As at 30 November 20X6	330

2. *Agreement with Eduaid and Bracos.* Textures entered into an agreement on 1 December 20X1 with Eduaid, a company that manufactured educational equipment, and Bracos, a South American lawyer, to set up under their joint control an unincorporated undertaking in South America to trade as Eurohelp.

   Textures had an effective 30% interest in Eurohelp. The statement of financial position of Textures as at 30 November 20X6 showed an investment at cost in Eurohelp of $750,000.

   The statement of financial position of Eurohelp for the year ended 30 November 20X6 showed:

	$'000
Non-current assets	7,500
Net current assets	1,100
	8,600
Capital account	
As at 30 November 20X5	6,750
Retained profit for the year	1,850
As at 30 November 20X6	8,600

3. *Agreement with Computer Control.* Textures entered into an agreement on 1 December 20X3 with Computer Control to jointly control Afrohelp, a company in which each company held a 50% interest. Afrohelp assembled mechanical products from Textures and automated them with control equipment from Computer Control.

   The joint venture has been equity accounted by each investor company. One of the newly appointed non-executive directors has questioned whether the investment in Afrohelp should be treated as a subsidiary.

   On 1 November 20X6 Textures sold inventory costing $110,000 to Afrohelp for $162,000. This inventory was unsold at 30 November 20X6.

   Textures adopts proportionate consolidation wherever permitted by IFRS.

Requirements

Explain how the investments in Textures & Pills Joint Venture and Eurohelp would be included in the consolidated financial statements of Textures and prepare appropriate extracts from the consolidated statement of financial position of the company as at 30 November 20X6. **(10 marks)**

Note: You should refer to the provisions of international accounting standards where relevant.

Question 8

Fair values in acquisition accounting is dealt with in IFRS 3 *Business Combinations*.

Requirements

(a) Explain why such an accounting standard was needed for fair values. **(4 marks)**

(b) Describe the main provisions of IFRS 3 as they relate to fair value. **(6 marks)**

(Total marks = 10)

Question 9

(a) On 1 January 20X1 J issues a zero-coupon bond for $10,000,000. The bond is repayable on 31 December 20X5 at a sum of $14,025,245. The bondholders receive no interest over the 5-year life of the bond.

Requirement

Explain, with reference to the appropriate international accounting guidance, how this financial instrument should be accounted for in the financial statements of J and calculate the amount of the finance charge that should be recognised by J in its financial statements for the year ending 31 December 20X2? **(5 marks)**

(b) J also issues 3,000 convertible bonds on 1 January 20X1 at par value of $2,000 per bond. The bonds are redeemable on 31 December 20X3 at par. The bonds pay interest annually in arrears at 4%. Under the terms of the bonds, each can be converted on maturity to 105 $1 shares.

The market rate of interest for a similar instrument with no conversion rights is 6%.

Requirement

Explain, with reference to the appropriate international accounting guidance, how this financial instrument should be accounted for in the financial statements of J and show prepare the accounting entry that would record this issue. **(5 marks)**

(Total marks = 10)

Question 10

(a) At 1 February 20X4, the beginning of its financial year, O has in issue 5,700,000 ordinary shares of $1 each. On 30 September 20X4, the entity raises a further $1,200,000 in capital by the issue of further ordinary shares at par.

Extract from O's consolidated income statement and statement of changes in equity at 31 January 20X5 shows the following:

	$
Consolidated profit before taxation	2,500,000
Tax	(750,000)
	1,750,000
Preference dividend	(200,000)
Ordinary dividend	(690,000)

Requirement

Calculate O's EPS for the year ending 31 January 20X5. **(3 marks)**

(b) Z has 3,000,000 shares in issue at 1 April 20X2. On 1 October 20X2 the entity makes a bonus issue of one share for every four held. On 1 October 20X3 Z makes a further bonus issue of one share for every three held.

Earnings attributable to ordinary shareholders for the year ending 31 March 20X3 were $810,000, and for the year ending 31 March 20X4 were $903,000.

Requirement

In the entity's financial statements for the year ending 31 March 20X4, what is the restated EPS comparative figure for 20X3. **(3 marks)**

(c) H has 3,000,000 shares in issue at 1 October 20X3. On 1 February 20X4 a rights issue of 1 for 6 is made at $1.62 per share. The market price of one share immediately prior to the rights issue was $1.90.

Earnings attributable to ordinary shareholders for the year ending 30 September 20X4 were $1,585,000.

Requirement

Calculate the EPS to be reported in the financial statements for the year ending 30 September 20X4. **(4 marks)**

(Total marks = 10)

Question 11

On 1 February 20X7 Jake sold a freehold interest in land to a financing institution for $5 million. The contractual terms require that Jake will repurchase the freehold in 3 years time for $8.82 million. Jake has the option to repurchase on 31 January 20X5 for $6 million or on 31 January 20X6 for $7.1 million. Prior to the disposal the land was recorded at its carrying value of $4 million in Jake's accounting records. The receipt of $5 million has been recorded with a credit to suspense account. No other accounting entries have been made in respect of this transaction.

At 31 January 20X5, Jake's directors decide not to take up the option to repurchase.

On 1 March 20X8 Jake issued 10 million $1 non-redeemable preference shares with a dividend rate of 5% which is accumulated if unpaid in any accounting period. The related transaction costs of $50,000 have been debited to share premium account. The proceeds of the issue have been credited to suspense as the accountant is unsure how to record the issue.

Requirement

Briefly explain the substance of both transactions, and prepare journal entries to record them correctly in the accounting records of Jake for the year ended 31 January 20X5.

(10 marks)

Question 12

Black has an available for sale investment with a carrying value of $1,130,000 as at the year end date, 31 December 20X6. The value of the investment at 31 December 20X7 is $1,150,000.

Black was concerned about the value of the shares falling and in order to mitigate this risk it entered into a derivative contract during 20X8 to hedge against the potential effect on the value of the shares of a general downturn in the market. The hedge is 100% effective and the contract has a positive value of $250,000 as at 31 December 20X8. The fall in the value of the available for sale investment was $270,000 as at 31 December 20X8, however $20,000 of that related to a change in the credit rating of the entity invested in.

Requirement

Briefly describe the treatment of the investments noted above and prepare the required journal entries for the years ended 31 December 20X7 and 20X8. **(10 marks)**

Question 13

You are the management accountant of Small. On 1 October 20X3 Small issued 10 million $1 preference shares at par, incurring issue costs of $100,000. The dividend payable on the preference shares was a fixed 4% per annum, payable on 30 September each year in arrears. The preference shares were redeemed on 1 October 20X8 at a price of $1.35 per share. The effective finance cost of the preference shares was 10%. The statement of financial position of the entity as at 30 September 20X8, the day before the redemption of the preference shares, was as follows:

Ordinary share capital (non-redeemable)	100.0
Redeemable preference shares	13.5
Share premium account	25.8
Retained earnings	59.7
	199.0
Net assets	199.0

Requirements

(a) Write a memorandum to your assistant which explains:
- how the total finance cost of the preference shares should be allocated to the income statement over their period of issue;

  Your memorandum should refer to the provisions of relevant accounting standards. **(5 marks)**

(b) Calculate the finance cost in respect of the preference shares for each of the 5 years ended 30 September 20X8. **(5 marks)**

(Total marks = 10)

Question 14

CBA is a listed entity that runs a defined benefit pension scheme on behalf of its employees. In the financial year ended 30 September 20X6 the scheme suffered an actuarial loss of $7.2 million. The entity's directors are aware that the relevant accounting standard, IAS 19 *Employee benefits*, was amended recently. They have asked you, the financial controller, to write a short briefing paper, setting out an outline of the options for accounting for the actuarial loss in accordance with the amended version of the standard.

Requirement

Prepare the briefing paper explaining the options and identifying, as far as possible from the information given, the potential impact on the financial statements of CBA of the two alternative accounting treatments. **(10 marks)**

Question 15

The IASB requires that a reporting entity's financial statements should report the substance of the transactions into which it has entered.

You are the management accountant of S. During the most recent financial year (ended 31 August 20X8), the company has entered into a factoring arrangement with F. The main terms of the agreement are as follows:

1. On the first day of every month S transfers (by assignment) all its trade receivables to F, subject to credit approval by F for each receivable transferred by S.
2. At the time of transfer of the receivables to F, S receives a payment from F of 70% of the gross amount of the transferred receivables. The payment is debited by F to a factoring account which is maintained in the books of F.
3. Following transfer of the receivables, F collects payments and performs any necessary follow-up work.
4. After collection by F, the cash received is credited to the factoring account in the books of F.
5. F handles all aspects of the collection of the receivables of S in return for a monthly charge of 1 % of the total value of the receivables transferred at the beginning of that month. The amount is debited to the factoring account in the books of F.
6. Any receivables not collected by F within 90 days of transfer are regarded as bad by F and are reassigned to S. The cash previously advanced by F in respect of bad receivables is recovered from S. The recovery is only possible out of the proceeds of other receivables which have been assigned to S. For example, if, in a particular month, S assigned trade receivables having a value of $10,000 and a debt of $500 was identified as bad, then the amounts advanced by F to S would be $6,650 (i.e., 70% × $10,000 − 70% × $500).
7. On a monthly basis, F debits the factoring account with an interest charge which is calculated on a daily basis on the balance on the factoring account.
8. At the end of every quarter, F pays over to S a sum representing any credit balance on its factoring account with S at that time.

Requirements

Draft guidance to the board of directors of S, explaining how the factoring arrangement will be reported in the financial statements of S. **(10 marks)**

Question 16

You are the chief accountant of Ant, an entity that prepares financial statements in accordance with International Accounting Standards. Your assistant has prepared the first draft of the consolidated financial statements for the year ended 31 October 20X3 and these show a profit after tax of $66 million, while the statement of financial position shows ownership interests (total assets less total liabilities, including non-controlling interests) of $450 million.

Your assistant has identified the following issues that require your review:

Issue (a)

On 1 November 20X2, Ant established a new subsidiary located in a jurisdiction where the unit of currency is the Franco. The initial investment was 40 million Francos (the initial net assets of the subsidiary). The investment was financed by a loan of 40 million Francos from a German bank. No capital repayments of the loan are due until 31 October 20Z2.

The exchange rate at 1 November 20X2 was 1.6 Francos to $1. On 31 October 20X3, the exchange rate was 1.5 Francos to $1. Due to large start-up costs, the subsidiary did not make a profit in the early months of trading and the net assets of the subsidiary at 31 October 20X3 remained at 40 million Francos.

In preparing the draft consolidated financial statements, your assistant has translated both the loan and the financial statements of the subsidiary at 1.6 Francos to $1 on the basis that the financing of the subsidiary was obtained when the exchange rate was 1.6 Francos to $1.

Issue (b)

On 1 November 20X2, Ant issued two million $100 loan notes at $90 per note. A merchant bank received $4 million to underwrite the issue and Ant incurred other costs of $500,000 relating to the issue of the notes. The notes pay no interest and are redeemable at $135 per note on 31 October 20X7. As an alternative to redemption, the notes can be converted into 50 Equity shares per $100 note on 31 October 20X7.

Your assistant has written off the issue costs of $4.5 million to the income statement for the year ended 31 October 20X3 as an administrative expense and credited the proceeds of issue ($180 million) to a convertible loan notes account. He proposes to show this in the capital and reserves section of the statement of financial position on the basis that the share price on 31 October 20X7 is likely to be at least $4, so conversion, rather than repayment, is likely to be a near certainty.

Your assistant has been informed that, at 1 November 20X2, the fair value of the options to convert the loan notes into shares on 31 October 20X7 was $22.5 million. However, he does not consider this information to be relevant and so has ignored it.

Requirement

For each of the issues, evaluate the treatment adopted by your assistant with reference to currently published Accounting Standards. Where you consider the treatment adopted to be incorrect, you should state the journal adjustment required to correct the error.

In all cases, you should give any supporting explanations you consider appropriate to justify your conclusions.

The allocation of marks to the issues is as follows:

Issue (a)	**(5 marks)**
Issue (b)	**(5 marks)**
	(Total marks = 10)

? Question 17

You are the financial controller of Jade, a entity which has recently established a pension scheme for its employees. It chose a defined benefit scheme rather than a defined contribution scheme.

Jade makes payments into the pension scheme on a monthly basis.

Jade prepares its financial statements to 31 December each year.

On 31 December 20X7 the market value of the scheme's assets was $40 million and the present value of the scheme's liability $44 million. Actuarial losses not yet recognised in the income statement amounted to $3 million. In 20X8 the following data is relevant:

- current service cost: $4 million,
- unwinding of discount: $3.6 million,
- expected return on pension plan assets: $4.8 million,
- contributions for the year: $3.4 million.

On 31 December 20X8 the market value of the scheme's assets was $42 million and the present value of the scheme's liability $25 million.

Jade's accounting policy is to defer actuarial gains and losses to future periods so far as is permissible under the requirements of IAS 19.

Requirement

Determine the total charge in the income statement for pensions (excluding amounts deducted from employees' gross salaries) and the amounts shown in the statement of financial position in respect of pensions.

Ignore deferred taxation. **(10 marks)**

Question 18

Make-it is a manufacturing entity. One of its subsidiaries, Do-it, operates in a country which experiences relatively high rates of inflation in its currency, the Do. Most entities operating in that country voluntarily present two versions of their financial statements: one at historical cost, and the other incorporating current cost adjustments. GFE complies with this accepted practice. Extracts from the income cp statement adjusted for current costs for the year ended 30 September 20X5 are as follows:

	Do 000	Do 000
Historical cost operating profit		1,500
Current cost adjustments:		
Cost of sales adjustment	130	
Depreciation adjustment	86	
Loss on net monetary position	32	
		248
Current cost operating profit		1,252

Requirements

(a) Explain the defects of historical cost accounting in times of increasing prices. **(4 marks)**

(b) Explain how each of the three current cost adjustments in GFE's financial statements contributes to the maintenance of capital. **(6 marks)**

Question 19

You have been asked by a colleague to present a brief paper to accounting students at the local university about recent attempts at convergence between International Financial Reporting Standards (IFRS) and US Generally Accepted Accounting Practice (GAAP). The students are knowledgeable about IFRS but have not studied US GAAP in any detail.

Requirement

Prepare the paper, describing the progress to date of the convergence project, including some examples of areas where convergence has taken place. **(10 marks)**

Question 20

It is becoming increasingly common for listed entities to provide non-financial disclosures intended to inform stakeholders about the business's environmental policies, impacts and practices. Supporters of such voluntary disclosures argue that stakeholders have a right to be informed about environmental issues in this way. However, there are also arguments against this type of disclosure.

Requirement

Identify and explain the principal arguments **against** voluntary disclosures by businesses of their environmental policies, impacts and practices.

Section B

The following questions are those that reflect exam standard questions worth 25 marks. These typically cover the syllabus areas of Sections A and C. There may also be areas of Sections B and D covered but they will not account for the majority of the marks.

Question 21

The statements of financial position of three entities, AD, BE and CF at 30 June 20X6, the year end of all three entities, are shown below:

	AD		*BE*		*CF*	
	$'000	$'000	$'000	$'000	$'000	$'000
ASSETS						
Non-current assets:						
Property, plant and equipment	1,900		680		174	
Financial asset: investments in shares	880		104		–	
Other financial asset	980		–		–	
		3,760		784		174
Current assets:						
Inventories	223		127		60	
Trade receivables	204		93		72	
Other current assets	25		–		–	
Cash	72		28		12	
		524		248		144
		4,284		1,032		318
EQUITY AND LIABILITIES						
Equity:						
Share capital ($1 shares)	1,000		300		100	
Retained earnings	2,300		557		122	
		3,300		857		222
Non-current liabilities		600		–		–
Current liabilities:						
Trade payables	247		113		84	
Income tax	137		62		12	
		384		175		96
		4,284		1,032		318

Notes

1. *Investment by AD in BE*
   AD acquired 80% of the ordinary shares of BE on 1 July 20X3 for $880,000 when BE's retained earnings were $350,000. Goodwill on acquisition continues to be unimpaired.

2. *Investment by BE in CF*
   BE acquired 40% of the ordinary shares of CF on 1 January 20X6 for $104,000. BE appoints one of CF's directors and since the acquisition has been able to exert significant influence over CF's activities. CF's retained earnings at the date of acquisition were $102,000.
   BE and CF are unquoted entities and their fair value cannot be reliably measured, as a result the investments held in the individual accounts of both AD and BE are classified as available for sale and are held at cost.
   The group's policy is to value non-controlling interest at the acquisition date at the proportionate share of the fair value of the subsidiary's identifiable net assets.
3. *Other financial asset*
   AD's other financial asset is a debt instrument with a fixed interest rate of 5%. The instrument was issued on 1 July 20X4 for proceeds of $1,000,000. The instrument is redeemable at a premium on 30 June 20X8; the applicable effective interest rate over the life of the instrument is 8%. The full annual interest amount was received and recorded by AD in June 20X5 and June 20X6, and the appropriate finance charge was recognised in the financial year ended 30 June 20X5. However, no finance charge has yet been calculated or recognised in respect of the financial year ended 30 June 20X6.
4. *Other current assets*
   Other current assets of $25,000 in AD represent a holding of shares in a major listed company. AD maintains a portfolio of shares held for trading. At 30 June 20X6 the only holding in the portfolio was 4,000 shares in DG, a major listed company with 2.4 million ordinary shares in issue. The investment was recognised on its date of purchase, 13 May 20X6, at a cost of 625 cents per share. At 30 June 20X6, the fair value of the shares had risen to 670 cents per share.
5. *Intra-group trading*
   BE supplies goods to CF. On 30 June 20X6 CF held inventories at cost of $10,000 that had been supplied to it by BE. BE's profit margin on the selling price of these goods is 30%. On 27 June 20X6 AD made a payment of $5,000 to BE, which was not received and recorded by BE until after the year end. The receivables of BE at the year end include $5,000 in respect of this intra-group balance.

Requirements

(a) Explain the accounting treatment in the statement of financial position and income statement for the financial asset and other current asset required by IAS 39 *Financial Instruments: Recognition and Measurement.* **(5 marks)**

(b) Prepare the consolidated statement of financial position for the AD Group at 30 June 20X6. **(20 marks)**

(Total marks = 25)

? Question 22

You are the accountant responsible for the Rag group consolidation. The income statements of Rag, Tag and Bobtail for the year ended 31 March 20X9 are given below.

	Rag	*Tag*	*Bobtail*
	$'000	$'000	$'000
Revenue *(note 1)*	65,000	50,000	100,000
Cost of sales	(35,000)	(28,000)	(82,000)
Gross profit	30,000	22,000	18,000
Other operating expenses	(15,000)	(11,000)	(9,000)
Operating profit	15,000	11,000	9,000
Investment income *(note 2)*	3,000	1,200	–
Interest payable	(3,200)	(1,800)	(1,200)
Profit before taxation	14,800	10,400	7,800
Taxation	(3,600)	(2,800)	2,400)
Profit for the period	11,200	7,600	5,400

Notes to the income statements

1. Rag supplies a component which is used by both Tag and Bobtail. Because of the close relationships between the three entities, the component is supplied at a mark-up of only 10% on cost. Details of inter-entity sales of the product for the year to 31 March 20X9 were as follows:
   - Rag to Tag $8 million
   - Rag to Bobtail $4 million

   Details of the inventory of the component supplied by Rag which were included in the books of Tag and Bobtail at the beginning and end of the year were:

	20X9	*20X8*
	$'000	$'000
Tag	2,200	1,980
Bobtail	1,100	990

2. Rag holds 75% of the issued share capital of Tag. Tag holds 40% of the issued share capital of Bobtail.

   Your assistant is responsible for preparing the draft consolidated financial statements for your review. She is aware that Tag will be dealt with as a 75% subsidiary but is unsure of the way of dealing with Bobtail.

   The group's policy is to value non-controlling interest at the acquisition date at the proportionate share of the fair value of the subsidiary's identifiable net assets.

Requirements

(a) Write a memorandum to your assistant which explains how Bobtail will be incorporated into the consolidated financial statements of Rag.

Your memorandum should refer to relevant accounting standards to support your explanations. **(5 marks)**

(b) Prepare a working schedule for the consolidated income statement of Rag for the year ended 31 March 20X9. You should start with the revenue and end with profit for the period. Do *not* prepare notes to the consolidated income statement. **(20 marks)**

(Total marks = 25)

Question 23

AX, a listed entity, is planning to acquire several smaller entities. In order to raise the cash for its programme of acquisitions, it has recently sold part of its stake in a subsidiary, CY, and has raised $10 million in a bond issue.

Summarised statements of financial position for AX, CY and the other member of the group, EZ, at 31 October 20X7 are given below:

	AX	*CY*	*EZ*
	$'000	$'000	$'000
ASSETS			
Non-current assets:			
Property, plant and equipment	20,000	8,900	5,000
Investment in subsidiaries (notes 1 & 2)	15,500	–	–
	35,500	8,900	5,000
Current assets	34,500	9,500	4,700
	70,000	18,400	9,700
EQUITY AND LIABILITIES			
Equity:			
Called up share capital ($1 shares)	20,000	4,000	3,000
Retained earnings	18,000	7,000	3,000
	38,000	11,000	6,000
Non-current liabilities	–	2,400	1,000
Current liabilities	18,000	5,000	2,700
Suspense account (notes 1 & 3)	14,000	–	–
	70,000	18,400	9,700

Notes:

1. The investment in 80% of CY's ordinary share capital was purchased several years ago for $8 million when CY's retained earnings were $3.5 million. There has been no change since then in the amount of CY's share capital, and goodwill has remained unimpaired. No adjustments to fair value of CY's net assets were made either at acquisition or subsequently.

   On 31 October 20X7 AX sold one quarter of its shareholding in CY to an unconnected party for $4 million. The retained earnings of CY totalled $6.5 million at the date of disposal. This amount has been debited to cash and credited to the suspense account. Ignore income tax implications.
2. The investment in 100% of EZ's ordinary share capital was purchased on 30 April 20X5 for $7.5 million when EZ's retained earnings were $1.5 million. Goodwill has remained unimpaired since the date of acquisition.

   Upon acquisition a revaluation exercise was carried out. Plant and equipment in EZ with a book value of $1 million was revalued to $1.5 million. There were no other adjustments in respect of fair value. The revaluation is treated as a consolidation adjustment only: EZ continues to recognise non-current assets at depreciated historic cost. The remaining useful life of the plant and equipment at 30 April 20X5 was estimated to be five years, of which thirty months had elapsed by 31 October 20X7.
3. AX issued $10 million of 5% convertible bonds on 31 October 20X7. The bonds were issued in units of $1,000 and are repayable on 31 October 20Y0 However, each bond is convertible into 250 ordinary shares at any time until maturity at the option of the bondholder. The market rate for similar, non-convertible, bonds is 7%. It can be

assumed that there were no issue costs. The $10 million raised by the issue was debited to cash and credited to the suspense account.

Requirements

(a) Explain the appropriate accounting treatment to record the issue of convertible bonds, discussing the reasons for the approach that is adopted by International Financial Reporting Standards for this type of financial instrument.

(b) Prepare the consolidated statement of financial position for the AX group at 31 October 20X7.

Question 24

Extracts from the consolidated financial statements of Holmes for the year ended 30 September 20X9 are given below.

1. Consolidated income statement for the year ended 30 September 20X9

	20X9	*20X8*
	$'m	$'m
Revenue	600	500
Cost of sales	(300)	(240)
Gross profit	300	260
Other operating expenses (N1)	(150)	(130)
Other income (N2)	10	–
Finance cost	(50)	(45)
Share of profit of associates	17	17
Profit before tax	127	102
Income tax expense	(35)	(25)
Profit for the period	92	77
Attributable to:		
Equity holders of parent	82	71
Non-controlling interest	10	6
	92	77

2. Summarised consolidated statement of changes in equity – year ended 30 September (amounts attributable to equity holders of parent)

	20X9	*20X8*
	$'000	$'000
Balance at the start of the year	242	196
Profit for the year	82	71
Dividends	(25)	(25)
	299	242

3. Consolidated statement of financial position as at 30 September

	20X9		*20X8*	
	$'m	$'m	$'m	$'m
Non-current assets				
Intangible assets (N3)		35		19
Property, plant and equipment (N4)		240		280
Investments in associates		80		70
		355		369
Current assets				
Inventories	105		90	
Receivables	120		100	
Investments	20		70	
Cash in hand	10		5	
		255		265
		610		634
Share capital		100		100
Revaluation reserve		–		20
Retained earnings		199		122
		299		242
Non-controlling interests		65		40
Non-current liabilities				
Obligations under finance leases	80		70	
Loans	–		90	
Deferred tax	30		24	
		110		184
Current liabilities				
Trade payables (N5)	71		60	
Tax	10		8	
Obligations under finance leases	25		20	
Bank overdraft	30		80	
		136		168
		610		634

Notes

1. *Other operating expenses*

	20X9	*20X8*
	$'m	$'m
Distribution costs	81	75
Administrative expenses	75	70
Investment income	(6)	(15)
	150	130

From time to time the group invests cash surpluses in highly liquid investments that are shown as current assets in the consolidated statement of financial position.

2. *Other income*

This represents the gain on sale of a large freehold property that was sold by Holmes during the year on 1 October 20X8 and leased back on an operating lease in line with the practice adopted by the rest of the group. The property was not depreciated in the current year. The property had been revalued in 20X0 and the revaluation surplus credited to a revaluation reserve. No other entries had been made in the revaluation reserve prior to the sale of the property.

3. *Intangible non-current assets*

This comprises the unimpaired balance of goodwill on consolidation. During the year ended 30 September 20X9 Holmes purchased 80% of the issued equity share capital of

Watson plc for $100 million payable in cash. The net assets of Watson plc at the date of acquisition were assessed as having fair values as follows:

	$'m
Plant and machinery – owned	50
Fixtures and fittings – owned	10
Inventories	30
Receivables	25
Cash at bank and in hand	10
Trade payables	(15)
Tax	(5)
	105

4. *Property, plant and equipment*

	30.9.X9	*30.9.X8*
	$'m	$'m
Freehold land and buildings	–	90
Plant and machinery – owned	130	100
Plant and machinery – leased	90	70
Fixtures and fittings – owned	20	20
	240	280

During the year the group entered into new finance lease agreements in respect of certain items of plant and machinery. The amounts debited to property, plant and equipment in respect of such agreements during the year totalled $40 million. No disposals of property, plant and equipment (owned or leased) took place during the year. Depreciation of property, plant and equipment for the year totalled $58 million.

5. *Trade payables*

Trade payables at 30.9.X9 and 30.9.X8 do not include any accrued interest.

Requirements

You are the management accountant of Holmes and you are in the process of preparing the consolidated cash flow statement. Your managing director is aware that the statement is required by IAS 7 *Cash Flow Statements*. She has a reasonable understanding of the rationale behind the cash flow statement but is not clear why it adds to the usefulness of financial statements since it is prepared from the income statement and the statement of financial position.

(a) Prepare the statement of cash flows for the Holmes group for the year ended 30 September 20X9 in the form required by IAS 7 *Cash Flow Statements*. Notes to the cash flow statement are *not* required but your workings must be clearly shown.

(20 marks)

(b) Write a brief memorandum to your managing director which explains the value that the cash flow statement adds to financial reports. **(5 marks)**

(Total marks = 25)

Question 25

AT holds investments in three other entities. The draft income statements for the four entities for the year ended 31 March 20X7 are as follows:

	AT	*BU*	*CV*	*DW*
	$'000	$'000	$'000	$'000
Revenue	2,450	1,200	675	840
Cost of sales	(1,862)	(870)	(432)	(580)
Gross profit	588	330	243	260
Distribution costs	(94)	(22)	(77)	(18)
Administrative expenses	(280)	(165)	(120)	(126)
Interest received	–	2	–	–
Finance costs	(26)	–	–	–
Profit before tax	188	145	46	116
Income tax	(40)	(50)	(12)	(37)
Profit for the period	148	95	34	79

Notes

1. *Investments in BU, CV and DW*
   Several years ago AT purchased 75% of the ordinary shares of BU. On 30 September 20X6 it purchased a further 5% of BU's ordinary shares. In 20X3 AT, together with two other investor entities, set up CV. Each of the three investors owns one-third of the ordinary shares in CV. All managerial decisions relating to CV are made jointly by the three investor entities. On 1 January 20X7, AT purchased 35% of the ordinary shares in DW. AT exerts significant influence over the management of DW, but does not control the entity.

   The group's policy is to value non-controlling interest at the acquisition date at the proportionate share of the fair value of the subsidiary's identifiable net assets.
2. *Intra-group trading*
   BU supplies inventories to AT, earning a gross profit margin of 20% on such sales. During the financial year ended 31 March 20X7, BU supplied a total of $80,000 at selling price to AT. Of these items, 25% remained in AT's inventories at the year end. AT supplies a range of administrative services to BU, at cost. $12,000 is included in BU's administrative expenses, and in AT's revenue, in respect of such services supplied during the year ended 31 March 20X7.
3. The group has a policy of adopting proportional consolidation wherever permitted by International Financial Reporting Standards.
4. Revenue and profits accrue evenly throughout the year, unless otherwise stated.
5. *Finance costs*
   The finance costs in AT's income statement are in respect of short-term bank borrowings only. Finance costs in respect of its long-term borrowings have not yet been included, and an appropriate adjustment must be made. On 1 April 20X4, AT issued bonds at par in the amount of $1,000,000. Issue costs were $50,000. The bonds carry a coupon rate of interest of 5% each year, payable on the last day of the financial year. The interest actually paid on 31 March 20X7 has been debited to a suspense account, which is included under current assets in AT's draft statement of financial position.

The bonds will be repaid on 31 March 20X9 at a premium of $162,000. The effective interest rate associated with the bonds is 9%, and the liability is measured, in accordance with IAS 39 *Financial Instruments: Recognition and Measurement*, at amortised cost.

6. *Financial asset*

   From time to time BU uses available cash surpluses to make short term investments in financial assets. Such assets are 'held-for-trading' and are invariably sold within a few months. At 31 March 20X7, BU held 4,000 shares in a listed entity, EX. The shares had been purchased on 20 January 20X7 at a price of 1332¢ per share. At 31 March 20X7, the market price per share was 1227¢. No adjustment has been made to the draft income statement above in respect of this financial asset.

Requirements

Prepare the consolidated income statement for the AT group for the financial year ended 31 March 20X7. Show full workings. **(25 marks)**

Note: 8 marks are available for the adjustments in respect of notes 5 and 6.

Work to nearest $100. For the purposes of this question it is not necessary to make any adjustments to income tax.

? Question 26

You advise a private investor who holds a portfolio of investments in smaller listed companies. Recently, she has received the annual report of the BZJ Group for the financial year ended 31 December 20X5. In accordance with her usual practice the investor has read the chairman's statement, but has not looked in detail at the figures. Relevant extracts from the chairman's statement are as follows:

'Following the replacement of many of the directors, which took place in early March 20X5, your new board has worked to expand the group's manufacturing facilities and to replace non-current assets that have reached the end of their useful lives. A new line of storage solutions was designed during the second quarter and was put into production at the beginning of September. Sales efforts have been concentrated on increasing our market share in respect of storage products, and in leading the expansion into Middle Eastern markets.

The growth in the business has been financed by a combination of loan capital and the issue of additional shares. The issue of 300,000 new $1 shares was fully taken up on 1 November 20X5, reflecting, we believe, market confidence in the group's new management. Dividends have been reduced in 20X5 in order to increase profit retention to fund the further growth planned for 20X6. The directors believe that the implementation of their medium- to long-term strategies will result in increased returns to investors within the next 2 to 3 years.'

The group's principal activity is the manufacture and sale of domestic and office furniture. Approximately 40% of the product range is bought in from manufacturers in other countries.

Extracts from the annual report of the BZJ Group are as follows:

BZJ Group: Income statement for the year ended 31 December 20X5

	20X5	*20X4*
	$'000	$'000
Revenue	120,366	121,351
Cost of sales	(103,024)	(102,286)
Gross profit	17,342	19,065
Operating expenses	(11,965)	(12,448)
Profit from operations	5,377	6,617
Interest payable	(1,469)	(906)
Profit before tax	3,908	5,711
Income tax expense	(1,125)	(1,594)
Profit for the period	2,783	4,117
Attributable to:		
Equity holders of the parent	2,460	3,676
Non-controlling interest	323	441
	2,783	4,117

BZJ Group: Summarised statement of changes in equity for the year ended 31 December 20X5

	Retained earnings	*Share capital*	*Share premium*	*Revaluation reserve*	*Total 20X5*	*Total 20X4*
	$'000	$'000	$'000	$'000	$'000	$'000
Opening balance	18,823	2,800	3,000		24,623	21,311
Surplus on revaluation of properties				2,000	2,000	
Profit for the period	2,460				2,460	3,676
Issue of share capital		300	1,200		1,500	–
Dividends paid 31 December	(155)				(155)	(364)
Closing balance	21,128	3,100	4,200	2,000	30,428	24,623

BZJ Group: Statement of financial position as at 31 December 20X5

	20X5		*20X4*	
	$'000	$'000	$'000	$'000
Non-current assets:				
Property, plant and equipment	40,643		21,322	
Goodwill	1,928		1,928	
Trademarks and patents	1,004		1,070	
		43,575		24,320
Current assets:				
Inventories	37,108		27,260	
Trade receivables	14,922		17,521	
Cash	–		170	
		52,030		44,951
		95,605		69,271
Equity:				
Share capital ($1 shares)	3,100		2,800	
Share premium	4,200		3,000	
Revaluation reserve	2,000		–	
Retained earnings	21,128		18,823	
		30,428		24,623
Non-controlling interest		2,270		1,947

Non-current liabilities:				
Interest bearing borrowings		26,700		16,700
Current liabilities:				
Trade and other payables	31,420		24,407	
Income tax	1,125		1,594	
Short-term borrowings	3,662		–	
		36,207		26,001
		95,605		69,271

Requirements

(a) Calculate the earnings per share figure for the BZJ Group for the years ended 31 December 20X5 and 20X4, assuming that there was no change in the number of ordinary shares in issue during 20X4. **(3 marks)**

(b) Produce a report for the investor that:

(i) analyses a nd interprets the financial statements of the BZJ Group, commenting upon the group's performance and position; **(17 marks)**

(ii) discusses the extent to which the chairman's comments about the potential for improved future performance are supported by the financial statement information for the year ended 31 December 20X5. **(5 marks)**

(Total marks = 25)

? Question 27

Spreader is a UK parent company with a number of wholly owned subsidiaries in Asia and Europe. Extracts from the consolidated financial statements of the group for the year ended 30 April 20X7 are given below.

Income statement – year ended 30 April

	20X7	*20X6*
	$'000	$'000
Revenue (note 1)	50,000	48,000
Cost of sales	(25,000)	(22,000)
Gross profit	25,000	26,000
Other operating expenditure	(15,000)	(14,200)
Operating profit	10,000	11,800
Interest payable	(1,000)	(900)
Profit before taxation (note 2)	9,000	10,900
Taxation	(2,800)	(3,600)
Profit for the period	6,200	7,300

Notes

1. *Analysis of turnover for the year by geographical segment*

	Spreader		*Asia*		*Europe*		*Total*	
	20X7	*20X6*	*20X7*	*20X6*	*20X7*	*20X6*	*20X7*	*20X6*
	$'000	$'000	$'000	$'000	$'000	$'000	$'000	$'000
Total revenue	15,000	20,000	10,000	8,000	30,000	25,000	55,000	53,000
Inter-segment revenue	(2,000)	(2,500)	(1,000)	(500)	(2,000)	(2,000)	(5,000)	(5,000)
Revenue from third parties	13,000	17,500	9,000	7,500	28,000	23,000	50,000	48,000

2. *Analysis of profit before tax for the year by geographical segments*

	Spreader		*Asia*		*Europe*		*Total*	
	20X7	*20X6*	*20X7*	*20X6*	*20X7*	*20X6*	*20X7*	*20X6*
	$'000	$'000	$'000	$'000	$'000	$'000	$'000	$'000
Segment profit	3,000	6,000	1,500	1,200	6,000	5,000	10,500	12,200
Common costs							(500)	(400)
Operating profit							10,000	11,800
Interest payable							(1,000)	(900)
Profit before taxation							9,000	10,900

3. *Analysis of net assets at end of year by geographical segment*

	Spreader		*Asia*		*Europe*		*Total*	
	20X7	*20X6*	*20X7*	*20X6*	*20X7*	*20X6*	*20X7*	*20X6*
	$'000	$'000	$'000	$'000	$'000	$'000	$'000	$'000
Segment net assets	15,000	13,500	6,000	5,000	20,000	20,000	41,000	38,500
Unallocated assets							2,000	1,800
Total net assets							43,000	40,300

4. *Dividends*

Amounts paid were: 20X7 $3 million; 20X6 $3.2 million.

Requirements

In your capacity as chief accountant of Spreader:

(a) prepare a report for the board of directors of the company which analyses the results of the group for the year ended 30 April 20X7; **(21 marks)**

(b) explain why the segmental data which has been included in the extracts may need to be interpreted with caution. **(4 marks)**

(Total marks = 25)

Question 28

You are the accounting adviser to a committee of bank lending officers. Each loan application is subject to an initial vetting procedure, which involves the examination of the application, recent financial statements, and a set of key financial ratios.

The key ratios are as follows:

- Gearing (calculated as debt/debt + equity, where debt includes both long- and short-term borrowings);
- Current ratio;
- Quick ratio;
- Profit margin (using profit before tax).

Existing levels of gearing are especially significant to the decision, and the committee usually rejects any application from an entity with gearing of over 45%.

The committee will shortly meet to conduct the initial vetting of a commercial loan application made by TYD, an unlisted entity. As permitted by national accounting law in its country of registration, TYD does not comply in all respects with International Financial Reporting Standards. The committee has asked you to interview TYD's finance director to determine areas of non-compliance. As a result of the interview, you have identified two significant areas for examination in respect of TYD's financial statements for the year ended 30 September 20X6.

1. Revenue for the period includes a sale of inventories at cost to HPS, a banking institution, for $85,000, which took place on 30 September 20X6. HPS has an option under the contract of sale to require TYD to repurchase the inventories on 30 September 20X8, for $95,000. TYD has derecognised the inventories at their cost of $85,000, with a charge to cost of sales of this amount. The inventories concerned in this transaction, are, however, stored on TYD's premises, and TYD bears the cost of insuring them.
2. Some categories of TYD's inventories are sold on a sale or return basis. The entity's accounting policy in this respect is to recognise the sale at the point of despatch of goods. The standard margin on sales of this type is 20%. During the year ended 30 September 20X6, $100,000 (in sales value) has been despatched in this way. The finance director estimates that approximately 60% of this value represents sales that have been accepted by customers; the remainder is potentially subject to return.

The financial statements of TYD for the year ended 30 September 20X6 are as presented below. (Note: at this stage of the analysis only one year's figures are considered).

TYD: Income statement for the year ended 30 September 20X6

	$'000
Revenue	600
Cost of sales	450
Gross profit	150
Expenses	63
Finance costs	17
Profit before tax	70
Income tax expense	25
Profit for the period	45

TYD: Statement of changes in equity for the year ended 30 September 20X6

	Share capital	*Retained earnings*	*Total*
	$'000	$'000	$'000
Balances at 1 October 20X5	100	200	300
Profit for the period	45	45	45
Balances at 30 September 20X6	100	245	345

TYD: Statement of financial position at 30 September 20X6

	$'000	$'000
ASSETS		
Non-current assets:		
Property, plant and equipment		527
Current assets:		
Inventories	95	
Trade receivables	72	
Cash	6	
		173
		700
EQUITY AND LIABILITIES		
Equity:		
Called up share capital	100	
Retained earnings	245	
		345

Non-current liabilities:		
Long-term borrowings		180
Current liabilities:		
Trade and other payables	95	
Bank overdraft	80	
		175
		700

Requirements

Prepare a report to the committee of lending officers that

(i) discusses the accounting treatment of the two significant areas identified in the interview with the FD, with reference to the requirements of International Financial Reporting Standards (IFRS) and to fundamental accounting principles; **(8 marks)**

(ii) calculates any adjustments to the financial statements that are required in order to bring them into compliance with IFRS (ignore tax); **(5 marks)**

(iii) analyses and interprets the financial statements, calculating the key ratios before and after adjustments, and making a recommendation to the lending committee on whether or not to grant TYD's application for a commercial loan. **(12 marks)**

(Total marks = 25)

Question 29

The directors of DPC, a listed entity, have been approached by three out of the five shareholders of PPS, an unlisted competitor. The PPS shareholders are nearing retirement age, and would like to realise their investment in the business. The two remaining shareholders do not object, but would like to retain between them at least a significant influence over the business.

The directors of DPC are currently concerned about the threat of a takeover bid for DPC itself. Although they would like to acquire an interest in PPS as it would help them to increase DPC's market share, they do not want to take any action that would adversely affect their financial statements and certain key accounting ratios (EPS, gearing [calculated as debt/equity], and non-current asset turnover).

There are two possibilities for consideration:

1. DPC could purchase 40% of the ordinary shares of PPS, giving it significant influence, but not control. The cost of this would be $3.5 million, to be settled in cash. DPC would pay $1 million out of its cash resources and would increase its existing long-term borrowings for the balance.
2. DPC could purchase 60% of the ordinary shares of PPS, giving it control. The cost of this would be $6 million, to be settled in cash. DPC would pay $3 million out of its cash resources, and would increase its existing long-term borrowings for the balances.

The purchase would take place on the first day of the new financial year, 1 January 20X8. Projected summary income statements for the 20X8 financial year, and projected summary statement of financial position at 31 December 20X8 are shown below. The DPC figures are consolidated to include its existing 100% held subsidiaries (it currently holds no interests in associates). The projected financial statements for PPS are for that entity alone.

Summary projected income statements for the year ended 31 December 20X8

	DPC consolidated Projected: 20X8	*PPS entity Projected: 20X8*
	$'000	$'000
Revenue	60,300	10,200
All expenses including income tax	(55,300)	(9,500)
Profit for the period attributable to equity holders	5,000	700

Summary projected statements of financial position at 31 December 20X8

	DPC consolidated Projected: 20X8	*PPS entity Projected: 20X8*	
	$'000	$'000	Notes
Non-current assets	50,400	9,800	2
Current assets	82,000	16,000	
	132,400	25,800	
Equity	31,400	4,000	3 & 4
Long-term liabilities	10,000	9,300	
Current liabilities	91,000	12,500	
	132,400	25,800	

Notes:

1. DPC's consolidated projected financial statements at 31 December 20X8 do not take into account the proposed acquisition of PPS.
2. DPC's non-current asset figure includes goodwill on acquisition of various subsidiaries.
3. PPS's equity comprises 100,000 ordinary shares of $1 each, $3,200,000 of retained earnings brought forward on 1 January 20X8 and $700,000 profit for the period.
4. DPC will have 10 million ordinary shares of $1 each on 1 January 20X8. No issues of shares will be made during 20X8.

Requirements

(a) Prepare draft projected financial statements for the DPC group for the year ending 31 December 20X8 under each of the following assumptions.

   (i) DPC acquires 40% of the ordinary shares of PPS on 1 January 20X8;

   (ii) DPC acquires 60% of the ordinary shares of PPS on 1 January 20X8.

   It can be assumed that no impairment of either investment would have taken place by 31 December 20X8. **(14 marks)**

(b) Calculate EPS, gearing and non-current asset turnover ratios based on the draft projected 31 December 20X8 financial statements for:

   (i) DPC and its existing subsidiaries;

   (ii) DPC including the acquisition of an associate interest in PPS;

   (iii) DPC including the acquisition of a subsidiary interest in PPS. **(6 marks)**

(c) Discuss the differences in the accounting ratios under the different scenarios, identifying reasons for the most significant differences. **(5 marks)**

(Total marks = 25)

 Question 30

You are the assistant to the Chief Financial Officer (CFO) of ABC, a light engineering business based in Bolandia. ABC, a listed entity, has expanded over the last few years with the successful introduction of innovative new products. In order to further expand its product range and to increase market share, it has taken over several small, unlisted, entities within its own country.

ABC's directors have recently decided to expand their markets by taking over entities based in neighbouring countries. As the first step in the appraisal of available investment opportunities the CFO has asked you to prepare a brief report on the position and performance of three possible takeover targets: entity W based in Winlandia, entity Y based in Yolandia and entity Z based in Zeelandia. These three countries share a common currency with Bolandia, and all three target entities identify their principal activity as being the provision of light engineering products and services. The report is to comprise a one page summary of key data and a brief written report providing an initial assessment of the targets. The format of the summary is to be based upon the one generally used by ABC for its first-stage assessment of takeover targets, but with the addition of:

(i) price/earnings ratio information (because all three target entities are listed in their own countries), and
(ii) so me relevant country-specific information.

You have produced the one-page summary of key data, given below, together with comparative information for ABC itself, based on its financial statements for the year ended 31 March 20X6.

	ABC	**W**	**Y**	**Z**
Country of operation	Bolandia	Winlandia	Yolandia	Zeelandia
Date of most recent annual report	31 March 20X6	31 January 20X6	30 June 20X5	30 June 20X5
Financial statements prepared in compliance with:	IFRS	IFRS	Yolandian GAAP	IFRS
Revenue	\$263.4m	\$28.2m	\$24.7m	\$26.3m
Gross profit margin	19.7%	16.8%	17.3%	21.4%
Operating profit margin	9.2%	6.3%	4.7%	8.3%
Return on total capital employed	11.3%	7.1%	6.6%	12.3%
Equity	\$197.8m	\$13.6m	\$14.7m	\$16.7m
Long-term borrowings	\$10.4m	\$6.2m	\$1.3m	\$0.6m
Average interest rate applicable to long-term borrowings by listed entities	7.5%	6%	8%	10%
Income tax rate	30%	28%	31%	38%
Inventories turnover	47 days	68 days	52 days	60 days
Receivables turnover	44 days	42 days	46 days	47 days
Payables turnover	46 days	50 days	59 days	73 days
Current ratio	1.4:1	0.7:1	1.1:1	0.9:1
P/E ratio	18.6	12.6	18.3	15.2

ABC has a cash surplus and would seek to purchase outright between 90% and 100% of the share capital of one of the three entities. The entity's directors do not intend to increase the gearing of the group above its existing level. Upon acquisition they would, as far as possible, retain the entity's management and its existing product range. However, they would also seek to extend market share by introducing ABC's own products.

Requirements

Prepare a report to accompany the summary of key data. The report should:

(a) Analyse the key data, comparing and contrasting the potential takeover targets with each other and with ABC itself. **(13 marks)**

(b) Discuss the extent to which the entities can be validly compared with each other, identifying the limitations of inter-firm and international comparisons. **(12 marks)**

(Total marks = 25)

Solutions to Revision Questions

Section A

Solution 1

(a) Consolidated current assets are \$400,000 + \$350,000 − \$40,000 + \$15,000 (cash in transit) = \$725,000.

Consolidated current liabilities are \$250,000 + \$100,000 − \$25,000 = \$325,000.

(b) The consolidated reserves are as follows:

	\$'000
Retained earnings of Peter as given	200
Own dividend paid	(40)
Dividend received from Paul	15
Share of post-acquisition retained earnings of Paul	45
[75% (\$180,000 − \$20,000 − \$100,000)]	220

(c)

	\$	\$
1. Adjust earnings:		
Earnings as stated		100,000
Interest saving:		
Finance cost	6,000	
Tax effect (6,000 × 30%)	(1,800)	
		4,200
Diluted earnings		104,200
2. Diluted ordinary shares		
\$50,000/100 × 12		6,000
Number of ordinary shares in issue		27,000
		33,000

Basic eps 5 10Diluted eps = 104,200/33,000 = 315.8¢ per share
Diluted eps = 104,200/33,000 = 315.8¢ per share

Solution 2

(a) The investment in Costello will be accounted for as a subsidiary under IAS27 and as such will be fully consolidated. The consideration paid will be compared to the fair value of the net assets acquired and the difference recognised as goodwill on acquisition.

The goodwill on consolidation is \$62 m − 80% (\$50 m + \$5 m + \$10 m) = \$10 million plus goodwill on non-controlling interest of \$1.3 m (\$6.2 m − 20% NA of \$52 m).

The total $11.3 of goodwill will be included in non-current assets in the consolidated statement of financial position.

The brand name is included within the goodwill figure rather than dealt with as a separate asset because it has no readily ascertainable market value.

(b) We can show the corrected post-acquisition reserves of Costello in the following table:

	Year end date	*Acquisition date*	*Post-acquisition*
	$'000	$'000	$'000
Share capital	25,000	25,000	
Retained earnings:			
Per accounts of Costello	35,000	25,000	
Contingent gain adjustment	–	5,000	
Property, plant and equipment adjustment	6,000	10,000	
Brand valuation adjustment	–	–	
	66,000	65,000	1,000

So the consolidated reserves are:

	$'000
Abbott	60,000
Costello (80% × $1,000,000)	800
	60,800

Solution 3

(a) Intra-group sales are eliminated in full from consolidated turnover and cost of sales. Recorded as:

Dr	Revenue	$6m
Cr	Cost of sales	$6m

Being elimination of intra-group sales

(b) The adjustment to gross profit is the *movement in* the provision for unrealised profit between the beginning and end of the year. This is 20% ($1,200,000 − $750,000) = $90,000. This will be charged to cost of sales and will therefore reduce gross profit by $90,000, recorded as:

Dr	Cost of sales/GP	$90,000
Cr	Inventories	$90,000

Being elimination of unrealised profit on inventories.

(c) The consolidated reserves of the Tea group are:

	$'000
Reserves of Tea	6,000
75% of reserves of Cup	3,000
75% of provision for unrealised profit ($1,200,000 × 20% × 75%)	(180)
	8,820

Solution 4

The effective interest of Frank in Sammy is 40% (2/3 × 60%). The effective date of acquisition is 31 December 20W5, when the accumulated profits of Sammy stood at $12 million.

The summary statement of financial position for the group as at 31 December 20X0 would be as follows:

	$000
ASSETS	
Goodwill on acquisition (W1)	733
Net assets ($40,000 + $30,000 + $32,000)	115,000
	115,733
EQUITY AND LIABILITIES	
Ordinary share capital	30,000
Retained earnings (W2)	48,733
	78,733
Non-controlling interest (W3)	37,000
	115,733

(W1) – **Goodwill on acquisition**

	$000	$000
Consideration transferred		32,000
Less net assets acquired:		
Dean – share capital	30,000	
Retained earnings at 20W5	22,000	
Less cost of investment in Sammy	(24,300)	
	27,700	
Group share 2/3		(18,467)
Sammy – share capital	20,000	
Retained earnings at 20W5	12,000	
	32,000	
Effective group share 40%		(12,800)
Goodwill on acquisition		733

(W2) – **Retained earnings**

	Frank $000	Dean $000	Sammy $000
Per SOFP 20X0	42,000	24,300	25,000
At acquisition	–	(22,000)	(12,000)
		2,300	
Group share of Dean	1,533		13,000
Effective share of Sam	5,200		
Consolidated	48,733		

(W3) – **Non-controlling interest**

NCI in Dean 1/3 × ($54,300 – cost of investment in Sammy $24,300)	= $10,000
NCI in Sammy (based on effective holdings) 60% × $45,000	= $27,000
Total	$37,000

Solution 5

(a) The dividends paid to non-controlling interest is:

	$m
Opening balance	50
Profit for the year	25
Increase due to acquisition ($100m × 20%)	20
Dividend paid (balancing figure)	**(15)**
Closing balance	80

The dividend paid to non-controlling interest will be included as an outflow under the heading 'cash flows from financing activities'. It will be shown separately from dividends paid to equity shareholders.

(b) The cash outflow is the *cash* paid ($20 million) *plus* the net bank overdrafts acquired ($10 million). Total: $30 million. This will be included as an outflow under the heading 'cash flows from investing activities'.

(c) The purchase of non-current assets is as follows:

	$m
Opening balance	10
Non-current of sub acquired	3
	13
depreciation	(2.6)
	10.4
Closing balance	14
Balancing fig is purchase of NCA	3.6

Solution 6

Memorandum

To: Assistant accountant
From: Management accountant
Date: 9 January 20X7

Accounting year ended 30 June 20X6 – adjustments to draft financial statements

The following are my views on how to correctly treat each of the transactions below.

(a) *Elimination of unrealised profits (IAS 27)*

Under IAS 27, all unrealised profits on inventory transferred between group companies at a market price must be eliminated as these can be realised only on their subsequent disposal to a third party. However, the IAS insists that the full amount of unrealised profit be eliminated from inventories with the minority shareholders being charged with their share.

The double entry would be recorded as follows:

Debit	Non-controlling interests	$2 m
	Retained earnings	$8 m
Credit	Inventory	$10 m

(b) *Intangible assets (IAS 38)*

A number of entities in the past have recorded brands on their statements of financial position but mostly when they have been acquired from other companies as a result of an acquisition.

IAS 38 states that internally generated goodwill, brands and other similar items should not be recognised as assets.

Solution 7

(a) The accounting treatment of joint ventures is set out in IAS 31 *Interests in Joint Ventures*. The treatment in the consolidated accounts depends on whether the form of the joint venture is that the venture comprises:

- jointly controlled operations
- jointly controlled assets
- jointly controlled entities.

The agreement with Pills appears to establish jointly controlled assets. The venture has no separate business of its own but both Textures and Pills have, on a 50:50 basis, contributed assets to it. Under these conditions each venturer will, in its individual financial statements, recognise its share of the assets and liabilities of the joint venture. These amounts will be classified according to the nature of the assets and liabilities. Since all assets are jointly controlled, \$150,000 will be included in non-current assets and \$15,000 in current assets. The treatment in the consolidated financial statements will be identical.

The agreement with Eduaid and Bracos establishes a jointly controlled entity. In the individual financial statements of the investors the amounts that have been contributed to the joint venture will be shown as an investment. In the consolidated financial statements the interest in the joint venture will be proportionally consolidated, irrespective of the actual amounts invested by each investor. Therefore, Textures will include \$2,250,000 (30% × \$7,500,000) in non-current assets and \$330,000 (30% × \$1,100,000) in current assets.

Solution 8

(a) The objective of IFRS3 is to ensure that when a business entity is acquired by another, all the assets and liabilities that existed in the acquired entity at the date of acquisition are recorded at fair values reflecting their condition at that date. The difference between the fair values of the net assets and the cost of the acquisition is recognised as goodwill or negative goodwill.

There is therefore a clear need for guidance as to which assets and liabilities would be permitted to be included in a fair value exercise and how these would be valued. This should help to ensure consistency and comparability in the calculations of fair values.

(b) The main relevant provisions of IFRS3 are as follows:

1. The assets and liabilities of a subsidiary acquires should be valued at their fair values. However, only those assets/liabilities that existed at the date of acquisition should be recognised. No attempt should be made to provide for any liability which would result from the acquirer's future intentions for the acquiree.
2. The acquiree should be valued using the acquirer's accounting policies.
3. The fair value of liabilities should also exclude provisions for future operating losses and reorganisation/restructuring costs.
4. The method of calculation of assets should be as follows:
   Non-monetary assets at lower of replacement cost or recoverable amount reflecting the current condition of the assets.

Monetary assets should be based on amounts expected to be received with the possibility of discounting long-term assets to their present value.

5. The fair value of the purchase consideration should represent the actual cash paid plus the present value of any deferred consideration plus the market value of the shares taken up on acquisition.

Solution 9

(a) The bond is repayable and so contains a present obligation to transfer future economic benefit, it is therefore a financial liability. In accordance with IAS 39 it will be held at amortised cost using the effective interest rate. The effective rate of interest attached to the zero-coupon bond is:

$$\$\frac{10,000,000}{14,025,245} = 0.713 = 7\%(\text{using PV tables})$$

Year	*Carrying value of instrument at 1 Jan.*	*Income statement charge*	*Carrying value of instrument at 31 Dec.*
	$	$	$
1	10,000,000	700,000 (7%)	10,700,000
2	10,700,000	749,000 (7%)	11,449,000

(b) This instrument is a hybrid, containing both a liability and an equity component. IAS 32 requires that the elements be recorded separately. The liability should be recorded at the value that is equivalent to the PV of a similar instrument that does not have conversion rights and then the difference is accounted for as equity.

It will be recorded as:

Dr	Bank	$6,000,000
Cr	Non-current liabilities (W1)	$5,681,520
Cr	Other reserves (within equity)	$641,520

Being the initial recording of the convertible instrument.

(W1) *Fair value of equivalent non-convertible instrument*
Simple rate for 3 years at 6% = 0.840
Cumulative rate for 3 years at 6% = 2.673

	$000
PV of principal repayable 31/12/X3	5,040,000
(3,000 × $2,000 × 0.840)	
PV of interest annuity for 3 years	641,520
	5,681,520
Equity element (balancing figure)	318,480
Total consideration received	6,000,000

Solution 10

(a) The weighted average of ordinary shares in issue:

To 30 September 20X4: 5,700,000 × 8/12	3,800,000
From 30 September 20X4 to 31 January 20X5: 6,900,000 × 4/12	2,300,000
	6,100,000

Earnings attributable to ordinary shareholders = \$1,750,000 − \$200,000 (preference share dividend) = \$1,550,000.

$$\text{Earnings per share} = \frac{\$1,550,000}{6,100,000} = 25.4¢$$

(b) 20X3 EPS as originally stated:

Shares in issue at 1 April 20X2	3,000,000
1 October 20X2: bonus issue 1 for 4	750,000
	3,750,000

$$\text{ESP} = \frac{810,000}{3,750,000} = 21.6¢$$

Restatement of 20X3 figure shown as comparative in the 20X4 financial statements – the 20X3 figure should be adjusted by the inverse of the bonus fraction.

Bonus fraction = 4/3
Inverse of bonus fraction = 3/4;
Restated EPS:3/4 × 21.6¢ = 16.2¢

(c) Theoretical ex-rights fair value per share:

	\$
6 shares at \$1.90	11.40
1 new share at \$1.62	1.62
	13.02

Theoretical ex-rights fair value per share: \$13.02/7 = \$1.86 per share.

$$\text{Bonus fraction} = \frac{\text{Fair value of one share prior to rights issue}}{\text{theoreticalex-rights fair value per share}} = \frac{1.90}{1.86}$$

1 October-1 Feb.: 4/12 × 1.90/1.86 × 3,000,000	1,021,505
1 Feb.–30 September: 8/12 × 3,500,000	2,333,333
	3,354,838

Solution 11

The substance of the transaction is that Jake has borrowed \$5 million against the security of a piece of freehold land. The land will be repurchased by Jake and the price it will pay increases over time. In this case, the increase each year in the repayable amount reflects an interest charge. IAS 39 *Financial Instruments: Recognition and Measurement* requires initial recognition of the liability, and the related interest expense should be recognised over the relevant period. This is accounted for in the year ended 31 January 20X5 as follows:

	\$'000	\$'000
DR Suspense account	5,000	
CR Non-current liabilities		5,000
DR Interest expense for year (\$6 m − 5 m)	1,000	
CR Non-current liabilities		1,000

The preference shares issued, while non-redeemable, contain a present obligation to transfer future economic benefit as the dividend is cumulative and will ultimately be paid. In accordance with IAS 32, the shares will therefore be included as a liability in the financial statements. IAS 39 requires that financial liabilities be initially recorded at the net proceeds ie total proceeds less transaction costs. The debit to share premium will be reversed and the shares recorded as:

Dr	Suspense	$10,000,000
Cr	Non-current liabilities	$9,950,000
Cr	Share premium	$50,000

Solution 12

This is an example of a fair value hedge. Black have entered into a hedging arrangement as it wants to minimise the risk of the value of the AFS investment falling as a result of a fall in value of the share price.

In 20X7 the available for sale asset is recorded as normal with the gain of $200,000 being recorded in reserves, in accordance with IAS 39:

Dr	Available for sale investment	$200,000
Dr	Other reserves	$200,000

This gain of $200,000 will be shown within other comprehensive income for the year ended 31 December 20X7.

In 20X8 an effective hedge exists to cover any fall in the value of the shares due to general market conditions. The derivative has a positive value and is therefore an asset held at fair value through profit or loss. This hedged item is the AFS but only the effective part of the hedge can be offset in the income statement. Any effective part or any loss not covered by hedge is recorded according to the normal rules for the available for sale asset, ie to reserves. The recording for 20X8 is:

Dr	Financial asset – derivative	$250,000
Cr	Gain on derivative (IS)	$250,000

Being the accounting for the derivative

Dr	Loss on hedged investment	$250,000
Dr	Other reserves	$20,000
Cr	Available for sale investment	$270,000

Being the accounting for the AFS investment

Solution 13

(a)

Memorandum

To: Assistant accountant

From: Management accountant

Date:

Subject: Financial instruments – preference shares

Preference shares are, in substance, similar to a debt instrument. They are issued on the understanding that they will receive a fixed dividend and will be redeemed at a specified amount on an agreed date. It is likely that IAS 32 would require these instruments to be recognised as a financial liability.

In the income statement, the finance charge should be calculated as the effective rate applied to the carrying value of the instrument. However, this charge represents the difference between the net proceeds and the total payments made during the life of the instrument. It will therefore incorporate not only interest charges but also the initial issue expenses, as well as any premiums payable at the end of the instrument's life.

The carrying value of the non-equity shares will increase each year by the difference between the effective interest charge and the dividends paid in cash. At the end of the instrument's life the amount outstanding on the statement of financial position should therefore represent the cash that must be paid to extinguish the full debt at the time.

Signed: Management accountant

(b) Short – finance cost for each of the 5 years to 30 September 20X8

	$'m	$'m
Total payments over the life of the instrument		
10m × $1.35		13.5
Dividends 0.4m × 5 years		2.0
		15.5
Net proceeds		
Proceeds on issue	10.0	
Less issue costs	0.1	
		9.9
Finance charge		5.6

The spreading of the annual finance cost is as follows:

	Opening balance	*Finance charge (10%)*	*Dividend cash flow*	*Closing balance*
	$'000	$'000	$'000	$'000
20X4	9,900	990	(400)	10,490
20X5	10,490	1,049	(400)	11,139
20X6	11,139	1,114	(400)	11,853
20X7	11,853	1,185	(400)	12,638
20X8	12,638	1,262*	(400)	13,500 redeemed
		5,600	2,000	

(*rounding)

 **Solution 14**

The amended version of IAS 19 permits alternative approaches in accounting for actuarial gains and losses:

1. The first option is the accounting treatment that was required by the original IAS 19. Actuarial gains and losses are not recognised immediately in the income statement except where they exceed certain parameters. Where the parameters in the standard are met, the gain or loss is recognised over the average remaining service lives of the employees. This may be a fairly lengthy period (for example, 10 or 15 years would not be unusual), so, even if the actuarial loss of $7.2 million were to exceed the parameters, the impact on the financial statements is likely to be very small.

   Where this option requires part of the loss to be recognised, it is recognised in the income statement, and so has a direct effect upon reported profit.

2. The standard permits entities to adopt any systematic method that results in faster recognition of actuarial gains and loss than stipulated in the first approach, provided that the same basis is applied to both gains and losses, and that the basis is applied consistently. Thus, entities are able to opt for a policy of recognising the whole of any actuarial gains or losses in the accounting period in which they occur. In CBA's case this would mean recognising the full amount of the $7.2 million loss in the financial year ended 30 September 20X6. In such cases (where actuarial gains and losses are recognised in full as they are incurred), the standard requires that such gains and losses should be recognised in a 'Other Comprehensive Income', within the statement of comprehensive income.

Solution 15

To: The board of directors of S
From: Management accountant
Subject: The determination of the economic substance of a transaction
Date: 25 November 20X8

(a) The substance of a transaction is determined by its likely effect on the assets and liabilities of the entity. A number of different scenarios are possible.
   (i) *An asset is created.* An asset must meet the definition provided in the IASB *Framework*, that is, the transaction will result in the creation of future economic benefits controlled by the entity as a result of a past transaction or event.
   (ii) *It is probable that future economic benefits will materialise.* If it is only possible that future benefits will materialise, then an asset would not be created even if it is likely that it may ultimately realise benefits to the reporting entity. (For example, revenue investments such as advertising, training, maintenance are expensed not capitalised.)
   (iii) *The cost or value of the asset can be reliably measured.* In order for an asset to be capitalised it must have a cost/value that can be reliably measured. For example, a home-grown brand may not pass the test.

   An additional aspect of applying the IASB *Framework* is considering to which party the 'risks' of ownership of the asset are attached. It is regarded as a 'significant indicator' of the party controlling the asset.

   Subsequently, the asset will be removed from the statement of financial position if the 'risks and rewards' of ownership are transferred to another party, that is, the asset is derecognised.

   If the risks and rewards are shared between two parties then the asset description and value may need to be changed. This occurs in a 'linked presentation' situation, for example, factoring of receivables, whereby advance non-returnable proceeds are paid to the original selling company. The proceeds are netted off on the face of the statement of financial position, usually in a boxed format.

(b) The appropriate accounting treatment of factoring depends on who bears the risks and rewards of ownership in the factoring contract. Questions such as who bears the risks of slow payments or bad debts and will the seller have to repay monies advanced by the factor must be answered.

   The terms of the agreement between S and F need to be investigated as follows:

(i) F only takes receivables after credit approval – risk is still with S.
(ii) Any debts not collected by F within 90 days are regarded as bad and reassigned to S with any advanced payments being recovered – risk is with S.
(iii) F charges interest, calculated on a daily basis on the outstanding balance – cost to S.
(iv) F administers the scheme and collects its fee from cash received from receivables – clearly a reward to F but little risk and S pays the cost.

In summary, it would appear that the seller, S, carries all the risks since there is a full recourse by F to S for any bad debts and slow payments. F is providing a loan to S on the security of its receivables. Legal title may have passed but the commercial reality of the transaction is that the receivables should be disclosed as an asset of S until such time as they are cleared by a payment to F. The amount advanced by F should be disclosed as a liability. The cost of interest, administration and bad debts suffered by S should be disclosed on the face of the income statement.

Solution 16

Issue (a)

The loan is a monetary liability in the statement of financial position of Ant and IAS 21 – *The Effects of Changes in Foreign Exchange Rates* – requires that monetary items be translated at the rate of exchange in force at the year end date. This would mean restating the loan from its original carrying value of $25 million (40 m Francos/1.6) to $26,666,667 (40 m Francos/1.5). The resulting exchange loss of $1,666,667 would be reported in the income statement as a financing item.

The net assets of the subsidiary would be translated using the rate of exchange in force at the year end date because the subsidiary is relatively independent of the parent on a day-to-day basis. Because the net assets of the subsidiary are the same as the loan balance, its closing dollar value would also be $26,666,667. There would be an exchange gain of $1,666,667 on the retranslation of the opening net assets which IAS 21 would require is taken to equity.

Where a foreign currency loan is used to finance a foreign currency equity investment then IAS 21 requires a form of hedge accounting to be used in the consolidated financial statements (as well as in the financial statements of the parent). Exchange differences arising on a monetary item that, in substance, forms part of the net investment in a foreign entity should be classified as equity until the disposal of the net investments. At that time they should be released to income along with the cumulative exchange differences on the relevant net investments.

The correcting journal entry will be:

DEBIT: Net assets
CREDIT: Long-term loans.

With $1,666,667, no net exchange differences will be reported because the exchanges differences on the loan and the net investment are both taken to equity and they are equal and opposite.

Issue (b)

The loan is a compound financial instrument and IAS 32 – *Financial Instruments: Presentation* – requires that such instruments be classified in two component parts in the statement of financial position of the issuer. This requirement is unaffected by the likelihood or otherwise that the holders of the instrument will exercise their conversion options. In this case, we are provided with the fair value of the option element (which does not change over the period) so the loan element can be derived by deducting the option element from the total initial carrying value of the instrument.

IAS 39 – *Financial Instruments: Recognition and Measurement* requires that financial liabilities should be initially measured at 'cost'. Cost is the proceeds received minus the issue costs. Therefore, in this case 'cost' is $175.5 million ($180 million – $4.5 m). The loan element of the instrument is $153 million ($175.5 m – $22.5 m). Since the loan is a held to maturity financial liability it should subsequently be re-measured at amortised cost using the effective interest method to measure the annual finance cost. The finance cost should be a constant percentage of the outstanding loan for each period.

In this case, the percentage can be found from tables:

- The initial loan amount is $153 million (A).
- The terminal loan amount with no interim payments is $270 million (B).
- A/B is 0.567.
- From tables this equates to an annual interest rate of 12%.

Therefore, the finance cost for the first year is $18,360,000 ($153 m × 12%) and the closing loan is $171,360,000. The correcting journal entry that is required is:

	DR	*CR*
	$'000	$'000
Shareholders funds – initial entry	180,000	
Shareholders funds – option element		22,500
Long-term loans		171,360
Income statement – admin expenses		4,500
Income statement – finance cost	18,360	

Solution 17

The charge to the income statement for 20X8 will be:

	$'000	$'000
Ongoing service cost		4,000
Unwinding of the discount	3,600	
Expected return on pension assets	(4,800)	
		(1,200)
Net charge to statement		2,800

The 'corridor' for recognition of actuarial losses from prior years is the greater of:

- 10% of the opening market value of the scheme's assets: $40 m × 10% = $4 m.
- 10% of the opening present value of the scheme's liabilities: $44 m × 10% = $4.4 m.

It is clear that the unrecognised actuarial losses are less than $4.4 million, so no recognition is appropriate for the current year.

The statement of financial position figures for the end of 20X8 will be:

	$'000	$'000
Market value of plan assets	42,000	
Present value of plan liability	(44,000)	
		(2,000)
Actuarial differences not yet taken to the income statement (see below)		600
So net liability		(1,400)

(W) *Actuarial differences*

	$'000
Net difference brought forward ($40 m–$44 m)	(4,000)
Net charge to income statement for the year (see above)	(2,800)
Contributions for the year	3,400
Actuarial difference for the year – to balance	400
Net difference carried forward ($42 m–$45 m)	(3,000)

This means that the end unrecognised actuarial losses at the end of the year are $600,000 ($1,000,000 – $400,000).

Solution 18

(a) In times of increasing prices, historical cost accounting displays the following defects:

(i) Revenues are stated at current values, but they tend to be matched with costs incurred at an earlier date. Therefore, profit is overstated.

(ii) Where historical cost accounting is applied consistently, asset values are stated at cost less accumulated depreciation. Current values of the assets may be considerably in excess of net book value, with the result that the historical cost depreciation charge does not constitute a realistic estimate of the value of the asset consumed.

(iii) By the time monetary liabilities are repayable, the amount of the outflow in current value terms is less than the original inflow. An entity can therefore gain by holding current liabilities, but historical cost accounting does not recognise these gains. The opposite effect is experienced in respect of monetary assets.

(iv) Typically, in a time of rising prices, profits are likely to be overstated, and capital to be understated, thus giving rise to unrealistic measurements of return on capital employed.

(b) The cost of sales adjustment comprises the additional amount of value, over and above value at historical cost, that is consumed at current cost. It represents an additional charge against profits, thus tending to reduce distributable earnings and ensuring that the business conserves the resources that allow it to continue to trade at current levels.

The depreciation adjustment is the difference between the historical cost accounting and current cost depreciation charges. Current cost depreciation is the value of the non-current asset consumption that has taken place during the year. In a time of rising prices it is a more realistic representation of the asset consumption. It tends to reduce distributable profits thus contributing to capital maintenance.

In the case of Do-it, there is a loss on net monetary position. As noted earlier in part (a) holding monetary liabilities in times of rising prices tends to give rise to gains, whereas holding monetary assets produces losses. Do-it appears, therefore, to have an excess of monetary assets over monetary liabilities, as the net effect is a loss.

The recognition of this loss produces a more realistic estimation of distributable profit, and thus contributes to capital maintenance.

Solution 19

The convergence project: progress to date

Traditionally, the US has adopted a 'rule-book' approach to financial reporting standard setting, whereas the approach taken by the IASB, and its predecessor body, has been to encourage adherence to principles. This fundamental difference in approach made it appear, for a long time, as though the US would never accept international standards. However, the rule-book approach was found wanting in a series of financial scandals in the US in the late 1990s and early years of the 21st century. The climate was therefore amenable to a change in approach which would make convergence possible between US and international financial reporting standards.

In September 2002 the US standard setter (Financial Accounting Standards Board – FASB) and the IASB agreed to undertake a project which would have the objective of converging their accounting practices, reducing the number of differences between US GAAP and IFRS. This agreement (the 'Norwalk agreement') committed the parties to making their existing standards fully compatible as soon as practicable, and to co-ordinating their future work programmes. In order to address the first commitment, a short-term project was undertaken to remove some of the differences between existing standards. The second commitment was to be met by collaborating on the development of standards.

A memorandum of understanding between FASB and the IASB sets out a 'Roadmap of Convergence between IFRS and US GAAP 2006–8'. This is aimed at removing the need for reconciliation to US GAAP requirement for those companies that use IFRS and are registered in the USA.

Progress to date has been impressive. Projects undertaken jointly between FASB and IASB have produced the following:

- IFRS 5 *Non-current Assets Held for Sale and Discontinued Operations*
- IFRS 3 *Business combinations*
- IFRS 8 *Operating Segments*
- IAS 1 *Presentation of Financial Statements: a revised presentation*

There are several on-going projects that will run into the longer-term. For example, the amendment to IAS 1 noted above represents just a first phase in a larger project on financial statement presentation. Subsequent phases will address fundamental issues in presenting information and the issue of interim reporting.

Other longer-term projects include convergence of the conceptual frameworks and revenue recognition.

Finally, despite the high level of activity on convergence, it should be noted that many significant differences remain between US GAAP and IFRS.

Solution 20

Arguments against voluntary disclosures by businesses in respect of their environmental policies, impacts and practices might include the following principal points:

The traditional view of the corporation is that it exists solely to increase shareholder wealth. In this view business executives have no responsibility to broaden the scope or nature of their reporting as doing so reduces returns to shareholders (because there is a cost associated with additional reporting).

From a public policy perspective, if governments wish corporations and similar entities to bear the responsibility for their environmental impacts, they should legislate accordingly. In the absence of such legislation, however, businesses bear no responsibility for environmental impacts, and in consequence there is no reporting responsibility either.

Voluntary disclosures of any type are of limited usefulness because they are not readily comparable with those of other entities. Therefore, it is likely that the costs of producing such disclosures outweigh the benefits to stakeholders.

The audit of voluntary disclosures is not regulated. Even where such disclosures are audited, the scope of the audit may be relatively limited, and moreover, its scope may not be clearly laid out in the voluntary report. Voluntary reports are not necessarily, therefore, reliable from a stakeholder's point of view.

Especially where voluntary disclosures are included as part of the annual report package, there is a risk of information overload: stakeholders are less able to identify in a very lengthy report the information that is relevant and useful to them.

Voluntary disclosures by business organisations, because they are at best lightly regulated, may be treated by the organisation in a cynical fashion as public relations opportunities. The view of the business's activities could very well be biased, but it would be quite difficult for most stakeholders to detect such bias.

It is questionable whether voluntary disclosures about environmental policies, impacts and practices would meet the qualitative characteristics of useful information set out in the IASB's Framework. The key characteristics are: understandability, reliability, relevance and comparability. Voluntary environmental disclosures might well fail to meet any of these characteristics and, if this is the case, it is highly questionable whether or not they merit publication.

Section B Solutions

Solution 21

Requirements

(a) The financial asset falls into the category of loans and receivables, and, according to the standard, should be accounted for using the amortised cost method. The effective interest rate inherent in the financial instrument is used to calculate the annual amount of interest receivable, which is credited to the income statement. If an annual amount of interest is receivable this is credited to the financial asset (with the related debit to cash or receivable).

The other current asset in this case falls into the category of 'held-for-trading' and should be accounted for at fair value through profit and loss account. Where securities are actively traded, the statement of financial position amount (at fair value) is likely to differ from the amount at which the asset was originally recognised. Fair value differences are debited or credited to profit or loss, and appear in the income statement.

(b)

AD: Consolidated statement of financial position as at 30 June 20X6

	$	$
ASSETS		
Non-current assets:		
Property, plant and equipment (1,900 + 680)	2,580,000	
Goodwill (W1)	360,000	
Investment in associate (W5)	106,160	
Financial asset (W2)	1,062,400	
		4,108,560
Current assets:		
Inventories (223 + 127)	350,000	
Trade receivables (204 + 93 − 5)	292,000	
Other current assets (W3)	26,800	
Cash in transit	5,000	
Cash (72 + 28)	100,000	
		773,800
		4,882,360
EQUITY AND LIABILITIES		
Equity:		
Share capital	1,000,000	
Retained earnings (W7)	2,555,240	
		3,555,240
Non-controlling interest (W6)		168,120
Non-current liabilities		600,000
Current liabilities:		
Trade payables (247 + 113)	360,000	
Income tax (137 + 62)	199,000	
		559,000
		4,882,360

Workings

(W1) *Goodwill on acquisition of BE*

	$
Cost of investment	880,000
Less: acquired (300,000 + 350,000) × 80%	(520,000)
	360,000

(W2) *Financial asset*

Calculation of finance charge for year ended 30 June 20X6:

	$
1 July 20X4 Proceeds of instrument	1,000,000
Year 1 finance charge 8%	80,000
Less: interest received ($1,000,000 × 5%)	(50,000)
At 30 June 20X5	1,030,000
Year 2 finance charge ($1,030,000 × 8%)	82,400
Less: interest received ($1,000,000 × 5%)	(50,000)
At 30 June 20X6	1,062,400

The balance is currently stated at $980,000 (i.e., $1,030,000 brought forward less the interest receipt of $50,000). The following adjustment is required:

DR Financial asset	82,400
CR Interest receivable	82,400

The credit to interest receivable increases retained earnings by $82,400 (see W7)

(W3) *Other current assets*

Increase in fair value: 670¢ − 625¢ = 45¢ × 4,000 shares = $1,800

DR Other current assets	1,800
CR Fair value adjustments	1,800

The credit to fair value adjustments increases retained earnings by $1,800 (see W7)

(W4) *Provision for unrealised profit*

Unrealised profit in BE: $10,000 × 30% × 40% = $1,200

This is deducted from the investment in associate (W5). The debit is split between group and minority shares:

	$
Group $1,200 × 80% (W7)	960
Minority $1,200 × 20% (W6)	240
	1,200

(W5) *Investment in associate*

Goodwill on acquisition	$
Investment at cost	104,000
Less: acquired (100,000 + 102,000) × 40%	(80,800)
Goodwill	23,200

The element relating to the non-controlling interest (20%) is excluded: $23,200 × 20% = $4,640

Investment in associate:	$
Cost of investment	104,000
Less: amount of goodwill relating to minority	(4,640)
Add: share of post-acquisition profit ($20,000 × 40%)	8,000
	107,360
Less: PURP (W4)	(1,200)
	106,160

(W6) *Non-controlling interest*

	$	$
Net assets in BE	857,000	
Less: cost of investment in CF	(104,000)	
Add: share of net assets in CF ($222,000 × 40%)	88,800	
	841,800 × 20%	168,360
Less: share of provision for unrealised profit (W5)		(240)
		168,120

(W7) *Retained earnings*

	$
AD's retained earnings	2,300,000
Group share of post-acquisition earnings in BE: ($557,000 − 350,000) × 80%	165,600
Group share of post-acquisition earnings in CF: ($122,000 − 102,000) × 32%	6,400
Financial asset interest credit (W2)	82,400
Fair value increase – other financial asset (W3)	1,800
	2,556,200
Less: group share of provision for unrealised profit (W5)	(960)
	2,555,240

Solution 22

(a) **Rag – memorandum**

To: Assistant accountant
From: Consolidation accountant
Date: 26 May 20X9
Subject: Treatment of Bobtail on consolidation

Assuming that all the shares in Tag and Bobtail carry equal voting rights at general meetings, the structure of the Rag group is as follows:

If Rag is actively involved in Bobtail's strategic decision-making, then a 40% shareholding should give Tag significant influence (per IAS 28) over the operating and financial policies of Bobtail. This means that Bobtail is an associate of Tag, by virtue of its direct shareholding.

Of greater importance to the Rag group is Rag's 30% indirect shareholding in Bobtail, which will need to be included in Rag's consolidated income statement under the equity accounting requirements of IAS 28. It has already been established that Rag has dominant influence over its subsidiary Tag. This means that Rag, indirectly through Tag, has significant influence over Bobtail, thereby making Bobtail an associate of Rag. The proportion of Bobtail's results not belonging to the Rag group will be automatically eliminated as part of the 25% non-controlling interest share of Tag's profits. This will leave the Rag group with its 30% share (75% × 40%) of the results of Bobtail, in accordance with its indirect shareholding. In this way, the significant influence that Rag has over Bobtail is reflected in Rag's consolidated income statement.

Signed: Consolidation accountant

(b) Working schedule for the consolidated income statement for the year ended 31 March 20X9

	Rag	*Tag*		*Group*	*Bobtail*
	$'000	$'000		$'000	$'000
Revenue	65,000	50,000		115,000	100,000
Less: Inter-group	(8,000)			(8,000)	
	57,000	50,000		107,000	
Cost of sales	(35,000)	(28,000)		(63,000)	(82,000)
Less: Inter-group	8,000			8,000	
	(27,000)	(28,000)		(55,000)	
Gross profit	30,000	22,000		52,000	18,000
Provision for unrealised profit on inventory	(20)	(4)		(24)	
	29,980	21,996		51,976	18,000
Other operating expenses	(15,000)	(11,000)		(26,000)	(9,000)
	14,980	10,996		25,976	9,000
Share of associate's operating profit		3,600	(40%)	3,600	
	14,980	14,596		29,576	
Interest payable	(3,200)	(1,800)		(5,000)	
Share of interest payable		(480)	(40%)	(480)	(1,200)
Profit before taxation	11,780	12,316		24,096	7,800
Taxation	(3,600)	(2,800)		(6,400)	
Share of associate's taxation		(960)	(40%)	(960)	(2,400)
Profit for the period	8,180	8,556		16,736	5,400

Workings

1. *Provisions for unrealised profit on inventory*

Rag to Tag and Tag to Bobtail

	Statement of financial position 20X9		*Statement of financial position 20X8*		*Income statement 20X9*	
Tag	2,200 × 1/11	200	1,980 × 1/11	180		20
Bobtail	1,100 = 1/11	100	990 × 1/11	90		10
			90 × 40%	36	× 40%	4

Solution 23

(a) The convertible bond issue is a compound or hybrid financial instrument, according to IAS 32 Financial Instruments: Presentation. It is a hybrid in the sense that is contains both a liability and an equity element. The liability embodies the issuer's obligation to pay interest and to redeem the bond. The equity element comprises the bond holder's right to claim a share of the issuer's equity. The appropriate accounting treatment is to determine the fair value of the liability element and to recognise this as part of liabilities. The residual difference between the proceeds of the instrument and the fair value of the liability portion should be recognised as part of equity.

The IASB Framework includes 'substance over form' as an important characteristic of financial statements. The required treatment of compound financial instruments follows this approach. The form of the convertible bond is that of a liability, but in substance the instrument contains elements of both debt and equity, and both should be recognised. Another important characteristic is 'faithful representation' and the IASB argues that the required accounting treatment in IAS 32 of this type of financial instrument is a more faithful representation.

(b) AX Group: Summary consolidated statement of financial position as at 31 October 20X7

	$'000	*Ref to workings*
ASSETS		
Non-current assets		
Goodwill	4,000	
PPE ($20,000 + $8,900 + $5,000 + $500 − $250 (W3))	34,150	
Current assets ($34,500 + $9,500 + $4,700)	48,700	
	86,850	
EQUITY & LIABILITIES		
Equity		
Called up share capital ($1)	20,000	
Equity component of bond issue	528	
Retained earnings	23,150	
	43,678	
Non-controlling interest	4,400	
Non-current liabilities (9,472 (W6) + 2,400 + 1,000)	12,872	
Current liabilities (18,000 + 5,000 + 2,700 + 400)	25,700	
	86,850	

Workings

1. Goodwill on acquisition

	$'000
Investment in CY	
Cost of investment	8,000
Acquired ($4,000 + $3,500) × 80%	(6,000)
Goodwill	2,000
Less disposed of	(500)
	1,500
Investment in EZ	
Cost of investment	7,500
Acquired ($3,000 + $1,500 + $500 FVA) × 100%	(5,000)
Goodwill	2,500

2. Adjustment to parent's equity on disposal of 20% of shareholding

	$'000
FV of consideration received	(4,000)
Increase in NCI in net assets at disposal date (20% × $11m (W3))	2,200
Adjustment to parent's equity	(1,800)

3. Net assets of CY at disposal date

	$'000
Share capital	(4,000)
Retained earnings at 31 October 20X7	6,500
	10,500)

4. Consolidated retained earnings

	$'000
AX's retained earnings	18,000
Adjustment to parent's equity on disposal of shareholding	1,800
Share of CY's post-acquisition profit ($7,000 − $3,500) × 60%	2,100
Share of EZ's post-acquisition profit ($3,000 − $1,500) × 100%	1,500
Additional depreciation on FV adjustment	(250)
	23,150)

5. Non-controlling interest 40% × $11,000 =$4,400

6. Hybrid financial instrument

	$'000
PV of capital element of bond issue	
Principal $10,000 × 0.816 (from tables)	8,160
Interest ($10,000 × 5%) × 2.624 (from tables)	1,312
Total to be recognised as a long-term liability	9,472
Equity element (balancing figure)	528
Total value of financial instrument	10,000

Solution 24

(a) Holmes: cash flow statement for the year ended 30 September 20X9

	$'m	$'m
Net cash flow from operating activities (W1)		105
Cash flow from investing activities		
Dividends received from associates (W5)	7	
Investment income	6	
Purchase of property, plant and equipment (W6)	(8)	
Sale of property	100	
Purchase of subsidiary (100 − 10)	(90)	
		15
Cash flow from financing activities		
Capital element of finance lease rentals (W7)	(25)	
Repayment of loan	(90)	
		(115)
Increase in cash and cash equivalents in period (W8)		5

Workings

1. *Cash flow from operating activities*

	$'m
Profit before tax from group entities (150 − 50 + 10 other income)	110
Exceptional item	(10)
Finance cost	50
Depreciation	58
Increase in inventory ($15 m − $30 m)	15
Increase in receivables ($20 m − $25 m)	5
Increase in payables ($11 m − $15 m)	(4)
Investment income	(6)
Interest payable	(50)
Dividends paid	
Holmes shareholders	(25)
Non-controlling interest (W3)	(6)
Tax paid (W4)	(32)
	105

2. *Reconciliation of non-controlling interest*

	$'m
Profit for the year	10
Increase due to acquisition of Watson	21
Movement in statement of financial position	(25)
Dividend for the year	6

3. *Cash flow relating to tax*

	$'m
Charge in income statement	35
Movement in liability	
Current	(2)
Deferred	(6)
Arising on acquisition	5
Paid	32

4. *Dividends received from associates*

	$'m
Share of profit after tax	17
Movement in investment	(10)
Dividend received	7

5. *Purchase of property, plant and equipment*

	$'m
Movement in assets	
Owned plant	30
Leased plant	20
Fixtures	–
Acquisitions under finance leases	(40)
Acquired with Watson	(60)
Depreciation	58
Purchased for cash	8

6. *Capital element of finance lease rentals*

	$'m
Increase in liability	
Current	5
Non-current	10
New debt	(40)
Capital repayments	(25)

7. *Increase in cash and cash*

	$'m
Cash in hand	5
Bank overdraft	50
Short-term investments	(50)
	5

(b) **Memorandum**

To: Managing director
From: Management accountant
Date:
Re: Cash flow statements

A cash flow statement is regarded as a key measure of performance. Even though it is often prepared from the other primary statements it presents information that is not readily available from the income statement and the statement of financial position. A particularly important function of the statement is that it shows how the entity has accumulated cash and how that cash has been used. This enables the user to see the extent to which financing and investment have been matched with each other.

Another key factor that makes the cash flow statement extremely useful is that the concept of 'cash flow' is well understood by users. Many users misunderstand the meaning of profit as they do not fully appreciate the matching principle that is involved in arriving at profit for the period. Cash flow, however, is something that is less open to misinterpretation. Therefore it has a key role to play in providing useful financial reports.

Signed: Management accountant

Solution 25

AT Group: consolidated income statement for the year ended 31 March 20X7

	$'000	*Ref to working*
Revenue	3,783	(1)
Cost of sales	(2,800)	(3)
Gross profit	983	
Distribution costs	(141.7)	(4)
Administrative expenses	(473)	(4)
Interest received	2	
Loss on investment in financial asset	(4.2)	(5)
Finance costs	(118.2)	(6)
Share of profit of associate	6.9	(7)
Profit before tax	254.8	
Income tax expense	(94)	(8)
Profit for the period	160.8	

Attributable to:	$'000	*Ref to working*
Equity holders of the parent	141.1	
Non-controlling interest	19.7	(9)
	160.8	

Workings

(W1) – Revenue

	$'000
AT	2,450
BU	1,200
CV (1/3 × 675)	225
	3,875
Less: Intra-group sales of inventories	(80)
Less: Intra-group sales of admin, services	(12)
	3,783

(W2) – Provision for unrealised profit

Closing intra-group inventories = $80,000 × 25% = 20,000.
Unrealised profit = 20% × $20,000 = $4,000.

(W3) – Cost of sales

	$'000
AT	1,862
BU	870
CV (1/3 × 432)	144
	2,876
Add: provision for unrealised profit (W2)	4
Less: Intra-group sales of inventories	(80)
	2,800

(W4) – Distribution costs and administrative expenses

	Distribution costs	*Administrative expenses*
	$'000	$'000
AT	94	280
BU	22	165
CV (1/3 × 77)/(1/3 × 120)	25.7	40
	141.7	485
Less: Intra-group purchases of admin services	–	(12)
	141.7	473

(W5) – Loss on investment in financial asset
Loss on investment in EX: 4,000 shares at (1332¢- 1227¢) = $4,200.

(W6) – Finance costs

Y/e 31 March	*Principal b/fwd*	*Effective interest @ 9%*	*Interest charge*	*C/fwd*
2005	950.0	85.5	(50)	985.5
20X6	985.5	88.7	(50)	1,024.5
20X7	1,024.5	92.2	(50)	1,066.4
2008	1,066.4	96.0	(50)	1,112.4
2009	1,112.4	100.1	(50)	1,162.5

The amount for inclusion in the income statement for the year ended 31 March 20X7 is $92.2 + interest of $26 on short term borrowings. Total = $118.2.

(W7) – Share of profit of associate
Profit after tax × 3/12 × 35% = $79 × 3/12 × 35% = $6.9

(W8) – Income tax

	$'000
AT	40
BU	50
CV (1/3 × 12)	4
	94

(W9) – Non-controlling interest

		6 months to 30 September20X6	*6 months to 31 March 20X7*
Adjusted profit of BU:			
Profit for the period, as stated	95		
Less: provision for unrealised profit	(4)		
	91		
Split 1:1		45.5	45.5
Less: loss on financial asset			(4.2)
		45.5	41.3

Minority share of profit:

6 months to 30 September 20X6:	45.5 × 25%	=	11.4
6 months to 31 March 20X7:	41.3 × 20%	=	8.3
			19.7

Solution 26

(a) Earnings per share for the year ended 31 December 20X4:

$$\frac{\$3{,}676{,}000}{2{,}800{,}000} = 131.3¢ \text{ per share}$$

Earnings per share for the year ended 31 December 20X5:

$$\frac{\$2,460,000}{2,850,000} = 86.3¢ \text{ per share}$$

(W1) Weighted average number of shares in issue

10/12 × 2,800,00	2,333,333
2/12 × 3,100,000	516,667
	2,850,000

(b)

Report

To: Investor
From: Adviser

The financial statements of the BZJ Group for the year ended 31 December 20X5

Financial performance

The performance of the group has declined sharply. Revenue has fallen by 0.8% between 20X4 and 20X5. Gross, operating and pre-tax profit margins are all substantially lower in 20X5 than in the previous year: gross profit has fallen from 15.7% to 14.4%; operating profit has fallen from 5.5% to 4.5%; pre-tax profit margin has fallen from 4.7% to 3.2%. The fall in revenue is particularly striking, given the large amount of investment in non-current assets that has taken place. Margins may have been adversely affected by additional depreciation charges arising because of the increase in non-current assets. It is also possible that the expansion into new markets and the new storage products will result in permanently lower margins. Return on equity (ROE) and return on total capital employed (ROTCE) have both dropped by significant margins: ROE has fallen from 21.5% to 12.0%, and ROTCE has fallen from 15.3% to 8.5%. Investors will be disappointed with the significant drop in the amount of dividend received. The dividend payout ratio is also substantially lower.

The amount of interest payable has increased by over $500,000 during the year, because of the large increase in borrowings intended, according to the chairman's statement, to fund business growth. Interest cover has halved, but the group's current levels of earnings cover the charge 3.7 times, which provides a reasonable margin of safety. However, it is worth noting that the average interest charge (taking interest payable as a percentage of long- and short-term borrowings) is less than 5% in 20X5. This may suggest that borrowings have reached their current level quite recently, and that the interest charge in the 20X6 financial statements will be significantly higher.

The analysis of financial performance suggests that, with falling margins and rising interest, potential returns from the business are likely to be more volatile in future.

Financial position

A very large increase in non-current assets has taken place. The increase of nearly $20 million appears to be mostly accounted for by purchases of new assets, although a revaluation of $2 million has taken place during the financial year. The investment in non-current assets has been financed in part by an increase in long-term borrowings of $10 million, and also by an issue of share capital at a premium which raised $1.5 million in funds. Current liabilities have increased by around $7 million and the business has moved from a position of holding cash at the end of 20X4 to quite substantial short-term borrowings at the end of 20X5.

Inventories have increased by almost $10 million, and the turnover period is much greater at 131.5 days than at the end of 20X4. It could be that the business is building up stocks of its new products; alternatively, it is possible that the new ranges have not sold as well as expected, in which case the build-up of inventories is a worrying sign. Receivables turnover has improved; this is the only element of working capital management that shows any sign of improvement.

The current ratio is probably adequate at its present level, but it, too, shows a significant decline from the previous year.

Even before the current year's expansion programme, gearing was at a high level. It has increased still further to the point where borrowings represent over 80% of equity. The business has no cash at the year end, and it may find that it becomes difficult and expensive to obtain further loan capital. There is an urgent need to improve working capital management and, especially, to start turning over inventories.

Chairman's comments

The chairman refers to 'growth in the business'. However, closer examination of the financial statements shows that the growth is all in statement of financial position items, especially inventories, trade and other payables and non-current assets. The increased investment in fixed and working capital has not, by the 20X5 year end, started to yield any benefits in terms of improved performance; the non-current asset turnover ratio has declined sharply from 4.99 in 20X4 to 2.76 in 20X5. All the performance indicators derived from the income statement are in decline. It is possible that the expansion into new markets and products had not begun to yield benefits by the end of 20X5, but investors and other stakeholders will expect the promised improvements to start to pay off in 20X6.

The chairman also refers to the successful issue of further ordinary shares only 2 months before the year end. This is, indeed, reassuring, as it suggests that investors are prepared to accept the high level of gearing, and that they are prepared to place confidence in the directors' strategies.

In summary, the business is in no immediate danger of failing, but the position could become critical if management's current expansionary policies do not succeed.

Solution 27

(a) **Memorandum**

To: The board of Spreader
From: Chief accountant
Date: 21 May 20X7
Subject: Financial performance of the Spreader group

Group revenue has risen by 4% on last year, but the cost of sales has increased by 13.6%, resulting in a reduction of gross profit of 3.8%. Operating costs are 5.6% up on last year and, consequently, operating profit is 15% down at $10 million. Analysed to business segments, this shows the following:

	Total		*Spreader*		*Asia*		*Europe*	
	20X7	*20X6*	*20X7*	*20X6*	*20X7*	*20X6*	*20X7*	*20X6*
Operating profit to external revenue, %	20.0	24.6	23.0	34.0	16.6	16.0	21.4	21.7
ROCE%	24.0	30.6	20.0	44.0	25.0	24.0	30.0	25.0

Spreader revenue has dropped by 25% ($5 million) but this has been more than replaced by increased revenue in Asia and Europe. More inter-segment sales in Asia have compensated for a reduction in Spreader sales within the group. Segment operating profit in Spreader has fallen by 50%, but in Asia and Europe it has increased by 25% and 20% respectively. Common costs have increased by 25% this year.

The fall in group profit is influenced by two major factors:

(i) Revenue lost by Spreader has been replaced by less profitable sales in Asia and Europe.
(ii) The profitability of sales by Spreader (26% of total revenue) has fallen significantly.

During the year, investment has been concentrated on Spreader (up by $1.5 million or 11%) and Asia (up by $1 million or 20%).

Investment has been targeted on Spreader where sales are falling, and Asia, where the profit margin is smallest. The ROCE on activity by Spreader shows a significant fall. The funds to finance this investment are adequately covered by retained profit, but interest has increased by 11% over last year.

Overall, net profit before tax is down by 17% and the tax charge is reduced to reflect lower profits and tax allowances on the new investment. Despite the fall in profit, the payout ratio has increased from 43% to 48% with a consequent impact on retained profit.

(b) Geographical segmental information should be interpreted with caution since economic conditions, terms of trade and levels of competition are not the same across the world. Transfer pricing decisions may also influence the profitability of inter-segment sales. The reliability of segmental analysis will be further limited by the fact that considerable common costs are not allocated, and there may be a defect in the logic on which geographical segments are identified.

Signed: Chief accountant

Solution 28

To: Members of the Lending Committee
From: Accounting Adviser
Subject: TYD's financial statements for the year ended 30 September 20X6

(i) *Treatment of two significant items in TYD's financial statements*

The principle at issue in the case of the first transaction is that of 'substance over form'. While there is currently no IFRS that deals specifically with substance over form, the principle is recognised as contributing to the reliability of financial statements in the IASB's *Framework* statement. Transactions and other events should be accounted for and presented in accordance with their substance and economic reality, and not merely their legal form. The legal form of this transaction, a sale and repurchase agreement, is that of a contract for sale of inventories. However, the 'sale' does not meet the criteria for treatment as a sale set out in IAS 18 *Revenue*. In substance, the transaction is a secured loan of $85,000 from HPS to TYD. The difference between the amount advanced at 30 September 20X6 ($85,000) and the amount for which the inventories will be repurchased after two years ($95,000) represents, effectively, the interest payable on the loan. The existence of the option, exercisable by the bank, to ensure repurchase after two years by TYD is a persuasive indicator of the true substance of the transaction. The facts that the inventories remain on TYD's premises, and that TYD bears the cost of insuring them, provide further supporting evidence that TYD continues to bear the risks and rewards of ownership of the inventories. The correct accounting treatment of this transaction is to treat it as a long-term loan.

The question of the transfer of the risks and rewards of ownership is also an issue in determining the true nature of the disposals of inventories on a sale or return basis. As noted above IAS 18 *Revenue* states that revenue can be recognised provided that a set of conditions have been satisfied. One of those conditions is that the risks and rewards of ownership have been transferred to the buyer. Another is that the selling entity should retain no effective control over the goods. Where the option is open to buyers to return the goods, it is likely that neither of these important conditions has been fulfilled, and that the sales cannot be recognised until and unless there is no possibility of the goods being returned.

(ii) *Adjustment of TYD's financial statements*

Both of these transactions are examples of creative accounting techniques that would not be permissible under IFRS regulation. In order to be able to fairly assess the loan application, it is necessary to adjust the financial statements, as follows:

TYD: Income statement for the year ended 30 September 20X6

	$'000	*Adjustment* $'000	*Trans ref*	*Adjusted* $'000
Revenue	600	−85	1	475
		(W1) − 40	2	
Cost of sales	450	(W1) − 32	2	333
		−85	1	
Gross profit	150			142
Expenses	63			63
Finance costs	17			17
Profit before tax	70			62
Income tax expense	25			25
Profit for the period	45	(W1) − 8	2	37

TYD: Statement of financial position at 30 September 20X6

	$'000	$'000	*Adjustment* $'000	*Trans ref*	*Adjusted* $'000
ASSETS					
Non-current assets:					
Property, plant and equipment		527			527
Current assets:					
Inventories	95		(W1) + 32	2	212
			+ 85	1	
Trade receivables	72		(W1) − 40	2	32
Cash	6				6
		173			
		700			777

EQUITY AND LIABILITIES					
Equity:					
Called up share capital	100				100
Retained earnings	245		(W1) − 8	2	237
		345			
Non-current liabilities:					
Long-term borrowings		180	+85	1	265
Current liabilities:					
Trade and other payables	95				95
Bank overdraft	80				80
		175			
		700			777

Workings

(W1) Sale or return items

40% of the sales cannot be recognised: 40% × \$100,000. Remove from trade receivables and from sales.

The related cost of sales figure is \$40,000 × 80% (that is, deducting profit margin) = \$32,000. Remove from cost of sales and add to inventories in the statement of financial position.

The net effect on profit is to remove \$8,000.

> **Examiner's note:**
>
> The income statement and statement of financial position have been adjusted to show the impact of the adjustments; however, there are many other valid ways of setting out the adjustments, for example, using journal entries, that might be quicker under exam conditions. Credit will be given for correct understanding of the adjustments, and not for a particular way of setting them out.

(iii) *Key ratio calculations and analysis*

The key ratio calculations are shown in the following table:

	Before adjustment		*After adjustment*	
Gearing				
$\frac{180 + 80}{(180 + 80 + 345)} \times 100$	43.0%		$\frac{265 + 80}{(265 + 80 + 337)} \times 100$	50.6%
Current ratio				
$\frac{173}{175}$	0.99:1		$\frac{(212 + 32 + 6)}{175}$	1.43:1
Quick ratio				
$\frac{(72 + 6)}{175}$	0.45:1		$\frac{(32 + 6)}{175}$	0.22:1
Profit margin				
$\frac{70}{600} \times 100$	11.7%		$\frac{62}{475} \times 100$	13.1%

It is clear from a very quick examination of the financial statements that TYD is quite highly geared. The gearing ratio before making any adjustments is 43%, close to the point where the application is likely to be rejected without discussion. After adjustment, gearing is at the unacceptably high level (for us) of 50.6%.

Although the current ratio improves substantially after adjustment, the already low quick ratio worsens. Also, it should be noted that the uplift in current assets relates to inventories which, after adjusting the financial statements, amount to 63% of cost of sales. It is quite likely that the inventories could not be rapidly realised in case of default, and so for our purposes, the quick ratio is likely to be a more useful guide.

The profit margin improves after adjustment. However, all other things being equal, it would be due to deteriorate in 20X7 and 20X8 because of the additional interest charge arising from the sale and repurchase agreement.

Taking these various points into consideration, the appropriate course of action is likely to be to reject TYD's application for loan finance.

Solution 29

(a) (i) DPC's summary projected financial statements to include the acquisition of an associate interest in PPS:

Summary projected income statement for the year ended 31 December 20X8

	Projected: 20X8
	$'000
Revenue	60,300
All expenses including income tax	(55,300)
Share of profit of associate (W1)	280
Profit for the period attributable to equity holders	5,280

Summary projected statement of financial position at 31 December 20X8

	Projected: 20X8
	$'000
Non-current assets	50,400
Investment in associate (W2)	3,780
Current assets (82,000 − 1,000)	81,000
	135,180
Equity (W3)	31,680
Long-term liabilities (10,000 + 2,500)	12,500
Current liabilities	81,000
	135,180

(ii) DPC's summary projected financial statements to include the acquisition of a subsidiary interest in PPS:

Summary projected income statement for the year ended 31 December 20X8

	Projected: 20X8 $'000
Revenue (60,300 + 10,200)	70,500
All expenses including income tax (55,300 + 9,500)	(64,800)
Non-controlling interest in PPS (700 × 40%)	(280)
Profit for the period attributable to equity holders	5,420

Summary projected statement of financial position at 31 December 20X8

	Projected: 20X8 $'000
Non-current assets (50,400 + 9,800 + 4,020 (W4)	64,220
Current assets (82,000 + 16,000 − 3,000)	95,000
	159,220
Equity (W5)	31,820
Non-controlling interest in PPS (4,000 × 40%)	1,600
Long-term liabilities (10,000 + 9,300 + 3,000)	22,300
Current liabilities (91,000 + 12,500)	103,500
	159,220

Workings

1. *Share of profits of associate:* $700,000 × 40% = $280,000
2. *Investment in associate:*

	$'000
Investment at cost	3,500
Share of post-acquisition profits	280
	3,780

3. *Equity*

	$'000
As given in the question	31,400
Share of post-acquisition profits in associate	280
	31,680

4. *Goodwill on acquisition*

	$'000
Investment at cost	6,000
Share of net assets acquired:	
([100 + 3,200] × 60%)	1,980
Goodwill on acquisition	4,020

5. *Equity*

	$'000
As given in the question	31,400
Share of post-acquisition profits in subsidiary	420
	31,820

(b)		*DPC existing*		*DPC + PPS associate*		*DPC + PPS subsidiary*
EPS	5,000/10,000	50¢	5,280/10,000	52.8¢	5,420/10,000	54.2¢
Gearing	10,000/31,400 × 100	31.8%	12,500/31,680 × 100	39.5%	22,300/33,420 × 100	66.7%
NCA turnover	60,300/50,400	1.20	Same	1.20	70,500/64,220	1.10

(d) Earnings per share would be improved under either acquisition scenario. Non-current asset turnover would be reduced if the investment in a subsidiary interest were to be acquired in PPS. However, it is the gearing ratio that shows the biggest potential differences. The gearing ratio if PPS were acquired as an associate worsens because of the additional borrowing of $2.5 million required to acquire the shareholding. If a subsidiary interest were to be purchased not only is there additional borrowing of $3 million to take into account in the gearing calculation, but, much more significantly, PPS's own borrowings have to be included in long-term liabilities. PPS is highly geared and so the impact on consolidation is very substantial. If an associate interest were acquired PPS's borrowing would be kept off statement of financial position.

Solution 30

Report

Takeover targets: W, Y and Z

(a) The three potential targets are similar in size, each producing revenue at the level of approximately 10% of ABC's revenue. In respect of performance, Z appears superior to the others: its gross profit margin and operating profit margins are significantly higher than those of W and Y. Y's operating profit margin is disappointing at 4.7%; however, there may be scope to improve control over its operating expenses. Z's return on capital employed is also impressive, at almost double that of entity Y, and it is better than that of ABC itself. However, it is relevant to note that the income tax rate in Zeelandia is significantly higher than that of the other countries, and this effect offsets some of its advantages.

The level of gearing in ABC itself is negligible with debt constituting only around 5% of equity. Gearing is also at a low level in Y and Z, but entity W is relatively more highly geared (debt constitutes 45.6% of equity). However, after takeover ABC's management would be able to control the level of gearing and to repay any long-term debt if it was felt necessary to do so. The economic environments in which the entities operate are, apparently, rather different from each other. As well as the differences in income tax rates already noted, interest rates vary from 6% in Winlandia to 10% in Zeelandia.

Working capital management varies between the entities. For ABC, the turnover in days for inventories, receivables and payables all lie in the mid-40s. Receivables turnover across the four entities is broadly similar, but there are some significant differences in respect of inventories and payables. Entity W appears to hold inventories for much longer than the other entities, and there may be problems with slow-moving or obsolete items. Payables turnover, on the other hand, is relatively fast in entity W, but at 73 days entity Z takes a long time to meet its payables obligations. This may be as a result of poor management, or deliberate policy. ABC has a relatively comfortable current ratio of 1.4:1, but the comparable ratio in all three target entities is less impressive.

The P/E ratios of the three targets and of ABC itself lie within a fairly narrow band. W's P/E is the lowest at 12.6; this could indicate that the share is relatively undervalued, that the most recent earnings figure was better than expected and the share price has not yet been adjusted upwards to reflect this, or that the investment is perceived as relatively risky in the market.

On the basis of the preliminary analysis, entity Z appears superior to the others in several aspects of performance. However, a great deal of further analysis will be required before reaching a conclusion, and, as noted below, there are many limitations in the analysis.

(b) There are several general limitations to any inter-firm comparisons. These limitations become even more important where international comparisons are made. The limitations include the following:

Accounting Standards and policies: in this case, entity Y prepares its financial statements in accordance with Yolandian GAAP. This may be very different from the International Standards that the other entities comply with. Even where the same or similar standards are adopted there is often scope for considerable variation in the choice of policies. For example, an entity can choose between valuing property, plant and equipment at depreciated cost, or at valuation. The policy selected by management may have a significant effect on the financial statements and upon accounting ratios such as return on capital employed.

Accounting reference date: there is a gap of 9 months between the accounting reference date of entities Y and Z on the one hand, and the accounting reference date of ABC on the other hand. A great deal of change can take place in a period of several months, both within the economy as a whole and in the activities of a single entity. The figures of Y and Z are, relatively speaking, out of date, and the comparison may be at least partially invalidated because of this effect.

Size of entities: the three target entities are of similar size, and so comparison between them is likely to have some validity. However, ABC is approximately ten times the size of each of the targets. Its expenses, for example, may be subject to economies of scale.

Differences between activities: all of the four entities being compared have the same principal activity. However, it is rarely, if ever, the case that entities are engaged in precisely the same sphere of activity, and there may be relatively minor supplementary activities that distort their performance. For example, one entity may derive part of its income through the hire or leasing of equipment. It is important to examine the details of entities' activities carefully in order to be sure that they are comparable with those of other entities.

Single period comparisons: there is always a risk that the results of a single period are not representative of the underlying trends within the business. Therefore, it is better, wherever possible, to examine the performance and position at several different dates.

Special problems of international comparison: where entities in different countries are being compared, it is even more important to be cautious about the value of the comparisons and conclusions drawn. National economies often experience cycles of economic growth and decline. These cyclical differences may have a significant effect upon the performance of entities. The entities in this case are, apparently, subject to different tax regimes. Such differences may very well be important factors in making decisions about investment. The size and nature of the stock markets may well differ considerably between different regimes. In a small, illiquid market, for example, share prices may be generally lower, reflecting the lack of liquidity in the investment. Lower prices would, of course, affect the P/E ratio, which is regarded as important.

Exam Q & As

At the time of publication there are no exam Q & As available for the 2010 syllabus. However, the latest specimen exam papers are available on the CIMA website.
Actual exam Q & As will be available free of charge to CIMA students on the CIMA website from summer 2010 onwards.

Index

Index